/100

"A riveting book that works like connective tissue, showing the shifts in events, ideology and personalities as they link and build toward 9/11. The reader, knowing the end, supplies the dread as Wright clears away the murk, untangles the particulars and tells a hapless, appalling and engrossing tale. The reporting in *The Looming Tower* is so good that it will matter in 100 years. Wright's determined, disciplined work has made his book indispensable."
—*The Plain Dealer*

"The current definitive history. . . . Wright relates the buildup [to 9/11] with the skill of a novelist and the solidly grounded information of a dedicated reporter."   —*Pittsburgh Post-Gazette*

"The most comprehensive, objective and readable guide to al-Qaeda's emergence."   —*The Economist*

"The perfect 9/11 book. . . . I don't know a book that does a better job—indeed a thrilling job—of illuminating the main human factors that went into producing the horrendous attack of [September 11]. . . . An unflaggingly compelling story."
—David Klinghoffer, *New York Post*

"A highly informative and gripping account, one that may well prove to be the definitive history of al-Qaeda for years to come. . . . Remarkable."   —*Associated Press*

"The library of books on al-Qaeda is by now vast and cavernous, but no other work succeeds so well in telling its extraordinary story or capturing its elusive character. . . . Wright's brilliantly constructed narrative is head and shoulders above the rest."
—*New Statesman*

"Absolutely riveting. . . . A masterful work. . . . Densely sourced yet driven by a strong narrative as it takes a compelling look at the rise of Osama bin Laden."   —*Daily News*

"An extensively researched, gripping tale of the growth of Islamic radicalism."   —*The Indianapolis Star*

"Brilliant. . . . More than a fascinating personal history, it also describes the contorted intellectual journey that has taken place among some Muslims which allows a holy book that appears to condemn suicide and the killing of innocents to be used to justify catastrophic terrorism."   —*Financial Times*

"Compulsively readable [and] deeply unnerving."   —*Time*

"Wright's *Tower* is not just fine reportage and writing, although both are exceptional. It's also an invaluable peek into the mindset of a gaggle of zealous misfits and malcontents who are bent on doing damage to the United States and the misfits and malcontents within the U.S. government who are trying to stop them."   —*The Kansas City Star*

"Fascinating and timely. . . . Wright's story sparkles with exquisite detail."   —*Houston Chronicle*

"Lawrence Wright's remarkable book, *The Looming Tower: Al-Qaeda and the Road to 9/11*, illuminates . . . like no volume before it. Wright synthesizes an array of figures and events into a riveting tableau. The book is a feat of exhaustive reporting and research, yet reads like a novel, thanks to Wright's vivid prose and instinct for dramatic detail."   —*Salon*

"A magisterial, beautifully crafted narrative of the path to September 11. . . . Wright untangles the anxieties, resentments, aspirations and ideals that have driven and defined radical Islamism."   —*Los Angeles Times*

"Compelling. . . . A comprehensive history of the people and ideas that led to that dark day."   —*The Daily Yomiuri* (Tokyo)

"Tense and fascinating. . . . A finely judged account of both collaboration among terrorists and rivalry between the CIA and the FBI."   —*The New York Review of Books*

"Wright describes the years of palm-greasing and back-stabbing that handed the responsibility for international jihad to a psychopath . . . with immense forensic skill, in the stripped-down prose of the best thriller-writers." —*The Daily Telegraph* (London)

"A gripping, lucid narrative [and] a deft guide to the divisions and infighting among the various Islamic sects."
—*The New York Observer*

"[Wright's] authoritative analysis is as unsettling as it is fascinating. . . . *The Looming Tower* might be the bracing splash of ice water that alerts the Great Satan America to how little it knows about the radical Islamic culture that spawned its bête noire Osama bin Laden and his global terrorist network, Qaeda al-Jihad."
—*Texas Monthly*

"A page-turner . . . encompassing religion, politics, economics and more. If you've been meaning to sharpen your understanding of what all led up to September 11, 2001, then Wright may have written just what you've been waiting for."
—*San Francisco Chronicle*

"Powerful and important. . . . A history of a man and a movement, replete with the accidents of history and historic inevitability."
—*St. Louis Post-Dispatch*

"Riveting. . . . Written with a cinematic clarity and vividness but yet it never lapses from the most rigorous standards of American history. It tells a story that is rich in analysis and cultural understanding and insistently commands the reader's attention."
—*The New York Sun*

"Deeply researched. . . . Immaculately crafted."
—*The Wall Street Journal*

Lawrence Wright

THE LOOMING TOWER

Lawrence Wright is a staff writer for *The New Yorker* and the author of eight previous works of nonfiction, including *In the New World*, *Remembering Satan*, *The Looming Tower*, *Going Clear*, and *Thirteen Days in September*, and one novel, *God's Favorite*. His books have received many prizes and honors, including the Pulitzer Prize for *The Looming Tower*. He is also a playwright and screenwriter. He and his wife are longtime residents of Austin, Texas.

www.lawrencewright.com

Lawrence Wright is available for select speaking engagements. To inquire about a possible speaking appearance, please contact Penguin Random House Speakers Bureau at speakers@penguinrandomhouse.com or visit www.prhspeakers.com.

THE
LOOMING
TOWER

THE
LOOMING
TOWER

Al-Qaeda and the Road to 9/11

Lawrence Wright

Vintage Books
A Division of Random House, Inc.
New York

FIRST VINTAGE BOOKS EDITION, SEPTEMBER 2007

The Library of Congress has cataloged the Knopf edition as follows:
Wright, Lawrence, [date]
The looming tower : Al-Qaeda and the road to 9/11 /
by Lawrence Wright.
p.   cm.
Includes bibliographical references and index.
1. September 11 Terrorist Attacks, 2001. 2. Qaida (Organization)
3. Terrorism—Government policy—United States.
4. Intelligence service—United States. I. Title.
HV6432.7.W75 2005
973.931—dc22   2006041032

Vintage ISBN: 978-1-4000-3084-2

Author photograph © Kenny Braun
Map by Mapping Specialists, Ltd.

www.vintagebooks.com

Printed in the United States of America
2 4 6 8 10 9 7 5 3

This is for my family,
Roberta, Caroline, Gordon & Karen

CONTENTS

Map   xi

    Prologue   3
1. The Martyr   9
2. The Sporting Club   38
3. The Founder   69
4. Change   97
5. The Miracles   114
6. The Base   139
7. Return of the Hero   165
8. Paradise   185
9. The Silicon Valley   200
10. Paradise Lost   213
11. The Prince of Darkness   230
12. The Boy Spies   242
13. Hijira   254
14. Going Operational   269
15. Bread and Water   278
16. "Now It Begins"   297

17. The New Millennium 325
18. Boom 340
19. The Big Wedding 376
20. Revelations 408

Afterword to the Vintage Books Edition (2011) 423
Principal Characters 433
Notes 445
Bibliography 499
Author Interviews 511
Acknowledgments and Notes on Sources 519
Index 529

Map of the Middle East

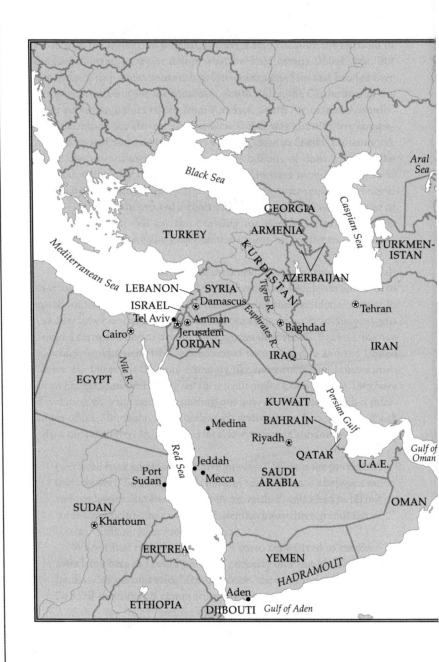

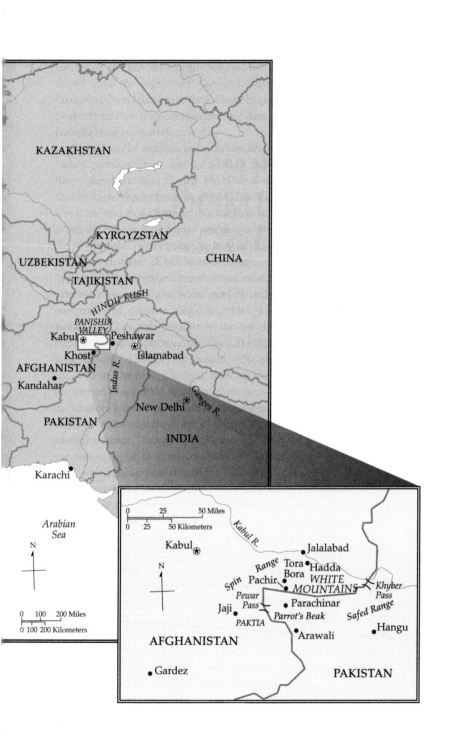

Prologue

ON SAINT PATRICK'S DAY, Daniel Coleman, an agent in the New York office of the Federal Bureau of Investigation handling foreign intelligence cases, drove down to Tysons Corner, Virginia, to report for a new posting. The sidewalks were still buried under gray banks of snow from the blizzard of 1996 a few weeks before. Coleman entered an undistinguished government office tower called the Gloucester Building and got off the elevator at the fifth floor. This was Alec Station.

Other stations of the Central Intelligence Agency are located in the various countries that they cover; Alec was the first "virtual" station, situated only a few miles from the headquarters building in Langley. On an organizational chart it was labeled "Terrorist Financial Links," a subsection of the CIA's Counterterrorist Center, but in practice it was devoted to tracking the activities of a single man, Osama bin Laden, whose name had arisen as the master financier of terror. Coleman first heard of him in 1993, when a foreign source spoke about a "Saudi prince" who was supporting a cell of radical Islamists who were plotting to blow up New York landmarks, including the United Nations, the Lincoln and Holland tunnels, and even 26 Federal Plaza, the building where Coleman worked. Now, three years later, the bureau had finally found time to send him to look over the intelligence the agency had compiled to see if there was any reason to pursue an investigation.

Alec Station already had thirty-five volumes of material on bin Laden, consisting mostly of transcripts of telephone conversations that had been sucked up by the electronic ears of the National Security Agency. Coleman found the material repetitive and inconclusive. Still, he opened an intelligence case on bin Laden, largely as a placeholder in case the "Islamist financier" turned out to be something more than that.

Like many agents, Dan Coleman had been trained to fight the Cold War. He joined the FBI as a file clerk in 1973. Scholarly and inquisitive, Coleman was naturally drawn to counterintelligence. In the 1980s, he concentrated on recruiting communist spies in the populous diplomatic community surrounding the United Nations; an East German attaché was a particular treasure. In 1990, however, when the Cold War had just ended, he found himself on a squad devoted to Middle Eastern terrorism. There was little in his background that prepared him for this new turn—but that was true of the bureau as a whole, which regarded terrorism as a nuisance, not a real threat. It was difficult to believe, in those cloudless days after the fall of the Berlin Wall, that America had any real enemies still standing.

Then, in August 1996, bin Laden declared war on America from a cave in Afghanistan. The stated cause was the continued presence of U.S. forces in Saudi Arabia five years after the first Gulf War. "Terrorizing you, while you are carrying arms in our land, is a legitimate right and a moral obligation," he stated. He presumed to speak on behalf of all Muslims, and even directed some of his lengthy fatwa to U.S. Secretary of Defense William Perry personally. "I say to you, William, that: These youths love death as you love life. . . . These youths will not ask you for explanations. They will sing out that there is nothing between us that needs to be explained, there is only killing and neck-smiting."

Other than Coleman, few in America—even in the bureau— knew or cared about the Saudi dissident. The thirty-five volumes in Alec Station painted a picture of a messianic billionaire from a sprawling, influential family that was closely connected to the rulers of the Kingdom of Saudi Arabia. He had made a name for himself in the jihad in Afghanistan against the Soviet occupation. Coleman had read enough history to understand the references in bin Laden's war cry to the Crusades and the early struggles of Islam. Indeed, one of the striking features of the document was that time seemed to have stopped a thousand years ago. There was now and there was then, but there was nothing in between. It was as if the Crusades were still going on in bin Laden's universe. The intensity of the anger was also difficult for Coleman to grasp. What did we do to him? he wondered.

Coleman showed the text of bin Laden's fatwa to prosecutors from the U.S. Attorney's Office for the Southern District of New York. It was droll, it was weird, but was it a crime? The lawyers puzzled over the language and found a rarely invoked seditious conspiracy statute from the Civil War era that forbids instigating violence and attempting to overthrow the U.S. government. It seemed a stretch to think that it might be applied to a stateless Saudi in a cave in Tora Bora, but on the basis of such meager precedent, Coleman opened a criminal file on the figure who would become the most wanted man in the FBI's history. He was still working entirely alone.

A few months later, in November 1996, Coleman traveled to an American military base in Germany with two U.S. attorneys, Kenneth Karas and Patrick Fitzgerald. There in a safe house was a jittery Sudanese informer named Jamal al-Fadl, who claimed to have worked for bin Laden in Khartoum. Coleman carried a briefing book with photographs of bin Laden's known associates, and Fadl quickly identified most of them. He was selling a story, but he clearly knew the players. The problem was that he kept lying to the investigators, embroidering his tale, depicting himself as a hero who only wanted to do the right thing.

"So why did you leave?" the prosecutors wanted to know.

Fadl said that he loved America. He had lived in Brooklyn and he spoke English. Then he said he had run away so he could write a best-selling book. He was keyed up and had a hard time sitting still. Obviously, he had a lot more to tell. It took several long days to get him to stop confabulating and admit that he had run off with more than $100,000 of bin Laden's money. When he did that, he sobbed and sobbed. It was the turning point in the interrogation.

Fadl agreed to be a government witness should a trial ever occur, but that seemed unlikely, given the modest charges that the government lawyers were considering.

Then, on his own initiative, Fadl began talking about an organization called al-Qaeda. It was the first time any of the men in the room had ever heard the term. He described training camps and sleeper cells. He talked about bin Laden's interest in acquiring nuclear and chemical weapons. He said that al-Qaeda had been responsible for a 1992 bombing in Yemen and for training the insurgents who shot down the American helicopters in Somalia that same year. He gave names and drew organizational charts. The investigators were stunned by his story. For two weeks, six or seven hours a day, they went over the details again and again, testing his responses to see if he was consistent. He never varied.

When Coleman got back to the bureau, no one seemed particularly interested. Fadl's testimony was chilling, they agreed, but how could they corroborate the testimony of a thief and a liar? Besides, there were other more pressing investigations.

For a year and a half, Dan Coleman continued his solitary investigation of bin Laden. Because he was posted to Alec Station, the bureau more or less forgot about him. Using wiretaps on bin Laden's businesses, Coleman was able to draw a map of the al-Qaeda network, which extended throughout the Middle East, Africa, Europe, and Central Asia. He was alarmed to realize that many of al-Qaeda's associates had ties to the United States. He concluded this was a worldwide terror organization dedicated to destroying America, but Coleman couldn't even get his superiors to return his phone calls on the matter.

Coleman was left to himself to puzzle out the questions that would later occur to everyone. Where had this movement come from? Why had it chosen to attack America? And what could we do to stop it? He was like a laboratory technician looking at a slide of some previously unseen virus. Under the microscope, al-Qaeda's lethal qualities began to reveal themselves. The group was small—only ninety-three members at the time—but it was part of a larger radical movement that was sweeping through Islam, particularly in the Arab world. The possibilities for contagion were great. The men who made up this group were well trained and battle hardened. They apparently had ample resources. Moreover, they were fanatically committed to their cause and convinced that they would be victorious. They were brought together by a philosophy that was so compelling that they would willingly—eagerly—sacrifice their lives for it. In the process they wanted to kill as many people as possible.

The most frightening aspect of this new threat, however, was the fact that almost no one took it seriously. It was too bizarre, too primitive and exotic. Up against the confidence that Americans placed in modernity and technology and their own ideals to protect them from the savage pageant of history, the defiant gestures of bin Laden and his followers seemed absurd and even pathetic. And yet al-Qaeda was not a mere artifact of seventh-century Arabia. It had learned to use modern tools and modern ideas, which wasn't surprising, since the story of al-Qaeda had really begun in America, not so long ago.

1

The Martyr

IN A FIRST-CLASS STATEROOM on a cruise ship bound for New York from Alexandria, Egypt, a frail, middle-aged writer and educator named Sayyid Qutb experienced a crisis of faith. "Should I go to America as any normal student on a scholarship, who only eats and sleeps, or should I be special?" he wondered. "Should I hold on to my Islamic beliefs, facing the many sinful temptations, or should I indulge those temptations all around me?" It was November 1948. The new world loomed over the horizon, victorious, rich, and free. Behind him was Egypt, in rags and tears. The traveler had never been out of his native country. Nor had he willingly left now.

The stern bachelor was slight and dark, with a high, sloping forehead and a paintbrush moustache somewhat narrower than the width of his nose. His eyes betrayed an imperious and easily slighted nature. He always evoked an air of formality, favoring dark three-piece suits despite the searing Egyptian sun. For a man who held his dignity so close, the prospect of returning to the classroom at the age of forty-two may have seemed demeaning. And yet, as a child from a mud-walled village in Upper Egypt, he had already surpassed the modest goal he had set for himself of becoming a respectable member of the civil service. His literary and social criticism had made him one of his country's most popular writers. It had also earned the fury of King Farouk, Egypt's dissolute monarch, who had signed an order for his arrest. Powerful and sympathetic friends hastily arranged his departure.

At the time, Qutb (his name is pronounced *kuh*-tub) held a comfortable post as a supervisor in the Ministry of Education. Politically, he was a fervent Egyptian nationalist and anti-communist, a stance that placed him in the mainstream of the vast bureaucratic middle class. The ideas that would give birth to what would be called Islamic fundamentalism were not yet completely formed in his mind; indeed, he would later say that he was not even a very religious man before he began this journey, although he had memorized the Quran by the age of ten, and his writing had recently taken a turn toward more conservative themes. Like many of his compatriots, he was radicalized by the British occupation and contemptuous of the jaded King Farouk's complicity. Egypt was racked by anti-British protests and seditious political factions bent on running the foreign troops out of the country— and perhaps the king as well. What made this unimposing, midlevel government clerk particularly dangerous was his blunt and potent commentary. He had never gotten to the front rank of the contemporary Arab literary scene, a fact that galled him throughout his career; and yet from the government's point of view, he was becoming an annoyingly important enemy.

He was Western in so many ways—his dress, his love of classical music and Hollywood movies. He had read, in translation, the works of Darwin and Einstein, Byron and Shelley, and had immersed himself in French literature, especially Victor Hugo. Even before his journey, however, he worried about the advance of an all-engulfing Western civilization. Despite his erudition, he saw the West as a single cultural entity. The distinctions between capitalism and Marxism, Christianity and Judaism, fascism and democracy were insignificant by comparison with the single great divide in Qutb's mind: Islam and the East on the one side, and the Christian West on the other.

America, however, stood apart from the colonialist adventures that had characterized Europe's relations with the Arab world. At the end of the Second World War, America straddled the political chasm between the colonizers and the colonized. Indeed, it was tempting to imagine America as the anticolonial paragon: a subjugated nation that had broken free and triumphantly outstripped its former masters. The country's power seemed to lie in its values, not in European notions of cultural superiority or privileged races and classes. And because America advertised itself as an immigrant nation, it had a permeable relationship with the rest of the world. Arabs, like most other peoples, had established their own colonies inside America, and the ropes of kinship drew them closer to the ideals that the country claimed to stand for.

And so, Qutb, like many Arabs, felt shocked and betrayed by the support that the U.S. government had given to the Zionist cause after the war. Even as Qutb was sailing out of Alexandria's harbor, Egypt, along with five other Arab armies, was in the final stages of losing the war that established Israel as a Jewish state within the Arab world. The Arabs were stunned, not only by the determination and skill of the Israeli fighters but by the incompetence of their own troops and the disastrous decisions of their leaders. The shame of that experience would shape the Arab intellectual universe more profoundly than any other event in modern history. "I hate those Westerners and despise them!" Qutb wrote after President Harry Truman endorsed the transfer of a hundred thousand Jewish refugees into Palestine. "All of them, without any exception: the English, the French, the Dutch, and finally the Americans, who have been trusted by many."

THE MAN IN THE STATEROOM had known romantic love, but mainly the pain of it. He had written a thinly disguised account of a failed relationship in a novel; after that, he turned his back on marriage. He said that he had been unable to find a suitable bride from the "dishonorable" women who allowed themselves to be seen in public, a stance that left him alone and unconsoled in middle age. He still enjoyed women—he was close to his three sisters—but sexuality threatened him, and he had withdrawn into a shell of disapproval, seeing sex as the main enemy of salvation.

The dearest relationship he had ever enjoyed was that with his mother, Fatima, an illiterate but pious woman, who had sent her precocious son to Cairo to study. His father died in 1933, when Qutb was twenty-seven. For the next three years he taught in various provincial posts until he was transferred to Helwan, a prosperous suburb of Cairo, and he brought the rest of his family to live with him there. His intensely conservative mother never entirely settled in; she was always on guard against the creeping foreign influences that were far more apparent in Helwan than in the little village she came from. These influences must have been evident in her sophisticated son as well.

As he prayed in his stateroom, Sayyid Qutb was still uncertain of his own identity. Should he be "normal" or "special"? Should he resist temptations or indulge them? Should he hang on tightly to his Islamic beliefs or cast them aside for the materialism and sinfulness of the West? Like all pilgrims, he was making two journeys: one outward, into the larger world, and another inward, into his own soul. "I have decided to be a true Muslim!" he resolved. But almost immediately he second-guessed himself. "Am I being truthful or was that just a whim?"

His deliberations were interrupted by a knock on the door. Standing outside his stateroom was a young girl, whom he described as thin and tall and "half-naked." She asked him in English, "Is it okay for me to be your guest tonight?"

Qutb responded that his room was equipped with only one bed.

"A single bed can hold two people," she said.

Appalled, he closed the door in her face. "I heard her fall on the wooden floor outside and realized that she was drunk," he recalled. "I instantly thanked God for defeating my temptation and allowing me to stick to my morals."

This is the man, then—decent, proud, tormented, self-righteous—whose lonely genius would unsettle Islam, threaten regimes across the Muslim world, and beckon to a generation of rootless young Arabs who were looking for meaning and purpose in their lives and would find it in jihad.

QUTB ARRIVED in New York Harbor in the middle of the most prosperous holiday season the country had ever known. In the postwar boom, everybody was making money—Idaho potato farmers, Detroit automakers, Wall Street bankers—and all this wealth spurred confidence in the capitalist model, which had been so brutally tested during the recent Depression. Unemployment seemed practically un-American; officially, the rate of joblessness was under 4 percent, and practically speaking, anyone who wanted a job could get one. Half of the world's total wealth was now in American hands.

The contrast with Cairo must have been especially bitter as Qutb wandered through the New York City streets, festively lit with holiday lights, the luxurious shop windows laden with appliances that he had only heard about—television sets, washing machines—technological miracles spilling out of every department store in stupefying abundance. Brand-new office towers and apartments were shouldering into the gaps in the Manhattan skyline between the Empire State Building and the Chrysler Building. Downtown and in the outer boroughs, vast projects were under way to house the immigrant masses.

It was fitting, in such a buoyant and confident environment, unprecedented in its mix of cultures, that the visible symbol of a changed world order was arising: the new United Nations complex overlooking the East River. The United Nations was the most powerful expression of the determined internationalism that was the legacy of the war, and yet the city itself already embodied the dreams of universal harmony far more powerfully than did any single idea or institution. The world was pouring into New York because that was where the power was, and the money, and the transforming cultural energy. Nearly a million Russians were in the city, half a million Irish, and an equal number of Germans—not to mention the Puerto Ricans, the Dominicans, the Poles, and the largely uncounted and often illegal Chinese laborers who had also found refuge in the welcoming city. The black population of the city had grown by 50 percent in only eight years, to 700,000, and they were refugees as well, from the racism of the American South. Fully a fourth of the 8 million New Yorkers were Jewish, many of whom had fled the latest European catastrophe. Hebrew letters covered the signs for the shops and factories on the Lower East Side, and Yiddish was commonly heard on the streets. That would have been a challenge for the middle-aged Egyptian who hated the Jews but, until he left his country, had never met one. For many New Yorkers, perhaps for most of them, political and economic oppression was a part of their heritage, and the city had given them sanctuary, a place to earn a living, to raise a family, to begin again. Because of that, the great emotion that fueled the exuberant city was hopefulness, whereas Cairo was one of the capitals of despair.

At the same time, New York was miserable—overfull, grouchy, competitive, frivolous, picketed with No Vacancy signs. Snoring alcoholics blocked the doorways. Pimps and pickpockets prowled the midtown squares in the ghoulish neon glow of burlesque houses. In the Bowery, flophouses offered cots for twenty cents a night. The gloomy side streets were crisscrossed with clotheslines. Gangs of snarling delinquents roamed the margins like wild dogs. For a man whose English was rudimentary, the city posed unfamiliar hazards, and Qutb's natural reticence made communication all the more difficult. He was desperately homesick. "Here in this strange place, this huge workshop they call 'the new world,' I feel as though my spirit, thoughts, and body live in loneliness," he wrote to a friend in Cairo. "What I need most here is someone to talk to," he wrote another friend, "to talk about topics other than dollars, movie stars, brands of cars—a real conversation on the issues of man, philosophy, and soul."

Two days after Qutb arrived in America, he and an Egyptian acquaintance checked into a hotel. "The black elevator operator liked us because we were closer to his color," Qutb reported. The operator offered to help the travelers find "entertainment." "He mentioned examples of this 'entertainment,' which included perversions. He also told us what happens in some of these rooms, which may have pairs of boys or girls. They asked him to bring them some bottles of Coca-Cola, and didn't even change their positions when he entered! 'Don't they feel ashamed?' we asked. He was surprised. 'Why? They are just enjoying themselves, satisfying their particular desires.' "

This experience, among many others, confirmed Qutb's view that sexual mixing led inevitably to perversion. America itself had just been shaken by a lengthy scholarly report titled *Sexual Behavior in the Human Male*, by Alfred Kinsey and his colleagues at the University of Indiana. Their eight-hundred-page treatise, filled with startling statistics and droll commentary, shattered the country's leftover Victorian prudishness like a brick through a stained-glass window. Kinsey reported that 37 percent of the American men he sampled had experienced homosexual activity to the point of orgasm, nearly half had engaged in extramarital sex, and 69 percent had paid for sex with prostitutes. The mirror that Kinsey held up to America showed a country that was frantically lustful but also confused, ashamed, incompetent, and astoundingly ignorant. Despite the evidence of the diversity and frequency of sexual activity, this was a time in America when sexual matters were practically never discussed, not even by doctors. One Kinsey researcher interviewed a thousand childless American couples who had no idea why they failed to conceive, even though the wives were virgins.

Qutb was familiar with the Kinsey Report, and referenced it in his later writings to illustrate his view of Americans as little different from beasts—"a reckless, deluded herd that only knows lust and money." A staggering rate of divorce was to be expected in such a society, since "Every time a husband or wife notices a new sparkling personality, they lunge for it as if it were a new fashion in the world of desires." The turbulent overtones of his own internal struggles can be heard in his diatribe: "A girl looks at you, appearing as if she were an enchanting nymph or an escaped mermaid, but as she approaches, you sense only the screaming instinct inside her, and you can smell her burning body, not the scent of perfume but flesh, only flesh. Tasty flesh, truly, but flesh nonetheless."

THE END OF THE WORLD war had brought America victory but not security. Many Americans felt that they had defeated one totalitarian enemy only to encounter another far stronger and more insidious than European fascism. "Communism is creeping inexorably into these destitute lands," the young evangelist Billy

Graham warned, "into war-torn China, into restless South America, and unless the Christian religion rescues these nations from the clutch of the unbelieving, America will stand alone and isolated in the world."

The fight against communism was being waged inside America as well. J. Edgar Hoover, the Machiavellian head of the FBI, claimed that one of every 1,814 people in America was a communist. Under his supervision, the bureau began to devote itself almost entirely to uncovering evidence of subversion. When Qutb arrived in New York, the House Un-American Activities Committee had begun hearing testimony from a *Time* magazine senior editor named Whittaker Chambers. Chambers testified that he had been part of a communist cell headed by Alger Hiss, a former Truman administration official, who was one of the organizers of the United Nations and was then president of the Carnegie Endowment for International Peace. The country was riveted by the hearings, which gave substance to the fears that communists were lurking in the cities and the suburbs, in sleeper cells. "They are everywhere," U.S. Attorney General Tom Clark asserted, "in factories, offices, butcher shops, on street corners, in private businesses—and each carries with him the germs of death for society." America felt itself to be in danger of losing not only its political system but also its religious heritage. "Godlessness" was an essential feature of the communist menace, and the country reacted viscerally to the sense that Christianity was under attack. "Either Communism must die, or Christianity must die, because it is actually a battle between Christ and the anti-Christ," Billy Graham would write a few years later—a sentiment that was very much a part of the mainstream Christian American consensus at the time.

Qutb took note of the obsession that was beginning to dominate American politics. He was himself a resolute anticommunist for similar reasons; indeed, the communists were far more active and influential in Egypt than in America. "Either we shall walk the path of Islam or we shall walk the path of Communism," Qutb wrote the year before he came to America, anticipating the same stark formulation as Billy Graham. At the same time, he saw in the party of Lenin a template for the Islamic politics of the future—the politics that he would invent.

In Qutb's passionate analysis, there was little difference between the communist and capitalist systems; both, he believed, attended only the material needs of humanity, leaving the spirit unsatisfied. He predicted that once the average worker lost his dreamy expectations of becoming rich, America would inevitably turn toward communism. Christianity would be powerless to block this trend because it exists only in the realm of the spirit— "like a vision in a pure ideal world." Islam, on the other hand, is "a complete system" with laws, social codes, economic rules, and its own method of government. Only Islam offered a formula for creating a just and godly society. Thus the real struggle would eventually show itself: It was not a battle between capitalism and communism; it was between Islam and materialism. And inevitably Islam would prevail.

No doubt the clash between Islam and the West was remote in the minds of most New Yorkers during the holiday season of 1948. But, despite the new wealth that was flooding into the city, and the self-confidence that victory naturally brought, there was a generalized sense of anxiety about the future. "The city, for the first time in its long history, is destructible," the essayist E. B. White had observed that summer. "A single flight of planes no bigger than a wedge of geese can quickly end this island fantasy, burn the towers, crumble the bridges, turn the underground passages into lethal chambers, cremate the millions." White was writing at the dawn of the nuclear age, and the feeling of vulnerability was quite new. "In the mind of whatever perverted dreamer might loose the lightning," he observed, "New York must hold a steady, irresistible charm."

SOON AFTER THE NEW YEAR BEGAN, Qutb moved to Washington, where he studied English at Wilson Teachers College.*

---

*Wilson Teachers College merged with three other schools to form the University of the District of Columbia in 1977.

"Life in Washington is good," he admitted in one letter, "especially as I live in close proximity to the library and my friends."
He enjoyed a generous stipend from the Egyptian government.
"A regular student can live well on $180 a month," he wrote. "I,
however, spend between $250 and $280 monthly."

Although Qutb came from a little village in Upper Egypt, it
was in America that he found "a primitiveness that reminds us of
the ages of jungles and caves." Social gatherings were full of
superficial chatter. Though people filled the museums and symphonies, they were there not to see or hear but rather out of a frantic, narcissistic need to be seen and heard. The Americans were
altogether too informal, Qutb concluded. "I'm here at a restaurant," he wrote a friend in Cairo, "and in front of me is this young
American. On his shirt, instead of a necktie, there is a picture of an
orange hyena, and on his back, instead of a vest, there is a char-
coal picture of an elephant. This is the American taste in colors.
And music! Let's leave that till later." The food, he complained,
"is also weird." He reports an incident at a college cafeteria when
he saw an American woman putting salt on a melon. He slyly told
her that Egyptians preferred pepper. "She tried it, and said it was
delicious!" he wrote. "The next day, I told her that some Egyptians
use sugar on their melons instead, and she found that tasty as
well." He even grouched about the haircuts: "Whenever I go to a
barber I return home and redo my hair with my own hands."

In February 1949 Qutb checked into the George Washington
University Hospital to have his tonsils removed. There, a nurse
scandalized him by itemizing the qualities she sought in a lover.
He was already on guard against the forward behavior of the
American woman, "who knows full well the beauties of her body,
her face, her exciting eyes, her full lips, her bulging breasts, her full
buttocks and her smooth legs. She wears bright colors that awaken
the primitive sexual instincts, hiding nothing, but adding to that
the thrilling laugh and the bold look." One can imagine what an
irresistible object of sexual teasing he must have been.

News came of the assassination of Hasan al-Banna, the
Supreme Guide of the Society of the Muslim Brothers, on February 12, in Cairo. Qutb relates that there was a hubbub in the street

outside his hospital window. He inquired about the reason for the festivities. "Today the enemy of Christianity in the East was killed," he says the doctors told him. "Today, Hasan al-Banna was murdered." It is difficult to credit that Americans, in 1949, were sufficiently invested in Egyptian politics to rejoice at the news of Banna's death. The *New York Times* did report his murder. "Sheikh Hasan's followers were fanatically devoted to him, and many of them proclaimed that he alone would be able to save the Arab and Islamic worlds," the paper noted. But for Qutb, lying in his hospital bed in a strange and distant country, the news came as a profound shock. Although they had never met, Qutb and Banna had known each other by reputation. They had been born within days of each other, in October 1906, and attended the same school, Dar al-Ulum, a teacher-training school in Cairo, although at different times. Like Qutb, Banna was precocious and charismatic, but he was also a man of action. He founded the Muslim Brothers in 1928, with the goal of turning Egypt into an Islamic state. Within a few years, the Brothers had spread across the country, and then throughout the Arab world, planting the seeds of the coming Islamic insurgence.

Banna's voice was stilled just as Qutb's book *Social Justice in Islam* was being published—the book that would make his reputation as an important Islamic thinker. Qutb had held himself pointedly apart from the organization that Banna created, even though he inclined to similar views about the political uses of Islam; the death of his contemporary and intellectual rival, however, cleared the way for his conversion to the Muslim Brothers. This was a turning point, both in Qutb's life and in the destiny of the organization. But at this pregnant moment, the heir apparent to the leadership of the Islamic revival was alone, ill, unrecognized, and very far from home.

As it happened, Qutb's presence in Washington was not completely overlooked. One evening he was entertained in the home of James Heyworth-Dunne, a British Orientalist and a convert to Islam, who spoke to Qutb about the danger of the Muslim Brothers, which he said was blocking the modernization of the Muslim world. "If the Brothers succeed in coming to power, Egypt will never progress and will stand as an obstacle to civilization," he reportedly told Qutb. Then he offered to translate Qutb's new book into English and pay him a fee of ten thousand dollars, a fantastic sum for such an obscure book. Qutb refused. He later speculated that Heyworth-Dunne was attempting to recruit him to the CIA. In any case, he said, "I decided to enter the Brotherhood even before I left the house."

GREELEY, COLORADO, was a flourishing agricultural community northeast of Denver when the recuperating Qutb arrived in the summer of 1949 to attend classes at the Colorado State College of Education.* At the time, the college enjoyed the reputation of being one of the most progressive teaching institutions in America. Summer courses were always swollen with teachers from around the country who came to take advanced degrees and enjoy the cool weather and the splendid mountains nearby. In the evenings, there were symphonies, lectures, Chautauqua programs, and outdoor theatrical presentations on the leafy commons of the college. The college set up circus tents to house the spillover classes.

Qutb spent six months in Greeley, the longest period he stayed in any one American town. Greeley offered an extreme contrast to his disagreeable experiences in the fast-paced cities of New York and Washington. Indeed, there were few places in the country that should have seemed more congenial to Qutb's sharpened moral sensibilities. Greeley had been founded in 1870 as a temperance colony by Nathan Meeker, the agricultural editor of the *New York Tribune*. Meeker had formerly lived in southern Illinois, near Cairo, above the convergence of the Ohio and the Mississippi, in the "Little Egypt" portion of that state. He had come to believe that the greatest civilizations were founded in river valleys, and so he established his colony in the rich delta between the Cache la Poudre and the South Platte rivers. Through irrigation, Meeker hoped to transform the "Great American Desert" into an

*Now the University of Northern Colorado.

agricultural paradise—just as Egyptians had done since the beginning of civilization. Meeker's editor at the *Tribune*, Horace Greeley, vigorously supported the idea, and his namesake city soon became one of the most highly publicized planned communities in the nation.

Greeley's early settlers were not youthful pioneers; they were middle class and middle-aged. They traveled by train, not by wagon or stagecoach, and they brought their values and their standards with them. They intended to establish a community that would serve as a model for the cities of the future, one that drew upon the mandatory virtues required of every settler: industry, moral rectitude, and temperance. Surely, on such a foundation, a purified and prosperous civilization would emerge. Indeed, by the time Sayyid Qutb stepped off the train, Greeley was the most substantial settlement between Denver and Cheyenne.

Family life was the center of Greeley society; there were no bars or liquor stores, and there seemed to be a church on every corner. The college boasted one of the finest music departments in the country, with frequent concerts that the music-loving Qutb must have enjoyed. In the evenings, illustrious educators spoke at the lyceum. James Michener, who had recently won the Pulitzer Prize for his novel *Tales of the South Pacific*, returned to teach a writing workshop at the school where he had studied and taught from 1936 to 1941. At last Qutb had stumbled into a community that exalted the same pursuits that he held so dear: education, music, art, literature, and religion. "The small city of Greeley that I now reside in is beautiful, beautiful," he wrote soon after he arrived. "Every house is like a flowering plant and the streets are like garden pathways. One observes the owners of these homes toiling away in their leisure time, watering their yards and manicuring their gardens. This is all they appear to do." The frantic pace of life that Qutb objected to in New York was far away. There was a front-page article in the *Greeley Tribune* that summer chronicling a turtle's successful crossing of a downtown street.

And yet even in Greeley there were disturbing currents under the surface, which Qutb soon detected. A mile south of campus there was a small community of saloons and liquor stores named Garden City. Here the teetotalers of Greeley held no sway. The town got its name during the Prohibition era, when local rumrunners hid bottles of liquor inside watermelons, which they sold to students at the college. Whenever there was a party, the students would visit "the garden" to stock up on supplies. Qutb would have been struck by the disparity between Greeley's sober face and the demimonde of Garden City. Indeed, the downfall of America's temperance movement earned Qutb's disdain because he believed that the country had failed to make a spiritual commitment to sobriety, which only an all-encompassing system such as Islam could hope to enforce.

America made him sharply aware of himself as a man of color. In one of the cities he visited (he doesn't say where) he witnessed a black man being beaten by a white mob: "They were kicking him with their shoes until his blood and flesh mixed in the public road." One can imagine how threatened this dark-skinned traveler must have felt. Even the liberal settlement of Greeley was on edge because of racial fears. There were very few black families in the town. Most of the Ute Indian population had been run out of the state after a battle that left fourteen cavalrymen dead and Nathan Meeker, the founder of Greeley, without his scalp. In the twenties, Mexican labor was brought in to work in the fields and slaughterhouses. Although the signs forbidding Mexicans to remain in town after dark had been taken down, the Catholic church still had a separate entrance for nonwhites, who were supposed to sit upstairs. In the handsome park behind the courthouse, Anglos kept to the south side and Hispanics to the north.

The international students at the college occupied an uneasy place in this charged racial environment. Students from Africa, Latin America, and Asia, as well as a number of Hawaiians, formed the core of the International Club, which Qutb joined. The college also hosted a small Middle Eastern community, including recent Palestinian refugees and several members of the Iraqi royal family. For the most part, they were well treated by the citizens of Greeley, who often invited them into their homes for meals and holidays. Once, Qutb and several friends were turned away from a movie theater because the owner thought they were black. "But we're Egyptians," one of the group explained. The owner apologized and offered to let them in, but Qutb refused, galled by the fact that black Egyptians could be admitted but black Americans could not.

Despite the tensions of the town, the college maintained a progressive attitude toward race. During the summer sessions students from the Negro teachers colleges of the South came to Greeley in abundance, but there were only a couple of black students during the regular school year. One of them was Jaime McClendon, the school's star football player, who was a member of the International Club and roomed with one of the Palestinians. Because the barbers in Greeley refused to serve him, he had to drive to Denver every month to get his hair cut. Finally, several of the Arab students escorted him to the local barbershop and refused to leave until McClendon was served. Qutb would later write that "racism had brought America down from the summit to the foot of the mountain—taking the rest of humanity down with it."

The 1949 football season was a dismal one for the Colorado State College of Education. McClendon sat out the season with an injury, and the team lost every game, including a memorable defeat (103–0) to the University of Wyoming. The spectacle of American football simply confirmed Qutb's view of its primitiveness. "The foot does not play any role in the game," he reported. "Instead, each player attempts to take the ball in his hands, run with it or throw it to the goal, while the players on the other team hinder him by any means, including kicking in the stomach, or violently breaking his arms or legs. . . . Meantime, the fans cry out, 'Break his neck! Crack his head!' "

It was the women, however, who posed the real threat to this lonely Egyptian bachelor. Far more than most settlements in the American West, Greeley expressed a powerfully feminine aesthetic. The city had not been settled by miners or trappers or railroad workers who lived in a world largely without women; from the beginning, Greeley had been populated by well-educated families. The female influence was evident in the cozy houses with their ample front porches, the convenient and well-ordered shops, the handsome public schools, the low-slung architecture, and the comparatively liberal political climate, but nowhere was it more powerfully expressed than in the college itself. Forty-two percent of the 2,135 students enrolled during the fall semester were women, at a time when the national average of female enrollment was about 30 percent. There were no departments of business or engineering; instead, three great schools dominated the college: education, music, and theater. City girls from Denver and Phoenix, country girls from the farms and ranches of the plains, and girls from the little mountain towns—all of them were drawn to the college because of its national reputation and the sense of entitlement that women were awarded on its campus. Here, among the yellow-brick buildings that embraced the great commons, the girls of the West could sample the freedom that most American women would not fully enjoy for decades to come.

In this remote Western town, Sayyid Qutb had moved ahead of his time. He was experiencing women who were living beyond most of their contemporaries in terms of their assumptions about themselves and their place in society—and consequently in their relations with men. "The issue of sexual relationships is simply biological," one of the college women explained to Qutb. "You Orientals complicate this simple matter by introducing a moral element to it. The stallion and the mare, the bull and the cow, the ram and the ewe, the rooster and the hen—none of them consider moral consequences when they have intercourse. And therefore life goes on, simple, easy and carefree." The fact that the woman was a teacher made this statement all the more subversive, in Qutb's opinion, since she would be polluting generations of young people with her amoral philosophy.

Qutb began his studies in the summer, auditing a course in elementary English composition. By fall, he was sufficiently confident of his English to attempt three graduate courses in education and a course in elocution. He was determined to master the language, since he harbored the secret goal of writing a book in English. One can appreciate the level of his achievement by

examining an odd and rather disturbing essay he wrote, titled
"The World Is an Undutiful Boy!", which appeared in the student
literary magazine, *Fulcrum,* in the fall of 1949, only a year after he
arrived in America. "There was an ancient legend in Egypt," he
wrote. "When the god of wisdom and knowledge created History,
he gave him a great writing book and a big pen, and said to him,
'Go walking on this earth, and write notes about everything you
see or hear.' History did as the god suggested. He came upon a
wise and beautiful woman who was gently teaching a young boy:

> History looked at her with great astonishment and cried,
> "Who is it?" raising his face to the sky.
> "She is Egypt," his god answered. "She is Egypt and that lit-
> tle boy is the world . . ."
> Why did those ancient Egyptians hold this belief? Because
> they were very advanced and possessed a great civilization before
> any other country. Egypt was a civilized country when other
> peoples were living in forests. Egypt taught Greece, and Greece
> taught Europe.
> What happened when the little boy grew up?
> When he grew up, he had thrown out his nurse, his kind
> nurse! He struck her, trying to kill her. I am sorry. This is not a
> figure of speech. This is a fact. This is what actually happened.
> When we came here [presumably, to the United Nations] to
> appeal to England for our rights, the world helped England
> against the justice. When we came here to appeal against Jews,
> the world helped the Jews against the justice. During the war
> between Arab and Jews, the world helped the Jews, too.
> Oh! What an undutiful world! What an undutiful boy!

Qutb was quite a bit older than most of the other students at
the school, and he naturally held himself somewhat apart. There
is a photograph of him in the campus bulletin showing a copy of
one of his books to Dr. William Ross, the president of the college.
Qutb is identified as "a famous Egyptian author" and "a noted
educator," so he must have been accorded some respectful notice
by his peers on the faculty, but he socialized mainly with the for-

eign students. One evening, the Arab students held an International Night, where they prepared traditional Arabian meals, and Qutb acted as host, explaining each dish. Otherwise, he spent most of his time in his room listening to classical records on his turntable.

There were polkas and square dances in town several times a week, and the college brought in well-known jazz bands. Two of the most popular songs that year were "Some Enchanted Evening" and "Bali Hai," both from the musical *South Pacific*, based on Michener's novel, and they must have been in the air constantly in Greeley. It was the end of the big band era; rock and roll was still over the horizon. "Jazz is the American music, created by Negroes to satisfy their primitive instincts—their love of noise and their appetite for sexual arousal," Qutb wrote, showing he was not immune to racial pronouncements. "The American is not satisfied with jazz music unless it is accompanied by noisy singing. As the volume increases, accompanied by unbearable pain to the ears, so does the excitement of the audience, their voices rising, their hands clapping, till one can hear nothing at all."

On Sundays the college did not serve food, and students had to fend for themselves. Many of the international students, including Muslims like Qutb, would visit one of the more than fifty churches in Greeley on Sunday evening, where, after services, there were potluck dinners and sometimes a dance. "The dancing hall was decorated with yellow, red and blue lights," Qutb recalled on one occasion. "The room convulsed with the feverish music from the gramophone. Dancing naked legs filled the hall, arms draped around the waists, chests met chests, lips met lips, and the atmosphere was full of love." The minister gazed upon this sight approvingly, and even dimmed the lights to enhance the romantic atmosphere. Then he put on a song titled "Baby, It's Cold Outside," a sly ballad from an Esther Williams movie that summer, *Neptune's Daughter*. "The minister paused to watch his young charges swaying to the rhythms of this seductive song, then he left them to enjoy this pleasant, innocent night," Qutb concluded sarcastically.

In December a new tone entered his letters to his friends. He began talking about his "estrangement," in both soul and body. By then he had withdrawn from all his classes.

Sayyid Qutb spent another eight months in America, most of that time in California. The America he perceived was vastly different from the way most Americans viewed their culture. In literature and movies, and especially in the new medium of television, Americans portrayed themselves as sexually curious but inexperienced, whereas Qutb's America was more like the one sketched by the Kinsey Report. Qutb saw a spiritual wasteland, and yet belief in God was nearly unanimous in the United States at the time. It was easy to be misled by the proliferation of churches, religious books, and religious festivals, Qutb maintained; the fact remained that materialism was the real American god. "The soul has no value to Americans," he wrote to one friend. "There has been a Ph.D. dissertation about the best way to clean dishes, which seems more important to them than the Bible or religion." Many Americans were beginning to come to similar conclusions. The theme of alienation in American life was just beginning to cast a pall over the postwar party. In many respects, Qutb's analysis, though harsh, was only premature.

CERTAINLY THE TRIP HAD NOT accomplished what Qutb's friends in Egypt had hoped. Instead of becoming liberalized by his experience in America, he returned even more radicalized. Moreover, his sour impressions, when published, would profoundly shape Arab and Muslim perceptions of the new world at a time when their esteem for America and its values had been high.

He also brought home a new and abiding anger about race. "The white man in Europe or America is our number-one enemy," he declared. "The white man crushes us underfoot while we teach our children about his civilization, his universal principles and noble objectives. . . . We are endowing our children with amazement and respect for the master who tramples our honor and enslaves us. Let us instead plant the seeds of hatred, disgust, and revenge in the souls of these children. Let us teach these children from the time their nails are soft that the white man is the enemy of humanity, and that they should destroy him at the first opportunity."

Oddly, the people who knew Qutb in America say he seemed to like the country. They remember him as shy and polite, political but not overtly religious. Once introduced, he never forgot anyone's name, and he rarely voiced any direct criticism of his host country. Perhaps he kept the slights to himself until he could safely broadcast them at home.

It is clear that he was writing not just about America. His central concern was modernity. Modern values—secularism, rationality, democracy, subjectivity, individualism, mixing of the sexes, tolerance, materialism—had infected Islam through the agency of Western colonialism. America now stood for all that. Qutb's polemic was directed at Egyptians who wanted to bend Islam around the modern world. He intended to show that Islam and modernity were completely incompatible. His extraordinary project, which was still emerging, was to take apart the entire political and philosophical structure of modernity and return Islam to its unpolluted origins. For him, that was a state of divine oneness, the complete unity of God and humanity. Separation of the sacred and the secular, state and religion, science and theology, mind and spirit—these were the hallmarks of modernity, which had captured the West. But Islam could not abide such divisions. In Islam, he believed, divinity could not be diminished without being destroyed. Islam was total and uncompromising. It was God's final word. Muslims had forgotten this in their enchantment with the West. Only by restoring Islam to the center of their lives, their laws, and their government could Muslims hope to recapture their rightful place as the dominant culture in the world. That was their duty, not only to themselves but also to God.

QUTB RETURNED TO CAIRO on a TWA flight on August 20, 1950. Like him, the country had become more openly radical.

Racked by corruption and assassination, humiliated in the 1948 war against Israel, the Egyptian government ruled without popular authority, at the whim of the occupying power. Although the British had nominally withdrawn from Cairo, concentrating their forces in the Suez Canal Zone, the hand of empire still weighed heavy on the restive capital. The British were present in the clubs and hotels, the bars and movie theaters, the European restaurants and department stores of this sophisticated, decadent city. As his people hissed, the obese Turkish king, Farouk, raced around Cairo in one of his two hundred red automobiles (his were the only cars in the country allowed to be red), seducing—if one can call it that—young girls, or else sailing his fleet of yachts to the gambling ports of the Riviera, where his debauchery tested historic standards. Meanwhile, the usual measures of despair—poverty, unemployment, illiteracy, and disease—grew recklessly out of control. Governments revolved meaninglessly as stocks fell and the smart money fled the teetering country.

In this rotten political environment, one organization steadily acted in the interests of the people. The Muslim Brothers created their own hospitals, schools, factories, and welfare societies; they even formed their own army and fought alongside other Arab troops in Palestine. They acted less as a countergovernment than as a countersociety, which was indeed their goal. Their founder, Hasan al-Banna, had refused to think of his organization as a mere political party; it was meant to be a challenge to the entire idea of politics. Banna completely rejected the Western model of secular, democratic government, which contradicted his notion of universal Islamic rule. "It is the nature of Islam to dominate, not to be dominated, to impose its law on all nations, and to extend its power to the entire planet," he wrote.

The fact that the Brothers provided the only organized, effective resistance to the British occupation ensured their legitimacy in the eyes of the members of Egypt's lower-middle class, who formed the core of Brothers membership. The government officially dissolved the Muslim Brothers in 1948, following the killing of the hated police chief Salim Zaki during a riot at the medical school of Cairo University; but by that time the Brothers had more than a million members and supporters—out of a total Egyptian population of 18 million. Although the Brotherhood was a mass movement, it was also intimately organized into cooperative "families"—cells that contained no more than five members each, giving it a spongy, clandestine quality that proved difficult to detect and impossible to eradicate.

There was a violent underside to the Society of the Muslim Brothers, which would become deeply rooted in the Islamist movement. With Banna's approval, a "secret apparatus" formed within the organization. Although most of the Brothers' activity was directed at the British and at Egypt's quickly dwindling Jewish population, they were also behind the bombings of two Cairo movie theaters, the murder of a prominent judge, and the actual assassinations—as well as many attempts—of several members of government. By the time the government murdered Banna, in an act of self-protection, the secret apparatus posed a powerful and uncontrollable authority within the Brotherhood.

In retaliation for raids against their bases, British forces assaulted a police barracks in the canal city of Ismailia in January 1952, firing at point-blank range for twelve hours and killing fifty police conscripts. Immediately upon hearing the news, agitated mobs formed on the streets of Cairo. They burned the old British haunts of the Turf Club and the famous Shepheard's Hotel. The arsonists, led by members of the Muslim Brothers' secret apparatus, slashed the hoses of the fire engines that arrived to put out the flames, then moved on to the European quarter, burning every movie house, casino, bar, and restaurant in the center of the city. By morning, a thick black cloud of smoke lingered over the ruins. At least 30 people had been killed, 750 buildings destroyed, fifteen thousand people put out of work, and twelve thousand made homeless. Cosmopolitan Cairo was dead.

Something new was about to be born, however. In July of that year, a military junta, dominated by a charismatic young army colonel, Gamal Abdul Nasser, packed King Farouk onto his yacht and seized control of the government, which fell without resistance. For the first time in twenty-five hundred years, Egypt was ruled by Egyptians.

QUTB HAD TAKEN UP his old job in the Ministry of Education and returned to his former home in the suburb of Helwan, which was once an ancient spa known for its healing sulfur waters. He occupied a two-story villa on a wide street with jacaranda trees in the front yard. He filled an entire wall of his salon with his collection of classical music albums.

Some of the planning for the revolution had taken place in this very room, where Nasser and the military plotters of the coup met to coordinate with the Muslim Brothers. Several of the officers, including Anwar al-Sadat, Nasser's eventual successor, had close ties to the Brotherhood. If the coup attempt failed, the Brothers were to help the officers escape. In the event, the government fell so easily that the Brothers had little real participation in the actual coup.

Qutb published an open letter to the leaders of the revolution, advising them that the only way to purge the moral corruption of the old regime was to impose a "just dictatorship" that would grant political standing to "the virtuous alone." Nasser then invited Qutb to become an advisor to the Revolutionary Command Council. Qutb hoped for a cabinet position in the new government, but when he was offered a choice between being the minister of education or general manager of Cairo radio, he turned both posts down. Nasser eventually appointed him head of the editorial board of the revolution, but Qutb quit the post after a few months. The prickly negotiation between the two men reflected the initial close cooperation of the Brothers and the Free Officers in a social revolution that both organizations thought was theirs to control. In fact, neither faction had the popular authority to rule.

In a story that would be repeated again and again in the Middle East, the contest quickly narrowed to a choice between a military society and a religious one. Nasser had the army and the Brothers had the mosques. Nasser's political dream was of

pan-Arab socialism, modern, egalitarian, secular, and industrial-
ized, in which individual lives were dominated by the overwhelming presence of the welfare state. His dream had little to do
with the theocratic Islamic government that Qutb and the Brothers espoused. The Islamists wanted to completely reshape society,
from the top down, imposing Islamic values on all aspects of life,
so that every Muslim could achieve his purest spiritual expression. That could be accomplished only through a strict imposition
of the Sharia, the legal code drawn from the Quran and the sayings of the Prophet Mohammed, which governs all parts of life.
Anything less than that, the Islamists argued, was not Islam; it
was *jahiliyya*—the pagan world before the Prophet received his
message. Qutb opposed egalitarianism because the Quran stated:
"We have created you class upon class." He rejected nationalism
because it warred with the ideal of Muslim unity. In retrospect, it
is difficult to see how Qutb and Nasser could have misunderstood
each other so profoundly. The only thing they had in common
was the grandeur of their respective visions and their hostility to
democratic rule.

Nasser threw Qutb in prison for the first time in 1954, but after
three months he let him out and allowed him to become the editor
of the Muslim Brothers magazine, *Al-Ikhwan al-Muslimin*. Presumably Nasser hoped his display of mercy would enhance his standing with the Islamists and keep them from turning against the
increasingly secular aims of the new government; he may also
have believed that Qutb had been chastened by his time in prison.
Like the former king, Nasser always underestimated his adversary's intransigence.

Qutb wrote a number of sharply critical editorials calling for
jihad against the British at the very time Nasser was negotiating a
treaty that would nominally end the occupation. In August 1954
the government shut the magazine down. By that time, ill will
between the Brothers and the military leaders had hardened into
cold opposition. It was clear that Nasser had no intention of insti-
tuting an Islamic revolution, despite his highly publicized pilgrimage to Mecca that same month. Qutb was so infuriated that

he formed a secret alliance with the Egyptian communists in an abortive effort to bring Nasser down.

The ideological war over Egypt's future reached a climax on the night of October 26, 1954. Nasser was addressing an immense crowd in a public square in Alexandria. The entire country was listening to the radio as a member of the Muslim Brothers stepped forward and fired eight shots at the Egyptian president, wounding a guard but missing Nasser. It was the turning point in Nasser's presidency. Over the chaos of the panicked crowd, Nasser continued speaking even as the gunshots rang out. "Let them kill Nasser! What is Nasser but one among many?" he cried. "I am alive, and even if I die, all of you are Gamal Abdul Nasser!" Had the gunman succeeded, he might have been hailed as a hero, but the failure gave Nasser a popularity he had never enjoyed until then. He immediately put that to use by having six conspirators hanged and placing thousands of others in concentration camps. Qutb was charged with being a member of the Muslim Brothers' secret apparatus that was responsible for the assassination attempt. Nasser thought he had crushed the Brothers once and for all.

STORIES ABOUT SAYYID QUTB'S SUFFERING in prison have formed a kind of Passion play for Islamic fundamentalists. It is said that Qutb had a high fever when he was arrested; nonetheless, the state-security officers handcuffed him and forced him to walk to prison. He fainted several times along the way. For hours he was held in a cell with vicious dogs, and then, during long periods of interrogation, he was beaten. "The principles of the revolution have indeed been applied to us," he said, as he raised his shirt to show the court the marks of torture.

Through confessions of other members of the Brotherhood, the prosecution presented a sensational scenario of a planned takeover of the government, involving the destruction of Alexandria and Cairo, blowing up all the bridges over the Nile, and numerous assassinations—an unprecedented campaign of terror, all in the service of turning Egypt into a primitive theocracy. The testimony also demonstrated, however, that the Brothers were too disorganized to accomplish any of these dreadful tasks. Three highly partisan judges, one of them Anwar al-Sadat, oversaw these proceedings. They sentenced Qutb to life in prison, but when his health deteriorated, the sentence was reduced to fifteen years.

Qutb was always frail. He had a weak heart, a delicate stomach, and sciatica, which gave him chronic pain. After a bout of pneumonia when he was thirty years old, he suffered from frequent bronchial problems. He experienced two heart attacks in prison, and bleeding in his lungs, which may have been an effect of torture, or tuberculosis. He moved to the prison hospital in May 1955, where he stayed for the next ten years, spending much of his time writing a lucid, highly personal, eight-volume commentary called *In the Shade of the Quran*, which by itself would have assured his place as one of the most significant modern Islamic thinkers. But his political views were darkening.

Some of the imprisoned Brothers staged a strike and refused to leave their cells. They were gunned down. Twenty-three members were killed and forty-six injured. Qutb was in the prison hospital when the wounded men were brought in. Shaken and terrified, Qutb wondered how fellow Muslims could treat each other in such a way.

Qutb came to a characteristically radical conclusion: His jailers had denied God by serving Nasser and his secular state. Therefore, they were not Muslims. In Qutb's mind, he had excommunicated them from the Islamic community. The name for this in Arabic is *takfir*. Although that is not the language he used, the principle of excommunication, which had been used to justify so much bloodshed within Islam throughout its history, had been born again in that prison hospital room.

Through family and friends, he managed to smuggle out, bit by bit, a manifesto called *Milestones* (*Ma'alim fi al-Tariq*). It circulated underground for years in the form of lengthy letters to his brother and sisters, who were also Islamic activists. The voice of the letters was urgent, passionate, intimate, and despairing.

When finally published in 1964, the book was quickly banned, but not before five printings had been run off. Anyone caught with a copy could be charged with sedition. Its ringing apocalyptic tone may be compared with Rousseau's *Social Contract* and Lenin's *What Is to Be Done?*—with similar bloody consequences.

"Mankind today is on the brink of a precipice," Qutb posits at the beginning. Humanity is threatened not only by nuclear annihilation but also by the absence of values. The West has lost its vitality, and Marxism has failed. "At this crucial and bewildering juncture, the turn of Islam and the Muslim community has arrived." But before Islam can lead, it must regenerate itself.

Qutb divides the world into two camps, Islam and *jahiliyya*, the period of ignorance and barbarity that existed before the divine message of the Prophet Mohammed. Qutb uses the term to encompass all of modern life: manners, morals, art, literature, law, even much of what passed as Islamic culture. He was opposed not to modern technology but to the worship of science, which he believed had alienated humanity from natural harmony with creation. Only a complete rejection of rationalism and Western values offered the slim hope of the redemption of Islam. This was the choice: pure, primitive Islam or the doom of mankind.

His revolutionary argument placed nominally Islamic governments in the crosshairs of jihad. "The Muslim community has long ago vanished from existence," Qutb contends. It was "crushed under the weight of those false laws and teachings which are not even remotely related to the Islamic teachings." Humanity cannot be saved unless Muslims recapture the glory of their earliest and purest expression. "We need to initiate the movement of Islamic revival in some Muslim country," he writes, in order to fashion an example that will eventually lead Islam to its destiny of world dominion. "There should be a vanguard which sets out with this determination and then keeps walking the path," Qutb declared. "I have written *Milestones* for this vanguard, which I consider to be a waiting reality about to be materialized." Those words would echo in the ears of generations of young Muslims who were looking for a role to play in history.

In 1964 President Abdul Salam Aref of Iraq personally prevailed

on Nasser to grant Qutb a parole, and invited him to Iraq, promising an important government post. Qutb declined, saying that
Egypt still needed him. He immediately returned to his villa in Helwan and began conspiring against the revolutionary government.

From prison, Qutb had been able to regenerate the secret
apparatus. The government of Saudi Arabia, fearing the influence
of Nasser's revolution, covertly supplied Qutb's group with
money and arms, but the movement was riddled with informers.
Two men confessed and named Qutb in a plot to overthrow the
government and assassinate public figures. Only six months after
Qutb left prison, the security police arrested him again at a beach
resort east of Alexandria.

The trial of Sayyid Qutb and forty-two of his followers opened
on April 19, 1966, and lasted nearly three months. "The time has
come for a Muslim to give his head in order to proclaim the birth
of the Islamic movement," Qutb defiantly declared when the trial
began. He bitterly acknowledged that the anticolonialist new
Egypt was more oppressive than the regime it had replaced. There
was little effort on the part of the judges to appear impartial;
indeed, the chief judge often took on the role of the prosecutor,
and hooting spectators cheered the grand charade. The only real
evidence produced against Qutb was his book, *Milestones.* He
received his death sentence gratefully. "Thank God," he declared.
"I performed jihad for fifteen years until I earned this martyrdom."

To the very end, Nasser misjudged his flinty adversary. As
demonstrators filled the Cairo streets protesting the impending
execution, Nasser realized that Qutb was more dangerous to him
dead than alive. He dispatched Sadat to the prison, where Qutb
received him wearing the traditional red burlap pajamas of a condemned man. Sadat promised that if Qutb appealed his sentence,
Nasser would show mercy; indeed, Nasser was even willing to
offer him the post of minister of education once again. Qutb
refused. Then Qutb's sister Hamida, who was also in prison, was
brought to him. "The Islamic movement needs you," she pleaded.
"Write the words." Qutb responded, "My words will be stronger
if they kill me."

Sayyid Qutb was hanged after dawn prayers on August 29, 1966. The government refused to surrender his corpse to his family, fearing that his grave would become a shrine to his followers. The radical Islamist threat seemed to have come to an end. But Qutb's vanguard was already hearing the music.

2

The Sporting Club

AYMAN AL-ZAWAHIRI, the man who would lead Qutb's vanguard, grew up in a quiet middle-class suburb called Maadi, five miles south of the noisy chaos of Cairo. It was an unlikely breeding ground for revolution. A consortium of Egyptian Jewish financiers, intending to create a kind of English village amid the mango and guava plantations and the Bedouin settlements on the eastern bank of the Nile, began selling lots in the first decade of the twentieth century. The developers regulated everything, from the height of the garden fences to the color of the shutters on the grand villas lining the streets. Like Nathan Meeker, the founder of Greeley, the creators of Maadi dreamed of a utopian society, one that was not only safe and clean and orderly but also tolerant and at ease in the modern world. They planted eucalyptus trees to repel flies and mosquitoes, and gardens to perfume the air with the fragrance of roses, jasmine, and bougainvillea. Many of the early settlers were British military officers and civil servants, whose wives started garden clubs and literary salons; they were followed by Jewish families, who by the end of World War II made up nearly a third of Maadi's population. After the war, Maadi evolved into a mélange of expatriate Europeans, American businessmen and missionaries, and a certain type of Egyptian— typically one who spoke French at dinner and followed the cricket matches.

The center of this cosmopolitan community was the Maadi Sporting Club. Founded at a time when the British still occupied

Egypt, the club was unusual in that it actually admitted Egyptians. Community business was often conducted on the all-sand eighteen-hole golf course, with the Giza pyramids and the palmy Nile as a backdrop. As high tea was being served to the Brits in the lounge, Nubian waiters bearing icy glasses of Nescafé glided among the pashas and princesses sunbathing at the pool. High-stepping flamingos waded through the lilies in the garden pond. The Maadi Club became an ideal expression of the founders' vision of Egypt—sophisticated, secular, ethnically diverse but married to British notions of class.

The careful regulations of the founders could not withstand the crush of Cairo's burgeoning population, however, and in the 1960s another Maadi took root within this exotic community. Road 9 ran beside the train tracks that separated the tony side of Maadi from the *baladi* district—the native part of town, where the irrepressible ancient squalor of Egypt unfurled itself. Donkey carts clopped along the unpaved streets past peanut vendors and yam salesmen hawking their wares and fly-studded carcasses hanging in the butcher shops. There was also, on this side of town, a narrow slice of the middle class—teachers and midlevel bureaucrats among them—who were drawn by Maadi's cleaner air and the nearly impossible prospect of crossing the tracks and being welcomed into the club.

In 1960 Dr. Mohammed Rabie al-Zawahiri and his wife, Umayma, moved from Heliopolis to Maadi. Rabie and Umayma belonged to two of the most prominent families in Egypt. The Zawahiri (pronounced za-*wah*-iri) clan was already on its way to becoming a medical dynasty. Rabie was a professor of pharmacology at Ain Shams University. His brother was a highly regarded dermatologist and an expert on venereal diseases. The tradition they established would continue in the next generation: a 1995 obituary in a Cairo newspaper for Kashif al-Zawahiri, an engineer, mentioned forty-six members of the family, thirty-one of whom were doctors or chemists or pharmacists scattered throughout the Arab world and the United States; among the others were an ambassador, a judge, and a member of parliament.

The Zawahiri name, however, was associated above all with

religion. In 1929 Rabie's uncle Mohammed al-Ahmadi al-Zawahiri became the rector of al-Azhar, the thousand-year-old university in the heart of Old Cairo, which is still the center of Islamic learning in the Middle East. The leader of that institution enjoys a kind of papal status in the Muslim world. Imam Mohammed is remembered as the institution's great modernizer, although he was highly unpopular at the time and eventually was driven out of office by student and faculty strikes protesting his policies. Rabie's father and grandfather were al-Azhar scholars as well.

Umayma Azzam, Rabie's wife, was from a clan that was equally distinguished, but wealthier and more political. Her father, Dr. Abdul Wahhab Azzam, was the president of Cairo University and the founder of King Saud University in Riyadh. Along with his busy academic life, he also served as the Egyptian ambassador to Pakistan, Yemen, and Saudi Arabia. He was the most prominent pan-Arab intellectual of his time. His uncle had been a founder and the first secretary-general of the Arab League.

Despite their remarkable pedigrees, Professor Zawahiri and Umayma settled into an apartment on Street 100, on the *baladi* side of the tracks. Later they rented a duplex at Number 10, Street 154, near the train station. Maadi society held no interest for them. They were religious, but not overtly pious. Umayma went about unveiled, but that was not unusual; public displays of religious zeal were rare in Egypt then and almost unheard-of in Maadi. There were more churches than mosques in the neighborhood, and a thriving Jewish synagogue as well.

Children quickly filled the Zawahiri home. The oldest, Ayman and his twin sister, Umnya, were born on June 19, 1951. The twins were at the top of their classes all the way through medical school. A younger sister, Heba, born three years later, also became a doctor. The two other children, Mohammed and Hussein, trained as architects.

Obese, bald, and slightly cross-eyed, Ayman's father had the reputation of being eccentric and absentminded, and yet he was beloved by his students and neighborhood children. He spent most of his time in the laboratory or in his private medical clinic.

Professor Zawahiri's research occasionally took him to Czechoslovakia, at a time when few Egyptians traveled because of currency restrictions. He always returned loaded with toys. He enjoyed taking the children to the movies at the Maadi Sporting Club, which were open to nonmembers. Young Ayman loved the cartoons and Disney films, which played three nights a week on the outdoor screen. In the summer, the extended family would go to the beach in Alexandria. Life on a professor's salary was often tight, however, especially with five ambitious children to educate. The family never owned a car until Ayman was grown. Like many Egyptian academics, Professor Zawahiri eventually spent several years teaching outside of Egypt—he went to Algeria—to earn a higher income. To economize, the Zawahiris kept hens and ducks behind the house, and the professor bought oranges and mangoes by the crate, which he pressed on the children as a natural source of vitamin C. Although he was a druggist by training, he was opposed to consuming chemicals.

For anyone living in Maadi in the fifties and sixties, there was one defining social standard: membership in the Maadi Sporting Club. All of Maadi society revolved around it. Because the Zawahiris never joined, Ayman would always be curtained off from the center of power and status. The family developed the reputation of being conservative and a little backward—*saeedis*, to use the term applied to them, referring to people from a district in Upper Egypt, which informally translates to "hicks."

At one end of Maadi, surrounded by green playing fields and tennis courts, was the private, British-built preparatory school for boys, Victoria College. The students attended classes in coats and ties. One of its best-known graduates was a talented cricket player named Michel Chalhub; after he became a film actor, he took the name Omar Sharif. Edward Said, the Palestinian scholar and author, attended the school, along with Jordan's future king, Hussein.

Ayman al-Zawahiri, however, attended the state secondary school, a modest, low-slung building behind a green gate on the opposite side of the suburb. It was for kids from the wrong side of Road 9. The students of the two schools existed in different worlds, never meeting each other even in sports. Whereas Victoria College measured its educational achievements by European standards, the state school had its back to the West. Inside the green gate, the schoolyard was run by bullies and the classrooms by tyrants. A physically vulnerable young boy such as Ayman had to create strategies to survive.

As a child, Ayman had a round face, wary eyes, and a mouth that was flat and unsmiling. He was a bookworm who excelled in his studies and hated violent sports—he thought they were "inhumane." From an early age he was known for being devout, and he would often attend prayers at the Hussein Sidki Mosque; an unimposing annex of a large apartment building, it was named after a famous actor who had renounced his profession because it was ungodly. No doubt Ayman's interest in religion seemed natural in a family with so many distinguished religious scholars, but it added to his image of being soft and otherworldly.

He was an excellent student, and invariably earned the respect of his teachers. His classmates thought he was a "genius," but he was introspective and often appeared to be daydreaming in class. Once, the headmaster sent a note to Professor Zawahiri saying that Ayman had skipped a test. The professor replied, "From tomorrow, you will have the honor of being the headmaster of Ayman al-Zawahiri. In the future, you will be proud." Indeed, Ayman earned perfect grades with little effort.

Although others saw Ayman as serious nearly all the time, he would show a more playful side at home. "When he laughed, he would shake all over—*yanni*, it was from the heart," said his uncle Mahfouz Azzam, an attorney in Maadi.

Ayman's father died in 1995. His mother, Umayma Azzam, still lives in Maadi, in a comfortable apartment above an appliance store. A wonderful cook, she is famous for her *kunafa*—a pastry of shredded phyllo filled with cheese and nuts and drenched in orange-blossom syrup. She was a child of the landed upper class and inherited several plots of rich farmland in Giza and the Fayoum Oasis from her father, which provide her with a modest independent income. Ayman and his mother shared an intense love of literature; she would memorize poems he sent—often odes of love for her.

Zawahiri's uncle Mahfouz, the patriarch of the Azzam clan, observed that although Ayman followed the Zawahiri medical tradition, he was actually closer to his mother's side of the family—the political side. Since the first Egyptian parliament, more than 150 years ago, there have been Azzams in government, but always in the opposition. Mahfouz carried on the tradition of resistance, having been imprisoned at the age of fifteen for conspiring against the government. In 1945 Mahfouz was arrested again, in a roundup of militants following the assassination of Prime Minister Ahmed Mahir. "I myself was going to do what Ayman has done," he boasted.

Sayyid Qutb had been Mahfouz Azzam's Arabic teacher in the third grade, in 1936, and Qutb and his young protégé formed a lifelong bond. Later, Azzam wrote for the Muslim Brothers magazine that Qutb published in the early years of the revolution. He then became Qutb's personal lawyer and was one of the last people to see him before his execution. Azzam entered the prison hospital where Qutb was preparing to die. Qutb was calm. He signed a power of attorney, awarding Azzam the authority to dispose of his property; then he gave him his personal Quran, which he inscribed—a treasured relic of the martyr.

Young Ayman al-Zawahiri heard again and again from his beloved uncle Mahfouz about the purity of Qutb's character and the torment he had endured in prison. The effect of these stories can be gauged by an incident that took place sometime in the middle 1960s, when Ayman and his brother Mohammed were walking home from the mosque after dawn prayers. The vice president of Egypt, Hussein al-Shaffei, stopped his car to offer the boys a ride. Shaffei had been one of the judges in the roundup of Islamists in 1954. It was unusual for the Zawahiri boys to ride in a car, much less with the vice president. But Ayman said, "We don't want to get this ride from a man who participated in the courts that killed Muslims."

His stiff-necked defiance of authority at such an early age

shows Zawahiri's personal fearlessness, his self-righteousness, and his total conviction of the truth of his own beliefs—headstrong qualities that would invariably be associated with him in the future and that would propel him into conflict with nearly everyone he would meet. Moreover, his contempt for the authoritarian secular government ensured that he would always be a political outlaw. These rebellious traits, which might have been chaotic in a less disciplined man, were organized and given direction by an abiding mission in his life: to put Qutb's vision into action.

"The Nasserite regime thought that the Islamic movement received a deadly blow with the execution of Sayyid Qutb and his comrades," Zawahiri later wrote. "But the apparent surface calm concealed an immediate interaction with Sayyid Qutb's ideas and the formation of the nucleus of the modern Islamic jihad movement in Egypt." Indeed, the same year that Sayyid Qutb went to the gallows, Ayman al-Zawahiri helped form an underground cell devoted to overthrowing the government and establishing an Islamist state. He was fifteen years old.

"WE WERE A GROUP OF STUDENTS from Maadi High School and other schools," Zawahiri later testified. The members of his cell usually met in each other's homes; sometimes they got together in mosques and then moved to a park or a quiet spot on the boulevard along the Nile. There were five of them in the beginning, and before long Zawahiri became the emir, or leader. He continued to quietly recruit new members to a cause that had virtually no chance of success and could easily have gotten them all killed. "Our means didn't match our aspirations," he conceded in his testimony. But he never questioned his decision.

The prosperity and social position enjoyed by the residents of Maadi, which had insulated them from the political whims of the royal court, now made them feel targeted in revolutionary Egypt. Parents were fearful of expressing their opinions even in front of their children. At the same time, clandestine groups such as the one Zawahiri joined were springing up all over the country. Made up mainly of restless and alienated students, these groups were small, disorganized, and largely unaware of one another. Then came the 1967 war with Israel.

After years of rhetorical attacks on Israel, Nasser demanded the removal of UN peacekeepers in the Sinai and then blockaded the Strait of Tiran to Israeli shipping. Israel responded with an overwhelming preemptive attack that destroyed the entire Egyptian air force within two hours. When Jordan, Iraq, and Syria joined the war against Israel, their air forces were also wiped out that same afternoon. In the next few days Israel captured all of the Sinai, Jerusalem, the West Bank, and the Golan Heights, while crushing the forces of the frontline Arab states. It was a psychological turning point in the history of the modern Middle East. The speed and decisiveness of the Israeli victory in the Six Day War humiliated many Muslims who had believed until then that God favored their cause. They had lost not only their armies and their territories but also faith in their leaders, in their countries, and in themselves. The profound appeal of Islamic fundamentalism in Egypt and elsewhere was born in this shocking debacle. A newly strident voice was heard in the mosques; the voice said that they had been defeated by a force far larger than the tiny country of Israel. God had turned against the Muslims. The only way back to Him was to return to the pure religion. The voice answered despair with a simple formulation: Islam is the solution.

There was in this equation the tacit understanding that God sided with the Jews. Until the end of World War II, there was little precedent in Islam for the anti-Semitism that was now warping the politics and society of the region. Jews had lived safely—although submissively—under Muslim rule for 1,200 years, enjoying full religious freedom; but in the 1930s, Nazi propaganda on Arabic-language shortwave radio, coupled with slanders by Christian missionaries in the region, infected the area with this ancient Western prejudice. After the war Cairo became a sanctuary for Nazis, who advised the military and the government. The rise of the Islamist movement coincided with the decline of fascism, but they overlapped in Egypt, and the germ passed into a new carrier.

The founding of the state of Israel and its startling rise to military dominance unsettled the Arab identity. In the low condition the Arabs found themselves in, they looked upon Israel and recalled the time when the Prophet Mohammed had subjugated the Jews of Medina. They thought about the great wave of Muslim expansion at the point of Arab spears and swords, and they were humbled by the contrast of their proud martial past and their miserable present. History was reversing itself; the Arabs were as fractious and disorganized and marginal as they had been in *jahiliyya* times. Even the Jews dominated them. The voice in the mosque said that the Arabs had let go of the one weapon that gave them real power: faith. Restore the fervor and purity of the religion that had made the Arabs great, and God would once again take their side.

The primary target of the Egyptian Islamists was Nasser's secular regime. In the terminology of jihad, the priority was defeating the "near enemy"—that is, impure Muslim society. The "distant enemy"—the West—could wait until Islam had reformed itself. To Zawahiri and his colleagues that meant, at a minimum, imposing Islamic law in Egypt.

Zawahiri also sought to restore the caliphate, the rule of Islamic clerics, which had formally ended in 1924 following the dissolution of the Ottoman Empire but which had not exercised real power since the thirteenth century. Once the caliphate was established, Zawahiri believed, Egypt would become a rallying point for the rest of the Islamic world, leading it in a jihad against the West. "Then history would make a new turn, God willing," Zawahiri later wrote, "in the opposite direction against the empire of the United States and the world's Jewish government."

NASSER DIED of a sudden heart attack in 1970. His successor, Anwar al-Sadat, desperately needing to establish his political legitimacy, quickly set about making peace with the Islamists. Calling himself the "Believer President" and "the first man of Islam," Sadat offered the Muslim Brothers a deal. In return for their support against the Nasserites and the leftists, he would allow them to preach and to advocate, so long as they renounced violence. He emptied the prisons of Islamists, without realizing the danger they posed to his own regime, especially the younger Brothers who had been radicalized by the writings of Sayyid Qutb.

In October 1973, during the fasting month of Ramadan, Egypt and Syria stunned Israel with simultaneous attacks across the Suez Canal into the occupied Sinai and on the Golan Heights. Although the Syrians were soon beaten back and the Egyptian Third Army was rescued only by UN intervention, it was seen in Egypt as a great face-saving victory, giving Sadat a badly needed political triumph.

Nonetheless, Zawahiri's underground cell began to grow—it had forty members by 1974. Zawahiri was now a tall and slender young man with large black glasses and a moustache that paralleled the flat line of his mouth. His face had grown thinner and his hairline was in retreat. He was a student in the Cairo University medical school, which was aboil with Islamic activism, but Zawahiri had none of the obvious attributes of a fanatic. He wore Western clothes—usually, a coat and tie—and his political involvement was almost completely unknown at the time, even to his family. To the few who knew of his activism, Zawahiri preached against revolution, which was an inherently bloody business, preferring a sudden military action designed to snatch the reins of government in a bold surprise.

He did not completely hide his political feelings, however. Egypt has always had a tradition of turning political misery into humor. A joke that his family recalls Zawahiri telling at this time concerned a poor woman who carried her plump little baby—in colloquial Egyptian Arabic, her *go'alos*—to see the king pass by in his royal procession. "I wish that God would grant that you will be seen in such glory," the woman prayed for her son. A military officer overheard her. "What are you saying?" he demanded. "Are you out of your mind?" But then, twenty years later, the same military officer saw Sadat passing by in a grand procession. "Oh, *go'alos*—you made it!" the officer cried.

In his last year of medical school, Zawahiri gave a campus

tour to an American newsman, Abdallah Schleifer, who later became a professor of media studies at the American University in Cairo. Schleifer was a challenging figure in Zawahiri's life. A gangly, wiry-haired man, six feet five inches tall, sporting a goatee that harked back to his beatnik period in the 1950s, Schleifer bore a striking resemblance to the poet Ezra Pound. He had been brought up in a non-observant Jewish family on Long Island. After going through a Marxist period, and making friends with the Black Panthers and Che Guevara, he happened to encounter the Sufi tradition of Islam during a trip to Morocco in 1962. One meaning of the word "Islam" is to surrender, and that is what happened to Schleifer. He converted, changed his name from Marc to Abdallah, and spent the rest of his professional life in the Middle East. In 1974, when Schleifer first went to Cairo as the bureau chief for NBC News, Zawahiri's uncle Mahfouz Azzam acted as a kind of sponsor for him. An American Jewish convert was a novelty; and Schleifer, for his part, found Mahfouz fascinating. He soon came to feel that he was under the protection of the entire Azzam family.

Schleifer quickly sensed the shift in the student movement in Egypt. Young Islamic activists were appearing on campuses, first in the southern part of the country, then in Cairo. They called themselves al-Gama'a al-Islamiyya—the Islamic Group. Encouraged by Sadat's acquiescent government, which covertly provided them with arms so that they could defend themselves against any attacks by Marxists and Nasserites, the Islamic Group radicalized most of Egypt's universities. Different branches were organized along the same lines as the Muslim Brothers, in small cells called *'anqud*—a bunch of grapes. Within a mere four years, the Islamic Group completely dominated the campuses, and for the first time in the living memory of most Egyptians, male students stopped trimming their beards and female students donned the veil.

Schleifer needed a guide to give him a better understanding of the scene. Through Mahfouz, Schleifer met Zawahiri, who agreed to show him around campus for an off-camera briefing. "He was scrawny and his eyeglasses were extremely prominent," said Schleifer, who was reminded of the radicals he had known in the United States. "I had the feeling that this is what a left-wing City College intellectual looked like thirty years ago." Schleifer watched students painting posters for the demonstrations and young Muslim women sewing hijabs, the headscarves that devout Muslim women wear. Afterward, Zawahiri and Schleifer walked along the boulevard through the Cairo Zoo to the University Bridge. As they stood over the massive, slow-moving Nile, Zawahiri boasted that the Islamist movement had found its greatest recruiting success in the university's two most elite faculties— the medical and engineering schools. "Aren't you impressed by that?"

Schleifer was patronizing. He noted that in the sixties those same faculties had been strongholds of the Marxist Youth. The Islamist movement, he observed, was only the latest trend in student rebellion. "Listen, Ayman, I'm an ex-Marxist. When you talk I feel like I'm back in the Party. I don't feel as if I'm with a traditional Muslim." Zawahiri listened politely, but he seemed puzzled by Schleifer's critique.

Schleifer encountered Zawahiri again soon thereafter. It was the Eid, the time of the annual feast, the holiest day of the year. There was an outdoor prayer in the beautiful garden of Farouk Mosque in Maadi. When Schleifer got there, he noticed Zawahiri with one of his brothers. They were very intense. They laid out plastic prayer mats and set up a microphone. What was supposed to be a meditative period of chanting the Quran turned into an uneven contest between the congregation and the Zawahiri brothers with their microphone. "I realized they were introducing the Salafist formula, which does not recognize any Islamic traditions after the time of the Prophet," Schleifer recalled. "It killed the poetry. It was chaotic."

Afterward, he went over to Zawahiri. "Ayman, this is wrong," Schleifer complained. Zawahiri started to explain, but Schleifer cut him off. "I'm not going to argue with you. I'm a Sufi and you're a Salafist. But you are making *fitna*"—a term for stirring up trouble that is proscribed in the Quran—"and if you want to do that, you should do it in your own mosque."

Zawahiri meekly responded, "You're right, Abdallah."

EVENTUALLY THE DISPARATE underground groups began to discover one another. There were five or six cells in Cairo alone, most of them with fewer than ten members. Four of these cells, including Zawahiri's, which was one of the largest, merged to form Jamaat al-Jihad—the Jihad Group, or simply al-Jihad. Although their goals were similar to those of the mainstream Islamists in the Muslim Brotherhood, they had no intention of trying to work through politics to achieve them. Zawahiri thought such efforts contaminated the ideal of the pure Islamic state. He grew to despise the Muslim Brotherhood for its willingness to compromise.

Zawahiri graduated from medical school in 1974, then served three years as a surgeon in the Egyptian Army, posted at a base outside Cairo. When he finished his military service, the young doctor established a clinic in the same duplex where he lived with his parents. He was now in his late twenties, and it was time for him to marry. Until then, he had never had a girlfriend. In the Egyptian tradition, his friends and relatives began making suggestions of suitable mates. Zawahiri was uninterested in romance; he wanted a partner who shared his extreme convictions and would be willing to bear the hardships his dogmatic personality was bound to encounter. One of the possible brides suggested to Ayman was Azza Nowair, the daughter of an old family friend.

Like the Zawahiris and the Azzams, the Nowairs were a notable Cairo clan. Azza had grown up in a wealthy Maadi household. She was extremely petite—like a young girl—but extraordinarily resolute. In another time and place she might have become a professional woman or a social worker, but in her sophomore year at Cairo University she adopted the hijab, alarming her family with the intensity of her newfound religious devotion. "Before that, she had worn the latest fashions," said her older brother,

Essam. "We didn't want her to be so religious. She started to pray a lot and read the Quran. And, little by little, she changed completely." Soon Azza went further and put on the *niqab*, the veil that covers a woman's face below the eyes. According to her brother, Azza would spend whole nights reading the Quran. When he woke in the morning, he would find her sitting on the prayer mat with the holy book in her hands, fast asleep.

The *niqab* imposed a formidable barrier for a marriageable young woman, especially in a segment of society that still longed to be a part of the westernized modern world. For most of Azza's peers, her decision to veil herself was a shocking abnegation of her class. Her refusal to drop the veil became a test of wills. "She had many suitors, all of them from prestigious ranks and wealth and elite social status," her brother said. "But almost all of them wanted her to drop the *niqab*. She very calmly refused. She wanted someone who would accept her as she was. Ayman was looking for that type of person."

According to custom, at the first meeting between Azza and Ayman, Azza lifted her veil for a few minutes. "He saw the face and then he left," Essam said. The young couple talked briefly on one other occasion after that, but it was little more than a formality. Ayman did not see his fiancée's face again until after the marriage ceremony.

He made a favorable impression on the Nowair family, who were a little dazzled by his distinguished ancestry but were put on guard by his piety. Although he was polite and agreeable, he refused to greet women, and he wouldn't even look at one if she was wearing a skirt. He never talked about politics with Azza's family, and it's not clear how much he revealed even to her. In any case, Azza must have approved of his underground activism. She told a friend that her greatest hope was to become a martyr.

Their wedding was held in February 1978, at the Continental-Savoy Hotel, a once-distinguished Anglo-Egyptian watering hole in Cairo's Opera Square, which had slipped from its days of grandeur into dowdy respectability. According to the wishes of the bride and groom, there was no music and photographs were forbidden. "It was pseudo-traditional," said Schleifer. "We were in the men's section, which was very somber, heavy, with lots of cups of coffee and no one cracking jokes."

"MY CONNECTION WITH AFGHANISTAN began in the summer of 1980 by a twist of fate," Zawahiri wrote in his brief memoir, *Knights Under the Prophet's Banner*. While he was covering for another doctor at a Muslim Brothers clinic, the director of the clinic asked if Zawahiri would like to accompany him to Pakistan to tend to the Afghan refugees. Hundreds of thousands were fleeing across the border after the recent Soviet invasion. Zawahiri immediately agreed. He had been secretly preoccupied with the problem of finding a secure base for jihad, which seemed practically impossible in Egypt. "The River Nile runs in its narrow valley between two deserts that have no vegetation or water," he observed in his memoir. "Such a terrain made guerrilla warfare in Egypt impossible and, as a result, forced the inhabitants of this valley to submit to the central government, to be exploited as workers, and compelled them to be recruited into its army." Perhaps Pakistan or Afghanistan would prove a more suitable location for raising an army of radical Islamists who could eventually return to take over Egypt.

Zawahiri traveled to Peshawar with an anesthesiologist and a plastic surgeon. "We were the first three Arabs to arrive there to participate in relief work," Zawahiri claims. He spent four months in Pakistan, working for the Red Crescent Society, the Islamic arm of the International Red Cross.

The name Peshawar derives from a Sanskrit word meaning "city of flowers," which it may have been during its Buddhist period, but it had long since sloughed off any refinement. The city sits at the eastern end of the Khyber Pass, the historic concourse of invading armies since the days of Alexander the Great and Genghis Khan, who left their genetic traces on the features of the diverse population. Peshawar was an important outpost of the British Empire, the last stop before a wilderness that stretched all the way to Moscow. When the British abandoned their cantonment in 1947, Peshawar was reduced to being a modest but unruly farming town. The war had awakened the ancient city, however, and when Zawahiri arrived it was teeming with smugglers, arms merchants, and opium dealers.

The city also had to cope with the influx of uprooted and starving Afghans. By the end of 1980, there were already 1.4 million Afghan refugees in Pakistan—a number that nearly doubled the following year—and most of them came through Peshawar, seeking shelter in the nearby camps. Many of the refugees were casualties of the Soviet land mines or the intensive bombing of towns and cities, and they desperately needed medical treatment. The conditions in the hospitals and clinics were degrading, however, especially at the beginning of the war. Zawahiri reported home that he sometimes had to use honey to sterilize wounds.

Writing to his mother, he complained of loneliness and pleaded for more frequent letters in return. In these notes, he would occasionally burst into poetry to express his despair:

> She met my evil actions with goodness,
> Without asking for any return . . .
> May God erase my ineptness and
> Please her despite my offenses . . .
> Oh God, may you have pity on a stranger
> Who longs for the sight of his mother.

Through his connection with local tribal chiefs, Zawahiri made several furtive trips across the border into Afghanistan. He became one of the first outsiders to witness the courage of the Afghan freedom fighters, who called themselves the "mujahideen"—the holy warriors. That fall, Zawahiri returned to Cairo full of stories about the "miracles" that were taking place in the jihad against the Soviets. It was a war few knew much about, even in the Arab world, although it was by far the bloodiest conflict of the 1980s. Zawahiri began going around to universities, recruiting for jihad. He had grown a beard and was affecting a Pakistani outfit—a long tunic over loose trousers.

At this point, there was only a handful of Arab volunteers, and when a delegation of mujahideen leaders came to Cairo, Zawahiri took his uncle Mahfouz to Shepheard's Hotel to meet them. The two men presented the Afghans with an idea that Abdallah Schleifer had proposed. Schleifer had been frustrated by the inability of Western news organizations to get close to the war. He had told Zawahiri to find him three bright young Afghans whom he could train as cameramen. That way, they could record their stories and Schleifer could provide the editing and narration. But he warned Zawahiri, "If we don't get the bang-bang, we don't get it on the air."

Soon after that, Schleifer paid a call on Zawahiri to learn what had happened to his proposal. He found his friend strangely formal and evasive. Zawahiri began by saying that Americans were the enemy and must be confronted. "I don't understand," Schleifer replied. "You just came back from Afghanistan where you're cooperating with the Americans. Now you're saying America is the enemy?"

"Sure, we're taking American help to fight the Russians," Zawahiri responded, "but they're equally evil."

"How can you make such a comparison?" said Schleifer, outraged. "There is more freedom to practice Islam in America than in Egypt. And in the Soviet Union, they closed down fifty thousand mosques!"

"You don't see it because you're an American," said Zawahiri.

Schleifer angrily told him that the only reason they were even having this conversation was that NATO and the American army had kept the Soviets from overrunning Europe and then turning their attention to the Middle East. The discussion ended on a bad note. They had debated each other many times, but always with respect and humor. This time Schleifer had the feeling that Zawahiri wasn't talking to him—he was addressing a multitude.

Nothing came of Schleifer's offer to instruct Afghan newsmen.

Zawahiri returned for another tour of duty with the Red Crescent Society in Peshawar in March of 1981. This time he cut short his stay and returned to Cairo after only two months. Later he would write that he saw the Afghan jihad as "a training course of the utmost importance to prepare the Muslim mujahideen to wage their awaited battle against the superpower that now has sole dominance over the globe, namely, the United States."

WHEN ZAWAHIRI RETURNED to his medical practice in Maadi, the Islamic world was still trembling from the political earthquakes of 1979, which included not only the Soviet invasion of Afghanistan but also the return of Ayatollah Ruhollah Khomeini to Iran and the toppling of the Peacock Throne—the first successful Islamist takeover of a major country. When Mohammed Reza Pahlavi, the exiled Shah of Iran, sought treatment for cancer in the United States, the Ayatollah incited student mobs to attack the American Embassy in Tehran. Sadat regarded Khomeini as a "lunatic madman . . . who has turned Islam into a mockery." He invited the ailing Shah to take up residence in Egypt, and the Shah died there the following year.

For Muslims everywhere, Khomeini reframed the debate with the West. Instead of conceding the future of Islam to a secular, democratic model, he imposed a stunning reversal. His intoxicating sermons summoned up the unyielding force of the Islam of a previous millennium in language that foreshadowed bin Laden's revolutionary diatribes. The specific target of his rage against the West was freedom. "Yes, we are reactionaries, and you are enlightened intellectuals: You intellectuals do not want us to go back 1,400 years," he said soon after taking power. "You, who want freedom, freedom for everything, the freedom of parties, you who want all the freedoms, you intellectuals: freedom that will corrupt our youth, freedom that will pave the way for the oppressor, freedom that will drag our nation to the bottom." As early as the 1940s, Khomeini had signaled his readiness to use terror to humiliate the perceived enemies of Islam, providing theological cover as well as material support. "Islam says: Whatever good there is exists thanks to the sword and in the shadow of the sword! People cannot be made obedient except with the sword! The sword is the key to paradise, which can be opened only for holy warriors!"

The fact that Khomeini came from the Shiite branch of Islam, rather than the Sunni, which predominates in the Muslim world outside of Iraq and Iran, made him a complicated figure among Sunni radicals.* Nonetheless, Zawahiri's organization, al-Jihad, supported the Iranian revolution with leaflets and cassette tapes urging all Islamic groups in Egypt to follow the Iranian example. The overnight transformation of a relatively wealthy, powerful, modern country such as Iran into a rigid theocracy showed that the Islamists' dream was eminently achievable, and it quickened their desire to act.

Islamism was by now a broad and variegated movement, including those who were willing to work within a political system, such as the Muslim Brothers, and those, like Zawahiri, who wanted to wreck the state and impose a religious dictatorship. The main object of the Islamists' struggle was to impose Islamic law—Sharia. They believe that the five hundred Quranic verses that constitute the basis of Sharia are the immutable commandments of God, offering a road back to the perfected era of the Prophet and his immediate successors—although the legal code actually evolved several centuries after the Prophet's death. These verses comment upon behavior as precise and various as how to respond to someone who sneezes and the permissibility of wearing gold jewelry. They also prescribe specific punishments for some crimes, such as adultery and drinking, but not for others, including homicide. Islamists say the Sharia cannot be improved upon, despite fifteen centuries of social change, because it arises directly from the mind of God. They want to bypass the long tradition of judicial opinion from Muslim scholars and forge a more authentically Islamic legal system that is untainted by Western influence or any improvisations caused by the engagement with

*The community of believers split after the death of Prophet Mohammed in 632 C.E. because of a quarrel over the line of succession. Those who call themselves Sunni supported the election of the caliphs, but another group, which became the Shia, believed that the caliphate should have passed through the Prophet's descendants, beginning with his cousin and son-in-law, Ali. Since then, the two branches have evolved numerous theological and cultural differences.

modernity. Non-Muslims and Islamic modernists, on the other hand, argue that the tenets of Sharia reflect the stringent Bedouin codes of the culture that gave birth to the religion and are certainly not adequate to govern a modern society. Under Sadat, the government had repeatedly pledged to conform to Sharia, but his actions showed how little that promise could be trusted.

Sadat's peace agreement with Israel united the disparate Islamist factions. They were also inflamed by a new law, sponsored by the president's wife, Jihan, that granted women the right to divorce, a privilege not provided by the Quran. In what would prove to be his final speech, Sadat ridiculed the Islamic garb worn by pious women, which he called a "tent," and banned the *niqab* from the universities. The radicals responded by characterizing the president as a heretic. It is forbidden, under Islamic law, to strike against a ruler unless he doesn't believe in God or the Prophet. The declaration of heresy was an open invitation to assassination.

In response to a series of demonstrations orchestrated by the Islamists, Sadat dissolved all religious student associations, confiscated their property, and shut down their summer camps. Reversing his position of tolerating, even encouraging, such groups, he now adopted a new slogan: "No politics in religion and no religion in politics." There could scarcely have been a more incendiary formulation in the Islamist mind.

Zawahiri envisioned not merely the removal of the head of state but a complete overthrow of the existing order. Stealthily, he had been recruiting officers from the Egyptian military, waiting for the moment when al-Jihad had accumulated sufficient strength in men and weapons to act. His chief strategist was Aboud al-Zumar, a colonel in military intelligence who was a hero of the 1973 war against Israel (a Cairo street had been renamed in his honor). Zumar's plan was to kill the main leaders of the country, capture the headquarters of the army and State Security, the telephone exchange building, and of course the radio and television building, where news of the Islamic revolution would then be broadcast, unleashing—he expected—a popular uprising against secular authority all over the country. It was, Zawahiri later testified, "an elaborate artistic plan."

Another key member of Zawahiri's cell was a daring tank commander named Essam al-Qamari. Because of his valor and intelligence, Major Qamari had been promoted repeatedly over the heads of his peers. Zawahiri described him as "a noble person in the true sense of the word. Most of his sufferings and sacrifices that he endured willingly and calmly were the result of his honorable character." Although Zawahiri was the senior member of the Maadi cell, he often deferred to Qamari, who had a natural sense of command—a quality that Zawahiri notably lacked. Indeed, Qamari observed that there was "something missing" in Zawahiri, and once cautioned him, "If you are a member of any group, you cannot be the leader."

Qamari began smuggling weapons and ammunition from army strongholds and storing them in Zawahiri's medical clinic in Maadi, which was in a downstairs apartment in the duplex where his parents lived. In February of 1981, as the weapons were being transferred from the clinic to a warehouse, police officers arrested a young man carrying a bag loaded with guns, military bulletins, and maps that showed the location of all the tank emplacements in Cairo. Qamari, realizing that he would soon be implicated, dropped out of sight, but several of his officers were arrested. Zawahiri inexplicably stayed put.

Until these arrests, the Egyptian government had persuaded itself that the Islamist underground had been eliminated. That September, Sadat ordered the roundup of more than fifteen hundred people, including many prominent Egyptians—not only Islamists but also intellectuals with no religious leanings, Marxists, Coptic Christians, student leaders, journalists, writers, doctors in the Muslim Brothers syndicate—a potpourri of dissidents from various sectors. The dragnet missed Zawahiri but captured most of the other leaders of al-Jihad. However, a military cell within the scattered ranks of Jihad had already set in motion a hasty and opportunistic plan. Lieutenant Khaled Islambouli, who was twenty-three years old, proposed to kill Sadat during an appearance at a military parade the following month.

.   .   .

Zawahiri testified that he did not hear about the plan until nine o'clock on the morning of October 6, 1981, a few hours before the assassination was scheduled to take place. One of the members of his cell, a pharmacist, brought him the news. "I was astonished and shaken," Zawahiri told his interrogators. The pharmacist proposed that they must do something to help the hastily conceived plot succeed. "But I told him, 'What can we do? Do they want us to shoot up the streets and let the police detain us? We are not going to do anything.'" Zawahiri went back to his patients. When he learned, a few hours later, that the military exhibition was still going on, he assumed that the operation had failed and everyone connected with it had been arrested. He then went to the home of one of his sisters, who informed him that the exhibition had been halted and the president had left unharmed. The real news was yet to be heard.

Sadat had been celebrating the eighth anniversary of the 1973 war. Surrounded by dignitaries, including several American diplomats and Boutros Boutros-Ghali, the future secretary-general of the United Nations, Sadat was saluting the passing troops when a military vehicle veered toward the reviewing stand. Lieutenant Islambouli and three other conspirators leaped out and tossed grenades into the stand. "I have killed the Pharaoh!" Islambouli cried, after emptying the cartridge of his machine gun into the president, who stood defiantly at attention until his body was riddled with bullets.

The announcement of Sadat's death later that day met with little grief in the Arab world, which regarded him as a traitor for making peace with Israel. In Zawahiri's opinion, the assassination had accomplished nothing in the way of achieving an Islamic state. But perhaps there was still time, in the shaky interval following the event, to put the grand plan into effect. Essam al-Qamari came out of hiding and asked Zawahiri to put him in touch with the group that had carried out the assassination. At ten that night, only eight hours after Sadat's murder, Zawahiri and Qamari met with Aboud al-Zumar in a car outside the apartment where Qamari was hiding. Qamari had a daring proposal, this one with the chance to eliminate the entire government and many foreign leaders as well: an attack on Sadat's funeral. Zumar agreed, and asked Qamari to supply him with ten bombs and two guns. The very next day the group met again. Qamari brought the weapons, as well as several boxes of ammunition. Meanwhile, the new government, headed by Hosni Mubarak, was rounding up thousands of prospective conspirators. Aboud al-Zumar was arrested before the plan could be put into action.

Zawahiri must have known that his name would surface, but still he lingered. On October 23, he had finally packed his belongings for another trip to Pakistan. He went to say good-bye to some relatives. His brother Hussein was driving him to the airport when the police stopped them on the Nile Corniche. "They took Ayman to the Maadi police station, and he was surrounded by guards," his cousin Omar Azzam recalled. "The chief of police slapped him on the face—and Ayman slapped him back!" The family regards this incident with amazement, not only because of the recklessness of Zawahiri's response but also because until that moment he had never, in their memory, resorted to violence. Zawahiri immediately became known among the other prisoners as the man who struck back.

SECURITY FORCES GREETED the incoming prisoners by stripping them naked, blindfolding and handcuffing them, then beating them with sticks. Humiliated, frightened, and disoriented, they were thrown into narrow stone cells, the only light coming from a tiny square window in the iron door. The dungeon had been built in the twelfth century by the great Kurdish conqueror Saladin, using the labor of captured Crusaders. It was part of the Citadel, a massive fortress on a hill overlooking Cairo, that had served as the seat of government for seven hundred years.

The screams of fellow prisoners who were being interrogated kept many men in a state of near madness, even when they weren't tortured themselves. Because of his status, Zawahiri was subjected to frequent beatings and other ingenious and sadistic forms of punishment created by Intelligence Unit 75, which oversaw Egypt's inquisition.

One line of thinking proposes that America's tragedy on September 11 was born in the prisons of Egypt. Human-rights advocates in Cairo argue that torture created an appetite for revenge, first in Sayyid Qutb and later in his acolytes, including Ayman al-Zawahiri. The main target of the prisoners' wrath was the secular Egyptian government, but a powerful current of anger was also directed toward the West, which they saw as an enabling force behind the repressive regime. They held the West responsible for corrupting and humiliating Islamic society. Indeed, the theme of humiliation, which is the essence of torture, is important to understanding the radical Islamists' rage. Egypt's prisons became a factory for producing militants whose need for retribution— they called it justice—was all-consuming.

Montassir al-Zayyat, an Islamist attorney who was imprisoned with Zawahiri and later became his lawyer and biographer,* maintains that the traumatic experiences suffered by Zawahiri in prison transformed him from being a relatively moderate force in al-Jihad into a violent and implacable extremist. Zayyat and other witnesses point to what happened to his relationship with Essam al-Qamari, who had been his close friend and a man he keenly admired. Immediately after Zawahiri's arrest, officers in the Interior Ministry began grilling him about Major Qamari, who continued to slip their nets. He was now the most wanted man in Egypt. He had already survived a firefight with grenades and automatic weapons in which many policemen were killed or wounded. In their relentless search for Qamari, the security officers booted the distinguished Zawahiri family out of their house and tore up the floors and pulled down all the wallpaper looking for evidence. They also waited by the phone, betting that eventually the desperado would call. Two weeks later, the call finally came. The caller identified himself as "Dr. Essam" and asked to meet Zawahiri. Qamari was unaware that Zawahiri was in custody when he phoned, since it had been kept secret. A police officer,

---

*He wrote a damning biography titled *Ayman al-Zawahiri as I Knew Him*, which was withdrawn by his Cairo publisher because of pressure from Zawahiri's supporters.

pretending to be a family member, told "Dr. Essam" that Zawahiri was not there. The caller suggested, "Let him pray the *maghreb*"— the sunset prayer—"with me," at a mosque they both knew.

"Qamari had given him an appointment on the road to Maadi, but he noticed the security people, and he escaped again," said Fouad Allam, who was the head of the Interior Ministry's anti-terrorism unit at the time. He is an avuncular figure with a basso profundo voice, who has interrogated almost every major Islamic radical since 1965, when he questioned Sayyid Qutb. "I called Ayman al-Zawahiri to my office in order to propose a plan." Allam found Zawahiri "shy and distant. He doesn't look at you when he talks, which is a sign of politeness in the Arab world." According to Zawahiri's uncle Mahfouz, Zawahiri had already been brutally tortured, and he actually came to Allam's office wearing only one shoe, because of an injury inflicted to his foot. Allam arranged to have Zawahiri's telephone line transferred into his office, and he held Zawahiri there until Qamari finally called again. This time Zawahiri answered and made a date to meet at the Zawya Mosque in Embaba. As planned, Zawahiri went to the mosque and fingered his friend.

Zawahiri himself doesn't admit to this in his memoir, except obliquely, where he writes about the "humiliation" of imprisonment. "The toughest thing about captivity is forcing the *mujahid*, under the force of torture, to confess about his colleagues, to destroy his movement with his own hands, and offer his and his colleagues' secrets to the enemy."

Perversely, the authorities placed Qamari in the same cell with Zawahiri after Zawahiri testified against him and thirteen others. Qamari received a ten-year sentence. "As usual, he received the news with his unique calmness and self-composure," Zawahiri recorded. "He even tried to comfort me, and said, 'I pity you for the burdens you will carry.' " In 1988 Qamari was shot to death by police after escaping from prison.

Z A W A H I R I   W A S   D E F E N D A N T   number 113 of 302 who were accused of aiding or planning the assassination, as well as various other crimes (in Zawahiri's case, dealing in arms). Lieutenant Islambouli and twenty-three others charged with the actual assassination were tried separately. Islambouli and four conspirators were hanged. Nearly every notable Islamist in Egypt was implicated in the plot.* The other defendants, some of whom were adolescents, were crowded into a zoo-like cage that ran across one side of a vast improvised courtroom in the Exhibition Grounds in Cairo where fairs and conventions are often held. They came from various organizations—al-Jihad, the Islamic Group, the Muslim Brotherhood—that formed the fractious core of the Islamist movement. International news organizations covered the trial, and Zawahiri, who had the best command of English among the defendants, was their designated spokesman.

Video footage of the opening day of the trial, December 4, 1982, shows the three hundred defendants, illuminated by the lights of the TV cameras, chanting, praying, and calling out desperately to family members. Finally, the camera settles on Zawahiri, who stands apart from the chaos with a look of solemn, focused intensity. Thirty-one years old, he is wearing a white robe and has a gray scarf thrown over his shoulder.

At a signal, the other prisoners fall silent, and Zawahiri cries out, "Now we want to speak to the whole world! Who are we? Why do they bring us here, and what we want to say? About the first question, we are Muslims! We are Muslims who believe in their religion! We are Muslims who believe in their religion, both in ideology and practice, and hence we tried our best to establish an Islamic state and an Islamic society!"

The other defendants chant, in Arabic, "There is no God but God!"

Zawahiri continues, in a fiercely repetitive cadence, "We are not sorry, we are not sorry for what we have done for our religion, and we have sacrificed, and we stand ready to make more sacrifices!"

---

*Zawahiri's brother Mohammed was sentenced in absentia, but the charges were later dropped. The youngest brother, Hussein, spent thirteen months in prison before the charges against him were also dropped.

The others shout, "There is no God but God!"

Zawahiri then says, "We are here—the real Islamic front and the real Islamic opposition against Zionism, Communism, and imperialism!" He pauses, then: "And now, as an answer to the second question, why did they bring us here? They bring us here for two reasons! First, they are trying to abolish the outstanding Islamic movement . . . and, secondly, to complete the conspiracy of evacuating the area in preparation for the Zionist infiltration."

The others cry out, "We will not sacrifice the blood of Muslims for the Americans and the Jews!"

The prisoners pull off their shoes and raise their robes to expose marks of torture. Zawahiri talks about the abuse that took place in the "dirty Egyptian jails . . . where we suffered the severest inhuman treatment. There they kicked us, they beat us, they whipped us with electric cables, they shocked us with electricity! They shocked us with electricity! And they used the wild dogs! And they used the wild dogs! And they hung us over the edges of the doors"—here he bends forward to demonstrate—"with our hands tied at the back! They arrested the wives, the mothers, the fathers, the sisters, and the sons!"

The defendants chant, "The army of Mohammed will return, and we will defeat the Jews!"

The camera captures one particularly wild-eyed defendant in a green caftan as he extends his arms through the bars of the cage, screams, and then faints into the arms of a fellow prisoner. Zawahiri calls out the names of several prisoners who, he says, died as a result of torture. "So where is democracy?" he shouts. "Where is freedom? Where is human rights? Where is justice? Where is justice? We will never forget! We will never forget!"

Zawahiri's allegations of torture were later substantiated by forensic medical reports, which noted six injuries in various places on his body resulting from assaults with "a solid instrument." Zawahiri later testified in a case brought against Intelligence Unit 75, which had conducted the prison interrogations. He was supported by the testimony of one of the intelligence officers, who confessed that he witnessed Zawahiri in the prison, "his head shaved, his dignity completely humiliated, undergoing all sorts of torture." The officer went on to say that he had been in the interrogation room when another prisoner was brought into the chamber, chained hand and foot. The interrogators were trying to get Zawahiri to confess his involvement in the Sadat assassination. When the other prisoner said, "How would you expect him to confess when he knows the penalty is death?" Zawahiri replied, "The death penalty is more merciful than torture."

THE TRIAL DRAGGED ON for three years. Sometimes the defendants would go every day, but then more than a month might pass before they returned to the improvised courtroom. They were from various groups, and many had not even known of the others' existence before they found themselves locked up together. They naturally began to conspire. While some eagerly talked about rebuilding, there were also intensive discussions among the prisoners about the dismaying fact that so many of them had been arrested, the movement so quickly betrayed. "We were defeated, and so we became lost," Zawahiri admitted to one of his prison mates. They spent many days considering why the underground operations had failed and how they might have succeeded. "Ayman told me that he hadn't wanted the [Sadat] assassination to take place," Montassir al-Zayyat, his fellow prisoner and biographer, recalled. "He thought they should have waited and plucked the regime from the roots through a military coup. He was not that bloodthirsty."

His education, family background, and relative wealth made Zawahiri a notable figure. Every other day, a driver arrived with food from his family, which Zawahiri distributed among the other prisoners. He also helped out in the prison hospital.

During this time, Zawahiri came face-to-face with Egypt's best-known Islamist, Sheikh Omar Abdul Rahman, who had also been charged as a conspirator in the Sadat assassination. A strange and forceful man, blinded by diabetes in childhood but blessed with a stirring, resonant voice, Sheikh Omar had risen in Islamic circles because of his eloquent denunciations of Nasser, who had tossed him in jail for eight months without charges.

After Nasser's death, the blind sheikh's influence increased, especially in Upper Egypt, where he taught theology at the Asyut branch of al-Azhar University. He developed a following among the students and became the leader of the Islamic Group. Some of the young Islamists were financing their activism by shaking down Coptic Christians, who made up perhaps 10 percent of the Egyptian population but who included many shopkeepers and small-business owners. On a number of occasions, the young radicals stormed into Coptic weddings and robbed the guests. The theology of jihad requires a fatwa—a religious ruling—in order to consecrate actions that would otherwise be considered criminal. Sheikh Omar obligingly issued fatwas that countenanced the slaughter of Christians and the plunder of Coptic jewelry stores, on the premise that a state of war existed between Christians and Muslims.

After Sadat finally attempted to rein in the Islamists, the blind sheikh took a three-year sojourn to Saudi Arabia and other Arab countries, where he found wealthy sponsors for his cause. When he returned to Egypt, in 1980, he was not merely the spiritual advisor of the Islamic Group, he was the emir. In one of Sheikh Omar's first fatwas, he declared that a heretical leader deserved to be killed by the faithful. At his trial for conspiring in the assassination of Sadat, his lawyer successfully convinced the court that, because his client had not mentioned the Egyptian president by name, he was, at most, tangential to the plot. Six months after the sheikh's imprisonment, he was released.

Although members of the two leading militant organizations, the Islamic Group and al-Jihad, shared the common goal of bringing down the government, they differed sharply in their ideology and tactics. The blind sheikh preached that all humanity could embrace Islam, and he was content to spread this message. Zawahiri profoundly disagreed. Distrustful of the masses and contemptuous of any faith other than his own stark version of Islam, he preferred to act secretly and unilaterally until the moment his group could seize power and impose its totalitarian religious vision.

The Islamic Group and al-Jihad had collaborated under the leadership of Sheikh Omar, but those from al-Jihad, including Qamari and Zawahiri, sought to have one of their own in charge. In the Cairo prison, members of the two organizations had heated debates about the best way to achieve a true Islamic revolution, and they quarreled endlessly over who was the best man to lead it. Zawahiri pointed out that Sharia states that the emir cannot be blind. Sheikh Omar countered that Sharia also decrees that the emir cannot be a prisoner. The rivalry between the two men became extreme. Zayyat tried to moderate Zawahiri's attacks on the sheikh, but Zawahiri refused to back down. The result was that al-Jihad and the Islamic Group split apart once more. They would remain polarized by these two intransigent personalities.

ZAWAHIRI WAS CONVICTED of dealing in weapons and received a three-year sentence, which he had nearly finished serving by the time the trial concluded. Perhaps in response to his cooperation in testifying against other defendants, the government dropped several additional charges against him.

Released in 1984, Zawahiri emerged a hardened radical whose beliefs had been hammered into brilliant resolve. Saad Eddin Ibrahim, a prominent sociologist at the American University in Cairo, spoke to Zawahiri soon after he got out of prison, and he noted a pronounced degree of suspicion and an overwhelming desire for revenge, which was characteristic of men who have been abused in prison. Torture may have had other, unanticipated effects on these intensely religious men. Many of them said that after being tortured they had had visions of being welcomed by the saints into Paradise and of the just Islamic society that had been made possible by their martyrdom.

Ibrahim had done a study of political prisoners in Egypt in the 1970s. According to his research, most of the Islamist recruits were young men from villages who had come to the city for schooling. The majority were the sons of middle-level government bureaucrats. They were ambitious and tended to be drawn to the fields of science and engineering, which accept only the most qualified students. They were not the alienated, marginalized youth that a sociologist might have expected. Instead, Ibrahim wrote, they were "model young Egyptians. If they were not typical, it was because they were significantly above the average in their generation." Ibrahim attributed the recruiting success of the militant Islamist groups to their emphasis on brotherhood, sharing, and spiritual support, which provided a "soft landing" for the rural migrants to the city.

Zawahiri, who had read the study in prison, heatedly disagreed. He asserted that the recruits responded to the Islamist ideals, not to the social needs that the groups attended. "You have trivialized our movement by your mundane analysis," he told Ibrahim. "May God have mercy on you."

Ibrahim responded to Zawahiri's challenge by recalling an old Arabic saying, "For everyone who tries, there is a reward. If he hits it right, he gets two rewards. But if he misses, he still gets a reward for trying."

Zawahiri smiled and said, "You get one reward."

Once again, Dr. Zawahiri resumed his surgical practice; however, he was worried about the political consequences of his testimony in the torture case against Intelligence Unit 75. He thought of applying for a surgery fellowship in England. He arranged to work at the Ibn al-Nafees clinic in Jeddah, Saudi Arabia, even though the Egyptian government had forbidden him to leave the country for three years. Zawahiri secured a tourist visa to Tunisia, perhaps using a false passport. It seems obvious that he did not intend to return. He had shaved his beard after his release, which indicated that he was returning to his underground work.

As he was leaving, he ran into his friend Abdallah Schleifer at the Cairo airport. "Where are you going?" Schleifer asked.

"Saudi," Zawahiri confided. He appeared relaxed and happy.

The two men embraced. "Listen, Ayman, stay out of politics," Schleifer warned.

"I will!" Zawahiri replied. "I will!"

3

The Founder

AT THE AGE OF THIRTY-FOUR, Dr. Ayman al-Zawahiri was a formidable figure. He had been a committed revolutionary and the leader of an underground Islamist cell for more than half his life. His political skills had been honed by endless prison debates, and he emerged pious, bitter, and determined.

Saudi intelligence says that he arrived in the Kingdom in 1985 on a pilgrimage visa, which he converted to a work visa. He spent about a year practicing medicine in the Ibn al-Nafees clinic in Jeddah. Zawahiri's sister Heba, a professor of oncology at the National Cancer Institute at Cairo University, said that during this period he passed the first part of an examination for a surgery fellowship he was seeking in England. His mother and other members of his family were under the impression that he was planning to return to Cairo eventually, because he continued to pay rent on his clinic in Maadi. His brother Mohammed was also in the Kingdom, working as an architect in Medina.

Zawahiri's attorney, and former prison mate, Montassir al-Zayyat, passed through Jeddah on his way to Mecca, and he found Zawahiri sober and downcast. "The scars left on his body from the indescribable torture he suffered caused him no more pain," Zayyat later wrote, "but his heart still ached from it." In Zayyat's opinion, Zawahiri had fled Egypt because the guilt of betraying his friends weighed so oppressively on his conscience. By testifying against his comrades while he was in prison, Zawahiri had lost his claim to leadership of al-Jihad. He was looking for a place where he could redeem himself and where the radical Islamist movement could gain a foothold. "The situation in Egypt had been getting worse," Zawahiri later wrote, "you can say explosive."

Jeddah was the commercial center of the Kingdom, the port of entry for the millions of pilgrims who passed through on their way to Mecca each year. Every Muslim who is capable of making the journey, called the hajj, is required to do so at least once. Some who remained became the founders of the great banking and merchant families—the bin Mahfouzes, the Alirezas, and Khashoggis among them—who could trace their immigrant roots to Yemen and Persia and Turkey. This cosmopolitan heritage set the city apart from the culturally and ethnically isolated interior. Here, in Jeddah, it was the families, not the tribes, that mattered, and among the handful of names that dominated Jeddah society was that of bin Laden.

Zayyat contends that Zawahiri and bin Laden met in Jeddah, and although there is no record of their first encounter, it is certainly likely. Zawahiri had already been to Afghanistan twice, before prison, and intended to return as soon as possible. The pipeline to Afghanistan ran directly through bin Laden's apartment. Anyone who gave money or volunteered for the jihad would have known the enterprising young Saudi. In any case, they were bound to discover each other sooner or later in the intimate landscape of jihad.

IN ARABIC THE NAME JEDDAH MEANS "grandmother," and according to legend the city's name refers to Eve, the grandmother of the human race, who is said to be buried in a spacious walled compound in the working-class neighborhood where Osama bin Laden grew up. In the twelfth century, a cult formed around her supposed tomb, which traced the remains of her giant body, nearly five hundred feet long, marked by a domed shrine where her navel was said to be. Sir Richard Burton visited the grave in 1853 and surveyed the dimensions, remarking, "If our first parent measured a hundred and twenty paces from head to waist, and eighty from waist to heel, she must have presented much the appearance of a duck." The Wahhabis—the creed-bound sect that predominates in Saudi Arabia—who condemn the veneration of tombs, knocked the place down in 1928, soon after they occupied Jeddah, and today it is a typical Wahhabi graveyard, with long rows of featureless, unmarked graves like unplanted flower beds. Osama bin Laden's father was buried here after his death in an air crash in 1967 at the age of fifty-nine.

One cannot understand the scale of the son's ambition without appreciating the father's accomplishment. Remote and powerful but humble in manner, Mohammed bin Awahd bin Laden was a legend even before Osama was born. He presented a formidable model to a young man who idolized him and hoped to equal, if not surpass, his achievements. Mohammed had been born in a remote valley in central Yemen. This region, which is called the Hadramout, is known for its ethereal mud-brick towers, like sandcastles, that rise as high as twelve stories. These fantastic constructions have given the Hadramis their reputation as builders and architects. Mainly, however, the Hadramout is famous for the people who have left it. For millennia, they have worn a path through the Empty Quarter of southern Arabia and then along the sere mountains guarding the eastern coast of the Red Sea and into the Hijaz, the land where Islam was born. From there, many of them fanned out into the Levant and southeastern Asia, even into the Philippines, forming a broad fraternity of merchants, businessmen, and contractors. A catastrophic drought in the early 1930s cast thousands of Hadramis out of their country to seek not merely opportunities but existence itself. Mohammed was among them. After spending a brief time in Ethiopia, he took a boat to Jizan, on the southern Arabian coast, and from there he joined a camel caravan to Jeddah. He was twenty-three years old when he arrived.

Arabia in 1931 was one of the poorest, most desolate places in the world. It was not yet unified—the Kingdom of Saudi Arabia did not formally come into existence until the following year. The ruler of this fractious desert empire was Abdul Aziz bin Abdul Rahman bin Faisal al-Saud,* who lived in Riyadh, in a modest palace made of mud brick. He had just put down a vicious revolt by a group of religious fanatics called the Ikhwan, a direct predecessor of al-Qaeda. They had once formed Abdul Aziz's own shock troops, massacring thousands of innocent and unarmed villagers in their campaign to purify the peninsula in the name of Islam. The king tried to control the Ikhwan, attempting to prevent their murderous raids from spilling over into neighboring countries. The Ikhwan already detested the king's alliance with Britain and his extravagantly polygamous lifestyle, but they decisively turned against him because of his attempt to bridle jihad, which to them was limitless and obligatory, their duty to God.

Abdul Aziz had to get the permission of the religious establishment to rein in the murderous zealots. This was the defining political moment of modern Saudi Arabia. By awarding the king the sole power to declare jihad, the Wahhabi clerics reaffirmed their position as the arbiters of power in a highly religious society. The king finally defeated the Ikhwan's camel-mounted corps with the help of motorcars, machine guns, and British bombers. But the tension between the royal family and religious fanatics was a part of the social dynamic of modern Saudi Arabia from the very beginning.

Most Saudis reject the name Wahhabi; they either call themselves *muwahhidun*—unitarians—since the essence of their belief is the oneness of God, or Salafists, which refers to their predecessors (*salaf*), the venerated companions of the Prophet. The founder of the movement, Mohammed ibn Abdul Wahhab, was an eighteenth-century revivalist who believed that Muslims had drifted away from the true religion as it had been expressed during the Golden Age of the Prophet and his immediate successors. Among other theological innovations, Abdul Wahhab believed that God clothed Himself in a human form; he rejected the intercessory prayer of saints and expressions of reverence for the dead; and he demanded that Muslim men refuse to trim their beards.

*More familiarly known to Westerners as Ibn Saud.

He banned holidays, even the Prophet's birthday, and his followers destroyed many of the holy sites, which he considered idols. He attacked the arts as being frivolous and dangerous. He gave a warrant to his followers that they could kill or rape or plunder those who refused to follow his injunctions.

Other Muslims in Arabia at the time considered Abdul Wahhab a dangerous heretic. In 1744, driven out of the Najd, the central part of the peninsula, he sought protection from Mohammed bin Saud, the founder of the first Saudi state. Although the Ottomans soon crushed the Saudis, the partnership that was formed with Abdul Wahhab and bin Saud's descendants persevered. The essence of their understanding was that there was no difference between religion and government. Abdul Wahhab's extreme views would always be a part of the fabric of Saudi rule.

There was a second Saudi state in the nineteenth century, which quickly fell apart because of family infighting. When Abdul Aziz returned the Saudis to power in the twentieth century for a third time, the doctrines of Abdul Wahhab became the official state religion, and no other forms of Islamic worship were permitted. This was done in the name of the Prophet, who had decreed that there should be only one religion in Arabia. In the blinkered view of the Wahhabis, there was only one interpretation of Islam—Salafism—and all other schools of Muslim thought were heretical.

Mohammed bin Laden's career traced the same gradual then suddenly explosive growth as Saudi Arabia. When he arrived in 1931, the nascent Kingdom was in a state of perilous economic decline. The main source of revenue had been the annual stream of pilgrims coming for hajj in the holy cities of Mecca and Medina, but the Great Depression had choked off the flow of pilgrims and devastated even the modest income derived from the export of dates. The country's future promised to be, at best, as dreary and obscure as its past. At the king's desperate invitation, an American geologist, Karl Twitchell, had arrived in April of that same year to probe for water and gold. He would find neither, but he did think there was some potential for oil.

Twitchell's discovery opened the way for the partnership that eventually came to be known as the Arabian American Oil Company—Aramco. Over the next few years, a small colony of petroleum engineers and roughnecks set up an oil camp in the Eastern Province. Aramco was a modest enterprise at first, but there was so little economic life in the Kingdom that the company quickly dominated the development of the entire country. Mohammed bin Laden, who had begun as a dockworker in Jeddah, managed to get a job with Aramco, working as a bricklayer in Dhahran.

The first great oil boom in the early 1950s ignited the transformation of this barren peninsula. Desert princes who had lived all their lives on dates and camel's milk were suddenly docking their yachts in Monaco. But the wealth wasn't being entirely squandered in the casinos of the Riviera, despite the Saudis' new reputation as international spendthrifts. Foreign contracting giants, especially the American firm Bechtel, brought their behemoth machinery to the Kingdom and set about building the roads and schools and hospitals and ports and power plants that would give the Kingdom the facade of modernity. Aramco commissioned most of these early projects. No country had ever experienced such rapid, overwhelming transformation.

Bin Laden's fortunes began to lift as the American engineers, under pressure from the Saudi government to train and hire more local workers, began giving him projects that were too modest for the major firms. He was quickly recognized as an exacting and honest builder. He was a small, handsome man, with one glass eye—the result of a blow a teacher had given him in his first days of schooling. Bin Laden never returned to school, and as a result he was illiterate—"his signature was like that of a kid," one of his sons remembered. He was nonetheless brilliant with figures, which he could effortlessly calculate in his head, and he never forgot a measurement. An American who knew him in the 1950s described him as "dark, friendly, and energetic." Aramco began a program that granted employees a leave for a year in order to try their luck in business. If they failed, they could return to the company with no loss in status. The Mohammed bin Laden Company was one of many enterprises that got its start with Aramco sponsorship. Bin Laden insisted on working side by side with his men, which created strong ties of loyalty. "I was raised as a laborer, and I love work and living with the laborers," he said. "If it were not for my love of work, I would never have succeeded." He also knew the value of holding a team together, so he would sometimes accept unprofitable projects just to keep his men on the job. They called him *mu'alim,* a word that means both "craftsman" and "teacher."

Bin Laden was renovating houses in Jeddah when his work caught the eye of the minister of finance, Sheikh Abdullah bin Suleiman. The minister lauded his skills to King Abdul Aziz. Years later, Osama bin Laden would recall how his father won the favor of the old king, who was now largely confined to his wheelchair and wanted to add a ramp so that his automobile could be driven to his bedroom on the second floor of the Khozam Palace in Jeddah. When Mohammed bin Laden finished the job, he personally drove the king's car up the ramp to show that it would support the weight. In gratitude, the king awarded him contracts to build several new royal palaces, including the first concrete building in Riyadh. Eventually, the king made him an honorary minister of public works.

As bin Laden's reputation grew, he became increasingly close to the royal family and responsive to their whims. Unlike those who ran the foreign firms, he was willing to abruptly break off one job to build another, he was patient when the royal treasury was empty, and he never turned down a job. His loyalty was rewarded when a British contractor defaulted on a project to build a highway between Jeddah and Medina; the finance minister gave the job to bin Laden and agreed to pay the same fee that would have been paid to the foreign company.

Saudi Arabia needed roads. Even into the fifties, there was only one well-paved road, from Riyadh to Dhahran. Bin Laden looked at his giant rival, Bechtel, and realized that without equipment he could never compete for the really important contracts. He began acquiring machinery, and within a very brief span of time he was the largest customer of Caterpillar earth-moving equipment in the world. From now on, he would build nearly every important road in the Kingdom. His old sponsor, Aramco, donated the asphalt free of charge. Bin Laden moved with his family to Jeddah.

When Umm Kalthoum, the most popular singer in the Arab world, visited the Prophet's Mosque in Medina, she was alarmed by the creaky columns and the cracks in the vaulted ceilings. She began raising money for repairs, which galled the old king. He ordered bin Laden to fix the problem. The original mosque, made of mud brick and tree trunks, had been constructed in 622 C.E. and expanded on several occasions, but it had not been designed to accommodate pilgrims by the millions. Bin Laden tripled the size of the Prophet's Mosque during the first renovation, which got under way in 1953. But that was just the beginning of Mohammed bin Laden's imprint on the holiest places in Islam.

One of King Abdul Aziz's sons, Prince Talal, was the finance minister during the renovation of the Prophet's Mosque. He tried to impose some order on the process, but bin Laden was used to working without supervision, keeping his figures in his head and answering to no one but the king. Talal was shocked to find that he had not even filed the proper legal papers to begin construction. "We have to organize this!" Talal complained. Bin Laden refused. He said he would do it his way or walk off the job.

Prince Talal decided to create a council, nominally headed by the king himself, to oversee the renovation. Then he offered to put bin Laden on the council. "It was not really correct for him to be a part of the same body that was supposed to supervise him," Talal admitted. "Fortunately, he agreed. If I had stood my ground against him, the king would have asked me to leave and kept bin Laden."

After the death of Abdul Aziz in November 1953, he was succeeded by Saud, his eldest son, who set a standard for wasteful extravagance, creating a new Saudi stereotype almost single-handedly as he rode through the sandy streets throwing money into the air. The restraints, such as they were, against royal opportunism dropped away as members of the royal family muscled their way into all the contracts, commissions, concessions, and franchises they could get their hands on, despite the fact that they were already being lavishly supported by the oil allowances they awarded themselves.

It was, however, a wonderful time to be in the construction business. King Saud was on a building spree—palaces, universities, pipelines, desalination plants, airports—and bin Laden's company was growing at a fantastic rate. In 1954 the seat of government moved from Jeddah to Riyadh, which involved building an entire bureaucratic complex, as well as the embassies, hotels, residences, and highways that would accompany the new capital. The treasury was so overextended that the government had to pay bin Laden by giving him the Hotel al-Yamama, one of the two five-star hotels in Riyadh at the time.

Through clever alliances with powerful foreign corporations, bin Laden began diversifying. Binladen Kaiser became one of the largest engineering and construction companies in the world. Binladen Emco manufactured pre-cast concrete for mosques, hotels, hospitals, and stadiums. Al-Midhar Binladen Development Company provided consulting for foreign companies seeking entry into the Saudi market. Bin Laden Telecommunications Company represented Bell Canada, which got the plum government contracts in this field. Saudi Traffic Safety, another joint venture, was the largest highway-lane-marking company in the world. The empire grew to include manufacturing plants for brick, doors, windows, insulation, concrete, scaffolding, elevators, and air conditioners.

It was during this period that the monumental, almost Stalinesque Saudi architectural style began to assert itself. The immense, sometimes intimidating spaces fashioned of pre-stressed concrete announced the arrival in history of a new great power. And it was the Saudi Binladin Group,* as the company came to be called, that defined this colossal and highly ornamental aesthetic, which reached its apogee in the renovation of the Grand Mosque in Mecca—the most prestigious construction contract that could ever be granted in the Kingdom.

---

*The company styles the name slightly differently in variant English renderings, as do members of the family.

Surrounded by the lunar foothills of the al-Sarawat escarpment, which shield the city from the eyes of nonbelievers, Mecca
arose at the intersection of two ancient caravan routes and served
as a depot for silk, spices, and perfumes from Asia and Africa on
their way to the Mediterranean. Even before the advent of Islam,
this important trading center was esteemed as a holy site by
virtue of the empty cubical building called the Kaaba. In Muslim
tradition, the Kaaba is the center of the planet, the focus of all
Muslim prayer. It is said that Adam laid the first stone and that
the structure was rebuilt by the Prophet Ibrahim (Abraham in the
Jewish and Christian traditions) and his son Ishmael, the fore-
father of the Arabs, using the gray-blue rock from the enclosing
hills. Thus Mohammed bin Laden joined hands with the first man
and the progenitor of monotheism.

The renovation of the Grand Mosque took twenty years. Mohammed bin Laden would not live to see it finished; indeed, the
Saudi Binladin Group would renovate both the Grand Mosque
and the Prophet's Mosque a second time, at a total cost of more
than $18 billion. Bin Laden's original plan for the Grand Mosque is
a masterwork of crowd management, with forty-one main
entrances, bathroom facilities for 1,440 people, and escalators that
can transport 100,000 people per hour. Two wide galleries of
arches enclose a gargantuan open courtyard. During hajj, the
mosque can accommodate a million worshippers at once. Nearly
every surface—even the roof—is made of marble, lending the
building a final touch of cool, impersonal, formidable splendor—
the universal mark of modern Saudi religious architecture.

King Saud's rule was disastrous in so many ways that, in 1958,
Crown Prince Faisal effectively seized control of the government.
He later said that when he took over there was less than a hun-
dred dollars in the treasury. He couldn't meet the payroll or pay
the interest on the Kingdom's debt. The National Commercial
Bank turned down Faisal's application for a loan, citing King
Saud's miserable credit record. While the crown prince shopped
for another institution willing to bail out the government,
Mohammed bin Laden quietly fronted the money, a gesture that

sealed the ties between the bin Ladens and the royal family, and particularly between Faisal and his chief builder.

MOHAMMED BIN LADEN was one of the first people to view the country from above, rather than from the more modest vantage of the camel's back. He received special permission from the king to fly, an activity prohibited for private citizens, so he could survey his far-flung projects from the air. Most of his pilots were from the American military, which had begun training Saudi forces in 1953. The country is as big as the eastern half of the United States, but in the 1950s one could still fly from the Persian Gulf—or the Arabian Gulf, as the Arabs call it—to the Red Sea without seeing a single mark of civilization except for the occasional Mercedes trucks crisscrossing the desert floor along elusive caravan tracks. The imposing dunes flatten out and the wadis become dim tracings in the bright, buttery sand. There are no rivers, no large bodies of water, few trees. Development was confined largely to the oil fields in the salt flats of the Eastern Province. The entire lower portion of the country, an area the size of France, is called the Empty Quarter—a great forbidding vacancy, the largest sand desert in the world. Flying over the middle of the country, one sees a featureless graveled plain. In the northern section, the few pilots operating at the time would fly low to view the ruins of the Hijaz railroad, which the Arab forces, led by T. E. Lawrence, destroyed in the First World War.

As one flies west, however, the earth suddenly lurches up, forming the al-Sarawat Range, a steep mountain barrier that stretches a thousand miles, from Jordan to the southern coast of Yemen. There are peaks within the range over ten thousand feet high. The al-Sarawat escarpment divides the country into unequal halves, with the slender western portion, the cosmopolitan Hijaz, squeezed into the space between the mountains and the Red Sea, effectively cutting it off from the vastness and the radical spirituality of the interior.

Like a sentry on the mountain rim stands the ancient summer

resort of Taif. It is different from any other place in Arabia. The breeze from the Red Sea collides with the mountain barrier, creating a cooling updraft, which bathes the high plateau in fog and sudden violent rains. In the winter, there are occasional freezes. Before Islam, the region was noted for its vineyards, and later for its prickly pears and fruit trees—peaches, apricots, oranges, and pomegranates. Roses from Taif have such a potent aroma that they are used to make prized perfumes. Mountain lions once stalked herds of Arabian oryx in fields of wild lavender, but when the lions were hunted to near extinction, the local population of hamadryas baboons boomed out of control, roaming the upper reaches like a horde of demanding beggars. It was to Taif, surrounded by the cool gardens and the scent of eucalyptus, that the old king, Abdul Aziz, went to die, in November 1953.

Twice it has been Taif's unfortunate fate to stand in the way of the consolidation of Arabia, first spiritually and then politically. In 630 C.E., the Prophet Mohammed laid siege to the walled city, which until then had resisted his authority. The Muslim forces gained permission from their leader to use a catapult to breach the city's defenses despite the fact that women and children would be harmed. (Later, al-Qaeda would use this precedent to justify the killing of noncombatants on September 11, likening the use of airplanes to that of the catapult so long ago.) In that instance, the siege failed and Mohammed withdrew from the city, but within the year the town's leaders converted to Islam and the last outpost of paganism fell. Then again, in 1924, when Abdul Aziz was waging his campaign to unify Arabia, the city surrendered to the Ikhwan, only to see the town pillaged and more than three hundred men slaughtered, their throats slit, their corpses thrown into the public wells. With the fall of Taif, the rest of the Hijaz lay open to the Saudi forces.

In the aftermath of that massacre, Faisal, who was then one of the teenage warrior sons of Abdul Aziz, led the Saudis down the precipitous caravan trail that spiraled toward Mecca. He had a vision at the time that one day a genuine road would connect the Hijaz with the nation that his family was forging, however bloodily.

Until Faisal became king, however, a road to Taif remained an unattainable dream. The sheer mountain wall defied even the most muscular and sophisticated approaches of modern construction. A path could be blasted through the rock, but there was still the strategic problem of getting equipment to the site—the excavators, bulldozers, backhoes, dump trucks, and graders necessary for modern construction. Otherwise, the road would have to be built almost like a tunnel, with one segment completed before the next could be started. Faisal invited many foreign companies to bid on the project, but none of them could figure out how to do it, even with an extravagant budget. Then bin Laden offered to build the road. He even provided a timetable.

Bin Laden's brilliant solution for getting the equipment to the site was to disassemble the giant machines and mount the pieces on the backs of donkeys and camels. Once in place, the bulldozers and tractors were put back together and set to work.

In Taif, there is a legend that to establish the route, bin Laden pushed a donkey over the edge of the mountain and followed him as he picked his way down the course of the future highway. For twenty months, beginning in 1961, he lived with his men on the side of the mountain, personally setting the dynamite charges and marking the path for the bulldozers with chalk. Despite his timetable, work went slowly. Occasionally King Faisal would arrive at the site to inquire about the mounting unbudgeted expenses.

The two-lane road that bin Laden built tiptoes down the granite escarpment in long winding loops, past the circling raptors, through geological time zones. In the distance, the Red Sea underscores the horizon; just beyond lies the barren shore of Sudan. The craftsmanship of the workers is evident in the stone walls and bridges that echo the caravan trail nearby. About two-thirds of the way down the mountain, the granite turns into basalt, and then to sandstone; the road widens into four lanes and becomes less headlong; and then finally the highway breaks free, six lanes now, on the yellow desert floor. The road from Taif to Mecca is only fifty-five miles; when it was completed, Saudi

Arabia was finally united, and Mohammed bin Laden became a national hero.

IT IS THE CUSTOM IN THE KINGDOM THAT, during the fasting month of Ramadan, beggars bring their petitions to the princes and the wealthy members of society; it's a particularly intimate and direct expression of charity. Mohammed bin Laden was known to be pious and openhanded. He paid for the operation in Spain of a man who had lost his sight. On another occasion, a man sought his help in building a well for his village. Bin Laden not only provided the well, he also donated a mosque. He avoided the publicity that usually attends such notable gifts, saying that his intention was to please God, not to gain fame. "What I remember is that he always prayed on time and would inspire people around him to pray," his son Osama once recalled. "I do not remember him ever doing anything outside of Islamic law."

The extravagant side of Mohammed bin Laden's nature made itself evident when it came to women. Islam permits a man four wives at a time, and divorce is a simple matter, at least for a man, who only needs to declare, "I divorce you." Before his death, Mohammed bin Laden officially had fathered fifty-four children from twenty-two wives. The total number of wives he procured is impossible to determine, since he would often "marry" in the afternoon and divorce that night. An assistant followed behind to take care of any children he might have left in his wake. He also had a number of concubines, who stayed in the bin Laden compound if they bore him children. "My father used to say that he had fathered twenty-five sons for the jihad," his seventeenth son, Osama, later remembered.

Mohammed had already taken a Syrian wife from the port of Latakiya in the early fifties. He went to the region frequently on business, and in the summer of 1956 he met a fourteen-year-old girl named Alia Ghanem. Her family were citrus farmers living in two small villages outside the port, called Omraneya and Babryon. The region is a center of the Alawite sect, a branch of Shia Islam that claims 1.5 million adherents in Syria, including the ruling Assad family. Within Islam, the Alawites are often deni-grated as a cult since they incorporate certain Christian, Zoroas-trian, and pagan elements into their beliefs. They subscribe to the notion of reincarnation, believing that upon death a person may be transformed into another being or even a star. They also prac-tice *taqiyya*, or religious dissimulation—denying, for instance, that they are members of the sect to outsiders so they can blend into the mainstream.

Alia joined bin Laden's household as the fourth wife—a posi-tion that is sometimes called the "slave wife," especially by the wives with more tenure. It must have been all the more difficult for a girl of fourteen, taken from her family and placed in the highly restricted environment that bin Laden imposed. By com-parison with the other wives, Alia was modern and secular, although like all of bin Laden's wives she was fully veiled in pub-lic, not even letting her eyes show through the several layers of black linen.

Mohammed bin Laden and Alia's only child was born in Riyadh in January 1958, named Osama, "the Lion," after one of the com-panions of the Prophet. When he was six months old, the entire extended family moved to the holy city of Medina, where bin Laden was beginning renovation of the Prophet's Mosque. For most of Osama's young life, however, he lived in Jeddah. Though his father was by now prosperous and esteemed, the family occu-pied a large, ramshackle house in al-Amariyya, a modest neighbor-hood with small shops and lines of laundry hanging off the balconies. It was Jeddah's first suburb, built just outside the bound-ary of the old city walls. The house is gone now, replaced by a mosque, but Mohammed bin Laden's office across the street still stands—a dingy, one-story stucco building with a long row of barred windows. It bespeaks the modesty of a man who despised the show of wealth that was so characteristic of the newly rich nation. "Rest his soul, my father was very strict, and he would pay no attention to appearances," Osama said. "Our house was of a lower standard than most of the houses of the people working for us."

Osama spent his early years among a horde of children in his father's house. Mohammed ran the family like a corporation, with each wife reporting on her division. The children rarely saw the great man, who was often away on business. Whenever he returned, he would call them into his office and gaze upon his vast brood. During the Islamic feasting days, he would kiss them and give each child a gold coin; otherwise, he rarely spoke to them. "I remember reciting a poem to him, and he gave me a hundred riyals, which was a huge amount of money in those days," Osama remembered. The children sought to either please him or run from him. It is not surprising that the remote and powerful father stirred deep currents of longing in his shy and willowy son, even though their exchanges were rare.

Mohammed frequently entertained distinguished male guests in his modest home, especially during the hajj, when pilgrims from all over the world passed through Jeddah on their way to worship at the holy sites. In typical Saudi manner, the men would sit barefoot on the carpeted floor, resting one arm against a bolster, as Mohammed's younger sons passed wordlessly among them, serving dates and pouring weak cardamom coffee from long-spouted silver pots. The patriarch enjoyed religious debates, and he would bring together the most notable clerics in the Kingdom to discuss often very obscure points of theology.

By now, the bin Laden construction empire extended well beyond Saudi Arabia. One of Mohammed's major projects outside the Kingdom was the renovation of the Al Aqsa Mosque in Jerusalem, which meant that the three holiest spots in Islam all bore his mark. "He gathered his engineers and asked them to estimate the cost of the project, without profit," Osama later stated. "Because of God's graciousness to him, sometimes he prayed in all three mosques in one single day."

Mohammed bin Laden had a custom of marrying off ex-wives who had borne him children to employees of his company. The wives had little or no say in the matter. They sometimes found themselves marrying below what they now considered their station—to a driver, for instance—an arrangement that influenced the future standing of their children in the family. Alia was fortunate when Mohammed decided to divorce her. He awarded her to one of his executives, Mohammed al-Attas, who was a descendant of the Prophet. Osama was four or five years old. He moved with his mother a few blocks away, to a modest two-story villa on Jabal al-Arab Street. The house was white stucco with a small courtyard and a black filigree iron gate in front of the garage. On top of the flat roof was a towering television antenna. Over one of the front entrances there was a brown-and-white-striped awning—the doorway that women used; the men entered through the gate into the courtyard.

Soon after Osama moved to the new house, Mohammed bin Laden died in a plane crash on his way to take another teenage bride. His body was so charred he could only be identified by his wristwatch. At the time of his death, Mohammed was still an active, vigorous man, not yet sixty years old, at the peak of his astonishing career. "King Faisal said upon the death of my father that today I have lost my right arm," Osama once remarked. Mohammed's sons were not yet old enough to take control of the family enterprise, so the king appointed three trustees who ran the company for the next ten years. One of the men, Sheikh Mohammed Saleh Bahareth, also oversaw the education of bin Laden's children. Their inheritance was withheld until they were twenty-one—and in any case, most of the value was tied up in the ownership of the construction empire their father had created.

THE MARRIAGE BETWEEN ALIA and her second husband proved to be an enduring match. Attas was kind and calm, but his relation to his stepson was somewhat compromised by the fact that Osama was the child of his employer. As for Osama, he went from being in a house full of children to one in which he was the only child. Eventually three younger half brothers and a half sister would be born, and Osama oversaw them almost as a third parent. "If his stepfather wanted something done, he would tell Osama," remembered Khaled Batarfi, who lived across the street and became his childhood companion. "His brothers say they didn't fear their father as much as they did Osama." Only with his mother did Osama let down his mask of authority. "She was the only person he would talk to about the small things," said Batarfi, "like what he had for lunch today."

Khaled Batarfi and Osama bin Laden were from the same large tribe, the Kendah, which has as many as 100,000 members. The tribe had originated in the Najd, the heart of the Kingdom, but then had migrated into the Hadramout in Yemen. "The Kendah are known to be bright," said Batarfi. "Usually they are fighters, well armed, and they have an air about them." Khaled found his new playmate "calm, shy, almost girlish. He was peaceful, but when he was angry, he was frightening."

Osama enjoyed television, especially westerns. *Bonanza* was his favorite show, and he adored *Fury,* a series about a boy and his silky black stallion. On summer mornings, after the dawn prayer, the boys would play soccer. Osama was an average player who could have been better if he had concentrated on the sport. But his mind was always somewhere else.

After the death of Mohammed bin Laden, the trustee sent most of the sons to Lebanon for their education. Only Osama remained behind, which would always mark him as the most provincial of the bin Laden boys. This was despite the fact that he enrolled in Jeddah's best school, called al-Thagr, on the road to Mecca. King Faisal had created the school in the early fifties for the education of his own sons. It was a free public school, but the standards were extremely high and the rector reported directly to the king. Students could gain admission only by passing a highly competitive examination. The goal was to have all classes of Saudi society represented, entirely on the basis of merit. This policy was so strictly adhered to that several sons of King Khalid were booted out while he was still on the throne.

Osama was a member of a class of sixty-eight students, only two of whom were members of the royal family. Fifty of his classmates went on to gain their doctorates. "He was a normal, not excellent, student," said Ahmed Badeeb, who taught Osama science courses for three years. The lives of these two men, bin Laden and Badeeb, would intertwine in unexpected ways in the future, as bin Laden was drawn to jihad and Badeeb became a member of Saudi intelligence.

All of the students dressed in Western clothes—a jacket and tie during the winter, pants and shirt during the rest of the school year. Osama stood out because he was tall and gangly and physically slow to mature. As his classmates began sporting moustaches and goatees, bin Laden remained clean-shaven because his beard was so light. His teachers found him shy and fearful of making mistakes.

In Osama's fourteenth year he experienced a religious and political awakening. Some ascribe the change to a charismatic Syrian gym teacher at the school who was a member of the Muslim Brothers. Osama stopped watching cowboy shows. Outside of school, he refused to wear Western dress. Sometimes he would sit in front of the television and weep over the news from Palestine. "In his teenage years, he was the same nice kid," his mother later related. "But he was more concerned, sad, and frustrated about the situation in Palestine in particular, and the Arab and Muslim world in general." He tried to explain his feelings to his friends and family, but his passion left them nonplussed. "He thought Muslims are not close enough to Allah, and Muslim youth are too busy playing and having fun," his mother concluded. He began fasting twice a week, on Mondays and Thursdays, in emulation of the Prophet. He went to bed right after *isha,* the evening prayer. In addition to the five prayers a day, he set his alarm for one in the morning and prayed alone every night. Osama became quite stern with his younger half siblings, especially about rising early to go to the mosque for the dawn prayer.

He was rarely angry except when sexual matters came up. When he thought one of his half brothers was flirting with a maid, Osama slapped him. Another time, when he was in a café in Beirut, one of his brother's friends produced a porno magazine. Osama made it clear that neither he nor any of his brothers would ever have anything to do with the boy again. There seems never to have been a moment in his entire life when he gave way to the sins of the flesh, venal or ribald behavior, the temptations of liquor, smoking, or gambling. Food held little interest for him. He loved adventure and poetry and little else but God.

Osama's mother watched the evolution of his religious convictions with alarm. She confided her anxiety to her younger sister, Leila Ghanem. "In the beginning of his path, being his mother, she was very concerned," her sister later said. "When she saw that this was his conviction, something he would not budge from, she said, 'God protect him.' "

On one occasion, Osama was riding with his family to Syria, to visit his mother's relatives, which they did every summer. The driver put on a cassette tape of the Egyptian diva Umm Kalthoum. Her powerful vibrato was so expressive of love and longing that it often brought her listeners to tears or involuntary gasps of desire. The lyrics called up the ancient verses of the desert bards:

You are more precious than my days, more beautiful than my dreams
Take me to your sweetness, away from the universe
Far, far away

Osama flared up. He ordered the driver to turn it off. The driver refused. "We are paying you," Osama reminded him. "If you don't shut the music off right now, you can take us back to Jeddah!" Everyone else in the car, including his mother and his stepfather, was silent in the face of Osama's anger. The driver relented.

His intransigent piety was unusual in his elevated social circle, but many young Saudis found refuge in intense expressions of religiosity. Exposed to so few alternative ways of thinking even about Islam, they were trapped in a two-dimensional spiritual world; they could only become more extreme or less so. Extremism had its consolations, as it always does; in Osama's case, it obviously shielded him from his teenage sexual urges. There was also in his nature a romance with the spirituality of the desert, humble and stripped of distraction. Throughout his life, he would hunger for austerity like a vice: the desert, the cave, and his as yet unspoken desire to die anonymously in a trench in warfare. But it was difficult to hold on to this self-conception while being chauffeured around the Kingdom in the family Mercedes.

At the same time, Osama made an effort not to be too much of a prig. Although he was opposed to the playing of musical instruments, he organized some of his friends into an a cappella singing group. They even recorded some of their tunes about jihad, which for them meant the internal struggle to improve themselves, not holy war. Osama would make copies and give them each a tape. When they played soccer, Osama would bring along tuna and cheese sandwiches for the other players, even on days when he was fasting. His commitment and composure commanded respect. Out of modesty, he stopped wearing regular soccer shorts and took to playing in long pants. In deference to his beliefs, the other players followed suit.

They would often go to play in the poorer districts of Jeddah. During lunch, even if he was fasting, Osama would divide his teammates into different groups, named after companions of the Prophet, and quiz them on the Quran. "The Abu Bakr group wins!" he would exclaim. "Now, let's have cakes."

He had an adventurous adolescence—mountain climbing in Turkey and big-game hunting in Kenya. On his family farm south of Jeddah, Osama kept a stable of horses, having as many as twenty at one time, including his favorite, a mare named al-Balqa. He liked to ride and shoot, just like the cowboys on his favorite television shows.

Osama began driving early, and he drove fast. In the mid-seventies, when he was sixteen or seventeen, he had a big white Chrysler that he accidentally ran into a culvert and destroyed. Amazingly, he was unhurt. After that, however, he made an effort to slow down. He began driving a Toyota jeep and a Mercedes 280S—the kind of car a respectable Saudi businessman would drive. But he still had trouble keeping his foot off the gas.

His science teacher, Ahmed Badeeb, noticed the change in his strong-willed young student. "At this time, Osama was trying to prove himself within the company," said Badeeb. "There is a law in the bin Laden family that if you prove yourself as a man, you can inherit." The Saudi Binladin Group had a contract for a large project in Jizan, near the Yemen border, and Osama badly wanted to be a part of it. "I decided to drop out of school to achieve my goals and dreams," bin Laden later related. "I was surprised at the major opposition to this idea, especially from my mother, who cried and begged me to change my mind. In the end, there was no way out. I couldn't resist my mother's tears. I had to go back and finish my education."

In 1974, while he was still in high school, Osama married for the first time. He was seventeen, she was fourteen—Najwa Ghanem, his cousin from his mother's village in Syria. She was unusually tall and quite beautiful. There was a small wedding party for the men in Osama's house, who never got to see the bride. Bin Laden's future sister-in-law, Carmen, described Najwa as meek and "constantly pregnant."

It was also during this time, in high school, that bin Laden joined the Muslim Brothers. The organization was very much an underground movement in Saudi Arabia in the 1970s. "Only nerds were in it," a fellow member recalled. The members were highly religious teenagers like bin Laden, and although they were not actively conspiring against the government, their meetings were secret and took place in private homes. The group sometimes went together on pilgrimages to Mecca, or on outings to the beach, where they would proselytize and pray. "We were hoping to establish an Islamic state anywhere," said Jamal Khashoggi, a friend of bin Laden's who joined the Brotherhood at about the same time. "We believed that the first one would lead to another, and that would have a domino effect which could reverse the history of mankind."

Bin Laden entered King Abdul Aziz University in Jeddah in 1976. He studied economics, but he was more involved in campus religious affairs. "I formed a religious charity at school, and we devoted a lot of time to interpreting the Quran and jihad," he later said.

In his first year in the university, bin Laden met Mohammed Jamal Khalifa, another member of the Brotherhood, who would become his closest friend. Jamal Khalifa was a year older than bin Laden. A gregarious young man with an easy smile, Khalifa came from a family of modest means, although he was able to trace his lineage back to the Prophet, which gave him a standing in Islamic society quite apart from his financial status. He and Osama played soccer together. Bin Laden, being tall and fast, was the striker, always in front. The two young men soon became inseparable.

On weekends, they would head out into the desert between Jeddah and Mecca, usually staying at the bin Ladens' family farm, an oasis called al-Barood. To keep the Bedouins from homesteading on his property, bin Laden erected a small cabin, little more than a kitchen and a toilet, and began farming. He kept a small herd of sheep and a stable of horses. Even in the summer he would cast off his shoes as soon as he arrived and walk barefoot through the scorching sand.

"Osama was very stubborn," Khalifa said. "We were riding horses in the desert, and we were really going very fast. I saw fine sand in front of us, and I told Osama this is dangerous, better stay away. He said no, and he continued. His horse turned over and he fell down. He got up laughing. Another time, we were riding in a jeep. Whenever he saw a hill, he would drive very fast and go over it, even though we didn't know what was on the other side. Really, he put us in danger many times."

It was a time of spiritual questioning for both of them. "Islam is different from any other religion; it's a way of life," said Khalifa. "We were trying to understand what Islam has to say about how we eat, who we marry, how we talk. We read Sayyid Qutb. He was the one who most affected our generation." Many of the professors at the university were members of the Brotherhood who had been run out of Egypt or Syria. They had brought with them the idea of a highly politicized Islam, one that fused the state and the religion into a single, all-encompassing theocracy. Bin Laden and Khalifa were drawn to them because they seemed more open-minded than the Saudi scholars and were willing to lead them to the books that would change their lives, such as Qutb's *Milestones* and *In the Shade of the Quran*. Each week, Mohammad Qutb, the younger brother of the martyr, would lecture at the school. Although bin Laden never formally studied with Qutb, he usually attended his public lectures. Qutb was extremely popular with the students, who noted his calm demeanor despite the fact that he had also endured the rigors of Nasser's prisons.

At that moment Mohammed Qutb was jealously defending his brother's reputation, which was under attack from moderate Islamists. They contended that *Milestones* had empowered a new, more violent group of radicals, especially in Egypt, who used Sayyid Qutb's writings to justify attacks on anyone they considered an infidel, including other Muslims. Foremost among Qutb's critics was Hasan Hudaybi, the Supreme Guide of the Muslim Brothers, who published his own prison book, *Preachers Not Judges*, to counter Qutb's seductive call to chaos. In Hudaybi's far more orthodox theology, no Muslim could deny the belief of another so long as he made the simple profession of faith: "There is no God but God, and Mohammed is His messenger." The debate, which had been born in the Egyptian prisons with Qutb and Hudaybi, was quickly spreading throughout Islam, as young Muslims took sides in this argument about who is a Muslim and who is not. "Osama read Hudaybi's book in 1978, and we talked about it," Jamal Khalifa recalled. "Osama agreed with him completely." His views would soon change, however, and it was this fundamental shift—from Hudaybi's tolerant and accepting view of Islam to Qutb's narrow and judgmental one—that would open the door to terror.

That same year, Osama and Najwa's son Abdullah was born. He was the first of their eleven children, and following Arab tradition, the parents came to be called Abu (the father of) Abdullah and Umm (the mother of) Abdullah. Unlike his own father, Osama was attentive and playful with his children—he loved to take his quickly expanding family to the beach—but he was also demanding. He had unyielding ideas about the need to prepare them for the tough life ahead. On the weekends, he brought both his sons and his daughters with him to the farm to live with camels and horses. They would sleep under the stars, and if it was cold, they would dig and cover themselves with sand. Bin Laden refused to let them attend school, instead bringing tutors into the house, so he could supervise every detail of their education. "He wanted to make them tough, not like other children," said Jamal Khalifa. "He thought other kids were spoiled."

Bin Laden's second son, Abdul Rahman, was born with a rare

and poorly understood birth defect called hydrocephalus, commonly called water on the brain. It results from an excess of cerebrospinal fluid building up inside the neural ventricles, which in turn causes the head to enlarge and the brain to shrink. After birth, the head continues to expand unless the fluid is drained. Abdul Rahman's condition was so serious that bin Laden himself took the baby to the United Kingdom for treatment—probably the only time that he traveled in the West. When the doctors told him that Abdul Rahman would need a shunt in his brain, bin Laden declined to let them operate. Instead, he returned to the Kingdom and treated the child himself, using honey, a folk remedy for many ailments. Unfortunately, Abdul Rahman became mildly retarded. As he grew older, he was prone to emotional outbursts. He had difficulty fitting in with the other children, especially in the robust outdoor life that bin Laden prescribed for them; often he would cry for attention or provoke fights if things weren't going as he wanted them to. Nonetheless, bin Laden always insisted on including Abdul Rahman, taking special care to make sure he was never left alone.

JAMAL KHALIFA also wanted to marry. The custom, in Saudi Arabia, is for the groom to pay a bride price and furnish a home before the wedding takes place. Khalifa found a suitable young woman, but he didn't have enough money to provide an apartment. Bin Laden owned a lot near the university, and he built a small home for his friend. Unfortunately, it was too spartan for Khalifa's bride.

Bin Laden did not take offense; indeed, he made an even more generous gesture. At that time, he was living in his mother's house with his stepfather and their children. Osama and his family occupied the first floor, which he divided in half by building a wall through the middle of the living room; then he invited Khalifa and his bride to move in. "You live on this side, and I'll live on the other," bin Laden said. Khalifa and his wife lived there until he graduated from King Abdul Aziz University in 1980.

While they were still in the university, Osama and Jamal made a resolution. They decided to practice polygamy. It had become socially unacceptable in Saudi Arabia. "Our fathers' generation was using polygamy in not a very good way. They would not give equal justice to their wives," Khalifa admitted. "Sometimes they would marry and divorce in the same day. The Egyptian media used to put this on television, and it made a very bad impression. So, we said, 'Let's practice this and show people we can do it properly.' " In 1982 bin Laden set an example by marrying a woman from the Sabar family in Jeddah who was descended from the Prophet. She was highly educated, with a Ph.D. in child psychology, and taught at the women's college of King Abdul Aziz University. Seven years older than Osama, she bore him one child, a son, and became known as Umm Hamza.

Managing two families wasn't easy, but bin Laden wasn't discouraged. He developed a theory of multiple marriages. "One is okay, like walking. Two is like riding a bicycle: it's fast but a little unstable. Three is a tricycle, stable but slow. And when we come to four, ah! This is the ideal. Now you can pass everyone!"

He bought a run-down four-unit apartment building on the corner of Wadi as-Safa Street and Wadi Bishah, about a mile from his mother's home. The units were in alternating gray and peach colors, and each had window air-conditioning units. There used to be an old pasta factory nearby, and because street numbers are rarely used in the Kingdom, bin Laden's new dwelling got to be known as the house on Macaroni Street. He put his two families in separate units. He married again a few years later a woman from the Sharif family in Medina, who was also highly educated—she held a doctorate in Arabic grammar and taught at the local teachers college. They would have three daughters and a son, so this wife was known as Umm Khaled. His fourth wife, Umm Ali, came from the Gilaini family in Mecca, and she bore him three children.

Academically undistinguished himself, and clearly uninterested, bin Laden would never pursue the respectable professions, such as law, engineering, or medicine, that might have given him independent standing. His brothers were being educated at the finest universities in the world, but the example that meant the most to him was that of his illiterate father. He spoke of him constantly and held him up as a paragon. He longed to achieve comparable distinction—and yet he lived in a culture where individuality was discouraged, or at least reserved for royalty. Like other members of the Saudi upper class, the bin Ladens prospered on royal favors, which they were loath to put at risk. Moreover, they were outsiders—still Yemenis, in the eyes of clannish Saudis. There was no political system, no civil society, no obvious route to greatness. Bin Laden was untrained for the clergy, which was the sole alternative to royal power in the Kingdom. His obvious future was to remain in the family company, far down the list in seniority, respected within his family ambit but never able to really make a mark.

Bin Laden continued to pester his older brothers to let him work for the company, and finally they gave him a part-time job in Mina, in the holy complex of Mecca. They expected it to take six months, but bin Laden declared, "I want to be like my father. I will work day and night with no rest." He was still trying to finish his studies, so after classes he would race to Mecca, where his job was to level hills to make room for the new highways and hotels and pilgrimage centers that the Saudi Binladin Group was building. He insisted on working directly with the laborers he was supposed to oversee, and he spent many hours operating bulldozers and earth-moving equipment. It had already become unusual to see Saudis doing physical labor—most such jobs were held by expatriates from the Philippines or the Indian subcontinent—so the sight of the founder's lanky scion caked with the sweat and dust of heavy construction made a startling impression. "I recall, with pride, that I was the only family member who succeeded in combining work and doing excellently in school," bin Laden later bragged; but, in truth, the schedule was unmanageable, even for him. At the end of the semester he dropped out of the university, a year short of graduation, and went to work for the company full-time.

He was just over six feet tall—not the giant that he was later made out to be. An acquaintance recalled meeting him in this period, before jihad changed everything. "Somebody died and we went to give condolences," the friend said. Bin Laden was in his early twenties, he was very handsome, with fair skin, a full beard, and broad, swollen lips. His nose was long and complex, being narrow and straight at the top, then abruptly spreading out into two broad wings with an upturned tip. He wore a black headband around his white headscarf, and under his scarf, his hair was short, black, and frizzy. He was gaunt from fasting and hard work. His high, reedy voice, and his demure and languid manner added to an impression of frailty. "He was confident and charismatic," the friend observed. Even though religious scholars were present, bin Laden presented himself almost as an equal. When he spoke, his composure was spellbinding. Everyone in the room was drawn to him. "What struck me is that he came from such a hierarchical family," said his friend, "but he broke the hierarchy."

4

Change

KING FAISAL SENT HIS SONS to America to be educated. The youngest, Turki, was packed off to the Lawrenceville School in New Jersey in 1959, when he was fourteen years old. It was an upper-class prep school, but for Turki it was an experience in American egalitarianism. On the first day, another student introduced himself by slapping the prince on the butt and asking his name. When Turki responded, the student asked, "Like a Thanksgiving turkey?" No one really understood or cared who he was, and this novel experience allowed him to be somebody new. His classmates called him Turk or Feaslesticks.

He was dashingly handsome, with a high forehead, wavy black hair, and a deep cleft in his chin. He had his father's hawkish features but not the ferocity that animated the old man's eyes; his aspect was more interior and bemused. Although he was president of the French Club, he was a sportsman, not a scholar. He played varsity soccer and represented the New Jersey fencing team in the 1962 Junior Olympics. He was highly intelligent but unfocused in his studies. When he graduated he went to college a few miles away at Princeton, but flunked out after one semester. He transferred to Georgetown University in Washington, D.C., where in 1964, one of his classmates approached him and asked, "Did you hear the news? Your father has become king."

From the safe distance of America, Turki followed the tumult in his country, including the financial rescue by Mohammed bin Laden—a timely gesture that allowed Faisal to reorganize and stabilize the Kingdom during a period of rising Arab socialism, when the royal family might well have been overthrown. The bond between the royal family and the bin Ladens was particularly strong with the children of King Faisal. They would never forget the favor that bin Laden had done for their father when he assumed the throne.

After Israel's victory in the 1967 Six Day War, the entire Arab world sank into a state of despondency. Turki became so depressed that he began skipping classes, then had to make up the work in summer school. One of his classmates, a gregarious young man from Arkansas named Bill Clinton, spent four hours coaching him for an ethics test. It was August 19, Clinton's twenty-first birthday. Turki got a B in the class, but he dropped out of Georgetown soon afterward without finishing his undergraduate degree. He continued taking courses at Princeton and Cambridge but was never really motivated to graduate.

Finally, in 1973, he returned to the Kingdom and went to ask his father what he should do next. The king understood him to be seeking a job. He raised his right eyebrow up to the sky and said, "Look, I didn't give any of your brothers a job. Go look for your own job." Of course, the king's youngest son had little to concern himself with, since his place in life was already assured by his family's immense wealth and his father's firm grip on the affairs of the Kingdom. Turki's maternal uncle, Sheikh Kamal Adham, offered him a post in the Foreign Liaison Bureau. "I had no interest in intelligence," Turki said. "I didn't even realize the job was in the intelligence field. I thought it had something to do with diplomacy." Quiet-spoken and intellectual, he seemed more suited to a profession that relied on ceremonial dinners and cordial negotiations on the tennis court than one that called on the darker skills. He married Princess Nouf bint Fahd al-Saud, from a neighboring branch of the royal family, and settled into a life of wealth that only a handful on the planet could match. But the plates of history were shifting, and the blissful existence he enjoyed was drifting toward a cataclysm.

.   .   .

PRINCE TURKI RETURNED to his homeland at a fateful juncture. Many Saudis were unprepared for the abrupt transformation
that their culture had endured since the first oil boom. In their
own lifetimes, they remembered a country that was starkly fundamental in every aspect. Most Saudis in the 1950s lived as their
ancestors had lived two thousand years before. Few actually
thought of themselves as Saudi, since the concept of nationality
meant little to them, and government occupied practically no
place in their lives. They were tribesmen without boundaries. The
enforced equality of poverty and meager expectations had created
a society as horizontal as the desert floor. Tribal codes of behavior,
coupled with the injunctions of the Quran, had governed individual thought and action. Many, perhaps the majority, had never
seen an automobile or a foreigner. There was little education
beyond the ritual memorization of the Quran, and scarce need for
more. The essential experience of living on the Arabian Peninsula
was that nothing changed. The eternal and the present were one
and the same.

Suddenly into this desert rushed a flood of change: roads,
cities, schools, expatriate workers, dollar bills, and an overriding
new awareness of the world and one's place in it. Their country—
and their lives—became alien to them. Thrown into the global
marketplace of ideas and values, many Saudis looking for something worthy in their own traditions found it in the unsparing
beliefs that informed their understanding of Islam. Wahhabism
provided a dam against the overwhelming, raging river of
modernity. There was a widespread feeling, not only among
extremists, that this torrent of progress was eroding the essential
quality of Arabia, which was its sacredness.

Unimaginable wealth had fallen on these austere desert
nomads—a gift from God because of their piety, they genuinely
believed. Paradoxically, this gift was undermining every facet of
their identity. Within twenty years of the first great oil boom in the
1950s, the average Saudi income was nearly equal to that of
the United States and increasing at a rate that promised to make
the Kingdom the largest economy in the world. Such tantalizing
expectations masked the fact that class divisions were shearing

apart a country that still fancied itself an extended tribal community. The spendthrift Saudi became a worldwide stereotype of
greed, gluttony, corruption, hypocrisy, and—even more offensive
to his dignity—a figure of fun. The sheer waste of fortunes at the
gaming tables, the drinking, the whoring, the avarice of the Saudi
women with their silver minks and their shopping bags on the
Champs-Elysées, the casual buying of jewels that could capsize
national economies, amused a world that was also shaken by the
prospect of a future in which the Saudis owned practically everything. This anxiety was sharpened by the 1973 oil embargo, which
caused prices to skyrocket and created genuine problems for a
Saudi government that simply didn't know how to spend all its
money. The wholesale squandering of wealth, both public and
private, only demonstrated the bottomless pocket that Saudi Arabia had become—at least, for the royal family.

They not only ruled the country, they essentially owned it. All
unclaimed land belonged to the king; he alone decided who could
acquire property. As the country expanded, the king's uncles and
aunts, brothers and sisters, nieces, nephews, and cousins grabbed
the richest parcels. Still not sated, the princes forced themselves
into business deals as "agents" or "consultants," raking in billions
in the form of kickbacks and bribes. This toll on commerce came
despite the fact that Al Saud—the royal family—had already
appropriated 30 or 40 percent of the country's oil profits in the
form of allowances for family members. Al Saud personified all
the venal changes in the Saudi identity, and it was natural that
their subjects would consider revolution.

Nonetheless, in a society with so few institutions, the royal
family was a conspicuously progressive force. In 1960, against
powerful resistance from the Wahhabi establishment, Crown
Prince Faisal had introduced female education; two years later he
formally abolished slavery. He prevailed upon President John F.
Kennedy to send American forces to protect the Kingdom during
the border war against Yemen. He brought television to the Kingdom, although one of his nephews was killed while leading a
protest against the opening of the broadcast station in 1965. He

was freer to act than his predecessor because his own piety was unquestioned, but he was wary of extremists who were constantly policing the thoughts and actions of mainstream Saudi society. From the point of view of some fervent believers, the most insidious accomplishment of Faisal's reign was to co-opt the ulema—the clergy—by making them employees of the state. By promoting moderate voices over others, the government sought to temper the radicalism spawned by the tumultuous experience of modernization. Faisal was such a powerful king that he was able to force these changes on his society at a stunning pace.

His sons helped the king consolidate his power. Turki became the Kingdom's spymaster, and his older brother, Prince Saud, was appointed the foreign minister. Between these two American-educated princes, Saudi Arabia began to assert itself in the world community. The Kingdom's stupendous wealth would ease the disorientation of rapid change and the resentment of royal corruption; and the creation of a sophisticated, technologically savvy elite would open the shutters on this deeply suspicious, fervently religious society. But in 1975 King Faisal was murdered by his nephew (the brother of the man who protested the opening of the television station), and that promising future died with him.

IN THE EARLY MORNING of November 20, 1979, Turki received a summons from King Khaled, his father's successor. Turki was in Tunis with Crown Prince Fahd, attending the Arab Summit. Turki was thirty-four years old, and he was about to face the biggest crisis in the brief history of Saudi Arabia.

That morning at dawn, the aged imam of the Grand Mosque of Mecca, Sheikh Mohammed al-Subayil, had been preparing to lead the prayers of fifty thousand Muslims gathered for the final day of hajj. As he approached the microphone, he was shoved aside, and a burst of gunfire echoed in the holy sanctuary. A ragged band of insurgents standing among the worshippers suddenly pulled rifles from under their robes. They chained the gates closed, trapping the pilgrims inside, and killed several policemen.

"Your attention, O Muslims!" a rough-looking man with an untrimmed beard cried. *"Allahu akhbar!"*—God is great—"The Mahdi has appeared!"

"The Mahdi! The Mahdi!" the armed men cried.

It was New Year's Day of the Islamic year 1400—the bloody inauguration of a turbulent new century. In some of the disputed oral traditions of Islam, the Mahdi ("the one who guides") will appear shortly before the end of time. The concept of the Mahdi is a controversial one, especially in Wahhabi Islam, since this messiah is not mentioned in the Quran. Tradition says that the Mahdi will be a descendant of the Prophet and will carry his name (Mohammed bin Abdullah), and that he will appear during the hajj. Eventually, Jesus will return and ask his people to adhere to Islam. Together, Jesus and the Mahdi will fight the Antichrist and restore justice and peace to the earth.

The man claiming to be the Mahdi was Mohammed Abdullah al-Qahtani, but the real leader of the revolt was Juhayman al-Oteibi, a fundamentalist preacher and former corporal in the National Guard. The two men had been imprisoned together for sedition, and it was during that time, Oteibi claimed, that God had revealed to him in a dream that Qahtani was the Mahdi.

Qahtani was persuaded by Oteibi's dream that he must be the chosen one. When the two men got out of prison, he married Oteibi's sister. Soon they began attracting followers with their messianic message, especially young theology students from the Islamic University in Medina, a center of Muslim Brothers radicalism. Thanks to donations from wealthy adherents, Oteibi's disciples were well armed and trained. Some, like Oteibi himself, were members of the Saudi National Guard, which is charged with protecting the royal family. Their goal was to seize power and institute theocratic rule, in expectation of the rapidly approaching apocalypse.

Jamal Khalifa, who was living in bin Laden's house at the time, used to see Oteibi and his followers preaching in different mosques, often making blunders in their recitations of the Quran. Bin Laden would have seen them as well. People were stunned to hear them speaking openly against the government. They even tore riyals in half because the bills bore the picture of the king.

These were unheard-of actions in a country that was so strictly controlled; and yet there was an ingrained reluctance on the part of the government to confront religious extremists. At some point, members of the ulema cross-examined Oteibi and Qahtani to discover any signs of heresy, but they were let go. They were seen as rustic throwbacks to the Ikhwan fanatics, the shock troops of King Abdul Aziz; indeed, Oteibi was the grandchild of one of those men. No one imagined that they posed a real threat to the established order.

Just before the insurgents cut the telephone lines, an employee of the bin Laden organization, which was still renovating the Grand Mosque, called the company headquarters and reported what had happened; then a representative of the company notified King Khaled.

Turki returned from Tunis to Jeddah at nine o'clock that night and drove his own car to Mecca. The entire city had been evacuated, and the streets were spookily vacant. The giant stadium lights that usually illuminated the immense mosque were cut off, along with all power, so the building loomed mountainously in shadow. Turki went to a hotel where his uncle, Prince Sultan, who was the minister of defense, was waiting for him. As Turki entered the hotel, a shot rang out from one of the rebel snipers in the minarets, shattering the glass door in his hands.

Later that evening, Turki moved to the command post, a hundred meters from the mosque, where he would remain for the next two weeks. Most of the hostages had been let go, but an undetermined number of them were still locked in the sanctuary. No one knew how many insurgents there were, how many weapons they had, what kinds of preparations had been made. About a hundred security officers from the Interior Ministry had made an initial attempt to regain the mosque. They were immediately gunned down.

Forces from the Saudi Army and the National Guard soon joined the surviving security officers. Before the princes on the scene could order a military assault on the mosque, however, they first had to gain permission from the Saudi clerical establishment, and there was no certainty that they would receive that blessing. The Quran forbids violence of any kind within the Grand Mosque—not even a plant can be uprooted—so the prospect of a gun battle within the holy confines posed a dilemma for both the government and the ulema. The king would face revolt from his own men if he ordered them to open fire within the sanctuary. On the other hand, if the ulema refused to issue a fatwa endorsing the government's right to reclaim the mosque, they could be seen as siding with the rebels. The historic compact between the royal family and the clergy would be broken, and who could guess the outcome?

The leader of the ulema was Abdul Aziz bin Baz, blind, seventy years old, an eminent religious scholar but a man who was suspicious of science and hostile to modernity. He claimed that the sun rotated around the earth and that the manned landing on the moon had never occurred. Now bin Baz found himself in an awkward and compromised position: Oteibi had been his student in Medina. Whatever bargain was struck during the meeting between the ulema and King Khaled, the government emerged with a fatwa authorizing the use of lethal force. With this decree, Prince Sultan ordered an artillery barrage followed by frontal assaults on three of the main gates. They never got close to breaching the rebel defenses.

Inside the mosque were four or five hundred insurgents, including some women and children. They included not only Saudis but also Yemenis, Kuwaitis, Egyptians, and even some American Black Muslims. In the weeks leading up to the hajj, they had stolen automatic weapons from the armory of the National Guard and smuggled them into the compound on biers on which the dead were commonly brought for ritual washing. The rebels had hidden their arms and supplies within the hundreds of tiny underground chambers beneath the courtyard that were used as hermitages for pilgrims on retreat. Now they were well fortified, and they had taken up commanding positions in the upper stories of the mosque. Snipers were picking off Saudi forces whenever they showed themselves.

In the field headquarters outside the mosque, a number of senior princes and the generals of rival services congregated, and their reckless orders, compounded by abundant contradictory advice from the military attachés from the United States and Pakistan, were causing confusion and needless fatalities. In the middle of the day, Sultan directed a suicidal helicopter assault in which troops were lowered on ropes into the vast courtyard in the center of the mosque. They were slaughtered. At that point, the king turned to the young Prince Turki, putting him in charge.

Turki worked out a strategy that would minimize casualties and damage to the holy shrine. The first priority was intelligence, and for that he called on the bin Ladens. The brothers had maps and electrical layouts and all the technical information about the mosque that would be critical for the assault that Turki was contemplating.

Salem bin Laden, the oldest of the brothers and the head of the clan, arrived on the hood of a car brandishing a machine gun. Salem was a wonderful character, so much the opposite of his pious, remote, and taciturn father. He was known throughout the Kingdom for his bravado and his nutty humor, traits that endeared him to the king, who loved him despite the practical jokes that Salem sometimes played on him. A daredevil pilot, Salem would buzz the ruler's desert camp and carry on such antics in the sky that the king eventually banned him from flying.* Once, according to family legend, Salem had a hemorrhoid operation, and he had a videotape of the procedure sent to the king. In this stoic culture, few people—perhaps no one else—exercised such rough liberties.

Oteibi and his followers had control of the mosque's public address system, and they were using this opportunity to broadcast their message to the world. Despite the government's efforts to marginalize the insurgents as religious fanatics upset by the spread of video games and football, Oteibi's brazen demands echoed through the streets of Mecca, electrifying the coffee houses and sheesha bars of the Kingdom.

*Like his father, Salem died in an air crash. He was piloting an ultralight craft outside San Antonio, Texas, when he died in 1988.

Oteibi insisted on the adoption of Islamic, non-Western values and the rupture of diplomatic relations with Western countries, thus rolling back the changes that had opened the society to modernity. The Saudi Arabia these men wanted to create would be radically isolated. The royal family would be thrown out of power, and there would be a full accounting of the money that they had taken from the Saudi people. Not only the king but also the ulema who countenanced his rule would be denounced as sinful and unjust. Oil exports to the United States would be cut off, and all foreign civilian and military experts would be expelled from the Arabian Peninsula. These demands foreshadowed those that Osama bin Laden would make fifteen years later.

BY FRIDAY, the fourth day of the siege, Saudi forces had regained the upper stories of the Grand Mosque and two of the minarets. Battles flared in the covered corridors surrounding the Kaaba, and the stench of death clouded the air. The bodies of dead rebels had been mutilated—their faces shot off by female insurgents—to keep them from being identified. One of the bodies government troops recovered more or less intact was that of Mohammed Abdullah al-Qahtani, the purported Mahdi, whose jaw was blown away. But even the death of the Mahdi did not put an end to the rebellion.

Using maps of the compound provided by Salem, Turki oversaw a series of reconnaissance probes by Special Security Forces, who slipped in and out among the hundred doors, retrieving bodies of fallen soldiers. But Turki wanted to see for himself. He exchanged his ministerial robes for the khaki uniform of an ordinary soldier; then he and a handful of men, including his brother, Prince Saud, and Salem bin Laden, entered the holy mosque.

The mosque's lengthy arcades and grand plaza were eerily vacant. Turki and his companions discovered that the main body of rebels had taken refuge in the warren of underground prayer rooms carved into the lava that underlay the great courtyard. The subterranean hive that the rebels now occupied was easily defended. The government had no idea how long the insurgents could hold out on the dates and water they had cached in the storerooms; nor was there any possibility of an assault upon this labyrinth, which offered infinite opportunities for ambush. Thousands of soldiers and an unknown number of hostages would die. For half an hour, the two sons of Faisal and the eldest son of Mohammed bin Laden crept about, sketching the sight lines of the rebels' positions and their probable lines of defense. The Kingdom itself weighed in the balance of their actions, for if they failed to secure the holy ground, they would lose the trust of the Saudi people. Nothing in the world was more sacred to them and to Muslims everywhere than this mosque. Now it was a surreal battlefield. The early bombardment had done appalling damage. Turki noticed that even the pigeons had fled; from the earliest accounts by pilgrims, pigeons were constantly circumnavigating the holy mosque in the same counterclockwise manner. It seemed to him that the devotion of nature had been interrupted by this bloody human quarrel.

One of the ideas the government entertained was to flood the underground chambers, then electrocute everyone inside with high-voltage cables. Such a plan, however, did not distinguish the hostages from their captors, and besides, Turki realized, "you would need the entire Red Sea to fill it." Another notion was to put explosive-laden saddles on dogs and detonate them by remote control.

With such hopeless alternatives in front of him, Turki could have called upon the American Central Intelligence Agency, which was training Saudi Army Special Forces in the nearby city of Taif. But he had found that when immediate action was needed, the French were less complicated than the Americans. He consulted the legendary spy Count Claude Alexandre de Marenches, who was then head of the French secret service. A huge, commanding presence, de Marenches recommended gas. Turki agreed, but insisted that it be nonlethal. The idea was to render the insurgents unconscious. A team of three French commandos from the Groupe d'Intervention de la Gendarmerie Nationale (GIGN) arrived in Mecca. Because of the prohibition against non-Muslims entering the holy city, they converted to Islam in a brief, formal ceremony. The commandos pumped gas into the underground chambers, but perhaps because the rooms were so bafflingly inter-connected, the gas failed and the resistance continued.

With casualties climbing, Saudi forces drilled holes into the courtyard and dropped grenades into the rooms below, indis-criminately killing many hostages but driving the remaining rebels into more open areas where they could be picked off by sharpshooters. More than two weeks after the assault began, the surviving rebels finally surrendered.

Oteibi was among them, looking like a wild man with his mat-ted hair and beard, which jutted defiantly toward the television cameras that recorded the emergence of the rebels stumbling out of the underground chambers. His defiance had faded once the tragedy concluded. Turki went to see him in the hospital, where his wounds were being attended. Oteibi jumped off the bed, grabbed the prince's hand, and kissed it. "Please ask King Khaled to forgive me!" he cried. "I promise not to do it again!"

Turki was too startled to answer at first. "Forgiveness?" he finally said. "Ask forgiveness of God."

The government divided Oteibi and sixty-two of his disciples among eight different cities where, on January 9, 1980, they were beheaded. It was the largest execution in Saudi Arabian history.

The Saudi government admitted that 127 of its men had been killed in the uprising and 461 injured. About a dozen worshippers were killed, along with 117 rebels. Unofficial accounts, however, put the number of dead at more than 4,000. In any case, the King-dom was traumatized. The holiest place in the world had been defiled—by Muslims. The authority of the royal family had been openly challenged. After this, nothing could remain the same. Saudi Arabia had come to a place where it would have to change, but in which direction? Toward openness, liberality, tolerance, modernity, and Western ideas of democratic progress, or toward greater authoritarianism and religious repression?

In the early days of the siege, Osama bin Laden and his brother Mahrous were arrested. They were driving home from Al-Barood, the family farm off the road from Jeddah to Mecca. Authorities spotted the dust trail of their car coming out of the desert and thought they were fleeing rebels. At the time of their arrest, the brothers professed to be unaware that the siege had taken place. They stayed in custody for a day or two, but their social prominence protected them. Osama remained secluded in his house for a week. He had been opposed to Oteibi and the extreme Salafists who surrounded him. Five years later, however, he would tell a fellow mujahideen in Peshawar that Oteibi and his followers were true Muslims who were innocent of any crime.

IN THE MONTH between the surrender of the rebels and their mass execution, there was a new shock to the Islamic world: on Christmas Eve 1979 Soviet troops entered Afghanistan. "I was enraged and went there at once," bin Laden later claimed. "I arrived within days, before the end of 1979." According to Jamal Khalifa, bin Laden had never even heard of the country of Afghanistan until that point and did not actually go there until 1984, which is when he first became noticed in Pakistan and Afghanistan. Bin Laden explained that the trips he made before then were "a big secret, so that my family wouldn't find out." He became a courier, he said, delivering charitable donations from wealthy Saudis. "I used to hand over the money and head straight back, so I wasn't really familiar with what was going on."

The most influential figure in bin Laden's involvement with the Afghan cause was a charismatic Palestinian scholar and mystic named Abdullah Azzam. Born in Jenin in 1941, Azzam fled to Jordan after Israel captured the West Bank in 1967. He went to al-Azhar University in Cairo, where he gained a doctorate in Islamic jurisprudence in 1973, two years behind his friend Omar Abdul Rahman, the blind sheikh. He then joined the faculty of the University of Jordan, but his Palestinian activism got him dismissed in 1980. Soon he found a job leading prayers in the school mosque at King Abdul Aziz University in Jeddah.

For aroused young Muslims such as Osama bin Laden, Sheikh Abdullah Azzam* embodied in a modern fashion the warrior

*He is not related to Ayman al-Zawahiri's mother's family, the Azzams of Cairo.

priest—a figure that was as well established in Islamic tradition as the samurai in Japan. Azzam combined piety and learning with a serene and bloody intransigence. His slogan was "Jihad and the rifle alone; no negotiations, no conferences, no dialogues." Around his neck he wore the black-and-white Palestinian kaffiyeh, or scarf—a reminder of his reputation as a freedom fighter. By the time he arrived in Jeddah, he was already well known for his courage and oratory. Tall and sturdy, with an impressive black beard distinctively forked by two bright streaks of white and dark eyes that radiated conviction, he mesmerized audiences with his vision of an Islam that would dominate the world through the force of arms.

Despite his growing body of followers, Azzam was restless in Jeddah and eager to participate in the nascent Afghan resistance. "Jihad for him was like water for a fish," his wife, Umm Mohammed, said. He soon found a position for teaching the Quran and Arabic language at the International Islamic University in Islamabad, Pakistan, and moved there as soon as he could, in November 1981.

Soon he was spending each weekend in Peshawar, which had become the headquarters of the Afghan resistance against the Soviet occupation. He visited the refugee camps and saw appalling suffering. He met with the leaders of the mujahideen— the "holy warriors"—who made Peshawar their base. "I reached Afghanistan, and I could not believe my eyes," Azzam would later recall in his countless videos and speeches around the world. "I felt as if I had been reborn." In his renderings, the war was primeval, metaphysical, fought in a landscape of miracles. The Afghans, in his tableau, represented humanity in a pristine state—a righteous, pious, pre-industrial people—struggling against the brutal, soulless, mechanized force of modernity. In this war, the believers were aided by the invisible hands of angels. Azzam spoke of Russian helicopters being snared by ropes, and he claimed that flocks of birds functioned as an early-warning radar system by taking wing when Soviet jets were still over the horizon. Repeatedly in his stories mujahideen discover bullet holes in their clothes when they themselves are not injured, and the bodies of those who are martyred do not putrefy but remain pure and sweet-smelling.

The struggle of Islam, as Qutb had framed it, and as Azzam deeply believed, was against *jahiliyya*—the world of unbelief that had existed before Islam, which was still corrupting and undermining the faithful with the lures of materialism, secularism, and sexual equality. Here in this primitive land, so stunted by poverty and illiteracy and patriarchal tribal codes, the heroic and seemingly doomed Afghan jihad against the Soviet colossus had the elements of an epochal moment in history. In the skillful hands of Sheikh Abdullah Azzam, the legend of the Afghan holy warriors would be packaged and sold all over the world.

Azzam returned to Jeddah frequently, staying in bin Laden's guest flat on his trips to the Kingdom. He held recruiting sessions in bin Laden's apartment, where he magnetized young Saudis with his portraits of the suffering of the refugees and the courage of the Afghan mujahideen. "You *have* to do this!" he told them. "It is your duty! You have to leave everything and go!"

Bin Laden revered Azzam, who provided a model for the man he would become. For his part, Azzam was enchanted by his well-connected young host with his monastic habits. "He lives in his house the life of the poor," Azzam marveled. "I never did see a single table or chair. Any Jordanian or Egyptian laborer's house was better than the house of Osama. At the same time, if you asked him for a million riyals for the Mujahideen, he would write you out a check on the spot." Still, Azzam was a little discomfited when, in the sweltering Saudi heat, bin Laden left the air conditioner off. "If you have it, why don't you use it?" he asked petulantly. Bin Laden reluctantly accommodated his guest's request.

Soon Jeddah became a transit station for young men who were answering Sheikh Abdullah's call to "join the caravan" of the Afghan jihad. Paid agents rounded up prospects, pocketing half of the money—typically, several hundred dollars—that the recruits received when they signed up. Young Muslim pilgrims were particular targets. To get them to the front, agents promised them jobs with aid organizations that never materialized. Fugitives from Algeria and Egypt slipped into the country and were provided with false papers by Saudi intelligence. The Saudi Binladin Group, which maintained an office in Cairo for hiring skilled laborers to work on the two holy mosques, became known as a pipeline for radicals who wanted to fight in Afghanistan. It is probable that Zawahiri connected to the Egyptians coming through Jeddah, and that would have brought him into bin Laden's realm.

Bin Laden opened a halfway house for the recruits and even put them up in his own apartment. In the summers, he ran special military camps for high school and college students. Despite his youth, he rapidly emerged as a talented fund-raiser. Wealthy individuals, including members of the royal family, eagerly contributed. The Saudi government encouraged these efforts by offering steep discounts on the national airline for flights to Pakistan, the dropping-off point for jihad. Crown Prince Abdullah personally donated dozens of trucks for the cause. It was a thrilling national effort, although it established charitable habits and associations that would later become ruinous. The people who rallied to the Afghan jihad felt that Islam itself was threatened by the advance of communism. Afghanistan meant little to most of them, but the faith of the Afghan people meant a great deal. They were drawing a line against the retreat of their religion, which was God's last word and the only hope of human salvation.

Jamal Khalifa was completely persuaded by Azzam's arguments. Later, he spoke to his friend Osama and declared that he had decided to go to Afghanistan. As a sign of his approval, bin Laden proposed that Jamal marry his favorite sister, Sheikha. She was divorced and several years older than Osama, who was taking care of her and her three children. Because Jamal wasn't allowed to see her at first, his friend extravagantly praised her pleasant nature, her humor, and her piety.

"What are you talking about?" Khalifa said. "Suppose I go to die?"

But he agreed to meet her as soon as it could be properly arranged. When he did, he decided that Sheikha was "the best I ever met in my whole life." He put off the marriage for a year, however, in case he was martyred in Afghanistan.

Bin Laden also wanted to go openly to Afghanistan, but he

could not get permission from the authorities. "The Saudi govern-ment asked me officially not to enter Afghanistan due to how close my family is to the Saudi leadership," bin Laden later said. "They ordered me to stay in Peshawar, because if the Russians arrested me that would be proof of our support against the Soviet Union. I didn't obey their order. They thought my entry into Afghanistan was damning to them. I didn't listen."

He would have to defy another authority as well, which was even more difficult for him. His mother forbade him to go. He begged for her permission, saying that he would be going there only to take care of the families of the mujahideen. He said he would call every day. Finally he promised, "I won't even get near Afghanistan."

5

The Miracles

ONE MONTH AFTER THE SOVIET INVASION, Prince Turki al-Faisal paid a visit to Pakistan. He was shaken by the Soviet takeover of Afghanistan, which he saw as the first step in a march toward the warm waters of the Persian Gulf. Pakistan would be next. He believed the Soviet Union's ultimate target was to control the Strait of Hormuz at the base of the Gulf, where Oman reaches toward Iran like a fishhook for an open mouth. From there, the Soviets could control the supply route for the super-tankers that ferried the petroleum from Saudi Arabia, Iraq, Kuwait, and Iran. Whoever commanded the strait had a knife at the throat of the world's oil supply.

Turki's colleagues in the Pakistani Inter-Services Intelligence (ISI) briefed him on the Afghan resistance, then took him to the refugee camps outside Peshawar. Turki was appalled by the scale of the suffering. He went back to the Kingdom vowing to dedicate more money to the mujahideen, although he believed that these ragged soldiers could never defeat the Red Army. "Afghanistan was gone," he decided. He only hoped to delay the inevitable Soviet invasion of Pakistan.

Similar thinking was going on in Washington, especially by Zbigniew Brzezinski, who was the U.S. national security advisor for the Carter administration. Brzezinski, however, saw the invasion as an opportunity. He wrote to Carter immediately, saying, "Now we can give the USSR its own Vietnam war." Looking for an ally in this endeavor, the Americans naturally turned to the

Saudis—that is, to Turki, the American-educated prince who held the Afghan account.

Turki became the key man in the covert alliance of the United States and the Saudis to funnel money and arms to the resistance through the Pakistani ISI. It was vital to keep this program secret in order to prevent the Soviets from having the excuse they sought to invade Pakistan. Until the end of the war, the Saudis would match the Americans dollar for dollar, starting with only seventy-five thousand dollars but growing into billions.

The immediate problem Turki faced was that the mujahideen were little more than disorganized mobs. There were about 170 armed Afghan militias in the mid-1980s. In order to manage this chaos, the ISI anointed six major émigré parties as the designated recipients for aid. Afghan refugees, who numbered 3.27 million by 1988, had to sign up with one of the six official parties to qualify for food and supplies. The two largest of these, headed by Gulbuddin Hekmatyar and Burhanuddin Rabbani, each had 800,000 people in Peshawar under their authority. Turki forcibly created a seventh official party that would better represent Saudi interests. Ittihad-e-Islami (Islamic Union) was privately funded through bin Laden and others and headed by Abdul Rasul Sayyaf. An imposing and dashing Afghan warlord, six feet three inches tall, who draped himself in colorful blankets, Sayyaf spoke excellent classical Arabic from his years studying at al-Azhar University in Cairo. His devout Wahhabi beliefs were out of step with the Sufi traditions that predominated in Afghanistan before the war, but they were very much attuned to the interests of the Saudi Arabian government and its religious establishment. These seven mujahideen leaders came to be known, by the CIA and other intelligence agencies that were their principal means of support, as the Seven Dwarves.

Turki saw trouble ahead with the greedy and contentious Dwarves, and he repeatedly urged these competing groups to unify under a single command. In 1980 he brought the mujahideen leaders to Mecca. Ahmed Badeeb, Turki's assistant, escorted them. Badeeb discovered that the most expedient way of silencing the discord among the resistance leaders was to lock them up in a jail in Taif until they agreed to pick Sayyaf—Turki's man—as their leader. But as soon as they left the Kingdom, the jailhouse agreement fell apart. "They went back to their old ways," Turki complained.

"FEAR OF BODILY PARTICIPATION" kept bin Laden well away from the battlefield in the early years of the war, a fact that later caused him great shame. He limited his trips in Pakistan to Lahore and Islamabad, not even venturing as far as Peshawar, then shuttling back home to Jeddah. These frequent excursions eventually cost him his job. By walking away from the Saudi Bin-ladin Group's reconstruction of the Prophet's Mosque in Medina, he forfeited his share of the profit—an amount that Abdullah Azzam calculated was 8 million riyals, about $2.5 million.

In 1984 Azzam persuaded him to cross the frontier into Jaji, where Sayyaf had a camp high in the mountains above a major Soviet outpost. "I was surprised by the sad state of the equipment and everything else—weapons, roads, and trenches," bin Laden recalled. "I asked forgiveness from God Almighty, feeling that I had sinned because I listened to those who advised me not to go. . . . I felt that this four-year delay could not be pardoned unless I became a martyr."

At seven in the morning on June 26, 1984, during the month of Ramadan, most of the mujahideen in the Jaji camp were still sleeping, since they had been praying and eating late into the night after fasting during the day. The sound of a Soviet jet rudely brought them back to consciousness. The men dove for the shallow trenches. "The mountains were shaking from the bombardment," bin Laden noted. He was shocked by how low the planes flew as they attacked. "The missiles that landed outside the camp were making a huge noise that covered the sound of the mujahideen cannon as if they did not exist. Bear in mind that if you heard these sounds alone, you might say that there could not be anything louder! As to the missiles that landed inside the camp, thanks to God, they did not explode. They landed as iron lumps on the land. I felt closer to God than ever."

Bin Laden recorded that the mujahideen shot down four Soviet aircraft that morning. "I saw with my own eyes the remains of [one of] the pilots," he marveled. "Three fingers, a part of a nerve, the skin of one cheek, an ear, the neck, and the skin of the back. Some Afghan brothers came and took a photo of him as if he were a slaughtered sheep! We cheered." He also noted admiringly that the Afghans had not bothered to jump into the trenches with the frightened Arabs when the attack began. "Not one of our brothers had been injured, thank God. This battle gave me in fact a big push to continue in this matter. I become more convinced of the fact that no one could be injured except by God's will."

Bin Laden immediately returned to Saudi Arabia, and before the end of Ramadan he raised a fortune for the mujahideen—"between five and ten million dollars," Abdullah Azzam airily recalled. "I don't remember for sure." More than $2 million of that came from one of bin Laden's half sisters. Until now bin Laden had been seen mainly as a promising acolyte of Sheikh Abdullah's, but suddenly he eclipsed his mentor as the chief private financier of the jihad.

Azzam reacted by officially joining forces with his protégé. In September 1984, during the hajj, the two men met in Mecca. Although he was quiet and deferential, bin Laden already had his own plan. Perhaps it had been born in that attack in Jaji, when the Arabs all dove for the trenches. He had observed that the Afghans treated them as "glorified guests," not as real mujahideen. He suggested to Azzam that "we should take on the responsibility of the Arabs, because we know them better and can provide more rigorous training for them." The two men agreed to create a more formal role for the Arabs in Afghanistan, although there were few Arabs actually fighting the jihad at that time. Bin Laden undertook to change that by offering a ticket, a residence, and living expenses for every Arab—and his family—who joined their forces. That amounted to about three hundred dollars per month for each household.

Azzam added to bin Laden's stunning announcement by issuing a fatwa that electrified Islamists everywhere. In a book eventually published under the title *Defense of Muslim Lands,* Azzam argued that jihad in Afghanistan was obligatory for every able-bodied Muslim.* He had given an advance copy of the text to Sheikh Abdul Aziz bin Baz, Saudi Arabia's chief cleric, who wrote a preface to the book and pronounced his own supporting fatwa in the bin Laden family mosque in Jeddah.

Azzam's fatwa draws a distinction between a *fard ayn* and a *fard kifaya.* The first is an individual religious obligation that falls upon all Muslims, like praying and fasting. One cannot avoid such duties and be considered a good Muslim. If nonbelievers invade a Muslim land, it is *fard ayn*—a compulsory duty—for the local Muslims to expel them. If they fail, then the obligation expands to their Muslim neighbors. "If they, too, slacken, or there is again a shortage of manpower, then it is upon the people behind them, and on the people behind them, to march forward. This process continues until it becomes *fard ayn* upon the whole world." A child does not need permission from his parents, nor a debtor from his creditor, nor even a woman from her husband to join the jihad against the invader. *Fard kifaya,* on the other hand, is a duty of the community. Azzam gives the example of a group of people walking along a beach. "They see a child about to drown." The child, he suggests, is Afghanistan. Saving the drowning child is an obligation for all the swimmers who witness him. "If someone moves to save him, the sin falls from the rest. But, if no one moves, all the swimmers are in sin." Thus Azzam argues that the jihad against the Soviets is the duty of each Muslim individually, as well as of the entire Muslim people, and that all are in sin until the invader is repelled.

Bolstered by the imprimatur of bin Baz and other distinguished clerics, news of the fatwa circulated immediately through

---

*Interestingly, this former Palestinian guerrilla makes the case that Afghanistan takes precedence over the Palestinian struggle against Israel. The war in Afghanistan was intended to bring forth an Islamic state, he says, whereas the Palestinian cause has been appropriated by various groups, including "communists, nationalists, and modernist Muslims," who were fighting for a secular state.

Islamic communities everywhere. Although it's true that the Arab Afghan movement began with these two events—bin Laden's announcement of financial support for Arab mujahideen and Azzam's searing fatwa—one would have to say that their initial efforts were largely a failure. Rather few Arabs actually obeyed the summons, and many who did were drawn as much by bin Laden's money as by the obligation to defend Islam in the manner that Azzam prescribed.

As soon as they returned to Pakistan, bin Laden and Sheikh Abdullah Azzam set up what they called the Services Bureau (Makhtab al-Khadamat) in a house bin Laden was renting in the University Town section of Peshawar. Bin Laden provided twenty-five thousand dollars a month to keep the office running. The house also served as a hostel for Arab mujahideen and the headquarters of Azzam's magazine and book publishing efforts. The Services Bureau was essentially a repository for the money that the two men were sweeping in through their intensive fund-raising efforts. Jamal Khalifa joined bin Laden and Azzam in the Services Bureau, and they struggled to ensure that the donations, which often came in suitcases full of cash, actually got into the hands of the refugees. Azzam's long-standing membership in the Muslim Brothers gave him an international circuit to call upon for his ceaseless promotion of the insurgency. Still, his efforts did not compare with those of bin Laden, whom he called "this heaven-sent man," with a direct connection to the Saudi royal family and the petro-billionaires of the Gulf.

Bin Laden also drew from his connection to Prince Turki. Twice a month Turki's chief of staff, and bin Laden's former science teacher, Ahmed Badeeb, traveled to Peshawar to deliver cash to the mujahideen leaders. The Saudi government contributed $350 to $500 million per year for the Afghan jihad. This money was placed in a Swiss bank account controlled by the United States government, which used it to support the mujahideen; but the Saudis also ran their own programs privately, raising millions of dollars for their favored commanders. More than a tenth of the private money went to supplement bin Laden's unofficial activities.

Turki says he first met bin Laden in 1985 or 1986 in Peshawar. They met again soon afterward at a Saudi Embassy party in Islamabad. Bin Laden would dutifully report his activities to Turki, such as bringing in heavy equipment and engineers to build fortifications. He struck the prince as shy, soft-spoken, friendly, "almost gentle," and highly useful. Through bin Laden, Turki could recruit young Arabs to the jihad, as well as provide training and indoctrination outside ISI control. Moreover, bin Laden was raising large sums of money off the books—a trove that a skillful intelligence operator could put to use.

The Services Bureau became a registry for young Arabs who turned up in Peshawar looking for a way to get into the war. It offered these men—or, often enough, high school students—guesthouses to stay in and directed them to the training camps. In a place where magical legends sprouted so easily, bin Laden soon became a part of jihadi lore. Many of the Arab Afghans swore fealty to Azzam, but it was bin Laden who was paying their rent. His wealth and his charity immediately distinguished him. He passed through hospital wards, a lanky, singular figure, handing out cashews and chocolate to the wounded fighters while carefully noting their names and addresses. He built a theological library for the edification of the mujahideen who were killing time in the city, and he tutored at least one young Afghan warrior in Arabic. He gave money to Sayyaf to start the University of Dawa al-Jihad just outside Peshawar in the Tribal Areas, which would become internationally known as a terrorist training academy. He also pitched in at *Jihad*, the Arabic-language magazine that Azzam published. He was not politically sophisticated, like some of the others in the bureau, but he was tireless—"an activist with great imagination," Abdullah Anas, an Algerian who worked with him in the Services Bureau, observed. "He ate very little. He slept very little. Very generous. He'd give you his clothes. He'd give you his money."

Bin Laden did not, however, make much of an impression as a charismatic leader, especially in the shadow of Abdullah Azzam. "He had a small smile on his face and soft hands," a hardened Pakistani mujahid recalled. "You'd think you were shaking hands with a girl." He was shy and serious, and he struck many as naïve. When he laughed, he covered his mouth with his hand. A Syrian who eventually became a confidant of bin Laden remembered their first meeting: "It was in November 1985. He had no name at the time. We were in a prayer hall in a guesthouse. People asked him to talk, so he talked about horses. He said if you love a horse, he will respond to you. That's what was in his mind, horses."

SHEIKH ABDULLAH called the small band of Arabs who gathered in Peshawar the "Brigade of the Strangers." The Arabs kept to themselves, establishing their own mosques and schools and newspapers. Some had arrived with nothing in their pockets but a telephone number. Thanks to bin Laden's generous subsidy, many of them settled in the suburb of Hayatabad, a neighborhood of two-story tract houses at the edge of the Tribal Areas, provided with all the modern conveniences—refrigerators, washing machines, dryers, and so on. Indeed, many of them lived more comfortably than bin Laden.

Across the Khyber Pass was the war. The young Arabs who came to Peshawar prayed that their crossing would lead them to martyrdom and Paradise. As they passed the time, they traded legends about themselves, about the call that had drawn young Muslims to free their brothers in Afghanistan. In fact the war was being fought almost entirely by the Afghans themselves. Despite Azzam's famous fatwa and bin Laden's subsidies, there were never more than three thousand of these outsiders—who came to be known as the Arab Afghans—in the war against the Soviets, and most of them never got out of Peshawar.

The Arab Afghans were often unwanted renegades in their own countries, and they found that the door closed behind them as soon as they left. Other young Muslims, prompted by their own governments to join the jihad, were stigmatized as fanatics when they did so. It would be difficult for many of them ever to return home. These abandoned idealists were naturally looking for a leader. They had little to cling to except their cause and each other. As stateless persons they naturally revolted against the very idea of the state. They saw themselves as a borderless posse empowered by God to defend the entire Muslim people. That was exactly bin Laden's dream.

In Peshawar, they adopted new identities. Few people in the Arab community used their actual names, and it was rude to ask. In this incognito underground, a child often did not know his father's real identity. The alias usually reflected the name of the mujahid's firstborn male child or some quality that suited his personality. A common jihadi name, such as Abu Mohammed, would be followed by his nationality—al-Libi, for instance, "the Libyan." It was a simple code but difficult to decipher, since one had to know a man's reputation or his family in order to catch the reference.

It was death, not victory in Afghanistan, that summoned many young Arabs to Peshawar. Martyrdom was the product that Azzam sold in the books, tracts, videos, and cassette tapes that circulated in mosques and Arabic-language bookstores. "I traveled to acquaint people with jihad," Azzam said, recalling his lectures in mosques and Islamic centers around the world. "We were trying to satisfy the thirst for martyrdom. We are still in love with this." Azzam visited the United States each year—Kansas City, St. Louis, Dallas, all over the heartland and the major cities as well—looking for money and recruits among the young Muslims who were mesmerized by the myths he spun.

He told stories of the mujahideen who defeated vast columns of Soviet troops virtually single-handed. He claimed that some of the brave warriors had been run over by tanks but survived; others were shot, but the bullets failed to penetrate. If death came, it was even more miraculous. When one beloved mujahid expired, the ambulance filled with the sound of humming bees and chirping birds, even though they were in the Afghan desert in the middle of the night. Bodies of martyrs uncovered after a year in the grave still smelled sweet and their blood continued to flow. Heaven and nature conspired to repel the godless invader. Angels rode into the battle on horseback, and falling bombs were intercepted by birds, which raced ahead of the jets to form a protective canopy over the warriors. The miracle stories naturally proliferated as word spread that Sheikh Abdullah was paying for mujahids who brought him wonderful tales.

The lure of an illustrious and meaningful death was especially powerful in cases where the pleasures and rewards of life were crushed by government oppression and economic deprivation. From Iraq to Morocco, Arab governments had stifled freedom and signally failed to create wealth at the very time when democracy and personal income were sharply climbing in virtually all other parts of the globe. Saudi Arabia, the richest of the lot, was such a notoriously unproductive country that the extraordinary abundance of petroleum had failed to generate any other significant source of income; indeed, if one subtracted the oil revenue of the Gulf countries, 260 million Arabs exported less than the 5 million Finns. Radicalism usually prospers in the gap between rising expectations and declining opportunities. This is especially true where the population is young, idle, and bored; where the art is impoverished; where entertainment—movies, theater, music—is policed or absent altogether; and where young men are set apart from the consoling and socializing presence of women. Adult illiteracy remained the norm in many Arab countries. Unemployment was among the highest in the developing world. Anger, resentment, and humiliation spurred young Arabs to search for dramatic remedies.

Martyrdom promised such young men an ideal alternative to a life that was so sparing in its rewards. A glorious death beckoned to the sinner, who would be forgiven, it is said, with the first spurt of blood, and he would behold his place in Paradise even before his death. Seventy members of his household might be spared the fires of hell because of his sacrifice. The martyr who is poor will be crowned in heaven with a jewel more valuable than the earth itself. And for those young men who came from cultures where women are shuttered away and rendered unattainable for someone without prospects, martyrdom offered the conjugal pleasures of seventy-two virgins—"the dark-eyed houris," as the Quran describes them, "chaste as hidden pearls." They awaited the martyr with feasts of meat and fruit and cups of the purest wine.

The pageant of martyrdom that Azzam limned before his worldwide audience created the death cult that would one day form the core of al-Qaeda. For the journalists covering the war, the Arab Afghans were a curious sideshow to the real fighting, set apart by their obsession with dying. When a fighter fell, his comrades would congratulate him and weep because they were not also slain in battle. These scenes struck other Muslims as bizarre. The Afghans were fighting for their country, not for Paradise or an idealized Islamic community. For them, martyrdom was not such a high priority.

Rahimullah Yusufzai, the Peshawar bureau chief for the *News*, a Pakistani daily, observed a camp of Arab Afghans that was under attack in Jalalabad. The Arabs had pitched white tents on the front lines, where they were easy marks for Soviet bombers. "Why?" the reporter asked incredulously. "We want them to bomb us!" the men told him. "We want to die!" They believed that they were answering God's call. If they were truly blessed, God would reward them with a martyr's death. "I wish I could raid and be slain, and then raid and be slain, and then raid and be slain," bin Laden later declared, quoting the Prophet.

THE QURAN IS FULL of references to jihad; some of them have to do with the inner striving for perfection, which the Prophet had called the "greater jihad," but others explicitly command the believers to "slay the idolaters wherever you find them" and to "fight those who do not believe in God . . . until they pay the tax in acknowledgement of superiority and they are in a state of subjection." Some Islamic scholars explain these injunctions by saying that they apply only when war is initiated by the infidels, or when Muslims are persecuted, or when Islam itself is threatened. The Quran, these thinkers point out, also bids the Muslims to "fight in the way of God against those who fight against you, and be not aggressive; surely God loves not the aggressors."

Under the spell of the Afghan struggle, many radical Islamists came to believe that jihad never ends. For them, the war against the Soviet occupation was only a skirmish in an eternal war. They called themselves jihadis, indicating the centrality of war to their religious understanding. They were the natural outgrowth of the Islamist exaltation of death over life. "He who dies and has not fought and was not resolved to fight, has died a *jahiliyya* death," Hasan al-Banna, the founder of the Muslim Brothers, had declared. He added, with a bit of residual Sufi mysticism, "Death is art."

The Quran explicitly states that "there is no compulsion in religion." That would seem to forbid waging war against non-Muslims and against Muslims who believe differently. Sayyid Qutb, however, scorned the notion that jihad is just a defensive maneuver to protect the community of faith. "Islam is not merely 'belief,' " he wrote. "Islam is a declaration of the freedom of man from servitude to other men. Thus it strives from the beginning to abolish all those systems and governments which are based on the rule of man over men." Qutb makes the argument that life without Islam is slavery; therefore real freedom cannot be achieved until *jahiliyya* is eliminated. It is only when the rule of man has been eradicated and Sharia imposed that there will be no compulsion in religion, because there is only one choice: Islam.

Yet the declaration of jihad was tearing the Muslim community apart. There was never a consensus that the jihad in Afghanistan was a genuine religious obligation. In Saudi Arabia, for instance, the local chapter of the Muslim Brotherhood refuted the demand to send its members to jihad, although it encouraged relief work in Afghanistan and Pakistan. Those who did go were often unaffiliated with established Muslim organizations and therefore more open to radicalization. Many concerned Saudi fathers went to the training camps to drag their sons home.

The fierce idealists who did respond to Azzam's message viewed Afghanistan as the beginning of Islam's return to international dominance, which would see not only the liberation of the Afghans but also the eventual recapture of all the territory, from Spain to China, that had been under enlightened Muslim domination while Europe was mired in the Middle Ages. The restoration of the former empire was only the first step, however. The next stage was final war against unbelievers, culminating in the Day of Judgment.

The Arab Afghans were not all suicidal or apocalyptic thinkers. They included as well the curious, the holiday fighters, the students looking for an exciting way to spend their break. Others were seeking significance that their ordinary lives didn't provide.

"I was not a believer," Mohammed Loay Baizid, a Syrian immigrant to the United States, remembered. Twenty-four years old in 1985, he thought of himself as a typical young middle-class American man, used to shopping malls and fast food, but he had run across a mimeographed tract by Abdullah Azzam and decided that if there were miracles he would have to see them. He was studying engineering at a community college in Kansas City, Missouri, at the time. No one could tell him how to get to the war from Kansas City, so he took a plane to Islamabad and called the number on the tract. If Azzam had not answered, he didn't know what he would have done.

Baizid only planned to stay for three months, but he was captivated by the strangeness of the place and the camaraderie of men who courted martyrdom. His expressive black eyebrows and constant stream of wisecracks were strikingly out of place in this sober group of holy warriors. "I went to Afghanistan with a blank mind and a good heart," he said. "Everything was totally strange. It was like I was born just now, like I was an infant, and I have to learn everything new. It was not so easy after that to leave and go back to your regular life." He took the jihadi name Abu Rida al-Suri.

Untrained but eager for action, the Brigade of Strangers agitated until Azzam agreed to take them into Afghanistan to join forces with the Afghan commander Gulbuddin Hekmatyar, who was fighting the Soviets near Jihad Wal. Bin Laden and sixty Arabs rode across the border with a single Afghan guide. Thinking that they were headed directly into battle, they had stuffed their pockets with raisins and chickpeas, most of which they consumed during the long drive. They began referring to themselves as the Brigade of the Chickpeas. Around ten that night, they finally arrived at the Afghan camp, only to learn that the Soviets had retreated.

"Your presence is no longer needed," Hekmatyar impatiently told them the following morning, "so go back."

Azzam immediately consented, but bin Laden and some of the other Arabs expressed their dismay. "If they have withdrawn, aren't we supposed to at least chase them?" they asked. Azzam set up some targets on fence posts so the men could have some shooting practice. Afterward, the Arabs surrendered their weapons to an Afghan commander and caught buses back to Peshawar. They began calling themselves the Brigade of the Ridiculous. When they got back to the city, they disbanded.

IN 1986 BIN LADEN BROUGHT his wives and children to Peshawar, where they joined the small but growing community of Arabs responding to Sheikh Abdullah Azzam's fatwa. It was clear by then that the Afghans were winning the war. Admitting that Afghanistan was "a bleeding wound," Mikhail Gorbachev, the general secretary of the Communist Party of the Soviet Union, offered a timetable for the complete withdrawal of Soviet troops. That was also the year that the American-made Stinger, the hand-fired missile that proved so deadly for Russian aircraft, was introduced, decisively tipping the balance in favor of the mujahideen. Although it would take another three bloody years for the Soviets to finally extricate themselves, the presence of several thousand Arabs—and rarely more than a few hundred of them actually on the field of battle—made no real difference in the tide of affairs.

Arms shipments poured into the port of Karachi. The ISI, which divvied the weapons among the Afghan commanders, needed a repository, preferably outside of Pakistan but not within the grasp of the Soviets. There is a distinctive portion of the Tribal Areas that juts into Afghanistan along a range of mountains southwest of the Khyber Pass known as the Parrot's Beak. The northern slope of the Parrot's Beak is called Tora Bora. The name means "black dust." Remote and barren, the place is rich in caves made of super-hard quartz and feldspar. Bin Laden expanded the caverns and constructed new ones to serve as armories. It was here, in the warren of ammunition caves that he built for the mujahideen, that bin Laden would one day make his stand against America.

In May 1986, bin Laden led a small group of Arabs to join Afghan forces in Jaji, in Sayyaf's territory near the Pakistani border. One night the Arab tents were pelted with what seemed to be rocks, perhaps debris thrown from the occasional distant bombs. When a Yemeni cook got up to prepare the pre-dawn meal, there was a huge explosion. "God is great! God is great!" the cook cried out. "My leg! My leg!" The Arabs awakened to find mines strewn around their encampment, although they were difficult to see because they were green and disappeared in the grass. As they were evacuating the site, a guided missile struck a few yards from bin Laden. Then a huge explosion on the mountaintop spewed boulders and splintered wood upon the besieged Arabs. Three were wounded and one, an Egyptian graduate student, was killed. The Arabs were thrown into panic, and they were further humiliated when the Afghan forces asked them to leave because they were so useless.

Despite this sorry display, bin Laden financed the first permanent all-Arab camp at the end of 1986, also at Jaji. This action put him at odds with his mentor, Azzam, who strongly opposed the plan. Each man was beset by a powerful and impractical dream. Azzam longed to erase the national divisions that kept the Muslim people from uniting. For that reason, he always sought to disperse the Arab volunteers among the various Afghan commands, even though few Arabs spoke the local languages or had received any practical training. They were cannon fodder. On the other hand, a fixed target such as the camp bin Laden envisioned was an extravagant waste of money and lives in the hit-and-run guerrilla warfare that the Afghans were waging. Bin Laden was already thinking of the future of jihad, and the Jaji camp was his first step toward the creation of an Arab legion that could wage war anywhere. Until now, he had subordinated his dream to the goals of the older man, but he was beginning to feel the tug of destiny.

Desperate to stop bin Laden's drift from his orbit, Azzam dispatched Jamal Khalifa to reason with him. No one could speak more frankly or with more authority to bin Laden than his old friend and brother-in-law. Khalifa rode across the Afghan border with Sayyaf, who controlled the mountainous territory around Jaji. The camp was high and cold and exposed to merciless wind. Osama—the Lion—called the place Maasada, the Lion's Den. He said he had been inspired by the lines of the Prophet's favorite poet Hassan Ibn Thabit, who wrote of another fortress of the same name:

> *Whoever wishes to hear the clash of swords,*
> *let him come to Maasada,*
> *where he will find courageous men ready to die*
> *for the sake of God.*

At the time, bin Laden's version of Maasada looked nothing like the elaborate cavernous training center it eventually became. Khalifa had been a devoted Boy Scout, and in his experienced eye this filthy and disorganized site hidden in the pine trees was far below even the standards of a children's encampment. There was a bulldozer, Egyptian knockoffs of Kalashnikovs, mortars, some small anti-aircraft guns they had bought in the markets in Peshawar, and Chinese rockets without launchers. To fire a rocket, the mujahid would rest it on a rock, string a wire, and set it off from some distance away—a crazily dangerous and inaccurate procedure.

Through binoculars Khalifa surveyed the Soviet base in a broad valley only three kilometers away. The Arabs were isolated and vulnerable. They had a single car that they used to smuggle water and supplies during the night, but they could easily be trapped and wiped out. They were already being carelessly expended under bin Laden's command. Khalifa was furious at the needless risk and the waste of lives.

He stayed for three days, talking to the people around bin Laden—mainly Egyptians associated with Zawahiri's al-Jihad and Saudi high school students, including Khalifa's own student

Wali Khan, an academic star in the biology class he taught in Medina. Khalifa learned that they had appointed bin Laden—rather than Azzam or Sayyaf—their leader. That news stunned him. He had never thought of his friend as one who would seek power.

Khalifa wondered if Osama was being manipulated by the Egyptians. These suspicions mounted when Abu Ubaydah and Abu Hafs, bin Laden's tall and commanding Egyptian tenders, cornered Khalifa to sound him out about his politics. They started talking about how the leaders of the Arab countries are *kafrs*—a term that means infidels or unbelievers, but when applied to other Muslims signifies that they are apostates who have rejected their religion. Such traitors should be killed, many fundamentalists believe. When Khalifa disagreed with them, they tried to screen him off from bin Laden. Khalifa brushed past them; he would not be managed by strangers.

Khalifa and bin Laden slept together in a foxhole with canvas sides and a wood ceiling, which had soil piled on top. His friend was so evasive that Khalifa decided he was hiding something from him. On the third day, Khalifa finally spoke out. "Everybody is angry—they are against this place," Khalifa said. "Even the people who are with you. I've talked to them."

Bin Laden was shocked. "Why don't they talk to me?" he asked.

"This is a question you have to ask yourself," Khalifa responded. "But everyone in Afghanistan is against this idea!"

Bin Laden reiterated his vision of creating an Arab force that would defend Muslim causes everywhere. That's what he was trying to establish in this miserable mountain camp.

"We came here to help the Afghans, not to form our own party!" Khalifa reminded him. "Besides, you're not a military man, so why are you here?"

As they talked, their voices began to rise. In the ten years that they had known each other, they had never had an argument. "This is jihad!" bin Laden cried. "This is the way we want to go to heaven!"

Khalifa warned him that the lives of these men were his responsibility. "God will ask you about every drop of their blood.

And since I am your friend, I cannot accept that you stay. You have to leave, or else I will leave you."

Bin Laden coldly refused. Khalifa left the camp. They would never be close again.

ALTHOUGH HE REJECTED the entreaties of Khalifa and others, bin Laden was concerned about the repeated failures of the Arab brigade and the dangers his men faced in the Lion's Den. "I began thinking about new strategies, such as digging caves and tunnels," he said. He borrowed an array of bulldozers, loaders, dump trucks, and trenching machines from the Saudi Binladin Group, along with skilled engineers, to craft seven man-made caverns, well disguised and perched above the main supply line from Pakistan. Some of the caves would be more than a hundred yards long and twenty feet high, serving as air-raid shelters, dormitories, hospitals, and arms dumps.

Bin Laden's men were impatient with construction work and continually pestered him for new opportunities to attack the Russians. The most vehement among them was an obese, forty-five-year-old Palestinian, Sheikh Tameem al-Adnani, a former English teacher who had become the imam at the air force base in Dhahran, Saudi Arabia, until he was expelled because of his radical views. A pale, fleshy man with a patchy fringe of beard that was turning gray at the temples, Sheikh Tameem turned to the lecture circuit, raising millions of dollars for the mujahideen. His scholarship and worldliness, plus his ardent longing for martyrdom, gave him an authority that rivaled that of bin Laden. Abdullah Azzam, who doted on him, called him "the Lofty Mountain."

Sheikh Tameem weighed nearly four hundred pounds. His corpulence was a source of amusement to the young Arab fighters, most of whom were not over eighteen years old. They would sometimes have to tow him up the steep mountain paths with ropes, joking that the horses had memorized his face and refused to carry him any longer. But Sheikh Tameem's commitment to jihad inspired them. He trained with the others despite his age and his poor physical condition. He was constantly pushing bin

Laden to throw the men into battle, giving voice to the bold and heedless elements in the camp who were lusting for death. Bin Laden managed to put him off, citing the men's lack of training and the pressing need to finish construction, but Tameem never let up.

At the end of March 1987, bin Laden returned to Saudi Arabia, and Sheikh Tameem took advantage of the moment. He cajoled Abu Hajer al-Iraqi, whom bin Laden had left in charge of the Lion's Den, to attack a small Soviet outpost nearby. Abu Hajer protested that he didn't have the authority to make such a decision, but Sheikh Tameem's persistence wore him down, and Abu Hajer reluctantly gave his assent. The sheikh quickly assembled fourteen to sixteen young men, who piled their heavy weapons onto a horse and began trekking down the mountain. The weapons kept sliding off the horse's back into the snow. Tameem had no plan other than to attack the Soviets and immediately retreat, nor was he entirely sure where he was going. If the Arabs actually engaged in a firefight with the enemy, Sheikh Tameem would be unable to run back up the mountain with the lithe young fighters who accompanied him. But, as usual, caution was not a feature of his scheme.

Suddenly, Abu Hajer's voice crackled on the walkie-talkie. Bin Laden had returned and he was alarmed. He ordered the men back to camp immediately.

"Tell him that I will not return," Sheikh Tameem responded.

Bin Laden took the radio. "Sheikh Tameem, return at once!" he commanded. "If you do not, then you will be sinful, for I am your commander, and I am ordering you to return."

Tameem grudgingly agreed to give up his battle plan, but he swore that he would fast until he had the opportunity to participate in a battle. For three days after his return to the Lion's Den, he refused to eat or drink. He became so weak that bin Laden finally arranged for a small action so that Tameem could fulfill his pledge, at least symbolically. He allowed the sheikh to climb a peak and fire mortars and machine guns toward the enemy. But Sheikh Tameem continued to present a challenge to bin Laden's authority, since many of the Arabs sided with him, saying that they had come for jihad, not for camping in the mountains. "I was afraid that some of the brothers might return to their countries and tell their people that they had stayed here for six months without ever shooting a single gun," bin Laden admitted. "People might conclude that we don't need their support." He had to prove that the Arabs were not just tourists, that they were capable of making a genuine contribution to the Afghan jihad. It was unclear how long he could keep men under his command if he failed to let them fight.

On April 17, 1987, before the snows had fully melted, bin Laden led a force of 120 fighters to harass an Afghan government outpost near Khost. He chose to attack on a Friday because he believed Muslims all over the world would be praying for the mujahideen. Both Sayyaf, the Arabic-speaking Afghan commander, and Hekmatyar agreed to provide covering artillery fire. The attack was set for six o'clock in the evening—time enough for a quick strike, followed by darkness that would protect the men from the Soviet aircraft that would soon be raining bombs upon them. Sheikh Tameem begged to be a part of the action, but bin Laden ordered him to remain in the Lion's Den.

The impending battle was months in the planning and had been well advertised back in Peshawar. "I heard about this attack and decided to join," Abu Rida, the Kansas City mujahid, later recalled. "I took my car. I didn't know much about the plan, but I found so many donkeys and horses carrying weapons in the valley." When he arrived at the staging area, he discovered chaos among the Arabs. At the time of the scheduled attack, none of the positions had been supplied with ammunition, which was stuck in a car at the end of a road some distance away. The men were frantically transporting rockets and mortars on their backs or on the four mules they had available. Some fighters were already so exhausted that they slipped back to the Lion's Den to sleep, and those who stayed were famished and upset because the food had run out. At the last minute, one of the commanders discovered that no one had brought the electrical wire to connect the rockets to the detonators. He dispatched a man on a horse to gallop back to camp. On top of this, bin Laden was ill—as he often was before battle—although he tried to remain composed in front of his men.

Sheikh Abdullah Azzam gave a rousing speech about the need to stand firm, but before the Arabs were ready to charge, an Afghan government soldier overheard their preparations and single-handedly kept them pinned down till nightfall with a Gorjunov machine gun. Bin Laden ordered his troops to withdraw. Amazingly, only one Arab was killed and two badly injured, but their pride was shattered—they had been defeated by one man! The Afghan mujahideen were laughing at them. As a result of this fiasco, the Pakistanis began closing down the Arab guesthouses in Peshawar. It seemed that the Arab Afghan misadventure had come to an ignominious finale.

The following month, a small band of Arabs engaged in another skirmish, this one planned by their Egyptian military commander, Abu Ubaydah, who led a flanking maneuver against a group of Soviet troops. "There were nine of them and myself," bin Laden later recounted. "No one hesitated." The Soviets fell back, and the Arabs were jubilant. But their brief victory prompted a stern Soviet counterattack against the Lion's Den. According to Abdullah Azzam's myth-making account, the Soviets assembled nine or ten thousand troops—including Soviet Special Forces and Afghan regulars—against only seventy mujahideen.

Sheikh Tameem pleaded with bin Laden to place him on the front lines, but bin Laden told him he was too fat for active fighting. He consigned Tameem to the communications room deep in an underground chamber. The Arabs waited until the entire Soviet convoy was within range of their three mortars. When bin Laden cried, *"Allahu akhbar!"* the Arabs opened fire, and the surprised Russians fell back. "The brothers were in a state of elation and total ecstasy," Azzam wrote. They watched ambulances arriving to collect the fallen soldiers, who included the military commander of the Jaji district.

Expecting another, larger Soviet counterattack, bin Laden divided his force in half, stationing thirty-five men to guard the

Lion's Den. He and nine others advanced to the top of a hill, where they observed two hundred Russian Special Forces creeping toward the camp. "Suddenly, mortar rounds began to pour on us like rain," said bin Laden. Miraculously, the Arabs escaped harm. An hour later, the Russians confidently resumed their advance. "When they reached the peak, we began our attack," bin Laden continued. "A few of them were killed, and the rest fled."

For weeks, the Soviets shelled the mujahideen position around the Lion's Den with 120 mm mortars and napalm bombs, which caused such devastation that Azzam wept and prayed for the safety of the fighters. The trees burned, even in the rain, illuminating the night. One morning, in this storm of shrapnel and fire, Sheikh Tameem emerged from the communications cave with his Quran in hand and began to wander around in the clearing, ignoring the pleas of his comrades as he recited the Quran and prayed aloud for martyrdom, his round wire-rimmed glasses tilted toward the sky. The ground shook and bullets and explosions tore the forest around him. It was near the end of Ramadan, and Tameem believed that his death on such an occasion would be especially blessed.

This mad excursion seemed to have a calming effect on the others. "We came under fire quickly," bin Laden recalled. "When the fire stopped for about thirty seconds, I told the people I was with that I thought we were going to die. But within minutes, the fire started again and I was reading the Holy Quran until we were saved and were able to move to a different location. We hadn't moved seventy meters when we were hit again, but we felt completely safe, as if we were in an air-conditioned room."

Despite the bravado, bin Laden worried that his men would all be killed if they stayed any longer. He would have to abandon the Lion's Den. It was the worst defeat he had ever suffered. His men were shocked at his decision. When one of them protested, bin Laden "shouted at me and told me some words which I heard for the first time from him." Sheikh Tameem bellowed and pulled the hair from his beard. "I thought he was possessed," recalled bin Laden. He scolded Tameem, saying that he was endangering all the fighters by his intransigence. "Sheikh Tameem, the men are in the car," bin Laden warned him. "If a single one of them is killed the sin will fall on your neck and you will be responsible for his blood on Judgment Day." Sobbing, Sheikh Tameem joined the other men in the van.

Those who were able to walk followed behind, after destroying much of the Lion's Den so that there would be nothing for the Soviets to pillage. They rolled their cannons into the ravines and buried their automatic weapons. One of the men threw a grenade into the pantry. The camp that they had labored so mightily to construct was now a ruin. A small squad stayed behind to provide cover for the retreating guerrillas.

Once again, bin Laden was ill. "I was very tired, and could barely walk twenty meters before I had to stop and drink water. I had been under great emotional and physical duress." His ordeal had only just begun.

Sayyaf was fuming when the bedraggled Arabs reached his camp. By now he had come to see the value of the Lion's Den, which overlooked a strategic caravan route for the supply of the mujahideen. He abruptly countermanded bin Laden's order and told the Arabs to return; he also sent some of his reliable Afghan warriors back to the camp with them to make sure that they held the position.

Embarrassed and exhausted, the fighters returned to the Lion's Den in groups of five or ten. Dawn found twenty-five Arabs and twenty Afghans gathered in the ruins of the camp, dismally celebrating the feast day at the end of Ramadan. There was practically nothing to eat since the kitchen had been blown up. Each man received three lemons. Later in the morning, Bin Laden returned with ten more fighters. Chastened and unwilling to assert his authority, he let his Egyptian military commander, Abu Ubaydah, take charge. The sight of the needless destruction of his camp at his own hand must have been unbearable.

Abu Ubaydah decided to give him something to do. "Go and guard the left side of the camp," Abu Ubaydah told him. "I think they will only enter from this place because it is the shortest path."

Bin Laden led the men to a promontory and spread them out

among the trees. They could see a Russian force only seventy meters away. Bin Laden called out to his men to advance, but his voice was hoarse and they didn't realize he was talking to them. He climbed a leafless tree so that they could hear him and immediately drew fire. A rocket-propelled grenade nearly knocked him out of the tree. "It passed by me and exploded nearby," bin Laden said in one account, "but I was not affected by it at all—in fact, by the Grace of Allah, the Exalted, it was as though I had merely been covered by a handful of mud from the ground. I descended calmly and informed the brothers that the enemy was in the central axis and not on the left wing." In another retelling, bin Laden's most intense experience of combat seems less composed. "There was a terrible battle, which ended up with me half sunk in the ground, firing at anything I could see."

Bin Laden and his men were pinned down all day by enemy mortar fire. "I was only thirty meters from the Russians and they were trying to capture me," he said. "I was under bombardment but I was so peaceful in my heart that I fell asleep." The story of bin Laden's nap is often told as evidence of his grace under fire. He may simply have fainted. He suffered from low blood pressure, which often made him light-headed. He always carried a bag of salt with him, and whenever he felt dizzy, he would wet a finger and stick it in the bag, then suck on the salt to keep his blood pressure from sinking.

Amazingly, by five o'clock in the afternoon, the Arab forces, led by Abu Ubaydah, succeeded in outflanking the enemy. Without air support, the main body of the Soviet troops withdrew. "There were only nine brothers against one hundred Russian Spetsnaz Special Forces troops, but out of sheer fright and panic in the dense forest, the Russians were unable to make out the number of brothers," bin Laden related. "All in all, about thirty-five Spetsnaz soldiers and officers were killed, and the rest fled. . . . The morale of the mujahideen soared, not only in our area, but in the whole of Afghanistan."

He had achieved his greatest victory immediately following his worst defeat. After the battle of the Lion's Den, Abu Ubaydah gave bin Laden a trophy from a dead Russian officer—a small

Kalikov AK-74 assault rifle, with a walnut stock and a distinctive rusty red ammunition magazine that marked it as the advanced paratroop version of the weapon. In the future, it would always be on his shoulder.

The entire action lasted three weeks. It was actually waged more by Sayyaf (who then took over the Lion's Den) than bin Laden, but the Arabs gained a reputation for courage and recklessness that established their legend, at least among themselves. Their guesthouses quietly reopened in Peshawar. From the Soviet perspective, the battle of the Lion's Den was a small moment in the tactical retreat from Afghanistan. In the heightened religious atmosphere among the men following bin Laden, however, there was a dizzying sense that they were living in a supernatural world, in which reality knelt before faith. For them, the encounter at the Lion's Den became the foundation of the myth that they defeated the superpower. Within a few years the entire Soviet empire fell to pieces—dead of the wound the Muslims inflicted in Afghanistan, the jihadis believed. By then they had created the vanguard that was to carry the battle forward. Al-Qaeda was conceived in the marriage of these assumptions: Faith is stronger than weapons or nations, and the ticket to enter the sacred zone where such miracles occur is the willingness to die.

6

The Base

BY 1986 MILLIONS OF AFGHAN REFUGEES had flooded into Pakistan's North-West Frontier Province, turning Peshawar, the capital, into the prime staging area for the jihad against the Soviet invasion. The streets of the city were a welter of languages and national costumes, achieving a strange and exhilarating cosmopolitanism that cast a spell over everyone who passed through it. Aid workers and freelance mullahs and intelligence agents from around the world set up shop. The underground flow of money and arms created an economic boom in a town that had always feasted on contraband. Already the treasures of the Afghan national museum—statuary, precious stones, antiquities, even entire Buddhist temples—were being slipped into the Smugglers' Market, an openly run bazaar on the outskirts of the city, and into the gift shops of the shabby hotels where the throng of international journalists holed up to cover the war. Afghan warlords moved their families into University Town, where the professional class lived among the eucalyptus and the magnolia trees. The warlords became rich by skimming off the subsidies that the Americans and the Saudis were providing. Their murderous rivalries, along with weekly bombings and assassinations by the KGB and KHAD (the Afghan intelligence service), made the death toll of Afghan commanders higher in Peshawar than on the field of battle. In a city that moved around mainly on handpainted private buses and smoky motorcycle rickshaws that ripped the air like chain saws, suddenly there were new Mercedes

Sedans and Toyota Land Cruisers navigating among the donkey carts. The air was a blue soup of diesel smoke. "Peshawar was transformed into this place where whoever had no place to go went," Osama Rushdi, one of the young Egyptian jihadis, remembered. "It was an environment in which a person could go from a bad place to a worse place, and eventually into despair."

After finishing his contract with the medical clinic in Jeddah in 1986, Dr. Ayman al-Zawahiri joined the growing Arab community in Peshawar. Rounder now than he had been during his previous visits before his prison years, he boasted that Pakistan was like a "second home" to him, since he had spent time as a child in the country when his maternal grandfather served there as the Egyptian ambassador. He quickly adapted to wearing the *shalwar kameez*, the traditional long shirt and loose-fitting pants of the region. His brother Mohammed, who had loyally followed him since childhood, joined him in Peshawar. The brothers had a strong family resemblance, though Mohammed was darker and slightly taller and thinner than Ayman. Soft-spoken and deferential, Mohammed set up al-Jihad's financial pipeline, which ran from Cairo to Pakistan via Saudi Arabia.

Zawahiri established his medical practice at a Kuwaiti-backed Red Crescent hospital, which, like most of the aid institutions in the city, was dominated by members of the Muslim Brotherhood. They hated him because of a lengthy diatribe he wrote, called *Bitter Harvest*, in which he attacked the Brothers for collaborating with infidel regimes—that is to say, all Arab governments. He called the Brotherhood "a tool in the hands of tyrants." He demanded that they publicly renounce "constitutions and man-made laws, democracy, elections, and parliament," and declare jihad against the regimes they formerly supported. Privately funded, this handsomely produced book appeared all over Peshawar. "They were available free of charge," one of the Brothers, who was working in Peshawar at the time, recalls. "When you would go to get food, the clerk would ask if you wished to have one of these books, or two?"

Another of Zawahiri's colleagues from the underground days in Cairo arrived, a physician named Sayyid Imam, whose jihadi moniker was Dr. Fadl. They worked in the same hospital in Peshawar. Like Zawahiri, Dr. Fadl was a writer and theoretician. Because he was older and had been the emir of al-Jihad during Zawahiri's imprisonment, he took over the organization once again. Zawahiri also adopted a nom de guerre: Dr. Abdul Mu'iz (in Arabic, *abd* means "slave," and *mu'iz* means "the bestower of honor," one of the ninety-nine names of God). He and Dr. Fadl immediately set about reestablishing al-Jihad by recruiting new members from the young Egyptians among the mujahideen. At first they called themselves the Jihad Organization, then they changed the name again, to Islamic Jihad. But it was still the same al-Jihad.

The Kuwaiti-backed Red Crescent hospital became the center of a divisive movement within the Arab Afghan community. Under the influence of an Algerian, Dr. Ahmed el-Wed, known for his bloody-minded intellect, the hospital turned into an incubator for a murderous new idea, one that would split the mujahideen and justify the fratricidal carnage that would spread through the Muslim Arab countries immediately after the Afghan war.

The heresy of *takfir*, or excommunication, has been a problem in Islam since its early days. In the mid seventh century, a group known as the Kharijites revolted against the rule of Ali, the fourth caliph. The particular issue that triggered their rebellion was Ali's decision to compromise with a political opponent rather than to wage a fratricidal war. The Kharijites decreed that they were the only ones who followed the true tenets of the faith, and that anyone who did not agree with them was an apostate, and that included even Ali, the Prophet's beloved son-in-law, whom they eventually assassinated.

In the early 1970s a group surfaced in Egypt called Takfir wa Hijira (Excommunication and Withdrawal), a forerunner of al-Qaeda. Their leader, Shukri Mustafa, a graduate of the Egyptian concentration camps, attracted a couple of thousand followers. They read Qutb and plotted the day when they would gain sufficient strength in exile to return to annihilate the unbelievers and bring on the final days. Meanwhile, they wandered in Egypt's Western Desert, sleeping in mountain grottoes.

The Cairo press called Mustafa's followers *ahl al-kahf*, "people of the cave," a reference to the Seven Sleepers of Ephesus. This Christian folktale recounts the story of seven shepherds who refused to renounce their faith. In punishment, the Roman emperor Decius had them walled up inside a cave in present-day Turkey. Three centuries later, according to the legend, the cave was discovered and the sleepers awakened, thinking they had slept only one night. There is an entire sura, or chapter, in the Quran, "The Cave," that refers to this story. Like Shukri Mustafa, bin Laden would fasten onto the imagery that the cave evokes for Muslims. Moreover, the modus operandi of withdrawal, preparation, and dissimulation that would frame the culture of al-Qaeda's sleeper cells was established by Takfir wa Hijira as early as 1975.

Two years later, members of the group kidnapped a former minister of religious endowments in Cairo, Sheikh Mohammed al-Dhahabi, a humble and distinguished scholar who often spoke at the Masjid al-Nur, a mosque Zawahiri had frequented in his youth. When the Egyptian government spurned Shukri Mastafa's demands for money and publicity, Mustafa murdered the old sheikh. His body was found on a Cairo street, hands bound behind him, part of his beard torn away.

The Egyptian police quickly rounded up most of the members of Takfir wa Hijira and brought dozens of them to a hasty trial. Shukri Mustafa and five others were executed. With that, the revolutionary concept of expelling Muslims from the faith—and thereby justifying their killing—seemed to have been stamped out. But in the subterranean discourse of jihad, a mutated form of *takfir* had taken hold. It still smoldered in Upper Egypt, where Shukri Mustafa had proselytized in his early years (and where Dr. Fadl was reared). Remnants of the group supplied Zawahiri's comrades in al-Jihad with the grenades and ammunition used to assassinate Anwar Sadat. Some adherents carried the heresy into North African countries, including Algeria, where Dr. Ahmed learned of it.

Takfir is the mirror image of Islam, reversing its fundamental principles but maintaining the semblance of orthodoxy. The Quran explicitly states that Muslims shall not kill anyone, except as punishment for murder. The murderer of one innocent, the Quran warns, is judged "as if he had murdered all of mankind." The killing of Muslims is an even greater offense. He who commits such an act, says the Quran, will find that "his repayment is Hell, remaining in it timelessly, forever." How, then, could groups such as al-Jihad and the Islamic Group justify using violence against fellow Muslims in order to come to power? Sayyid Qutb had pointed the way by declaring that a leader who does not impose Sharia on the country must be an apostate. There is a well-known saying of the Prophet that the blood of Muslims cannot be shed except in three instances: as punishment for murder, or for marital infidelity, or for turning away from Islam. The pious Anwar Sadat was the first modern victim of the reverse logic of *takfir*.

The new takfiris, such as Dr. Fadl and Dr. Ahmed, extended the death warrant to encompass, for instance, anyone who registered to vote. Democracy, in their view, was against Islam because it placed in the hands of people authority that properly belonged to God. Therefore, anyone who voted was an apostate, and his life was forfeit. So was anyone who disagreed with their joyless understanding of Islam—including the mujahideen leaders they had ostensibly come to help, and even the entire population of Afghanistan, whom they regarded as infidels because they were not Salafists. The new takfiris believed that they were entitled to kill practically anyone and everyone who stood in their way; indeed, they saw it as a divine duty.

Until he arrived in Peshawar, Zawahiri had never endorsed wholesale murder. He had always approached political change like a surgeon: A speedy and precise coup d'état was his lifelong ideal. But while he was working in the Red Crescent hospital with Dr. Fadl and Dr. Ahmed, the moral bonds that separated political resistance from terrorism became more elastic. His friends and former prison mates noticed a change in his personality. The modest, well-mannered doctor who had always been so exacting in his arguments was now strident, antagonistic, and strangely illogical. He would seize on innocent comments and interpret them in a weird and malicious manner. Perhaps for the first time in his adulthood, he faced a crisis of identity.

In a life as directed and purposeful as Zawahiri's, there are few moments that can be said to be turning points. One was the execution of Sayyid Qutb when Zawahiri was fifteen; indeed, that was the point of origin for all that followed. Torture did not so much change Zawahiri as purify his resolve. Each step of his life was in the service of fulfilling his goal of installing an Islamic government in Egypt as bloodlessly as possible. But the takfiri doctrine had shaken him. The takfiris convinced themselves that salvation for all of humanity lay on the other side of moral territory that had always been the certain province of the damned. They would shoulder the risks to their eternal souls by assuming the divine authority of deciding who was a real Muslim and who was not, who should live and who should die.

Zawahiri stood at this great divide. On one side, there lay before him the incremental process of rebuilding his movement in exile, waiting for the opportunity, if it ever came, of returning to Egypt and taking control. This was his life's goal. But it was only a small step toward the apocalypse, which seemed so much closer at hand when he viewed the other side of the divide. There, across what he must have known was an ocean of blood, was the promise of the universal restoration of true Islam.

For the next ten years, Zawahiri would be pulled in both directions. The Egyptian option was al-Jihad, which he had created and defined. The universal option had not yet been named, but it was already taking shape. It would be called al-Qaeda.

ZAWAHIRI'S WIFE, Azza, set up housekeeping in Hayatabad, Pakistan, where many of the other Arabs were living. The wives of al-Jihad kept themselves apart, wearing black abayas and covering their faces in public. The Zawahiris rented a four-bedroom villa and kept one room always available for the many visitors who passed through. "If they had money left over, they gave it to the needy," Azza's brother Essam said. "They were happy with very little."

Azza's mother, Nabila Galal, visited Azza and Ayman in Pakistan on three occasions. She brought boxes of Fisher-Price toys to her grandchildren. She thought they were "an unusually close family, and always moved together as one unit." But the man her pious daughter had chosen still confounded her. He seemed always to be drawing his wife and children deeper into danger. Nabila was helpless to stop this fatal drift, which had begun in 1981 when Zawahiri went to prison just as his first child, Fatima, was born. Nabila had taken care of his wife and child until he got out three years later. After Zawahiri escaped from Egypt and relocated to Jeddah, Nabila dutifully came to attend the birth of Umayma, who was named after Zawahiri's mother. During those visits, Azza privately confessed to her mother how much she missed Egypt and her family. Again and again, Nabila fretted over the direction that Azza's life was taking.

"One day, I got a letter from Azza, and I felt intense pain as I read the words," Nabila said. "She wrote that she was to travel to Pakistan with her husband. I wished that she would not go there, but I knew that nobody can prevent fate. She was well aware of the rights her husband held over her and her duty toward him, which is why she was to follow him to the ends of the earth."

In Peshawar, Azza gave birth to Nabila, her mother's namesake, in 1986, and to a fourth daughter, Khadija, the following year. In 1988 the Zawahiris' only son, Mohammed, was born, so Ayman was at last accorded the honor of being called Abu Mohammed. Nabila came for her final visit soon after that. She would never forget the sight of Azza and her daughters waiting for her at the airport, all wearing hijabs and smiling at her. That was the last time she would ever see them.

BIN LADEN SOMETIMES CAME to lecture at the hospital where Zawahiri worked. Although the two men had different goals at the time, they had in common much that drew them together. They were both very modern men, members of the educated and technological class, despite their fundamentalist religious views. From a young age, bin Laden had managed large teams of workers on sophisticated construction projects, and he was at ease in the world of high finance. Zawahiri, seven years older, was a surgeon, immersed in contemporary science and medical technology. They were both from families that were well known throughout the Arab world. They were quiet-spoken, devout, and politically stifled by the regimes in their own countries.

Each man filled a need in the other. Zawahiri wanted money and contacts, which bin Laden had in abundance. Bin Laden, an idealist given to causes, sought direction; Zawahiri, a seasoned propagandist, supplied it. They were not friends but allies. Each believed he could use the other, and each was pulled in a direction he never intended to go. The Egyptian had little interest in Afghanistan except as a staging area for the revolution in his own country. He planned to use the Afghan jihad as an opportunity to rebuild his shattered organization. In bin Laden, he found a wealthy, charismatic, and pliable sponsor. The young Saudi was a devout Salafist but not much of a political thinker. Until he met Zawahiri, he had never voiced opposition to his own government or other repressive Arab regimes. His main interest was in expelling the infidel invader from a Muslim land, but he also nursed an ill-formed longing to punish America and the West for what he believed were crimes against Islam. The dynamic of the two men's relationship made Zawahiri and bin Laden into people they would never have been individually; moreover, the organi-zation they would create, al-Qaeda, would be a vector of these two forces, one Egyptian and one Saudi. Each would have to com-promise in order to accommodate the goals of the other; as a result, al-Qaeda would take a unique path, that of global jihad.

During one of his lectures at the hospital, bin Laden spoke about the need to boycott American products as a way of support-ing the Palestinian cause. Zawahiri warned him that by attacking America he was steering into dangerous water. "As of now, you should change the way in which you are guarded," Zawahiri said. "You should alter your entire security system because your head is now wanted by the Americans and the Jews, not only by the communists and the Russians, because you are hitting the snake on its head."

To back up his proposal, Zawahiri offered a highly disciplined cadre of mujahideen. They were different from the teenagers and drifters who made up so much of the Arab Afghan community. Zawahiri's recruits were doctors, engineers, and soldiers. They were used to working in secret. Many of them had been through prison and had already paid a hideous price for their beliefs. They would become the leaders of al-Qaeda.

IT WAS SNOWING IN FEBRUARY 1988 when an Egyptian film-maker, Essam Deraz, and his hurriedly assembled crew arrived at the Lion's Den. Mujahideen wearing bandoliers and carrying Kalashnikovs guarded the entrance to the main cave, under an overhanging cliff. The sight of the video cameras alarmed them. Deraz explained that he had permission from bin Laden to visit the Lion's Den and film the Arabs, but he and his crew were forced to wait outside for an hour in the bitter cold. Finally a guard said that Deraz could enter, but his team would have to stay outside. Deraz indignantly refused. "Either we all come in or we all stay out," he said.

In a few minutes, Zawahiri appeared, identifying himself as Dr. Abdul Mu'iz. He apologized for the ungracious welcome and invited the men inside for tea and bread. That night Deraz slept on the floor of the cave, next to Zawahiri, who was there to over-see the building of a hospital in one of the tunnels.

The Egyptians maintained their own camp within the Lion's Den complex. Bin Laden had put them on his payroll, giving each man 4,500 Saudi riyals (about $1,200) per month, to support their families. Among the Egyptians was Amin Ali al-Rashidi, who had taken the jihadi name of Abu Ubaydah al-Banshiri. Abu Ubaydah was a former police officer whose brother had participated in the Sadat assassination. Zawahiri had introduced him to bin Laden, who found him so irreplaceable that he made him the military leader of the Arabs. Abu Ubaydah had already earned a reputa-tion for bravery on the battlefield, fighting first under Sayyaf's banner and then bin Laden's. He was credited with the Arabs' mythic victory over the Soviets several months before. He seemed to Deraz as shy as a child. Second in command under Abu

Ubaydah was another former police officer, Mohammed Atef, who was called Abu Hafs. He had dark skin and shining green eyes.

A moody hothead named Mohammed Ibrahim Makkawi had recently arrived expecting to be awarded the military command of the Arab Afghans because of his experience as a colonel in the Egyptian Army's Special Forces. A small, dark man, Makkawi kept his clean-shaven military look despite the fundamentalist beards all around him. "The other Arabs hated him because he acted like an officer," said Deraz. He struck some of the Islamists as being dangerously unbalanced. Before he left Cairo in 1987, Makkawi deliberated whether he should go to the United States and join the American army or to Afghanistan and wage jihad. At the same time, he told an Egyptian lawmaker about a scheme to crash an airliner into the Egyptian parliament. Makkawi may be the same man who took the nom de guerre Saif al-Adl. Only their common determination to overthrow the Egyptian government kept Makkawi and Zawahiri together.

Deraz became bin Laden's first biographer. He soon came to notice how the Egyptians formed a barrier around the curiously passive Saudi, who rarely ventured an opinion of his own, preferring to solicit the views of others in his company. This humility, this apparent artlessness, on bin Laden's part elicited a protective response from many, including Deraz. He claims he sought to counter the influence of his countrymen, but whenever he tried to speak confidentially to bin Laden, the Egyptians would surround the Saudi and drag him into another room. They all had designs on him. Deraz thought bin Laden had the potential to be "another Eisenhower" by turning his wartime legend into a peaceful political life. But that wasn't Zawahiri's plan.

IN MAY 1988 the Soviets began a staged withdrawal from Afghanistan, signaling the end of the war. Slowly, Peshawar shrank back into its shabby former self, and the Afghan mujahideen leaders started stockpiling weapons, preparing to confront their inevitable new enemies—each other.

Bin Laden and his Egyptian handlers were also surveying the

future. Zawahiri and Dr. Fadl constantly fed him position papers outlining the "Islamic" perspective, which reflected their takfiri tendencies. One of bin Laden's close friends paid a call on him in Peshawar during this period and was told that bin Laden was unavailable because "Dr. Ayman was giving him a class in how to become the leader in an international organization."

As he groomed bin Laden for the role that he envisioned for him, Zawahiri sought to undermine Sheikh Abdullah Azzam, the single great competitor for bin Laden's attention. "I don't know what some people are doing here in Peshawar," Azzam complained to his son-in-law Abdullah Anas. "They are talking against the mujahideen. They have only one point, to create *fitna*"—discord—"between me and these volunteers." He singled out Zawahiri as one of the troublemakers.

Azzam recognized that the real danger was *takfir*. The heresy that had infected the Arab Afghan community was spreading and threatened to fatally corrupt the spiritual purity of jihad. The struggle was against nonbelievers, Azzam believed, not within the community of faith, however fractured it might be. He issued a fatwa opposing the training of terrorists with money raised for the Afghan resistance, and he preached that the intentional killing of civilians, especially women and children, was against Islam.

And yet Azzam himself was in favor of forming a "pioneering vanguard" along the lines called for by Sayyid Qutb. "This vanguard constitutes the solid base"—*qaeda*—"for the hoped-for society," Azzam wrote in April 1988. Upon this base the ideal Islamic society would be built. Afghanistan was just the beginning, Azzam believed. "We shall continue the jihad no matter how long the way, until the last breath and the last beat of the pulse—or until we see the Islamic state established." The property he surveyed for the future of jihad included the southern Soviet republics, Bosnia, the Philippines, Kashmir, central Asia, Somalia, Eritrea, and Spain—the entire span of the once-great Islamic empire.

First, however, was Palestine. Azzam helped create Hamas, the Palestinian resistance group, which he saw as the natural extension of the jihad in Afghanistan. Based on the Muslim Brotherhood, Hamas was meant to provide an Islamic counterweight to Yasser Arafat's secular Palestine Liberation Organization. Azzam sought to train brigades of Hamas fighters in Afghanistan, who would then return to carry on the battle against Israel.

Azzam's plans for Palestine, however, ran counter to Zawahiri's intention of stirring revolution within Islamic countries, especially in Egypt. Azzam fiercely opposed a war of Muslim against Muslim. As the war against the Soviets wound down, this dispute over the future of jihad was defined by these two strong-willed men. The prize they fought over was a rich and impressionable young Saudi who had his own dreams.

WHAT DID BIN LADEN WANT? He did not share either Zawahiri's or Azzam's priorities. The tragedy of Palestine was a constant theme in his speeches, yet he was reluctant to participate in the intifada against Israel. Like Azzam, bin Laden hated Yasser Arafat because he was a secularist. Nor did he relish the prospect of war against Arab governments. At the time, he envisioned moving the struggle to Kashmir, the Philippines, and particularly the Central Asian republics where he could continue the jihad against the Soviet Union. Notably, the United States was not yet on anyone's list. The vanguard he would create was primarily to fight against communism.

One fateful day in Peshawar, August 11, 1988, Sheikh Abdullah Azzam called a meeting to discuss the future of jihad. Bin Laden, Abu Hafs, Abu Ubaydah, Abu Hajer, Dr. Fadl, and Wa'el Julaidan were present. These men were bound by uncommon experiences but profoundly divided by their goals and philosophies. One of Azzam's objectives was to make sure that, in the event of an Afghan civil war, the Arabs were not involved. His former stance of scattering the Arabs among the various commanders could prove disastrous if the Afghans began fighting each other. He had come to agree with bin Laden about the need to establish a separate Arab group, although they differed on the direction it should take. The takfiris—Hafs, Ubaydah, and Fadl— were mainly interested in taking over Egypt, but they wanted to have a say in the latest venture. Abu Hajer, the Iraqi Kurd, was always suspicious of the Egyptians and inclined to oppose them on principle, but he was also the most militant among them, and it was difficult to know which side he would support. Although Azzam chaired the meeting, the comments were directed at bin Laden, because everyone understood that the fate of jihad was in his hands, not theirs.

According to Abu Rida's sketchy handwritten notes of the meeting, the men began with three general talking points:

a. *Did you take the opinion of Sheikh Abdullah*
   → *knowing that the Sheikh's military gang has ended.*
b. *This future project is in the interest of the Egyptian brothers.*
c. *The next stage is our foreign work*
   → *disagreement is present*
   → *weapons are plenty.*

The men observed that it had been more than a year since the construction of the Lion's Den, but it was little more than a training camp. Arabs were still excluded from the real fighting. Educating the youth is important, the men admitted, but it was time to take the next step. "We should focus on the original idea we came here for," Abu Rida noted in his pinched handwriting. "All this is to start a new project from scratch."

In response, bin Laden, who was now being called the Sheikh in deference to his increased stature among the Arabs, reflected on his experience in Afghanistan so far: "I am only one person. We have started neither an organization nor an Islamic group. It was a space of a year and a half—a period of education, of building trust, of testing the brothers who came, and a period of proving ourselves to the Islamic world. Although I began all these matters in the darkest of circumstances and in such a brief time, we still made huge gains." He gave no credit to Azzam, the real progenitor of the Arab Afghans; it was bin Laden's saga now. One can hear for the first time the epic tone that began to characterize his speech—the sound of a man in the grasp of destiny.

"As for our Egyptian brothers," bin Laden continued, mentioning what was obviously a contentious subject with many of his followers, "their standing with us in the worst of times cannot be ignored."

One of the men then said that although the main goals of the Arabs had not yet been achieved, "we worked with what we had," but "we lost a lot of time."

"We have progressed well," bin Laden responded, perhaps defensively. He pointed to the "trained, obedient and faithful youth" who could readily be put to use.

Although the notes don't reflect it, a vote was taken to form a new organization aimed at keeping jihad alive after the Soviets were gone. It is difficult to imagine these men agreeing on anything, but only Abu Hajer voted against the new group. Abu Rida summarized the meeting by saying that a plan must be established within a suitable time frame and qualified people must be found to put the plan into effect. "Initial estimate, within 6 months of al-Qaeda, 314 brothers will be trained and ready." For most of the men in the meeting, this was the first time that the name al-Qaeda had arisen. The members of the new group would be drawn from the most promising recruits among the Arab Afghans, but it was still unclear what the organization would do or where it would go after the jihad. Perhaps bin Laden himself didn't know.

Few people in the room realized that al-Qaeda had already been secretly created some months before by a small group of bin Laden insiders. Bin Laden's friend from Jeddah, Medani al-Tayeb, who had married his niece, had joined the group on May 17, the day after Ramadan, so the organizational meeting on August 11 only brought to the surface what was already covertly under way.

On Saturday morning, August 20, the same men met again to establish what they called al-Qaeda al-Askariya (the military base). "The mentioned al-Qaeda is basically an organized Islamic faction, its goal is to lift the word of God, to make His religion victorious," the secretary recorded in his minutes of the meeting. The founders divided the military work, as they termed it, into two parts: "limited duration," in which the Arabs would be trained and placed with Afghan mujahideen for the remainder of the war;

and "open duration," in which "they enter a testing camp and the best brothers of them are chosen." The graduates of this second camp would become members of the new entity, al-Qaeda.

The secretary listed the requirements of those who sought to join this new organization:

- *Members of the open duration.*
- *Listening and obedient.*
- *Good manners.*
- *Referred from a trusted source.*
- *Obeying statutes and instructions of al-Qaeda.*

In addition, the founders wrote an oath that the new members would recite upon joining al-Qaeda: "The pledge of God and his covenant is upon me, to energetically listen and obey the superiors who are doing this work, rising early in times of difficulty and ease."

"The meeting ended on the evening of Saturday, 8/20/1988," the secretary noted. "Work of al-Qaeda commenced on 9/10/1988, with a group of fifteen brothers." At the bottom of the page, the secretary added, "Until the date 9/20, Commandant Abu Ubaydah arrived to inform me of the existence of thirty brothers in al-Qaeda, meeting the requirements, and thank God."

Bin Laden attached no special meaning to the name of the new group. "Brother Abu-Ubaydah al-Banshiri—God rest his soul—formed a camp to train youth to fight against the oppressive, atheist, and truly terrorist Soviet Union," he later stated. "We called that place al-Qaeda—in the sense that it was a training base—and that is where the name came from."

Bin Laden's associates had mixed reactions to the formation of al-Qaeda. Abu Rida al-Suri, the mujahid from Kansas City, claims that when he first heard about the international Arab legion that bin Laden was creating, he asked doubtfully how many had joined. "Sixty," bin Laden lied.

"How are you going to transport them?" Abu Rida asked. "Air France?"

The formation of al-Qaeda gave the Arab Afghans something

else to fight over. Every enterprise that arose in the sparsely populated cultural landscape was contested, and any head that rose
above the crowd was a target. The ongoing jihad in Afghanistan
became an afterthought in the war of words and ideas that was
being fought in the mosques. Even the venerable Services
Bureau, which bin Laden and Azzam had established to assist
the Arabs in their desire to join the jihad, was slandered as a CIA
front and Azzam as an American stooge.

At the root of these quarrels was the usual culprit—money.
Peshawar was the funnel through which cash poured into the
jihad and the vast relief effort to help the refugees. The main pool
of funds—the hundreds of millions of dollars from the United
States and Saudi Arabia doled out by the Pakistani Inter-Services
Intelligence (ISI) each year to the Afghan warlords—was drying
up as the Soviets prepared to leave. Scarcity only fed the frenzy
over what remained: the international aid agencies, private charities, and bin Laden's pockets.

From the beginning, the Egyptians who were sponsoring bin
Laden saw Azzam as a formidable obstacle. No one among the
Arabs enjoyed equal prestige. Most of the young men who had
gravitated to jihad were responding to his fatwa, and they
regarded Azzam with awe. "He was an angel, worshipping all
night, crying and fasting," recalled his former assistant, Abdullah
Anas, who married Azzam's daughter just to be close to his mentor. For most of the Arabs who passed through Peshawar, Azzam
was the most famous man they had ever met. Many of them—
including bin Laden—had spent their first nights in Peshawar
sleeping on his floor. They spoke movingly of his wisdom, generosity, and courage. He had come to personify the noble spirit of
the Arab Afghans, and his shadow reached around the world.
Destroying such a celebrated icon would be a treacherous task.

The Egyptians were not the only ones interested in bringing
down Azzam. The Saudis worried that the charismatic leader
would convert their young jihadis to the Muslim Brothers. They
wanted an "independent body"—one that was run by a Saudi—
that could be entrusted to manage the affairs of the mujahideen
while keeping the Kingdom's interests in mind. Bin Laden and al-

Qaeda were seen as a proper Salafist alternative managed by a loyal son of the Saudi regime.

Abdullah Anas, the greatest exemplar of the Arab Afghan warriors, had just returned to Peshawar after fighting beside Ahmed Shah Massoud in northern Afghanistan. He was astounded to learn that there was to be a meeting among the Arab leaders to replace his father-in-law, Abdullah Azzam. When Anas talked to him about it, Azzam assured him that the election was strictly cosmetic. "The Saudi authorities are not pleased that I am leading the Arabs in Afghanistan," Azzam explained. "All the money that comes for orphans and widows and schools comes from Saudi Arabia. They are unhappy to see the young Saudis being organized under my leadership. They fear they will become a part of the Muslim Brotherhood." The Saudis wanted one of their own in charge. With Osama bin Laden as the new emir, Azzam continued, the Saudis would feel safe. "They will relax, because when they feel Osama is out of control, they can stop him. But I am a Palestinian. They have no way of stopping me."

It was even more difficult for Azzam to persuade his old friend Sheikh Tameem to support this proposal. Although Azzam had told him the election was only a charade to gain Saudi approval, it was clear that others in the meeting had a different agenda. They heatedly used the occasion to slander Azzam's reputation with charges of theft and corruption and mismanagement of the Services Bureau. Sheikh Tameem was outraged and turned to bin Laden. "Say something," he demanded.

"I'm the emir of this meeting," bin Laden responded. "Wait for your round."

"Who told you that you are my emir?" Tameem began weeping. "Sheikh Abdullah persuaded me to support you, but how do you let these people say these things?" Tameem refused to endorse the vote, which overwhelmingly selected bin Laden as the Arabs' new leader.

Azzam was philosophical and apparently unconcerned. "Osama is limited," he reassured his supporters. "What can Osama do to organize people? Nobody knows him! Don't worry."

Azzam was more weakened than he realized. One of

Zawahiri's men, Abu Abdul Rahman, a Canadian citizen of Egyptian origin, lodged a complaint against Azzam. Abu Abdul Rahman headed a medical and educational project in Afghanistan. He alleged that Azzam's men had snatched the project out of his hands by confiscating the funds that were earmarked for it. He further accused Azzam of spreading rumors that he was trying to sell the humanitarian project to the American embassy or a Christian organization.

The charges created a sensation in Peshawar. Placards were handed out and posters pasted on the walls demanding that Azzam be brought to trial. Fights broke out in the mosques among the different camps of supporters. Behind the charges being thrown at Azzam were the takfiri doctors at the Kuwaiti Red Crescent hospital—Zawahiri and his colleagues. They had already managed to expel him from the leadership of the hospital's mosque, and now they were gleefully predicting his downfall. "Soon we will see the hand of Abdullah Azzam cut off in Peshawar," Dr. Ahmed el-Wed, the Algerian, exclaimed in a meeting.

They formed a court to hear the charges, with Dr. Fadl acting as the prosecutor and the judge. This takfiri court had sat before to consider another mujahid whom they judged guilty of being an apostate. His body was found, chopped to pieces, inside a burlap bag on a street in Peshawar.

On the second day of the trial, after midnight, bin Laden rushed out to fetch his closest Saudi friend, Wa'el Julaidan, who was in bed with chills and a high fever, suffering from malaria. Bin Laden insisted that Julaidan come at once. "We cannot trust the Egyptians," he declared. "I swear by God those people, if they have the chance to make a resolution against Dr. Abdullah Azzam, they will kill him." Julaidan followed bin Laden back to the meeting, which lasted another couple of hours. The judges found against Azzam and ordered the charity returned to Abu Abdul Rahman's control, but thanks to bin Laden's intervention, they spared Azzam the disgrace of public mutilation. From the perspective of Azzam's enemies, however, it was an inconclusive verdict, since it allowed Azzam to remain as a figurehead, and they were determined to finish him off.

GENERAL BORIS V. GROMOV, the commander of Soviet forces in Afghanistan, walked across the Friendship Bridge into Uzbekistan on February 15, 1989. "There is not a single Soviet soldier or officer left behind me," the general remarked. "Our nine-year stay ends with this." The Soviets had lost fifteen thousand lives and suffered more than thirty thousand casualties. Between a million and two million Afghans perished, perhaps 90 percent of them civilians. Villages were razed, crops and livestock destroyed, the landscape studded with mines. A third of the population sheltered in refugee camps in Pakistan or Iran. The Afghan communist government remained in Kabul, however, and the jihad entered a confusing new period.

The end of the occupation coincided with a sudden and surprising influx of Arab mujahideen, including hundreds of Saudis who were eager to chase the retreating Soviet bear. According to Pakistan government statistics, more than six thousand Arabs came to take part in the jihad from 1987 to 1993, twice the number who came for the war against the Soviet occupation. These young men were different from the small cadre of believers who had been lured to Afghanistan by Abdullah Azzam. They were "men with large amounts of money and boiling emotions," an al-Qaeda diarist noted. Pampered kids from the Persian Gulf came on excursions, staying in air-conditioned cargo containers; they were supplied with RPGs and Kalashnikovs, which they could fire into the air, and then they could return home, boasting of their adventure. Many of them were newly religious high school or university students with no history and no one to vouch for them. Chaos and barbarism, which always threatened to overwhelm the movement, sharply increased as bin Laden took the helm. Bank robberies and murders became even more commonplace, justified by absurd religious claims. A group of takfiris even held up a truck from an Islamic aid agency, absolving their action by saying that the Saudis were infidels.

Now that he was the emir of the Arabs, bin Laden held himself above the riotous competition for recruits among the rival Islamic groups that were elbowing each other at the airport as they hustled the newcomers onto their buses. The wrangling was especially nasty among the Egyptians. The two main Egyptian organizations— the Islamic Group, led by Sheikh Omar Abdul Rahman, and Zawahiri's al-Jihad—set up competing guesthouses, and they began publishing magazines and broadsides with little purpose other than to vilify each other. Among the accusations made by the Islamic Group against Zawahiri were that he had sold arms for gold, which he deposited in a Swiss bank account, and that he was an agent for the Americans—the universal charge of treason. In turn, Zawahiri wrote a tract attacking Sheikh Omar titled "The Blind Leader," in which he recapitulated their prison quarrels for control of the radical Islamist movement. The unstated cause of these slanderous salvos was the question of who was going to control bin Laden, the golden Saudi goose. Bin Laden made his preference known by awarding $100,000 to al-Jihad to begin its operations.

Meantime, a new battle was taking shape in Jalalabad, the strategic entry point on the Afghan side of the Khyber Pass, where all the roads and valleys and footpaths converged. The adversary was no longer the Soviet superpower. Now it was the communist Afghan government, which refused to collapse as so many had predicted. (One of the ugly ironies of the Arab Afghan crusade is that it was made up, by a large majority, of Muslims who came to fight Muslims, not Soviet invaders.) The siege of Jalalabad was supposed to close the curtain on communist rule in Afghanistan. Emboldened by the Soviet withdrawal, the mujahideen had contemptuously decided to mount a frontal assault on the Afghan position. The city, which stood behind a river and a wide corridor of Russian mines, was defended by thousands of Afghan government troops, who were demoralized by the articles in the Pakistani press of the impending mujahideen attack and the inevitable rapid victory that was supposed to follow.

The initial assault came in March 1989, with five to seven thousand Afghan mujahideen charging down Highway 1. Eight different commanders led the men, not counting the Arabs, who followed bin Laden. After overrunning the airport on the outskirts of town, the mujahideen fell back against a powerful counterattack; then matters settled into an unexpected stalemate, with the various mujahideen commanders involved in the siege refusing to coordinate with one another.

Bin Laden and his military staff occupied a small cave in the mountains, four kilometers above the city. He had fewer than two hundred men under his command. Once again, he was ill.

His biographer, Essam Deraz, arrived, bringing with him a supply of vitamins and twelve boxes of Arcalion, a drug bin Laden always requested. He told Deraz that it was to help with his concentration. Arcalion is normally prescribed for a marked decrease in muscle strength or stamina, which might be caused by vitamin deficiencies or lead poisoning, among other things. Bin Laden's health, which had been so robust when he was a desert youth, had endured several blows in the harsh mountain environs. Like many of the men, he had contracted malaria; then in the severe winter of 1988–89, he nearly died of pneumonia when an intense snowfall buried him and several companions in their vehicle for a few days. The prolonged and unanticipated siege of Jalalabad taxed his weakened constitution further, and he was nagged increasingly by puzzling spells of back pain and paralyzing fatigue.

Zawahiri, who had developed a reputation among the Arab fighters as being a medical genius, drove over from Peshawar two or three times a week to treat the injured. His main patient, of course, was bin Laden, who needed intravenous glucose treatments to keep from fainting. Bin Laden would lie for hours on the floor of the cave, in pain and unable to move. The diagnosis was low blood pressure, which is usually a symptom of another ailment.* Whatever bin Laden's health problems were,

*One candidate, in bin Laden's case, is Addison's disease, a disorder of the endocrine system marked by low blood pressure, weight loss, muscle fatigue, stomach irritability, sharp back pains, dehydration, and an abnormal craving for salt. This is purely speculation, but bin Laden manifested all of these symptoms. Although the disease can be controlled with steroids, an addisonian crisis, as bin Laden may have been experiencing, can be fatal if the patient is not treated with saline and glucose immediately.

the friendship between him and Zawahiri would always be complicated by the fact that one placed his life in the hands of the other.

Afghan bombers flew twenty sorties a day, pummeling the mujahideen infantry with cluster bombs. Bin Laden and his men were dug into a trench between two mountain positions. On one occasion, bin Laden was awaiting a glucose transfusion from Zawahiri, who set up a metal pole to hold the bottle and then inserted the IV tube into the bottle. Bin Laden rolled up his sleeve and waited for his doctor to slip the cannula into his vein. Just then, a bomber roared overhead at a low altitude, followed by explosions that shook the mountains. Smoke and dust blanketed the mujahideen, who crept out of the trench to see what had been hit. As it turned out, the bombs had fallen on the peak above them, but the hail of rocks had knocked over the glucose stand.

Zawahiri calmly set the stand back up and untangled the IV tube. He got another sterile cannula, but once again, just as bin Laden stretched out his arm, a series of explosions pelted the men with rocks and blasted the wooden beams supporting the walls of the trench. The bombs were right on top of them. The men hugged the earth and waited until the aircraft disappeared. Then Zawahiri collected the stand and the same glucose bottle, which this time had been hurled across the trench. By now the men had become fixated on the bottle, "as if it were a living entity with a secret," Deraz recalled.

One of the men complained to Zawahiri, "Don't you see? Every time you put that bottle on the stand, we are bombed!"

Zawahiri laughed and refused to switch to another glucose bottle. "It's merely a coincidence," he said. But as he prepared to insert the needle, yet another terrifying series of explosions shattered the landscape and sent the men diving to the ground, crying out and mumbling verses from the Quran. The timbers holding the roof were blown apart and the trench was opened to the sky. Then came a cry that they were being attacked with poison gas. They quickly put on their gas masks. In the midst of the smoke and fear and confusion, Zawahiri patiently reassembled the metal stand, and again he picked up the glucose container.

Everyone in the trench began to shout at him, "Throw the bottle outside! Don't touch it!"

Bin Laden tried to remind them that evil omens are forbidden in Islam, but as Zawahiri started to attach the IV tube, one of the Saudis stood up and wordlessly took the glucose bottle out of Zawahiri's hands and hurled it out of the trench. Everyone laughed, even bin Laden, but they were all happy to see the bottle gone.

THERE WAS A YOUNG MAN fighting beside bin Laden during the siege of Jalalabad named Shafiq. Less than five feet tall, weighing perhaps ninety pounds, he was one of the few original Saudis who remained loyal despite the Egyptian entourage that encircled his leader. Jamal Khalifa, who was his teacher in Medina, remembered Shafiq as a polite, neatly groomed young man who had dropped out of school when he was sixteen to join the jihad. His father had soon come to Afghanistan to fetch him home. Khalifa was shocked when he saw his former student once again in Saudi Arabia. His hair was matted and hanging over his shoulders, and he wore dirty shoes and Afghan pants. The schoolboy had been completely transformed into a toughened warrior who couldn't wait to return to battle. Only a few weeks had passed before Shafiq snatched his passport from where his father had hidden it and returned to the war—a decision that had historic consequences.

One day a sentry in Jalalabad noticed Afghan army helicopters bearing down on the Arab position, followed by tanks and infantry. They were being led by a traitorous mujahid who had sold them out. The sentry called to bin Laden's men to evacuate the cave where they were hunkered down, but by that time the armored units were upon them, ready to annihilate the entire outpost.

Bin Laden hurried away with the rest of his soldiers except for Shafiq, who single-handedly covered their retreat with a small mortar. Without the few moments of relief that Shafiq provided, bin Laden would likely have died in Jalalabad, along with his unrealized dream. Eighty other Arabs did die there, including Shafiq, in the greatest disaster of the Arab Afghan experience.

AL-QAEDA HELD its first recruitment meeting in the Farouk camp near Khost, Afghanistan, shortly after the debacle in Jalal-abad. Farouk was a *takfir* camp, established by Zawahiri and Dr. Fadl, devoted entirely to training the elite Arab mujahideen being groomed to join bin Laden's private army. Although the Lion's Den was just across the mountain, the Farouk camp was kept iso-lated from the others so that the young men could be closely watched. Those chosen were young, zealous, and obedient. They were given a bonus and were told to bid farewell to their families.

The majority of the leadership council set up to advise bin Laden were Egyptians, including Zawahiri, Abu Hafs, Abu Ubay-dah, and Dr. Fadl. Also represented were members from Algeria, Libya, and Oman. The organization opened an office in a two-story villa in Hayatabad, the suburb of Peshawar where most of the Arabs resided.

New recruits filled out forms in triplicate, signed their oath of loyalty to bin Laden, and swore themselves to secrecy. In return, single members earned about $1,000 a month in salary; married members received $1,500. Everyone got a round-trip ticket home each year and a month of vacation. There was a health-care plan and—for those who changed their mind—a buyout option: They received $2,400 and went on their way. From the beginning, al-Qaeda presented itself as an attractive employment opportunity for men whose education and careers had been curtailed by jihad.

The leaders of al-Qaeda developed a constitution and by-laws, which described the utopian goals of the organization in clear terms: "To establish the truth, get rid of evil, and establish an Islamic nation." This would be accomplished through education and military training, as well as coordinating and supporting jihad movements around the world. The group would be led by a commander who was impartial, resolute, trustworthy, patient, and just; he should have at least seven years of jihad experience and preferably a college degree. Among his duties were appoint-

ing a council of advisors to meet each month, establishing a budget, and deciding on a yearly plan of action. One can appreciate
the ambition of al-Qaeda by looking at its bureaucratic structure,
which included committees devoted to military affairs, politics,
information, administration, security, and surveillance. The military committee had subsections dedicated to training, operations,
research, and nuclear weapons.

After the failure of Jalalabad, the Afghan mujahideen succumbed to a cataclysmic civil war. The strongest parties in this
fratricide were Gulbuddin Hekmatyar and Ahmed Shah Massoud. Both were ruthless, charismatic leaders from the north, bent
on establishing an Islamic government in Afghanistan. Hekmatyar, the more skilled politician, was a Pashtun, the dominant
tribe in both Pakistan and Afghanistan. He had the backing of the
Pakistan ISI, and therefore of the United States and Saudi Arabia.
Massoud, one of the most talented guerrilla leaders of the twentieth century, was Tajik, from the Persian-speaking tribe that is the
second-largest ethnic group in Afghanistan. Based in the Panjshir
Valley north of Kabul, Massoud rarely traveled to Peshawar, the
hotbed of intelligence agencies and international media.

Most of the Arabs sided with Hekmatyar, excepting Abdullah
Anas, the son-in-law of Abdullah Azzam. Anas talked the sheikh
into visiting Massoud, to see for himself what kind of man he was.
The trip to visit the Lion of Panjshir required eight days of walking across four peaks in the Hindu Kush Mountains. As they
hiked through the mountains, Azzam reflected on the Jalalabad fiasco. He worried that the Afghan jihad had been a disorganized,
misguided failure. The Soviets were gone and now the Muslims
were fighting each other.

Massoud and a guard of a hundred men met them on the Pakistan border and led them down into the Panjshir Valley. Massoud
lived in a cave with two bedrooms—"like a Gypsy," said Anas,
who translated for the two men. Azzam was charmed by Massoud's modesty and admired the discipline of his troops, which
stood in such contrast to the other mujahideen irregular forces.
"We are your soldiers," Azzam pledged. "We love you and we are
going to help you."

When he returned to Peshawar, Azzam made no secret of his revised opinion of Massoud. He even traveled to Saudi Arabia and Kuwait, saying, "I have seen the true Islamic jihad. It is Massoud!" Hekmatyar was enraged by Azzam's turnaround, which could cost him the support of his Arab backers.

Azzam had already accumulated many enemies with dark hearts and bloody hands. Bin Laden begged Azzam to stay away from Peshawar, which had become too dangerous for his former mentor. One Friday, Hekmatyar's men discovered and disarmed a powerful bomb in the mosque near Azzam's house. It was an anti-tank mine planted under the rostrum that Azzam stood upon when he led prayers. Had it exploded, hundreds of worshippers could have been killed.

Confused and despondent because of the civil war among the mujahideen, and still suffering from the embarrassment of Jalalabad, bin Laden returned to Saudi Arabia for consultations with Saudi intelligence. He wanted to know which side to fight on. Prince Turki's chief of staff, Ahmed Badeeb, told him, "It's better to leave."

Before he quit Peshawar entirely, bin Laden returned to say farewell to Azzam. Bin Laden's rise had left Azzam vulnerable, but somehow their friendship had survived. They embraced for a long time, and both men shed many tears, as if they knew that they would never see each other again.

On November 24, 1989, Azzam rode to the mosque with two of his sons, Ibrahim and Mohammed, who was the driver. As Mohammed was parking, a roadside bomb made from twenty kilograms of TNT exploded with such force that the car shattered. Body parts were strewn over the trees and power lines. A leg of one of his children flew through a shop window a hundred yards away. But Azzam's body, it is said, was found peacefully resting against a wall, completely intact, not at all disfigured.

Earlier that Friday, on the streets of Peshawar, Azzam's main rival, Ayman al-Zawahiri, had been spreading rumors that Azzam was working for the Americans. The next day, he was at Azzam's funeral, praising the martyred sheikh, as did his many other jubilant enemies.

7

Return of the Hero

FAME CREATES ITS OWN AUTHORITY, even in Saudi Arabia, where humility is prized and prestige is carefully pruned among non-royals. It is a country that forbids the public display of portraits, except for the faces of the omnipresent ruling princes, who also name the streets and hospitals and universities after themselves, hoarding whatever glory is available. So when bin Laden returned to his hometown of Jeddah in the fall of 1989, he presented a dilemma that was unique in modern Saudi history. Only thirty-one years old, he commanded an international volunteer army of unknown dimensions. Because he actually believed the fable, promoted by the Saudi press, that his Arab legion had brought down the mighty superpower, he arrived with certain unprecedented expectations of his future. He was better known than all but a few princes and the upper tier of Wahhabi clergy— the Kingdom's first real celebrity.

He was rich, although not by royal standards or even those of the great merchant families of the Hijaz. His share of the Saudi Binladin Group at the time amounted to 27 million Saudi riyals— a little more than $7 million. He also received a portion of the annual earnings from the company that ranged from half a million to a million riyals a year. He settled back into the family business, helping to build roads in Taif and Abha. He kept a house in Jeddah and another in Medina, the city he had always loved the most, where he could be close to the Prophet's Mosque.

The young idealist returned to the Kingdom with a sense of

divine mission. He had risked death and had been, he thought, miraculously spared. He had gone as an acolyte of an iconic Muslim warrior, and he returned as the undisputed leader of the Arab Afghans. He had a commanding air of confidence, which was all the more seductive because of his instinctive humility. In a time when Saudis were increasingly uncertain about their identity in the modern world, bin Laden appeared as an unsullied archetype. His piety and humble manner reminded Saudis of their historic image of themselves as shy and self-effacing, but also fierce and austere. Some of his young admirers called him "the Othman of his age," a reference to one of the early caliphs, a wealthy man known for his righteousness.

Inevitably, bin Laden's fame cast an unwelcome light on the behavior of the Saudi royal family, led by King Fahd, who was known for his boozing and carousing in the ports of the French Riviera, where he docked his 482-foot yacht, the $100 million *Abdul Aziz*. The ship featured two swimming pools, a ballroom, a gym, a theater, a portable garden, a hospital with an intensive-care unit and two operating rooms, and four American Stinger missiles. The king also liked to fly to London in his $150 million 747 jet, equipped with its own fountain. He lost millions in the casinos on these excursions. One night, upset with the curfew imposed by British gaming laws, he hired his own blackjack and roulette dealers so that he could gamble in his hotel suite all night long. Other Saudi princes enthusiastically followed his example, notably King Fahd's son Mohammed, who accepted more than $1 billion in bribes, according to British court documents, which he spent on "whores, pornography; fleets of more than 100 high-performance cars; palaces in Cannes and Geneva; and such luxuries as powerboats, chartered jets, ski-chalets, and jewelry."

Oil prices collapsed in the mid-1980s, sending the Saudi economy into a deficit, but the royal family continued taking massive personal "loans" from the country's banks, which they rarely repaid. Every substantial business deal required "commissions"—kickbacks—to the royal mafia to lubricate the agreement. Individual princes confiscated land and muscled in on private businesses; this was in addition to the secret, but substantial, monthly allowance that each member of the family received. "Al Saud" became a byword for corruption, hypocrisy, and insatiable greed.

The attack on the Grand Mosque ten years before, however, had awakened the royal family to the lively prospect of revolution. The lesson the family drew from that gory standoff was that it could protect itself against religious extremists only by empowering them. Consequently, the *muttawa*, government-subsidized religious vigilantes, became an overwhelming presence in the Kingdom, roaming through the shopping malls and restaurants, chasing men into the mosques at prayer time and ensuring that women were properly cloaked—even a strand of hair poking out from under a hijab could rate a flogging with the swagger sticks these men carried. In their quest to stamp out sinfulness and heresy, they even broke into private homes and businesses; and they waged war on the proliferating satellite dishes, often shooting at them with government-issued weapons from government-issued Chevrolet Suburbans. Officially known as representatives of the Committee for the Promotion of Virtue and the Prevention of Vice, the *muttawa* would become the models for the Taliban in Afghanistan.

PRINCE TURKI PRESENTED a striking contrast to the public image of the royal family. Courteous, charming, and soft-spoken, he was the kind of man many people knew and liked; but he was also guarded and private, and he kept the various parts of his life so carefully separated that no one knew him well. He enjoyed the royal prerogatives of power, but within the Kingdom he lived in an appealingly humble manner. He occupied a comparatively modest, one-story house in Riyadh with his wife, Princess Nouf, and their six children; and on weekends, he retreated to his desert ranch, where he raised ostriches. He wore the invariable Saudi garments: the ankle-length white gown, called a *thobe*, and a red-checked headscarf. The fundamentalists respected him because he was an Islamic scholar, but he was also an advocate of women's rights, so the progressives saw him as a possible champion. He ran an intelligence service in the Middle East, which is usually a watchword for torture and assassination, but he had quickly gained a reputation for valuing clean hands. His father was the martyred king; his beloved mother, Effat, was the only woman in Saudi history ever called queen. All that, plus his youth and his important career, meant that Turki would have to be considered when the grandsons of Abdul Aziz finally have the opportunity to contend for the crown.

Outside the Kingdom, Turki lived a different life. He kept a house in London and an elaborate flat in Paris. He cruised the Mediterranean on his yacht, *White Knight*. In the drawing rooms of London and New York, he was known to favor the occasional banana daiquiri, but he was not a gambler or a lush. Because he fit comfortably into several different worlds, he had the quality of reflecting the virtues that others longed to see in him.

The CIA worked closely with Turki and his service during the Afghan jihad, and he had impressed the agency with his insight, the range of his knowledge, and his easy familiarity with American customs. There was an assumption on the part of some members of the U.S. intelligence community that Turki was Our Man in Riyadh, but others found him deceitful and reluctant to share information. These reactions mirrored the thorny relationship the Americans and the Saudis found themselves entangled in.

One Friday Turki went to a mosque in Riyadh where the imam had spoken out against certain female charitable organizations, including one that was overseen by five members of the Faisal family. Turki had listened to a tape recording of the sermon in which the imam had called the women running the charity whores. It was an astounding breach of the ancient bargain between Al Saud and the Wahhabi clergy. The following week Turki sat in the front row of the mosque, and when the imam rose to speak Turki furiously confronted him. "This man has defamed my family!" Turki shouted into the microphone. "My sisters! My daughter-in-law! Either he proves it, or I'm going to sue." A witness to the event says that Turki actually threatened to kill the man on the spot.

The daring slander and Prince Turki's furious response threw the country into turmoil. The governor of Riyadh, Prince Salman, placed the offending imam under arrest. He quickly offered his apology, which Turki accepted. But Turki realized that the balance of power between the two factions had begun to shift. Many of his family members were cowed by the religious posse that roamed the malls and streets with policemen at their command. The super-piety of the *muttawa* was bound to focus itself on the conspicuous depravity of some members of the royal family; now, however, they had even attacked the charitable works of popular and upstanding princesses who sought to advance women's causes. Clearly, the royal family could not abide such an insult, but the fact that such things were being said in public demonstrated that the *muttawa* were emboldened enough to preach revolution right under the noses of the ruling princes.

Like the CIA, Turki's intelligence service was not supposed to operate inside the homeland; that was the province of Prince Naif, Turki's truculent uncle, who ran the Interior Ministry and who jealously guarded his territory. Turki decided that the situation inside the country was too dangerous to be ignored, even if it meant intruding into Naif's domain. He secretly began monitoring members of the *muttawa*. He learned that many of them were ex-convicts whose only job qualification was that they had memorized the Quran in order to reduce their sentences. But they had become so powerful, Turki believed, that they now threatened to overthrow the government.

LIFE IN SAUDI ARABIA had always been marked by abstinence, submissiveness, and religious fervor, but the reign of the *muttawa* stifled social interaction and imposed a dangerous new orthodoxy. For centuries, the four main schools of Islamic jurisprudence—Hanafi, Maliki, Shafei, and Hanbali—were taught and studied in Mecca. The Wahhabis ostensibly held themselves above such doctrinal divisions, but in practice they ruled out other interpretations of the faith. The government forbade the Shia, who form a substantial minority in Saudi Arabia, from building new mosques or expanding existing ones. Only Wahhabis worshipped freely.

Not content to cleanse its own country of the least degree of religious freedom, the Saudi government set out to evangelize the Islamic world, using the billions of riyals at its disposal through the religious tax—*zakat*—to construct hundreds of mosques and colleges and thousands of religious schools around the globe, staffed with Wahhabi imams and teachers. Eventually, Saudi Arabia, which constitutes only 1 percent of the world Muslim population, would support 90 percent of the expenses of the entire faith, overriding other traditions of Islam.

Music disappeared in the Kingdom. Shortly after the 1979 attack on the Grand Mosque in Mecca, Umm Kalthoum and Fayrouz, the songbirds of the Arab world, were banished from the Kingdom's television stations, which were already dominated by bearded men debating fine points of religious law. There had been a few movie theaters in Saudi Arabia before the mosque attack, but they were quickly shut down. A magnificent concert hall was completed in Riyadh in 1989, but it never hosted a single performance. Censorship smothered art and literature, and intellectual life, which had scarcely had the chance to blossom in the young country, withered. Paranoia and fanaticism naturally occupy minds that are closed and fearful.

For the young, the future in this already joyless environment promised even less than the present. Only a few years earlier, Saudi Arabia had been on its way to becoming the wealthiest country, per capita, in the world, thanks to the bounty of its oil wealth. Now the declining price of oil crushed such expectations. The government, which had promised jobs to university graduates, withdrew its guarantees, creating the previously unknown phenomenon of unemployment. Despair and idleness are dangerous companions in any culture, and it was inevitable that the young would search for a hero who could voice their longing for change and provide a focus for their rage.

Neither a cleric nor a prince, Osama bin Laden assumed this new role, even though there was no precedent for such an independent agent in the Kingdom. He offered a conventional, Muslim Brothers critique of the plight of the Arab world: The West, particularly the United States, was responsible for the humiliating failure of the Arabs to succeed. "They have attacked our brothers in Palestine as they have attacked Muslims and Arabs elsewhere," he said one spring night in the bin Laden family mosque in Jeddah, just after evening prayers. "The blood of Muslims is shed. It has become too much. . . . We are only looked upon as sheep, and we are very humiliated."

Bin Laden wore a white robe with a gauzy camel-colored cloak draped over his shoulders. He spoke in a sleepy monotone, sometimes wagging his long, bony index finger to make a point, but his manner was relaxed and his gestures were limp and wan. Already, the messianic stare into the middle distance that would characterize his later pronouncements was on display. Before him hundreds of men sat cross-legged on the carpet. Many of them had fought with him in Afghanistan, and they sought a new direction in their lives. Their old enemy, the Soviet Union, was falling to pieces, but America did not seem to offer such an obvious substitute.

At first, it was difficult to grasp the basis of bin Laden's complaint. The United States had never been a colonial power, nor for that matter had Saudi Arabia ever been colonized. Of course, he was speaking for Muslims in general, for whom American support of Israel was a cause of anguish, but the United States had been a decisive ally in the Afghan jihad. The sense of humiliation he expressed had more to do with the stance of Muslims in the modern world. Their lives were sold at a discount, bin Laden was telling his hometown audience, which confirmed their sense that other lives—Western, American lives—were fuller and more worthwhile.

Bin Laden gave them a history lesson. "America went to Vietnam, thousands of miles away, and began bombing them in planes. The Americans did not get out of Vietnam until after they suffered great losses. Over sixty thousand American soldiers were killed until there were demonstrations by the American people. The Americans won't stop their support of Jews in Palestine until we give them a lot of blows. They won't stop until we do jihad against them."

There he stood, on the threshold of advocating violence against the United States, but he suddenly stopped himself.

"What is required is to wage an economic war against America," he continued. "We have to boycott all American products. . . . They're taking the money we pay them for their products and giving it to the Jews to kill our brothers." The man who had made his name in combat against the Soviets now invoked Mahatma Gandhi, who brought down the British Empire "by boycotting its products and wearing non-Western clothes." He urged a public-relations campaign. "Any American we see, we should notify of our complaints," bin Laden meekly concluded. "We should write to American embassies."

BIN LADEN WOULD LATER SAY that the United States had always been his enemy. He dated his hatred for America to 1982, "when America permitted the Israelis to invade Lebanon and the American Sixth Fleet helped them." He recalled the carnage: "blood and severed limbs, women and children sprawled every-where. Houses destroyed along with their occupants and high rises demolished over their residents. . . . The situation was like a crocodile meeting a helpless child, powerless except for his screams." This scene provoked an intense desire to fight tyranny, he said, and a longing for revenge. "As I looked at those demolished towers in Lebanon, it entered my mind that we should punish the oppressor in kind and that we should destroy towers in America in order that they taste some of what we tasted."

His actions at the time belied this public stance. Privately, bin Laden approached members of the royal family during the Afghan jihad to express his gratitude for American participation in that war. Prince Bandar bin Sultan, the Saudi ambassador to the United States, remembered bin Laden coming to him and saying, "Thank you. Thank you for bringing the Americans to help us get rid of the secularist, atheist Soviets."

Bin Laden had never shown himself to be an interesting or original political thinker—his analysis, until then, was standard Islamist boilerplate, uninformed by any deep experiences in the West. And yet, wrapped in the mystique that had been spun around him, bin Laden held a position in Saudi society that gave weight to his pronouncements. The very fact that his American critique was being uttered at all—in a country where speech was so curtailed—suggested to other Saudis that there must be royal consent behind the anti-American campaign that bin Laden had launched.

Few countries in the world were so different from each other, and yet so dependent on one another, as America and Saudi Arabia. Americans built the Saudi petroleum industry; American construction companies, such as Bechtel, built much of the country's infrastructure; Howard Hughes's company, Trans World Airlines, built the Saudi passenger air service; the Ford Foundation modernized Saudi government; the U.S. Army Corps of Engineers built the country's television and broadcast facilities and oversaw the development of its defense industry. Meantime, Saudi Arabia sent its top students to American universities—more than thirty thousand per year during the 1970s and 1980s. In return, more than 200,000 Americans have lived and worked in the Kingdom since the discovery of oil. Saudi Arabia needed American investment, management, technology, and education to guide it into the modern world. America, for its part, became increasingly reliant on Saudi oil to sustain its economic and military supremacy. In 1970 the United States was the tenth greatest importer of Saudi oil; a decade later, it was number one.

By that time, Saudi Arabia had replaced Iran as America's main ally in the Persian Gulf. The Kingdom depended on U.S. arms and defense agreements for its protection. Thus the apparent complicity on the part of the royal family in bin Laden's escalating verbal attack on America seemed a suicidal paradox. But so long as bin Laden remained focused on an external enemy, he diverted popular attention from the princely looting of the oil wealth and the spiral of religious fanaticism. Events would soon give bin Laden the excuse he sought to make America into the enemy he needed.

In 1989 bin Laden approached Prince Turki with a bold plan. He would use his Arab irregulars to overthrow the Marxist government of South Yemen. Bin Laden was enraged by the communist rule in his ancestral home, and he saw an opportunity to exploit his partnership with the Saudi government to purge the Arabian Peninsula of any secular influences. It would be bin Laden's first opportunity to put al-Qaeda into action.

Saudi Arabia had always had an uneasy relationship with its smaller, poorer, and more populous southern neighbors, the Yemens. The quarreling twins posed a strategic problem as well. Reaching across the southern tip of the Arabian Peninsula, with its thumb on the throat of the Red Sea, South Yemen was the only Marxist entity in the Arab world. North Yemen was a pro-Western military regime, but it was constantly engaged in boundary disputes with the Kingdom.

Turki listened to bin Laden's offer and declined. "It's a bad idea," he told him. The Saudis had a long history of meddling in the affairs of both Yemens, so Turki's demurral wasn't a matter of propriety. Bin Laden spoke of "my mujahideen" and of liberating South Yemen from the *kafrs*. The grandeur of bin Laden's manner put Turki off.

Shortly after the meeting between bin Laden and the Saudi intelligence chief, North and South Yemen came to an unexpected agreement to merge their countries into an entity that would be called the Republic of Yemen. Oil had been discovered in the ill-defined border region between the two impoverished countries, and now there was an incentive to resolve their arguments through politics rather than arms.

Bin Laden, however, was not reconciled to peace. He became convinced that the Americans had a secret agreement with the socialists to create a military base in Yemen, and therefore he set out to wreck this alliance by financing a guerrilla war. Soon Yemeni veterans of the Afghan jihad began showing up at his apartment house in Jeddah and leaving with suitcases full of cash to supply the rebellion.

Ahmed Badeeb, bin Laden's old teacher, went to pay a call on him, no doubt at Turki's direction. Bin Laden was managing investments in Jeddah at the time. As they spoke, Badeeb took the measure of anger in his former student's voice and realized something was going to happen. Bin Laden simply could not tolerate the fact that there were any communists in the coalition government at all. He insisted on imposing his own ill-defined notions of Islamic government in place of the peaceful and practical political solution that the Yemens had agreed upon. In bin Laden's mind, the entire peninsula was sacred and had to be cleansed of foreign elements. The fact that his father was born in the Hadramout, in the southern part of the country, fortified his fervent desire to liberate his kinsmen from any vestige of communist rule. He made a number of trips to the new republic, speaking in mosques to incite the opposition. His al-Qaeda brigade worked with tribal leaders in the north to carry out raids in the cities of the south and to assassinate socialist leaders.

These murderous forays had an effect. With the brittle union in danger of breaking apart into civil war once again, the new president of the Republic of Yemen, Ali Abdullah Saleh, traveled to Saudi Arabia to plead with King Fahd to keep bin Laden under control. The king firmly instructed bin Laden to stay out of Yemen's affairs. Bin Laden denied that he was involved, but soon he was back in Yemen, making more speeches and campaigning against the communists. The frustrated and irate Yemeni president returned to Saudi Arabia to press his case once again before King Fahd, who was unused to being disobeyed by his subjects, much less openly lied to. He turned to the family enforcer.

The minister of the interior, Prince Naif, an imperious figure often compared to J. Edgar Hoover, summoned bin Laden to his office. The ministry occupies a strangely unsettling building—an inverted pyramid—that looms on the perimeter of downtown Riyadh. Tubular black elevator columns rise inside the vast and disorienting marble atrium, which seems specially designed to diminish anyone who stands there. Bin Laden had reported to Naif in this building many times during the Afghan jihad, scrupulously keeping the government informed of his activities. He had always received respectful treatment in the past, due to his family, his status, and the loyalty to the royal family that he had displayed over the years.

This time was different. Naif spoke to him harshly and

demanded his passport. The prince didn't want to hear any more about bin Laden's personal foreign policy.

It was a cold splash of reality, but bin Laden felt double-crossed. "I was working for the sake of the Saudi government!" he complained to his friends.

AS THE RICHEST COUNTRY in the region, surrounded by envious neighbors, Saudi Arabia was also the most anxious. When King Faisal commissioned the country's first census in 1969, he was so shocked by how small the population actually was that he immediately doubled the figure. Since then, the statistics in the Kingdom have been distorted by this fundamental lie. By 1990 Saudi Arabia claimed a population of more than 14 million, nearly equal to that of Iraq, although Prince Turki privately estimated the Kingdom's population to be a little over 5 million. Always fearful of being overrun and plundered, the Saudi government spent billions of dollars on weapons, buying the most sophisticated equipment on the market from the United States, Britain, France, and China and further enriching members of the royal family with lucrative kickbacks. In the 1980s the Kingdom built a $50 billion air-defense system; the U.S. Army Corps of Engineers moved its foreign headquarters from Germany to Saudi Arabia in order to construct bases, schools, and headquarters complexes for the Saudi army, air force, navy, and National Guard. After the U.S. Congress passed laws prohibiting American companies from participating in bribery and kickbacks with foreign agents, the Saudi government concluded the largest arms deal in history with Great Britain. By the end of the decade, the Kingdom should have been well equipped to defend itself against the immediate threats in its neighborhood. It had the weapons; all it lacked was training and troops—an actual army, in other words.

In 1990 bin Laden warned of the danger that the murderous tyrant in Iraq, Saddam Hussein, posed to Saudi Arabia. He was treated as a Cassandra. "I said many times in my speeches at the mosques, warning that Saddam will enter the Gulf," bin Laden lamented. "No one believed me." Much of the Arab world was elated by Saddam's anti-Western rhetoric and his threats to "burn half of Israel" with chemical weapons. He was especially popular in Saudi Arabia, which maintained cordial relations with its northern neighbor. Nonetheless, bin Laden continued his lonely campaign against Saddam and his secular Baath Party.

Once again the king was annoyed by bin Laden, a dangerous position for any Saudi subject to find himself in. The Kingdom had signed a non-aggression pact with Iraq, and Saddam had personally assured Fahd that he had no intention of invading Kuwait, even as he was moving Republican Guard divisions to the border. The Saudi government warned bin Laden once again to mind his own business, then followed up on the threat by sending the National Guard to raid bin Laden's farm and arrest several of his workers. Bin Laden protested this outrage to Crown Prince Abdullah, the commander of the National Guard, who denied knowing about the incident.

On July 31 King Fahd personally chaired a meeting between representatives of Iraq and Kuwait to arbitrate the disputes between the two countries, which concerned the ownership of the invaluable oil fields on the border. Saddam also contended that Kuwait's high rate of production was driving down the price of petroleum and ruining the Iraqi economy, already bankrupted by a disastrous war with Iran that Saddam had provoked in 1980, which ended eight years later after a million casualties. Despite the king's mediation, talks between Iraq and Kuwait quickly fell apart. Two days later, the formidable Iraqi army rolled over the tiny nation, and suddenly all that stood between Saddam Hussein and the Saudi oil fields was a few miles of sand and the superbly equipped but cowed and undermanned Saudi military. One battalion of the Saudi National Guard—fewer than a thousand men—guarded the oil fields.

The royal family was so shocked that it forced the government-controlled media to wait a week before announcing the invasion. Moreover, after years of paying billions of dollars to cultivate the friendship of neighboring countries, the royal family was stunned to discover how isolated it was in the Arab world. The Palestinians, Sudanese, Algerians, Libyans, Tunisians, Yemenis, and even the Jordanians openly supported Saddam Hussein.

With the Iraqi army poised on the Saudi border, bin Laden wrote a letter to the king beseeching him not to call upon the Americans for protection; he followed this with a frenzied round of lobbying the senior princes. The royal family itself was divided about the best course of action, with Crown Prince Abdullah strongly opposing American assistance and Prince Naif seeing no obvious alternative.

The Americans had already made a decision, however. If, after snacking on Kuwait, Saddam gobbled up the Eastern Province of Saudi Arabia, he would then control the bulk of the world's available oil supply. That was an intolerable threat to the security of the United States, not just the Kingdom. U.S. Secretary of Defense Dick Cheney flew to Jeddah with a team of advisors, including General Norman Schwarzkopf, to persuade the king to accept American troops to defend Saudi Arabia. Schwarzkopf showed satellite images of three armored Iraqi divisions inside Kuwait, followed by ground troops—far more manpower, he contended, than the number needed to occupy such a small country. The Saudis had intelligence that several Iraqi reconnaissance teams had already crossed the Saudi border.

Crown Prince Abdullah advised against letting the Americans enter the country for fear they would never depart. In the name of the president of the United States, Cheney pledged that the troops would leave as soon as the threat was over, or whenever the king said they should go. That promise decided the matter.

"Come with all you can bring," the king implored. "Come as fast as you can."

In early September, weeks after American forces began arriving, bin Laden spoke to Prince Sultan, the minister of defense, in the company of several Afghan mujahideen commanders and Saudi veterans of that conflict. It was a bizarre and grandiose replication of General Schwarzkopf's briefing. Bin Laden brought his own maps of the region and presented a detailed plan of attack, with diagrams and charts, indicating trenches and sand traps along the border to be constructed with the Saudi Binladin

Group's extensive inventory of earth-moving equipment. Added to this, he would create a mujahideen army made up of his colleagues from the Afghan jihad and unemployed Saudi youth. "I am ready to prepare one hundred thousand fighters with good combat capability within three months," bin Laden promised Prince Sultan. "You don't need Americans. You don't need any other non-Muslim troops. We will be enough."

"There are no caves in Kuwait," the prince observed. "What will you do when he lobs missiles at you with chemical and biological weapons?"

"We will fight him with faith," bin Laden responded.

Bin Laden also made his presentation to Prince Turki. He was one of the few princes who had agreed with bin Laden's assessment of Saddam as a threat to the Kingdom; in fact, over the years, Turki had made several proposals to the CIA about removing Saddam through covert means, but each time he was spurned. When the invasion of Kuwait occurred, Turki had been in Washington, D.C., on vacation. He was in a theater watching *Die Hard* 2 when he was summoned to the White House. He spent the rest of the night at the Central Intelligence Agency, helping to coordinate the campaign to repel the Iraqis from Kuwait. In his opinion, if Saddam were allowed to stay in Kuwait, he would enter the Kingdom at the slightest provocation.

So when bin Laden approached him with his plan, Turki was taken aback by the naïveté of the young Afghan veteran. There were only fifty-eight thousand men in the entire Saudi army. Iraq, on the other hand, had a standing army of nearly a million men—the fourth-largest army in the world—not counting its reserves and paramilitary forces. Saddam's armored corps counted 5,700 tanks, and his Republican Guards included the most fearsome and well-trained divisions in the Middle East. That did not impress bin Laden. "We pushed the Soviets out of Afghanistan," he said.

The prince laughed in disbelief. For the first time, he was alarmed by the "radical changes" he saw in bin Laden's personality. He had gone from being "a calm, peaceful and gentle man" whose only goal was to help Muslims, to being "a person who believed that he would be able to amass and command an army to liberate Kuwait. It revealed his arrogance and his haughtiness."

SPURNED BY THE GOVERNMENT, bin Laden turned to the clergy for support. His case against American assistance rested on the Prophet's remark, as he lay dying, "Let there be no two religions in Arabia." The meaning of this remark has been disputed ever since it was uttered. Prince Turki argued that the Prophet meant only that no other religion should dominate the peninsula. Even during the Prophet's lifetime, he pointed out, Jews and Christians were traveling through Arabia. It was not until 641 C.E., the twentieth year of the Muslim calendar, that Caliph Omar began removing the indigenous Christians and Jews from some parts of Arabia. They were resettled in Iraq, Syria, and Palestine. Since then, the holy cities of Mecca and Medina have been off-limits for non-Muslims. To bin Laden and many other Islamists, that wasn't enough. They believed that the Prophet's deathbed injunction is clear: All non-Muslims should be expelled from the entire peninsula.

Nonetheless, recognizing the danger that the foreign troops posed to their legitimacy, the Saudi government pressured the clergy to issue a fatwa endorsing the invitation of non-Muslim armies into the Kingdom on the excuse that they were defending Islam. This would give the government the religious cover it needed. Bin Laden furiously confronted the senior clerics. "This is inadmissible," he told them.

"My son Osama, we cannot discuss this issue because we are afraid," one of the sheikhs replied, pointing to his neck and indicating that his head would be cut off if he talked about the matter.

Within weeks, half a million American GIs streamed into the Kingdom, creating what many Saudis feared would be a permanent occupation. Although the Americans—and other coalition forces—were stationed mainly outside the cities in order to stay out of view, Saudis were mortified by the need to turn to Christians and Jews to defend the holy land of Islam. That many of these foreign soldiers were women only added to their embar-

rassment. The weakness of the Saudi state and its abject dependence on the West for protection were paraded before the world,
thanks to the 1,500 foreign journalists who descended on the
Kingdom to report on the buildup to the war. For such a private
and intensely religious people, with a press that had been entirely
under government control, the scrutiny was disorienting—at
times both shameful and exhilarating. There was a combustible
atmosphere of fear, outrage, humiliation, and xenophobia, but
instead of rallying behind their imperiled government, many
Saudis saw this as a one-time-only opportunity to change it.

At this awkward moment in Saudi Arabia's history, with the
world peering through the windows, Saudi progressives were
sufficiently emboldened to press their modest agenda. In November, forty-seven women decided it was time to challenge the Kingdom's informal ban on female driving. As it turned out, there was
no actual law forbidding it. The women met in front of the Safe-
way in Riyadh and ordered their drivers out of their cars, then
took a defiant fifteen-minute spin through the capital city. A
policeman stopped them, but he had no legal reason to hold them.
Prince Naif instantly banned the practice, however, and Sheikh
Abdul Aziz bin Baz, the chief cleric, helpfully added a fatwa, calling female driving a source of depravity. The women lost their
passports, and several of them, who had been professors in the
women's college of King Saud University, were fired after their
own female students protested that they did not want to be taught
by "infidels."

In December, reformers circulated a petition requesting an end
to discrimination based on tribal affiliation, the establishment of a
traditional council of advisors to the king (called a *shura*), more
press freedom, the introduction of certain basic laws of governance, and some kind of oversight on the proliferation of religious
fatwas.

A few months later, the religious establishment fired back with
its own vehement "Letter of Demands." It was an open bid for
Islamic control of the Kingdom, containing a barely disguised
attack on the predominance of the royal family. The four hundred
religious scholars, judges, and professors who signed the letter

called for strict conformity with the Sharia throughout society, including a ban on the payment of interest, the creation of an Islamic army through universal military training, and "purifying" the media in order to better serve Islam. The royal family was more shocked by this letter than by Saddam Hussein's invasion of Kuwait. Many of the demands of the religious dissidents echoed those of the leaders of the 1979 attack on the Grand Mosque. They became the basis of bin Laden's political agenda for the Kingdom.

The American mission quickly grew from protecting Saudi Arabia to repelling the Iraqis from Kuwait. The war began on January 16, 1991. By then, most Saudis were resigned to the presence of the Americans and the troops of thirty-four other countries that formed the coalition against Iraq. Hundreds of thousands of Kuwaiti citizens had taken refuge in the Kingdom, and they told affecting stories about the looting of their country; the kidnapping, torture, and murder of civilians; and the rape of Kuwaiti women by the Iraqi troops. When Iraqi Scud missiles began raining down, however fecklessly, on Riyadh, even the Islamists held their tongues. But to many Saudis, the presence of the foreign "crusaders," as bin Laden characterized the coalition troops, in the sanctuary of Islam posed a greater calamity than the one that Saddam was already inflicting on Kuwait.

"Tonight in Iraq, Saddam walks amidst ruin," President George H. W. Bush was able to boast on March 6. "His war machine is crushed. His ability to threaten mass destruction is itself destroyed." Although Saddam remained in power, that seemed to be a footnote to the awesome display of American military force and the international coalition that rallied behind U.S. leadership. The president was exultant. With the fall of the Soviet Union followed by this lightning victory, American hegemony was undisputed. "We can see a new world coming into view," Bush told Congress, "in which there is the very real prospect of a new world order. . . . A world where the United Nations, freed from cold war stalemate, is poised to fulfill the historic vision of its founders. A world in which freedom and respect for human rights find a home among all nations."

These words, uttered so hopefully, found a bitter audience in

Osama bin Laden. He also wanted to create a new world order, one that was ruled by Muslims, not dictated by America and enforced by the UN. The scale of his ambition was beginning to reveal itself. In his fantasy he would enter history as the savior of Islam.

BIN LADEN WAGED a high-level campaign to retrieve his passport. He argued that he needed to return to Pakistan in order to help mediate the civil war among the mujahideen, which the Saudi government was keenly interested in resolving. "There's a role I can play," bin Laden pleaded. Many prominent princes and sheikhs interceded on his behalf. Eventually, Prince Naif backed down and returned bin Laden's travel documents, but only after making the nettlesome warrior sign a pledge that he would not interfere with the politics of Saudi Arabia or any Arab country.

In March 1992, bin Laden arrived in Peshawar. In the three years since his departure, the communist government in Afghanistan had managed to hang on to power, but it was on the verge of being overrun. Rival mujahideen forces, led by Ahmed Shah Massoud and Gulbuddin Hekmatyar, were already engaged in a bloody struggle to determine who was going to seize power. The great powers that had chosen to use Afghanistan as a venue for the existential battle between communism and capitalism were notably absent in the chaotic aftermath of the war. Prince Turki hoped to establish a provisional government in Afghanistan that would unite the warring commanders and stabilize the country. He led the negotiations in Peshawar, along with Pakistani prime minister Nawaz Sharif.

Worried about the influence of Iran on Afghanistan's western border, Turki was inclined to support the more intransigent and fundamentalist Sunni elements, led by Hekmatyar. Bin Laden, on the other hand, attempted to play the role of the honest broker. He arranged a telephone conference call between Massoud and Hekmatyar, in which he begged Hekmatyar to come to the bargaining table. Hekmatyar was unyielding—knowing, no doubt, that he had Turki's blessing. But, in the middle of the night, Massoud's forces slipped into the city. The next morning, the surprised Hek-matyar furiously lobbed rockets into Kabul and began the siege of the capital. The Afghan civil war had begun.

By opposing Turki in the negotiations, bin Laden believed that he had crossed a line. He told some of his companions that Saudi Arabia had recruited Pakistani intelligence to kill him. The old alliances formed by the jihad were falling apart. He and Prince Turki were now deadly antagonists.

Before he left Afghanistan, bin Laden put on a disguise and checked into a clinic in Karachi for some unknown ailment. His doctor, Zawahiri, was in Yemen, but they would soon be reunited.

8

Paradise

ALTHOUGH THE FIGHTING never paused after the fall of Kabul, the curtain came down on the Afghan jihad. Some Arabs remained, caught up in the civil war, but most of them moved on. They were largely unwelcome in their home countries, which had perceived them as misfits and extremists even before they went to Afghanistan. These same governments had advertised for young men to go to jihad, and subsidized their travel, hoping that the troublemakers would bleed away in a doomed cause. Little thought was given to the prospect of thousands of these young men returning, now trained in guerrilla-warfare tactics and empowered by the myth of their victory. Like any returning warriors, they brought home psychological problems and memories that were difficult to live with. Even those who had little actual experience of combat were indoctrinated with the culture of martyrdom and *takfir*. They strutted around the mosque, often wearing Afghan garb to signal their special status.

Saudi intelligence guessed that between fifteen and twenty-five thousand Saudi youths trained in Afghanistan, although other estimates are far lower. Those who came back to the Kingdom were taken directly to jail for two or three days of interrogation. Some countries simply refused to let the fighters return. They became a stateless, vagrant mob of religious mercenaries. Many of them took root in Pakistan, marrying local women and learning to speak Urdu. Some went to fight in Kashmir, Kosovo, Bosnia, or Chechnya. The cinders of the Afghan conflagration were drifting across the globe, and soon much of the Muslim world would be aflame.

For those free-floating but ideologically charged veterans, a new home awaited them. In June 1989, at the same time that the jihad was ending in Afghanistan, Islamists staged a military coup d'état against the civilian, democratic government of Sudan. The leader of the coup was Brigadier General Omar Hasan al-Bashir, but the prime mover was Hasan al-Turabi, one of Africa's most complex, original, charismatic, and devious characters.

Like bin Laden and Zawahiri, Turabi attributed the failures of the Arab world to the fact that its governments were insufficiently Islamic and too dependent on the West. But unlike those other men, Turabi was a Quranic scholar who was well acquainted with Europe and the United States. A Sudanese student in 1960, he wandered across America, staying with ordinary families—"even with Red Indians and farmers"—an adventure that would inform his piercing critique of secularism and capitalism. He had gained his master's degree in law from the London School of Economics in 1961 and a doctorate in law from the Sorbonne in Paris three years later.

Turabi envisioned the creation of an international Muslim community—the *ummah*—headquartered in Sudan, which would then spill into other countries, carrying the Islamist revolution in an ever-widening circle. Sudan, until then a cultural backwater in the Muslim world, would be the intellectual center of this reformation and Turabi its spiritual guide. In order to carry out this plan, he opened the doors of his country to any Muslim, regardless of nationality, no questions asked. Naturally, the people who responded to his invitation tended to be those who were welcome nowhere else.

The government of Sudan began its courtship of bin Laden by sending him a letter of invitation in 1990, and followed it up by dispatching several members of the Sudanese intelligence service to meet with him. Essentially, he was being offered an entire country in which to operate freely. At the end of that year, bin Laden sent four trusted associates to investigate the business opportunities that the Sudanese government had promised. Turabi dazzled these representatives with his erudition, and they brought back an enthusiastic report. "What you are trying to do, it is Sudan!" they told bin Laden. "There are people with minds, with professions! You're not mixing with the goats."

Soon, another bin Laden emissary appeared in Khartoum with a bundle of cash. Jamal al-Fadl, a Sudanese member of al-Qaeda, rented a number of houses and bought several large parcels of land that would be used for training. Al-Jihad was already in Sudan, and Zawahiri personally gave Fadl $250,000 to buy a farm north of the capital. The neighbors began complaining about the sound of explosions coming from the untilled fields.

As an additional inducement, the Saudi Binladin Group got the contract to build an airport in Port Sudan, which brought Osama frequently into the country to oversee the construction. He finally moved to Khartoum in 1992, flying from Afghanistan with his four wives and—at that point—seventeen children. He also brought bulldozers and other heavy equipment, announcing his intention to build a three-hundred-kilometer road in eastern Sudan as a gift to the nation. The leader of Sudan greeted him with garlands of flowers.

TWO MEN WITH SUCH SIMILAR DREAMS as bin Laden and Turabi could scarcely be more different. As terse and laconic as bin Laden was, Turabi was fluent and endlessly theoretical, a brilliant windbag. He held soirees in his house, where on any evening heads of state or distinguished clerics would be perched on the green corduroy settees pressed against the walls of Turabi's salon, drinking tea and listening to his prolonged monologues. He could speak without pause for hours, unprompted except for the presence of an audience, gesturing with both hands and punctuating his witticisms with nervous laughter. He was slight and very dark, which, contrasted with his immaculate white robe and turban and his bright, toothy grin, made him appear all the more vivid.

Nearly every month bin Laden would attend one of these events, more out of courtesy than curiosity. He disagreed with

almost everything Turabi said, but he was no match for the professor in his drawing room. The Islam that Turabi was straining to
create in such a radical, nondemocratic fashion was, in fact, surprisingly progressive. Turabi advocated healing the ancient
breach between the Sunni and the Shia branches of Islam, which
was heresy in bin Laden's eyes. Turabi spoke about integrating
"art, music, singing" into religion, offending bin Laden's Wahhabi
sensibilities. Early in his career, Turabi had made his reputation as
an Islamic thinker by his advocacy of women's rights. He thought
that Muslim women had suffered a long retreat from the comparative equality they once enjoyed. "The Prophet himself used to
visit women, not men, for counseling and advice. They could lead
prayer. Even in his battles, they are there! In the election between
Othman and Ali to determine who will be the successor to the
Prophet, they voted!"

Now that he was finally living in a radical Islamist state, bin
Laden would ask practical questions, such as how the Islamists
intended to apply Sharia in Sudan and how they proposed to han-
dle the Christians in the south. Often he did not like the answers.
Turabi told him that Sharia would be applied gradually and only on
Muslims, who would share power with Christians in a federal sys-
tem. Bin Laden would stay ten to thirty minutes and then slip away.
He couldn't wait to get out of there. "This man is a Machiavelli," bin
Laden confided to his friends. "He doesn't care what methods he
uses." Although they still needed one another, Turabi and bin
Laden soon began to see themselves as rivals.

KHARTOUM BEGAN AS THE HAPPIEST PERIOD in bin
Laden's adult life. He opened a small downtown office on Mek
Nimr Street in a sagging, single-story building with nine rooms, a
low ceiling, and a heavy air conditioner that dripped on the sidewalk. Here he started Wadi El Aqiq, the holding company for his
many enterprises, named after a river in Mecca. Across the street
was the Ministry of Islamic Affairs, in a building that had been a
famous brothel during the British occupation. "Osama just
laughed when I told him that," recalled Hasan Turabi's son Issam.

Bin Laden and Issam became friends because of their common passion, riding. There are four million horses in Sudan, a country that relies on them for transportation and farm work but loves them for sport. Although Issam was only twenty-five when bin Laden arrived in Sudan, he was already one of the country's top breeders, and he kept a stable at the Khartoum track. One Friday bin Laden came shopping for a mare, and Issam showed him around the fly-ridden stalls. Issam was very struck by his Saudi visitor. "He was not tall, but he was handsome—his eyes, his nose—he was beautiful." Bin Laden settled on a stately thoroughbred from another breeder, and Issam arranged to buy the horse without asking a commission. Bin Laden was so used to people taking advantage of his money that this simple courtesy impressed him. He decided to quarter his horses with Issam. He added four more Sudanese thoroughbreds for himself and bought his children about ten local horses, which he bred to some Arabians he had flown in from the Kingdom. Issam was disdainful of what he saw as bin Laden's romantic attachment to native stock. "Here we are trying to go toward the thoroughbred, away from the Arabian. But he wanted to establish a breeding scheme of his own."

The Khartoum track is a chaotic bowl of dust. Wild dogs romp across the grassless infield, chasing after the horses. The rickety grandstand is divided between the lower half, where the common people stand, and the upper half, with the superior view, where the social elite and horse owners sit in relative comfort. Osama insisted on watching the races in the lower part, even though Issam was on the track's board of directors and enjoyed a prime box. In Sudan, the races are wild and the audiences are boisterous, given to dancing and singing. The famous mujahid would plug his ears with his fingers whenever the band played. It ruined the experience for him. When he asked people to stop singing, they told him to get lost.

"It's not your fault the music is there," Issam would gently remind bin Laden. "You didn't rent the band." Bin Laden was unappeased. "Music," he declared, "is the flute of the devil." Eventually he stopped coming to the races altogether.

He bought a three-story red stucco villa in a district of Khartoum called Riyadh. Across the unpaved street, he acquired an unfurnished guesthouse that he used for entertaining. The neighbors claimed he received fifty people a day, starting at five in the afternoon, most of them Arabs wearing calf-length *thobes* and long beards—a parade of fundamentalists. His barefoot young sons would pass among the men, offering sweetened hibiscus tea. Every day he slaughtered a lamb for his expected visitors, but he ate very little himself, preferring to nibble what his guests left on their plates, believing that these abandoned morsels would gain the favor of God.

Sometimes bin Laden would take his sons for picnics on the shore of the Nile, with sandwiches and sodas, and in the packed sand along the river bank he taught them to drive. Bin Laden adopted humble Sudanese attire, a white turban and gallabea, and he carried a typical walking stick with a *V*-shaped handle. "He was becoming Sudanese," Issam observed. "It seems he wanted to stay here forever." Bin Laden was finally at peace. He kept members of al-Qaeda busy working in his burgeoning enterprises, since there was little else for them to do. On Fridays after prayers, the two al-Qaeda soccer teams squared off against each other. There was training going on, but at a low level, mainly refresher courses for men who had already been in Afghanistan. Al-Qaeda had become largely an agricultural organization.

IN SUDAN, bin Laden had the opportunity to imitate his father's career as a road builder and businessman. He was "the great Islamic investor," as Turabi called him at a reception he gave soon after bin Laden arrived. Although it was true that he was Sudan's major tycoon, he was also practically the only one. The Sudanese dinar was sinking and the government was constantly in arrears. The ongoing civil war between the largely Arab, Islamic north and the black Christian south was draining the treasury and scaring away investors, who were already appalled by the confluence of terrorists and the experimental nature of Islamist rule. That bin Laden was willing to put his money into such an economy made him all the more prized. Exaggerated rumors about his wealth were circulating; people said that he was investing $350 million—or more—in the country, which would certainly be its salvation. It was said that he capitalized a bank with $50 million, which was well beyond his financial capacity.

Through al-Hijira, his construction company, bin Laden built several major roads in Sudan, including one to Port Sudan. When the government was unable to pay him, he took large plots of land in trade. One parcel alone was "larger than Bahrain," he bragged to his brothers. The government also threw in a tannery in Khartoum, where bin Laden's employees prepared leather for the Italian market. Another bin Laden venture, al-Qadurat, imported trucks and machinery from Russia and Eastern Europe.

But it was farming that captivated his imagination. The government barter had made him perhaps the largest landowner in the country. He had a million acres in the Gash River Delta in northeast Sudan; a large plot in Gedarif, the most fertile province in the eastern section, and another in Damazine, which lies along the western bank of the Blue Nile near the Ethiopian border. Through his agricultural company, al-Thimar al-Mubaraka, bin Laden enjoyed a near monopoly on Sudan's major farm exports—sesame, white corn, and gum arabic. Other bin Laden subsidiaries produced sorghum, honey, peanuts, chickens, livestock, and watermelons. He declared that Sudan could feed the entire world if it were properly managed, and to prove the point he showed off a prize sunflower he had grown in Gedarif. "It could be in the Guinness Book of World Records," he told the minister of state.

He was a comparatively generous employer by Sudanese standards, paying $200 per month to most of his workers, with senior managers making from $1,000 to $1,500. He imposed corporate management techniques on his organization, requiring that forms be filled out in triplicate to purchase tires, for instance. Those employees who were actual members of al-Qaeda received a monthly bonus, between $50 and $120, depending on the size of the member's family and his nationality—Saudis got more and Sudanese got less—along with free housing and medical care. There were about five hundred people working for bin Laden in

Sudan, but there were never more than a hundred of them who were active members of al-Qaeda.

Bin Laden shied away from the intractable conflict in the southern region of Sudan that was costing the impoverished Sudanese government $1 million a day and would eventually claim more than a million lives. Issam, a veteran, considered the war a jihad, and it seemed wrong to him that the famous Islamic warrior held himself apart from it. Bin Laden explained that he was through with warfare. He said he resolved to quit al-Qaeda altogether and become a farmer.

He made similar statements to many of his friends. He was at a crossroads. Life in Sudan was pleasantly monotonous. In the mornings he walked to his local mosque to pray, followed by a gaggle of acolytes and admirers; he lingered to study with the holy men, often breakfasting with them before going to his office, or to visit one of the various factories that were part of his expanding portfolio, or to hop on a tractor and plow the fields on one of his massive estates. Although he was the CEO of a burgeoning empire, he continued his lifelong habit of fasting on Mondays and Thursdays. Before Friday prayers, he would sometimes speak in the main Khartoum mosque, urging his fellow Muslims to discover the blessings of peace.

There was one galling fact that prevented bin Laden from relaxing into the life of business and of spiritual contemplation that so strongly beckoned: the continued presence of American troops in Saudi Arabia. King Fahd had pledged that the nonbelievers would be gone as soon as the war was over, and yet months after the Iraqi defeat coalition forces were still entrenched in Saudi air bases, monitoring the cease-fire agreement. Bin Laden agonized over what he believed was a permanent occupation of the holy land. Something had to be done.

COINCIDENTALLY, AMERICAN TROOPS were stopping over in Yemen on their way to Somalia. The famine had drawn international attention, and the United States sent a modest force to protect the United Nations aid workers against the marauding local clans.

The strategists in al-Qaeda felt encircled, however, and they read this latest development as a direct assault: Americans already controlled the Persian Gulf, and now they were using the excuse of the famine in Somalia to occupy the Horn of Africa. Yemen and Somalia were the gateposts to the Red Sea, which could easily be pinched off. After all the plans al-Qaeda had nurtured to spread an Islamist revolution, it was America that appeared to be waxing in influence across the region, seizing control of the pressure points of the Arab world and pushing into al-Qaeda's arena. The net was closing. Sudan could be next. This thinking took place at a time when the United States had never heard of al-Qaeda, the mission to Somalia was seen as a thankless act of charity, and Sudan was too inconsequential to worry about.

Every Thursday evening, al-Qaeda members would gather in bin Laden's Khartoum guesthouse to hear lectures from their leaders. On one of these Thursdays at the end of 1992, they discussed the threat of the expanded U.S. presence. Al-Qaeda as a terrorist organization was really born in the decisions that bin Laden and his *shura* council would make in this brief period when bin Laden was wavering—the lure of peace being as strong as the battle cry of jihad.

Bin Laden's religious advisor was his close friend Mamdouh Salim, also known as Abu Hajer al-Iraqi. He was a dashing, hard-headed Kurd who made a striking impression on everyone he met. Solemn and imperious, with a trim goatee and penetrating black eyes, Abu Hajer had been a colonel in Saddam's army during the war with Iran, specializing in communications, until he deserted and fled to Iran. He and bin Laden were the same age (thirty-four in 1992). They had worked together in the Services Bureau in Peshawar and fought together in Afghanistan, forging such powerful bonds that no one could get between them. Unlike nearly everyone around bin Laden in Sudan, Abu Hajer had never sworn fealty to him; he saw himself as an equal, and bin Laden treated him as such. Because of his piety and learning, Abu Hajer led the prayers; his voice, singing the verses of the Quran in a melancholy Iraqi style, was so lyrical that it made bin Laden weep.

Besides being bin Laden's friend, Abu Hajer was his imam. There were remarkably few among the members of al-Qaeda who had any extensive religious training. Despite their zealotry, they were essentially theological amateurs. Abu Hajer had the greatest spiritual authority, by virtue of having memorized the Quran, but he was an electrical engineer, not a cleric. Nonetheless, bin Laden made him head of al-Qaeda's fatwa committee—a fateful choice. It was on Abu Hajer's authority that al-Qaeda turned from being the anti-communist Islamic army that bin Laden originally envisioned into a terrorist organization bent on attacking the United States, the last remaining superpower and the force that bin Laden and Abu Hajer believed represented the greatest threat to Islam.

Why did these men turn against America, a highly religious country that so recently had been their ally in Afghanistan? In large part, it was because they saw America as the locus of Christian power. Once, the piety of the Muslim mujahideen and the Christian leaders of the U.S. government had served as a bond between them. Indeed, mujahideen leaders had been considerably romanticized in the American press and had made tours through American churches, where they were lauded for their spiritual courage in the common fight against Marxism and godlessness. But Christianity—especially the evangelizing American variety—and Islam were obviously competitive faiths. Viewed through the eyes of men who were spiritually anchored in the seventh century, Christianity was not just a rival, it was the archenemy. To them, the Crusades were a continual historical process that would never be resolved until the final victory of Islam. They bitterly perceived the contradiction embodied by Islam's long, steady retreat from the gates of Vienna, where on September 11— that now resonant date—in 1683, the king of Poland began the battle that turned back the farthest advance of Muslim armies. For the next three hundred years, Islam would be overshadowed by the growth of Western Christian societies. Yet bin Laden and his

Arab Afghans believed that, in Afghanistan, they had turned the tide and that Islam was again on the march.

Now they faced the greatest military, material, and cultural power any civilization had ever produced. "Jihad against America?" some of the al-Qaeda members asked in dismay. "America knows everything about us. It knows even the label of our underwear." They saw how weak and splintered their own governments were—empowered only by the force of America's need to maintain the status quo. The oceans, the skies, even the heavens were patrolled by the Americans. America was not distant, it was everywhere.

Al-Qaeda economists pointed to "our oil" that fueled America's rampant expansion, feeling as if something had been stolen from them—not the oil, exactly, although bin Laden felt it was underpriced—but the cultural regeneration that should have come with its sale. In the woefully unproductive societies they lived in, fortunes melted away like snow in the desert. What remained was a generalized feeling of betrayal.

Of course, oil had brought wealth to some Arabs, but in the process of becoming rich hadn't they only become more Western? Consumerism, vice, and individuality, which the radical Islamists saw as the hallmarks of modern American culture, threatened to destroy Islam—even the idea of Islam—by blending it into a globalized, corporate, interdependent, secular commercial world that was part of what these men meant when they said "America." But by defining modernity, progress, trade, consumption, and even pleasure as Western assaults on Islam, al-Qaeda thinkers left little on the table for themselves.

If America owned the future, the Islamic fundamentalists laid claim to the past. They were not rejecting technology or science; indeed, many of the leaders of al-Qaeda, such as Ayman al-Zawahiri and Abu Hajer, were men of science themselves. But they were ambivalent about the way in which technology weakened the spirit. This was reflected in bin Laden's interest in earthmoving machinery and genetic engineering of plants, on the one hand, and his rejection of chilled water on the other. By returning the rule of Sharia, radical Islam could draw the line against the encroaching West. Even the values that America advertised as being universally desirable—democracy, transparency, the rule of law, human rights, the separation of religion from governance—were discredited in the eyes of the jihadis because they were Western and therefore modern. Al-Qaeda's duty was to awaken the Islamic nation to the threat posed by the secular, modernizing West. In order to do that, bin Laden told his men, al-Qaeda would drag the United States into a war with Islam—"a large-scale front which it cannot control."

INDIGENOUS SALAFIST MOVEMENTS were arising spontaneously across the Arab world and parts of Africa and Asia. These movements were largely nationalist, but they needed a place to organize. They found safe harbor in Khartoum, and naturally they mingled and learned from one another.

Among these groups were the two main Egyptian organizations, Zawahiri's al-Jihad and Sheikh Omar Abdul Rahman's Islamic Group, as well as nearly every other violent radical group in the Middle East. The Palestinian group Hamas aimed to destroy Israel and replace it with a Sunni Islamist state; it was known for murdering Israeli citizens, and torturing and killing Palestinians who it believed had been collaborating with Israel. Another Palestinian group, the Abu Nidal Organization, was even more violent and rejectionist, having killed more than nine hundred people in twenty different countries, aiming mainly at Jews and moderate Arabs. Its best-known operations included the machine-gunning of a synagogue in Vienna, the grenade attack on a Parisian restaurant, the bombing of a British Airways office in Madrid, the hijacking of an EgyptAir flight to Malta, and bloody attacks on the airports of Rome and Vienna. Hezbollah, which aimed to set up a revolutionary Shia state in Lebanon, had murdered more Americans than any other terrorist organization at the time. Sponsored by Iran, Hezbollah specialized in kidnapping and hijacking, although it was also responsible for a series of bombings in Paris. The most wanted terrorist in the world, Ilich Ramírez Sánchez, known as Carlos the Jackal, also took up residence in Khartoum, posing as a French arms dealer. A Marxist and a member of the Popular Front for the Liberation of Palestine, Carlos had kidnapped eleven members of the oil-producers' cartel, OPEC, in Vienna in 1975 and flown them to Algiers for ransom. Having lost faith in communism, he now believed that radical Islam was the only force sufficiently ruthless to destroy America's cultural and economic dominion. Wanted all over the world, Carlos could easily be found in the mornings drinking coffee and eating croissants at Khartoum's Meridien Hotel.

Although bin Laden distrusted Turabi—hated him, even—he experimented with one of Turabi's most progressive and controversial ideas: to make common cause with Shiites. He had Abu Hajer advise the members of al-Qaeda that there was only one enemy now, the West, and the two main sects of Islam needed to come together to destroy it. Bin Laden invited Shiite representatives to speak to al-Qaeda, and he sent some of his top people to Lebanon to train with the Iranian-backed group Hezbollah. Imad Mugniyah, the head of Hezbollah's security service, came to meet bin Laden and agreed to train members of al-Qaeda in exchange for weapons. Mugniyah had planned the 1983 suicide car bombings of the U.S. Embassy and the U.S. Marine Corps and French paratrooper barracks in Beirut, which killed more than three hundred Americans and fifty-eight French soldiers and had led to the prompt withdrawal of American peacekeeping forces from Lebanon. That precedent had made a profound impression on bin Laden, who saw that suicide bombers could be devastatingly effective and that, for all its might, America had no appetite for conflict.*

*Most of al-Qaeda's relationship with Iran came through Zawahiri. Ali Mohammed told the FBI that al-Jihad had planned a coup in Egypt in 1990. Zawahiri had studied the 1979 overthrow of the Shah of Iran, and he sought training from the Iranians. He offered information about an Egyptian government plan to storm several islands in the Persian Gulf that both Iran and the United Arab Emirates lay claim to. According to Mohammed, in return for this information, the Iranian government paid Zawahiri $2 million and helped train members of al-Jihad in a coup attempt that never actually took place.

On December 29, 1992, a bomb exploded in the Mövenpick Hotel in Aden, Yemen, and another blew up prematurely in the parking lot of a nearby luxury hotel, the Goldmohur. The bombers had targeted American troops who were on their way to Somalia to participate in Operation Restore Hope, the international famine relief effort. In fact, the soldiers were staying in a different hotel altogether. Bin Laden would later claim credit for this blundered attack, which was barely noticed in the United States, since no Americans died. The troops went on to Somalia as scheduled, but the triumphant leaders of al-Qaeda told themselves that they had frightened the Americans away and scored an easy victory.

And yet it had come at a price. Two people died, an Australian tourist and a Yemeni hotel worker, and seven others, mostly Yemenis, were severely injured. Behind the delirious, self-congratulatory chatter in Sudan, moral questions posed themselves, and members of al-Qaeda began to wonder exactly what kind of organization they were becoming.

One Thursday evening, Abu Hajer addressed the ethics of killing innocent people. He spoke to the men about Ibn Tamiyyah, a thirteenth-century scholar who is one of the primary references for Wahhabi philosophy. In his day, Ibn Tamiyyah confronted the problem of the Mongols, who savaged Baghdad but then converted to Islam. Was it proper to take revenge against fellow Muslims? Ibn Tamiyyah argued that just because the Mongols had made the profession of faith, they were still not true believers, and therefore they could be killed. Moreover, as Abu Hajer explained to the thirty or forty al-Qaeda members who were sitting on the carpet in bin Laden's salon, propping their elbows on the bolsters and sipping mango juice, Ibn Tamiyyah had issued a historic fatwa: Anyone who aided the Mongols, who bought goods from them or sold to them or was merely standing near them, might be killed as well. If he is a good Muslim, he will go to Paradise; if he is bad, he will go to hell, and good riddance. Thus the dead tourist and the hotel worker would find their proper reward.

A new vision of al-Qaeda was born. Abu Hajer's two fatwas,

the first authorizing the attacks on American troops and the second, the murder of innocents, turned al-Qaeda into a global terrorist organization. Al-Qaeda would concentrate not on fighting armies but on killing civilians. The former conception of al-Qaeda as a mobile army of mujahideen that would defend Muslim lands wherever they were threatened was now cast aside in favor of a policy of permanent subversion of the West. The Soviet Union was dead and communism no longer menaced the margins of the Islamic world. America was the only power capable of blocking the restoration of the ancient Islamic caliphate, and it would have to be confronted and defeated.

9

The Silicon Valley

IN THE EARLY MORNING, when the sun hit the towers of the World Trade Center, the twin shadows stretched across the entire island of Manhattan. The object of the buildings was to be noticed. They were the two tallest towers in the world when they were finished in 1972 and 1973, a record that didn't last long, since architectural egos are always straining for the sky. Vanity was their most obvious quality; otherwise, the buildings were bland and impractical. Tenants felt isolated; just descending to earth and going out to lunch meant a time-consuming drop through several elevators and a brisk walk across the concourse to what was, finally, the welcome smell and clatter of the city. The "tube" construction that held up these stupendous stilts required columns spaced only twenty-two inches apart, which gave the impression, inside the offices, of being in a cage. But the vistas were glorious: the endless snake of lights on the New Jersey Turnpike; the bustling harbor with the diminutive Statue of Liberty; tankers and cruise ships slicing through the bending horizon of the Atlantic; the gray shores of Long Island; the trees beginning to turn in Connecticut; and recumbent Manhattan stretched out like a queen on her great bed between the rivers. Such momentous constructions are bound to intrude on the subconscious, as they are meant to do—"those awesome symbolic towers that speak of liberty, human rights and humanity"—as bin Laden labeled them.

The most impressive view of the Trade Center was just across the Hudson River in Jersey City; there, in a neighborhood known as Little Egypt, followers of Omar Abdul Rahman, the blind sheikh, conspired to bring the towers down. Abdul Rahman was seeking asylum in the United States, despite being listed as a terrorist on the State Department watch list. As he had done in Egypt, he issued a fatwa in America that permitted his followers to rob banks and kill Jews. He traveled widely in the United States and Canada, arousing thousands of young immigrant Muslims with his sermons, often directed against Americans, who he said are "descendants of apes and pigs who have been feeding from the dining tables of the Zionists, Communists, and colonialists." He called on Muslims to assail the West, "cut the transportation of their countries, tear it apart, destroy their economy, burn their companies, eliminate their interests, sink their ships, shoot down their planes, kill them on the sea, air, or land."

And indeed his followers were laboring to bring about this apocalypse. They hoped to paralyze New York by assassinating several political figures and destroying many of its most important landmarks—the George Washington Bridge, the Lincoln and Holland tunnels, Federal Plaza, and the United Nations—in simultaneous bombings. They were reacting to American support for the Egyptian president, Hosni Mubarak, whom they intended to kill when he came to New York. The FBI later learned that Osama bin Laden was financially backing the blind sheikh's efforts.

Few Americans, even in the intelligence community, had any idea of the network of radical Islamists that had grown up inside the country. The blind sheikh may as well have been speaking in Martian as Arabic, since there were so few Middle East language specialists available to the FBI, much less to the local police. Even if his threats had been heard and understood, the perception of most Americans was dimmed by their general insulation from the world's problems and clouded by the comfortable feeling that no one who lived in America would turn against it.

Then, on February 26, 1993, a rented Ford Econoline van entered the World Trade Center's massive basement parking garage. Inside the truck was Ramzi Yousef. It is unclear if bin Laden sent him, but he was a product of an al-Qaeda camp in

Afghanistan, where he had learned his bomb-craft. He had come to America to oversee the construction of what the FBI later determined was the largest improvised explosive device the bureau had ever encountered. Yousef lit four twenty-foot-long fuses and fled to a vantage point just north of Canal Street, from which he expected to see the buildings fall.

Yousef was dark and slender, with one eye that wandered in its socket and burn marks on his face and hands—the result of accidental explosions. His real name was Abdul Basit Mahmoud Abdul Karim. The son of a Palestinian mother and a Pakistani father, he had grown up in Kuwait City, then studied electrical engineering in Wales. He had a wife and child and another on the way in Quetta, the capital of the Pakistani province of Baluchistan. He was not a particularly devout Muslim—he was motivated mainly by his devotion to the Palestinian cause and his hatred of Jews—but he was the first Islamist terrorist to attack the American homeland. More important, his dark and grandiose imagination was the cocoon in which the movement would transform itself. Until Yousef arrived in America, the Brooklyn cell had been experimenting with pipe bombs. It was Yousef's ambition and skill that radically changed the nature of terror.

By placing the bomb in the southern corner of the garage, Yousef intended to topple one tower onto the other, bringing the entire complex down and killing what he hoped would be 250,000 people—a toll he thought equaled the pain the Palestinians had experienced because of America's support of Israel. He had hoped to maximize the casualties by packing the device, made of ammonium nitrate and fuel oil, with sodium cyanide, or by making a dirty bomb with radioactive material smuggled out of the former Soviet Union, which would contaminate much of lower Manhattan.

The explosion blew through six stories of structural steel and cement, all the way down to the PATH train station below the garage and up to the Marriott ballroom above it. The shock was so great that tourists felt the ground shudder a mile away on Ellis Island. Six people were killed and 1,042 were injured, generating the greatest number of hospital casualties of any event in American history since the Civil War. The towers shook and swayed, but the mighty buildings did not fall. When Lewis Schiliro, the head of the FBI office in New York at the time, surveyed the two-hundred-foot-wide crater in the subterranean heart of the mighty complex, he was astonished. He told a structural engineer, "This building will stand forever."

Yousef flew back to Pakistan, and soon after that, he moved to Manila. There he began concocting extraordinary schemes to blow up a dozen American airliners simultaneously, to assassinate Pope John Paul II and President Bill Clinton, and to crash a private plane into CIA headquarters. It is interesting to note, at this early date, the longing on the part of the Islamists to accomplish complex, highly symbolic attacks that were unlike anything ever achieved by any other terrorist group. Theater is always a feature of terror, and these were terrorists whose dramatic ambition was unrivaled. But Ramzi Yousef and the followers of the blind sheikh were not merely seeking attention for a cause; they were hoping to humiliate an enemy by killing as many people as possible. They had an eye on vulnerable economic targets that were bound to provoke a ferocious response, and they actually courted retaliation as a prod to other Muslims. One could not say, however, that they had a cogent political plan. Revenge for many varied injustices was their constant theme, even though most of the conspirators were enjoying freedoms and opportunities in America not accorded in their own countries. They had a network of willing conspirators who were inflamed and eager to strike. The only thing that the jihadi terrorists lacked to carry off a truly devastating attack on America was the organizational and technical skills employed by Ayman al-Zawahiri and al-Jihad.

A MONTH AFTER THE TRADE CENTER BOMBING, Zawahiri appeared on the speaker circuit in several California mosques. He came from Bern, Switzerland, where al-Jihad maintained a safe house. (Zawahiri's uncle was a diplomat in Switzerland.) Although he entered the United States under his real name, Zawahiri was traveling under his nom de guerre, Dr. Abdul

Mu'iz, posing as a representative of the Kuwaiti Red Crescent. He said he was raising money for Afghan children who had been injured by Soviet land mines from the time of jihad.

For years, the United States had been one of the main fundraising destinations for Arab and Afghan mujahideen. Sheikh Abdullah Azzam blazed a trail through the mosques of Brooklyn, St. Louis, Kansas City, Seattle, Sacramento, Los Angeles, and San Diego—altogether there were thirty-three cities in America that opened branches of bin Laden and Azzam's organization, the Services Bureau, in order to support the jihad. The war against the Soviet Union had also created an international network of charities, especially dense in the United States, which remained in operation after the Soviet Union broke into splinters and the Afghans turned against each other. Zawahiri hoped to tap this rich American vein for al-Jihad.

Zawahiri's guide in the United States was a singular figure in the history of espionage, Ali Abdelsoud Mohammed. Six-foot-one, two hundred pounds, and exceptionally fit, Mohammed was a martial artist and a skilled linguist who spoke fluent English, French, and Hebrew in addition to his native Arabic. He was disciplined, clever, and gregarious, with a marked facility for making friends—the kind of man who was going to get to the top of any organization. He had been a major in the same unit of the Egyptian Army that produced Sadat's assassin, Khaled Islambouli, and the government rightly suspected him of being an Islamic fundamentalist (he was already a member of al-Jihad). When the Egyptian Army cashiered him, Zawahiri gave him the daunting task of penetrating American intelligence.

In 1984 Mohammed boldly walked into the Cairo station of the CIA to offer his services. The officer who assessed him decided he was probably a plant by Egyptian intelligence; however, he cabled other stations and headquarters to see if there was any interest. The Frankfurt station, which hosted the Iranian office of the agency, responded, and soon Ali found himself in Hamburg as a novice intelligence man. He entered a mosque associated with Hezbollah and immediately told the Iranian cleric in charge that he was an American spy assigned to infiltrate the community. He didn't realize that the agency had already penetrated the mosque; his declaration was immediately reported.

The CIA says that it terminated Mohammed, sent out cables labeling him highly untrustworthy, and placed him on the State Department watch list to prevent him from entering the United States. By that time, however, Mohammed was already in California on a visa-waiver program that was sponsored by the agency itself, one designed to shield valuable assets or those who have performed important services for the country. In order to stay in the United States, he would need to become a citizen, so he married a California woman, Linda Sanchez, a medical technician, whom he met on the transatlantic flight to the United States.

A year after Mohammed arrived, he returned to his military career, this time as an enlisted man in the U.S. Army. He managed to get stationed at the John F. Kennedy Special Warfare Center and School at Fort Bragg, North Carolina. Even though he was only a supply sergeant, Mohammed made a remarkable impression, gaining a special commendation from his commanding officer "for exceptional performance" and winning fitness awards in competition against some of the most highly trained soldiers in the world. His awed superiors found him "beyond reproach" and "consistently accomplished."

Perhaps the secret to preserving his double identity was that he never disguised his beliefs. He began each morning with dawn prayers, followed by a long run while listening on his Walkman to the Quran, which he was trying to memorize. He cooked his own meals to make sure they followed Islamic dietary rules. In addition to his military duties, he was pursuing a doctorate in Islamic studies. The American army was so respectful of his views that it asked him to help teach a class on Middle East politics and culture and to make a series of videotapes explaining Islam to his fellow soldiers. According to Mohammed's service records, he "prepared and executed over 40 country orientations for teams deploying to the Middle East." Meantime, he was slipping maps and training manuals off base to downsize and copy at Kinko's. He used these to write the multivolume terrorist training guide that became al-Qaeda's playbook. On weekends he commuted to

Brooklyn and Jersey City, where he trained Muslim militants in military tactics. Among them were members of al-Jihad, including el-Sayyid Nosair, a fellow Egyptian who would kill Rabbi Meir Kahane, the Jewish extremist, in 1990.

In 1988 Mohammed casually informed his superior officers that he was taking some leave time to go "kill Russians" in Afghanistan. When he came back, he showed off a couple of belt buckles he said he took from Soviet soldiers he killed in ambush. In fact, he had been training the first al-Qaeda volunteers in techniques of unconventional warfare, including kidnappings, assassinations, and hijacking planes, which he had learned from the American Special Forces.

Mohammed left active military service in 1989 and joined the U.S. Army Reserve. He and his wife settled in the Silicon Valley. He managed to hold a job as a security guard (for a defense contractor that was developing a triggering device for the Trident missile system) despite the fact that he sometimes disappeared for months, ostensibly to "buy rugs" in Pakistan and Afghanistan. Meanwhile, he continued his attempts to penetrate American intelligence. He had applied for a position as a translator at both the CIA and the FBI while in North Carolina.

Then in May 1993, an FBI agent in San Jose named John Zent approached Mohammed, inquiring about the trade in fake driver's licenses. Still hoping to get recruited by American intelligence, Mohammed steered the conversation toward radical activities in a local mosque, and he told some eye-opening tales about fighting the Soviets in Afghanistan. Because of the military nature of these revelations, Zent contacted the Department of Defense, and a team of counterintelligence specialists from Fort Meade, Maryland, came to San Jose to talk to Mohammed. They spread out maps of Afghanistan on the floor of Zent's office, and Mohammed indicated the mujahideen training camps. He mentioned the name of Osama bin Laden, who Mohammed said was preparing an army to knock off the Saudi regime. Mohammed also spoke about an organization, al-Qaeda, which was operating training camps in Sudan. He even admitted that he was providing the members instruction in hijacking and espionage. The interrogators apparently made nothing of these revelations. It would be three critical years before anyone else in American intelligence would hear of al-Qaeda.

Perhaps Mohammed was revealing these details because of some psychological need to elevate his importance. "He saw himself as a James Bond," an FBI agent who later talked to him observed. But it is more likely that this highly directed operative was seeking to fulfill Zawahiri's assignment of penetrating American intelligence. Al-Jihad and al-Qaeda were still separate entities in the spring of 1993, and Zawahiri had not yet signed on to bin Laden's campaign against America. Apparently Zawahiri was willing to sell out bin Laden in order to get access to American intelligence that would benefit his own organization.

If the FBI and the Department of Defense's counterintelligence team had responded to Mohammed's overture, they would have had a very dangerous, formidably skilled double agent on their hands. Mohammed openly revealed himself as a trusted member of bin Laden's inner circle, but that meant nothing to investigators at the time. Agent Zent filed a report, which went to FBI headquarters and was forgotten. Later, when the bureau sought to retrieve the notes of the conversation with the counterintelligence specialists from Fort Meade to find out what else had been discussed, the Defense Department said they had been lost.

MONEY FOR AL-JIHAD was always in short supply. Many of Zawahiri's followers had families, and they all needed food and housing. A few had turned to theft and shakedowns to support themselves. Zawahiri strongly disapproved of this; when members of al-Jihad robbed a German military attaché in Yemen, he investigated the incident and expelled those responsible. But the money problem remained. He hoped to raise enough money in America to keep his organization alive.

Zawahiri had none of the blind sheikh's charisma or fame, so when he appeared after evening prayers at the al-Nur Mosque in Santa Clara, presenting himself as "Dr. Abdul Mu'iz," nobody knew who he actually was. Ali Mohammed introduced him to Dr.

Ali Zaki, a gynecologist in San Jose, and asked him to accompany them on Dr. Mu'iz's tour of the Silicon Valley. Zaki took Zawahiri to mosques in Sacramento and Stockton. The two doctors spent most of their time discussing medical problems that Zawahiri encountered in Afghanistan. "We talked about the injured children and the farmers who were missing limbs because of all the Russian mines," Zaki recalled. "He was a well-balanced, highly educated physician."

At one point, the two men had a tiff over what Zaki thought was Zawahiri's narrow-minded view of Islam. Like most jihadis, Zawahiri followed the Salafist teachings of Ibn Tamiyyah, the thirteenth-century reformer who had sought to impose a literal interpretation of the Quran. Zaki told Zawahiri that he was leaving out the other two streams of Islam: the mystical, which was born in the writings of al-Harith al-Muhasibi, the founder of Sufism; and the rationalist school, which was reflected in the thought of the great sheikh of al-Azhar, Mohammed Abdu. "Your brand of Islam will never prevail in the West, because the best thing about the West is the freedom to choose," Zaki said. "Here you see the mystical movement spreading like fire, and the Salafis didn't even convert a single person to Islam!" Zawahiri was unmoved.

Zaki estimated that, at most, the donations produced by these visits to California mosques amounted to several hundred dollars. Ali Mohammed put the figure at two thousand dollars. Whatever the case, Zawahiri returned to Sudan facing a dispiriting choice: whether to maintain the independence of his bootstrap organization that was always struggling financially or to formally join forces with bin Laden.

When they had met nearly a decade before, Zawahiri was by far the more powerful figure; he had an organization behind him and a clear objective: to overthrow the government of Egypt. But now bin Laden, who had always had the advantage of money, also had his own organization, one that was much more ambitious than al-Jihad. In the same way that he ran multiple businesses under a single corporate tent, bin Laden sought to merge all Islamic terrorist groups into one multinational consortium, with common training and economies of scale and departments devoted to everything from personnel to policymaking. The protégé had begun to outstrip his mentor, and both men knew this.

Zawahiri also faced the prospect of being overshadowed by the blind sheikh and the activities of the Islamic Group. Despite the fact that Zawahiri had assembled a capable and dedicated cadre, many of them well-educated, skilled operatives like Ali Mohammed, who moved easily from the suburbs of Silicon Valley to the dusty streets of Khartoum, al-Jihad had not undertaken a single successful operation. Meanwhile, the blind sheikh's followers had undertaken an unparalleled rampage of murder and pillage. In order to weaken the government and prod the masses into rebellion, they chose to attack tourism, the tent pole of the Egyptian economy, because it opened the country to Western corruption. The Islamic Group initiated a war on Egypt's security forces by announcing the goal of killing a policeman every day. They also targeted foreigners, Christians, and particularly intellectuals, beginning with the shooting death in 1992 of Farag Foda, a secular columnist who had suggested in his final article that the Islamists were motivated less by politics than sexual frustration. The blind sheikh also issued a fatwa against Egypt's Nobel Prize–winning writer, Naguib Mahfouz, calling him an infidel, and in 1994 Mahfouz suffered a near-fatal stabbing. There was a sad irony in this attack: It was Sayyid Qutb who first discovered Mahfouz; later, when Mahfouz was famous, he returned the favor by visiting Qutb in prison. Now Qutb's progeny were savaging the intellectual circle that Qutb had, to some extent, produced.

Zawahiri thought such actions pointless and self-defeating. In his opinion, they succeeded only in provoking the security forces and reducing the opportunity to make an immediate, total change by a military coup, his lifelong goal. In fact, the government crackdown on militants that followed these attacks nearly eliminated both organizations in Egypt.

Zawahiri had imposed a blind-cell structure on al-Jihad, so that members in one group would not know the identities or activities of those in another; however, Egyptian authorities fortuitously captured the one man who had all the names—the organization's membership director. His computer contained a database with every member's address, his aliases, and his potential hideouts. Supplied with this information, the security forces reeled in hundreds of suspects and charged them with sedition. The press labeled the group "Vanguards of Conquest," but it was actually a faction of al-Jihad. Although the evidence against them was thin, the judicial standards weren't very rigorous.

"The government newspapers were elated about the arrest of 800 members of the al-Jihad group without a single shot being fired," Zawahiri bitterly recounted in his brief memoir. All that remained of the organization he had struggled to build were scattered colonies in other countries—in England, America, Denmark, Yemen, and Albania, among others. He realized he had to make a move in order to keep the fragments of his organization together. To do that he needed money.

Despite Jihad's financial precariousness, many of its remaining members were suspicious of bin Laden and had no desire to divert their efforts outside Egypt. Moreover, they were incensed by the roundup of their colleagues in Cairo and the show trial that resulted. They wanted to strike back. Nonetheless, around this time, most of the members of al-Jihad went on the al-Qaeda payroll. Zawahiri viewed the alliance as a temporary marriage of convenience. He later confided to one of his chief assistants that joining with bin Laden had been "the only solution to keeping the Jihad organization abroad alive."

ZAWAHIRI HAD CERTAINLY NOT ABANDONED his dream of capturing Egypt. Indeed, Sudan was an ideal spot from which to launch attacks. The long, trackless, and almost entirely unguarded border between the two countries facilitated secret movements; ancient caravan trails provided convenient routes for smuggling weapons and explosives into Egypt on the backs of camels; and the active cooperation of Sudan's intelligence agency and its military forces guaranteed a sanctuary for Zawahiri and his men.

Al-Jihad began its assault on Egypt with another attempt on

the life of the interior minister, Hasan al-Alfi, who was leading the crackdown on Islamic militants. In August of 1993 a bomb-laden motorcycle exploded next to the minister's car, killing the bomber and his accomplice. "The Minister escaped death, but his arm was broken," Zawahiri lamely noted.

It was another failure, but a significant one, because with this action Zawahiri introduced the use of suicide bombers, which became the signature of al-Jihad assassinations and later of al-Qaeda "martyrdom operations." The strategy broke a powerful religious taboo against suicide. Although Hezbollah, a Shiite organization, had employed suicide truck bombers to attack the American Embassy and the U.S. Marine barracks in Beirut in 1983, such actions had never been undertaken by a Sunni group. In Palestine, suicide bombings were virtually unknown until the mid-nineties, when the Oslo Accords began to unravel.* Zawahiri had been to Iran to raise money, and he had sent Ali Mohammed, among others, to Lebanon to train with Hezbollah, so it is likely that the notion of suicide bombings came from this source. Another of Zawahiri's innovations was to tape the bomber's vows of martyrdom on the eve of his mission. Zawahiri distributed cassettes of the bomber's voice justifying his decision to offer his life.

In November, during the ongoing trials of al-Jihad, Zawahiri attempted to kill Egypt's prime minister, Atef Sidqi. A car bomb exploded as the minister was driven past a girls' school in Cairo. The minister, in his armored car, was unhurt, but the explosion injured twenty-one people and killed a young schoolgirl, Shayma Abdel-Halim, who was crushed by a door blown loose in the blast. Her death outraged Egyptians, who had seen more than 240 people killed by the Islamic Group in the previous two years. Although there was only this one by al-Jihad, little Shayma's death captured people's emotions as nothing else had. When her coffin was borne through the streets of Cairo, people cried, "Terrorism is the enemy of God!"

---

*On April 6, 1994, the first Palestinian suicide bomber blew up a bus in Afula, Israel.

Zawahiri was shaken by the popular outrage. "The unintended death of this innocent child pained us all, but we were helpless and we had to fight the government," he wrote in his memoir. He offered to pay blood money to the girl's family. The Egyptian government arrested 280 more of his followers; 6 were eventually given a sentence of death. Zawahiri wrote: "This meant that they wanted my daughter, who was two at the time, and the daughters of other colleagues, to be orphans. Who cried or cared for our daughters?"

Sayyid Qutb, the educator and writer whose book *Milestones* ignited the radical Islamist movement, is shown here displaying one of his books (probably *Social Justice in Islam*) to the president of Colorado State College of Education, Dr. William Ross.

Greeley, Colorado, from the air in the 1940s. "The small city of Greeley, in which I am staying, is so beautiful that one may easily imagine that he is in paradise," Qutb wrote. But he also saw the darker side of America.

Qutb on trial, circa 1965. He was hanged in 1966. "Thank God," he said when his death sentence was pronounced. "I performed jihad for fifteen years until I earned this martyrdom."

Ayman al-Zawahiri grew up in Maadi, a middle-class suburb of Cairo. A solitary child, his classmates regarded him as a genius. He is shown in his childhood in a Cairo park.

Zawahiri as a schoolboy, *right*, and as a medical student at Cairo University, *below*

Opposite bottom: Ayman al-Zawahiri was defendant number 113 of the 302 who were charged with aiding or planning the October 1981 assassination of Anwar al-Sadat. He became spokesperson for the defendants because of his superior English. He is shown here delivering his lecture to the world press in December 1982. Many blame the torture of prisoners in the Egyptian prisons for the savagery of the Islamist movement. "They kicked us, they beat us, they whipped us with electric cables! They shocked us with electricity! And they used the wild dogs!"

The defendants on trial

Left: Sheikh Omar Abdul Rahman, "the blind sheikh," was one of the defendants. He was the emir of the Islamic Group at the time.

Left: Mohammed bin Laden came to Saudi Arabia in 1931 as a penniless Yemeni laborer and rose to become the king's favorite contractor and the man who built much of the infrastructure of the modern Kingdom. He gestures here to Prince Talal bin Abdul Aziz during a tour of the renovation of the Grand Mosque in Mecca, circa 1950.

Right: Mohammed bin Laden and King Faisal. During the construction of the road to Taif, King Faisal would often come to examine the progress and ask about cost overruns. When the road was completed, the Kingdom was finally united and Mohammed bin Laden became a national hero.

Left: The renovation of the Grand Mosque took twenty years. During the hajj it can accommodate a million worshippers at once.

Jamal Khalifa, bin Laden's college friend and later his brother-in-law, moved into bin Laden's house with his first wife. Their friendship broke apart over the issue of creating an all-Arab legion in Afghanistan, which was the predecessor of al-Qaeda.

Osama moved to this house in Jeddah with his mother after Mohammed bin Laden divorced her.

Osama bin Laden's second house in Jeddah, a four-unit apartment building, which he acquired after he became a polygamist

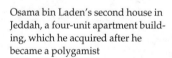

Opposite, bottom: Juhayman al-Oteibi, the leader of the attack on the mosque in 1979, a turning point in the history of Saudi Arabia. The demands of the insurgents foreshadowed bin Laden's agenda. When Oteibi begged for forgiveness after his capture, Prince Turki, head of Saudi intelligence, told him, "Ask forgiveness of God!"

Abdullah Azzam, who issued a fatwa in 1984 that called upon Muslims everywhere to "join the caravan" of the Afghan jihad. He and bin Laden set up the Services Bureau in Peshawar to facilitate the movement of Arabs into the war.

Bin Laden in a cave in Jalalabad in 1988, at about the time that he began al-Qaeda

Below: Azzam in the Panjshir Valley in 1988, where he traveled to meet with Ahmed Shah Massoud, the greatest of the Afghan commanders in the war against the Soviet invasion. Massoud sits next to Azzam with his arm around Azzam's son Ibrahim. Shortly after this visit Azzam and two of his sons, including Ibrahim, were assassinated in a bombing that has never been solved.

General Hamid Gul, who ran the Pakistani Inter-Services Intelligence during the Afghan jihad. The United States and Saudi Arabia funneled hundreds of millions of dollars through the ISI, which was largely responsible for creating the Taliban when the Soviets withdrew from Afghanistan.

Right: Prince Turki al-Faisal, head of Saudi intelligence, held the file on Afghanistan and worked with bin Laden. Later he negotiated with Mullah Mohammed Omar, the Taliban leader, but came away empty-handed.

Prince Turki after the Soviet occupation, negotiating among the warring mujahideen. He is on the far left, next to Burhanuddin Rabbani, the head of Ahmed Shah Massoud's political party. Pakistani prime minister Nawaz Sherif sits on the right.

The World Trade Center as seen from New Jersey, where the followers of Sheikh Omar Abdul Rahman plotted to bring it down

Ramzi Yousef was the mastermind of the first World Trade Center bombing. It was his dark imagination that gave shape to al-Qaeda's ambitious agenda.

Hasan al-Turabi, the loquacious and provocative ideologue who organized the Islamist coup in Sudan and courted bin Laden to invest in the country. "Bin Laden hated Turabi," a friend confided. "He thought he was a Machiavelli." Bin Laden came to Sudan a wealthy man; he left with little more than his wardrobe.

While bin Laden was in Sudan, the king of Saudi Arabia revoked bin Laden's citizenship and sent an emissary to collect his passport. Bin Laden threw it at the man. "Take it, if having it dictates anything on my behalf!"

In the mornings, bin Laden walked to the mosque, followed by acolytes, and would linger to study with holy men, often breakfasting with them before going to his office.

Osama bin Laden returned to Afghanistan in 1996. He habitually carried the Kalikov AK-74 that had been awarded to him in the jihad against the Soviets.

Opposite, top: Zawahiri and bin Laden holding a press conference in Afghanistan in May 1998. In Afghanistan, the destinies of bin Laden and Zawahiri became irrevocably intertwined, and eventually their terrorist organizations, al-Qaeda and al-Jihad, merged into one.

Taliban fighters headed to the front to fight against the Northern Alliance in 2001. The Taliban arose out of the chaos of mujahideen rule in 1994 and swiftly moved to consolidate their control of Afghanistan. At first, bin Laden and his followers had no idea who they were— there were rumors that they were communists.

The Dar-ul-Aman Palace, Kabul. The palace was caught between the lines during the civil war that followed the Soviet withdrawal. After twenty-five years of continuous warfare, much of Afghanistan was left in ruins.

Above: The ruins of the American Embassy in Nairobi, Kenya, which was bombed on August 7, 1998—al-Qaeda's first documented terrorist strike. The attack killed 213 people and injured thousands. More than 150 people were blinded by flying glass.

Right: The American Embassy in Dar es Salaam, Tanzania, was bombed nine minutes later, killing 11 and wounding 85.

Left: The Clinton administration responded by destroying several al-Qaeda training camps in Afghanistan and the al-Shifa pharmaceutical plant in Khartoum, pictured here. A night watchman was killed in the plant, which later proved to have nothing to do with producing chemical or biological weapons.

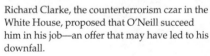

The USS *Cole* after a suicide attack by two al-Qaeda operatives in a fishing skiff in October 2000. The attack nearly sank one of the most invulnerable ships in the U.S. Navy. Seventeen sailors died. "The destroyer represented the capital of the West," said bin Laden, "and the small boat represented Mohammed."

Michael Scheuer, who created Alec Station, the CIA's virtual Osama bin Laden station. He and the FBI's John O'Neill were bitter rivals.

Richard Clarke, the counterterrorism czar in the White House, proposed that O'Neill succeed him in his job—an offer that may have led to his downfall.

Valerie James saw John O'Neill in a bar in Chicago in 1991 and bought him a drink because "he had the most compelling eyes." O'Neill was married at the time, a fact he failed to reveal to the many women he courted.

While he was dating Valerie in Chicago, O'Neill asked for an "exclusive relationship" with Mary Lynn Stevens in Washington, D.C.

In Washington, O'Neill also became involved with Anna DiBattista. "That guy is never going to marry you," her priest warned her.

John O'Neill said good-bye to Daniel Coleman and his FBI teammates at a farewell coffee on the occasion of his retirement from the bureau on August 22, 2001. The next day he started work at the World Trade Center.

Above: After gaining the names of the hijackers from al-Qaeda suspects in Yemen, Ali Soufan (left, with Special Agent George Crouch) traveled to Afghanistan. Here he stands in the ruins of what was bin Laden's hideout in Kabul.

O'Neill's funeral was the catastrophe of coincidence that he had always dreaded. Here his mother, Dorothy, and his wife, Christine, leave St. Nicholas of Tolentine Church in Atlantic City. They were among a thousand mourners.

The ruins of the World Trade Center burned for a hundred days. John O'Neill's body was found ten days after the 9/11 attack.

10

Paradise Lost

YOUNG MEN FROM MANY COUNTRIES came to the dusty and obscure Soba Farm, ten kilometers south of Khartoum. Bin Laden would greet them, and then al-Qaeda trainees would begin their courses in terrorism. Their motivations varied, but they had in common a belief that Islam—pure and primitive, unmitigated by modernity and uncompromised by politics—would cure the wounds that socialism or Arab nationalism had failed to heal. They were angry but powerless in their own countries. They did not see themselves as terrorists but as revolutionaries who, like all such men throughout history, had been pushed into action by the simple human need for justice. Some had experienced brutal repression; some were simply drawn to bloody chaos. From the beginning of al-Qaeda, there were reformers and there were nihilists. The dynamic between them was irreconcilable and self-destructive, but events were moving so quickly that it was almost impossible to tell the philosophers from the sociopaths. They were glued together by the charismatic personality of Osama bin Laden, which contained both strands, idealism and nihilism, in a potent mix.

Given the diversity of the trainees and their causes, bin Laden's main task was to direct them toward a common enemy. He had developed a fixed idea about America, which he explained to each new class of al-Qaeda recruits. America appeared so mighty, he told them, but it was actually weak and cowardly. Look at Vietnam, look at Lebanon. Whenever soldiers start coming home in body bags, Americans panic and retreat. Such a country needs only to be confronted with two or three sharp blows, then it will flee in panic, as it always has. For all its wealth and resources, America lacks conviction. It cannot stand against warriors of faith who do not fear death. The warships in the Gulf will retreat to the oceans, the bombers will disappear from the Arabian bases, the troops in the Horn of Africa will race back to their homeland.

The author of these sentiments had never been to America, but he liked to have people around him—such as Abu Rida al-Suri, Wa'el Julaidan, Ali Mohammed—who had lived there. They reinforced the bloated and degenerate America of his imagination. Bin Laden could scarcely wait to drive a spear into the heart of the last superpower. He saw his first opportunity in Somalia.

In the triumphant months following the defeat of Saddam Hussein, Somalia arose as the initial test of America's new world order. The UN was overseeing the international effort to end the Somali famine, which had already taken 350,000 lives. As in the Gulf War, there was an international coalition crowded under the UN umbrella and backed by American power. This time, however, there was no large Iraqi army to face, no Republican Guard, no armored divisions, only disorganized mobs with machine guns and RPGs. But the threat they posed was convincingly demonstrated by an ambush that killed twenty-four Pakistani soldiers.

Bin Laden claimed that he sent 250 men to Somalia to fight against U.S. troops. According to Sudanese intelligence, the actual number of al-Qaeda fighters was only a handful. The al-Qaeda guerrillas provided training and tried to fit into the anarchic clan war that was raging within the tableau of starvation that the hostilities had caused. Little the al-Qaeda men did impressed their hosts; for instance, the Arabs built a car bomb to attack the UN, but the bomb failed. "The Somalis treated us in a bad way," one of the Arabs complained. "We tried to convince them that we were messengers for people behind us, but they were not convinced. Due to the bad leadership situation there, we decided to withdraw."

One night in Mogadishu a couple of al-Qaeda fighters saw two

U.S. helicopters get shot down. The return fire struck the house next to where the men were hunkered down. Terrified that the Americans would capture them, they left Somalia the next day. The downing of those two American helicopters in October 1993, however, became the turning point in the war. Enraged Somali tribesmen triumphantly dragged the bodies of the dead crewmen through the streets of Mogadishu, a sight that prompted President Clinton to quickly withdraw all American soldiers from the country. Bin Laden's analysis of the American character had been proven correct.

Even though his own men had run away, bin Laden attributed to al-Qaeda the downing of the helicopters in Somalia and the desecration of the bodies of U.S. servicemen. His influence was magnified because of insurgent successes—as in Afghanistan and Somalia—that he really had little to do with. He simply appropriated such victories as his own. "Based on the reports we received from our brothers who participated in the jihad in Somalia," bin Laden boasted on al-Jazeera, "we learned that they saw the weakness, frailty, and cowardice of U.S. troops. Only eighteen U.S. troops were killed. Nonetheless, they fled in the heart of darkness, frustrated after they had caused great commotion about the New World Order."

BIN LADEN LURED various nationalist groups under his umbrella by offering weapons and training. He had instructors with years of combat experience. Zawahiri's double agent, Ali Mohammed, taught a course on surveillance, using the techniques he had picked up from the U.S. Special Forces (bin Laden himself took Mohammed's first course as a student). The weapons came from the storehouses of leftover mujahideen arms in Tora Bora, which bin Laden was able to smuggle into Sudan. Bin Laden also provided seed money for revolution. It must have been gratifying to see how much he could accomplish with so little.

In Algeria in 1992, a military coup prevented the election that an Islamist party, the Front Islamique du Salut (FIS) was expected to win. The following year, bin Laden sent Qari el-Said, an Algerian who was on the *shura* council of al-Qaeda, to meet with some of the rebel leaders who had taken refuge in the mountains. At that time, the Islamists were trying to pressure the unpopular military government to negotiate with them. The al-Qaeda emissary brought forty thousand dollars of bin Laden's money. He warned the Islamist leaders that they were making jihad merely for politics, not for God, and that was a sin. There was no room for compromise with an impious government, he told them. Total war was the only solution. "This simple argument destroyed us," recalled Abdullah Anas, who was part of the resistance. Those, like Anas, who favored dialogue with the government were pushed aside by other Arab Afghans in their midst who had been indoctrinated by *takfir* philosophy.

The young, poor, and largely urban guerrillas drawn to the Algerian revolt coalesced under the banner of the Groupe Islamique Armé (GIA). For the next five years they drenched the country in blood. The progression followed a predictable *takfiri* path. The Islamists began by killing non-Muslims, concentrating on priests and nuns, diplomats, intellectuals, feminists, doctors, and businessmen. According to the logic of GIA, democracy and Islam were incompatible; therefore, anyone who had a voting card was against Islam and deserved to be killed. The warrant was extended to include anyone who worked in establishments allied with the government, such as public schools. In two months of 1994 alone, thirty teachers and principals were killed and 538 schools were torched. The GIA terrorists were not only killing teachers and democrats, however. The inhabitants of entire villages were slain in midnight massacres. These atrocities were celebrated in GIA's weekly newspaper, *Al-Ansar*, published in London, which featured headlines such as "Thank God, We Have Cut 200 Throats Today!" and "Our Brother Beheaded His Father for the Sake of Allah." The religious madness culminated in a declaration that condemned the entire population of Algeria. A GIA communiqué stated the equation starkly: "There is no neutrality in the war we are waging. With the exception of those who are with us, all others are apostates and deserve to die." This formulation was appealingly available to those who saw the conflict in apocalyptic terms.

Even bin Laden recoiled—if not from the violence itself, then from the international revulsion directed at the Islamist project. He sought to create a "better image of the jihad." When some of the leaders of GIA came to Khartoum to beg for more funds, they had the temerity to criticize him for being "too flexible" with democrats, which made him appear "weak." Bin Laden was furious and withdrew his support entirely. But his forty thousand dollars had already helped to create a catastrophe. More than a hundred thousand people would die in the Algerian civil war.

AT THE END OF 1993, a rumor raced through Khartoum that a Sudanese general had gotten his hands on some black market uranium. Bin Laden was already interested in acquiring more powerful weapons to match his enlarged vision of al-Qaeda as an international terrorist organization. He was working with the Sudanese government to develop chemical agents that could be used against the Christian rebels in the south and smuggling weapons from Afghanistan on Sudan Airways cargo planes. He bought an American military jet, a T-39, specifically to transport more Stingers. So, naturally, when word of the uranium reached him, he was excited. He sent Jamal al-Fadl to negotiate the price.

By his own account Fadl was the third person to pledge allegiance to al-Qaeda, giving him a special claim on bin Laden's affections. He was a wiry and nimble athlete who played center on bin Laden's soccer team. Fadl was always smiling, and he had an infectious horse laugh that caught people by surprise. Like many of al-Qaeda's inner circle, he had come to jihad from America, having worked in the Services Bureau office on Brooklyn's Atlantic Avenue. Because Fadl was Sudanese and knew the local real estate market, bin Laden had entrusted him with the money to buy the property for al-Qaeda's farms and houses before the organization relocated to Khartoum.

The general wanted $1.5 million for the uranium plus a commission. He produced a cylinder, two and a half feet long and about six inches in diameter, and some documents showing that the canister had come from South Africa. Bin Laden was satisfied by this information and paid Fadl ten thousand dollars for his part of the exchange. As it turned out, the canister was filled with a substance called red mercury—also known as cinnabar—that physically resembles uranium oxide although chemically it is quite different. Red mercury has been used in nuclear scams for more than twenty-five years. Despite this expensive lesson, bin Laden continued his search for enriched uranium or Russian nuclear warheads that were said to be available in the ruins of the Soviet Union.

At this point, in the early nineties, bin Laden was still refining the concept of al-Qaeda. It was only one of his many enterprises, but it offered him a potentially extraordinary base of power. His actions, such as his foray into Somalia, were small and speculative; but with sufficiently powerful tools—nuclear or chemical weapons, for example—al-Qaeda could change the course of human events.

BY 1994 BIN LADEN'S LIFE had reached a pinnacle. His first two years in Sudan had been full of pleasure and good fortune. His wives and families were all together in his large villa; his business interests were expanding; al-Qaeda was gaining energy and momentum—but also raising alarms. Although Western intelligence agencies were still largely unaware of bin Laden, or simply failed to appreciate the scale of his enterprise, the Saudis and the Egyptians had taken notice of the activities in Sudan. Al-Qaeda proved difficult to penetrate, however. Loyalty, kinship, and fanaticism were formidable barriers against curious outsiders.

On Fridays, bin Laden normally went to pray in the Ansar al-Sunnah Mosque, across the Nile from Khartoum in the suburb of Omdurman. It was a Wahhabi mosque, frequented by Saudis. On February 4, a small group of takfiris, armed with Kalashnikovs and headed by a Libyan named Mohammed Abdullah al-Khilaifi, brazenly broke into two police stations, killing two policemen and seizing weapons and ammunition. Khilaifi and two companions then went to the mosque just as the evening prayers concluded. They fired indiscriminately into the crowd, killing sixteen people at once and wounding about twenty others. The killers hid out behind the airport. The next day, driving around Khartoum seeking other targets, they shot at policemen on the streets and at some of bin Laden's employees in the Wadi El Aqiq office downtown. They were wild and undisciplined, but it seemed clear that they were gunning for bin Laden.

At five in the afternoon, when he normally opened his salon to visitors, bin Laden was having a dispute with his eldest son, Abdullah. Since childhood, Abdullah had suffered from asthma, and the experience in Peshawar and Khartoum had been difficult for him. He was sixteen years old, and he longed to be with his friends and his cousins in Jeddah, just across the slender ribbon of the Red Sea. Abdullah was, after all, a member of a very wealthy clan, and in Jeddah he could enjoy the family beach resort, the yachts, the parties, the cars, and all the luxuries that his father abhorred. He also worried that his father's home tutorials had left him far behind his peers—in fact, the bin Laden children of his first wife could scarcely read. Osama believed that his family was already much too comfortable in Sudan. He wanted to make their lives more austere, not less.

As the father and son were talking in bin Laden's house, his guests began arriving at his office across the street. "At that moment, I heard the sound of a shotgun coming from the direction of the guesthouse," bin Laden recounted. "Then several shots were fired at the house." He took his pistol out of the pocket of his gallabea and handed another weapon to Abdullah.

The killers had driven into the street between bin Laden's two houses and immediately opened fire. Khilaifi and his two companions had expected bin Laden to be entertaining at his office. "They had targeted the spot where I used to sit," bin Laden said. He and Abdullah, along with Sudanese security men who were patrolling the area, shot at the attackers. Three of bin Laden's guests were hit and several of the guards. Khilaifi was wounded and both of his companions killed.

Bin Laden obliquely blamed "regimes in our Arabic region"

for the assaults. When his old friend Jamal Khashoggi asked him what he meant by that, bin Laden pointed to Egyptian intelligence. The CIA believed that the Saudis were behind the attempt. Turki's chief of intelligence, Saeed Badeeb, said, "We never tried to assassinate him. We only wanted to cool him down."

This near murder offered Zawahiri a superb opportunity to expand his influence with bin Laden. Zawahiri called in his own man, Ali Mohammed, to investigate the assassins. Mohammed learned that Khilaifi was a Libyan who had trained in Lebanon and then traveled to Peshawar in 1988. There he joined the mujahideen and met bin Laden. But he had also come under the influence of the takfiris. Khilaifi was a sociopath who used this philosophy to justify the murder of anyone he labeled an infidel. It was no different, except in the less ambitious scale of the enterprise, from what Zawahiri and bin Laden were doing. *Takfir* was a weapon that could blow up in anyone's face.

Zawahiri arranged for Ali Mohammed to train bin Laden's bodyguards, and he made sure that they were largely Egyptians—drawing even tighter the noose of influence he was casting around the Saudi. As for bin Laden, he gloomily concluded that his Sudanese idyll had come to an end. The picnics on the Nile, the meditative strolls to the mosque, the Friday horse races—all that was part of the past. He traveled in convoys now, and he always carried the Kalikov AK-74 that he had been awarded on the field of combat.

LIFE AT HOME also changed for bin Laden. As stern as he was toward his children, he was surprisingly permissive toward his career-oriented wives. Umm Hamza, the professor of child psychology, and Umm Khaled, who taught Arabic grammar, kept their university jobs and commuted to Saudi Arabia during the Sudan years. Umm Hamza lived on the ground floor of the Khartoum house, where she offered lectures to women about the teachings of Islam.

For Umm Abdullah, however, life in Khartoum was not so rewarding. Two of her sons, Abdullah and Omar, hated the deprivation and the hazards that their father imposed on them. And there was the ongoing problem of caring for Abdul Rahman, the retarded son, whose emotional outbursts were all the more difficult to deal with in the cramped household.

The fourth wife, Umm Ali, asked for a divorce. Bin Laden had expected this. "We have not been on good terms since the beginning," he confessed to Jamal Khalifa. When Osama and Jamal decided back in their university days to become polygamists, they had made a pledge that they would never abuse their moral code by being the one to ask for a divorce. Instead of marrying scores of women, like his father had done, bin Laden intended to fulfill the Quranic injunction to treat his four wives equally. But that meant he had to wait patiently for Umm Ali to make the request herself and put years of unhappiness behind them.

Under Islamic law, children younger than seven stay with their mothers; after that, the daughters go to their fathers. Sons over seven years old may choose between their parents. Eight-year-old Ali, the oldest, decided to stay with his mother. Umm Ali took her three children and returned to her family in Mecca. The daughters stayed with her, even as they grew.

Bin Laden valued loyalty; indeed, nearly all those around him had formally pledged themselves to him. He lived as feudal lord, controlling the destinies of hundreds of people. Betrayal, until now, was practically unknown in his dominion. The sudden desertion by several members of his family was a crushing loss to a man who held himself out as an exemplar of Islamic family values. The spartan virtues that he had pressed upon his children had turned some of them against him. And yet he willingly let them go.

BIN LADEN also longed for home. The only times he got to see his mother or other members of his family were when the Saudi royal court sent them to Khartoum to command him to return. King Fahd was beside himself with this continuing display of disloyalty. Algeria and Yemen were furiously pressing the Saudis to put a stop to the man they saw as a source of the insurgencies in their countries. It was Egypt, however, that finally forced the Kingdom to choose between its prodigal son and continued good relations with a powerful ally. The Egyptians were fed up with the violence spilling out of Sudan and protested again and again that bin Laden was behind it. Finally, on March 5, 1994, Fahd personally decided to revoke bin Laden's Saudi citizenship.

Saudi Arabia is an intimate nation, with large families and tribes complexly knitted together. To be expelled from the country was to be banished from these intricate relationships that are so much a part of every Saudi's identity. Citizenship is a closely guarded property, rarely awarded to foreigners, and the fact that the bin Laden family, of Yemeni origin, were full members of Saudi society indicated the honored—but vulnerable—place they held. Immediately after the king canceled bin Laden's citizenship, Bakr bin Laden, the eldest brother, publicly condemned Osama, turning the family's back to him. Many of bin Laden's countrymen date the moment of his total radicalization to the announcement of the king's decision. An emissary traveled to Sudan to formally deliver the news and demand bin Laden's passport. Bin Laden threw it at the man. "Take it, if having it dictates anything on my behalf!" he declared.

Bitter and reproachful, bin Laden authorized his representatives to establish an office in London. (He considered seeking asylum in Britain himself, but upon hearing of that possibility, the British home secretary immediately banned him.) The office, called the Advice and Reformation Committee, was run by Khaled al-Fawwaz, a Saudi, and two Egyptian members of al-Jihad. They sent faxes by the hundreds to prominent Saudis, who were stunned by bin Laden's open denunciations of royal corruption and the family's under-the-table deals with the Islamic clergy. These dispatches caused a sensation at a time when the fever for reform was already blazing. Bin Laden published an open letter to Sheikh bin Baz, chief of the Saudi ulema, denouncing his fatwas authorizing the royal family to keep the American forces in the holy land and to lock up dissident Islamic scholars.

"Bring this man to heel," the Saudi king ordered Prince Turki. Assassination plots were considered, but the Saudis were not clever killers, nor did Turki have the stomach for such risky ventures. Instead, the Interior Ministry ordered bin Laden's family to cut him off, and it seized his share of the company—about $7 million. As predictable as such moves were, bin Laden was taken by surprise. He depended on the monthly stipend the company paid him—in fact, it was his only real source of income.

His business career was a terrible failure. He had started his life in Sudan by spreading money around, loaning the government hard currency to purchase wheat, for instance, when an acute shortage caused breadlines to form; helping to build the Sudanese radio and television facilities; and occasionally picking up the tab for the nation's oil imports when the government was short. In such an impoverished country, bin Laden's modest fortune almost constituted a second economy. But he cared little about running his companies or overseeing his investments. Though he had an office with a fax machine and a computer, he rarely spent much time there, preferring to tinker with his agricultural projects during the day and entertain dignitaries and mujahideen in his evening salons.

He had sunk much of his money into enterprises he knew little about. His interests now included rock-crushing machines, insecticides, soap making, leather tanning—dozens of unrelated projects. He set up accounts in banks in Khartoum, London, Malaysia, Hong Kong, and Dubai, each in the names of different al-Qaeda members, which made them difficult for intelligence agencies to trace, but also nearly impossible to manage. He drifted into projects without much thought. When one of his aides thought it would be a clever investment to import cheap bicycles from Azerbaijan to Sudan, where no one rides them, all that was needed was to have three al-Qaeda managers sign a form and bin Laden was in the bicycle business.

These extremely diverse enterprises were haphazardly grouped under various corporate entities. From the first, the men who oversaw bin Laden's business interests realized that there was trouble ahead. In a 1992 meeting with bin Laden, Jamal al-Fadl and Abu Rida al-Suri asked him if it was really necessary for his companies to make money. "Business is very bad in Sudan," they warned him. Inflation was over 150 percent, and the Sudanese currency was constantly losing value against the dollar, undermining the entire portfolio. "Our agenda is bigger than business," bin Laden carelessly replied—a statement that ran a sword through any responsible management practices. When bin Laden's Saudi allowance was suddenly cut off, he had to confront a river of deficits and no reliable stream of income. "There were five different companies, and nothing worked," Abu Rida, his main business advisor, said. "All these companies lost. You cannot run a business on remote control."

The crunch came at the end of 1994. Bin Laden told the members of al-Qaeda that he would have to reduce their salaries because he had "lost all my money." When L'Houssaine Kherchtou, one of bin Laden's pilots, mentioned that he needed to go to Kenya to renew his pilot's license, which he had gained after three years of study on al-Qaeda's payroll, bin Laden told him to "forget about it." A few months later, Kherchtou's pregnant wife needed a Caesarean section, and he asked the al-Qaeda paymaster for $500 for the operation. "There is no money," the man told him. "We can't give you anything."

Suddenly Kherchtou felt expendable. The camaraderie that sustained the men of al-Qaeda rested on the financial security that bin Laden provided. They had always seen him as a billionaire, an endless font of wealth, and bin Laden had never sought to correct this impression. Now the contrast between that exaggerated image of bin Laden's resources and the new destitute reality caused some of the men to begin looking out for themselves.

Jamal al-Fadl, who was one of bin Laden's most popular and trusted men, had been chafing at the differential pay scale, which favored the Saudis and the Egyptians. When bin Laden refused to give him a raise, the Sudanese secretary reached into the till. He used the money to buy several plots of land and a car. In the narrow circles of Khartoum, such a burst of affluence was quickly noticed. When confronted, Fadl admitted to taking $110,000. "I don't care about the money, I care about you. You are one of the best people in al-Qaeda," bin Laden told him. "If you need money, you should come to us." Bin Laden pointed to other members of the organization who had been given a new car or a house when they asked for help. "You didn't do that," said bin Laden. "You just stole the money."

Fadl begged bin Laden to forgive him, but bin Laden said that would not happen "until you bring all the money back."

Fadl considered the offer, then disappeared. He would become al-Qaeda's first traitor. He offered to sell his story to various intelligence agencies in the Middle East, including the Israelis. He eventually found a buyer when he walked into the American Embassy in Eritrea in June 1996. In return for nearly $1 million, he became a government witness. While in protective custody, he won the New Jersey Lottery.

AFRICA WAS BLEEDING in the mid-1990s. Major wars and civil conflicts in Liberia, Angola, Sierra Leone, Congo, Nigeria, Rwanda, Burundi, and Zimbabwe took millions of lives. For bin Laden, the strife represented an opportunity to spread al-Qaeda's influence. He sent Ali Mohammed to Nairobi, the Kenyan capital, to conduct surveillance on American, British, French, and Israeli targets. They were chosen because of their involvement with Operation Restore Hope in Somalia, which was still going on at the time.

Ali Mohammed walked around Nairobi posing as a tourist. Among the possible targets he considered were the French Cultural Center and the British-owned Norfolk Hotel, one of the great artifacts of the colonial period. The Israeli Embassy was too heavily fortified, and the El Al office in a local strip mall was surrounded by security.

The American Embassy stood out as a rich, vulnerable target. There was no setback from the road, making it easy for a car bomb to get close enough to do great damage. Mohammed carried two cameras, one around his neck, like a tourist, and another, a tiny Olympus, that he cupped in his hand. For four or five days he passed by the building, snapping pictures at different times of the day, noticing the traffic patterns and the rotation of the security guards. He spotted the closed-circuit television cameras and determined their range. He developed the photos himself and then buried them in a stack of other pictures so they would appear inconspicuous. He drew up a plan of attack, which he placed on an Apple PowerBook 140; then he returned to Khartoum to make a presentation to bin Laden.

"Bin Laden looked at the picture of the American Embassy and pointed to where a truck could go as a suicide bomber," Mohammed eventually testified. But when the international community withdrew from Somalia and that miserable country collapsed back into a hopelessness from which it has yet to recover, al-Qaeda lost its pallid excuse for attacking the embassy in Nairobi. The plan was not forgotten, however; it was only filed away.

IN 1995 BIN LADEN began to have second thoughts about his life. He was struggling to keep his businesses afloat and his organization from flying apart. He could no longer afford to be a dilettante, but he was unwilling to cut loose his unprofitable projects and was paralyzed by the unfamiliar predicament of being broke. He was also pining for the familiar. "I am tired," he told one of his followers. "I miss living in Medina. Only God knows how nostalgic I am."

Al-Qaeda so far had come to nothing. It was another of his tantalizing enthusiasms that had no leadership and no clear direction. Al-Qaeda's treasurer, Medani al-Tayeb, who had married Osama's niece, had been urging bin Laden to reconcile with the king as a way of rectifying the organization's dire finances. The Saudi government sent several delegations to see him in Khartoum. According to bin Laden, the government offered to return his passport and his money provided that "I say through the media that the king is a good Muslim." He also claimed that the Saudis offered two billion riyals ($533 million) to his family if he abandoned jihad. He was torn between his righteous stance against the king and his sudden need for funds to keep al-Qaeda alive. When he rejected the offer, Tayeb defected, causing panic among the members when he turned up back in Saudi Arabia.

Some accounted for his shocking desertion by saying that he was under a magical spell.

Bin Laden wanted to go home as well, but his loathing for King Fahd was so great he could never call him a "good Muslim." During this time he had a dream of being in Medina, where he heard the sound of a great celebration. He looked over a mud wall and saw that Prince Abdullah was arriving. "It means that Abdullah will become king," he told Abu Rida. "That will be a relief to the people and will make them happy. If Abdullah becomes king, then I will go back."

But Abdullah was still crown prince. Bin Laden wrote a cagey and conciliatory note to him, trying to sound him out. He learned that the Saudi government was agreeable to his return if he pledged to give up jihad; otherwise, he would be jailed or put under house arrest.

His family heard about his yearning to come home, and they turned to a longtime friend of his, the journalist Jamal Khashoggi, who had covered bin Laden's exploits in Afghanistan. Khashoggi's job was to get Osama to grant an interview in which he renounced violence. That would be a very public signal to the government that he accepted its terms.

Bin Laden cheerfully received his friend. Khashoggi had visited him several times before in Khartoum. Previously, when Osama was beginning his press campaign against the Saudi government, Khashoggi found him surrounded by young Saudi dissidents, who fetched newspaper clippings for him whenever he wanted to make a point. This time there were no articles. Bin Laden was subdued and introspective, and he kept his automatic weapon beside him. They had dinner on the terrace beside his house, next to the garden. There were a couple of Saudis, a Sudanese, and Abu Hajer, the Iraqi. They ate around nine, when the temperature became just bearable. Sudanese servants spread plastic on the ground and laid out a platter of rice and lamb, Saudi style.

Khashoggi explained his mission, and in clear, unambiguous language, bin Laden condemned the use of violence inside the

Kingdom. Khashoggi pulled out his tape recorder. "Why don't you say that on the record?" he asked.

"Let's do that tomorrow night," said bin Laden.

The next day, bin Laden took Khashoggi to visit his genetics laboratory, where he spent hours discoursing on the Muslims' duty to aquire technology to improve their lives. For example, the Dutch have a monopoly on the best banana pods. Why can't Muslims devote themselves to horticulture with the same level of sophistication? Here, in this laboratory, bin Laden was trying to develop high-quality seeds appropriate for Sudan. He also discussed another major highway he was about to construct. He seemed to be utterly engaged in his projects—buoyant, content, peaceful, but homesick.

Then at dinner, bin Laden unexpectedly began boasting about al-Qaeda. He said he was convinced that the Americans could be easily driven out of the Arabian Peninsula. He gave the example of Yemen. "We hit them in Aden and they left," he said proudly. "We hit them in Somalia, and they left again."

"Osama, this is very dangerous," Jamal replied. "It is as if you are declaring war. You will give the right to the Americans to hunt for you."

Bin Laden just smiled.

Again, Khashoggi pulled out his tape recorder. Again, his friend declined to speak on the record.

The following night, Khashoggi came to dinner for the last time. They sat once more on the floor of the terrace. It was exactly the same simple meal he had enjoyed the previous nights—rice and lamb. Bin Laden sometimes ate with a spoon, but he preferred to use the fingers of his right hand, because it was Sunna— the way the Prophet did it. He rhapsodized about how much he missed Medina and how he would like to go back and settle there. Khashoggi responded that all he had to do was state on the record what he'd already said privately—that he renounced the use of violence.

Just then someone approached bin Laden and whispered in his ear. Osama stood up and went into the garden. In the shadows, Khashoggi could see two or three men quietly speaking in

Egyptian accents. Five minutes later, bin Laden returned, and Khashoggi posed the question again.

"What will I get for that?" bin Laden asked.

Khashoggi was caught by surprise. Osama had never acted like a politician before, negotiating for a personal advantage. "I don't know," Khashoggi admitted. "I'm not representing the government. Just say something, break the ice! Maybe there will be a positive reaction. Don't forget you said a few nasty things about the Kingdom."

Bin Laden smiled. "Yes, but a move like that has to be calculated." He aired a couple of possible sweeteners: a full pardon for him, a timetable for the complete withdrawal of the American forces from the peninsula.

Khashoggi had the feeling that his friend was losing his hold on reality. Bin Laden began to speak fondly about Sudan, saying what great investment opportunities there were. He asked Khashoggi about a couple of mutual friends, and suggested that they should come investigate the agricultural prospects. He would be happy to show them around.

"Osama, any Saudi person would be afraid to be seen with you in public," said Jamal. "Why can't you see that?"

Bin Laden just gave him the same old smile that Khashoggi had always seen. He didn't seem to realize what he had done or become in the eyes of his compatriots.

Exasperated, Khashoggi told bin Laden that he was going to leave the next day. If Osama wanted to do the interview, he should call him at the Hilton.

Bin Laden never called.

11

The Prince of Darkness

ON A SUNDAY MORNING in February 1995, Richard A. Clarke, the national coordinator for counterterrorism in the White House, went to his office to review intelligence cables that had come in over the weekend. One of the reports noted that Ramzi Yousef, the suspected mastermind behind the World Trade Center bombing two years earlier, had been spotted in Islamabad. Clarke immediately called FBI headquarters, although in his experience there was rarely anyone there on Sundays. A man whose voice was unfamiliar to him answered the phone. "O'Neill," he growled.

"Who are you?" Clarke asked.

"I'm John O'Neill," the man replied. "Who the fuck are you?"

O'Neill had just been appointed chief of the FBI's counterterrorism section. He had been transferred from the bureau's Chicago office. After driving all night, he had gone directly to headquarters that Sunday morning without dropping off his bags. Alone in the massive J. Edgar Hoover Building, except for security guards, O'Neill was not even supposed to start work until the following Tuesday. Clarke informed him that Ramzi Yousef, the FBI's most wanted terrorist, had tripped a wire nine thousand miles away. It was now O'Neill's responsibility to put together a team that would bring the suspect back to New York, where he had been indicted for the 1993 World Trade Center bombing and a conspiracy to bomb American airliners.

O'Neill walked down the empty hallway and opened the

Strategic Information and Operations Center (SIOC). The windowless room is set up for secure videoconferences with the White House, the State Department, and other branches of the FBI. It is the nerve center of the bureau, opened only during emergencies. O'Neill began making calls. He wouldn't leave FBI headquarters for the next three days.

A "rendition"—as the bureau terms the legal kidnapping of suspects in foreign lands—is a complex and time-consuming procedure, usually planned months in advance. O'Neill would need an airplane to fly the suspect home. Because of the $2 million reward on Yousef's head, there had been a flood of false reports concerning his whereabouts, so one of O'Neill's first concerns was to make sure he actually had his man. He would have to have a fingerprint expert, whose job would be to determine that the suspect was, in fact, Ramzi Yousef. He needed a medical doctor to attend Yousef in case he was injured or had some unknown condition that required treatment. He would have to push the State Department to get permission from the Pakistani government to perform the snatch immediately. Under ordinary circumstances, the host country would be asked to detain the suspect until extradition paperwork had been signed and the FBI could place the man in custody. There was no time for that. Yousef was planning to board a bus for Peshawar in a few hours. Unless he was quickly apprehended, he would soon be over the Khyber Pass and into Afghanistan, out of reach.

Gradually the room filled with agents in casual weekend clothes or churchgoing finery. A contingent from the New York office flew in; they would be the ones to make the actual arrest if Yousef was captured, since he had been indicted in their district.

For many of the agents in the room, O'Neill was an unfamiliar face, and no doubt it was odd to be suddenly taking orders from a man they had never before met. But most had heard of him. In a culture that favors discreet anonymity, O'Neill cut a memorable figure. Darkly handsome, with slicked-back hair, winking black eyes, and a big round jaw, O'Neill talked tough in a New Jersey accent that many loved to imitate. He had entered the bureau in the J. Edgar Hoover era, and throughout his career he had something of the old-time G-man about him. He wore a thick pinky ring and carried a 9-mm automatic strapped to his ankle. He favored Chivas Regal and water with a twist, along with a fine cigar. His manner was bluff and profane, but his nails were buffed and he was always immaculately, even fussily, dressed: black double-breasted suits, semitransparent black socks, and shiny loafers as supple as ballet slippers—"a nightclub wardrobe," as one of his colleagues labeled it.

He had wanted to work for the bureau since boyhood, when he watched Efrem Zimbalist, Jr., star as the buttoned-down Inspector Lewis Erskine in the TV series *The F.B.I.* He got a job as a fingerprint clerk with the bureau as soon as he graduated from high school in Atlantic City, New Jersey, and he put himself through American University and a master's program in forensics at George Washington University by serving as a tour guide at FBI headquarters. In 1976 he became a full-time agent in the bureau's office in Baltimore, and in 1991 he was named assistant special agent in charge of the Chicago office. Nicknames—Satan, the Prince of Darkness—followed him around from his days in Chicago, which spoke about his remorseless intensity, his sleeplessness, and the fear that he often inspired in those who worked with him. Time meant little to him; he kept the shades down in his office and seemed to live in eternal night.

In SIOC, O'Neill walked around with a phone at each ear, coordinating the rendition team on one line and arranging for an Air Force transport on the other. Because Pakistan would not permit an American military aircraft to land on its soil, O'Neill ordered the Air Force to paint its jet in civilian colors—immediately! He also demanded that, if Yousef was captured, the flight home would be refueled in midair, fearing that Yousef might claim asylum if the aircraft had to land in another country. O'Neill was operating well outside his authority, but he was reckless and domineering by nature. (The Pentagon later sent him a bill for $12 million for the midair refueling and the paint job. The bill went unpaid.)

As the news spread of Yousef's sighting, Attorney General Janet Reno and the director of the FBI, Louis Freeh, came into

SIOC. Many critical operations had been conducted in this room, but none so urgent and complex. The policy of renditions had only recently been instituted through an executive order that extended the reach of the FBI outside the borders of the United States, turning it into an international police agency; in practice, however, the bureau was still learning—not only how to operate in foreign environments but also how to beat a path through the U.S. government agencies abroad, each of which needed to be bullied or appeased. Such diplomacy normally required lengthy negotiations. But there was no time for talk. If Yousef escaped, few doubted that he would attempt to carry out his scheme of blowing up American airliners or even crashing a plane into CIA headquarters, as he had once planned.

O'Neill got the rendition team in the air, but he still needed to put a snatch team in place. There was only one FBI agent in Pakistan who could be pressed into service. O'Neill located several agents from the Drug Enforcement Administration and the State Department Bureau of Diplomatic Security who were also in the country. They enlisted a couple of Pakistani soldiers and rushed to the motel to grab Yousef before he got on the bus.

At 9:30 a.m. Pakistani time on February 7, the agents entered the Su-Casa Guest House in Islamabad and knocked on the door of room 16. A sleepy Yousef was immediately thrown to the floor and handcuffed. Moments later, the news reached the jubilant agents at FBI headquarters.

During the three days he was in SIOC, John O'Neill turned forty-three years old. He finally took his luggage to his new apartment. It was Tuesday, his first official day on the job.

IN WASHINGTON, O'Neill became part of a close-knit group of terrorism experts that formed around Dick Clarke. In the web of federal agencies concerned with terrorism, Clarke was the spider. Everything that touched the web eventually came to his attention. He was the first coordinator for counterterrorism on the National Security Council, a position he crafted for himself through the powerful force of his personality. The members of this inner circle, which was known as the Counterterrorism Security Group (CSG), were drawn mainly from the CIA, the National Security Council, and the upper tiers of the Defense Department, the Justice Department, and the State Department. They met every week in the White House Situation Room.

The FBI had always been a problematic member of the CSG. Its representatives tended to be close-mouthed and unhelpful, treating all intelligence as potential evidence that couldn't be compromised, whether there was an actual criminal case or not. O'Neill was different. He cultivated his counterparts in other agencies rather than pulling down the bureaucratic shutters. In Clarke's experience, most federal law-enforcement officers were dull and slow. By the time they had risen to the upper ranks of management, they were already at their maximum pay rank and were marking time toward their retirement. Against this drab background, O'Neill leaped out—charismatic, improvisatory, outspoken, and intriguingly complicated.

Clarke and O'Neill were both relentless infighters, and they made enemies easily. But each recognized in the other qualities he could use. Clarke had always groomed key allies who protected him against changes in administration and armed him with inside information. After more than two decades in government—beginning as a management intern at the Pentagon in 1973—he had protégés scattered all over Capitol Hill. He was brilliant but solitary, living alone in a blue clapboard house in Arlington, Virginia, with azaleas surrounding the front porch and an American flag flying from the second story. He spoke in emphatic, declarative sentences that brooked no argument. Ambitious and impatient, he had little time for life outside of his office on the third floor of the Old Executive Office Building, overlooking the West Wing of the White House. It was rare that someone interested him as a rival. He could push competitive bureaucrats aside for sport, since he played the game better than all but a few.

Although Clarke was shrewd and formidable, he was also socially awkward, tending to look past people when he spoke to them. He had the pallor of a redhead—now gone gray—and the tight, inappropriate smile of the superrealist. He spotted O'Neill as someone who shared his obsession about the threat posed by terrorism at a time when few in Washington considered it real. They had in common the resentment of the unprivileged outsider who had escaped the narrow expectations of his upbringing. O'Neill still had a strong whiff of the Jersey streets about him, which Clarke, the son of a nurse and a factory worker, valued. And, like Clarke, O'Neill saw through the political burlesque.

The two men worked to establish clear lines of responsibility among the intelligence agencies, which had a long history of savage bureaucratic warfare. In 1995 their efforts resulted in a presidential directive giving the FBI the lead authority in both investigating and preventing acts of terrorism wherever in the world Americans or American interests were threatened. After the bombing in Oklahoma City in April of that year, O'Neill formed a separate section for domestic terrorism, while he concentrated on redesigning and expanding the foreign branch. He organized a swap of deputies between his office and the CIA's Counterterrorist Center despite resistance from both organizations.

To younger agents who gave him what he demanded, which was absolute loyalty, he became a kind of consigliere. In the fiefdoms of the bureau, O'Neill was a powerful sponsor. He would often put his arms around his employees and tell them he loved them, and he showed it by going to extraordinary lengths to help when any of his people faced health problems or financial difficulties. On the other hand, he could be brutal, not only with subordinates but also with his superiors, when they failed to meet his expectations. Many who began by hating him became his most devoted followers, "Sons of John," as they still call themselves in the bureau. Others held their tongues and stood out of the way. Those who tried to keep pace with him would find themselves wondering what else they were willing to sacrifice—their marriages, their families, their private lives, everything except the bureau. These were sacrifices O'Neill had made long before.

O'NEILL'S TENURE IN THE FBI coincided with the internationalization of crime and law enforcement. Since 1984 the FBI had exercised the authority to investigate crimes against Americans abroad, but that mandate had been handicapped by a lack of connection with foreign police agencies. O'Neill made a habit of entertaining every foreign cop or intelligence agent who entered his orbit. He called it his "night job." In Clarke's opinion, O'Neill was like an Irish ward boss, who governed through interlocking friendships, debts, and obligations. He was constantly on the phone, doing favors and massaging contacts, creating a personal network that would facilitate the bureau's international responsibilities. Within a few years, O'Neill was perhaps the most widely known policeman in the world. He would also become the man most identified with the pursuit of Osama bin Laden.

Few people in American law enforcement or intelligence, including O'Neill, had any experience with Islam or much understanding of the grievances that had already given rise to the attack on the World Trade Center and other plots against the United States. Indeed, in a country as diverse as America, the leadership of the FBI was stunningly narrow in its range. It was run by Irish and Italian Catholic men. The backgrounds of many agents in the bureau, particularly in the upper ranks, were monotonously repetitive, very much like O'Neill's—Jersey boys, or Philly, or Boston. They called each other by boyish nicknames—Tommy, Danny, Mickey—that they had picked up when they were altar boys or playing hockey for Holy Cross. They were intensely patriotic and were trained from childhood not to question the hierarchy.

The bureau's culture had grown up in the decades when the FBI was fighting the Mafia, an organization created by people from very similar origins. The bureau knew its enemy then, but it was deeply uninformed about this new threat. The radical Islamists came from places few agents had ever been to, or even heard of. They spoke a language that only a handful in the bureau understood. Even pronouncing the names of suspects or informants was a challenge. It was hard to believe in those days that people who were so far away and so exotic posed a real threat. There was a sense in the bureau that because they were not like us, they were not a very appealing enemy.

What distinguished O'Neill early in his new posting was his

recognition of the fact that the nature of terrorism had changed; it had gone global and turned murderous. In the recent past, terror in America had been largely a domestic product, produced by underground associations such as the Ku Klux Klan, the Black Panthers, or the Jewish Defense League. The bureau had faced foreign elements before on American soil, notably the Fuerzas Armadas de Liberación Nacional (FALN), a Puerto Rican independence group that carried out approximately 150 terrorist acts in the United States during the seventies and early eighties. But deaths from those attacks were accidental, or at least beside the point. O'Neill's realization, shared by few, was that the radical Islamists had a wider dramatic vision that included murder on a large scale. He was one of the first to recognize the scope of their enterprise and their active presence inside the United States. It was O'Neill who saw that the man behind this worldwide network was a reclusive Saudi dissident in the Sudan with a dream to destroy America and the West. Early in O'Neill's career as the bureau's counterterrorism chief, his interest in bin Laden became such an obsession that his colleagues began to question his judgment.

O'Neill was separated from bin Laden by many layers of culture and belief, but he devoted himself to trying to understand this new enemy in the darkened mirror of human nature. They were quite different men, but O'Neill and bin Laden were well-matched opponents: ambitious, imaginative, relentless, and each eager to destroy the other and all he represented.

ON THE OTHER SIDE OF THAT MIRROR, bin Laden looked at America as something other than an ordinary country or even a superpower. He saw it as the vanguard of a global crusade on the part of Christians and Jews to crush the Islamic resurgence. Although he may not have read Samuel P. Huntington's 1993 treatise on the "clash of civilizations," he seized the idea and would refer to it later in interviews, saying it was his duty to promote such a clash. History moved in long, slow waves, he believed, and this contest had been going on continuously since the founding of Islam. "This battle is not between al-Qaeda and the U.S.," bin

Laden would later explain. "This is a battle of Muslims against the global Crusaders." It was a theological war, in other words, and the redemption of humanity was at stake.

In August 1995 bin Laden made a decisive break with his homeland. In what he labeled a "frank manifesto," bin Laden attacked King Fahd directly in one of his faxed commentaries. This was ostensibly a response to the reshuffling of the Saudi cabinet the week before, which, like most political events in the Kingdom, was designed to give the appearance of reform without any real change. In a lengthy preamble, bin Laden made a legalistic case, based upon the Quran and the commentaries of Islamic scholars, that the king himself was an infidel. The takfiri influence is clear, although some of his argument was obscure and wild-eyed. For instance, bin Laden cited article 9 of the charter of the Gulf Cooperation Council, which was set up to resolve trade conflicts between Arab countries in the Persian Gulf. Article 9 states that the council will follow the rules of its constitution, international law and norms, and the principles of Islamic law. "What mockery of Allah's religion!" bin Laden exclaimed. "You have put the Islamic law only at the end."

But many of the points bin Laden made in his diatribe were already deeply believed by large numbers of Saudis and echoed the pleas that Islamic reformers had made in a far more polite petition, one that resulted in the imprisonment of several leading clerics. "The main reason for writing this letter to you is not your oppression of people and their rights," bin Laden began. "It's not your insult to the dignity of our nation, your desecration of its sanctuaries, and your embezzlement of its wealth and riches." Bin Laden gestured to the economic crisis that had followed the Gulf War, to the "insane inflation," the overcrowding in the classroom, and the spread of unemployment. "How can you ask people to save power when everyone can see your enchanting palaces lit up night and day?" he demanded. "Do we not have the right to ask you, O King, where has all the money gone? Never mind answering—one knows how many bribes and commissions ended in your pocket."

He then turned to the galling presence of American troops in the Kingdom. "It is unconscionable to let the country become an

American colony with American soldiers—their filthy feet roaming everywhere—for no reason other than protecting your throne and protecting oil sources for their own use," he wrote. "These filthy, infidel Crusaders must not be allowed to remain in the Holy Land."

The king's tolerance of man-made laws and the presence of infidel troops proved to bin Laden that the king was an apostate and must be toppled. "You have brought to our people the two worst calamities, blasphemy and poverty," he wrote. "Our best advice to you now is to submit your resignation."

One can imagine the shock that such a letter must have visited on the Saudi people, much less the king. In a society where no one could speak freely, the thunder of bin Laden's language jolted and titillated his mute countrymen. But he did not call for revolution. Although he accused several leading princes of corruption and incompetence, he was not asking for the overthrow of the royal family. Except for the king's abdication, he didn't propose any solutions to the problems he cited. He pointedly made no reference at all to Crown Prince Abdullah, next in line to the throne. Despite the incendiary tone of the document, it was essentially modest in its ambition. Bin Laden showed himself to be a loyal reformer with little to offer in the way of useful political ideas. His insurrectionary zeal was directed toward the United States, not toward his homeland.

Many Saudis shared his hostility to the continuing American presence in the Kingdom, especially after Dick Cheney's well-known pledge that they would leave. Ostensibly, the troops remained in order to enforce the UN-mandated no-fly zone over Iraq. By 1992, however, and certainly by 1993, there were enough new basing agreements in the region that the Americans could have withdrawn without jeopardizing their mission. But the Saudi bases were convenient and well appointed, and there didn't seem to be a sufficiently pressing need to leave.

THE WEEK FOLLOWING bin Laden's insulting letter to the king, Prince Naif announced the execution of Abdullah al-Hudhaif. Hudhaif, an Arab Afghan, was not under a death sentence; he had been given twenty years for spraying acid in the face of a security officer who was reputed to have been a torturer. The Saudis were now being advised by the former Egyptian minister of the interior, who had led a brutal crackdown on dissidents in his own country. There was a widespread feeling in the Kingdom that the stakes had been raised, and that this summary execution was a message to bin Laden and his followers. Hudhaif's Arab Afghan comrades, for their part, were calling for revenge against the regime.

In downtown Riyadh, Saudi Arabia, on Telateen Street, across from the Steak House restaurant, there was a communications center for the Saudi National Guard. The mission of the guard was to protect the royal family and enforce stability. Because those goals were also important to the United States, there was an agreement between the two countries that the U.S. Army, along with the Vinnell Corporation, an American defense contractor, would train the guard in the monitoring and surveillance of Saudi citizens.

Shortly before noon on November 13, 1995, Colonel Albert M. Bleakley, an engineer who had lived for three years in the Kingdom, walked out of the center to his truck, parked on the street outside. Suddenly a hot blast blew him backward several feet. When he was able to stand, he could see a line of cars burning, including the demolished remnants of his Chevrolet Yukon. "Why would my car blow up?" he wondered. "There are no bombs here."

The assassins had parked a van containing a hundred pounds of Semtex explosive outside the three-story building, which was now shattered and burning. Bleakley staggered into the ruin. He was bleeding from the neck and his ears were ringing from the deafening blast. Three dead men lay in the snack bar, crushed by a concrete wall. Four others were killed and sixty people injured. Five of the dead were Americans.

The Saudi government reacted by rounding up Arab Afghans and torturing confessions out of four men. Three of the four suspects had fought in Afghanistan, and one had also fought in Bosnia. The purported leader of the group, Muslih al-Shamrani, had trained at al-Qaeda's Farouk camp in Afghanistan. The men read their nearly identical confessions on Saudi television, admitting that they had been influenced by reading bin Laden's speeches and those of other prominent dissidents. Then they were taken to a public square and beheaded.

Although bin Laden never publicly admitted authorizing the attack or training the men who carried it out, he called them "heroes" and suggested they were responding to his fatwa urging jihad against the American occupiers. "They have pulled down the disgrace and submissiveness off the forehead of their nation," he said. He noted the fact that the number of U.S. troops in the Kingdom was reduced as a consequence—another proof of the truth of his analysis of American weakness.

The summary executions foreclosed the opportunity of learning exactly what connections there were between al-Qaeda and the perpetrators. Bin Laden himself privately confided to the editor of *Al-Quds al-Arabi* that he had activated a sleeper cell of Afghan veterans when the Saudi government failed to respond to his protest of American troops on Arabian soil. John O'Neill suspected that the executed men had nothing to do with the crime. He had sent several agents to try to question the suspects, but they had been executed before the Americans got the chance to talk to them. Whatever al-Qaeda's actual connection to the attack, Prince Turki would later describe the National Guard bombing as bin Laden's "first terrorist blow."

12

The Boy Spies

HOSNI MUBARAK, THE EGYPTIAN PRESIDENT, is a squat, neckless man with a heavy lower lip that juts forward when he talks, fleshy cheeks, and thickly lidded eyes, like a clay rendering that has not been fully formed. He was sixty-seven years old in 1995, but his wavy hair was dyed a brilliant black, and the billboards bearing his visage in Cairo showed a man twenty years younger—changelessness being the most obvious feature of his rule. He had stood beside Anwar al-Sadat on the reviewing platform when the assassins struck, and upon assuming the presidency he declared a state of emergency that was still in effect fourteen years later. His early efforts at liberalizing the political process were answered by the victories of the Muslim Brothers and then by the terror campaign of the radical Islamists in the nineties. Mubarak showed himself to be as pitiless as the insurgents, but the violence had not yet reached its climax.

In April, Egyptian intelligence learned that Zawahiri had chaired a meeting of al-Jihad in Khartoum that included leading members of the rival Islamic Group—a troublesome development. The reports said that the two organizations were working together to restart terror activities in Egypt, and that they were being aided by the Sudanese government, which was supplying them with arms and false papers. But as yet there was no word on how they would strike, or where.

Hasan al-Turabi's grand Islamist revolution had been stymied, unable to spread beyond Sudan. Egypt was of course the ultimate target, but Mubarak had the country in an iron grip. If he were eliminated, Zawahiri and the plotters reasoned, that would create a power vacuum, and in the upcoming parliamentary elections alternative Islamist movements could take charge.

Mubarak was flying to Addis Ababa on June 26 for a meeting of the Organization of African Unity. The Egyptian radicals had been anticipating this event for more than a year, placing members of the cell charged with carrying out the killing in the Ethiopian capital. Some of them married local women and ostensibly became a part of the community.

Working with assassins from the Islamic Group, Sudanese intelligence smuggled weapons into their embassy in Ethiopia. The leader of the plot was Mustafa Hamza, a senior Egyptian member of al-Qaeda and commander of the military branch of the Islamic Group. At a farm north of Khartoum, Zawahiri gave a motivational talk to the nine terrorists who were going to carry out the plot, and then he went on to Ethiopia to inspect the killing ground.

The plan was to station two cars along the airport road, the only route into the capital. When Mubarak's limousine approached the first car, the assassins would strike with automatic weapons and rocket-propelled grenades. If Mubarak escaped the first trap, another car would be waiting down the road.

Mubarak's plane arrived an hour early, but delays in getting his entourage and bodyguards together gave the assassins time to get into place. The limousine appeared, the shooters opened fire, but the grenade launcher malfunctioned. Two of Mubarak's Ethiopian bodyguards were killed in the exchange, and five of the assailants. Mubarak probably saved his own life when he ordered his driver to return to the airport, thus avoiding the second ambush.

Three of the assassins were captured, and one fled back to Sudan.

The Ethiopian police quickly pieced together the plot, exposing the complicity of the Sudanese government. The debacle led to a unanimous vote in the United Nations to impose stiff economic sanctions on Sudan. The Sudanese representative denied the charges, but the Sudanese delegation was already in disfavor, having been implicated only two years earlier in a plot to blow up UN headquarters, a part of the blind sheikh's plan to destroy New York City landmarks. The international community had had enough of Turabi's revolution, but Turabi managed to make things worse by praising the attempted murder of Mubarak. "The sons of the Prophet Moses, the Muslims, rose up against him, confounded his plans, and sent him back to his country," he said. As for his future relations with the Egyptian president, Turabi remarked, "I found the man to be very far below my level of thinking and my views, and too stupid to understand my pronouncements."

There was a reckoning coming, as everyone knew.

MUBARAK'S SECURITY FORCES fanned out all across Egypt, from the slums of Cairo to the mud-brick villages of the upper Nile, to destroy the radical Islamist movement. Houses were burned. Suspects disappeared. Sometimes a mother was dragged out on the street and stripped naked, and her children were warned that she would be raped if their brother was not present the next time they came. Mubarak instituted an anti-terrorism law that made it a crime to even express sympathy for terrorist movements. Five new prisons were built to house the thousands of suspects that were rounded up, many of whom were never charged.

To deal with Zawahiri, Egyptian intelligence agents devised a fiendish plan. They lured a thirteen-year-old boy named Ahmed into an apartment with the promise of juice and videos. Ahmed was the son of Mohammed Sharraf, a well-known Egyptian fundamentalist and a senior member of al-Jihad. The boy was drugged and sodomized; when he awakened, he was confronted with photographs of the homosexual activity and threatened with the prospect of having them shown to his father. For the child, the consequences of such a disclosure were overwhelming. "It could even be that the father would kill him," a source close to Zawahiri admitted.

Egyptian intelligence forced him to recruit another child,

Mus'ab, whose father, Abu al-Faraj, was also in al-Jihad and served as the treasurer for al-Qaeda. Mus'ab endured the same humiliating initiation of drugs and sexual abuse and was forced to turn against his family. The agents taught the boys how to plant microphones in their own homes and photograph documents. A number of arrests followed because of the information produced by the boy spies.

The Egyptian agents then decided to use the boys to kill Zawahiri. They gave Mus'ab a bomb to place inside a five-story apartment building where Zawahiri's family lived. But Zawahiri was not there, and Sudanese intelligence discovered the bomb. The other child, Ahmed, was in the hospital, suffering from malaria. He had not yet been revealed as a spy. His physician was Zawahiri, who visited him every day. The Egyptian agents learned from Ahmed what time to expect his doctor. The next day an assassination team was waiting, but for whatever reason, Zawahiri didn't come.

An even better opportunity arose, however: Egyptian intelligence learned of a meeting of al-Jihad's *shura* council. An agent gave Mus'ab a suitcase bomb and instructed him to place it in the office where Zawahiri and his companions would be meeting. As the boy got out of the agent's car, however, both the Sudanese intelligence and Jihad security were waiting for him. The Egyptian agent sped away, leaving the boy to his fate.

Al-Jihad and Sudanese intelligence quarreled over who would take custody of Mus'ab. Finally, Zawahiri was allowed to question the boy. He promised to return him safely. He soon placed his young patient, Ahmed, under his arrest as well. Then Zawahiri convened a Sharia court.

Many members of al-Jihad and al-Qaeda objected to putting children on trial, saying it was against Islam. In response, Zawahiri had the boys stripped naked to determine whether they had attained puberty, which they had. The helpless boys confessed everything. The court convicted them of sodomy, treason, and attempted murder.

Zawahiri had the boys shot. To make sure he got his point across, he videotaped their confessions and their executions and distributed the tapes as an example to others who might betray the organization.

When Turabi and his people learned of the firing squad, they were incensed. The Sudanese government accused al-Jihad of behaving like a "state within a state" and ordered Zawahiri and his organization out of the country immediately. They did not even get time to pack. "All we did was to apply God's Sharia," Zawahiri complained. "If we fail to apply it to ourselves, how can we apply it to others?"

Al-Jihad scattered, mainly to Afghanistan, Jordan, and Yemen. Many members broke away, scandalized by the cold-blooded execution of the two young boys. In Zawahiri's hands, al-Jihad had splintered into angry and homeless gangs. There were fewer than a hundred members left in the organization, and many of the men were still trying to collect their families and their belongings from Khartoum. "These are bad times," Zawahiri admitted in Yemen, where he had taken refuge. He confided to some of his colleagues that he was developing an ulcer.

His disillusioned followers often reflected on the pronouncement, made during the prison years by the man Zawahiri betrayed, Major Essam al-Qamari, that some vital quality was missing in Zawahiri. Qamari was the one who had told him, "If you are the member of any group, you cannot be the leader." That now sounded like prophecy.

Zawahiri had few resources remaining other than bin Laden's backing. He was determined to strike back quickly against the Egyptian authorities in order to redeem his reputation and keep the remnants of his organization intact. His views had undergone a powerful shift from those of the young man who spurned revolution because it was too bloody. He now believed that only violence changed history. In striking the enemy, he would create a new reality. His strategy was to force the Egyptian regime to become even more repressive, to make the people hate it. In this he succeeded. But the Egyptian people did not turn to him or to his movement. They only became more miserable, more disenchanted, frightened, and despairing. In the game Zawahiri had begun, however, revenge was essential; indeed, it was the game itself.

FIRST ACTIONS often set the course of future events. On November 19, 1995, the eighteenth anniversary of Anwar al-Sadat's trip to Jerusalem, Zawahiri's men bombed the Egyptian Embassy in Islamabad, Pakistan. Although the bombing was an al-Jihad operation, it would become the prototype of future al-Qaeda attacks, in terms of both the target and the means of destroying it. One of Zawahiri's men, known as Abu Khabab, was an Egyptian cab driver who had studied chemistry and had become an explosives instructor. He created a powerful new bomb. Two men approached the embassy, one of them carrying a Samsonite briefcase filled with weapons. He threw grenades to frighten off the security guards. A pickup truck packed with a 250-pound explosive rushed into the compound. Then the driver set off the bomb. The embassy crumbled. Many other buildings within a half-mile radius of the bomb were severely damaged. Sixteen people died, not counting the two suicide bombers, and sixty were wounded.

This act of mass murder was al-Jihad's first success under Zawahiri's administration. "The bomb left the embassy's ruined building as an eloquent and clear message," Zawahiri wrote in his memoir. Bin Laden had not approved the operation, however; nor was he happy about it. Pakistan still offered the best route into Afghanistan and, until then, had provided sanctuary to many Arab Afghans who had lingered after the war. Now the government rounded up nearly two hundred of them and locked them in a wedding hall in Peshawar, pending deportation to their home countries. The authorities were surprised when bin Laden appeared at the wedding hall with airline tickets to Sudan for the detainees. He suddenly had on his hands a dedicated group of terrorists, who were now dependent on him but loyal to Zawahiri.

Zawahiri also alienated many of his remaining followers, who

were alarmed both by the death of innocents and by the use of suicide bombers. These issues would always plague the conversation about the morality of global jihad. In responding to these
objections, Zawahiri created the theoretical framework to justify
the Islamabad bombing and similar al-Qaeda attacks that followed.

He explained that there were no innocents inside the embassy.
Everyone who worked there, from the diplomats to the guards,
was a supporter of the Egyptian regime, which had detained
thousands of fundamentalists and blocked the rule of Islam.
Those who carried out the duties of the government must shoulder responsibility for its crimes. No true Muslim could work for
such a regime. In this, Zawahiri was repeating the *takfir* view that
had been carried to its logical extreme in Algeria. Yes, he admitted, there might have been innocent victims—children, true
believers—who also died, but Muslims are weak and their enemy
is so powerful; in such an emergency, the rules against the slaughter of innocents must be relaxed.

The question of suicide was even more problematic. There is
no theological support for such an action in Islam; indeed, it is
expressly prohibited. "Do not kill yourselves," the Quran states.
The hadith, or sayings of the Prophet, are replete with instances in
which Mohammed condemns the action. The specific punishment
for the suicide is to burn in hell and to be forever in the act of
dying by means of the same instrument that was used to take his
life. Even when one of his bravest warriors was severely
wounded in battle and hurled himself upon his own sword only
to relieve his terrible suffering, Mohammed declared that he was
damned. "A man may do the deeds of the people of the Fire while
in fact he is one of the people of Paradise, and he may do the
deeds of the people of Paradise when in fact he belongs to the
people of Fire," the Prophet observed. "Verily, (the rewards of)
the deeds are decided by the last actions."

In his defense of the bombing, Zawahiri had to overcome this
profound taboo. The bombers who carried out the Islamabad
operation, Zawahiri said, represent "a generation of mujahideen
that has decided to sacrifice itself and its property in the cause of

God. That is because the way of death and martyrdom is a weapon that tyrants and their helpers, who worship their salaries instead of God, do not have." He compared them to the martyrs of early Christianity. The only example he could point to in Islamic tradition was that of a group of Muslims, early in the history of the faith, who were captured by "idolaters" and forced to choose between recanting their religion or being killed by their captors. They chose to become martyrs to their beliefs.

It was, Zawahiri argued, a suicidal choice. Other Muslims did not condemn them at the time because they were acting for the glory of God and the greater good of Islam. Therefore, anyone who gives his life in pursuit of the true faith—such as the bombers in Islamabad—is to be regarded not as a suicide who will suffer the punishment of hell but as a heroic martyr whose selfless sacrifice will gain him an extraordinary reward in Paradise.

With such sophistry, Zawahiri reversed the language of the Prophet and opened the door to universal murder.

"DO YOU REMEMBER THAT CHAP, bin Laden?" Hasan al-Turabi asked his son in early 1996.

"Of course!" Issam replied. "We're stable mates."

"Some people in my party want to throw him out," said the father.

When Issam next saw bin Laden, he was surprised at how depressed he appeared. Zawahiri and al-Jihad had been expelled, removing the Egyptian core of bin Laden's organization, and he was crippled by the loss. The relaxed and playful character Issam had known was gone. Rumors were racing through Khartoum that bin Laden was "the next Carlos." The Sudanese government had allowed French intelligence to kidnap Carlos the Jackal while he was undergoing an operation on his right testicle. Now Sudanese intelligence cleverly put out a false story that the French had issued a similar indictment for bin Laden—intending, no doubt, to scare him out of the country.

Without the Egyptians, bin Laden was isolated and uncertain. There was no one he could trust. He knew that something might happen to him. He was already looking for another sanctuary, just in case.

"You shouldn't leave Sudan," Issam advised his friend. "If you go, who is going to manage your investments?" Bin Laden had no answer.

Issam pitied his predicament. He knew how merciless Sudanese politics could be, especially to a naïve foreigner with much to lose. "I loved that man by that time," Issam said, "because of so many ideas I see in him. There was no hypocrisy in his character. No divergence between what he says and what he does. Unfortunately, his IQ was not that great."

THE CATASTROPHE that the radical Islamist leaders of Sudan had created for themselves finally made itself starkly apparent. The government's complicity in the terror plots against New York and the attempted assassination of Mubarak guaranteed international sanctions, which took effect in April 1996. By that time the U.S. Embassy in Khartoum had already moved its American staff, along with the CIA's Khartoum Station, to Kenya. It was part of a general withdrawal of the diplomatic community. Sudan was being pushed into the freezer, and its leaders were struggling to find a way out.

On his final night in Sudan, the American ambassador, Timothy Carney, had dinner with the Sudanese vice president, Ali Othman Taha. They discussed what Sudan could do to improve its reputation. Sending Osama bin Laden back to Saudi Arabia was one of Carney's suggestions. He had already spoken to a senior Saudi official who had assured him that bin Laden could still return to the Kingdom "if he apologizes."

A month later, the Sudanese minister of state for defense, Major General Elfatih Erwa, met Carney and covert operatives of the CIA in a Rosslyn, Virginia, hotel room. Erwa communicated his government's desire to get off the State Department's list of state sponsors of terror. He wanted a written checklist of measures that would satisfy the U.S. government. The CIA responded with a memorandum, which among other things proposed that

Sudan turn over the names of all the mujahideen that bin Laden had brought into that country, along with their passport numbers and dates of travel. In later meetings, the Americans pushed the Sudanese representative to expel bin Laden. Erwa told the agency that it was better for him to stay in Sudan, where the government could keep an eye on him; however, he said, if the United States wanted to bring charges against bin Laden, "We are ready to hand him to you."

The Clinton administration still perceived bin Laden as a wealthy nuisance, not a mortal threat. His name had arisen as a financier of terror mainly because of his support of the blind sheikh. There was a consensus that he needed to be pushed out of his sanctuary in Sudan, because the country was overrun with Islamic terrorists, and they were far more dangerous with money than without. There was no real debate about the consequences of expelling him, however. Nor was there any point in forcing Sudan to hand him over to U.S. authorities, because there was no evidence so far that he had harmed American citizens. Administration officials briefly nurtured the fantasy that the Saudis would accept their wayward son and simply cut off his head. The president of Sudan, Omar al-Bashir, went to the Kingdom on hajj, and while he was there he met with Crown Prince Abdullah. Bashir offered to turn over bin Laden if the Saudis would guarantee that he would not be imprisoned or prosecuted. The crown prince rejected those terms. The Egyptian government, which held bin Laden responsible for financing the attempted assassination of Mubarak, also pressured the Saudis to bring bin Laden to justice. This time it was Prince Turki who demurred. There was no solid proof that bin Laden was involved in the operation, he contended. Ahmed Badeeb, Turki's deputy, privately told the Egyptians, "Give us proof and we will kidnap him." But the Saudis made it obvious to everyone that they were washing their hands of bin Laden. Bin Laden wasn't yet a wanted man, but he certainly was an unwanted one.

The Americans continued pushing the Sudanese government. "Ask him to leave the country," they told General Erwa. "Just don't let him go to Somalia."

"He will go to Afghanistan," Erwa warned.

"Let him," the Americans responded.

HASAN AL-TURABI and bin Laden argued heatedly late into the night over a period of three consecutive days. Bin Laden said that after all he had invested in the country, the government had no right to throw him out. He had committed no crimes against Sudan, and there was no other place in the world that was ready to receive him. Turabi replied that bin Laden had only two choices: to leave or to remain and keep his mouth shut. Bin Laden said he couldn't remain silent as long as young Islamists were unjustly imprisoned in Saudi Arabia. Finally, he agreed to leave.

But where in the world could he go? He no longer had a Saudi passport, which gave him entry anywhere in the world; now he was traveling as a rather notorious Sudanese businessman and alleged sponsor of terror. Some members of al-Jihad offered to arrange for him to have plastic surgery and then smuggle him into Egypt, but Zawahiri, who reportedly was lying low in Bulgaria, advised against it. He had always maintained that Egypt was too transparent and lacked the natural retreats—caves, mountains—where a revolution could nurture itself. Somalia was a possibility, but the hostility of the local population toward the Arabs made the country too untrustworthy.

As the Sudanese had warned, Afghanistan was the most obvious destination—perhaps the only one. Turabi did bin Laden the favor of calling the Sudanese ambassador to Afghanistan to ease bin Laden's return. Then the rulers of Sudan sat down to divvy up bin Laden's investments.

The government still owed him for the $20 million, 450-mile highway from Khartoum to Port Sudan. Bin Laden had agreed to accept the tannery, which the government valued at $5 million, as partial payment, but now he had to suffer the indignity of selling it back to the government at a fraction of its worth. He liquidated his other businesses as quickly as possible, hoping to regain some portion of his fortune, but he was forced to virtually give away nearly everything he owned. The government confiscated his heavy equipment—the Caterpillars, steamrollers, and cranes that were the key assets of his construction company, worth approximately $12 million by themselves. The spreading acres that he had cultivated with so much anticipation and pleasure were snatched away for next to nothing. He sold his horses to Issam for a few hundred dollars. The net loss, he ruefully admitted, was more than $160 million.* Turabi's Islamist party, bin Laden concluded, was "a mixture of religion and organized crime."

The imminent departure of its leader threw al-Qaeda into a panic. Some members were invited to join bin Laden in Afghanistan in the future; others were told the organization could no longer support them. Each of them got a check for $2,400 and a plane ticket home.

Having shorn bin Laden of most of his net worth, the Sudanese government thoughtfully chartered him an antique Soviet Tupolev jet. Saif al-Adl, later to become al-Qaeda's military chief, sat in the copilot's seat holding a map so he could direct the Russian pilot, who didn't speak Arabic and whom they didn't trust. Two of bin Laden's young sons, Saad and Omar, were with him, and a couple of bodyguards. Bin Laden left on May 18, 1996. His family was scattered and broken. The organization that he had built was torn apart. He held America responsible for the crushing reversal that had led him to this state.

*Bin Laden told Abdel Bari Atwan that he was able to recover about 10 percent of his investment after the Sudan government offered to repay him in grain and cattle that he could resell to other countries (Atwan, *Secret History*, 52). Mohammed Loay Baizid told me that bin Laden invested only $20 million in Sudan, and that he probably left the country with about fifty thousand dollars. Hassabulla Omer, who held the al-Qaeda file for Sudanese intelligence, places bin Laden's total investment at $30 million and says he left the country with "nothing."

13

Hijira

SUDAN WAS BEHIND HIM. Bin Laden flew across the bright, narrow sea, and soon Jeddah and Mecca passed below, and the al-Sarawat escarpment, and then the great yellow desert, marked only by the roads his father had built across it. He was thirty-eight years old. He had been famous, a hero, and now he was a refugee, forbidden to touch down in his own country. He refueled in the United Arab Emirates, where he was briefly greeted by emissaries of the government who may have given him money. He had been rich all of his life, but he had poured his savings into poor invest-ments, which were, in any case, essentially stolen from him. Now he accepted the charity of those who remembered his name.

He flew over the suckling supertankers docked beside the massive refineries lining the ports of the Persian Gulf, the source of so much wealth and trouble. Beyond Iran lay the blank south-ern desert of Afghanistan, and then Kandahar, surrounded by the ruins of its irrigation canals and pomegranate orchards. Now there were only poppy fields, the last resource worth the risk of cultivating in a country so devastated by twenty years of warfare. The savagery of the Soviets was forgotten in the convulsion of the civil war. Authority had broken down everywhere. The roads were given over to highwaymen who demanded tolls and some-times abducted children when money was insufficient. Tribes were fighting tribes, warlords against warlords; drug gangs and the transport mafia dominated the barren economy. The cities had been pounded so hard they were disaggregated into piles of bricks and stones. Electrical posts, turned to lace after two decades of flying armament and long since stripped of wire, ran along the roadsides as ghostly reminders of a time when Afghanistan had taken its first turn toward modernity. Millions and millions of land mines contaminated the countryside, having disabled 4 percent of the population, according to a UN survey, and rendering much of the arable land useless.

As bin Laden passed over Kabul, the capital was under siege once again, this time by the Taliban. They had arisen in 1994 as a small group of students, most of them orphans who had been raised in the refugee camps and who were outraged by the chaos and depravity of the rule of the mujahideen. The liberators in the war against the Soviets had turned out to be more barbaric rulers than their enemy. Stirred to action by the misery that victory had brought to Afghanistan, the Taliban arose with stunning swiftness. Thanks to the support of Pakistani intelligence, they were transformed from a populist militia into a formidable, highly mobile guerrilla army, on the verge of consolidating their rapid rise to power as they stood on the outskirts of Kabul, raining rockets into the ruins.

In the next valley, at the base of the Hindu Kush Mountains, was Jalalabad. Bin Laden landed at the same airport that he had laid siege to in 1989. He was greeted by three former mujahideen commanders, then he moved into an old lodge above the river that had once served as a Soviet military post. A few weeks later he moved again, to a tumbledown farm five miles south of Jalalabad. It was owned by one of bin Laden's old sponsors, Younis Khalis, an elderly warlord with a taste for teenage brides.

AFGHANISTAN IS A LARGE AND RUGGED COUNTRY, divided from east to west by the Hindu Kush Mountains, its population split into four major ethnic groups and numerous tribes and dialects. It is a difficult country to govern even in peacetime, although peace was such a distant memory that many Afghans had never experienced it. The longing for order was so great that almost any strong, stabilizing power would have been welcomed.

The Taliban rapidly captured nine out of Afghanistan's thirty provinces. President Burhanuddin Rabbani tried to negotiate with them, but they simply demanded his resignation. The wily and experienced commander, Ahmed Shah Massoud, managed to push the young insurgents out of southern Kabul and then roll back their advance in some of the other provinces. After observing the anarchy that came with mujahideen rule and deciding that the Taliban offered the best chance to impose order, Saudi Arabia and Pakistan rebuilt the Taliban forces, providing training, weapons, and vehicles—mainly Datsun four-wheel-drive pickup trucks with heavy machine guns, cannons, anti-aircraft guns, or multiple-barreled rocket launchers mounted in the beds. The Taliban moved swiftly, in swarms, making up in speed and daring what they lacked in organization and discipline. They hired pilots and commanders from the former communist regime as mercenaries. Opposition leaders acknowledged the flow of events and used the opportunity to stuff their pockets with Taliban bribes. Jalalabad, which had fended off the mujahideen for months, suddenly surrendered to four Talibs in a jeep. The Taliban now commanded the gateway to the Khyber Pass. They also found themselves in charge of a famous refugee.

The Taliban had not invited bin Laden to return to Afghanistan and had no obligation to him. They sent a message to the Saudi government asking what they should do with him. They were told to hold on to him and keep him quiet. Thus bin Laden came under the control of a political hermit named Mullah Mohammed Omar, who had only recently declared himself "the ruler of all Muslims."

Mullah Omar had lost his right eye in an artillery shell explosion in the battle of Jalalabad in 1989, which also marred his cheek and forehead. Thin but tall and strongly built, he was well known as a crack marksman who had destroyed many Soviet tanks during the Afghan War. Unlike most of the Afghan mujahideen, he spoke passable Arabic, and he became devoted to the lectures of Sheikh Abdullah Azzam. Piety, modesty, and courage were the main features of his personality. He was little noticed in Azzam's lectures, except for the occasional shy smile buried within his heavy black beard and for his knowledge of the Quran and the hadith; he had studied Islamic jurisprudence in Pakistan.

After the Soviets withdrew from Afghanistan, Omar returned to teach at a madrassa (religious boarding school) in a small village near Kandahar. The fighting, however, did not end, not even when the communist government finally fell to the mujahideen in April 1992. The violence had no limits. Warring tribes and bandits roamed the countryside. Ancient ethnic hatreds combined with mutual calls for revenge in the escalating savagery. A local commander orchestrated the gang rape of several young boys. Such indecencies were common. "Corruption and moral disintegration had gripped the land," Omar later stated. "Killing, looting, and violence had become the norm. Nobody had ever imagined that the situation could get this bad. Nobody thought it could be improved, either."

In this desperate moment, Omar received a vision. The Prophet appeared to him and instructed this simple village mullah to bring peace to his country. With the fearlessness of total religious commitment, Omar borrowed a motorcycle and began visiting students in other madrassas in the province. The students (the word in Pashtu is "taliban") all agreed that something had to be done, but few were willing to leave their studies and join Omar in his risky quest. He eventually gathered fifty-three of the bravest of them. His old commander in the war against the Soviets, Haji Bashar, humbled by Omar's vision of the Prophet, helped by raising money and arms, and personally donated two cars and a truck. Soon, with about two hundred adherents, the Taliban took over the administration of the Maiwand district in Kandahar province. The local commander surrendered, along with 2,500 men, a large supply of weapons, some helicopters and armored vehicles, and six MiG-21 fighter jets. Desperate for order, many Afghans rallied to the Taliban, who advertised themselves as fervent and incorruptible servants of God.

There were three streams that fed the Taliban, which flooded across Afghanistan with such extraordinary rapidity. One was the material support—money and arms—from Saudi Arabia and Pakistan. Some of the Taliban had been students in a vocational

school that Ahmed Badeeb, Prince Turki's chief of staff, had established during the war; so from the beginning there was an intimate connection between Saudi intelligence and the young
insurgents.

The second stream drew from the madrassas across the Pakistan border, such as the one that Ahmed Badeeb had established,
which were crammed full with the sons of Afghan refugees. Such
schools were desperately needed because Pakistan, with one of
the highest illiteracy rates in the world, had failed to create a public school system that would adequately instruct its own children,
much less those of the three million Afghan refugees who had fled
to Pakistan after the Soviet invasion. (There was an equal number
of refugees in Iran.) Typically, the madrassas were funded by
charities from Saudi Arabia and other Gulf countries, which chan-
neled the money through local religious parties. As a result, many
of the indigenous Sufi shrines were closed down and turned into
schools that taught the Wahhabi doctrine. Naturally, the madrassas created a powerful political constituency for the local Wahhabi
parties, since they not only provided free room and board but
actually paid a monthly stipend—a vital source of support for
many of the students' families.

These boys had grown up in an exclusively male world, separated from their families for long periods of time. The traditions
and customs and lore of their country were distant to them. They
were stigmatized as beggars and sissies, and often preyed upon
by men who were isolated from women. Entrenched in their studies, which were rigidly concentrated on the Quran and Sharia and
the glorification of jihad, the talibs imagined a perfect Islamic
society, while lawlessness and barbarity ran rampant all around
them. They lived in the shadow of their fathers and older brothers, who had brought down the mighty superpower, and they
were eager to gain glory for themselves. Whenever the Taliban
army required reinforcements, the madrassas in Peshawar and
the Tribal Areas simply shut down classes and the students went
to war, praising God as the buses ferried them across the border.
Six months after Kandahar surrendered, there were twelve thou-

sand fighters in the Taliban, and twice again that number six months later.

The third stream was opium. Immediately after capturing Kandahar, the Taliban consolidated control of Helmand province, the center of opium cultivation. Under the Taliban, Afghanistan became the largest poppy grower in the world. The smugglers and drug barons depended on the Taliban to keep the roads clear of bandits; in return, they paid a 10 percent tax, which became a principal source of income for the Taliban.

In Kandahar there is a shrine that houses what is said to be the cloak of the Prophet Mohammed. The ancient robe is removed from its silver box only during periods of catastrophe—the last time had been during a cholera epidemic seventy years before. On April 4, 1996, Omar took the Prophet's cloak to a mosque in the center of the city. Having announced on the radio that he would display the relic in public, he climbed on the roof of the mosque and for thirty minutes paraded around with his hands in the sleeves of the cloak, while a delirious crowd cheered his designation as Amir-ul-Momineen, the leader of the faithful. Some people in the crowd fainted; others threw their hats and turbans into the air, hoping that they would brush against the sacred garment.

Of course, it was the dream of Islamists everywhere that their religion would again be unified under the rule of a single righteous individual. Kings and sultans had bid for the role, but none had wrapped himself in the mantle of the Prophet as had this obscure mullah. It was a gesture both preposterous and electrifying. Omar gained the political authority he needed to pursue the war; but more than that, the action symbolically promised that the Taliban, as a moral force, would roll through Afghanistan and then magnify itself throughout the Islamic world.

BIN LADEN'S FAMILIES and some of his followers arrived in Jalalabad to find rudimentary quarters: tents for the wives, with latrines and drainage ditches, set inside a barbed-wire enclosure. When winter arrived, bin Laden secured new housing for the families on a former Soviet collective farm, which he called Najm al-Jihad (star of the holy war). The men bunked nearby in the old ammunition storage cavern that bin Laden had excavated in Tora Bora. He outfitted the main cave with an armory of Kalashnikovs, a theological library, an archive of press clippings, and a couple of mattresses draped across several crates of hand grenades.

He went back into business, setting up a modest trade in honey, but Afghanistan has almost no commercial infrastructure, so there was little he could actually do. The three wives who stayed with him were accustomed to hardship, which bin Laden, naturally, embraced. He no longer slaughtered a lamb every day to serve his guests; now he rarely ate meat, preferring to live on dates, milk, yoghurt, and flatbread. Electricity was available for only three hours a day, and because there was no international telephone service his wives were completely cut off from their families in Syria and Saudi Arabia. Bin Laden had a satellite phone, but he spoke on it sparingly, believing that the Americans were monitoring his calls. He was suspicious of mechanical devices in general, even clocks, which he thought might be used for surveillance.

Mainly, however, he was worried about the Taliban. He had no idea who they were. The anxious tribesmen in the northern region of Afghanistan spread rumors that the Taliban were a huge army of communists. When two of his mujahideen sponsors, Governor Mehmoud and Maulvi Saznoor, were killed in an ambush soon after Jalalabad fell, bin Laden taught his wives how to shoot.

The Taliban knew something about bin Laden, though, and they were just as worried about him as he was about them. "We don't want subversive actions to be launched from here against any other countries," the Taliban's acting information minister declared. "In areas under Taliban control, there are no terrorists." But they had heard about the millions he had poured into Sudan, and they assumed he was still a wealthy Islamic philanthropist. They hoped to use his money and expertise to rebuild their shattered country. Mullah Omar was also mindful of the pledge he had given, no doubt supported by many millions of Saudi riyals, to keep his guest silent and out of trouble.

After Jalalabad fell, the Taliban finally entered Kabul. The victorious young fighters broke into the UN compound where Najibullah, the former president of Afghanistan from its communist era, had taken refuge since the fall of his government four years before. He and his brother were beaten and tortured, castrated, dragged behind a jeep, shot, then hanged from a traffic pole in downtown Kabul. Cigarettes were placed in their mouths and money was stuffed in their pockets. There was little to mourn about a man who had begun his career as a torturer in the secret police, but the immediate disregard for international protocols, the casual savagery, the mutilation of the body—forbidden in Islam—and the absence of any court of justice set the stage for the carnival of religious tyranny that characterized the Taliban era. The Saudis and the Pakistanis, the Taliban's chief backers, quickly recognized the new government. During the entire Taliban reign, only one other country—the United Arab Emirates—recognized their rule as legitimate.

"Women you should not step outside your residence," the new government ordered. Women were a particular target, as might be expected from men who had so little experience of their company. "If women are going outside with fashionable, ornamental, tight and charming clothes to show themselves," the decree continued, "they will be cursed by the Islamic Sharia and should never expect to go to heaven." Work and schooling for women were halted at once, which destroyed the health-care system, the civil service, and effectively eliminated elementary education. Forty percent of the doctors, half of the government workers, and seven out of ten teachers were women. Under the Taliban, many of them would become beggars.

The Taliban also turned their attention to ordinary pleasure. They forbade kite flying and dog racing. Trained pigeons were slaughtered. According to the Taliban penal code, "unclean things" were banned, an all-purpose category that included: "pork, pig, pig oil, anything made from human hair, satellite dishes, cinematography, any equipment that produces the joy of music, pool tables, chess, masks, alcohol, tapes, computers, VCRs, televisions, anything that propagates sex and is full of music, wine, lobster, nail polish, firecrackers, statues, sewing catalogs, pictures, Christmas cards."

The fashion dictators demanded that a man's beard be longer than the grip of his hand. Violators went to jail until they were sufficiently bushy. A man with "Beatle-ly" hair would have his head shaved. Should a woman leave her home without her veil, "her home will be marked and her husband punished," the Taliban penal code decreed. The animals in the zoo—those that had not been stolen in previous administrations—were slain or left to starve. One zealous, perhaps mad, Taliban jumped into a bear's cage and cut off his nose, reputedly because the animal's "beard" was not long enough. Another fighter, intoxicated by events and his own power, leaped into the lion's den and cried out, "I am the lion now!" The lion killed him. Another Taliban soldier threw a grenade into the den, blinding the animal. These two, the noseless bear and the blind lion, together with two wolves, were the only animals that survived the Taliban rule.

"Throw reason to the dogs," read a sign posted on the wall of the office of the religious police, who were trained by the Saudis. "It stinks of corruption." And yet the Afghan people, so exhausted by war, initially embraced the imposition of this costly order.

WHILE BIN LADEN was setting up in Jalalabad, his friend and military chief, Abu Ubaydah, was in East Africa, overseeing the al-Qaeda cell that had been established two years before. The former Egyptian policeman was a revered figure in al-Qaeda. His courage was legendary. He had been with bin Laden during the war against the Soviets, all the way from the battle of the Lion's Den to the siege of Jalalabad. Some said that if Zawahiri had taken over bin Laden's brain, Abu Ubaydah had his heart. He was bin Laden's most trusted emissary, often serving as a mediator between al-Qaeda and al-Jihad. He trained mujahideen in Bosnia, Chechnya, Kashmir, and Tajikistan, drawing valuable recruits to the Qaeda camps. In Kenya, he had taken a new identity and married a local woman, claiming to be in the mining business while he was actually preparing al-Qaeda's first great strike against America.

On May 21, three days after bin Laden left Sudan for Afghanistan, Abu Ubaydah and his Kenyan brother-in-law, Ashif Mohammed Juma, were in a second-class cabin in an overloaded ferry on Lake Victoria, traveling to Tanzania. One of the ballast tanks was empty, and in the early morning the ferry capsized in rough water. Juma managed to get through the door of the cabin into the corridor, but the five other passengers crammed into the tiny compartment were trapped. The door was now above them, and water was gushing in from an open portal. Passengers were screaming, luggage and mattresses were falling on top of them, and they clawed at each other in order to reach the door, their only escape. Juma grabbed Abu Ubaydah's hand and pulled him halfway out of the room, but suddenly the door was ripped from its hinges and al-Qaeda's military chief was pulled back into the cabin by his doomed companions.

THIS WAS THE NADIR of bin Laden's career.

Abu Ubaydah was not his only loss. Others, such as Abu Hajer, chose not to follow bin Laden back to Afghanistan. The Saudi was isolated, stripped of his once great wealth, dependent on the hospitality of an unknown power, and yet he was not broken or even subdued. His life was lived in two spheres, the existential and the sacred. His flight to Jalalabad and the scandal of his current circumstances must have struck him, on one level, as a nearly hopeless exile; but in spiritual terms it recapitulated a critical moment in the Prophet's life when, in 622, ostracized and ridiculed, he was expelled from Mecca and fled to Medina. The *hijira,* or retreat, as the event is called, was such a significant turning point that it begins the Islamic calendar. The *hijira* transformed Mohammed and his demoralized followers. Within a few years, their nascent religion burst out of Medina and spread from Spain to China in a blinding flash of conversion and conquest.

Since childhood, bin Laden had consciously modeled himself on certain features of the Prophet's life, choosing to fast on the days the Prophet fasted, to wear clothes similar to those the Prophet may have worn, even to sit and to eat in the same postures that tradition ascribes to him; and although none of this is unusual for a strict Muslim, bin Laden instinctively referenced the Prophet and his era as the template of his own life and times. Intervening history meant little to him. Naturally, he would turn to the Prophet's example for consolation during his own period of defeat and withdrawal. However, he was also savvy enough to recognize the symbolic power of his own *hijira* and its usefulness as a way of inspiring his followers and beckoning to other Muslims to join his sacred retreat. He brilliantly reframed the disaster that had fallen upon him and his movement by calling up images that were deeply meaningful to many Muslims and practically invisible to those who were unfamiliar with the faith.

Afghanistan was already marked by miracles, the deaths of martyrs, and the defeat of the superpower. Bin Laden now called this country Khorasan, referring to the ancient Muslim empire that once encompassed much of Central Asia. His followers adopted names that harked back to the companions of the Prophet or to famous warriors of early Islam. There is a disputed hadith that states that in the last days the armies of Islam will unfold black banners (like the flag of the Taliban) and come out of Khorasan. Their names will be aliases, and they will carry the names of their cities—in the same manner that al-Qaeda's legion followed. All of these references were in the service of connecting with a former greatness and reminding Muslims of their devastating loss.

The key symbol of bin Laden's *hijira*, however, was the cave. The Prophet first encountered the angel Gabriel, who revealed to him, "You are the Messenger of God," in a cave in Mecca. Again, in Medina, when Mohammed's enemies pursued him, he hid in a cave that was magically concealed by a spiderweb. Islamic art is replete with images of stalactites, which reference both the sanctuary and the encounter with the divine that caves provided the Prophet. For bin Laden, the cave was the last pure place. Only by retreating from society—and from time, history, modernity, corruption, the smothering West—could he presume to speak for the true religion. It was a product of bin Laden's public-relations genius that he chose to exploit the presence of the ammunition caves of Tora Bora as a way of identifying himself with the Prophet in the minds of many Muslims who longed to purify Islamic society and restore the dominion it once enjoyed.

On the existential plane, bin Laden was marginalized, out of play, but inside the chrysalis of myth that he had spun about himself he was becoming a representative of all persecuted and humiliated Muslims. His life and the symbols in which he cloaked himself powerfully embodied the pervasive sense of dispossession that characterized the modern Muslim world. In his own miserable exile, he absorbed the misery of his fellow believers; his loss entitled him to speak for theirs; his vengeance would sanctify their suffering. The remedy he proposed was to declare war on the United States.

"YOU ARE NOT UNAWARE OF THE INJUSTICE, repression, and aggression that have befallen Muslims through the alliance of Jews, Christians, and their agents, so much so that Muslims' blood has become the cheapest blood and their money and wealth are plundered by the enemies," bin Laden said, on August 23, 1996, in his "Declaration of War Against the Americans Occupying the Land of the Two Holy Places." The latest indignity—"one of the worst catastrophes to befall the Muslims since the death of the Prophet"—was the presence of American and coalition troops in Saudi Arabia. The purpose of his treatise was "to talk, work, and discuss ways of rectifying what has befallen the Islamic world in general and The Land of the Two Holy Mosques in particular."

"Everyone is complaining about everything," bin Laden observed, adopting the voice of the Islamic man on the street. "People have been greatly preoccupied with matters of their livelihood. Talk of economic decline, high prices, massive debts, and overcrowded prisons is widespread." As for Saudi Arabia, "everyone agrees that the country is moving toward a deep abyss." Those brave few Saudis who confronted the regime demanding change were disregarded; meanwhile, the war debt had caused the state to impose taxes. "People are wondering: Is ours really the largest oil exporting country? They feel that God is tormenting them because they kept quiet about the regime's injustice."

He then taunted the American secretary of defense, William Perry, by name. "O William, tomorrow you will know which young man is confronting your misguided brethren. . . . Terrorizing you, while you carry weapons in our land, is a legitimate and moral obligation."

He was so far from being able to carry out such threats that one might conclude that the author of this document was utterly mad. Indeed, the man in the cave had entered a separate reality, one that was deeply connected to the mythic chords of Muslim identity and in fact gestured to anyone whose culture was threatened by modernity and impurity and the loss of tradition. By declaring war on the United States from a cave in Afghanistan, bin Laden assumed the role of an uncorrupted, indomitable primitive standing against the awesome power of the secular, scientific, technological Goliath; he was fighting modernity itself.

It did not matter that bin Laden, the construction magnate, had built the cave using heavy machinery and that he had proceeded to outfit it with computers and advanced communications devices. The stance of the primitive was appealingly potent, especially to people who had been let down by modernity; however, the mind that understood such symbolism, and how it could be manipulated, was sophisticated and modern in the extreme.

SOON AFTER BIN LADEN set up his camp in Tora Bora, he agreed to meet a visitor named Khaled Sheikh Mohammed. He had known Mohammed slightly during the anti-Soviet jihad, when Mohammed worked as a secretary for bin Laden's old sponsor, Sayyaf, and also for Abdullah Azzam. Far more significantly, Khaled Sheikh Mohammed was also the uncle of Ramzi Yousef, who had bombed the World Trade Center in 1993. Now Yousef was under arrest and his uncle was on the run.

Except for their hatred of America, Khaled Sheikh Mohammed and Osama bin Laden had almost nothing in common. Mohammed was short and squat; pious but poorly trained in religion; an actor and a cutup; a drinker and a womanizer. Whereas bin Laden was provincial and hated travel, especially in the West, Mohammed was a globe-trotter fluent in several languages, including English, which he perfected while studying mechanical engineering at North Carolina Agricultural and Technical State University, a mostly black school in Greensboro.

In Tora Bora, Mohammed briefed bin Laden about his life since the anti-Soviet jihad. Inspired by Ramzi Yousef's attack on the World Trade Center, Mohammed joined his nephew for a month in the Philippines in 1994. They came up with an extraordinary plan to bomb twelve American jumbo jets over the Pacific. They called it Operation "Bojinka"—a nonsense word that Mohammed had picked up when fighting in Afghanistan. Ramzi Yousef, the master bomb-maker, had perfected a small nitroglycerine device that was undetectable by airport security. He tested it out on a flight from Manila to Tokyo. Yousef got off the flight in Cebu, a city on one of the central islands of the Philippine archipelago. The passenger who took his seat was Haruki Ikegami, a twenty-four-year-old Japanese engineer. Two hours later, the bomb under Ikegami's seat detonated, tearing him apart and nearly bringing the aircraft down. The assault that Yousef and Mohammed were planning would bring international air travel to a complete standstill.

Although bin Laden claims he did not know Yousef personally, he had sent a messenger to Manila to ask Yousef to do him the favor of assassinating President Bill Clinton when he came to Manila in November 1994. Yousef and the others mapped out the president's route and sent to bin Laden diagrams and sketches of possible points of attack; finally, however, Yousef decided that the security was too tight. The men thought instead to kill Pope John Paul II when he came to the city the following month—even going so far as to get priests' cassocks—but that plan, too, came to nothing. The Manila police caught on to them after chemicals in their apartment caught fire, and Yousef fled, leaving behind his computer with all their plans encrypted on the hard drive.

The plans were still in Khaled Sheikh Mohammed's mind, however. He came to bin Laden with a portfolio of schemes for future attacks against America, including one that would require training pilots to crash airplanes into buildings. Bin Laden was noncommittal, although he did formally ask Mohammed to join al-Qaeda and move his family to Afghanistan. Mohammed politely declined. But the seed of September 11 had been planted.

14

Going Operational

ON JUNE 25, 1996, John O'Neill arranged a private retreat for FBI and CIA agents at the bureau's training center in Quantico, Virginia. There were hamburgers and hot dogs, and O'Neill even let the CIA officers on the firing range, since they rarely had the opportunity to shoot. It was a lovely day. O'Neill went out to play a round of golf on the Quantico course. Suddenly everyone's beepers went off.

There had been a catastrophic explosion in Saudi Arabia, at the Khobar Towers military-housing complex in Dhahran. The building served as the barracks for the 4404th Airlift Wing, which was enforcing the no-fly zone in Iraq. Nineteen American soldiers had died and nearly four hundred other people were injured. O'Neill assembled a team of more than a hundred agents, support personnel, and members of various police agencies. The next day they were on an Air Force transport plane to Saudi Arabia. A few weeks later, O'Neill himself joined them, along with the director of the FBI, Louis Freeh.

A slender and sober man, Freeh was temperamentally O'Neill's opposite in many ways. The director prided himself on being a family man, usually leaving the office at six in order to be home with his wife and children. Unlike O'Neill, who was fascinated by gadgetry and always had the latest electronic organizer or mobile phone in his pocket, Freeh was bored by technology. One of his first actions on taking office in 1993 was to jettison the computer on his desk. The bureau was technologically crippled even before Freeh arrived, but by the time he left not even church groups would accept the vintage FBI computers as donations. Like most of his male agents, Freeh inclined toward cheap suits and scuffed shoes, posing quite a contrast to O'Neill, his subordinate, in his Burberry pinstripes and his Bruno Magli loafers.

It was evening when the two men, along with a small executive team, arrived in Dhahran. The disaster site was a vast crater, eighty-five feet wide and thirty-five feet deep, illuminated by lights on high stanchions; nearby lay charred automobiles and upended Humvees. Looming above the debris were the ruins of the housing complex. The bomb was larger by far than the car bomb that had destroyed the Saudi National Guard training center the year before and even more powerful than the explosives that had killed 168 people in Oklahoma City in 1995. O'Neill walked through the rubble, embracing exhausted agents who were sifting sand for evidence and painstakingly bagging personal effects. Body parts still lay in the sand, indicated by circles of red paint. Under a tarp nearby, investigators were gradually reconstructing fragments of the truck that had carried the bomb.

The agents on the ground were demoralized by the obstacles that Saudi investigators put in their path. They were not allowed to interview witnesses or question suspects. They couldn't even leave the bomb site. In the opinion of the agents, the Saudis were obstructing the investigation because they didn't want to expose the existence of internal opposition in the Kingdom. The impression, quickly formed by agents with little experience in the Middle East, was that the Saudi royal family was hanging on to power by their fingernails.

Freeh was initially optimistic that the Saudis would cooperate, but O'Neill became more and more frustrated as the late-night meetings drifted on a sea of pleasantries. As they were flying home after one of their several trips to the Kingdom together, Freeh was upbeat. "Wasn't that a great trip? I think they're really going to help us."

O'Neill replied, "You've got to be kidding. They didn't give us anything. They were just shining sunshine up your ass."

For the remainder of the flight, Freeh refused to speak to him. But, recognizing O'Neill's passion and talents, he sent him back to Saudi Arabia to continue lobbying for cooperation. O'Neill met with Prince Naif and other officials. They listened grudgingly to his pleas. Intelligence agencies across the world are jealous and insular organizations, not inclined to share information, which O'Neill appreciated. He was used to cadging what he could through charm and persistence, but the Saudis were seemingly immune to his wooing. They were far more close-mouthed than any other police organization he had ever worked with. The Americans were infuriated to learn that a few months earlier Saudi authorities had intercepted a car from Lebanon that was stuffed with explosives and headed for Khobar. It was Naif who decided not to inform his U.S. counterparts.

In addition to their ingrained cultural reticence, the Saudis had legal reasons to be cautious in dealing with the Americans. Because the Kingdom is governed by Sharia law, clerical judges have complete discretion to throw out any evidence they don't care to hear, such as material provided by foreign agencies. The Saudis were worried that the involvement of the FBI would taint the case. O'Neill worked out an agreement that allowed the FBI agents to interview suspects through mirrored glass, which gave the bureau access while preserving the appearance of separation that the Saudis insisted upon.

As the evidence began to point to Iranian-backed terrorists as being the most likely perpetrators of the bombing, however, the Saudis became reluctant to pursue the investigation. They worried what the Americans would do if Iran were implicated, which soon became the case. The Saudi's own investigation pointed to a branch of Hezbollah inside the Kingdom. Economic and diplomatic sanctions against Iran appeared unlikely, because the Europeans wouldn't go along. "Maybe you have no options," one of the Saudis told O'Neill. "If it is a military response, what are you going to bomb? Are you going to nuke them? Flatten their military facilities? Destroy their oil refineries? And to achieve what? We are next door to them. You are six thousand miles away."

In the new era of a globalized FBI, O'Neill learned, it was one thing to solve the case, another to gain justice.

O'NEILL LONGED TO GET OUT OF WASHINGTON and "go operational." He wanted to supervise cases again. In January 1997 he became special agent in charge of the National Security Division in New York, the bureau's largest and most prestigious field office. When he arrived, he dumped four boxes of Rolodex cards on the desk of his new secretary, Lorraine di Taranto. Then he handed her a list of everyone he wanted to meet—the mayor, the police commissioner, the deputy police commissioners, the heads of the federal agencies, and religious and ethnic leaders in all five boroughs. Within six months, he had checked off all the people on his list.

By then it seemed as if he had lived in New York his entire life. The city was a great stage upon which O'Neill claimed a title role. He stood with John Cardinal O'Connor, the archbishop of New York, on the steps of St. Patrick's Cathedral during the Saint Patrick's Day parade. He prayed with imams in Brooklyn. Sports figures and movie stars, such as Robert De Niro, consulted him and called him their friend. "John, you've got this town wired," one of his buddies said after a late night when it seemed that everyone had bowed in O'Neill's direction. O'Neill replied, "What's the point of being sheriff if you can't act like one?"

O'Neill was now in charge of counterterrorism and counterintelligence in a city that was full of émigrés, spies, and shady diplomats. The particular squad responsible for the Middle East was called, in the noncommittal bureaucratic vernacular, I-49. Its personnel spent the bulk of their time covering the Sudanese, Egyptians, and Israelis, all of whom were actively recruiting in New York.

Most members of the squad were native New Yorkers who had stayed close to home. They included Louis Napoli, an NYPD detective, who had been assigned to I-49 through the Joint Terrorism Task Force. Napoli still lived in the same house in Brooklyn that he had grown up in. The Anticev brothers, John and Mike, also from Brooklyn, were the children of Croatian immigrants. Richard Karniewicz was a Brooklyn son of Polish immigrants who played polkas on his accordion. Jack Cloonan grew up in Waltham, Massachusetts, and it was not only his accent that set him apart: He was an English and Latin major who joined the bureau in 1972 on the day its director, J. Edgar Hoover, died. Carl Summerlin was a black New York State trooper and former tennis champion. Kevin Cruise was a West Point graduate and former captain in the Eighty-second Airborne. Mary Deborah Doran was the daughter of an FBI agent; she had worked for the Council on Foreign Relations before going to Northern Ireland for graduate work in Irish history. Their supervisor was Tom Lang, a blunt, profane, and quick-tempered Irishman from Queens who had known O'Neill from the days when they both served as tour guides at headquarters. Some members of the squad, like Lang and the Anticev brothers, had been working on terrorism for years. Others, like Debbie Doran, were new to the squad; she had joined the bureau in 1996 and was assigned to New York the month before O'Neill took over. This squad would soon grow much larger, but the nucleus was these seven agents, one state trooper, and a city police detective. The other member of the squad was Dan Coleman, who was assigned to Alec Station and who had been laboring alone on the bin Laden case.

When O'Neill arrived, however, most of the I-49 squad had been diverted to work on the crash of TWA Flight 800, which occurred off the coast of Long Island in July 1996. Dozens of witnesses reported having seen an ascending flare that culminated in a midair explosion. It appeared to have been one of the worst acts of terror in American history, and the bureau mobilized all its impressive resources to solve the crime as quickly as possible. The Khobar Towers bombing and TWA 800 investigations were absorbing all the bureau's available manpower without any resolution in sight.

At the outset, investigators believed that the plane had been bombed or shot down in retaliation by followers of Sheikh Omar Abdul Rahman, who was on trial in New York at the time. But after three months they came to the conclusion that the aircraft had suffered a freakish mechanical failure. The case had become largely a public-relations problem: In the face of vivid eyewitness testimony, the bureau simply didn't know how to explain its conclusions to a skeptical public. Demoralized agents continued to comb through the wreckage of the plane, which was being put back together piece by piece in a hangar on Long Island.

O'Neill needed his squad back. Together with the Defense Department, O'Neill determined the height of TWA 800 and its distance from shore at the time of the explosion. He demonstrated that it was out of range of a Stinger missile—the most likely explanation at the time of the apparent vapor trail that witnesses noted. O'Neill proposed that the flare could have been caused by the ignition of leaking fuel from the aircraft, and he persuaded the CIA to do a video simulation of this scenario, which proved to be strikingly similar to the witnesses' accounts. Now he could get to work on bin Laden.

ALEC STATION WAS NAMED after the adopted Korean son of O'Neill's temperamental CIA counterpart, Michael Scheuer. For the first time, the bureau and the agency were working in tandem on a single project, an unprecedented but awkward partnership. As far as Scheuer was concerned, the FBI simply wanted to place a spy inside Alec Station in order to steal as much information as possible. Yet Scheuer grudgingly came to respect Dan Coleman, the first bureau man to be posted inside his domain. Coleman was overweight and disheveled, with a brushy moustache and hair that refused to stay combed. He was as cantankerous as a porcupine (his FBI colleagues called him "Grumpy Santa" behind his back), but he had none of the macho FBI swagger that Scheuer so despised. It would have been easy to dismiss Coleman as another nebbishy bureaucrat, except for his intelligence and decency, the very qualities Scheuer most admired. But there was a fundamental institutional conflict that friendship could not bridge: Coleman's mission, as an FBI agent, was to gather evidence with the eventual goal of convicting bin Laden of a crime. Scheuer, the CIA officer, had determined early on that the best strategy for dealing with bin Laden was simply to kill him.

Although Coleman dutifully reported to his superiors at the FBI, the only person genuinely interested in what he was learning was O'Neill, whom he first met at one of Dick Clarke's briefings in the White House. O'Neill was fascinated by the Saudi dissident at a time when it was rare to meet anyone, even in the bureau, who knew who Osama bin Laden was. Then, a couple of months before O'Neill arrived in New York, Coleman had interrogated Jamal al-Fadl, the al-Qaeda defector, who revealed the existence of the terror organization and its global ambitions. In the several weeks he had spent with Fadl in a safe house in Germany, learning about the structure of the group and the personalities of its leaders, Coleman had come to the conclusion that America faced a profound new threat; and yet, his reports met with little response outside a small circle of prosecutors and a few people in the agency and the bureau who took an interest—mainly Scheuer and O'Neill.

They were the two men most responsible for putting a stop to bin Laden and al-Qaeda, and yet they disliked each other intensely—an emotion that reflected the ingrained antagonism of the organizations they represented. From the start, the response of American intelligence to the challenge presented by al-Qaeda was hampered by the dismal personal relationships and institutional warfare that these men exemplified. Coleman was caught between these two bullheaded, tempestuous, talented individuals, who constantly battled each other over a subject—bin Laden—that neither of their organizations really cared about.

In his cubicle in Alec Station, Dan Coleman continued to pursue leads that had been turned up from the Fadl interviews. He examined telephone transcripts from the wiretapped phones that were tied to bin Laden's businesses in Khartoum. One frequently called number belonged to bin Laden's former secretary, Wadih el-Hage, in Nairobi, Kenya. Most of Hage's conversations had been translated from Arabic, but others were in English, especially when he was talking to his American wife. He often made awkward attempts at speaking in code, which his wife obstinately refused to understand.

"Send ten green papers, okay?" Hage said in one exchange.

"Ten red papers?" she asked.

"Green."

"You mean money," she concluded.

"Thank you very much," he responded sarcastically.

Coleman took an interest in Hage, who seemed, despite his clumsy tradecraft, to be an attentive father and a caring husband. Whenever he was away, he would call his children and caution his wife about letting them watch too much television. He was ostensibly running a charity called Help Africa People, while making a living as a gem dealer.

The CIA thought Hage might be recruited as an agent. As Coleman studied the transcripts, he decided Hage was unlikely to turn, but he agreed to go to Kenya, thinking that at least he might find some evidence to substantiate the existence of this organization, al-Qaeda, that Fadl had described.

In August 1997, Coleman and two CIA officers appeared at Hage's home in Nairobi with a search warrant and a nervous Kenyan police officer carrying an AK-47. The house sat behind a high cinder-block wall covered with broken glass, guarded by a scrawny German shepherd on a rope. Hage's American wife, April Brightsky Ray, and her six children were there, along with April's mother, Marion Brown. Both women, Islamic converts, were wearing hijabs.

It was odd to see them in person after having studied them from such a distance. Coleman put the women in the same category as mob wives, knowledgeable in some general way that unlawful actions were going on, but not legally complicit. April was a heavy woman with a pleasant, round face. She said her husband was out of the country on business (actually, he was in Afghanistan talking to bin Laden), but he would be back that evening. Coleman showed her his warrant to search for what he said were stolen documents.

The place was filthy and swarming with flies. One of the children had a high fever. While the agency people talked to April in another room, Marion Brown closely watched Coleman going through their drawers and closets.

"Would you like some coffee?" Brown asked.

Coleman took a look at the kitchen and declined.

"That's good, because I might be trying to poison you," she said.

There were papers and notebooks stacked everywhere, gas receipts that were eight years old, and business cards for bankers, lawyers, travel agents, and exterminators. On the top shelf of the bedroom closet, Coleman found an Apple PowerBook computer.

Later that day Wadih el-Hage returned. A slender, bearded man with a withered right arm, Hage had been born in Lebanon but had gained American citizenship through his wife. He was a convert to Islam from Catholicism, and he had his own ideas about recruitment: He arrived at the meeting with the agents carrying religious tracts and spent the evening trying to get Coleman and the CIA officers to accept Islam.

That night in Nairobi, however, one of the CIA men was able to retrieve several deleted documents on the PowerBook's hard drive that substantiated many of the allegations that Jamal al-Fadl had made about the existence of al-Qaeda and its terrorist goals. The criminal case against bin Laden remained unfocused, however.

Coleman and the agency men went through the documents, piecing together Hage's travels. He had bought some guns for bin Laden in Eastern Europe and seemed to be making frequent trips to Tanzania. Al-Qaeda was up to something, but it was unclear what that was. In any case, it was certainly a low-end operation, and the exposure of the safe house in Nairobi had no doubt put an end to it.

15

Bread and Water

MULLAH OMAR SENT a delegation to Tora Bora to greet bin Laden and learn more about him. Bin Laden's declaration of war and the subsequent international media storm had shocked and divided the Taliban. Some of them pointed out that they had not invited bin Laden to Afghanistan in the first place and were not obliged to protect a man who was endangering their relations with other countries. The Taliban had no quarrel at the time with the United States, which was nominally encouraging their stabilizing influence on the country. Moreover, bin Laden's attacks on the Saudi royal family were a direct violation of a pledge Mullah Omar had made to Prince Turki to keep his guest under control.

On the other hand, the Taliban were hopeful that bin Laden could help rebuild Afghanistan's ravaged infrastructure and provide jobs to revivify the dead economy. They flattered him, saying that they considered themselves like the supporters of the Prophet when he took refuge in Medina. They emphasized that so long as he refrained from attacking their sponsor, Saudi Arabia, or speaking to the press, he would be welcome to remain under their protection. In return, bin Laden endorsed their rule unconditionally, although he immediately broke their trust.

In March 1997, a television crew for CNN was driven into the frigid mountains above Jalalabad to a blanket-lined mud hut to meet with Osama bin Laden. Since arriving in Afghanistan, the exiled Saudi had already spoken with reporters from the London-based newspapers the *Independent* and *Al-Quds al-Arabi*, but this was the first television interview he had ever granted. Peter Bergen, the producer, observed that bin Laden seemed to be ill. He walked into the room using a cane and coughed softly throughout the interview.

It is possible that, until now, bin Laden had not killed an American or anyone else except on the field of battle. The actions in Aden, Somalia, Riyadh, and Dhahran may have been inspired by his words, but it has never been demonstrated that he commanded the terrorists who carried them out. Although Ramzi Yousef had trained in an al-Qaeda camp, bin Laden was not connected to the 1993 World Trade Center bombing. Bin Laden told the London-based Palestinian editor Abdel Bari Atwan that al-Qaeda was responsible for the ambush of American forces in Mogadishu in 1993, the National Guard Training Center bombing in Riyadh in 1995, and the Khobar Towers bombing in 1996, but there is no evidence to substantiate these claims. He was certainly surrounded by men, like Zawahiri, who had plenty of blood on their hands, and he supported their actions in Egypt. He was, as the CIA characterized him at the time, a terrorist financier, albeit a financier without much money. Declaring war on America, however, proved to be a dazzling advertisement for himself and his cause—and irresistible for a man whose fortunes had been so badly trampled upon. Of course, his Taliban hosts forbade such publicity, but once bin Laden had gotten hold of the world's attention, he would allow nothing to pull it out of his grasp.

Peter Arnett, the CNN reporter, began by asking bin Laden to state his criticism of the Saudi royal family. Bin Laden said that they were subservient to the United States, "and this, based on the ruling of Sharia, casts the regime outside the religious community." In other words, he was declaring *takfir* against the royal family, saying that they were no longer to be considered Muslims and therefore could be killed.

Arnett then asked, what kind of society he would create if the Islamic movement were to take over Saudi Arabia. Bin Laden's exact response was this: "We are confident, with the permission of God, praise and glory be to Him, that Muslims will be victorious in the Arabian Peninsula and that God's religion, praise and glory be to Him, will prevail in this peninsula. It is a great pride and a big hope that the revelation unto Mohammed, peace be upon him, will be resorted to for ruling. When we used to follow Mohammed's revelation, peace be upon him, we were in great happiness and in great dignity, to God belongs the credit and praise."

What is notable about this response, filled as usual with ritual-istic locutions, is the complete absence of any real political plan, beyond imposing Sharia, which of course was already in effect in Saudi Arabia. The happiness and dignity that bin Laden invoked lay on the other side of history from the concepts of nationhood and the state. The radical Islamist movement has never had a clear idea of governing, or even much interest in it, as the Taliban would conclusively demonstrate. Purification was the goal; and whenever purity is paramount, terror is close at hand.

Bin Laden cited American support for Israel as the first cause of his declaration of war, followed by the presence of American troops in Arabia. He added that American civilians must also leave the Islamic holy land because he could not guarantee their safety.

In the most revealing exchange, Arnett asked whether, if the United States complied with bin Laden's demands to leave Arabia, he would call off his jihad. "The reaction came as a result of the aggressive U.S. policy toward the entire Muslim world, not just the Arabian Peninsula," bin Laden said. Therefore, the United States has to withdraw from any kind of intervention against Muslims "in the whole world." Bin Laden was already speaking as the representative of the Islamic nation, a caliph-in-waiting. "The U.S. today has set a double standard, calling whoever goes against its injustice a terrorist," he complained. "It wants to occupy our countries, steal our resources, impose on us agents to rule us . . . and wants us to agree to all these. If we refuse to do so, it will say, 'You are terrorists.' "

THIS TIME MULLAH OMAR sent a helicopter to Jalalabad and summoned bin Laden to Kandahar. It wasn't clear whether bin

Laden would prove to be an ally or a rival. In either case, Omar couldn't afford to leave him in Jalalabad, on the opposite side of the country, in an area that the Taliban only marginally controlled. The talkative Saudi obviously had to be restrained or expelled.

The two men met at the Kandahar airport. Omar told bin Laden that the Taliban intelligence service claimed to have uncovered a plot by some tribal mercenaries to kidnap him; whether or not the story was true, it provided the excuse for Mullah Omar to order bin Laden to evacuate his people from Jalalabad and relocate to Kandahar, where the Taliban could keep an eye on him. Omar personally extended his protection to bin Laden, but he said that the interviews must come to a stop. Bin Laden said he had already decided to freeze his media campaign.

Three days later, bin Laden flew all of his family members and supporters to Kandahar, and he followed by car. Once again his entire movement had been uprooted; once again discouraged followers drifted away. Omar gave bin Laden and al-Qaeda the choice of occupying a housing complex built for the workers of the electric company, which had all the necessary utilities, or an abandoned agricultural compound called Tarnak Farms, which had none, not even running water. Bin Laden chose the dilapidated farm. "We want a simple life," he said.

Behind the ten-foot walls of the compound were about eighty mud-brick or concrete structures, including dormitories, a small mosque, storage facilities, and a crumbling six-story office building. Bin Laden's three wives were all crowded into a walled compound where they lived, according to one of bin Laden's bodyguards, "in perfect harmony." Outside the walls, the Taliban stationed two T-55 Soviet tanks.

As always, bin Laden drew strength from privation and seemed oblivious to the toll such circumstances took on others. When a Yemeni jihadi, Abu Jandal, went to his chief complaining that there was nothing for the men to eat, bin Laden replied, "My son Jandal, we have not yet reached a condition like that of the Prophet's companions, who placed stones against their middles and tightened them around their waists. The Messenger of Allah used two stones!"

"Those men were strong in faith and God wished to test them," Abu Jandal protested. "We, on the other hand, have sinned, and God would not test us."

Bin Laden laughed.

Meals were often little more than stale bread and well water. Bin Laden would dip the hard bread in the water and say, "May God be praised. We are eating, but there are millions of others who wish that they could have something like this to eat." There was little money to buy provisions. One of the Arabs came to bin Laden asking for funds for an emergency trip abroad; bin Laden went into the house, collected all the cash he could find, and emerged with about $100. Realizing that bin Laden was emptying the treasury, Abu Jandal complained, "Why did you not leave a part of that money for us? Those who are staying here are more deserving than those who are leaving." Bin Laden replied, "Do not worry. Our livelihood will come to us." But for the next five days, there was nothing to eat in the camp except the green pomegranates that grew around bin Laden's house. "We ate raw pomegranates with bread, three times a day," Abu Jandal recalled.

AFTER ZAWAHIRI LEFT SUDAN IN 1996, he became a phantom. Egyptian intelligence agents tracked him to Switzerland and Sarajevo. He allegedly sought asylum in Bulgaria, but an Egyptian newspaper also reported that he was living luxuriously in a Swiss villa near the French border and that he had $30 million in a secret account. At the same time, Zawahiri nominally edited the al-Jihad newspaper, *Al-Mujahideen,* which had its office in Copenhagen. Neither Swiss nor Danish intelligence knows whether Zawahiri was ever actually in either country during this time. A fake passport he was using shows that he traveled to Malaysia, Taiwan, Singapore, and Hong Kong. He was reported to have been in Holland talking about establishing a satellite television channel. He said he was backed by wealthy Arabs who wanted to provide a fundamentalist alternative to the al-Jazeera network recently launched in Qatar. Zawahiri's plan was to broadcast ten hours a day to Europe and the Middle East, using only male presenters, but he never pursued it.

Zawahiri also traveled to Chechnya, where he hoped to establish a new home base for al-Jihad. "Conditions there were excellent," he wrote in a memo to his colleagues. The Russians had begun to withdraw from Chechnya earlier that year after achieving a cease-fire with the rebellious, largely Muslim region. To the Islamists, Chechnya offered an opportunity to create an Islamic republic in the Caucasus from which they could wage jihad throughout Central Asia. "If the Chechens and other Caucasian mujahideen reach the shores of the oil-rich Caspian Sea, the only thing that will separate them from Afghanistan will be the neutral state of Turkmenistan," Zawahiri observed in his memoir. "This will form a mujahid Islamic belt to the south of Russia that will be connected in the east to Pakistan, which is brimming with mujahideen movements in Kashmir." Thus the caliphate would begin to re-create itself. The world he was making seemed very much at hand.

At four in the morning on December 1, 1996, Zawahiri crossed into Russia in a minivan with two of his closest assistants—Mahmoud Hisham al-Hennawi and Ahmed Salama Mabruk, who was head of the al-Jihad cell in Azerbaijan. Traveling without visas, they were detained at a roadblock and taken to the Federal Security Service, which charged them with entering the country illegally. Zawahiri carried four passports, each from a different country and with a different name. The Russians were never able to establish his real identity. They found $6,400 in cash; some other forged documents, including graduation certificates for "Mr. Amin" from the medical school of Cairo University; a number of medical textbooks; and a laptop, fax, and satellite phone. At the trial, Zawahiri posed as a Sudanese merchant. He claimed he was unaware that he had crossed the border illegally and maintained that he had come to Russia "to find out the price for leather, medicine, and other goods." The judge sentenced Zawahiri and his companions to six months in jail. They had nearly completed the term by the time of the trial, and a few weeks later they were taken to the border of Azerbaijan and sent on their way. "God blinded them to our identities," Zawahiri boasted in an account of his trip to his disgruntled supporters, who had wondered where he was.

This fiasco had a profound consequence. With even more defectors from his membership and no real sources of income, Zawahiri had no choice but to join bin Laden in Kandahar. Each man saw an advantage in linking forces. Al-Qaeda and al-Jihad were both very much reduced from their salad days in Sudan. However, the Pakistani intelligence service had persuaded the Taliban to return the al-Qaeda camps in Khost and elsewhere to bin Laden's control in order to train militants to fight in Kashmir. With ISI subsidizing the cost, the training camps had become an important source of revenue. Moreover, bin Laden was still able to call upon a few of his donors from the days of the Soviet jihad. So at least there was a modest income, enough for bin Laden to be able to purchase some expensive vehicles for Mullah Omar and his top commanders, which made him more welcome. Despite the still dire financial circumstances, Zawahiri believed that his fortunes were better served with bin Laden than without him.

MANY OF THE EGYPTIANS REGROUPED in Afghanistan, including Abu Hafs, who was appointed the al-Qaeda military chief after Abu Ubaydah's drowning. Al-Qaeda was able to provide only a hundred-dollar-per-month stipend, half of what it had paid in Sudan. The leaders of the Islamic Group came, and some other Islamists from Pakistan and Bangladesh. At first they gathered in Jalalabad in the same compound with the al-Qaeda families—about 250 people altogether—and most of them followed bin Laden when he moved to Kandahar. They were dismayed by the squalor, the awful food, the noxious water, and especially the lack of facilities. Hepatitis and malaria were epidemic. "This place is worse than a tomb," one of the Egyptians wrote home. Eventually their leader, Zawahiri, joined them.

Since there was no more schooling in Afghanistan, the children spent a lot of time with each other. Zaynab Ahmed Khadr, a

Canadian citizen and the strong-willed daughter of one of Zawahiri's prominent supporters, was upset when her family left Peshawar, where they had lived comfortably for fifteen of her eighteen years. Afghanistan was just across the steep ridge of mountains that blocked the sunset, and yet it seemed anchored in another century. Although she already covered herself completely, even wearing gloves and a *niqab* over her face, she detested the burka, which Afghan women were forced to wear. Her parents promised that she would be happy in this country, where the true Islam was being practiced, and that she would soon find new friends to replace the schoolmates she'd grown up with. Zaynab moodily declared that she didn't want to make any friends.

Two days later, her mother said they were going to meet the bin Ladens. "I don't want to meet *anybody!*" she said defiantly.

"If you don't behave yourself, you'll never dream of going to Peshawar again," her father said impatiently.

As it turned out, bin Laden's daughters became some of Zaynab's closest friends. Fatima, the oldest, who was fourteen in 1997, was the daughter of Umm Abdullah, and Khadija, thirteen, was the daughter of Umm Khaled. (Fatima was the name of one of the Prophet's daughters, and Khadija the name of his first wife.) The age difference between Zaynab and the bin Laden girls was something she simply accepted, since they were living in such a small community.

Bin Laden's three wives and their children lived in separate houses inside their compound. All the children of al-Qaeda were dressed in rags, and the effort to keep even minimal levels of cleanliness often came to naught. Zaynab observed that each of the bin Laden houses was clean and distinctly different. Umm Abdullah was poorly educated but fun and good-hearted, and she loved to decorate. Whereas the houses of the other wives were neat and well scrubbed, hers was also beautiful. There were flowers and posters, and coloring books for the younger children. Her daughter Fatima had to do a lot of cleaning, Zaynab noticed, because the mother "was not raised to work."

Fatima was fun but a little slow. She confided to Zaynab that she would never marry any of the men around her father, because "he'd be wanted everywhere in the world."

"His crime would be marrying you, Fatima," Zaynab said.

"Oh, right."

Zaynab was not joking. In the world the girls lived in, marriage was a union of families, not just individuals. It seemed to Zaynab that Fatima had forgotten who she was. (Of course, Fatima had no say about whom she would marry; her eventual husband—one of bin Laden's followers—would be killed four years later in the evacuation of Kandahar.)

Life was very different in Umm Khaled's house—quieter and more organized. Unlike Umm Abdullah, Umm Khaled made an attempt to educate her three daughters and one son. A private school for the Arab boys started up in the compound, but the girls studied at home. Umm Khaled, who had a doctorate in the subject, helped Zaynab study Arabic grammar, and she often pitched in with the girls to make dinner. Bin Laden taught his daughters math and science, spending time with them every day. Sometimes he would give them quizzes to make sure they were keeping up.

Umm Khaled's oldest daughter, Khadija, liked to read history and biography. Although in Zaynab's opinion none of the children were well educated, she thought that Khadija was "very, very bright."

Umm Hamza had only one child—a son—but in Zaynab's opinion, compared to the other wives "Umm Hamza was the greatest." She was also the oldest, and seven years older than her husband. Her eyesight was weak and her constitution frail. She suffered frequent miscarriages. As a Saudi woman from a wealthy and distinguished family, she exuded a regal quality, but she was deeply committed to the cause. When bin Laden had proposed to her, Umm Hamza's family was deeply offended because she would be his second wife, but she consented because she wanted to marry a true mujahid. Umm Hamza was very popular in the al-Qaeda community. Other women felt that they could go to her, and she would talk to them as if their problems were important to her. "We knew things might collapse around us, and we'd get depressed," said Zaynab. "She'd keep everybody going."

Bin Laden also depended on her. Although he tried to treat his wives equally, as the Quran commands, everyone knew that Umm Hamza was his favorite. She was not beautiful, but she was sensible and devoted. Her house was always the neatest. There was a bed in the house and a box that contained all her clothes. She would have a *shalwar kameez* (the typical Afghan gown) on the back of the door clean and ready for bin Laden. In the bathroom there was a small shelf with a bottle of perfume for her and one for her husband.

Umm Abdullah was extremely jealous of their relationship. Although she was first in the rank of wives, and the mother of eleven of bin Laden's children, she was also the youngest and least educated. Her beauty was her only advantage, and she worked hard to keep herself attractive. Whenever other women traveled, especially to Western countries, Umm Abdullah gave them a shopping list of brand-name cosmetics and lingerie, preferring American products that no one else would consider buying. Bin Laden's wives all lived within a small inner court in the larger compound, and Umm Abdullah would put on a jogging suit and run around the perimeter to keep in shape. "She would always be fighting with Osama," her friend Maha Elsamneh recalled. "I would tell her this man could be taken away from you in the blink of an eye. You should enjoy him while he is with you. Don't make him so miserable every time he's around."

The girls sometimes played childish pranks on each other. On one occasion, when Fatima didn't want Zaynab to go home, she cajoled her younger sister Iman into hiding Zaynab's shoes and her head covering until the curfew sounded, so she was stuck there all night.

Bin Laden's children did not see him as being nearly as pious and intransigent as the rest of the community did. When Fatima wanted to borrow several cassette tapes, Zaynab told her, "I'll give them to you on one condition. Your dad shouldn't hear them, because some men are very strict."

"My dad is not going to destroy them," Fatima protested. "He's not really that hard. He just acts like that in front of the men."

"He actually listens to songs?" Zaynab asked, amazed.

"Oh, yeah, he doesn't mind."

Reflecting his love of horses, bin Laden kept a library of books on the subject in Umm Khaled's house, and even tolerated coloring books and calendars with pictures of horses on them, although no one else in the community allowed pictures on the walls. Zaynab concluded, "The Sheikh was pretty broad-minded."

The older bin Laden boys were usually with their father nearby in Tora Bora. Among the teenagers, there was a strange, unstable mix of boredom and mortal danger. Unlike the girls, the boys had the opportunity to go to school, but they did little other than memorize the Quran all day. Bin Laden let his younger sons play Nintendo because there was not much else to entertain them. The boys were quite wild and inclined to reckless behavior to escape the monotony. One of Zaynab's younger brothers, Abdul Rahman, became friends with bin Laden's son by the same name. They were the only two boys in the compound whose fathers could afford a horse for them. Sometimes, instead of riding, they would goad their animals into fighting each other. Abdul Rahman bin Laden's horse was a spirited Arabian, but when Abdul Rahman Khadr brought a stronger horse that nearly killed the Arabian, the bin Laden boy chambered a bullet in his gun and pointed it at Khadr, saying he would shoot him if he didn't pull his horse off. Murder and mayhem were always brewing.

In the afternoons, the boys often played volleyball, and Osama would sometimes join in the game. He was apparently in excellent health. Once, he bought a horse from the Taliban, who said they had captured it from Ahmed Shah Massoud. It was a large golden stallion with three white stockings. Nobody could ride it until bin Laden jumped on its back and galloped off. Twenty-five minutes later, he rode back into the compound with the horse completely under his control.

The men who were so feared and despised in the rest of the world did not seem so terrifying in their own homes, where they roughhoused with the children and helped with their homework. Zaynab remembered one occasion when her family was at the Zawahiris' house in Kandahar and the father came in carrying his machine gun. As he was going up the stairs, Zaynab's ten-year-old brother grabbed Zawahiri's legs and begged him to give it to him. "Abdul Kareem, just wait until we go to the room!" said Zawahiri. The boy wouldn't let go; he kept begging and grabbing for the weapon. Zawahiri finally relented and let the boy examine his weapon. This struck Zaynab and the others as a tender moment. "And this is the man, they make him seem like a monster!" she exclaimed.

The four Zawahiri daughters were bright, outspoken, and beautiful, particularly Nabila. When she turned twelve, she became a subject of intense interest among the bride-shopping mothers in the community. Mohammed, the Zawahiris' only son, was also very attractive, the pet of his older sisters. As he got older, however, he was spending more time with the men and with his classmates. It was a rough environment for such a delicate, well-mannered boy, and he was constantly teased and bullied. He preferred to stay at home and help his mother.

The Zawahari girls would often get together for games or exercise. Azza, their mother, liked to have small parties, although there was little to offer her guests—sometimes no more than noodles and tomatoes. When Zaynab visited the Zawahiris for the engagement of their second daughter, Umayma, the girls talked and talked through breakfast, lunch, and dinner. Late at night, they were still singing, making so much noise that they couldn't hear Dr. Ayman knocking on the door asking them to keep it down. "I thought about how this guy scares the whole world but he doesn't even scream at us. We see them as nice and gentle."

Despite her modest manner, Zawahiri's wife insisted on retaining a certain elegance. Azza sewed her own clothes, preferring classical styles. She obtained some patterns from Iran, and she taught herself enough Persian to understand the instructions. She also sewed nightgowns to raise money, usually donating a portion of her income to various needful projects. She and the girls made floral strands out of candy wrappers and strung them on the wall, and arranged stones in a pleasing design in front of their humble mud cottage.

In 1997 Azza had a surprise: She was pregnant again, almost a decade after the birth of her last child. The baby was born in the winter, severely underweight. Dr. Ayman realized at once that his fifth daughter suffered from Down syndrome. Azza, already pressed by the responsibility of taking care of a large family in extraordinary circumstances, accepted this new burden as well. They named the baby Aisha. Everyone loved her, but Azza was the only one who could attend to all her needs.

Looking back at her friendships with the bin Laden and the Zawahiri children, Zaynab observed that the families "had their ups and downs, but they were pretty much normal kids. They had pretty much a normal childhood."

IN JULY 1997, two months after Zawahiri returned to Afghanistan, he was infuriated by a development in Egypt that threatened to undermine his entire movement. The Islamist lawyer Montassir al-Zayyat had brokered a deal between the Islamic Group and the Egyptian government. The nonviolence initiative, as it was called, had originated in the same prisons where Zayyat and Zawahiri had been incarcerated together sixteen years before. With twenty thousand Islamists in Egyptian custody, and thousands of others who had been cut down by the security forces, the fundamentalist movement had been paralyzed, and it was clear to the leaders of the Islamic Group that unless they formally renounced violence they would never see daylight.

After the initiative was declared, Sheikh Omar Abdul Rahman added his imprimatur from his prison cell in the United States. While denying that a deal had been struck, the government released two thousand members of the Islamic Group within the following year. Many senior members of Zawahiri's own al-Jihad joined the movement to reconcile with the regime.

At first, Zawahiri was alone in his dissent. "The political translation of this initiative is surrender," he raged. "In which battle is a fighter forced to end his fighting and incitement, accept captivity, and turn in his men and weapons—in exchange for nothing?" The barrage of letters over this matter between Zawahiri and other Islamists to the editor of an Arabic paper in London came to be called the War of the Faxes. Zawahiri said he understood the suffering of the imprisoned leaders, but "if we are going to stop now, why did we start in the first place?"

Zawahiri's stance divided the Egyptian Islamists between those still in the country, who wanted peace, and those outside Egypt, who opposed reconciliation. Zawahiri enlisted Mustafa Hamza, the new emir of the rival Islamic Group, and its military leader, Rifai Ahmed Taha, both of whom were in Afghanistan, to join him. (As for the blind sheikh's participation in the initiative, he may have thought of it as a bargaining chip with the Americans, who he hoped would set him free. When it later became clear that would not happen, he retracted his support.) The Egyptian exiles decided to justify the continuing use of violence through a single transformative blow.

The attack may have been intended for a performance of *Aida*, Verdi's opera of ancient Egypt, which was staged in October 1997 in front of Queen Hatshepsut's temple on the west bank of the Nile near Luxor. The splendid ruin is one of the great artifacts of the New Kingdom. Suzanne Mubarak, the president's wife, hosted the opening-night gala.

The Islamic Group's strategy was to attack tourism, the life force of the Egyptian economy and the main source of foreign exchange, in order to provoke the government into repressive, unpopular responses. Al-Jihad had always disdained this approach as counterproductive. But with so many VIPs and government officials in attendance, including the president himself, the performance also presented the opportunity to accomplish al-Jihad's goal of decapitating the government. The presence of three thousand security officers initially deterred this attack, however.

On November 17, 1997, the glorious ruin looked out on the amber sand of the southern desert as it had for thirty-five centuries—long before Jesus or Mohammed or even Abraham, the father of the great monotheistic religions. The summer heat had ebbed, marking the beginning of the high season, and hundreds of tourists were strolling through the grounds, some in groups with Egyptian guides, others snapping photos and shopping in the kiosks.

Six young men dressed in black police uniforms and carrying vinyl bags entered the temple precinct shortly before nine in the morning. One of the men shot a guard, and then they all put on red headbands identifying themselves as members of the Islamic Group. Two of the attackers remained at the gate to await the shoot-out with the police, who never arrived. The other men criss-crossed the terraced temple grounds, mowing down tourists by shooting their legs, then methodically finishing them off with close shots to the head. They paused to mutilate some of the bodies with butcher knives. One elderly Japanese man was eviscerated. A pamphlet was later found stuffed in his body that said, "No to tourists in Egypt." It was signed "Omar Abdul Rahman's Squadron of Havoc and Destruction—the Gama'a al-Islamiyya, the Islamic Group."

Caught inside the temple, cowering behind the limestone colonnades, the tourists tried to hide, but there was no escape. It was a perfect trap. The screams of the victims were echoed by cries of "Allahu akhbar!" as the attackers reloaded. The killing went on for forty-five minutes, until the floors streamed with blood. The dead included a five-year-old British child and four Japanese couples on their honeymoons. The ornamented walls were splattered with brains and bits of hair.

When the job was done, the attackers hijacked a bus, looking for more tourists to kill, but at last they ran into a police check-point. In the shoot-out that followed, one of the attackers was wounded. His companions killed him, then fled into the hills, chased by tour guides and villagers on scooters and donkeys, who had little more to fight with than shovels and stones.

The attackers' bodies were later found in a cave, arranged in a circle. The Egyptian press speculated that they had been murdered by the outraged village posse, but they apparently killed themselves in a ritualistic suicide. One of the men had a note in his pocket, apologizing for not carrying out the operation sooner.

Fifty-eight tourists and four Egyptians had died, not counting the attackers. It was the worst act of terror in modern Egyptian history. The majority of the victims—thirty-five of them—were Swiss; others came from Japan, Germany, the United Kingdom, France,

Bulgaria, and Colombia. Seventeen other tourists and nine Egyptians were wounded. One Swiss woman had seen her father's head cut off in front of her eyes.

The following day, the Islamic Group claimed credit for the attack. Rifai Taha said that the attackers were supposed to take hostages in order to free the imprisoned Islamist leaders, but the systematic slaughter put the lie to that claim. The death of the killers showed the influence of Zawahiri; until this point, the Islamic Group had never engaged in suicide operations. The Swiss federal police later determined that bin Laden had financed the operation.

Egypt was in shock. Revolted and ashamed, the population decisively turned against the Islamists, who suddenly began issuing retractions and pointing fingers in the usual directions. From prison, the blind sheikh blamed the Israelis, saying that Mossad had carried out the massacre. Zawahiri blamed the Egyptian police, who he said had done the actual killing, but he also held the victims responsible for coming to the country. "The people of Egypt consider the presence of these foreign tourists to be aggression against Muslims and Egypt," he said. "The young men are saying that this is our country and not a place for frolicking and enjoyment, especially for you."

Luxor proved to be the turning point in the counterterrorist campaign in Egypt. Whatever the strategists in Afghanistan had thought would come of their one great blow, the consequences had landed on them, not on their adversaries. Their support evaporated, and without the consent of the population, there was nowhere for them to hide. In the five years before Luxor, Islamist terror groups in Egypt had killed more than 1,200 people, many of them foreigners. After Luxor, the attacks by the Islamists simply stopped. "We thought we'd never hear from them again," one Cairo human-rights worker observed.

PERHAPS, IN THEIR ISOLATION IN KANDAHAR, the jihadi leaders, especially the Egyptians, could not appreciate the nature of their defeat. They were locked into a logic of their own making.

They spoke mainly to each other, fortifying their opinions with selected verses from the Quran and lessons from hadith that made their destiny appear inescapable. They lived in a country so brutalized by endless violence that the horror of Luxor could not have seemed all that significant; indeed, the Taliban revolution had inspired them to become even bloodier and more intransigent. And yet, immediately after Luxor, there was a period of introspection among the leaders, who analyzed their predicament and prescribed a strategy for the triumph of Islam and the final showdown with the unbelievers.

The main point of their diagnosis was that the Islamic nation was in misery because of illegitimate leadership. The jihadis then asked themselves who was responsible for this situation. They pointed to what they called the Christian-Jewish alliance that had emerged following the 1916 Sykes-Picot Agreement, in which Britain and France divided Arab lands between them, and the Balfour Declaration the following year, which called for a Jewish homeland in Palestine. Soon thereafter the Ottoman Empire collapsed, and with it the Islamic caliphate. This was all seen as an ongoing campaign by the Christian-Jewish alliance to suffocate Islam, using such tools as the United Nations, compliant Arab rulers, multinational corporations, satellite channels, and international relief agencies.

Radical Islamist groups had risen in the past, only to fail because of disunity and the lack of a clear plan. In January 1998, Zawahiri began writing a draft of a formal declaration that would unite all of the different mujahideen groups that had gathered in Afghanistan under a single banner. It would turn the movement away from regional conflicts and toward a global Islamic jihad against America.

The language was measured and concise, in comparison with bin Laden's declaration of war two years before. Zawahiri cited three grievances against the Americans. First, the continuing presence of American troops in Saudi Arabia seven years after the end of the Gulf War. "If some people have formerly debated the fact of the occupation, all the people of the peninsula have now acknowledged it," he observed. Second, America's intention to destroy Iraq, as evidenced by the death of what he said was more than a million civilians. Third, the American goal of propping up Israel by incapacitating the Arab states, whose weakness and disunion are Israel's only guarantee of survival.

All this amounted to a "war on God, his messenger, and the Muslims." Therefore, the members of the coalition were issuing a fatwa: "The ruling to kill the Americans and their allies—civilian and military—is an individual duty for every Muslim who can do it in any country in which it is possible to do it."

On February 23, *Al-Quds al-Arabi* in London published the text of the fatwa by the new coalition, which called itself the International Islamic Front for Jihad Against Jews and Crusaders. It was signed by bin Laden, individually; Zawahiri, as leader of al-Jihad; Rifai Taha, as leader of the Islamic Group; the Pakistani opposition figures Sheikh Mir Hamzah, secretary of the Jamiat-ul-Ulema; and Fazlul Rahman, head of Harakat al-Ansar; and Sheikh Abdul Salam Mohammed Khan, the leader of the Bangladeshi group Harakat al-Jihad. The name al-Qaeda was not used. Its existence was still a closely held secret.

Outside of Afghanistan, members of the Islamic Group greeted the declaration with disbelief. After the catastrophe of Luxor, they were appalled to find themselves part of a coalition that they hadn't been asked to join. Taha was forced to withdraw his name from the fatwa, lamely explaining to fellow members of the Islamic Group that he had only been asked over the telephone to join in a statement of support for the Iraqi people.

Al-Jihad was also in an uproar. Zawahiri called a meeting of his supporters in Afghanistan to explain the new global organization. The members accused him of turning away from their primary goal of taking over Egypt, and they protested al-Jihad's being drawn into bin Laden's grandiose war with America. Some objected to bin Laden personally, saying he had a "dark past" and could not be trusted as the head of this new coalition. Zawahiri responded to the attacks on bin Laden by e-mail: "If the Contractor [bin Laden] made promises in the past he did not carry out, then now the man has changed. . . . Even at this time, almost everything we enjoy comes to us from God first and then from him." His attachment to bin Laden by now was total. Without bin Laden's money, however scarce it had become, there was no al-Jihad.

In the end, Zawahiri pledged to resign if the members failed to endorse his actions. The organization was in such disarray because of arrests and defections, and so close to bankruptcy, that the only choice was to follow Zawahiri or abandon al-Jihad. Many members chose the latter option, among them Zawahiri's own brother Mohammed, who was also his military commander. The two brothers had been together from their underground days. They had sometimes been at odds with each other—on one occasion, Ayman denounced Mohammed in front of his colleagues for mismanaging the group's paltry finances. But Mohammed was popular, and, as deputy emir, he had run the organization whenever Ayman was off on his lengthy travels or in jail. The alliance with bin Laden was too much for Mohammed, however. His defection was a shocking blow.

Several members of the Islamic Group tried to have the blind sheikh named emir of the new Islamic Front, but the proposal was brushed aside, since Sheikh Omar was in prison in America. Bin Laden had had enough of the infighting between the Egyptian factions. He told both groups that their operations in Egypt were ineffectual and too expensive and that it was time for them to "turn their guns" on the United States and Israel. Zawahiri's assistant, Ahmed al-Najjar, later told Egyptian investigators, "I myself heard bin Laden say that our main objective is now limited to one state only, the United States, and involves waging a guerrilla war against all U.S. interests, not only in the Arab region but also throughout the world."

16

"Now It Begins"

AL-QAEDA'S FORTUNES began to improve after the coalition's fatwa to kill Americans wherever they might be found. Until then, bin Laden's name and his cause had been obscure outside of Saudi Arabia and Sudan, but news of the fatwa excited a new generation of fighters. Some came from the madrassas in Pakistan, others from the streets of Cairo or Tangier. The call was heard also in Muslim enclaves in the West. In March 1998, only a month after the fatwa, Ahmed Ressam came from Montreal. A petty thief of Algerian origin who would later be arrested for trying to blow up the Los Angeles International Airport, Ressam was one of about thirty Algerians in the Khaldan camp, the entry point for al-Qaeda trainees in Afghanistan. That same month, Zacarias Moussaoui, a French citizen of Moroccan descent who was living in London, arrived; he would later plead guilty to planning to attack the United States. Young men from Yemen, Saudi Arabia, Sweden, Turkey, and Chechnya came to Khaldan, and each nationality had its own emir. They created cells that they could then transplant to their own or adopted countries. Some went to fight in Kashmir and Chechnya. Many fought for the Taliban.

Publicity was the currency bin Laden was spending, replacing his wealth with fame, and it repaid him with recruits and donations. Despite his pledge to Mullah Omar to remain silent, bin Laden followed up the fatwa with a series of press conferences and interviews, first with a group of fourteen Pakistani journalists, who were driven around in circles for two days before

landing in an al-Qaeda camp only miles from where they had
started. They stood around idly waiting for bin Laden to make his
appearance. Suddenly there was a barrage of gunfire and rocket
grenades to herald bin Laden's arrival in a convoy of four pickup
trucks, accompanied by bodyguards with their faces covered. A
dog ran amok, looking for cover, and skidded behind a tree.

The event struck the Pakistani reporters as staged and cartoonish. They weren't interested in bin Laden's declaration of war
against America, which seemed like an absurd publicity stunt.
India had just tested a nuclear device, and they wanted bin Laden
to declare jihad against India instead. Frustrated, bin Laden tried
to steer the reporters back to his agenda. "Let's talk about real
problems," he pleaded.

"Terrorism can be commendable and it can be reprehensible,"
bin Laden philosophized in response to a planted question from
one of his followers. "Terrifying an innocent person and terrorizing him is objectionable and unjust, also unjustly terrorizing people is not right. Whereas, terrorizing oppressors and criminals
and thieves and robbers is necessary for the safety of people and
for the protection of their property. . . . The terrorism we practice
is of the commendable kind."

After the formal interview, Rahimullah Yusufzai, the reporter
for the *News* in Islamabad, drew bin Laden aside and asked if he
would talk a bit about his life. For instance, how many wives and
children did he have?

"I've lost count," bin Laden said, laughing.

"Maybe at least you know about your wives," Yusufzai suggested.

"I think I have three wives, but I have lost count of my children," bin Laden said.

Yusufzai then asked bin Laden how much money he had. Bin
Laden put his hand on his heart and smiled. "I am rich here," he
said. He continued to evade personal questions.

As soon as Yusufzai got back to Peshawar, he received a call
from a furious Mullah Omar. "Bin Laden holds a press conference
announcing jihad and he doesn't even tell me?" he exclaimed.

"There can only be one ruler in Afghanistan, either me or bin Laden."

THESE INTERVIEWS always took a toll on bin Laden's voice, although he drank copious amounts of tea and water. The next day he wouldn't speak at all, communicating by gesture, because his vocal cords were so inflamed. His bodyguard contended that this was the lingering effect of a Soviet chemical weapon, but some of the reporters concluded that he must be suffering from kidney disease—the origin of a persistent and unsubstantiated legend.

Two days after speaking to the Pakistani press, bin Laden received reporter John Miller and an ABC news crew. Beforehand, the irrepressible American correspondent had sat on the floor of a hut with Zawahiri and explained the needs of his crew. "Doc, we need shots of bin Laden going around the camps, interacting with the men, watching them train or whatever, so we'll have some footage over which we can narrate his story," Miller said. Zawahiri nodded knowingly. "You need some 'B' roll," he said, using the technical term for such coverage. He chuckled and continued, "Mr. Miller, you have to understand that this is not like your Sam Donaldson walking with the president in the Rose Garden. Mr. bin Laden is a *very important man.*"

It occurred to Miller at the time that Zawahiri might be the real power behind al-Qaeda, but then bin Laden himself arrived, with the same staged, awe-inspiring fusillade as before. Over the chirping of crickets outside the mud hut, Miller asked bin Laden if his fatwa was directed at all Americans or just the military. "Through history, America has not been known to differentiate between the military and the civilians, or between men and women or adults and children," bin Laden quietly responded. He cast shy, doe-eyed glances at the American, as if he worried about giving offense. "We anticipate a black future for America. Instead of remaining united states, it shall end up separated states"—just like the old Soviet Union. Bin Laden wore a white turban and a green military jacket. Looming behind his head was a large map of Africa, an unremarked clue.

"You are like the Middle East version of Teddy Roosevelt," Miller concluded.

During the interview, many of bin Laden's followers crowded into the hut. Two Saudis, Mohammed al-'Owhali and "Jihad Ali" Azzam, were preparing for al-Qaeda's first big operation the following month. After Miller's crew finished the taping, bin Laden's technical experts erased the Saudis' faces from the videotape before giving it to the Americans.

DURING THE INTERVIEW, Miller asked about Wali Khan Amin Shah, who had been arrested in Manila. "American authorities believe he was working for you, funded by you, setting up training camps there and part of this plan was . . . the assassination or the attempted assassination of President Clinton during his trip to Manila," said Miller. Wali Khan was "a close friend," bin Laden mildly replied. "As to what you said about him working for me, I have nothing to say. We are all together in this."

The fact that Khan was in American custody was supposed to be a closely held secret, but someone had leaked that information to Miller. Some people in the FBI and the U.S. Attorney's Office were enraged when Khan's name was mentioned directly to bin Laden on television. They knew that John O'Neill was a friend of Christopher Isham, an investigative producer for ABC News; they often drank together at Elaine's. Patrick Fitzgerald, the assistant prosecutor in New York's Southern District, was so angry that he threatened to indict O'Neill. Both Isham and Miller denied that O'Neill was their source and volunteered to take lie-detector tests to prove it. Fitzgerald backed off, but the allegation that O'Neill talked carelessly to reporters lingered as a slur on his reputation. It didn't help that some journalists' investigations of bin Laden were more creative than those of the American intelligence community.

.   .   .

THE FACT WAS THAT THE CIA had no one inside al-Qaeda or the Taliban security that surrounded bin Laden. The agency did have some contacts with a few Afghan tribesmen—leftover assets from the jihad against the Soviets. At Alec Station, Mike Scheuer came up with a plan to use them to kidnap bin Laden. The Afghans were supposed to enter through a drainage ditch that ran under the back fence of Tarnak Farms. Another group of Afghans would sneak through the front gate, using silenced pistols to kill whoever got in the way. When they found bin Laden, they would stash him in a cave thirty miles away. If they were caught, there would be no American fingerprints on the abduction; if they were not, then the Afghans would turn bin Laden over to the Americans a month or so later, after the search parties had given up.

The CIA had outfitted what appeared to be a commercial shipping container that would fit in the cargo hull of a civilian version of a C-130 aircraft. Inside the container was a dentist's chair with restraints modeled for a very tall man (the CIA was under the impression that bin Laden was six feet five inches tall); there would be a doctor inside the box as well, and he would have a wide array of medical equipment available to him, including a dialysis machine in case bin Laden actually did have kidney problems. The agency had even built a landing strip on a private ranch near El Paso, Texas, in order to practice landing at night with no lights, the pilots using night-vision goggles.

It was Scheuer's plan to drop bin Laden in Egypt, where he could be rudely questioned and then quietly disposed of. John O'Neill furiously objected to this idea. He was a lawman, not a killer. He wanted bin Laden arrested and tried in America. He made his case to Janet Reno, the U.S. attorney general, who agreed to let the bureau take possession of bin Laden should he actually be captured. Soon Dan Coleman found himself in El Paso, rehearsing his role as the arresting officer. The plane would land, the cargo door would open, and then the container with the manacled terrorist inside would be loaded into the bay. Coleman would enter the container and find Osama bin Laden strapped to the dentist's chair. Then he would read him his rights.

But for that, he needed an indictment. A federal grand jury in

New York was listening to evidence even as the training was under way. One of the documents Coleman found on Wadih el-Hage's computer in Nairobi made a tentative link between al-Qaeda and the killing of American servicemen in Somalia, and that became the basis of the criminal indictment that was eventually returned against bin Laden in New York in June 1998. Those specific charges against him were later dropped, however, and no testimony in subsequent terrorist trials ever proved that al-Qaeda or bin Laden had been responsible for the murder of Americans—or anyone else—before August of that year. Had he been captured at that time, it's unlikely that bin Laden would have been convicted.

The dispute between the FBI's O'Neill and the CIA's Scheuer, along with the reluctance of the National Security Council to endorse what might be an embarrassing and bloody fiasco, paralyzed the plan. In desperation, George Tenet, the director of Central Intelligence, flew to the Kingdom twice in May 1998 to beg for the help of the Saudis. According to Scheuer, Crown Prince Abdullah made it clear that if the Saudis succeeded in getting bin Laden from the Taliban, American intelligence "would never breathe a word."

The Saudis had their own concerns about bin Laden. Prince Turki had learned that he had attempted to smuggle weapons to his followers inside the Kingdom in order to attack police stations. The Saudis repeatedly complained to the Taliban about bin Laden's meddling with Saudi internal affairs, to no effect. Finally, in June 1998, the king summoned Turki and told him, "Finish this."

Turki flew into the Kandahar airport, directly over the fortress-like Tarnak Farms. Until then, Turki had never met Mullah Omar. The prince was taken to a decrepit guesthouse, the former home of a wealthy merchant, a remnant of what had once been a graceful city. Mullah Omar limped forward to greet him. The one-eyed leader appeared thin and pale, with a long beard, and some kind of infirmity in one of his hands, which he clutched to his chest. War wounds and other afflictions were surpassingly common in Afghanistan; most of the Taliban cabinet members and governors were amputees or severely handicapped in multiple ways, and it was rare for any male assemblage to have a full complement of arms, legs, or eyes. Turki shook hands and sat opposite him on the floor of the salon. Behind Omar were French doors that looked out onto a semicircular terrace, and beyond that, to a dusty, barren yard.

Even during such an important ceremonial occasion as this, there was a casually disconcerting atmosphere of chaos. The room was full of people, young and old, entering at their leisure. Turki was grateful at least for the single air conditioner, which moderated the stifling heat of the Afghan summer.

Turki had brought with him Sheikh Abdullah Turki, a renowned Islamic scholar and the former minister for religious endowments, which was a lucrative source of contributions to the Taliban. In addition to serving as a reminder of Saudi support, Sheikh Abdullah's authoritative presence would instantly resolve any religious or legal questions that might be posed about bin Laden's status. Reminding Omar of his pledge to keep bin Laden from launching attacks of any kind against the Kingdom, Turki then asked Mullah Omar to hand over bin Laden, who had inconveniently left town for the duration of Turki's visit.

Mullah Omar professed to be totally surprised. "I can't just give him to you to put on the plane," Omar complained. "After all, we provided him shelter."

Prince Turki was stupefied by this turnabout. Mullah Omar then lectured him on the Pashtu tribal code, which he said was quite strict about betraying guests.

Sheikh Abdullah Turki offered the opinion that if a guest breaks his word, as bin Laden had done repeatedly by granting press interviews, that action absolves the host who is protecting him. The Taliban leader was unconvinced.

Thinking that Omar needed a face-saving compromise, Prince Turki suggested that the two of them set up a committee that would explore ways to formally hand over bin Laden. Then Prince Turki and his party got up to leave. As he did so, Turki asked specifically, "Are you agreed in principle that you will give us bin Laden?"

Mullah Omar said he was.

After the meeting, Saudi Arabia reportedly sent four hundred four-wheel-drive pickup trucks and other financial aid to the Taliban as a down payment for bin Laden. Six weeks later, the money and the trucks allowed the Taliban to retake Mazar-e-Sharif, a bastion of a Persian-speaking, Shiite minority, the Hazaras. Among the Taliban fighters were several hundred Arabs sent by bin Laden. Well-placed bribes left a force of only 1,500 Hazara soldiers guarding the city, and they were quickly killed. Once inside the defenseless city, the Taliban continued raping and killing for two days, indiscriminately shooting anything that moved, then slitting throats and shooting dead men in the testicles. The bodies of the dead were left to wild dogs for six days before survivors were allowed to bury them. Those citizens who fled the city on foot were bombed by the Taliban air force. Hundreds of others were loaded into shipping containers and baked alive in the desert sun. The UN estimated the total number of victims in the slaughter to be between five and six thousand people. They included ten Iranian diplomats and a journalist, whom the Taliban rounded up and shot in the basement of the Iranian consulate. Four hundred women were taken to be concubines.

But the massacre of Mazar was immediately overshadowed by other tragedies far away.

AFTER THE FORMATION OF THE ISLAMIC FRONT, American intelligence agencies took a greater interest in Zawahiri and his organization, al-Jihad, which was still separate from al-Qaeda but closely allied. In July 1998 CIA operatives kidnapped Ahmed Salama Mabruk and another member of Jihad outside a restaurant in Baku, Azerbaijan. Mabruk was Zawahiri's closest political confidant. The agents cloned his laptop computer, which contained al-Qaeda organizational charts and a roster of Jihad members in Europe—"the Rosetta Stone of al-Qaeda"—as Dan Coleman called it, but the CIA refused to turn it over to the FBI.

It was a typical, pointless bureaucratic standoff of the sort that had handicapped counterterrorism efforts at both organizations from the start, made worse by the personal vindictiveness that several senior agency people, including Scheuer, felt toward O'Neill. Overvaluing information for its own sake, the agency was a black hole, emitting nothing that was not blasted out of it by a force greater than gravity—and it recognized that O'Neill was such a force. He would *use* the information—for an indictment, a public trial—and it would no longer be secret, no longer be intelligence; it would be evidence, it would be news, and it would become useless as far as the agency was concerned. The agency treated the exposure of any bit of intelligence as a defeat, and it was in its nature to clutch the Mabruk computer as if it were the crown jewels. Such high-quality information was difficult to come by and, when acquired, even more difficult to act upon. Because of decades of cutbacks on human intelligence assets, there were only two thousand real operatives—spies—in the agency to cover the entire world.

O'Neill was so angry that he sent an agent to Azerbaijan to demand the actual computer from the president of the country. When that failed, he persuaded Clinton to appeal personally to the Azerbaijani president. Eventually the FBI got the computer, but the ill will between the bureau and the agency continued unabated, damaging both in their attempts to round up the al-Qaeda network.

The CIA moved against another al-Jihad cell in Tirana, Albania, which had been created by Mohammed al-Zawahiri in the early nineties. Albanian agents, under CIA supervision, kidnapped five members of the cell, blindfolded them, interrogated them for several days, and then sent the Egyptian members to Cairo. There they were tortured and put on trial with more than a hundred other suspected terrorists. Their ordeal produced twenty thousand pages of confessions. Both Zawahiri brothers were given death sentences in absentia.

On August 6, a month after the breakup of the Albanian cell, Zawahiri sent the following declaration to the London newspaper *Al Hayat:* "We are interested in briefly telling the Americans that their message has been received and that the response, which we hope they will read carefully, is being prepared, because, with

God's help, we will write it in the language that they understand."

DESPITE THE BLUSTER, the media, the lurid calls for jihad, al-
Qaeda had really done nothing so far. There were grand plans,
and there were claims of past successes that al-Qaeda had little or
no part of. Although al-Qaeda had already existed for ten years, it
was still an obscure and unimportant organization; it didn't compare to Hamas or Hezbollah, for instance. Thousands of young
men had trained in al-Qaeda camps and returned to their home
countries to create havoc; because of their training, they would be
called, by intelligence agencies, "al-Qaeda linked." Unless they
had pledged their loyalty to bin Laden, however, they were not
formally a part of the organization. There were fewer actual al-
Qaeda members in Kandahar than there had been in Khartoum
because bin Laden could no longer support them. The fireworks
displays he put on for reporters were accomplished with rented
mujahideen. Like blowfish, al-Qaeda and bin Laden made themselves appear larger than they actually were. But a new al-Qaeda
was about to make its debut.

It was August 7, 1998, the same day the slaughter commenced
in Mazar-e-Sharif and the anniversary of the arrival of American
troops in Saudi Arabia eight years before.

In Kenya, an Egyptian bomb-maker called "Saleh"—one of
Zawahiri's men—oversaw the construction of two huge explosive
devices. The first, made of two thousand pounds of TNT, aluminum nitrate, and aluminum powder, was stuffed in boxes that
were wired to batteries, then loaded into a brown Toyota cargo
truck. The two Saudis who sat in on the ABC interview,
Mohammed al-'Owhali and Jihad Ali, drove the truck through
downtown Nairobi toward the American Embassy. At the same
time, in Tanzania, Saleh's second bomb was on its way to the
American Embassy in Dar es Salaam. This bomb was similar in
construction except that Saleh had added a number of oxygen
tanks or gas canisters to provide additional fragmentation. The
delivery vehicle was a gasoline truck driven by Ahmed Abdullah,

an Egyptian whose nickname was Ahmed the German because of his fair hair. The bombings were scheduled for ten thirty on a Friday morning, a time when observant Muslims were supposed to be in the mosque.

Al-Qaeda's first documented terrorist strike bore the hallmarks of its future actions. The novelty of multiple, simultaneous suicide bombings was a new and risky strategy, given the increased likelihood of failure or detection. If they succeeded, al-Qaeda would make an unrivaled claim on the world's attention. The bombings would be worthy of bin Laden's grandiose and seemingly lunatic declaration of war on the United States, and the suicide of the bombers would provide a scanty moral cover for operations intended to murder as many people as possible. In this, al-Qaeda was also unusual. Death on a grand scale was a goal in itself. There was no attempt to spare innocent lives, since the concept of innocence was subtracted from al-Qaeda's calculations. Although the Quran specifically forbids killing women and children, one of the reasons the embassy in Kenya was targeted was that the death of the female American ambassador, Prudence Bushnell, would garner more publicity.

Each part of the operation betrayed al-Qaeda's inexperience. As Jihad Ali drove into the rear parking lot of the embassy, 'Owhali jumped out and charged toward the guard station. He was supposed to force the unarmed guard to raise the drop bar, but the guard refused. 'Owhali had left his pistol in his jacket in the truck. He did carry out a portion of his mission, which was to throw a stun grenade into the courtyard. The noise drew the interest of people inside the buildings. One of the lessons Zawahiri had learned from his bombing of the Egyptian Embassy in Islamabad three years before was that an initial explosion brought people rushing to the windows, and many were decapitated by flying glass when the real bomb went off.

'Owhali abruptly faced a moral choice that he believed would determine his eternal fate—at least, that was what he later told an FBI agent. He had expected to be a martyr; his death in the operation would assure him his immediate place in Paradise. But he realized that his mission of setting off the stun grenade had already been accomplished. If he were to go forward to his own certain death, that would be suicide, he explained, not martyrdom. Damnation would be his fate, not salvation. Such is the narrow bridge between heaven and hell. To save his soul, 'Owhali turned and ran, failing in his main task of raising the drop bar so that the truck could get closer to the building.

'Owhali didn't get far. The blast knocked him to the sidewalk, shredding his clothes and pounding shrapnel into his back. When he managed to stand, in the weird silence after the blast, he could see the results of his handiwork.

The face of the embassy had sheared off in great concrete slabs. Dead people still sat at their desks. The tar-covered street was on fire and a crowded bus was in flames. Next door, the Ufundi Building, containing a Kenyan secretarial college, had completely collapsed. Many were pinned under the rubble, and soon their cries arose in a chorus of fear and pain that would go on for days, until they were rescued or silenced by death. The toll was 213 dead, including 12 Americans; 4,500 were injured, more than 150 of them blinded by the flying glass. The ruins burned for days.

Nine minutes later, Ahmed the German drove his truck into the parking lot of the American Embassy in Dar es Salaam and pushed the detonator wired into the dashboard. Fortuitously, between him and the embassy there was a water tanker truck. It was blown three stories high and came to rest against the chancery of the embassy, but it prevented the bomber from getting close enough to bring the building down. The toll was 11 dead and 85 wounded, all of them Africans.

Beyond the obvious goal of calling attention to the existence of al-Qaeda, the point of the bombings was vague and confusing. The Nairobi operation was named after the Holy Kaaba in Mecca; the Dar es Salaam bombing was called Operation al-Aqsa, after the mosque in Jerusalem; neither had an obvious connection to the American embassies in Africa. Bin Laden put forward several explanations for the attack. He initially said that the sites had been targeted because of the "invasion" of Somalia; then he described an American plan to partition Sudan, which he said was hatched in the embassy in Nairobi. He also told his followers that the genocide in Rwanda had been planned inside the two American embassies.

Muslims all over the world greeted the bombings with horror and dismay. The deaths of so many people, most of them Africans, many of them Muslims, created a furor. Bin Laden said that the bombings gave the Americans a taste of the atrocities that Muslims had experienced. But to most of the world and even to some members of al-Qaeda, the attacks seemed pointless, a showy act of mass murder with no conceivable effect on American policy except to provoke a massive response.

But that, as it turned out, was exactly the point. Bin Laden wanted to lure the United States into Afghanistan, which was already being called the graveyard of empires. The usual object of terror is to draw one's opponent into repressive blunders, and bin Laden caught America at a vulnerable and unfortunate moment in its history.

"Now it begins," Assistant U.S. Attorney Pat Fitzgerald told Coleman when the news of the bombings came. It was 3:30 in the morning in New York when he called. Coleman got out of bed and drove immediately to Washington. Two days later his wife met him at a Dairy Queen on I-95 to drop off his medicine and a change of clothes. She knew he would be at SIOC for a long time.

FBI headquarters assigned the embassy bombings case to the Washington field office, which normally handles overseas investigations. O'Neill passionately wanted control. New York had a sealed indictment of bin Laden, which gave that office the right to claim the case if he indeed was behind it; but bin Laden was still obscure, even in the upper reaches of the FBI, and the term "al-Qaeda" was almost unknown. Several possible perpetrators were under discussion, Hezbollah and Hamas among them. O'Neill had to prove to his own bureau that bin Laden was the prime mover.

He snatched a young Lebanese American agent named Ali Soufan from another squad. Soufan was the only FBI agent in New York who actually spoke Arabic, and one of eight in the entire country. On his own, he had studied bin Laden's fatwas and interviews, so when a claim of responsibility was sent to several press organizations the same day of the bombing from a group no one had ever heard of before, Soufan immediately recognized bin Laden as the author. The language was exactly the same as in his previous declarations. Thanks to Soufan, O'Neill was able to send a teletype to headquarters the very day of the bombing outlining the damning similarities between bin Laden's past statements and the demands expressed in the pseudonymous claim.

Thomas Pickard, then head of the criminal division at headquarters, was temporarily in charge of the bureau while Director Freeh was on vacation. He spurned O'Neill's request to give the New York office control of the investigation. Pickard wanted to keep the probe under the supervision of the Washington office, which he formerly headed. O'Neill frantically enlisted every powerful contact he could, including Attorney General Reno and his friend Dick Clarke. Eventually, the bureau bowed to the strong-arm pressure that this subordinate was able to apply, but as punishment O'Neill was not allowed to go to Kenya personally to oversee the investigation. The bruises left by this internecine conflict would never heal.

Only eight hours after the bombings, dozens of FBI investigators were on their way to Kenya. Eventually, almost five hundred would be working the two cases in Africa, the largest deployment in the history of the bureau. On the way into Nairobi, the airport bus carrying the agents stopped for a Masai tribesman herding his cattle across the road. The agents stared at the congested streets, crammed with bicycles and donkey carts, dizzying scenes that were at once beautiful, exotic, and full of shocking poverty. Many of the agents were unfamiliar with the world beyond America; indeed, some had not even been given passports until the day of their departure, and here they were, nine thousand miles away. They knew little about the laws and customs of the countries they were working in. They were anxious and watchful, knowing that they were now likely targets of al-Qaeda as well.

Stephen Gaudin, a stocky redhead from the North End of

Boston, took out his short-stock machine gun and placed it on his lap. Until recently, his FBI career had been spent in a two-person office in upstate New York above a Dunkin' Donuts. He had never heard of al-Qaeda. He had been brought along to provide protection, but he was staggered by the immense number of people surrounding the embassy. They dwarfed any crowd he had ever seen. Nothing looked familiar to him. How could he protect the other agents when he had no idea what was going on?

The bus dropped them off in front of the smoldering ruins of the embassy. The scale of devastation was overwhelming. The building was gutted from one end to the other; next door, the Kenyan secretarial school was completely flattened. Rescuers were digging into the rubble with their bare hands, trying to reach the wounded. Steve Gaudin gaped at the ruins and wondered, "What the hell are we going to do?" The FBI had never solved an overseas bombing.

One of the people buried under the secretarial school was named Roselyn Wanjiku Mwangi—Rosie, as everyone called her. The rescuers could hear her talking to another victim whose leg was crushed, trying to keep his spirits up. For two days Rosie's encouraging voice inspired the rescuers, who worked relentlessly. Finally they reached the man with the crushed leg and carefully worked him free of the debris. They promised Rosie they would have her loose in less than two hours, but when they finally did reach her, it was too late. Her death was a heartbreaking blow to the exhausted workers.

The bombings were an audacious assault on America's place in the world. The level of coordination and technical sophistication required to carry out nearly simultaneous explosions was surprising, but more troubling was the willingness of al-Qaeda to escalate the level of violence. The FBI eventually discovered that five American embassies had been targeted—luck and better intelligence had saved the other three. The investigators were stunned to learn that nearly a year earlier an Egyptian member of al-Qaeda had walked into the U.S. Embassy in Nairobi and told the CIA about the bombing plot. The agency had dismissed this intelligence as unreliable. This was not an isolated incident. All through the spring there had been a drumroll of threats and fat-was from bin Laden, but few had taken them seriously. Now the consequence of that neglect was starkly evident.

THREE DAYS AFTER THE BOMBING, Steve Gaudin's chief, Pat D'Amuro, told him to check out a lead. "There's a guy in a hotel outside of Nairobi," said D'Amuro. "He doesn't fit in."

"That's it?" Gaudin asked. "He doesn't 'fit in'? What does that mean?"

"If you don't like it, I got a hundred other leads," said D'Amuro.

Gaudin and a couple of other agents drove to a shantytown largely inhabited by Somali refugees. Their truck inched along through a staring crowd and stopped in front of a decrepit hotel. "Whatever you do, don't get out of the truck," their Kenyan colleague warned. "They hate Americans here."

While the agents nervously waited for the Kenyan cop to return, a man in the crowd leaned against the truck with his back to the window. "I told you not to come here," he said under his breath. "You're going to get killed."

Gaudin guessed the man was the tipster. "Can you help us?" he asked.

"He's not here," the man hissed. "He's in another hotel."

At the next hotel, the agents found a man who didn't fit in: a slender young Arab with several jagged stitches on his forehead and bandages on his hands that were leaking blood. He identified himself as Khaled Saleem bin Rasheed from Yemen. He said he was in the country researching business opportunities—he was a nut merchant—and that he had stopped at a bank near the embassy when the "accident" happened. The only items in his pocket were eight brand-new hundred-dollar bills.

"How did you wind up at this hotel?" the interrogator asked.

Bin Rasheed said that when he got out of the hospital, a cab driver took him there, knowing that he didn't speak Swahili. It was a place where Arabs sometimes stayed.

"Where are the rest of your things—your clothes, your identi-fication documents?"

"Everything was lost in the explosion," bin Rasheed explained. "These are the clothes I was wearing that day."

As Gaudin listened to the young Arab responding to the American interrogators, he thought the story was plausible. It wasn't Gaudin's place to ask questions; more experienced agents handled that. Still, Gaudin noticed that bin Rasheed's clothes were a lot neater than his own. Although Gaudin had been in the country only a couple of days, he was rumpled and coated in dust; and yet bin Rasheed, who claimed to have lost everything in a catastrophic bombing, looked comparatively spiffy. But why would he lie about his clothes?

Gaudin couldn't sleep that night, he was so troubled by an improbable thought that played in his mind. The next morning when the investigation resumed, Gaudin asked the lead inter-rogator if he could ask a couple of questions. "I spent six years in the army," he told bin Rasheed. He said that he had gone through specialized training in counterinterrogation techniques at the John F. Kennedy Special Warfare Center. It had been a brutal expe-rience. Soldiers learned what to expect if they were ever taken prisoner. They were beaten and intimidated; they were also coached on how to tell a convincing cover story. "I think you got the same training," Gaudin asserted. "Now, if you remember your instruction, when you lie you must tell a single logical story. But you made a mistake. You said one thing that was illogical."

Instead of laughing in disbelief, bin Rasheed pulled his chair closer. "Where was I illogical?" he asked.

"Here's where your story falls apart," said Gaudin, who was staring pointedly at bin Rasheed's shoes, which were scuffed and filthy like Gaudin's own. "You got cuts on both hands, but there's not a drop of blood on your green denim pants. In fact, you're per-fectly clean."

"Arab men are much cleaner than American men," bin Rasheed responded.

"I'll give you that," said Gaudin, still staring at his shoes.

"And maybe you've got a magic soap that gets the blood out of your clothes."

"Yes."

"You've got a gash on your back as well. I suppose there was some way a piece of glass fell from a building and went down your shirt without tearing it."

"Anything is possible," said bin Rasheed.

"I'll give you that, too. Then you wash your bloody shirt with your magic soap and it looks like new. But there are two things you don't wash."

Bin Rasheed followed Gaudin's stare. "Of course, I don't wash my shoes!"

"No," said Gaudin, leaning forward and putting his hand on bin Rasheed's knee. "But I said there were two things you don't wash, and here's where you forgot your training." Gaudin stood up and put his hands on his belt, which was worn and faded. "You don't wash a belt! Look at yours. It's pristine! Stand up and take it off!"

Bin Rasheed stood up like a soldier obeying an order. As soon as he undid his belt, everyone in the room noticed the price tag.

Although bin Rasheed quickly recovered his poise, the interrogation now moved to a different level. Gaudin brought in John Anticev, one of the original members of the I-49 squad. Anticev has a calm manner, but his blue eyes are as vivid as searchlights. He began by politely asking if bin Rasheed had had a chance to pray. This led to a discussion of Sayyid Qutb, Abdullah Azzam, and the blind sheikh. Bin Rasheed relaxed. He seemed to relish the opportunity to lecture a Westerner about the importance of these men. They chatted until late in the evening.

"There's one other person we haven't talked about," Anticev observed. "Osama bin Laden."

Bin Rasheed's eyes narrowed and he stopped talking. A small smile appeared on his face.

Anticev, who had been listening like a captivated student, suddenly thrust a pen and paper into bin Rasheed's hand. "Write down the first telephone number you called after the bombing!"

Once again, bin Rasheed obeyed the order. He wrote "967-1-200578," a number in Yemen. It belonged to a jihadi named Ahmed al-Hada. Bin Rasheed had called the number both before and after the bombing—as had Osama bin Laden, investigators quickly learned. This Yemeni telephone number would prove to be one of the most important pieces of information the FBI would ever discover, allowing investigators to map the links of the al-Qaeda network all across the globe.

After giving up the number, bin Rasheed stopped cooperating. Gaudin and other agents decided to leave him alone, hoping he would think he wasn't so important to them. Meanwhile, they began to check out his story. They went to the hospital to see if they could find the doctor who treated his wounds, but there were nearly five thousand injured the day of the bombing, and few of the staff remembered any faces in the sea of blood and pain. Then a janitor asked the agents if they had come because of the bullets and the keys he had found. The items had been stashed on a window sill above a toilet stall. The key fit the model of truck used in the bombing.

At the airport, the agents discovered bin Rasheed's landing card, which gave as his address in Nairobi the hotel where he had been discovered—so he was lying about the cab driver taking him there after the bombing. Phone records led them to a large villa where a call had been placed to the Hada phone in Yemen half an hour before the bombing. When the evidence team arrived, their swabs lit up with explosive residue. It was here the bomb had been made.

"You want to blame this on me?" bin Rasheed shouted when Gaudin confronted him with the evidence. "It's your fault, your country's fault for supporting Israel!" He was sputtering with fury. Flecks of foam were flying from his mouth. It was a startling turnaround from the controlled demeanor the investigators had witnessed for the past few days. "My tribe is going to kill you and your entire family!" he promised.

Gaudin was also angry. The death toll had been rising all through the week as badly injured people succumbed to their awful wounds. "Why did these people have to die?" he asked. "They had nothing to do with the United States and Israel and Palestine!"

Bin Rasheed didn't answer directly; instead, he said something surprising: "I want a promise that I'll be tried in America. Because America is my enemy, not Kenya. You get me that promise, and I'll tell you everything."

Gaudin brought Patrick Fitzgerald, the prosecutor from the Southern District of New York, into the room. Fitzgerald drew up a contract pledging that the investigators would do everything in their power to get the suspect extradited to the United States.

"My name is not Khaled Saleem bin Rasheed," the suspect now said. "I am Mohammed al-'Owhali, and I'm from Saudi Arabia."

He said he was twenty-one years old, well educated, from a prominent merchant family. He had become very religious as a teenager, listening to sermons on audiocassettes and reading books and magazines that glorified martyrdom. A tape by Sheikh Safar al-Hawali that talked about "Kissinger's Promise"—a purported plan of former American secretary of state Henry Kissinger's to occupy the Arabian Peninsula—particularly affected him. Inflamed by this spurious information, 'Owhali made his way to Afghanistan to join the jihad.

He took basic training at the Khaldan camp, learning how to use automatic weapons and explosives. 'Owhali performed so well that he was granted an audience with bin Laden, who counseled him to get more instruction. 'Owhali went on to learn techniques for kidnapping, hijacking planes and buses, seizing buildings, and gathering intelligence. Bin Laden kept an eye on him, reassuring him that he would eventually get a mission.

While 'Owhali was fighting with the Taliban, Jihad Ali came to him and said that they had finally been approved for a martyrdom operation, but it was to be in Kenya. 'Owhali was crestfallen. "I want to attack *inside* the U.S.," he pleaded. His handlers told him that the embassy strikes were important because they would keep America distracted while the real attack was being prepared.

"We have a plan to attack the U.S., but we're not ready yet," the suspect told Gaudin and the other investigators. "We need to hit you outside the country in a couple of places so you won't see what is going on inside. The big attack is coming. There's nothing you can do to stop it."

WORKING FOR O'NEILL sometimes felt like being in the Mafia. The other agents observed that O'Neill's dress and manners, not to mention his Atlantic City background, gave him a mobbed-up air. The founding director of the FBI, J. Edgar Hoover, was sufficiently concerned about the young agent when he first entered the bureau that he drew O'Neill aside to ask about his "connections." The only link was that O'Neill, like the Mafia, was a product of a culture that thrived on personal loyalty. Nor was he above issuing threats to ruin the careers of agents who crossed him.

After the embassy bombings, O'Neill scheduled meetings at four o'clock each afternoon, and typically he arrived as much as an hour late. His chronic tardiness aroused a lot of angry chatter among the married agents, who had children to attend. O'Neill would finally enter the conference room, then go around the table and shake the hands of each team member—another time-consuming ritual.

On one of these occasions, Jack Cloonan, a member of the I-49 squad, kissed the massive FBI ring on O'Neill's finger. "Thank you, Godfather," he said.

"Fuck you," O'Neill snapped.

Dan Coleman was explaining a piece of intelligence in one of the meetings when O'Neill broke in. "You don't know what you're talking about," he said to the man who, more than anyone in America, with the exception of Mike Scheuer, had studied bin Laden and his organization.

"Fine," said Coleman.

"I'm just kidding."

"You know what? I'm just Joe Shit the Ragman," Coleman said heatedly. "You're the SAC. I can't defend myself in a position like this."

The next day O'Neill came by Coleman's desk and apologized. "I shouldn't have done that," he said.

Coleman accepted the apology, although he afforded himself the opportunity to lecture O'Neill on the responsibility of being a boss. O'Neill listened, then observed, "You look like you comb your hair with a hand grenade."

"Maybe I should use some of that oil you dump on your hair," said Coleman.

O'Neill laughed and walked away.

After that, Coleman slyly began to study O'Neill. The key, Coleman decided, was that "he had come from nowhere." O'Neill's mother still drove a cab in Atlantic City during the day, and his father operated the same cab at night. O'Neill's uncle, a piano player, helped support them when the casino economy died. O'Neill had left home as soon as he could. On his first job, when he was a tour guide at FBI headquarters, he would carry a briefcase to work—as if he needed one—and he immediately attempted to exert control over the other guides. They resentfully called him "Stinky" because he was always in a sweat.

Coleman had a sense of the empty space between the public O'Neill and the private one. The flashy suits, the gleaming finger-nails, concealed a man of humble background and modest means. It was a front O'Neill could scarcely afford on a government salary. Belligerent and belittling at times, O'Neill was also anx-ious and insecure, frequently seeking reassurance and dragging a long tail of debt. Few knew how precarious his career was, how fragmented his private life, how unsettled his spirit. Once, when an agent got so angry at O'Neill in a meeting that he began screaming, O'Neill stalked out of the room and calmed himself down by making calls on his cell phone. "You can't do that," Cole-man told the agent. "Tell him you're sorry—you didn't mean to disrespect him." O'Neill was as emotionally dependent on respect as any gangster.

But he was also capable of extravagant and almost alarming gestures of caring, quietly raising money for victims of the bomb-ings he investigated and personally making sure his employees got the best doctors in the city when they fell ill. One of O'Neill's friends in Washington had bypass surgery during a blizzard. Traffic in the city was shut down, but he awakened to see O'Neill at his bedside. He had tramped through eighteen inches of snow. Every morning he insisted on bringing coffee and a pastry to his secretary from a kiosk on the street, and he always remembered birthdays. These gestures, large and small, spoke to his own longing to be noticed and attended.

TEN DAYS AFTER THE EMBASSY BOMBINGS Jack Cloonan got a call from one of his intelligence contacts in Sudan telling him that two men involved in the case were in Khartoum. They had rented an apartment overlooking the American Embassy there. Cloonan gave the information to O'Neill, who called Dick Clarke at the National Security Council the following day. "I want to work with the Sudanese," he told Clarke. O'Neill was well aware that the country was on the State Department's terror list, but at least they were making an overture.

"John, there's something I can't tell you," Clarke said on the phone. He suggested that O'Neill come to Washington to talk to the attorney general. She informed him that it was out of the question for him to work for the Sudanese: in a few hours the United States was going to bomb that country in retaliation for the attacks on the embassies in East Africa. The missiles were already spinning in their tubes, preparatory to launch, in American warships stationed in the Red Sea.

O'Neill landed in Washington the same day that Monica Lewinsky, a former White House intern, testified before a Washington grand jury that she had provided oral sexual favors for the president of the United States. Her story would be a deciding factor in the articles of impeachment that followed. In the minds of Islamists and, indeed, many Arabs, the relationship between the president and his intern perfectly symbolized Jewish influence in America, and any military response to the bombings was likely to be seen as an excuse to punish Muslims and divert attention from the scandal. "No war for Monica!" was a sign seen in many Arab streets. But Clinton's crippled presidency offered him few options.

The CIA suspected that bin Laden was developing chemical

weapons in Sudan. The information had come from Jamal al-Fadl, bin Laden's former assistant who was now a U.S. government witness. But Fadl had left Sudan two years before, about the same time that bin Laden had been expelled from the country. Unconvinced by the sincerity of the Sudanese government's repeated overtures to the United States to get itself removed from the State Department blacklist, the agency hired a spy from an Arab country to secure a soil sample from an area close to al-Shifa, a pharmaceutical plant suspected of being a secret chemical-weapons facility and thought to be owned in part by bin Laden. The sample, taken in June 1998, purportedly showed traces of EMPTA, a chemical that was essential in making the extremely potent nerve gas VX; indeed, it had few other uses. On August 20, on the basis of this information, President Clinton authorized the firing of thirteen Tomahawk cruise missiles into Khartoum as the first part of the American retaliation for the embassy bombings. The plant was completely destroyed.

It developed that the plant actually made only pharmaceuticals and veterinary medicines, not chemical weapons. No other traces of EMPTA were ever found in or around the site. The chemical might have been a product of the breakdown of a commercially available pesticide widely used in Africa, which it closely resembles. Moreover, bin Laden had nothing to do with the plant. The result of this hasty strike was that the impoverished country of Sudan lost one of its most important manufacturers, which employed three hundred people and produced more than half of the country's medicines, and a night watchman was killed.

Sudan let the two accomplices in the East Africa bombings escape, and they've never been seen again. O'Neill and his team lost an invaluable opportunity to capture al-Qaeda insiders.

AT THE SAME TIME that the warheads were exploding in northern Khartoum, sixty-six U.S. cruise missiles were in flight toward two camps around Khost, Afghanistan, near the Pakistan border.

Zawahiri happened to be talking on bin Laden's satellite phone at the time to Rahimullah Yusufzai, a distinguished reporter for BBC and the Pakistani paper the *News*. Zawahiri told him, "Mr. bin Laden has a message. He says, 'I have not bombed the American embassies in Kenya and Tanzania. I have declared jihad, but I was not involved.' "

The best way American intelligence had of detecting bin Laden's and Zawahiri's movements at the time was by tracking their satellite phone. If surveillance aircraft had been positioned in the region, Zawahiri's call to the reporter would have given agents his exact location. But the strike was delivered so quickly that there was little time to prepare. Still, American intelligence knew in general where bin Laden and Zawahiri were hiding, so the fact that surveillance aircraft were not available prior to the strike is inexplicable. Had they pinpointed Zawahiri prior to launch there is little question that he would have been killed in the strike. On the other hand, it takes several hours to prepare a missile for firing, and the flight time from the warships in the Arabian Sea across Pakistan to eastern Afghanistan was more than two hours. By the time Zawahiri picked up the phone the missiles were probably already on their way and it was already too late.

Although the National Security Agency was able to monitor calls on the satellite phone, it refused to share the raw data with the FBI or the CIA or Dick Clarke in the White House. When the CIA learned from one of its own employees, who was posted at the NSA, that al-Qaeda's phones were being monitored, it demanded the transcripts. The NSA refused to hand them over; instead, it offered narrative summaries that were often out of date. The CIA then turned to its own director of science and technology to construct a device that would monitor the transmissions of satellite phones from that portion of Afghanistan. They were able to receive only one side of the conversation, but based on one of the partial intercepts the CIA determined that bin Laden and others were going to be in Khost.

The information was timely and relevant. Bin Laden had made the decision to go to Khost only the night before. But as he and his companions were driving through Vardak province, they happened to pause at a crossroads.

"Where do you think, my friends, we should go?" bin Laden asked. "Khost or Kabul?"

His bodyguard and others voted for Kabul, where they could visit friends.

"Then, with God's help, let us go to Kabul," bin Laden decreed—a decision that may have saved his life.

AT THE AGE OF FIFTEEN, Abdul Rahman Khadr was the youngest trainee in the Farouk camp near Khost. There were between 70 and 120 men training there, he estimated, and about an equal number in the Jihad Wal camp nearby. After the evening prayer, he was walking back from the washroom, carrying a bucket, when bright lights punctured the sky just above him. He threw the bucket aside, but before it hit the ground the missiles began to explode.

The first twenty explosions were at Jihad Wal. Abdul Rahman dove for cover as the next wave followed, detonating all around him. He glanced up to see the air pulsing with explosive waves. When the rain of rocks and pebbles subsided, he walked around the smoking ruins to see what was left.

The administration building was destroyed. Abdul Rahman concluded that the trainers must be dead. But then he heard shouting, and he walked over to Jihad Wal, where he discovered that the trainers had gathered for a meeting. Amazingly, they were all alive. None of al-Qaeda's leaders were harmed.

There were five injured men, whom Abdul Rahman loaded into a four-by-four. Despite his youth, he was the only one who could drive, so he rushed them to the hospital in Khost. He stopped along the way to give water to one of the badly injured, and the man died in his arms.

Abdul Rahman returned to the camp to help bury the dead. One body was so mutilated it was impossible to identify. "Can you at least find his feet?" Abdul Rahman asked. Someone discovered one of them, and by the birthmark on a toe Abdul Rahman was able to identify his friend, a Canadian citizen of Egyptian background like himself. There were four other dead men, whom they buried as surveillance aircraft flew overhead recording the damage.

IN THE BIG-CHESTED PARLANCE of U.S. military planners, the failed strikes were dubbed Operation Infinite Reach. Designed to be a surgical and proportional response to the terrorist acts—two bombings, two decisive replies—the missile attacks exposed the inadequacy of American intelligence and the futility of military power, which rained down nearly three-quarters of a billion dollars' worth of armament on two of the poorest countries in the world.

According to General Hamid Gul, the former head of the ISI, more than half of the missiles fell in Pakistani territory, killing two Pakistani citizens. Although Abdul Rahman Khadr buried only five men in the al-Qaeda camp, not counting the one who died in his arms, there were many false claims. Sandy Berger, Clinton's national security advisor, said that "twenty or thirty al-Qaeda operatives were killed." The Taliban later complained that twenty-two Afghans had also been killed and more than fifty gravely wounded. Bin Laden's bodyguard observed the damage, however, and agreed with Abdul Rahman's assessment. "Each house was hit by a missile but they did not destroy the camp completely," he reported. "They hit the kitchen of the camp, the mosque, and some bathrooms. Six men were killed: a Saudi, an Egyptian, an Uzbek, and three Yemenis."

The attacks did have other profound consequences, however. Several of the Tomahawk missiles failed to detonate. According to Russian intelligence sources, bin Laden sold the unexploded missiles to China for more than $10 million. Pakistan may have used some of the ones found on its territory to design its own version of a cruise missile.

The main legacy of Operation Infinite Reach, however, was that it established bin Laden as a symbolic figure of resistance, not just in the Muslim world but wherever America, with the clamor of its narcissistic culture and the majestic presence of its military forces, had made itself unwelcome. When bin Laden's exhilarated voice came crackling across a radio transmission—"By the grace of God, I am alive!"—the forces of anti-Americanism had found their champion. Those Muslims who had objected to the slaughter of innocents in the embassies in East Africa were cowed by the popular support for this man whose defiance of America now seemed blessed by divine favor. Even in Kenya and Tanzania, the two countries that had suffered the most from al-Qaeda's attacks, children would be spotted wearing bin Laden T-shirts.

The day after the strikes, Zawahiri called Yusufzai again. "We survived the attack," Zawahiri informed him. "Tell the Americans that we aren't afraid of bombardment, threats, and acts of aggression. We suffered and survived the Soviet bombings for ten years in Afghanistan, and we are ready for more sacrifices. The war has only just begun; the Americans should now await the answer."

17

The New Millennium

Two days after the American missile attacks, Mullah Omar placed a secret call to the U.S. State Department. He had a piece of advice. The strikes would only arouse anti-American sentiment in the Islamic world and provoke more acts of terrorism, he said. The best solution was for President Clinton to resign.

The unflappable State Department official who fielded the call, Michael E. Malinowski, pointed out that there was considerable evidence that bin Laden was behind the bombings in East Africa. Malinowski added that he appreciated the tribal code that required Omar to shelter bin Laden, but the Saudi was behaving like a guest who was shooting at neighbors from the host's window. As long as bin Laden stayed in Afghanistan, Malinowski warned, there would be no reconstruction aid. Although the conversation resolved nothing, it was the first of many such candid and informal talks between the United States and the Taliban.

Mullah Omar certainly realized that he had a problem. Bin Laden's declaration of war against the United States had split the Taliban. There were those who said that America had always been Afghanistan's friend, so why turn it into a powerful and unnecessary enemy? They pointed out that no one in bin Laden's inner circle, including bin Laden himself, had the religious authority to pronounce any fatwa, much less a jihad. Others felt that America had made itself Afghanistan's enemy when it launched the missiles.

Omar was furious at bin Laden's defiance of his authority, but the American attack on Afghanistan soil placed him in a quandary. If he surrendered bin Laden, he would be seen to be caving in to American pressure. He judged that the Taliban could not survive in power if he did so. And, of course, there was the deal that Mullah Omar had struck with Prince Turki, who would soon be returning to Kandahar to collect bin Laden and take him back to the Kingdom.

Once again Omar summoned bin Laden. "I shed tears," bin Laden later admitted. "I told Mullah Omar that we would leave his country and head toward God's vast domain, but that we would leave our children and wives in his safekeeping. I said we would seek a land which was a haven for us. Mullah Omar said that things had not yet reached that stage."

Bin Laden then made a pledge of personal fealty, much like the one that members of al-Qaeda swore to him. He acknowledged Omar as the leader of the faithful. "We consider you to be our noble emir," bin Laden wrote. "We invite all Muslims to render assistance and co-operation to you, in every possible way they can."

With this promise in his pocket, Mullah Omar's attitude changed. He no longer viewed bin Laden as a threat. A friendship developed between them. From now on, when other members of the Taliban complained about the Saudi, Mullah Omar proved to be bin Laden's strongest defender. They often went fishing together below a dam west of Kandahar.

"THIS TIME, why don't *you* come with me?" Prince Turki asked his Pakistani colleague, General Naseem Rana, head of the ISI, in mid-September. "That way, Mullah Omar can see that both of us are serious."

On the basis of their own intelligence, the Pakistanis had informed Turki that bin Laden was behind the embassy bombings and that Saudi citizens had actually carried out the attack in Nairobi. Turki gloomily realized that he was no longer negotiating for a mere dissident but for a master terrorist. Surely the Taliban's two strongest allies—Saudi Arabia and Pakistan—would be able to persuade the Afghan to surrender his nettlesome guest.

Turki and General Rana came to the same Kandahar guesthouse where Mullah Omar had received the Saudi prince before. Turki greeted the Taliban ruler, then reminded him of his pledge. Before answering, Omar abruptly stood up and left the room for about twenty minutes. Turki wondered if he was consulting with his *shura* council or even with bin Laden himself. Finally, the Leader of the Faithful returned and said, "There must have been a translator's mistake. I never told you we would hand over bin Laden."

"But, Mullah Omar, I did not say this only one time," Turki sputtered. He pointed to Omar's main advisor and de facto foreign minister, Mullah Wakil Ahmed Muttawakil, who, Turki remarked, had come to the Kingdom only the month before to negotiate the handover. How could Omar pretend otherwise?

Omar's voice was shrill, and he began to perspire. Turki began to wonder if he was on drugs. Omar screamed at the prince, telling him that bin Laden was "a man of honor, a man of distinction" who only wanted to see the Americans run out of Arabia. "Instead of seeking to persecute him, you should put your hand in ours and his, and fight against the infidels." He called Saudi Arabia "an occupied country" and became so personally insulting that the translator hesitated.

"I'm not going to take any more of this," Turki said furiously. "But you must remember, Mullah Omar, what you are doing now is going to bring a lot of harm to the Afghan people."

Turki and General Rana rode back to the airport in stunned silence. It was particularly galling to once again pass by Tarnak Farms, bin Laden's dilapidated citadel. From now on, not only Turki's personal reputation but also Saudi Arabia's place in the world would be held hostage by the man inside.

ALTHOUGH THE AMERICAN STRIKE had damaged the Afghan training camps, they were easily relocated—this time near the population centers of Kandahar and Kabul. But the

attack had left a residue of paranoia, and the members of the al-
Qaeda community, who were always suspicious of outsiders,
turned on each other. Saif al-Adl, the head of bin Laden's security
force, was certain that there was a traitor in his camp. After all, bin
Laden and key members of the *shura* council would have been in
Khost when the missiles struck had it not been for the last-minute
decision to turn off on the road to Kabul.

Bin Laden still sat with the men in his same casual manner,
and it was easy for anyone to approach him. On one occasion, a
Sudanese named Abu al-Sha'tha came into the circle and spoke
rudely to bin Laden in front of the other leaders. One of the men,
Abu Jandal, recognized the man as a takfiri and offered to sit
between him and bin Laden. "There is no need," bin Laden
assured him, but he put his hand on his pistol while he talked.

When the Sudanese takfiri made a sudden movement, Abu
Jandal pounced on him and pulled his hands behind his back, sitting on the man until he could no longer move. Bin Laden
laughed and said, "Abu Jandal, let the man be!"

But bin Laden and his Egyptian security men had been
impressed by the alertness and strength of this loyal follower. Bin
Laden gave Abu Jandal a pistol and made him his personal bodyguard. There were only two bullets in the gun, meant to kill bin
Laden in the face of capture. Abu Jandal took care to polish the
bullets every night, telling himself, "These are Sheikh Osama's
bullets. I pray to God not to let me use them."

After the humiliation of Prince Turki by Mullah Omar, both
the Taliban and bin Laden's security force were on edge about an
expected Saudi response. The Taliban caught a young Uzbek in
Khost who was acting strangely. His name was Siddiq Ahmed,
and he had grown up in the Kingdom as an expatriate. He admitted that Prince Salman, the governor of Riyadh, had hired him to
kill bin Laden (Prince Salman denies this). In return, the assassin
would receive two million Saudi riyals and Saudi citizenship.
"Did you expect that you would be able to kill Sheikh Osama bin
Laden and escape from fourteen highly trained guards armed
with automatic weapons?" Abu Jandal demanded. The boy was

only eighteen, but he looked like a child. "I made a mistake," he cried. He was dazed and pathetic. Finally, bin Laden said, "Release him."

IN EARLY FEBRUARY 1999, bin Laden floated into Mike Scheuer's sights once again. The CIA received intelligence that bin Laden was camping with a group of royal falconers from the United Arab Emirates in the desert south of Kandahar. The tip came from the bodyguard of one of the princes. They were hunting the houbara bustard, an endangered bird legendary for its speed and cunning, as well as its potency as an aphrodisiac. The princes arrived in a C-130, carrying generators, refrigerated trucks, elaborate air-conditioned tents, towering masts for their communications equipment and televisions, and nearly fifty four-by-four pickups, which they would leave behind for their Taliban hosts as gratuities. Scheuer could see the encampment vividly on reconnaissance photos. He could even make out the falcons roosting on their poles. But he could not find bin Laden's smaller camp, which he knew must be nearby.

Whenever bin Laden set foot in the royal camp, the Emirati bodyguard would report to his American handler in Pakistan, and the information would be on Scheuer's desk within the hour. Afghan spies placed in a wide circle around the camp confirmed the Saudi's comings and goings.

Scheuer is tall and rumpled, with glasses and a bristling brown beard. One can imagine his portrait on the wall of a nineteenth-century Prussian estate. He is a driven and demanding person, who sleeps only a few hours a night. Coleman used to notice the employee sign-in sheets with "2:30 a.m." or some such hour marked by Scheuer's name. He would usually linger till eight at night. A pious Catholic of the type Coleman knew well, Scheuer had a cold detachment about the job he needed to do. Only a couple of months before, Scheuer had gotten intelligence that bin Laden would be spending the night in the governor's residence in Kandahar. When Scheuer proposed an immediate cruise missile strike, the military objected, saying that as many as three hundred people might die and a nearby mosque would likely be damaged. Such considerations enraged Scheuer.

Convinced that the sighting in the bustard camp was the best chance he would ever get to assassinate bin Laden, Scheuer accompanied CIA director George Tenet to meet with Dick Clarke in the White House. Once again, the Pentagon was readying cruise missiles—America's chosen means of assassination—for a strike the following morning. Coincidentally, Clarke had recently returned from the Emirates, where he had helped negotiate the sale of American-built fighter aircraft worth $8 billion. He had personal ties to the UAE royal family. No doubt the image of dead princes scattered in the sand played in his mind, along with the failures of Operation Infinite Reach. Moreover, the CIA could not guarantee that bin Laden was actually in the camp.

Clarke rejected the mission. Tenet also voted against it. Scheuer felt betrayed. The considerations that turned the men against the project seemed petty and mercenary compared to the opportunity to kill bin Laden. "I'm not a big consequences guy," Scheuer admitted, and to prove it he sent out a series of wounded, recriminating e-mails. Talk in the hallways of the agency suggested that he had suffered a breakdown, that his obsession with bin Laden had gotten the best of him. In the meantime, he blew up at a senior FBI manager in Alec Station, which elicited an angry phone call from Director Freeh to Tenet. In May, Scheuer was dismissed as the head of Alec. "You're burned out," his boss told him.

He was expected to retire and accept the intelligence medal that had been struck for him. "Stick it in your ass," said Scheuer. He reported at his usual dizzying time on Monday morning and occupied a desk in the library. He remained there month after month, with no duties, waiting for the agency to come to him when it was ready to kill, not to dither over a few dead princes.

O'NEILL'S OFFICE was in the northeast corner of the twenty-fifth floor of New York's 26 Federal Plaza, overlooking the

Chrysler and Empire State buildings through one window and the Brooklyn Bridge through the other. He made sure that there was no other FBI office like it. He cleaned out the prison-made government-issue furniture and brought in a lavender couch. On his flame mahogany coffee table was a book about tulips—*The Flower That Drives Men Wild*—and he filled the room with plants and seasonal cut flowers. He kept two computers, one the antiquated and handicapped version supplied by the bureau and the other his own high-speed PC. In the background CNN ran constantly on a small television. Instead of the usual family pictures that adorn office walls and desktops, O'Neill had prints of French Impressionists.

Few people in the bureau knew that he had a wife and two children (John Junior and Carol) in New Jersey, who did not join him when he moved to Chicago in 1991. Shortly after he arrived in that city, he met Valerie James, a fashion sales director who was divorced and had two children of her own. She was tall and beautiful, with a level gaze and a sultry voice. She saw O'Neill at a bar and bought him a drink because "he had the most compelling eyes." They stayed up talking till five in the morning.

O'Neill sent Valerie flowers every Friday, the weekly anniversary of the day they met. He was a terrific dancer and allowed that he had been on *American Bandstand* when he was a teenager. Whenever Valerie had to travel on business, she would find a bottle of wine waiting for her in her hotel room. "Are you sure you're not married?" Valerie asked.

Just before O'Neill moved to Washington, a female agent pulled Valerie aside at the bureau Christmas party and told her about O'Neill's family in New Jersey. "That's not possible," said Valerie. "We're getting married. He asked my father for my hand."

While he was courting Valerie, O'Neill had a girlfriend in Washington, Mary Lynn Stevens, who worked at the Pentagon Federal Credit Union. He had asked her for an "exclusive" relationship two years before, when she visited him in Chicago on New Year's Eve. Mary Lynn found out about Valerie when she happened to hear a message on O'Neill's answering machine. She confronted him, and he dropped to his knees begging forgiveness, promising he would never see Valerie again. But when Mary Lynn got back to Washington, her hairdresser, who happened to be from Atlantic City, filled her in about O'Neill's wife. O'Neill explained that he was still talking to the lawyers; he hadn't wanted to endanger his relationship with Mary Lynn by revealing a marriage that was over except for the last legal details. He had said much the same to Valerie James.

Soon after he got to Washington, he met another woman, Anna DiBattista, a stylish blonde who was working in the defense industry. She knew he was married from the beginning—a coworker informed her—but O'Neill never let her know about his other women. Anna's priest warned her, "That guy is never going to marry you. He's never going to get an annulment." And yet one day O'Neill told her he had gotten the annulment after all, which was a lie. "I know how much that means to you," he told her. Often he spent part of the night with Mary Lynn and the rest of it with Anna. "I don't think he ever stayed later than five or six a.m.," said Mary Lynn. "I never made him breakfast." In the meantime, he kept his relationship with Valerie in Chicago alive. All three women were under the impression that he intended to marry them. He was also obsessed with a beautiful, high-powered woman in the Justice Department who was married, a fact that caused him endless despair.

In an odd way, his protean domestic drama paralleled that of his quarry, Osama bin Laden. Perhaps, if O'Neill had lived in a culture that sanctioned multiple marriages, he would have created such a harem. But he was furtive by nature, thriving on dangerous secrets and innovative lies. His job, of course, gave him the perfect cover, since he could always disappear for days on some "classified" mission.

There was a side of him that sought the solace of a committed relationship, which he seemed closest to achieving with Valerie James. When O'Neill moved to New York, Val joined him. They got an apartment in Stuyvesant Town. He was so fond of her two grown children that friends mistook them for his, and when her first grandchild came along, and needed babysitting, O'Neill stayed home with the baby so Val could go to work. They settled into a routine. On Tuesday mornings, they left their clothes at the Laundromat and went for a run. Every Saturday morning, O'Neill would treat himself to a haircut and a hot shave. On Sundays, he and Val experimented with churches and sometimes explored the city on bicycles. Often when he came in late at night, smashed after entertaining cops from Venezuela or Uzbekistan, he would crawl into bed with a glass of milk and a plate of chocolate-chip cookies. He loved handing out candy on Halloween.

But there was a restlessness in him that seemed frightened of simple arrangements. When Anna DiBattista got a job offer in New York in 1999 that threatened to complicate his life beyond reason, O'Neill actually pleaded for her to come. "We can get married!" he said. But when she arrived, he told her she couldn't move in with him right away. He said there were "linguists" staying in his apartment.

With each woman, he lived a different life. He managed to keep his social circles separate, so one group of friends knew him with Val, another with Anna, another with Mary Lynn. He took them to different restaurants and even to different countries on vacation. "Jazz was his thing," said Val. With Anna, he listened to Andrea Bocelli. "Our song was 'Time to Say Goodbye,' " she recalled. Mary Lynn introduced him to grand opera. "He flew all the way from California when I invited him to *Mephisto*." His politics were also flexible, tending to conform to the views of his companion at the time, a moderate Democrat with one, a moderate Republican with another.

On holidays, he went home to New Jersey to visit his parents and to see his wife and children. Although he had been separated from Christine for many years, he never got a divorce. He explained to his friends who knew about his family that it was a "Catholic thing." He continued to support them, and he spoke to his children frequently on the phone. But Atlantic City was part of his life that he shared with very few. Because the women in his life sensed that they could never trust him, they couldn't give him the unqualified love and devotion that he sought. He remained isolated by his compulsive deceptions.

Inevitably, the complexity took a toll. He left his Palm Pilot in Yankee Stadium; it was filled with police contacts from all over the world. Fortunately, the Yankees security force found it. Then he left his cell phone in a cab. In the summer of 1999, he and Valerie were driving to the Jersey shore when his Buick broke down near the Meadowlands. His bureau car happened to be parked nearby at a secret off-site location, so O'Neill switched cars, although the bureau bans the use of an official vehicle for personal reasons. Still, O'Neill's infraction might have been overlooked had he not let Valerie enter the building to use the toilet. She had no idea what the place was. When the FBI learned about the violation, apparently from a spiteful agent who had been caught using the site as an auto-repair shop, O'Neill was reprimanded and docked fifteen days' pay.

That was a penalty O'Neill could scarcely afford. He had always been a showy host, grabbing every tab, even going so far as to tear another agent's money in half when he offered to split the bill. These gestures mounted up. An agent who did his taxes noted O'Neill's credit-card debt and observed, "Gee, John, you'd be a candidate for recruitment." O'Neill was also paying the mortgage on his wife's house and dipping into his retirement funds and borrowing money from wealthy friends, who held promissory notes that he had to disclose. Anyone with that much liability would normally come under scrutiny as a security risk.

He was insecure, deceptive, and potentially compromised. He was also driven, resourceful, and brilliant. For better or worse, this was the man America now depended on to stop Osama bin Laden.

IRAQ WAS AN UNLIKELY ALLY in al-Qaeda's war on the West, but there had been a series of contacts between Iraq and al-Qaeda since the end of the first Gulf War. Saddam Hussein sought allies to salvage his shattered regime, and the radical Islamists at least shared his longing for revenge. In 1992 Hasan al-Turabi arranged a meeting between the Iraqi intelligence service and al-Qaeda with the goal of creating a "common strategy" for deposing pro-

Western Arab governments. The Iraqi delegation met with bin Laden and flattered him, claiming that he was the prophesied Mahdi, the savior of Islam. They wanted him to stop backing anti-Saddam insurgents. Bin Laden agreed, but in return he asked for weapons and training camps inside Iraq. That same year, Zawahiri traveled to Baghdad, where he met the Iraqi dictator in person. But there is no evidence that Iraq ever supplied al-Qaeda with weapons or camps, and soon bin Laden resumed his support of Iraqi dissidents.

Talks continued intermittently, however. When bin Laden issued his fatwa against America in 1998, Iraqi intelligence officials flew to Afghanistan to discuss with Zawahiri the possibility of relocating al-Qaeda to Iraq. Bin Laden's relations with the Taliban were strained at the time, and several senior members of al-Qaeda were in favor of seeking a new haven. Bin Laden opposed this notion, since he didn't want to be indebted to the Iraqi tyrant.

In September 1999, Zawahiri went to Baghdad again with a false passport to attend the Ninth Islamic People's Congress, an international consortium of clerics and activists under the sponsorship of the Iraqi government. Coincidentally, a Jordanian jihadi named Abu Musab al-Zarqawi arrived in Baghdad at about the same time. Zarqawi was not a member of al-Qaeda, but he ran a training camp in Herat, Afghanistan. He saw himself as a competitor to bin Laden, but he had close ties to al-Jihad. Iraqi intelligence may have assisted Zawahiri and Zarqawi in setting up a terror organization of Kurdish fundamentalists called Ansar al-Islam, which was inspired by Iran's sponsorship of Hezbollah.* (Zarqawi would later become the leader of the al-Qaeda insurgency against the American forces following the invasion of Iraq in 2003.)

O'NEILL WAS PARTICULARLY CONCERNED THAT, as the millennium approached, al-Qaeda would seize the moment to

---

*These suppositions are based on remarks made by the former interim Iraqi prime minister Iyad Allawi, who claims to have discovered the information in the archives of the Iraqi secret service.

dramatize its war with America. He was certain that Islamic terrorists had established a beachhead in America. This view was very much different from the one that the leadership of the bureau endorsed. Director Freeh repeatedly stressed in White House meetings that al-Qaeda posed no domestic threat. Bin Laden did not even make the FBI's Most Wanted list until June 1999.

O'Neill had come to feel that there was a pace to the al-Qaeda attacks, and he told friends, "We're due." That feeling was very much on him in the second half of 1999. He knew how much timing and symbols meant to bin Laden, and the millennium presented an unparalleled opportunity for theatrical effect. O'Neill thought the target would be some essential piece of the infrastructure: the drinking water, the electrical grid, perhaps the transportation system. The intelligence to support that hypothesis was frustratingly absent, however.

In December, Jordanian authorities arrested sixteen suspected terrorists believed to be planning to blow up a Radisson Hotel in Amman and a number of tourist sites frequented by Westerners. One of the plotters was Abu Musab al-Zarqawi, although he was not captured. The Jordanians also discovered a six-volume al-Qaeda training manual on CD-ROM. The Jordanian cell included several Arab Americans.

The CIA warned of multiple attacks inside the United States but provided few details. With the FAA, the Border Patrol, the National Guard, the Secret Service, and every sheriff's office and police department in the country on high alert, there was still no actual sign of any forthcoming attack. The fears of a terrorist strike were wrapped up in the general Y2K hysteria—the widespread concern about the possible failure of most computers to accommodate the millennial change in the calendar, leading to a collapse of the technological world.

Then on December 14, a border guard in Port Angeles, Washington, stopped an Algerian man, Ahmed Ressam, whose obvious anxiety aroused her suspicion. She asked him to step out of the car. Another guard opened his trunk and said, "Hey, we've got something here." A customs officer grabbed the back of Ressam's coat and guided him to the trunk of the car. Inside were four timers, more than a hundred pounds of urea, and fourteen pounds of sulfate—the makings of an Oklahoma City–type bomb.

Ressam bolted, leaving his coat in the hands of the customs officer. The guards gave chase and caught him four blocks away trying to break into a car stopped at a traffic light.

It developed that Ressam's target was Los Angeles International Airport. For all the precautions that had been taken, if that one border guard had not been sufficiently curious about Ressam's nervousness, the millennium might have gotten started with a major catastrophe. But luck chose a different venue.

Ressam was not really an al-Qaeda operative, although he had learned to build bombs in one of bin Laden's camps in Afghanistan. He was a freelance terrorist sailing under al-Qaeda colors, the sort that would proliferate after 9/11. A thief with little religious training, he could be called a harbinger. Trained and empowered by al-Qaeda, he formed his own ad hoc cell in Montreal. He had called Afghanistan before the attack to inquire if bin Laden would like to take credit for the act, but he never heard back.

John O'Neill was certain that Ressam had confederates in the United States. Who were they? Where were they? He felt that there was a ticking clock, counting down to New Year's, when an al-Qaeda attack would be most noticeable.

In Ressam's pocket litter, Washington State authorities found a slip of paper with a name, Ghani, on it, as well as several telephone numbers. One of them had a 318 area code, but when Jack Cloonan called it, a child in Monroe, Louisiana, answered. Cloonan looked again at the number. Perhaps it could be a 718 area code instead, he decided. When he checked, he found that the number belonged to Abdul Ghani Meskini, an Algerian who lived in Brooklyn.

O'Neill oversaw the stakeout of Meskini's residence from the FBI's Brooklyn command post. A wiretap picked up a call that Meskini made to Algeria in which he spoke about Ressam and another suspected terrorist in Montreal. On December 30, O'Neill arrested Meskini on conspiracy charges and a number of other suspected terrorists on immigration violations. Eventually, both

Meskini and Ressam would become cooperating witnesses for the government.

On that frigid New Year's Eve, O'Neill stood with two million people in Times Square. At midnight he spoke to Clarke in the White House to let him know he was standing under the giant ball while the bells tolled the new millennium. "If they're gonna do anything in New York, they're gonna do it here," he told Clarke. "So I'm here."

AFTER THE MILLENNIUM ROUNDUP, O'Neill concluded that al-Qaeda had sleeper cells buried in America. The links between the Canadian and the Jordanian cells all led back to the United States; and yet, even after the attacks on the American embassies and the attempt to bomb the Los Angeles airport, the bureau hierarchy continued to view al-Qaeda as a distant and manageable threat. Dale Watson, the assistant director of the Counterterrorism Division, was an exception. O'Neill and Watson met with Dick Clarke over the next few months to create a strategic plan called the Millennium After-Action Review, which specified a number of policy changes designed to root out al-Qaeda cells. They included increasing the number of Joint Terrorism Task Force groups around the country, assigning more agents from the Internal Revenue Service and the Immigration and Naturalization Service to monitor the flow of money and personnel, and creating a streamlined process for analyzing information obtained from wiretaps. But such changes were not sufficient to overcome the bureaucratic lassitude that fell upon Washington after the millennium passed.

THE NIGHT OF POWER, near the end of the fasting month of Ramadan, commemorates the date that the Prophet Mohammed began to receive the word of God in a cave on Mount Hira. On that auspicious date, January 3, in 2000, five men broke their fast in Aden, Yemen, then walked down to the shore. They saw the oddest thing: a fiberglass fishing skiff swamped in the surf. Their eyes fell on the new 225-horsepower Yamaha outboard motor. The men talked about this apparition and decided that it was a gift from heaven. Since they were in a state of ritual purity, they believed they were being rewarded for their devotion, and so they proceeded to strip the boat of whatever they could find, beginning with the six-hundred-pound motor, which was worth more than $10,000. When they disconnected the massive motor it plunged into the salt water. They had to roll it to shore, and by then it was ruined.

Then one of the men opened the hatch. It was stacked with strange bricks. He thought they must be hashish, but there were wires running between them and a battery. The man pulled one of the bricks loose and smelled it. It had a strange oily odor, not at all like hashish. The men decided that the bricks must be valuable, whatever they were, so they formed a line from the boat to the shore and began tossing the bricks to each other.

Suddenly, a couple of al-Qaeda operatives in a small SUV drove up and demanded to know what the men were doing with their boat. When the operatives saw the Yemeni men throwing the bricks they backed away in alarm.

Later, American investigators would learn that the fiberglass skiff was to have been used in a suicide attack on an American destroyer, USS *The Sullivans*, that was refueling in Aden harbor. The al-Qaeda operatives who had overloaded the boat with C-4 explosives had removed the flotation devices from the craft, which caused it to sink in the soft sand as soon as it slid off the trailer. They eventually were able to retrieve the boat using a marine crane, and soon it would be ready for another operation.

18

Boom

THE MEN WHO CAME TO TRAIN in Afghanistan in the 1990s were not impoverished social failures. As a group, they mirrored the "model young Egyptians" who formed the terrorist groups that Saad Eddin Ibrahim had studied in the early eighties. Most of the prospective al-Qaeda recruits were from the middle or upper class, nearly all of them from intact families. They were largely college-educated, with a strong bias toward the natural sciences and engineering. Few of them were products of religious schools; indeed, many had trained in Europe or the United States and spoke as many as five or six languages. They did not show signs of mental disorders. Many were not even very religious when they joined the jihad.

Their histories were more complicated and diverse than those of their predecessors who fought the Soviets. The previous generation had included many middle-class professionals—doctors, teachers, accountants, imams—who had traveled to Afghanistan with their families. The new jihadis were more likely to be young, single men, but there were also criminals among them whose skills in forgery, credit card fraud, and drug trafficking would prove to be useful. The former group had been predominantly from Saudi Arabia and Egypt; many of the new recruits spilled out of Europe and Algeria. There were practically none from Sudan, India, Turkey, Bangladesh, or even Afghanistan or Pakistan. In the jihad against the Soviets, some Shia Muslims had participated; there had even been a Shia camp in bin Laden's outpost of

Maasada. This new group of jihadis was entirely Sunni. Their immediate goal was to prepare themselves for combat in Bosnia or Chechnya and then to return to their own homelands and establish Islamist governments. Between ten and twenty thousand trainees passed through the Afghan camps from 1996 until they were destroyed in 2001.

The recruits were interviewed about their background and special skills. The information gathered was useful in determining what kinds of assignments they would be given; for instance, Hani Hanjour, a young Saudi, noted that he had studied flying in the United States. He would become a part of the 9/11 plot.

In addition to the strenuous physical training the new recruits endured, they were also indoctrinated with the al-Qaeda worldview. The class notes of some of the trainees spelled out the utopian goals of the organization:

1. *Establishing the rule of God on Earth.*
2. *Attaining martyrdom in the cause of God.*
3. *Purification of the ranks of Islam from the elements of depravity.*

These three precisely stated goals would frame al-Qaeda's appeal and its limitations. They beckoned to idealists who did not stop to ask what God's rule would look like in the hands of men whose only political aim was to purify the religion. Death, the personal goal, was still the main attraction for many of the recruits.

They studied past operations, both the successful ones, such as the embassy bombings, and the unsuccessful, like the attempt on Mubarak's life. Their text was a 180-page manual, *Military Studies in the Jihad Against the Tyrants,* which included chapters on counterfeiting, weapons training, security, and espionage. "The confrontation that we are calling for with the apostate regimes does not know Socratic debates . . . Platonic ideals . . . nor Aristotelian diplomacy," the manual begins. "But it does know the dialogue of bullets, the ideals of assassination, bombing and destruction, and the diplomacy of the cannon and machine gun."

There were three main stages in the training. The raw recruits spent a period of fifteen days in boot camp, where they were pushed to total exhaustion, with only a couple of hours of sleep some nights. During the second phase, lasting forty-five days, the recruits received basic military training in map reading, trenching, celestial navigation, and the use of an extraordinary variety of weapons, including light machine guns, Claymore mines, mortars, shoulder-fired rockets, and anti-aircraft missiles. The targets were always Americans, either U.S. soldiers or vehicles, but there were other "enemies of Islam," according to the handwritten notes of a student in an al-Qaeda ideology class:

1. *Heretics (the Mubaraks of the world)*
2. *Shiites*
3. *America*
4. *Israel*

The diversity of enemies would always plague al-Qaeda, especially as new actors with different priorities came upon the stage.

Graduates of the second phase could choose to attend the guerrilla warfare school, which also lasted forty-five days. There were specialty camps in hijacking and espionage, and a ten-day course in assassination. One al-Qaeda trainee recorded in his diary that he had learned "shooting the personality and his guard from a motorcycle" on one day and "shooting at two targets in a car from above, front and back" on the next. Another camp specialized in making bombs, and still another, called the Kamikaze Camp, was reserved for suicide bombers, who wore special white or gray clothes and lived alone, speaking to no one.

There was a well-supplied library of military books, including *Revolt,* the autobiography of the Israeli terrorist and eventual prime minister Menachem Begin. Another book, on the establishment of the U.S. Marines Rapid Deployment Force, included a scenario in which a tanker carrying liquefied natural gas would be blown up in the Straits of Hormuz at the mouth of the Persian Gulf, leading to a massive rise in the price of oil. The trainees were captivated by this notion and spent considerable time planning how to pull off such a maneuver. At night they would often watch Hollywood thrillers, looking for tips. The movies of Arnold Schwarzenegger were particular favorites.

Zawahiri was particularly keen on the use of biological and chemical warfare. He noted that "the destructive power of these weapons is no less than nuclear weapons." He established a program, code-named Zabadi—"curdled milk"—to explore the use of unconventional techniques for mass murder, and he pored over medical journals to research various poisons. "Despite their extreme danger, we only became aware of them when the enemy drew our attention to them by repeatedly expressing concern that they can be produced simply," he wrote. One of his men, named Abu Khabab, set up a laboratory near Jalalabad, where he experimented on dogs with homemade nerve gas and videotaped their agonizing deaths. It often took them more than five hours to die. Abu Khabab explained to his trainees that humans were much more susceptible, not having as powerful antibodies as the dogs. Zawahiri set up another laboratory near Kandahar, where a Malaysian businessman, Yazid Sufaat, spent months attempting to cultivate biological weapons, particularly anthrax. Sufaat had a degree in chemistry and laboratory science from California State University in Sacramento.

Bin Laden was cool at first to the use of biological or chemical weapons, but he found himself at odds with Abu Hafs, who led the hawks in the al-Qaeda debate about the ethics and consequences of using such indiscriminate agents. Would they be used in Muslim lands? Would civilians be targeted? The doves argued that the use of any weapon of mass destruction would turn the sympathy of the world against the Muslim cause and provoke a massive American response against Afghanistan. Bin Laden clearly preferred nuclear bombs over the alternatives, but that posed additional moral considerations. The hawks pointed out that the Americans had already used the nuclear bomb twice, in Japan, and they were currently using bombs in Iraq that contained depleted uranium. If the United States decided to use nuclear weapons again, who would protect the Muslims? The UN? The

Arab rulers? It was up to al-Qaeda to create a weapon that would inoculate the Muslim world against Western imperialism.

WHAT THE RECRUITS tended to have in common—besides their urbanity, their cosmopolitan backgrounds, their education, their facility with languages, and their computer skills—was displacement. Most who joined the jihad did so in a country other than the one in which they were reared. They were Algerians living in expatriate enclaves in France, Moroccans in Spain, or Yemenis in Saudi Arabia. Despite their accomplishments, they had little standing in the host societies where they lived. Like Sayyid Qutb, they defined themselves as radical Muslims while living in the West. The Pakistani in London found that he was neither authentically British nor authentically Pakistani; and this feeling of marginality was just as true for Lebanese in Kuwait as it was for Egyptians in Brooklyn. Alone, alienated, and often far from his family, the exile turned to the mosque, where he found companionship and the consolation of religion. Islam provided the element of commonality. It was more than a faith—it was an identity.

The imams naturally responded to the alienation and anger that prompted these men to find a spiritual home. A disproportionate number of new mosques in immigrant communities had been financed by Saudi Arabia and staffed by Wahhabi fundamentalists, many of whom were preaching the glories of jihad. Spurred by the rhetoric and by the legend of the victory against the Soviets, young men made the decision, usually in small groups, to go to Afghanistan.

Such was the case of four young men in Hamburg.

The most prosperous city in Germany, with more millionaires per capita than any other metropolitan area in Europe, Hamburg was, in 1999, a bourgeois, libertarian stronghold. The city liked to think of itself as more British than German—aloof but polite, patrician but multicultural. It had become a popular destination for foreign students and political refugees, with about 200,000 Muslims among them. Mohammed Atta arrived in the fall of 1992 and enrolled as a graduate student of urban planning at the Technical University of Hamburg-Harburg. Foreign students in Germany could stay as long as they wanted, paid no tuition, and could travel anywhere in the European Union.

The scars of history were easy to detect, not only in the reconstructed portion of the Old City, but also in the laws of the country and the character of the German people. The new Germany had carefully enshrined tolerance in its constitution, including the most openhanded political asylum policy in the world. Acknowledged terrorist groups were allowed to operate legally, raising money and recruits—but only if they were foreign terrorists, not domestic. It was not even against the law to plan a terrorist operation so long as the attack took place outside the country. Naturally, many extremists took advantage of this safe harbor.

In addition to the constitutional barriers that stood in the way of investigating the radical groups, there were internal cautions as well. The country had suffered in the past from xenophobia, racism, and an excess of police power; any action that summoned up such ghosts was taboo. The federal police preferred to concentrate their efforts on native right-wing elements, paying little attention to the foreign groups. Germany feared itself, not others. The unspoken compact that the Germans made with the radical foreign elements inside their country was that if Germans themselves were not attacked, they would be left alone. In recoiling from its own extremist past, Germany inadvertently became the host of a new totalitarian movement.

The radical Islamists had little in common with the Nazi enterprise. Although they would often be accused of being a fascistic cult, the resentment that burned inside the al-Quds mosque, where Atta and his friends gathered, had not been honed into a keen political agenda. But like the Nazis, who were born in the shame of defeat, the radical Islamists shared a fanatical determination to get on top of history after being underfoot for so many generations.

Although Atta had only vaguely socialist ideas of government, he and his circle filled up the disavowed political space that the Nazis left behind. One of Atta's friends, Munir al-Motassadeq, referred to Hitler as "a good man." Atta himself often said that the Jews controlled the media, banks, newspapers, and politics from their world headquarters in New York City; moreover, he was convinced that the Jews had planned the wars in Bosnia, Kosovo, and Chechnya as a way of holding back Islam. He believed that Monica Lewinsky was a Jewish agent sent to undermine Clinton, who had become too sympathetic to the Palestinian cause.

The extreme rigidity of character that everyone detected in Atta was a Nazi trait, and no doubt it was reinforced in him by the need to resist the lure of this generous city. The young urban planner must have admired the cleanliness and efficiency of Hamburg, which was so much the opposite of the Cairo where he had grown up. But the odious qualities that Sayyid Qutb had detected in America—its materialism, its licentiousness, its spiritual falsity—were also spectacularly on display in Hamburg, with its clanging casinos, prostitutes in shop windows, and magnificent, empty cathedrals.

During World War II, Hamburg was a great shipbuilding center; the *Bismarck* had been built here, as well as the German U-boat fleet. Naturally it became a prime target of Allied bombing. In July 1943, Operation Gomorrah—the destruction of Hamburg—was the heaviest aerial bombardment in history until that time. But the attack went far beyond the destruction of the factories and the port. The firestorm created by the day and night attacks killed forty-five thousand people in a deliberate campaign to terrorize the population. Most of the workers in the shipyards occupied row houses in Harburg, across the Elbe River, and the Allied bombing was particularly heavy there. Atta lived in an apartment at 54 Marienstrasse, a reconstructed building on a street that had been almost entirely destroyed by the terror bombings.

Atta was a perfectionist; in his work he was a skilled but not creative draftsman. Physically, there was a feminine quality to his bearing: He was "elegant" and "delicate," so that his sexual orientation—however unexpressed—was difficult to read. His black eyes were alert and intelligent but betrayed little emotion. "I had a difficult time seeing the difference between his iris and his pupil, which in itself gave him the appearance of being very, very scary," one of his female colleagues recalled. "He had an unusual habit. When he'd ask a question, and then when he was listening to your response, he pressed his lips together."

On April 11, 1996, when Atta was twenty-seven years old, he signed a standardized will he got from the al-Quds mosque. It was the day Israel attacked Lebanon in Operation Grapes of Wrath. According to one of his friends, Atta was enraged, and by filling out his last testament during the attack he was offering his life in response.

Although the sentiments in the will represent the tenets of his community of faith, Atta constantly demonstrated an aversion to women, who in his mind were like Jews in their powerfulness and corruption. The will states: "No pregnant woman or disbelievers should walk in my funeral or ever visit my grave. No woman should ask forgiveness of me. Those who will wash my body should wear gloves so that they do not touch my genitals." The anger that this statement directs at women and its horror of sexual contact invites the thought that Atta's turn to terror had as much to do with his own conflicted sexuality as it did with the clash of civilizations.

MOHAMMED ATTA, Ramzi bin al-Shibh, Marwan al-Shehhi, and Ziad Jarrah, the four friends from Hamburg, arrived in the Khaldan camp in November 1999 for a preliminary training course. They came at a propitious moment.

In the three years since Khaled Sheikh Mohammed had proposed his "planes operation" to bin Laden in a cave in Tora Bora, al-Qaeda had been researching a plan to strike the American homeland. Mohammed envisioned two waves of hijacked planes, five from the East Coast and five from Asia. Nine of the planes would crash into selected targets, such as the CIA, the FBI, and nuclear plants. Khaled Sheikh Mohammed himself would pilot the last plane. He would kill all the men aboard, then make a proclamation condemning American policy in the Middle East; finally, he would land the plane and set the women and children free.

Bin Laden rejected this last conceit, but in the spring of 1999 bin Laden summoned Mohammed back to Kandahar and gave him the go-ahead to put his plan into operation.

A few months later bin Laden, Khaled Sheikh Mohammed, and Abu Hafs gathered in Kandahar to pick potential targets. The three men were the only ones involved. Their goal was not only to inflict symbolic damage. Bin Laden imagined that America—as a political entity—could actually be destroyed. "America is a great power possessed of tremendous military might and a wide-ranging economy," he later conceded, "but all this is built upon an unstable foundation which can be targeted, with special attention to its obvious weak spots. If it is hit in one hundredth of those spots, God willing, it will stumble, wither away and relinquish world leadership." Inevitably, he believed, the confederation of states that made up America would dissolve.

It was natural, then, that bin Laden wanted to strike the White House and the U.S. Capitol. He also put the Pentagon on his list. If he succeeded in destroying the American seat of government and the headquarters of its military, the actual dismemberment of the country would not seem such a fantasy. Khaled Sheikh Mohammed nominated the World Trade Center, which his nephew Ramzi Yousef had failed to bring down in the bombing six years earlier. The Sears Tower in Chicago and the Library Tower (now called the U.S. Bank Tower) in Los Angeles were also discussed. Bin Laden decided that the attack on the American cities on the West Coast could wait.

There was little money to work with but plenty of willing martyrs. When the plan merely envisioned blowing up the planes in midair, there was no need for trained pilots, but as the concept evolved and took on the brilliance of its eventual design, it became clear that the planes operation would require a disciplined group with skills that might take years to develop.

Bin Laden assigned four of his most reliable men to be a part of the operation. Yet none of the four men could fly; nor could they speak English, which was required for a pilot's license. They had no experience living in the West. Mohammed tried to tutor them. He taught them English phrases and collected brochures for flight schools in the United States. They played flight simulator computer games and watched Hollywood movies featuring hijackings, but the gap between the abilities of the men involved and the grandeur of the mission must have been deflating.

Nawaf al-Hazmi was one of those men. He had come to Afghanistan in 1993 when he was seventeen years old. He was strongly built, with a quick and handsome smile. His father was a wealthy grocer in Mecca. His boyhood friend Khaled al-Mihdhar was also from a prominent Meccan family. Following bin Laden's example, these two rich Saudi boys had fought together in Bosnia and then with the Taliban against the Northern Alliance—the loose group of mujahideen and former Afghan government supporters who were led by Ahmed Shah Massoud. Although he held Saudi citizenship, Mihdhar was originally from Yemen. He married Hoda al-Hada, the sister of one of his Yemeni comrades in arms, and fathered two daughters by her. In fact, it was her family's phone that the FBI had turned up in the embassy bombings investigation and that would prove so important in understanding the scope of al-Qaeda. The movements of these two men, Hazmi and Mihdhar, offered the most realistic hope for American intelligence to uncover the 9/11 conspiracy.

Because they were Saudi citizens, both Hazmi and Mihdhar easily obtained U.S. visas. They didn't even have to apply in person. For the other two prospective hijackers, both Yemenis, the situation was different. Immigration authorities believed that Yemenis were far more likely to disappear into the illegal underground once they arrived in the United States, so they were routinely turned down when they sought visas. Stymied by the inability to get all of his men into America, bin Laden sent them instead to Southeast Asia, to study the possibility of carrying out Khaled Sheikh Mohammed's scheme of simply blowing up American airliners in midair. At that point, the grand plan of attacking the American homeland seemed to have been shelved.

That is the moment when Mohammed Atta and his friends first showed up in Afghanistan. Their arrivals were staggered over a two-week period at the end of November, when the leaves were dropping and Ramadan was about to begin. Abu Hafs spotted them immediately: educated, technical men, with English skills ranging from rudimentary to fluent. They did not need to be told how to live in the West. Visas would be no problem. All they needed was to learn how to fly and to be willing to die.

By the time bin al-Shibh arrived, Atta, Jarrah, and Shehhi told him that they had been picked for a secret, undisclosed mission. The four of them were invited to a Ramadan feast with bin Laden himself. They discussed the Taliban, and bin Laden asked about the conditions of Muslims living in Europe. Then he informed them that they would be martyrs.

Their instructions were to return to Germany and apply to flight schools in the United States.

THERE WERE NOW two separate teams on the rapidly changing planes operation, each of which would lead to a major attack. The Hamburg cell reported their passports lost or stolen in order to cover up their trip to Afghanistan. Meantime, the four men who had originally been selected for the planes operation went to Kuala Lumpur. Besides Khaled al-Mihdhar and Nawaf al-Hazmi, there were the two Yemenis: Abu Bara and Tewfiq bin Attash, who adopted the name Khallad.

Khallad was another elusive but highly significant figure in al-Qaeda. He wore a metal prosthesis in place of the right leg he had lost while fighting against Ahmed Shah Massoud's Northern Alliance. Although he was born in Yemen, he was raised in Saudi Arabia, and he had known bin Laden since he was a child. He had been part of the embassy bombing and the failed attempt to blow up USS *The Sullivans* in the Aden harbor, and he would be the mastermind behind the bombing of the USS *Cole* ten months later.

At the end of 1999, Khallad telephoned Mihdhar and summoned him to a meeting in Kuala Lumpur. It was the only time that members of the two teams would be together. The NSA picked up a conversation from the phone of Mihdhar's father-in-law, Ahmad al-Hada, in Yemen—the one that al-Qaeda used as a message board—in which the forthcoming meeting in Malaysia was mentioned, along with the full name of Khaled al-Mihdhar and the first names of two other participants: Nawaf and Salem. The NSA had information from the same phone that Nawaf's last name was Hazmi, although the agency did not check its own database. "Something nefarious might be afoot," the NSA reported, but it did not pursue the matter further.

The CIA already had the names of Mihdhar and Hazmi, however. Saeed Badeeb, Prince Turki's chief analyst in Saudi intelligence, had previously alerted his American colleagues that they were members of al-Qaeda in one of the monthly meetings in Riyadh. Armed with this knowledge, the CIA broke into Mihdhar's hotel room in Dubai, where he had stopped on his way to Malaysia. The American agents photographed his passport, then faxed it to Alec Station. Inside the passport was the critical information that Mihdhar had a multi-entry American visa, due to expire in April. Alec Station notified various intelligence agencies around the world saying, "We need to continue the effort to identify these travelers and their activities . . . to determine if there is any true threat posed." The same cable said that the FBI had been alerted to the Malaysia meeting and that the bureau had been given copies of Mihdhar's travel documents. That turned out not to be true.

The CIA asked Malaysian authorities to provide surveillance of the meeting in Kuala Lumpur, which took place on January 5 at a secluded condominium in a resort overlooking a golf course designed by Jack Nicklaus. The condo was owned by Yazid Sufaat, the Malaysian businessman who had worked with Zawahiri to cultivate anthrax spores. The meeting was not wiretapped, so the opportunity to discover the plots that culminated in the bombing of the USS *Cole* and the 9/11 attack was lost. Without Mike Scheuer's sleepless vigilance, Alec Station had lost its edge. He was still sitting in the library, waiting to be used.

There was a cable that same day from Riyadh Station to Alec Station concerning Mihdhar's American visa. One of the FBI agents assigned to Alec, Doug Miller, read the cable and drafted a memo requesting permission to advise the FBI of the Malaysia meeting and the likelihood that one or more of the terrorists would be traveling soon to the United States. Such permission was required before transmitting intelligence from one organization to another. Miller was told, "This is not a matter for the FBI." Miller followed up a week later by querying Tom Wilshire, a CIA deputy chief who was assigned to FBI headquarters; Wilshire's job was ostensibly to facilitate the passage of information from the agency to the bureau. Miller sent him the memo he had drafted and asked, "Is this a no go or should I remake it in some way?" Wilshire never responded. After that, Miller forgot about the matter.

Special Branch, the Malaysian secret service, photographed about a dozen al-Qaeda associates entering the condo and visiting Internet cafés. On January 8, Special Branch notified the CIA station chief in Thailand that three of the men from the meeting— Mihdhar, Hazmi, and Khallad—were flying to Bangkok. There, as it happened, Khallad would meet with the bombers of the USS *Cole*. But the CIA failed to alert anyone that the men should be followed. Nor did the agency notify the State Department to put Mihdhar's name on a terror watch list so that he would be stopped or placed under surveillance if he entered the United States.

Three months later, the CIA learned that Hazmi had flown to Los Angeles on January 15, 2000. Had it checked the flight manifest, it would have noticed that Mihdhar was traveling with him. The agency neglected to inform either the FBI or the State Department that at least one known al-Qaeda operative was in the country.

Why would the CIA—knowing that Mihdhar and Hazmi were al-Qaeda operatives, that they had visas to the United States, and that at least one of them had actually arrived on American soil— withhold this information from other government agencies? As always, the CIA feared that prosecutions resulting from specific intelligence might compromise its relationship with foreign services, but there were safeguards to protect confidential information, and the FBI worked routinely with the agency on similar operations. The CIA's experience with John O'Neill, however, was that he would demand complete control of any case that touched on an FBI investigation, as this one certainly did. There were many in the agency—not just the sidelined Scheuer—who hated O'Neill and feared that the FBI was too blundering and indiscriminate to be trusted with sensitive intelligence. And so the CIA may have decided to hide the information in order to keep O'Neill off the case. Several of O'Neill's subordinates strongly endorse this theory.

There may have been other reasons the CIA protected information that it was obliged to give to the bureau. Some other members of the I-49 squad would later come to believe that the agency was shielding Mihdhar and Hazmi because it hoped to recruit them. The CIA was desperate for a source inside al-Qaeda; it had completely failed to penetrate the inner circle or even to place a willing partner in the training camps, which were largely open to anyone who showed up. Mihdhar and Hazmi must have seemed like attractive opportunities; however, once they entered the United States they were the province of the FBI. The CIA has no legal authority to operate inside the country, although in fact the bureau often caught the agency running backdoor operations in the United States. This was especially true in New York City, where there are so many foreign delegations. On many occasions, O'Neill complained to the CIA's chief of station in New York about shenanigans that the I-49 squad had discovered. It is also possible, as some FBI investigators suspect, the CIA was running a joint venture with Saudi intelligence in order to get around that restriction. Of course, it is also illegal for foreign intelligence services to operate in the United States, but they do so routinely.

These are only theories about the CIA's failures to communicate vital information to the bureau, which can perhaps be better explained by the fact that the agency was drowning in a flood of threats and warnings. Alec Station had begun with twelve employees in 1996, a number that had grown to about twenty-five when the Malaysia meeting occurred. There were another thirty or so analysts in the Counterterrorist Center who worked on all forms of terrorism worldwide, but al-Qaeda was not their primary responsibility. The analysts at Alec Station were a junior group, with about three years of experience on average. Most of them were women, which counted against them in the very masculine culture that surrounded the Near East Division of the agency. These young women analysts were the ones primarily charged with preventing a terrorist attack on the United States, a burden that weighed so heavily on them that they came to be seen in the agency as fanatics—"the Manson Family" some called them, after Charles Manson, the convicted psycho-killer. But they were sounding an alarm that the older generation of civil servants did not care to hear.

The atmosphere inside Alec Station was poisoned as a result of the attitude of the CIA analysts who held O'Neill responsible for the firing of Mike Scheuer, the driven leader of Alec from its inception. Only a few months before, the senior FBI agent assigned to Alec had demanded the authority to release CIA information to the bureau, and the quarrel over this matter had gone all the way to Freeh and Tenet, the respective heads of the two institutions. Scheuer was forced to step down, but the FBI agent who did gain that authority developed cancer and had to resign only a few days before the Malaysia meeting. None of the three FBI agents remaining in Alec had the seniority to release information, and consequently they had to rely on the agency to give them permission for any transfer of classified cable traffic. This was true until July 2000, when a more senior agent, Charles E. Frahm, was assigned to Alec. He never saw a single memo or cable or heard any discussion about withholding information from the FBI. When he later learned about the Malaysia meeting, he concluded that the fact that it hadn't been transmitted to the bureau was a mistake, accounted for by the abundance of threats that had occurred during the millennium period.

Many critical events occurred in the interim.

When Mihdhar and Hazmi arrived in Los Angeles, on January 15, 2000, they were supposed to enroll in flight school. They must have been overwhelmed by their assignment. Even finding a place to live would have presented a formidable challenge, since neither of them spoke English. Soon after their arrival, however, they became acquainted with Omar Bayoumi, a forty-two-year-old student who rarely attended classes and was supported by a stipend from a Saudi government contractor. He had drawn the attention of the local FBI office in 1998 because of the suspicions of the manager of the apartment complex where he lived. One of the bureau's sources in San Diego asserted that Bayoumi was an agent for the Saudi government, but that meant little to the FBI investigators, since Saudi Arabia was seen as a loyal ally. In any case, the agents were called off the investigation by their supervisor, who worried that the Bayoumi inquiry would intrude on a major counterterrorism operation then under way.

As Bayoumi later told investigators, he drove up from San Diego on February 1, 2000, to handle some visa matters at the Saudi consulate. From there he went directly to lunch at a halal restaurant nearby and overheard Gulf Arabic being spoken. He talked briefly with Mihdhar and Hazmi, who complained that they were having a hard time in Los Angeles, so he invited them to San Diego. Three days later they showed up. He let them stay in his apartment, then found them another place across the street and lent them money for the first two months' rent. He held a party to introduce them to other members of the Muslim community.

If Bayoumi was sent to oversee the two men, who sent him? Perhaps he was their al-Qaeda contact. They certainly needed a caretaker. The fact that Bayoumi went directly from the Saudi consulate to the restaurant, however, suggests to some investigators that the two future hijackers were already under surveillance by Saudi government officials, who were aware of their membership in al-Qaeda. The CIA is the only government agency that knew who Hazmi and Mihdhar were and that they were in America. The CIA had tracked Mihdhar and Hazmi from Kuala Lumpur to Bangkok to Los Angeles. Perhaps the agency decided that Saudi intelligence would have a better chance of recruiting these men than the Americans. That would leave no CIA fingerprints on the operation as well.

This is the view of some very bitter FBI investigators, who wonder why they were never informed of the existence of al-Qaeda operatives inside America. Mihdhar and Hazmi arrived nineteen months before 9/11. The FBI had all the authority it needed to investigate these men and learn what they were up to, but because the CIA failed to divulge the presence of two active members of al-Qaeda, the hijackers were free to develop their plot until it was too late to stop them.

THE HEAD OF THE NEW YORK BUREAU, Louis Schiliro, retired soon after the turn of the millennium, and O'Neill badly wanted his job. Because of the size and importance of the New York office, he would be an assistant director of the FBI, a position he held temporarily while the bureau considered two candidates for the post—O'Neill and Barry Mawn, the head of the Boston office. Mawn had more experience and O'Neill had more enemies. Moreover, O'Neill's record, which had been unblemished, was now clouded by the incident of letting Valerie James use the bathroom in the offsite facility. Thomas Pickard, the deputy director of the bureau, reputedly told O'Neill that his career was going nowhere. The job went to Mawn.

Mawn was still feeling bruised by the campaign O'Neill had waged against him when the two men happened to meet at a seminar at the FBI academy in Quantico, just after the decision was announced. Mawn answered a knock at his door and found O'Neill holding two beers. "I understand you're an Irishman," O'Neill explained.

Wary about the prospect of working together, Mawn told O'Neill that he was going to need people in the office who were loyal to him. "I'm not sure I can depend on you," he stated flatly, offering to find O'Neill another job, possibly in the New Jersey bureau.

O'Neill pleaded to stay in New York for "family reasons." He said that if Mawn would keep him on, "I'll be more loyal to you than your closest friend."

"You'll still have to prove yourself to me," Mawn warned.

O'Neill agreed. "The only thing I ask in return is that you be supportive of me," he said.

Mawn made the bargain, but he soon learned that supporting O'Neill would be a full-time job.

·   ·   ·

THERE IS AN ANECDOTE that counterterrorism officials often tell about the rendition of Ramzi Yousef. After being captured in Pakistan, he was flown into Stewart Airport in Newburgh, New York, and then transferred to an FBI helicopter for the trip to the Metropolitan Correctional Center next to Federal Plaza in Lower Manhattan. "Two huge guys carried him off the plane, shackled and blindfolded," remembered Schiliro. "After we got airborne and were flying down the Hudson River, one of the SWAT guys asks me, 'Can we take off his blindfold?' It took Yousef a minute to focus his eyes. Ironically, the helicopter was alongside the World Trade Center. The SWAT guy gives him a nudge and says, 'You see, it's still standing.' And Yousef says, 'It wouldn't be if we had had more money.' "

Because it was still standing, however, the Trade Center had become a symbol of the success of New York's Joint Terrorism Task Force, a coalition of the FBI, the CIA, the New York City Police Department, the Port Authority, and various other regional and federal agencies. In September 2000 the JTTF chose to celebrate its twentieth anniversary there, in the famous Windows on the World banquet room. Some of the representatives looked a little out of place in black tie, but this was a night to congratulate themselves. Mayor Rudy Giuliani, a former U.S. attorney for the Southern District of New York, was present, as was Mary Jo White, his successor in that job. She praised the task force for "your close-to-perfect record of successful investigations and convictions," which included Yousef and six other World Trade Center bombers, as well as Sheikh Omar Abdul Rahman and nine of his followers who had planned to assassinate public officials and blow up New York City landmarks. The people in the room had seen the world of terrorism move from the relatively innocent days of Croatian nationalists and anti-Castro Cubans, who had been more interested in publicity than terror, to the sobering new world of deliberate mass murder.

It was a misty night, and the clouds obscured the view from the 106th floor of the tower. O'Neill seemed at ease as he wandered through the room, although some might have wondered why Mary Jo White had omitted his name from the list of FBI officials she chose to acknowledge. Mark Rossini, the new I-49 representative at Alec Station, was there; he had just gotten engaged, and he introduced his fiancée to his boss, a man he idolized. Rossini was one of the Sons of John. He studied everything about O'Neill, including his taste in cigars and restaurants; he even dressed like O'Neill. But Rossini had no idea that his mentor's career had been thrown further into turmoil because of a troubling incident that had occurred two months earlier.

O'Neill had attended a mandated pre-retirement conference in Orlando that July. He had no intention of retiring and was impatient that he had been forced to attend, but since he was in Florida, he asked Valerie James to join him so they could spend the weekend in Miami.

During the conference O'Neill got a page, and he left the room to return the call. When he returned a few minutes later, the other agents had broken for lunch. His briefcase was missing. O'Neill first called the local police, then Mawn. He admitted that the briefcase contained some classified e-mails and one highly sensitive document, the Annual Field Office Report, which contained an itemized breakdown of every national security operation in New York. Both the director of the FBI and the attorney general would have to be notified.

"It's hideous," O'Neill told Valerie when he came back to the room. He was ashen.

Police found the briefcase a couple of hours later in another hotel. A Montblanc pen had been stolen, along with a silver cigar cutter and an expensive lighter. The papers were intact, and fingerprint analysis soon established that they had not been touched, but it was another careless mistake at a pregnable moment in his career.

Even though O'Neill immediately reported the theft and none of the information had been compromised, the Justice Department ordered a criminal inquiry. Mawn thought that was absurd. He would have recommended an oral reprimand or, at worst, a letter of censure. People took work home all the time, he observed; they just never had it stolen. He felt guilty because he had been pushing O'Neill to get the AFOR completed, and O'Neill was just doing what he'd asked.

Despite their competition for the top job in New York, Mawn had become O'Neill's staunchest defender. Mawn appreciated that excellence was the enemy of any bureaucracy and that a forceful personality was essential to fight off the interagency rivalries and departmental jealousies that sap the will of the best people. They were the ones who needed to be protected and encouraged; only then, behind a powerful and visionary leader, could a heartless bureaucracy like the FBI achieve anything remarkable. O'Neill was such a leader. He had made the New York office the most effective branch in the bureau, but it had come at great cost, as Mawn slowly realized. The enemies that O'Neill had accumulated in his polarizing bureaucratic struggle were eager to destroy him, and now he had given them an opening.

AL-QAEDA HAD DEVELOPED a management philosophy that it called "centralization of decision and decentralization of execution." Bin Laden decided on the targets, selected the leaders, and provided at least some of the funding. After that, the planning of the operation and the method of attack were left to the men who would have the responsibility of carrying it out.

That approach had worked well in the embassy bombings, but the operations scheduled for the millennium had gone awry. One had been a comical fiasco: the attempted bombing of USS *The Sullivans* at the end of Ramadan, when the fiberglass skiff that was supposed to attack the destroyer had foundered so ignominiously in Aden's harbor.

Originally, the intention had been to attack an oil tanker off the coast of Yemen. Bin Laden, characteristically, urged the planners to be more ambitious. He wanted them to sink an American warship. When that failed, bin Laden demanded that the two suicide bombers be replaced. The local supervisor of that operation, Abdul Rahim al-Nashiri, stoutly disagreed with bin Laden. He argued that one of the bombers had been injured in the cruise missile attack on the al-Qaeda training camps, and it would be unjust to take away the opportunity to strike an American ship that might well have been a participant in that attack. Moreover, the team had trained together for a year and a half, and Nashiri had built a sophisticated new bomb, one with shaped charges that would concentrate the force of the explosion in one direction. Everything was ready for the next U.S. Navy warship to call at the Yemeni port.

Bin Laden relented and let his supervisor retain control of the operation. He also released a video in which he threatened America with another assault. As in the interview with ABC before the embassy bombings, he included a teasing clue: This time he wore a distinctive, curved Yemeni dagger in his belt. Next to him, Zawahiri declared, "Enough of words. It is time to take action."

ADEN PERCHES ON THE SLOPE of a former volcano, the collapsed cone of which forms one of the finest deepwater ports in the world. The name derives from the belief that this is the site of the Garden of Eden. It is also said to be the spot where Noah launched his ark, and where Cain and Abel are buried. Steeped in legend and antiquity, the city had known prosperity during the British era, which ended in 1967, when the country split apart and the People's Democratic Republic of Yemen began its rocky experiment with secular socialism. The lines of fracture were still evident in 1994, after the war had ended and the country was reunited. Decades of violence and instability had left Aden much reduced from the cosmopolitan port it once had been.

Docked at a fueling buoy was the USS *Cole,* a billion-dollar guided-missile destroyer. Using advanced stealth technology, the sleek warship was designed to be less visible to radar, but it was starkly evident in the Aden harbor: more than five hundred feet long, displacing 8,300 tons, with its swirling antenna scanning the skies for any foreseeable threat. The *Cole* was one of the U.S. Navy's most "survivable" ships, with seventy tons of armor shielding its vital spaces; passive protection for chemical, biological, or nuclear attack; and a hull capable of withstanding an explosion of fifty-one thousand pounds per square inch. In addition to Tomahawk cruise missiles, which it had launched in Operation Infinite Reach, the *Cole* carried anti-ship and anti-aircraft missiles, a five-inch cannon, and the Phalanx Close-In Weapons System, which fires fifty 20-mm shells per second. The ship's network of computers and radars, called AEGIS, was capable of simultaneously tracking hundreds of incoming missiles or aircraft more than two hundred miles away. The *Cole* was superbly designed to fight the Soviet navy.

On October 12, 2000, at 11:15 a.m., as the *Cole* was preparing to get under way, a fiberglass fishing boat approached its massive prey. Some of the sailors were standing watch, but many were belowdecks or waiting in the chow line. Two men brought the tiny skiff to a halt amidships, smiled and waved, then stood at attention. The symbolism and the asymmetry of this moment were exactly what bin Laden had dreamed of. "The destroyer represented the capital of the West," he said, "and the small boat represented Mohammed."

The shock wave of the enormous explosion in the harbor knocked over cars onshore. Two miles away, people thought there was an earthquake. In a taxi in the city, the concussion shook Fahd al-Quso, a member of the al-Qaeda support team who was running late; he was supposed to have videotaped the attack, but he slept through the page on his phone that would have notified him to set up the camera.

A fireball rose from the waterline and swallowed a sailor who had leaned over the rail to see what the men in the little boat were up to. The blast opened a hole forty feet by forty feet in the port side of the ship, tearing apart sailors who were waiting for lunch. Seventeen of them perished, and thirty-nine were wounded. Several of the sailors swam through the blast hole to escape the flames. The great modern man-of-war was gaping open like a gutted animal.

WITHIN HOURS OF THE ATTACK on the *Cole,* Barry Mawn called headquarters and demanded that the New York office gain control of the investigation. "It's al-Qaeda," he told Tom Pickard. He wanted O'Neill to be the on-scene commander.

As he had during the embassy bombings investigation, Pickard declined, saying there was no proof that al-Qaeda was involved. He intended to send the Washington Field Office instead. Mawn went over his head, appealing the decision to Louis Freeh, who immediately agreed that it was New York's case. But the question of sending O'Neill was controversial.

"John's my guy," Mawn insisted. There was no one else with O'Neill's experience and commitment. He was told, "If it falls on bad times, it's your ass."

"I can live with that," said Mawn.

O'Neill was overjoyed. It would be his best chance to break up the criminal enterprise of al-Qaeda and perhaps his last opportunity to redeem his career. "This is it for me," he told a friend in Washington.

O'Neill had learned many lessons since his first day on the job in Washington five years before, when he coordinated the Ramzi Yousef rendition. One of those lessons was to stockpile supplies on skids at Andrews Air Force Base so that a rapid-response team would be ready to go at any moment. In little more than twenty-four hours after the explosion, O'Neill and about sixty FBI agents and support staff were in the air.

They had to stop first in Germany to await clearance from the Yemen authorities, who were still claiming that the explosion had been an accident. Coincidentally, many of the injured sailors were also in Germany, having been flown to the Landstuhl Regional Medical Center, the largest American hospital outside the United States. O'Neill took his investigators directly to the ward where the sailors were being treated. While the bomb technicians swept the victims' hair and clothing for residue, O'Neill went through the room with a naval investigator, talking to the wounded sailors. They were young men and women, most of them not yet out of their teens, some of them missing limbs, some horribly burned. Three of the sailors were too badly wounded to be interviewed. One of them, petty officer Kathy Lopez, was completely swathed in bandages, but she insistently motioned that she wanted to say something. A nurse put her ear to the sailor's lips to hear the whispered words. She said, "Get them."

AS SOON AS ALI SOUFAN, the young Arabic-speaking agent recently assigned to the I-49 squad, got on the plane to Yemen, O'Neill told him that he was the case agent for the USS *Cole*—the biggest assignment of his career.

Soufan is a highly caffeinated talker, his voice carrying a hint of Lebanon, the country where he was born. He knew what it was like to live in lawlessness and chaos, to see cities destroyed. His family fled to America during the civil war, and he loved America because it allowed him to dream. In return, America embraced him. His experience was completely opposite to that of the alienated Muslims in the West who had turned to Islamism as a way of finding an identity. He never personally experienced prejudice because he was an Arab or a Muslim; on the contrary, he was elected president of his student body and presented with many academic awards. After gaining his master's degree in international relations at Villanova University, he planned to get his Ph.D. at Cambridge. But he had developed a fascination with the American Constitution, and like many naturalized citizens, he had a feeling of indebtedness for the new life he had been given. As he stood poised on the brink of an academic career, he decided—"as a joke"—to send his résumé to the FBI. He thought the chances that a Muslim American scholar of Arab extraction would be hired by the bureau were laughably remote, but he was drawn by the mystique, and obviously something inside him cried out to be saved from the classroom. As he was packing to go to England, the response came: report to the FBI Academy in two weeks.

O'Neill had drafted him on the squad because of his language ability, but he soon came to value Soufan's initiative, imagination, and courage. When the plane landed in Aden, the agents looked out upon a detachment of the Yemen Special Forces, wearing yellow uniforms with old Russian helmets, each soldier pointing an AK-47 at the plane. The jittery hostage rescue team, who had been sent along to protect the investigators, immediately responded by breaking out their M4s and their handguns. Soufan realized they were all going to die in a bloodbath on the tarmac if he didn't do something quickly.

He opened the plane's door. One man among the yellow uniforms was holding a walkie-talkie. Soufan walked directly toward him, carrying a bottle of water, while the guns followed him. It was about 110 degrees outside; behind their weapons, the Yemeni soldiers were wilting.

"You look thirsty," Soufan said in Arabic to the officer with the walkie-talkie. He handed him the bottle of water.

"Is it American water?" the officer asked.

Soufan assured him that it was; moreover, he told the man, he had American water for all the others as well. They treated it as such a precious commodity that some would not drink it.

With this simple act of friendship, the soldiers lowered their weapons and Soufan gained control of the airport.

O'Neill was a little puzzled to find the soldiers saluting as he disembarked. "I told them you were a general," Soufan confided.

One of the first things O'Neill noticed was a sign for "Bin Ladin Group International," a subsidiary of the Saudi Binladen Group, which had a contract to rebuild the airport after it was damaged in the 1994 civil war. It was a small reminder that he was playing on his opponent's court.

O'Neill had already spent some time studying the country. He was reading a book by Tim Mackintosh-Smith titled *Yemen: The Unknown Arabia*. He learned that Sanaa, the capital, claimed to be the world's first city and that the Hadramout, bin Laden's homeland, meant "death has come." He underlined these facts with his Montblanc ballpoint in a firm straight hand, as he always did when he was reading. He was determined not to be defeated by the exoticism.

His real adversary, however, turned out to be his own ambassador, Barbara Bodine. She had personally negotiated the agreements between the United States and Yemen two years before, which allowed American warships to refuel in Aden's harbor.

That now seemed a calamitous miscalculation. They met at six o'clock on the morning after O'Neill arrived. In his New Jersey accent, he remarked that he was looking forward to working with her in "Yay-man."

"Ye-men," she coldly corrected him.

From O'Neill's perspective, Yemen was filled with jihadis, and it was still quaking from the civil war. "Yemen is a country of 18 million citizens and 50 *million* machine guns," he later reported. Gunfire was a frequent distraction. The temperature often exceeded 120 degrees, and scorpions were as common as house-flies. Moreover, Yemen was full of spies who were well equipped with listening devices. One of the largest cells of Zawahiri's al-Jihad operated here, and there were many veterans who had fought with bin Laden in Afghanistan. When the rest of O'Neill's team arrived, he warned them, "This may be the most hostile environment the FBI has ever operated in."

Bodine, however, saw Yemen as a promising American ally in an unsettled but strategically crucial part of the world. The country was an infant democracy, far more tolerant than its neighbors; it even allowed women to vote. Unlike O'Neill, the ambassador had plenty of experience working in dangerous places. During the Iraqi invasion and occupation of Kuwait, she had served as deputy chief of mission and stayed through the 137-day siege of the American Embassy by Iraqi troops until all the Americans were evacuated. Moreover, Barbara Bodine was as forceful and blunt as John O'Neill.

Bodine thought she had an understanding with O'Neill that he would bring in a team of no more than fifty. She was furious when many more investigators and support staff arrived. In her mind, it was the same as if a military plane with "three hundred heavily armed people" arrived to take over Des Moines. (O'Neill's account, confirmed by other agents and news reports, said that there were only 150 personnel in his group, not 300.) She pleaded with O'Neill to consider the delicate diplomatic environment he was entering. O'Neill responded that he was here to investigate a crime, not to conduct diplomacy. That was the kind of answer Bodine had come to expect in her dealings with the FBI. "There was the FBI way, and that was it," she had concluded. "O'Neill wasn't unique. He was simply extreme."

Her goal was to preserve the delicate relations between the United States and Yemen, which she had worked hard to improve. Although one can understand that the State Department and the FBI might have two different agendas, in this case Bodine had been given clear directives by the secretary of state to ensure the safety of American investigators and to assist them in their investigation. Those were to be her top priorities, not protecting the relationship with the Yemen government; instead, she continually worked to lower the bureau's "footprint" by reducing the number of agents and stripping them of their heavy weapons, which she said was for their own safety. Meanwhile, on local television each night, the Yemeni parliament featured speakers who were openly calling for jihad against America.

Bodine ordered that the entire FBI team be moved to the Aden Hotel, which was crammed with other U.S. military and government employees. O'Neill's investigators were billeted three and four to a room. "Forty-five FBI personnel slept on mats on the hotel's ballroom floor," O'Neill reported. He set up a command center on the eighth floor of the hotel; fifty Marines guarded the sandbagged hallway. Outside, the hotel was ringed with machine-gun nests manned by Yemeni troops. It wasn't entirely clear what their purpose was, other than to make sure the Americans were confined to the hotel. "We were prisoners," one of the agents recalled.

Early on the morning after his arrival, O'Neill boarded a launch to the *Cole*, which was listing in the harbor a thousand yards offshore. The recovery of the dead was still under way, and bodies lined the deck, draped with American flags. Down below there were clumps of flesh mashed into the tangled mass of wire and metal of a ship that had once seemed so invulnerable. Through the blast hole, O'Neill could see divers searching for bodies and, in the background, the rocky city embracing the port like an ancient theater.

The sailor in charge of refueling the ship told investigators that it normally took about six hours for the ship to take on the 240,000 gallons of fuel it required. They were just forty-five minutes into the process when the bomb exploded. He'd thought the gas line had blown, and he immediately shut off the connection. Then a cloud of black liquid suddenly covered the ship. It was not oily. It was the residue of the bomb.

O'Neill spent much of his time coaxing the Yemeni authorities in the Political Security Organization—the equivalent of the FBI—to cooperate with the investigation. He was conscious of the need to build cases that would survive American standards of justice, so his agents would have to be present during interrogations by local authorities to assure U.S. courts that none of the suspects had been tortured. He also sought to gather eyewitness testimony from residents who had seen the explosion. Both the PSO and Bodine resisted these requests. "You want a bunch of six-foot-two Irish-Americans to go door-to-door?" Bodine asked O'Neill. "And, excuse me, but how many of your guys speak Arabic?"

Actually, there were only half a dozen Arabic speakers in the FBI contingent, and language was a constant source of misunderstanding. O'Neill kept Ali Soufan at his side most of the time. Once, when he was talking to an obstructionist colonel in Yemen intelligence, O'Neill exclaimed in frustration, "Christ, this is like pulling teeth!" When the colonel's personal translator repeated the remark in Arabic, the officer stood up, visibly angry. "What'd I say?" O'Neill asked Soufan. Soufan told him that the translator had told the colonel, "If you don't answer my questions, I'm going to pull out your teeth!"

The Yemeni authorities understandably felt encroached upon and unfairly treated. In exchange for the evidence O'Neill was demanding, they wanted access to any information the FBI gathered outside the country, which for legal reasons O'Neill could not provide. The Yemenis finally produced a videotape taken by a harborside security camera, but it appeared to have been edited to delete the crucial moment of the explosion. When O'Neill expressed his frustration to Washington, President Clinton sent a note to President Ali Abdullah Saleh. It had little effect. The FBI was convinced that the bombers had been tipped off about the arrival of the *Cole*, and they wanted to expand the investigation to include a member of the president's own family and a colonel in the PSO. There was scant interest on the part of the Yemen authorities in pursuing such leads.

O'Neill had spent his entire career romancing police from other countries. He had found that "coppers"—as he called them—formed a universal fraternity. And yet some of his requests for evidence mystified the local detectives, who were not acquainted with the advanced forensic techniques the bureau is famous for. Elementary procedures, such as fingerprinting, were rarely employed. They couldn't understand, for instance, why O'Neill was requesting a hat worn by one of the conspirators, which he wanted to examine for DNA evidence. Even the harbor sludge, which contained residue from the bomb and bits of the fiberglass fishing boat, was off-limits until the bureau paid the Yemeni government $1 million to dredge it. The debris was loaded onto barges and shipped to Dubai for examination.

Yemen was an intensely status-conscious society, and because Soufan had promoted O'Neill to "general," one of his counterparts was General Hamoud Naji, head of Presidential Security. General Naji finally agreed to take them to the site where the bombers had launched their boat. The police had discovered a twelve-year-old boy named Hani who had been fishing on the pier when the bombers unloaded their skiff. One of the men had paid him a hundred Yemeni riyals—about sixty cents—to watch his Nissan truck and boat trailer, but he never returned. The police had arrested Hani to make sure he didn't disappear, and then locked up his father as well to take care of him. "If this is how they treat their cooperating witnesses," O'Neill observed, "imagine how they treat the more difficult ones."

O'Neill also viewed the safe house where the bombers had been living. It was clean and neat. In the master bedroom was a prayer rug oriented to the north, toward Mecca. The bathroom sink was full of body hair that the bombers had shaved before going to their deaths. The investigators were solemn, imagining the scene of the ritual ablutions and the final prayers.

But cooperation was still very slow in coming. "This investigation has hit a rock," General Naji admitted. "We Arabs are very stubborn."

Ali Soufan teased him, saying, "You're dealing with another Arab, and I'm also stubborn."

When Soufan translated this exchange, O'Neill contended that the Arabs were not the equal of the Irish in that department. He told a story about the O'Neill clan in Ireland, who he said had the reputation of being the strongest men in their country. Every year there was a boat race to a giant stone in the middle of a lake, and the O'Neills always won. But one year, another clan was rowing faster and pulling ahead, and it appeared that they would touch the stone first. "But then my great-grandfather took his sword," said O'Neill, "and he cut off his hand and threw it at the rock. You got anything that can match that?"

Soufan and the general looked at each other. "We're stubborn," said Soufan, "but we're not crazy."

ONE OF THE PROBLEMS investigators faced was that the *Cole* was in real danger of sinking. Naval engineers were urgently trying to prevent this indignity. Finally an immense Norwegian semi-submersible salvage ship, with a middle deck designed to dip underwater and scoop up oil platforms, arrived to pick up the wounded warship and take it on its long journey home. The public-address system of the *Cole* broadcast "The Star-Spangled Banner" as it piggybacked out of the harbor, followed defiantly by Kid Rock's "American Bad Ass."

There were so many perceived threats that the agents often slept in their clothes and with their weapons at their sides. The investigators learned from a mechanic that a truck similar to one purchased by the bombers had been brought to his shop to have metal plates installed in a way that might be used to direct the force of an explosion. Certainly the most tempting target for such a bomb would be the hotel where the agents were staying.

Bodine thought these fears were overblown. The agents were suspicious of everyone, she observed, including the hotel staff. She assured O'Neill that the gunfire he frequently heard outside the hotel was probably not directed at the investigators but was simply the noise of wedding celebrations. Then one night, when O'Neill was running a meeting, shots were fired just outside the hotel. The hostage rescue team took positions. Once again, Soufan ventured out to talk to the Yemeni troops stationed in the street.

"Hey, Ali!" O'Neill said. "Be careful!" He had raced down the steps of the hotel to make sure Soufan was wearing his flak jacket. Frustration, stress, and danger, along with the enforced intimacy of their situation, had brought the two men closer. O'Neill had begun to describe Soufan as his "secret weapon." To the Yemenis, he simply called him "my son."

Snipers covered him as Soufan strolled outside. The Yemeni officer stationed there assured him that everything was "okay."

"If everything is okay, why are there no cars on the street?" Soufan asked.

The officer said there must be a wedding nearby. Soufan looked around and saw that the hotel was surrounded with men in traditional dress, some in jeeps, all carrying guns. They were civilians, not soldiers. Soufan was reminded of the tribal uprising in Somalia, which ended with dead American soldiers being dragged through the streets of Mogadishu. That could happen right here, right now, he thought.

O'Neill ordered the U.S. Marines to deploy two armored vehicles to block the street in front of the hotel. The night passed without further incident, but the next day O'Neill relocated his team to the USS *Duluth*, stationed in the Bay of Aden. He had to get permission from the Yemeni government to fly back to shore. The helicopter pilot had to take evasive maneuvers after the craft was painted by an SA-7 missle. O'Neill sent most of the investigators home. He and Soufan and four other agents moved back to the hotel, now practically empty because of bomb threats.

Relations between Bodine and O'Neill deteriorated to the point that Barry Mawn flew to Yemen to assess the situation. "It became clear that she simply hated his guts," Mawn observed, but what Bodine told him was that O'Neill couldn't get along with the Yemenis. For the next ten days Mawn spoke to members of the FBI team and American military officers. Every night, when the Yemen authorities did business, he would go with O'Neill and watch him interact with his counterparts. The meetings invariably went late, with O'Neill cajoling, pressuring, charming, entreating, doing whatever he could do to inch the process along. One such night O'Neill complained to General Ghalib Qamish of the PSO that he needed photographs of the suspects that the Yemenis had arrested. The discussion dragged on deep into the early-morning hours, with General Qamish politely explaining that the FBI was not needed on this case at all and O'Neill patiently describing the urgency of the situation. Mawn could barely keep his head up. But the following night the general announced, "I have your photos for you."

O'Neill thanked him, then went on to beg for the right to interview the suspects face-to-face, rather than feeding questions to the Yemeni interrogators. It was an endless and tortuous negotiation, but in Mawn's view it was carried out with respect and even affection on both sides. General Qamish referred to O'Neill as "Brother John." When Mawn returned, he reported to the director that O'Neill was doing a masterful job, adding that Bodine was his "only detractor." He said as much to Bodine on his way out of the country. He was not recalling O'Neill, he told her. Of course, Mawn was responsible for sending O'Neill in the first place. He may not have wanted to see Bodine's point of view. In any case, ambassadors have the final say over which Americans are allowed to remain in a foreign country, and O'Neill was not one of them.

THE YEMENIS ARRESTED FAHD AL-QUSO, the al-Qaeda cameraman who had overslept his assignment to videotape the bombing, at the end of October. Quso admitted that he and one of the suicide bombers had delivered five thousand dollars to "Khallad"—the one-legged mastermind of the *Cole* attack—in Bangkok. He said the money was to buy Khallad a new prosthesis. The transcript of the conversation was passed along to the FBI a month later.

Soufan remembered the name Khallad from a source he had

recruited in Afghanistan. The source had described a fighter with a metal leg who was the emir of a guesthouse in Kandahar—bin Laden's "errand boy," he had called him. Soufan and O'Neill faxed Khallad's passport photo to the Afghan source, who made a positive identification. That was the first real link between the *Cole* bombing and al-Qaeda.

Soufan wondered why money was leaving Yemen when a major operation was about to take place. Could there be another operation under way that he didn't know about? Soufan sent Khallad's photo to the CIA, asking for information about him and whether there might have been an al-Qaeda meeting in the region. The agency did not respond to his clearly stated request. The fact that the CIA withheld information about the mastermind of the *Cole* bombing and the meeting in Malaysia, when directly asked by the FBI, hampered the pursuit of justice in the death of seventeen American sailors. Much more tragic consequences were on the horizon.

A MONTH AFTER THE *COLE* INVESTIGATION BEGAN, assistant FBI director Dale Watson told the *Washington Post*, "Sustained cooperation" with the Yemenis "has enabled the FBI to further reduce its in-country presence. . . . The FBI will soon be able to bring home the FBI's senior on-scene commander, John O'Neill." It appeared to be a very public surrender to Bodine's complaints. The same day, the Yemeni prime minister told the *Post* that no link had been discovered between the *Cole* bombers and al-Qaeda.

O'Neill came home just before Thanksgiving. Valerie James was shocked when she saw him: He had lost twenty-five pounds. He said that he felt he was fighting the counterterrorism battle alone, without any support from his own government, and he worried that the investigation would grind to a halt without him. Indeed, according to Barry Mawn, Yemeni cooperation slowed significantly when O'Neill left the country. Concerned about the continuing threats against the remaining FBI investigators, O'Neill tried to return in January 2001, but Bodine denied his application. Meanwhile, the American investigators, feeling increasingly vulnerable, retreated behind the walls of the American Embassy in Sanaa.

Soufan finally was allowed to interview Fahd al-Quso, the sleeping cameraman, who was small and arrogant, with a wispy beard that he kept tugging on. Before the interview began, a colonel in the PSO entered the room and kissed Quso on both cheeks—a signal to everyone that Quso was protected. And indeed, whenever it seemed obvious that Quso was on the verge of making an important disclosure, the Yemeni colonel would insist that the session stop for meals or prayers.

Over a period of days, however, Soufan was able to get Quso to admit that he met with Khallad and one of the *Cole* bombers in Bangkok, where they stayed at the Washington Hotel. Quso confessed that his mission was to hand over thirty-six thousand dollars in al-Qaeda funds, not the five thousand he had mentioned before, nor was the money for Khallad's new leg. It now seems evident that the money was used to purchase first-class air tickets for the 9/11 hijackers Mihdhar and Hazmi and support them when they arrived in Los Angeles a few days later, which would have been obvious if the CIA had told the bureau about the two al-Qaeda operatives.

The FBI agents went through phone records to verify Quso's story. They found calls between the Washington Hotel in Bangkok and Quso's house in Yemen. They also noticed that there were calls to both places from a pay phone in Malaysia. It happened to be directly outside the condo where the meeting had taken place. Quso had told Soufan that he was originally supposed to have met Khallad in Kuala Lumpur or Singapore—he couldn't seem to get the two cities straight. Once again, Soufan sent an official teletype to the agency. He sent along a passport picture of Khallad. Do these telephone numbers make any sense? Is there any connection to Malaysia? Any tie to Khallad? Again, the agency had nothing to say.

If the CIA had responded to Soufan by supplying him with the intelligence he requested, the FBI would have learned of the Malaysia meeting and of the connection to Mihdhar and Hazmi. The bureau would have learned—as the agency already knew—

that the al-Qaeda operatives were in America and had been for more than a year. Because there was a preexisting indictment for bin Laden in New York, and Mihdhar and Hazmi were his associates, the bureau already had the authority to follow the suspects, wiretap their apartment, intercept their communications, clone their computer, investigate their contacts—all the essential steps that might have prevented 9/11.

In June 2001, Yemeni authorities arrested eight men who they said were part of a plot to blow up the American Embassy in Yemen, where Soufan and the remainder of the FBI investigators had taken refuge. New threats against the FBI followed, and Freeh, acting on O'Neill's recommendation, withdrew the team entirely.

THE STRIKE ON THE *COLE* had been a great victory for bin Laden. Al-Qaeda camps in Afghanistan filled with new recruits, and contributors from the Gulf states arrived carrying Samsonite suitcases filled with petrodollars, as in the glory days of the Afghan jihad. At last there was money to spread around. The Taliban leadership, which was still divided about bin Laden's presence in the country, became more compliant when cash appeared, despite the threat of sanctions and reprisals. Bin Laden separated his senior leaders—Abu Hafs to another location in Kandahar, and Zawahiri to Kabul—so that the anticipated American response would not kill the al-Qaeda leadership all at once.

But there was no American response. The country was in the middle of a presidential election, and Clinton was trying to burnish his legacy by securing a peace agreement between Israel and Palestine. The *Cole* bombing had occurred just as the talks were falling apart. Clinton maintains that, despite the awkward political timing, his administration came close to launching another missile attack against bin Laden that October, but at the last minute the CIA recommended calling it off because his presence at the site was not completely certain.

Bin Laden was angry and disappointed. He hoped to lure America into the same trap the Soviets had fallen into: Afghanistan. His strategy was to continually attack until the U.S. forces invaded; then the mujahideen would swarm upon them and bleed them until the entire American empire fell from its wounds. It had happened to Great Britain and to the Soviet Union. He was certain it would happen to America. The declaration of war, the strike on the American embassies, and now the bombing of the *Cole* had been inadequate, however, to provoke a massive retaliation. He would have to create an irresistible outrage.

One can ask, at this point, whether 9/11 or some similar tragedy might have happened without bin Laden to steer it. The answer is certainly not. Indeed, the tectonic plates of history were shifting, promoting a period of conflict between the West and the Arab Muslim world; however, the charisma and vision of a few individuals shaped the nature of this contest. The international Salafist uprising might have occurred without the writings of Sayyid Qutb or Abdullah Azzam's call to jihad, but al-Qaeda would not have existed. Al-Qaeda depended on a unique conjunction of personalities, in particular the Egyptians—Zawahiri, Abu Ubaydah, Saif al-Adl, and Abu Hafs—each of whom manifested the thoughts of Qutb, their intellectual father. But without bin Laden, the Egyptians were only al-Jihad. Their goals were parochial. At a time when there were many Islamist movements, all of them concentrated on nationalist goals, it was bin Laden's vision to create an international jihad corps. It was his leadership that held together an organization that had been bankrupted and thrown into exile. It was bin Laden's tenacity that made him deaf to the moral quarrels that attended the murder of so many and indifferent to the repeated failures that would have destroyed most men's dreams. All of these were qualities that one can ascribe to a cult leader or a madman. But there was also artistry involved, not only to achieve the spectacular effect but also to enlist the imagination of the men whose lives bin Laden required.

19

The Big Wedding

SOCIAL EVENTS WERE RARE in the al-Qaeda community, but bin Laden was in the mood to celebrate. He arranged a marriage between his seventeen-year-old son, Mohammed, and Abu Hafs's fourteen-year-old daughter, Khadija. She was a quiet, unlettered girl, and the women wondered what she and Mohammed would have to say to each other. They could just imagine the surprises that awaited her on her wedding night, since sexual matters were rarely discussed, especially with children.

For the occasion bin Laden had taken over a large hall—a former movie theater on the outskirts of Kandahar that had been gutted by the Taliban—to accommodate the five hundred men in attendance. (The women were in a separate facility with the young bride.) He began the festivities by reading a long poem, apologizing that it was not his own work, but that of his speechwriter. "I am not, as most of our brothers know, a warrior of the word," he said modestly. The poem included a tribute to the bombing of the *Cole:*

> *A destroyer, even the brave might fear,*
> *She inspires horror in the harbor and the open sea,*
> *She goes into the waves flanked by arrogance, haughtiness, and*
>   *fake might,*
> *To her doom she progresses slowly, clothed in a huge illusion,*
> *Awaiting her is a dinghy, bobbing in the waves.*

Two television cameras recorded the event, but bin Laden wasn't satisfied with the result—knowing that the poem would be featured on the Arabic satellite channels and an al-Qaeda recruitment video—so he had the cameras set up again the following morning to record his recitation a second time. He even stationed a few supporters in front of him to cry out praise, as if there were hundreds still in the hall, instead of a handful of reporters and cameramen. His image management extended to asking one of the reporters, who had taken a digital snapshot, to take another picture because his neck was "too full." He had dyed his beard to cover the streaks of gray, but he couldn't disguise the dark circles under his eyes that testified to the anxiety and sleeplessness that had become his steady companions.

Twelve-year-old Hamza, the only child of bin Laden's favorite wife, also read a poem at the wedding. He had long black eyelashes and his father's thin face, and he wore a white turban and a camouflage vest. "What crime have we committed to be forced to leave our country?" he asked solemnly, with impressive composure. "We will fight the *kafr* forever!"

"Allahu akhbar!" the men roared in response. Then they began to sing:

> *Our men are in revolt, our men are in revolt.*
> *We will not regain our homeland*
> *Nor will our shame be erased except through*
> *Blood and fire.*
> *On and on it goes.*
> *On and on it goes.*

Following afternoon prayer, the meal was served—meat, rice, and tomato juice. It was a rare extravagance for bin Laden. Some of the diners thought the food rather primitive, however, and his stepfather noticed something larval squirming inside his water glass.

"Eat! Eat!" the guests cried, as they peeled oranges for the young groom. "He has a long night ahead!" The men remarked how much the son's shy smile resembled his father's. They danced and sang more songs and lifted the boy up and cheered. Then they put him in a car and sent him to the family compound for his first night of married life.

A FEW MONTHS after the inauguration of George W. Bush, Dick Clarke met with Condoleezza Rice, the national security advisor for the incoming Bush administration, and asked to be reassigned. From the moment the new team had taken over, it was clear that terrorism had a lower priority. When Clarke first briefed her, in January, about the threat that bin Laden and his organization posed to the United States, Rice had given him the impression that she had never heard of al-Qaeda. She subsequently downgraded his position, that of the national coordinator for counterterrorism, so that he would now be reporting to deputies, not to principals. Clarke pressed his strategy of aiding Ahmed Shah Massoud and the Northern Alliance in their struggle against the Taliban and al-Qaeda, but Rice demurred, saying that the administration needed a broader strategy that would include other Pashtun opponents of the Taliban. But the planning for that dragged on for months, without much force. "Maybe you need someone less obsessive," Clarke now suggested, his irony lost on Rice and her deputy, Stephen Hadley. They were surprised and asked him to stay on until October. During that time, they told him, he should find "someone similar" to replace him.

"There's only one guy that fits that bill," said Clarke.

O'Neill viewed Clarke's job as a perfect fit for him. The offer came at a time when he was despairing about the government's tangled response to terrorism and distressed about his future. He had always harbored two aspirations—to become deputy director of the bureau in Washington or to take over the New York office. Freeh was retiring in June, so there would be some vacancies at the top; but the investigation into the briefcase incident would likely block any promotion in the bureau. As the nation's new terrorism czar, however, he would be personally vindicated, and he must have relished the prospect of having both the FBI and the CIA answer to him.

On the other hand, he was financially pressed, and he would still be at the same pay grade in the White House as in the bureau. The Justice Department inquiry had been a ruinous blow. In addition to his other debts, he now owed his attorney eighty thousand dollars, more than he took home in a year.

Throughout the summer, Clarke courted O'Neill, who agonized but refused to commit. He discussed the offer with a number of friends but became alarmed when he thought that FBI headquarters might hear of it. He called Clarke in a fit of anxiety and said that people in the CIA knew he was being considered. "You have to tell them it's not true," he pleaded. He was certain that if the agency knew, the bureau was sure to find out. Clarke dutifully called one of his friends in the CIA and said that, by the way, he was looking for names for his replacement since O'Neill had turned him down—even though O'Neill still wanted to be a candidate for that position. O'Neill also talked about the offer to Mawn, saying that he didn't want him to hear it through the grapevine, but he pointedly told Mawn he wasn't at all interested in the job.

Money would have been a barrier, but O'Neill—by now a veteran bureaucratic infighter—also understood the ruthlessness with which some powerful people in Washington would greet the news of his new position. Clarke's offer was tempting, but it was also dangerous.

FOR YEARS, Zawahiri had been battling elements inside al-Jihad who opposed his relationship with bin Laden. He spewed disdain on the Jihad members who found fault with him from comfortable perches in Europe. He called them "the hot-blooded revolutionary strugglers who have now become as cold as ice after they experienced the life of civilization and luxury." Increasingly, many of his former allies, exhausted and demoralized by years of setbacks, had become advocates of the initiative by Islamist leaders imprisoned in Egypt, who had declared a unilateral ceasefire. Others no longer wanted to endure the primitive living conditions in Afghanistan. Yet, even as the organization was disintegrating, Zawahiri rejected any thought of negotiating with the Egyptian regime or with the West.

In an angry moment he actually resigned as the emir of al-Jihad, but without him the organization was totally adrift. Several months later, his successor relinquished the post, and Zawahiri was back in charge. According to testimony given at the trial of the Albanian cell members, however, there were only forty members left outside Egypt, and within the country the movement had been eradicated. Al-Jihad was dying, and with it the dream that had animated Zawahiri's imagination since he was a teenager. Egypt was lost to him.

The end came in June 2001, when al-Qaeda absorbed al-Jihad, creating an entity formally called Qaeda al-Jihad. The name reflected the fact that the Egyptians still made up the inner circle; the nine-member leadership council included only three non-Egyptians. But it was bin Laden's organization, not Zawahiri's.

Naturally, the domination by the Egyptians was a subject of contention, especially among the Saudi members of al-Qaeda. Bin Laden tried to mollify the malcontents by explaining that he could always count on the Egyptians because they were unable to go home without being arrested; like him, they were men without a country.

Bin Laden turned to Zawahiri and the Egyptians with a particular task. He wanted them to kill Ahmed Shah Massoud. The Northern Alliance commander represented the only credible force keeping the Taliban from completely consolidating their hold on Afghanistan. Slender and dashing, Massoud was a brilliant tactician, and he was willing to match the Taliban in ruthlessness. Now that the Taliban had allied itself with al-Qaeda, Dick Clarke and others saw Massoud as the last chance for an Afghan solution to the bin Laden problem.

Massoud was an eager partner. He was himself a dedicated Islamist whose wife wore a burka and whose troops had committed more than one massacre. Like his competitors, he probably supported his militia on the opium trade. But he spoke a rudimentary French, which he learned in high school in Kabul, and he was well known for his love of Persian poetry, which made him seem like a civilized alternative to the Taliban. In February, Taliban goons had gone through the Kabul museum with sledgehammers, pulverizing the artistic heritage of the country; then in March, they used tanks and anti-aircraft weapons in Bamiyan Province to destroy two colossal images of the Buddha that had loomed above the ancient Silk Road for fifteen hundred years. To the degree that the Taliban were sinking in the world's estimation, Massoud was rising.

In a reflection of his increased international stature, Massoud addressed the European Parliament in Strasbourg, France, in April 2001. He spoke about the danger that al-Qaeda posed to the world. He also told American officials that his own intelligence had learned of al-Qaeda's intention to perform a terrorist act against the United States that would be vastly greater than the bombings of the American embassies in East Africa.

In July, Zawahiri composed a letter in poorly written French purporting to be from the Islamic Observation Centre in London. He requested permission for two journalists to interview Massoud. That letter was followed up by a personal recommendation from Abdul Rasul Sayyaf. Permission was granted.

Massoud was not alone in his warnings to America. In addition to the gleeful chatter that the NSA was picking up about a major attack ("spectacular," "another Hiroshima") that was in the works, intelligence agencies from Arab countries, with better human sources, issued dire advisories. Egyptian president Hosni Mubarak warned the United States that terrorists were planning to attack President Bush in Rome, "using an airplane stuffed with explosives," while he was on his way to the G-8 summit in Genoa that July. The Italian authorities put up anti-aircraft emplacements to prevent the attack. The Taliban foreign minister, Wakil Ahmed Muttawakil, confided to the American consul general in Peshawar and the United Nations in Kabul that al-Qaeda was planning a devastating strike on the United States. He feared that American retaliation would destroy his country. Around the same time, Jordanian intelligence overheard the name of the rumored operation, which it passed along to Washington: The Big Wedding. In the culture of suicide bombers, the day of a martyr's death is his wedding day, when he greets the maidens of Paradise.

BIN LADEN DECIDED to take another bride himself, a fifteen-year-old Yemeni girl named Amal al-Sada. One of bin Laden's bodyguards traveled to the mountain town of Ibb to pay a bride price of five thousand dollars. According to Abu Jandal, the wedding was a splendid celebration. "Songs and merriment were mixed with the firing of shots into the air."

Although the marriage seems to have been a political arrangement between bin Laden and an important Yemeni tribe, meant to boost al-Qaeda recruitment in Yemen, bin Laden's other wives were upset, and even his mother chastised him. Two of bin Laden's sons, Mohammed and Othman, angrily confronted Abu Jandal. "Why do you bring our father a girl of our age?" they demanded. Abu Jandal complained that he had not even known that the money he took to Yemen was to purchase a bride. He had thought it was for a martyrdom operation.

Najwa, bin Laden's first wife, left at about this time. After eleven children and twenty-seven years of marriage, she decided to return to Syria, taking her daughters and her retarded son, Abdul Rahman, with her. The man she had married was not a mujahid or an international terrorist; he was a rich Saudi teenager. The life she might have expected as bin Laden's wife was one of wealth, travel, society; an easy existence made more comfortable with the usual retinue of servants, a beach house, a yacht, perhaps an apartment in Paris. This was the minimum. Instead, she had lived a life on the run, deprived, often in squalor. She had sacrificed so much, but now she was free.

ON MAY 29, 2001, in a federal courtroom in Manhattan, a jury convicted four men in the bombings of the American embassies in East Africa. It was the capstone of a perfect record of twenty-five terrorist convictions accomplished by the prosecutors of the

Southern District of New York, which was headed by Mary Jo White, with her assistants Kenneth Karas and Patrick Fitzgerald. The struggle against Islamic terrorists had begun in 1993 with the first World Trade Center bombing. Eight years later, these convictions were practically the only victories that America could point to, and they were based upon the laborious investigations of the New York bureau of the FBI, particularly the I-49 squad.

O'Neill sat in on the closing arguments and after the verdict he drew Steve Gaudin aside. Gaudin was the agent who had broken Mohammed al-'Owhali, who had gotten his wish to be tried in America. O'Neill put his arm around Gaudin and told him he had a gift for him. "I'm sending you to a language school in Vermont. You're gonna learn Arabic."

Gaudin reeled at the thought.

"You know this fight ain't over," O'Neill continued. "What did al-'Owhali tell you? He said, 'We have to hit you outside so they won't see us coming on the inside.' "

O'Neill understood that the crime model was just one way to deal with terrorism, and that it had limits, especially when the adversary was a sophisticated foreign network composed of skilled and motivated ideologues who were willing to die. But when Dick Clarke had said to him during the millennium arrests, "We're going to kill bin Laden," O'Neill didn't want to hear about it. Although al-Qaeda posed a far greater challenge to law enforcement than the Mafia, or any criminal enterprise, had, the alternatives—military strikes, CIA assassination attempts—had accomplished nothing except to aggrandize bin Laden in the eyes of his admirers. The twenty-five convictions, on the other hand, were genuine and legitimate achievements that demonstrated the credibility and integrity of the American system of justice. But the jealous rivalry among government agencies, and the lack of urgency at FBI headquarters, hobbled the I-49 squad in New York, who had been rendered blind to the danger that, as it turned out, was already in the country.

As the embassy bombings trial was ending, nearly all of the nineteen 9/11 hijackers had settled in the United States. About this time, Tom Wilshire, who was the CIA's intelligence representative to the FBI's international terrorism section at FBI headquarters, was studying the relationship between Khaled al-Mihdhar and Khallad, the one-legged mastermind of the *Cole* bombing. The CIA had thought, because of the similarity of names, that they might be the same person, but thanks to Ali Soufan's investigations, the agency now knew that Khallad was part of bin Laden's security team. "OK. This is important," Wilshire noted in an e-mail to his supervisors at the CIA Counterterrorist Center. "This is a major-league killer, who orchestrated the *Cole* attack and possibly the Africa bombings." Wilshire already knew that Nawaf al-Hazmi was in the United States and that Hazmi and Mihdhar had traveled with Khallad. He also discovered that Mihdhar had a U.S. visa. "Something bad was definitely up," Wilshire decided. He asked permission to disclose this vital information to the FBI. The agency never responded to his request.

That summer, Wilshire asked that an FBI analyst assigned to the CTC, Margarette Gillespie, review the material about the Malaysia meeting "in her free time." She didn't get around to it until the end of July. Wilshire did not reveal the fact that some of the participants in the meeting might be in the United States. In fact he conveyed none of the urgency reflected in his note, even though he was privy to the reports that al-Qaeda was planning a "Hiroshima" inside America.

Wilshire did want to know, however, what the FBI knew. He gave Dina Corsi, another FBI analyst stationed at bureau headquarters, three surveillance photos from the Malaysia meeting to show to several I-49 agents. The pictures showed Mihdhar and Hazmi and a man who resembled Quso. Wilshire did not tell Corsi why the pictures had been taken, but he did say one of the men was named Khaled al-Mihdhar. Meantime, Maggie Gillespie researched the Intelink database about the Malaysia meeting, but the agency had not posted any reports about Mihdhar's visa or Hazmi's arrival in the country. There was NSA coverage of the events leading up to the Malaysia meeting, but Intelink advised her that such information was not to be shared with criminal investigators. On June 11, another CIA supervisor, Clark Shannon, along with Maggie Gillespie and Dina Corsi, went to New

York to talk with the agents on the *Cole* investigation—except for Soufan, who was out of the country. The meeting started in mid-morning with the New York FBI agents thoroughly briefing the others on the progress of their investigation. That went on for three or four hours. Finally, about two in the afternoon, Shannon, the CIA supervisor, asked Corsi to display the photographs to her colleagues. There were three high-quality surveillance photos. One, shot from a low angle, showed Mihdhar and Hazmi standing beside a tree. The supervisor wanted to know if the agents recognized anyone, and if Quso was in any of the pictures.

The FBI agents on the I-49 squad asked who was in the pictures, and when and where they were taken. "And were there any other photographs?" one of the agents demanded. Shannon refused to say. Corsi promised that "in the days and weeks to come" she would try to get permission to pass that information along. The meeting became heated; people began yelling at each other. The FBI agents knew that clues to the crimes they were trying to solve were being dangled in front of their eyes, but they couldn't squeeze any further information from Shannon or the two FBI analysts—except for one detail: Corsi finally dropped the name Khaled al-Mihdhar.

Steve Bongardt, a former Navy pilot and Annapolis graduate who was on the I-49 squad, asked the supervisor to provide a date of birth or a passport number to go with Mihdhar's name. A name by itself was not sufficient to put a stop on his entry into the United States. Bongardt had just returned from Pakistan with a list of thirty names of suspected al-Qaeda associates and their dates of birth, which he had given to the State Department as a precaution to make sure they didn't get into the country. That was standard procedure, the very first thing most investigators would do. But the CIA supervisor declined to provide the additional information.

One can imagine a different meeting, in which the CIA supervisor was authorized to disclose the vital details of Mihdhar's travel to the United States, his connection to the telephone in Yemen that was a virtual al-Qaeda switchboard, his association with Hazmi, who was also in America, their affiliation with al-Qaeda and with Khallad. The pictures that were laid out on the table in the New York office contained within them not only the answers to the planning of the *Cole* attack but also the stark fact that al-Qaeda was inside the United States and planning to strike.

There was a fourth photo of the Malaysia meeting, however, that the CIA supervisor did not produce. That was a picture of Khallad. The *Cole* investigators certainly knew who he was. They had an active file on him and had already talked to a grand jury, preparing to indict him. That fourth photo would have prompted O'Neill to go to Mary Margaret Graham, who headed the New York office of the CIA, which was located in the World Trade Center, and demand that the agency turn over all information relating to Khallad and his associates. By withholding the picture of Khallad standing beside the future hijackers, however, the CIA blocked the bureau's investigation into the *Cole* attack and allowed the 9/11 plot to proceed.

At the time, Mihdhar had returned to Yemen and then gone to Saudi Arabia, where presumably he had been herding the remaining hijackers into the United States. Two days after the frustrating meeting between the CIA supervisor and the I-49 squad, Mihdhar received a new American visa from the consulate in Jeddah. Since the CIA had not given his name to the State Department to post on its watch list, Mihdhar disembarked in New York on the Fourth of July.

THE JUNE 11 MEETING was the culmination of a bizarre trend in the U.S. government to hide information from the people who most needed it. There had always been certain legal barriers to the sharing of information. By law—Rule 6E of the Federal Rules of Criminal Procedure—information arising from grand jury testimony is secret. The bureau took that as a nearly absolute bar to revealing any investigative material at all. Every morning on Dick Clarke's classified computer there were at least a hundred reports, from the CIA, the NSA, and other intelligence branches, but the FBI never disseminated such information. Rule 6E also meant that agents could not talk about criminal cases with colleagues who were working intelligence—even if they were in the same squad.

But until the second Clinton administration, information derived from intelligence operations, especially if it might involve a crime, was freely given to criminal investigators. In fact, it was essential. Agents in the 26 Federal Plaza building would often go upstairs to a highly secure room where they could read NSA transcripts and get briefings by a CIA representative posted there. Such cooperation helped convict Sheikh Omar Abdul Rahman, for instance; the wiretaps that had been placed in his apartment during an intelligence-gathering operation proved that he authorized terrorist bombings in New York. But there was always the concern that intelligence operations would be compromised by the disclosure of sensitive information during a trial.

The Justice Department promulgated a new policy in 1995 designed to regulate the exchange of information between agents and criminal prosecutors, but not among the agents themselves. FBI headquarters misinterpreted the policy, turning it into a straitjacket for its own investigators. They were sternly warned that sharing intelligence information with criminal investigators could mean the end of an agent's career. A secret court in Washington, created by the 1978 Foreign Intelligence Surveillance Act, became the arbiter of what information could be shared— "thrown over the Wall," in the parlance of the court. Bureaucratic confusion and inertia allowed the policy to gradually choke off the flow of essential information to the I-49 counterterrorism squad.

The CIA eagerly institutionalized the barrier that separated it from the bureau. The formula used by the CIA supervisor in the June 11 meeting to justify not telling the agents the identities of the men in the photographs was that it would compromise "sensitive sources and methods." The source of their intelligence about the Malaysia meeting was the telephone in Yemen belonging to the al-Qaeda loyalist, Ahmed al-Hada, that was so central in mapping al-Qaeda's network. The Hada phone was an al-Qaeda clearinghouse and an intelligence bonanza. Ironically, it was the FBI's investigation in the embassy bombings case—headed by the New

York office—that had uncovered the Hada phone in the first place. Any information that had to do with the Hada household was crucial. The CIA knew that one of the men in the photographs of the Malaysia meeting—Khaled al-Mihdhar—was Hada's son-in-law, but the agency also kept this vital detail from the bureau.

The NSA, not wanting to bother with applying to the FISA court for permission to distribute essential intelligence, simply restricted its distribution. For example, in San Diego, Mihdhar made eight calls to the Hada phone to talk to his wife, who had just given birth, which the NSA did not distribute at all. There was a link chart on the wall of the "bullpen"—the warren of cubicles housing the I-49 squad—showing the connections between Ahmed al-Hada's phone and other phones around the world. It provided a map of al-Qaeda's international reach. Had the line been drawn from the Hada household in Yemen to Hazmi and Mihdhar's San Diego apartment, al-Qaeda's presence in America would have been glaringly obvious.

The I-49 squad responded to the constraints in several aggressive and creative ways. When the NSA began to withhold intercepts of bin Laden's satellite phone from the bureau and from prosecutors in the Southern District, the squad came up with a plan to build two antennae, one in the remote Pacific islands of Palau and another in Diego Garcia, in the Indian Ocean, that would capture the signal from the satellite. The NSA fought this scheme but finally coughed up 114 transcripts to prevent the antennae from being built. It kept a tight hold on other intercepts, however. The squad also constructed an ingenious satellite telephone booth in Kandahar for international calls, hoping to provide a convenient facility for jihadis wanting to call home. The agents could not only listen in on the calls, they received video of callers through a camera hidden in the booth. In Madagascar, I-49 agents built an antenna aimed at intercepting the phone calls of Khaled Sheikh Mohammed. Millions of dollars and thousands of hours of labor were consumed in replicating information that the U.S. government already had but refused to share.

The agents on the I-49 were so used to being denied access to intelligence that they bought a CD of a Pink Floyd song, "Another

Brick in the Wall." Whenever they received the same formulation about "sensitive sources and methods," they would hold up the phone to the CD player and push Play.

ON THE FIFTH OF JULY 2001, Dick Clarke assembled representatives of various domestic agencies—the Federal Aviation Administration, the Immigration and Naturalization Service, the Coast Guard, the FBI, and the Secret Service among them—to issue a warning. "Something really spectacular is going to happen here, and it's going to happen soon," he told them.

The same day, John O'Neill and Valerie James arrived in Spain, where he had been invited to address the Spanish Police Foundation. O'Neill decided to take a few days of vacation to decide what to do with his life. Although the Justice Department had dropped its inquiry into the briefcase incident, the bureau was conducting an internal investigation of its own, which kept the pressure on. Meantime, he had learned that the *New York Times* was preparing a story about the affair. The reporters not only knew about the classified material in the briefcase, they also had information about the previous incident with Val at the safe house parking garage and about O'Neill's personal debt. This information had been leaked to them by someone in the bureau or the Justice Department, along with highly sensitive details about the budget that O'Neill had been preparing. The very material that had caused the Justice Department and the bureau to investigate O'Neill had been freely given to reporters in order to further sabotage his career. The leak seemed to be timed to destroy his chances of being confirmed for Clarke's job in the NSC, which by now was an open secret.

Before leaving for Spain, O'Neill had met with Larry Silverstein, the president of Silverstein Properties, which had just taken over the management of the World Trade Center. Silverstein offered him a position as chief of security. It would pay more than twice his government salary. But O'Neill could not commit. He told Barry Mawn that he didn't want to resign from the FBI with his reputation still in question. He promised Silverstein an answer when he returned from Spain; he also had still not turned down Dick Clarke.

He and Val and her son, Jay, spent several days in Marbella, playing golf and reading. Mark Rossini, who often served as a liaison between the FBI and the Spanish police, had come along to translate. On July 8, O'Neill lit a cigar on the verandah of the villa where they were staying and told Rossini, "I'm K.M.A."

It was the twentieth anniversary of the day he became an FBI agent. That is the time when an FBI agent can retire with his full pension and finally tell the bureau, "Kiss my ass."

O'Neill was smiling, Rossini observed, but his eyes were sad. He was on the verge of making his choice. Rossini could see that O'Neill was saying good-bye to the man he had been, and to the man he might have been. There were dreams that would never be realized. For one, he would never catch Osama bin Laden.

All the time that O'Neill was in Spain, Mohammed Atta and Ramzi bin al-Shibh were also in the country, in a little coastal resort called Salou, reviewing the final details of the 9/11 strike.

IN THE SAME WAY that his dress and manners paid tribute to the FBI's traditional opponent, the mobster, O'Neill also displayed an affinity for the terrorist mind. His hero was the Irish nationalist Michael Collins, the martyred leader of Sinn Fein and the inventor of modern guerrilla warfare, who (like O'Neill) had been betrayed by his own people. Although O'Neill worked against the Irish Republican Army as an FBI agent, supervising several highly successful operations, he sympathized with its aspirations. He obviously saw something of himself in Michael Collins. But for the last decade he had found himself matched in a mortal contest against the most daring terrorist in history, whose goals appalled him but whose commitment and relentlessness were unequaled.

After the *Cole* investigation and the inquiry about the briefcase, O'Neill grasped that his reputation was so undermined that the NSC job was now out of the question. The usual course of a retired FBI executive is to become a security consultant in a high-paying corporate job, so that in the final years of his career he can finally cash in. O'Neill had applied for several positions of that sort, but the one that he settled on when he returned from Spain was the World Trade Center post. Some of his friends, including Mark Rossini, congratulated him, saying, "At least now you'll be safe. They already tried to bomb it." And O'Neill replied, "They'll try again. They'll never stop trying to get those two buildings." Once again, he was instinctively placing himself in the bull's-eye. And perhaps in this decision there was a certain acceptance of his fate.

One can imagine that John O'Neill's life exemplified, in the minds of Islamic radicals as well as believers of many faiths, the depravity that was characteristic of his country and his age. It was a time in America when, spiritually speaking, people were pushed to extremes. The comfortable morality of the center had decayed, along with the mainstream denominations, which were withering into irrelevance; meanwhile, rapidly growing funda- mentalist churches were transforming the political landscape. The sexual decadence of the Clinton presidency was replaced by the dogmatism of the religious right. O'Neill, too, was pulled between turpitude and extreme piousness. He was an adulterer, a philanderer, a liar, an egotist, and a materialist. He loved celebrity and brand names, and he lived well beyond his means. These qualities were exactly the stereotypes that bin Laden used to paint his portrait of America. But now O'Neill was reaching for a spiri- tual handhold.

He had moved away from the Catholic Church when he met Valerie. She was the daughter of a fundamentalist preacher in Chicago. O'Neill loved the fire-and-brimstone services, but at the same time he was leading a national FBI probe of the violence of anti-abortion protesters. Both he and Val became aware of the power and danger of fundamentalist beliefs. These were people who went to churches very similar to the ones they did, who were drawn to ecstatic experiences that more traditional faiths could not provide. The difference was that the protesters were willing to kill others in the name of God. When O'Neill and Val moved to New York, they attended the stately Marble Collegiate Church on

Fifth Avenue, which had been the pulpit of Norman Vincent Peale and his upbeat philosophy of "positive thinking." It was a safe harbor, but O'Neill was too unsettled for such sedate religion.

After the incident in the FBI parking garage, O'Neill began reading the Bible every day. In Yemen, he kept a Bible on his bedside table, along with a recent biography of Michael Collins. He returned to Catholicism in the spring of 2001, attending Mass every morning. He told Val that a priest was counseling him about getting a divorce. That August his wife, Christine, signed a property agreement, which gave her custody of the children and the house in Linwood, New Jersey. But his impending freedom seemed only to add to the spiritual burden he was carrying.

O'Neill bought a book titled *Brush Up on Your Bible!* As a preacher's daughter, Val knew the Bible far better than O'Neill did, no matter how hard he studied. They got into heated discussions about salvation. He believed that a soul was saved through good works; Val thought it was only through belief in Jesus Christ. She always had the sickening feeling that he was doomed.

Soon after he returned from Spain, O'Neill happened upon a children's book titled *The Soul Bird*. Val was in the bathroom getting ready for work when O'Neill came in to read it to her. She was only half paying attention. The story is about a bird that perches on one foot inside our soul.

> This is the soul bird.
> It feels everything we feel.

O'Neill, the tough guy, with his service automatic strapped on his ankle, read that the soul bird runs around in pain when someone hurts us, then swells with joy when we are embraced. Then he came to the part about the drawers:

> Do you want to know what the soul bird is made of?
> Well, it's really quite simple: it's made of drawers.
> These drawers can't be opened just like that—because each is locked with its own special key!

Valerie was taken aback as O'Neill began to weep. But he continued to read about the drawers—one for happiness, one for sadness, one for jealousy, one for contentment—until suddenly he was sobbing so hard that he couldn't finish. He was completely broken.

Immediately after that episode, he buried himself in prayer. He had a couple of prayer guides, and he marked his favorites with ribbons or Post-it notes. He was particularly drawn to the Psalms, including number 142:

> *On the way where I shall walk*
> *they have hidden a snare to entrap me.*
> *Look on my right and see:*
> *there is not one who takes my part.*
> *I have no means of escape,*
> *not one cares for my soul.*
> *I cry to you, O Lord.*
> *I have said: "You are my refuge,*
> *all I have left in the land of the living."*
> *Listen then to my cry*
> *for I am in the depths of distress.*

In the back of one of his red-leather breviaries, he clipped a schedule of Catholic prayer times, and on July 30 he began to obsessively check them off. It is now a rare practice for ordinary Catholics to pray four or five times a day, as Muslims do, but the ancient practice is still available to members of the clergy and extremely fervent believers. Perhaps in his worship O'Neill drew parallels between the early church and certain aspects of modern Islamism, since the church calendar is full of martyrs and stern ideologues who would be seen as religious extremists today. He began this regimen on the feast day of Peter Chrysologus, the bishop of Ravenna, who banned dancing and persecuted the heretics. The next day, July 31, celebrates Saint Ignatius of Loyola, the indomitable Spanish soldier who founded the Jesuit order. The vision these saints had of a society governed by God is far more like that of Sayyid Qutb than that of most modern Christians.

In his schedule, O'Neill checked off every prayer until Sunday, August 19, the day the article about the briefcase incident finally appeared in the *Times*. Then the marks abruptly stopped.

"THE DUTIES OF THIS RELIGION are magnificent and difficult," bin Laden said in a videotaped speech that was later discovered on the computer of a member of the Hamburg cell. "Some of them are abominable."

Bin Laden spoke about the Prophet, who warned the Arabs that they would become weak because of their love of life and their fear of fighting. "This sense of loss, this misery that has befallen us: all these are proof that we have abandoned God and his jihad," bin Laden said. "God has imposed inferiority on you and will not remove it from you until you return to your religion."

Recalling the Prophet's injunction on his deathbed that Islam should be the only religion in Arabia, bin Laden asked, "What answer do we have for God on the day of reckoning? . . . The *ummah* in this time have become lost and have gone astray. Now, ten years have passed since the Americans entered the land of the two holy places. . . . It becomes clear to us that shying away from the fight, combined with the love of earthly existence that fills the hearts of many of us, is the source of this misery, this humiliation, and this contempt."

These words reached into the hearts of nineteen young men, many of whom had skills, talent, and education, and were living comfortably in the West; and yet they still resonated with the sense of shame that bin Laden sang to them.

> *What do we want? What do we want?*
> *Don't we want to please God?*
> *Don't we want Paradise?*

He urged them to become martyrs, to give up their promising lives for the greater glory that awaited them. "Look, we have found ourselves in the mouth of the lion for over twenty years now," he said, "thanks to the mercy and favor of God: the Russian Scud missiles hunted us for over ten years, and the American Cruise missiles have hunted us for another ten years. The believer knows that the hour of death can be neither hastened nor postponed." Then he quoted a passage from the fourth sura of the Quran, which he repeated three times in the speech—an obvious signal to the hijackers who were on their way:

> *Wherever you are, death will find you,*
> *even in the looming tower.*

O'NEILL WAS A FLAWED AND POLARIZING FIGURE, but there was no one else in the bureau who was as strong and as concerned, no one else who might have taken the morsels of evidence that the CIA was withholding and marshaled a nationwide dragnet that would have stopped 9/11. The bureau was a timid bureaucracy that abhorred powerful individuals. It was known for its brutal treatment of employees who were ambitious or who fought conventional wisdom. O'Neill was right about the threat of al-Qaeda when few cared to believe it. Perhaps, in the end, his capacity for making enemies sabotaged his career, but those enemies also helped al-Qaeda by destroying the man who might have made a difference. Already the New York office was losing focus, and without O'Neill, terrible mistakes were made.

While O'Neill was in Spain, an FBI agent in Phoenix, Kenneth Williams, sent an alarming electronic communication to headquarters, to Alec Station, and to several agents in New York. "The purpose of this communication is to advise the bureau and New York of the possibility of a coordinated effort by Osama bin Laden to send students to the United States to attend civil aviation universities and colleges," the note said. Williams went on to advise headquarters of the need to make a record of all the flight schools in the country, interview the operators, and compile a list of all Arab students who had sought visas for flight training.

Jack Cloonan was one of the New York agents to read the

memo, which was printed out and distributed. He wadded it into a ball and threw it against a wall. "Who's going to conduct the thirty thousand interviews?" he asked the supervisor in Phoenix. "When the fuck do we have time for this?" But he did run a check on the several Arab names that the agent in Phoenix had listed. Nothing came up. The CIA, which has an office in Phoenix, also looked at the names and made no connections. As it turns out, a student the Phoenix agent had mentioned had been friendly with Hani Hanjour, one of the presumed pilots of 9/11, but there was little chance that an investigation such as the one the agent was suggesting would have led to the plot. At least, not by itself.

Then, in mid-August, a flight school in Minnesota contacted the local FBI field office to express concern about a student, Zacarias Moussaoui. He had asked suspicious questions about the flight patterns around New York City and whether the doors of a cockpit could be opened during flight. The local bureau quickly determined that Moussaoui was an Islamic radical who had been to Pakistan and probably to Afghanistan. The agents believed he might be a potential suicide hijacker. Because he was a French citizen who had overstayed his visa, the INS placed him under arrest. The FBI agents investigating the case sought permission from headquarters to examine Moussaoui's laptop, which was denied because the agents couldn't show a probable cause for their search. When the Minneapolis supervisor pressed the matter with headquarters, he was told he was trying to get people "spun up." The supervisor defiantly responded that he was "trying to keep someone from taking a plane and crashing into the World Trade Center"—a weird premonition that suggests how such thoughts were surging through the unconscious of those who were reading the threat reports.

Moussaoui was probably intended to be part of a second wave of al-Qaeda attacks that would follow 9/11, most likely on the West Coast. If the agents in Minneapolis had been allowed to thoroughly investigate Moussaoui, they would have made the connection to Ramzi bin al-Shibh, who was sending him money. Moussaoui carried a letter of employment from Infocus Tech, which was signed by Yazid Sufaat. That name meant nothing to the FBI, since the CIA kept secret the information about the meeting in Kuala Lumpur, which took place in Sufaat's condo. The bureau failed to put together the warning from its own office in Minneapolis with that of Kenneth Williams in Phoenix. Typically, it withheld the information from Dick Clarke and the White House, so no one had a complete picture.

ON AUGUST 22, O'Neill wrote an e-mail to Lou Gunn, who had lost his son on the *Cole*. "Today is my last day," O'Neill informed him. "In my thirty-one years of government service, my proudest moment was when I was selected to lead the investigation of the attack on the USS *Cole*. I have put my all into the investigation and truly believe that significant progress has been made. Unknown to you and the families is that I have cried with your loss. . . . I will keep you and all the families in my prayers and will continue to track the investigation as a civilian. God bless you, your loved ones, the families and God bless America."

O'Neill was packing boxes in his office when Ali Soufan came in to say good-bye. Soufan was headed back to Yemen later that day; in fact, O'Neill's last act as an FBI agent would be to sign the paperwork that would send his team back into the country. The two men walked across the street to Joe's Diner. O'Neill ordered a ham and cheese sandwich.

"You don't want to change your infidel ways?" Soufan kidded him, indicating the ham. "You're gonna go to hell." But O'Neill was not in a joking mood. He urged Soufan to come visit him in the Trade Center when he returned. "I'm going to be just down the road," he said. It was strange to have O'Neill pleading to be remembered.

Then Soufan confided that he was getting married. He was worried about how O'Neill would react. In the past, whenever they talked about women, O'Neill would make a wisecrack or somehow indicate how uncomfortable he was about the subject. "You know why it costs so much to get a divorce?" O'Neill once asked him. "Because it's worth it."

This time, O'Neill thought about it and remarked, "She has put up with you all this time. She must be a good woman."

The next day, O'Neill started work at the World Trade Center.

THE DAY AFTER O'NEILL RETIRED from the bureau, Maggie Gillespie, the FBI analyst at Alec Station who was reviewing coverage of the Malaysia meeting, notified INS, the State Department, Customs, and the FBI, asking them to put Khaled al-Mihdhar and Nawaf al-Hazmi on their watch lists. She had noticed that both men had arrived in Los Angeles in January 2000, about the same time as Ahmed Ressam had planned to blow up the L.A. airport. Since then, Mihdhar had left the country and returned. Gillespie passed the information to her colleague, the intelligence analyst Dina Corsi, at FBI headquarters.

Alarmed by the information, Corsi sent an e-mail to the supervisor of the I-49 squad titled "IT: al-Qaeda." "IT" means "international terrorism." The message urgently ordered the squad to investigate whether Khaled al-Mihdhar was still in the United States. There was little explanation about who he might be, except that his association with al-Qaeda and his possible involvement with the bombers of the *Cole* made him "a risk to the national security." The squad's orders were to "locate al-Mihdhar and determine his contact and reasons for being in the United States." But no criminal agents could be involved in the search, Corsi said. As it turned out, there was only one intelligence agent on the squad, and he was brand new.

Jack Cloonan was the temporary supervisor. He requested that criminal agents should carry out the investigation. Because of the existing bin Laden indictment, they would have far more freedom and resources to search for any al-Qaeda–related individuals. Corsi e-mailed the squad, "If al-Mihdhar is located, the interview must be conducted by an intel agent. A criminal agent CANNOT be present at the interview.... If at such time information is developed indicating the existence of a substantial federal crime, that information will be passed over the wall according to the proper procedures and turned over for follow-up investigation."

Corsi's original e-mail was accidentally copied to a criminal agent on the squad, however: Steve Bongardt, an aggressive investigator who had been Top Gun as a Navy fighter pilot. For more than a year he had been protesting the obstacles that were increasingly being put in the way of criminal investigators by the growing wall. "Show me where this is written that we can't have the intelligence," he demanded on a number of occasions from headquarters, but of course that was impossible, since the wall was largely a matter of interpretation. Since the June 11 meeting, Bongardt had been pressing Corsi to supply the information about the men in the photos, including Khaled al-Mihdhar. After Corsi's e-mail wound up on his computer, Bongardt called her. "Dina, you got to be kidding me!" he said. "Mihdhar is in the country?"

"Steve, you've got to delete that," she told him, referring to the e-mail. She said he had no right to the information. "We'll have a conference call about it tomorrow."

The next day Corsi called over the secure phone. A CIA supervisor at Alec Station was also on the line. They told Bongardt he would have to "stand down" in the effort to find Mihdhar. They explained how the wall prevented them from sharing any further information. Bongardt repeated his complaints that the wall was a bureaucratic fiction, and that it was preventing the agents from doing their work. "If this guy is in the country, it's not because he's going to fucking Disneyland!" he said. But he was told once again, not only by Corsi but also by her supervisor at the bureau, to stand down.

The next day Bongardt sent Corsi an angry e-mail: "Whatever has happened to this—someday somebody will die—and wall or not—the public will not understand why we are not more effective and throwing every resource we had at certain 'problems.' "

Rookie intelligence agent Rob Fuller got the assignment to track down Mihdhar, as well as Hazmi, whose name was linked to Mihdhar's on the watch list. Mihdhar had written on his landing card a month before that he would be staying at the "New York Marriott." The lone agent set out to find the two al-Qaeda operatives in the nine different Marriotts in the city. They were long gone.

ON AUGUST 30, eight days after O'Neill retired, Prince Turki relinquished his post as head of Saudi intelligence. It was the first time in decades that a senior prince had been pushed aside, reputedly because of Crown Prince Abdullah's impatience with Turki's failure to get bin Laden.

Turki says that he was not fired. "I left because I was tired," he said. "I thought new blood might be needed." He compared himself to "an over-ripened fruit. You know how it starts to smell bad, the skin peels and it deteriorates. So I asked to be relieved."

THE MOMENT O'NEILL LEFT THE FBI, his spirits lifted. People remarked that he seemed light on his feet for the first time in months, perhaps years. He talked about getting a new Mercedes to replace his aging Buick. He told Anna DiBattista that they could now afford to get married. On Saturday night, September 8, he attended a wedding at the Plaza Hotel with Valerie James, and they danced nearly every number. "I feel like a huge burden has been lifted from me," he told his former boss, Lewis Schiliro, who was at the wedding. To another friend within Val's hearing, he said, "I'm gonna get her a ring."

The next day, September 9, Ahmed Shah Massoud agreed to see two Arab television journalists who had been waiting in his camp for nine days for an interview. Massoud was without doubt the greatest of the Afghan commanders, having endured twenty-five years of warfare against the the Soviets, Afghan communists, rival mujahideen, and now the combined forces of the Taliban and al-Qaeda. Massoud's capacity for survival was a powerful feature of his legend. He was the best hope Afghanistan had of a moderate Islamist alternative to the Taliban.

Zawahiri's forged letter had gotten the two phony journalists into Massoud's office. The cameraman's battery pack was filled with explosives. The bomb tore the assassins apart, killed a translator, and drove two pieces of metal into Massoud's heart.

When Ali Soufan heard the news in Yemen, he told another agent, "Bin Laden is appeasing the Taliban. Now the big one is coming."

That day bin Laden and Zawahiri attended a wake for the father of the Taliban's former interior minister. Two Saudi members of al-Qaeda approached the deputy interior minister, Mullah Mohammed Khaksar, to tell him that Massoud was dead. The Northern Alliance had claimed that Massoud was only wounded. "No, believe me, he is gone," the Saudis informed the minister. They boasted that bin Laden had given the order to kill Massoud. Now the Northern Alliance was leaderless, the last obstacle to the Taliban's total control of the country removed by this significant favor.

On Monday, September 10, O'Neill called Robert Tucker, a friend and security-company executive, and arranged to get together that evening to talk about security issues at the World Trade Center. Tucker met O'Neill in the lobby of the north tower, and the two men rode the elevator up to O'Neill's new office on the thirty-fourth floor. O'Neill was proud of his domain: seven buildings on sixteen acres of land with nine million square feet of office space. They went up to Windows on the World for a drink, and then drove in a downpour to Elaine's to have dinner with their friend Jerry Hauer. O'Neill ate steak and pasta. Elaine Kaufman, the renowned doyenne of the establishment, remembered that O'Neill nursed a glass of iced coffee with dessert. "He wasn't an alcoholic like a lot of them," she said. Around midnight, the three men dropped in on the China Club, a nightspot in midtown. O'Neill told his friends that something big was going to happen. "We're overdue," he said again.

Valerie James had been out entertaining clients that evening. It was Fashion Week, and as the sales director for a major designer, she was harried. O'Neill had called her at the office earlier and promised to be home no later than ten thirty. She finally went to bed an hour later. She woke up at one thirty and he still wasn't home. Annoyed, she sat down at the computer and began playing a game. John came home around four and sat down next to her. "You play a mean game of solitaire, babe," he said. But Valerie felt spurned and they went to bed without speaking. The next morning she was still frosty. O'Neill came into the bathroom and put his arms around her. He said, "Please forgive me." She was touched and said, "I do forgive you." He offered to drive her to work and dropped her off at 8:13 in the flower district, where she had an appointment. Then he headed to the Trade Center.

BIN LADEN AND ZAWAHIRI and a small group of the inner corps of al-Qaeda fled into the mountains above Khost, near the Lion's Den, where bin Laden's Afghan adventure had begun. He told his men that something great was going to happen, and soon Muslims from around the world would join them in Afghanistan to defeat the superpower. The men carried a satellite dish and a television set.

Before 9/11, bin Laden and his followers had been beset by vivid dreams. Normally, after the dawn prayers, if a member of al-Qaeda had a dream during the night, he would recount it, and bin Laden would divine its meaning. People who knew nothing of the plot reported dreams of a plane hitting a tall building. "We were playing a soccer match. Our team against the Americans," one man told bin Laden. "But the strange thing is, I was wondering why Osama made our entire team up of pilots. Was this a soccer match or an airplane?" The al-Qaeda spokesman, Suleiman Abu Ghaith, dreamed he was watching television with bin Laden, which showed an Egyptian family at the dinner table and the eldest son dancing an Egyptian folk dance. A legend scrolled across the bottom of the screen: "To avenge the children of al-Aqsa [the mosque in Jerusalem], Osama bin Laden carries out attacks against the Americans." When he described this to bin Laden in front of fifty other men, bin Laden simply said, "Okay, I will tell you later." But then he abruptly banned all talk of dreams, especially those that envisioned airplanes flying into buildings, for fear that they would give the plan away. He personally dreamed of America in ashes, believing it was a prophecy.

Steve Bongardt was at his cubicle in the I-49 squad reading intelligence on his computer. There was a report that the al-Qaeda camps in Tora Bora were being revitalized. "That can't be good," he thought. Barry Mawn was in his office when he heard an ear-splitting roar. He looked out his window too late to see the plane passing, nearly at eye level, but he heard the explosion. He thought a jet hurtling down the Hudson River had broken the sound barrier. An instant later his secretary screamed, and Mawn ran to look out her window at the burning hole in the ninety-second floor of the north tower of the Trade Center, blocks away. Mawn immediately gathered his employees. He told the SWAT and evidence recovery teams that they needed to go assist the New York police and fire departments. As an afterthought, he also dispatched the terrorism task force.

John P. O'Neill, Jr., a computer expert for MBNA in Delaware, was on his way to New York to install some equipment in his father's new office. From the window of the train, O'Neill's son saw smoke coming from the Trade Center. He called his father on his cell phone. O'Neill told him he was okay. He said he was headed outside to assess the damage.

The plane, carrying about nine thousand gallons of jet fuel, had crashed fifty-eight floors above O'Neill's office. He made it to the concourse level. People weren't panicked, they were confused. Was there a bomb? an earthquake? Nothing made sense. Water poured out of the ceiling, puddling on the marble floor. The two-story cathedral windows were shattered, and a disconcerting breeze stirred the lobby. By now, the first jumpers had broken through the windows of the north tower above the burning jet fuel. Their flailing bodies landed like grenades. The plaza outside was set up for a noon concert, and pieces of bodies were draped over the chairs. Dozens of shoes were scattered across the tiles. There was a day-care center in the building, and O'Neill helped usher the children outside to safety.

In Afghanistan, members of al-Qaeda were having difficulty

getting a signal from the satellite. One of the men cupped the dish in his hands, aiming it toward the sky, but he found only static. Finally, someone tuned a radio to the BBC Arabic service. A newscaster was finishing a report when he said there was breaking news: A plane had struck the World Trade Center in New York! The members of al-Qaeda, thinking that was the only action, cried in joy and prostrated themselves. But bin Laden said, "Wait, wait."

Ali Soufan and a handful of other agents were in the American Embassy in Yemen. Barbara Bodine had been rotated out of the country and the new ambassador had not yet arrived. Soufan was talking to his fiancée on the phone when she told him that the Trade Center had been attacked. He asked permission of the deputy chief of mission to enter the ambassador's office to turn on the TV. Just as he did, the second plane hit.

Valerie James was arranging flowers in her office when "the phones started ringing off the hook." It was a little after nine in the morning. Her children were calling her in a panic. Finally, O'Neill called. "Honey, I want you to know I'm okay. My God, Val, it's terrible. There are body parts everywhere. Are you crying?" She was. He asked if she knew what had hit the building. She told him that her son had guessed it was a 747. Then he said, "Val, I think my employers are dead. I can't lose this job."

"They're going to need you more than ever," she told him.

In Afghanistan, bin Laden also wept and prayed. The accomplishment of striking the two towers was an overwhelming signal of God's favor, but there was more to come. Before his incredulous companions, bin Laden held up three fingers.

At 9:25, Anna DiBattista, who was driving to Philadelphia on business, received a call from O'Neill. The connection was good and then it decayed. O'Neill said he was safe and outside. "Are you sure you're out of the building?" she asked. O'Neill replied that he loved her. She absolutely knew he was going back in.

The cloudless sky filled with coiling black smoke and a blizzard of paper—memos, photographs, stock transactions, insurance policies—which fluttered for miles on a gentle southeasterly breeze, across the East River into Brooklyn. Debris spewed onto the streets of lower Manhattan, which were already covered with bodies. Some of them had been exploded out of the building when the planes hit. A man walked out of the towers carrying someone else's leg. Jumpers landed on several firemen, killing them instantly.

The air pulsed with sirens as firehouses and police stations all over the city emptied, sending the rescuers, many of them to their deaths. Steve Bongardt was running toward the towers, against a stream of people racing in the opposite direction. He heard the boom of the second collision. "There's a second plane!" somebody cried. Bongardt wondered what kind of aircraft it was, perhaps a private jet that had gotten off course. Then, three blocks away from the towers, he saw one of the massive engines that had blown all the way through the tower. It had landed on a woman, who was still alive and squirming underneath. Bongardt understood then that this was the work of bin Laden.

O'Neill went back into the north tower, where the fire department had set up a command post. The lobby stank of jet fuel, which was draining into the elevator shafts, creating an explosive well. Heavily laden firemen made their way up the stairs. They were used to disaster, but their eyes were filled with awe and uncertainty. Meanwhile, a slow-moving stream of people descended the escalators from the mezzanine, like a dream. They were wet and caked in slime. Some of them had come from the upper floors and were naked and badly burned. Police directed them to the underground tunnels to avoid the jumpers. A rumor raced through the room that a third plane was headed toward them. Suddenly one of the elevators, which had been paralyzed after the strike, popped open, disgorging a dozen dazed people who had been trapped since the first plane hit and had no idea what had happened.

Wesley Wong, an FBI communications expert, leaped into the lobby through one of the busted-out windows, narrowly escaping the plummeting body of a middle-aged man in blue pants and a white shirt. Wong and O'Neill had known each other for more than twenty years. Even in this confusion, O'Neill looked calm and dapper, wearing his usual dark suit with a white pocket handkerchief, only a smudge of ash on his back indicating that the bottom had fallen out of his world. O'Neill asked Wong if there was any information he could divulge, acknowledging the fact that he was now an outsider and not privy to such details. "Is it true the Pentagon has been hit?" he asked. "Gee, John, I don't know," said Wong. "Let me try to find out." But then O'Neill had trouble with the reception on his cell phone and started walking away. He said, "I'll catch up with you later." Wong last saw O'Neill walking toward the tunnel leading to the south tower.

At 9:38 a.m., the third plane had crashed into the headquarters of American military power and the symbol of its might. When news came of the Pentagon strike, bin Laden held up four fingers to his wonder-struck followers, but the final strike, on the U.S. Capitol, would fail.

Ali Soufan called O'Neill from Yemen, but could not get a connection.

Steve Gaudin, just back from language school in Vermont, picked up a piece of an airplane on the corner of Church and Vesey Streets and helplessly thought, "I just didn't ask enough questions." A few feet away, Barry Mawn was walking west on Vesey Street, toward the police emergency command center. He saw a woman's foot in the street with a pink sock and a white tennis shoe. Suddenly, the ground trembled. He looked up to see the south tower collapsing on top of itself, gathering momentum and force as it threw off a great gray cloud of pulverized concrete that spilled over the surrounding office towers in a massive cascade. It sounded like an express train roaring through the station, chased by a huge wind. Mawn, plagued by a herniated disk, hobbled after two firemen who ran through the shattered windows of 7 World Trade. There were six or seven men pressed together in the lobby, sheltering behind a single column. One of the firemen cried out that they should hold on to each other and not let go. Just then, the debris blew in like a bomb. If they hadn't been behind a column they would have been shredded. The room blacked out and the men choked on the acrid dust. Outside, everything was on fire.

Half a block away, Debbie Doran and Abby Perkins, who were on the I-49 squad, were in the basement of a building on the corner of Church and Vesey. They remembered Rosie, the woman rescue workers had failed to save in the rubble of the Nairobi bombing in 1998. She had died of dehydration. Now they expected to be buried under a building themselves, and they began filling trash cans with water.

Dan Coleman was in his bureau car next to St. Paul's Chapel, waiting for another member of the I-49 squad, when he saw a tornado coming up Broadway. It was incomprehensible. His partner ran past him, headed north. "Get in the car!" Coleman called out. Four policemen also jumped in; one of them was having a heart attack. Then the blackness of the cloud engulfed them. "Turn on the air conditioning!" one of the cops gasped. Coleman turned it on, and the car filled with smoke. He quickly switched it off.

Everybody was yelling at him to get out of there, but he couldn't see anything. He backed up and almost rolled into a subway entrance. Then an ambulance appeared and the cops got out. Coleman abandoned the car and went to find the rest of his squad.

He walked inside the cloud against the stream of fleeing people who were like ash-covered ghouls, as if they had been exhumed. He also was as white as a snowman, and the dust was beginning to harden, turning his hair into a helmet. The dust was a compound of concrete, asbestos, lead, fiberglass, paper, cotton, jet fuel, and the pulverized organic remains of 2,749 people who died in the towers.

Valerie heard screams in the rental office next door. She ran to see the large-screen TV. As soon as she saw the south tower collapsing, she slumped into a chair and declared, "Oh my God, John is dead."

20

Revelations

THE FBI ORDERED ALI SOUFAN and the rest of the team in Yemen to evacuate immediately. The morning after 9/11, the CIA's chief of station in Aden did them the favor of driving them to the airport in Sanaa. He was sitting in the lounge with them when he got a call on his cell phone. He told Soufan, "They want to talk to you."

One of the FBI communications specialists unpacked the satellite phone and set up the dish so Soufan could make the call. When he spoke to Dina Corsi at headquarters, she told him to stay in Yemen. He was upset. He wanted to get back to New York to investigate the attack on America—*right now!* "This is about that—what happened yesterday," she told him. "Quso is our only lead."

She wouldn't tell him any more. Soufan got his luggage off the plane, but he was puzzled. What did Quso, the sleeping cameraman in the *Cole* bombing, have to do with 9/11? Another investigator, Robert McFadden, and a couple of SWAT guys stayed with him for security.

The order from headquarters was to identify the hijackers "by any means necessary," a directive Soufan had never seen before. When they returned to the embassy, a fax came over a secure line with photos of the suspects. Then the CIA chief drew Soufan aside and handed him a manila envelope. Inside were three surveillance photos and a complete report about the Malaysia meeting— the very material Soufan had been asking for, which the CIA had denied him until now. The wall had come down. When Soufan realized that the agency and some people in the bureau had known for more than a year and a half that two of the hijackers were in the country, he ran into the bathroom and retched.

One of the photos showed a man who looked like Quso. Soufan went to General Ghalib Qamish, director of the Political Security Office, and demanded to see the prisoner Quso again. "What does this have to do with the *Cole?*" Qamish wanted to know.

"I'm not talking about the *Cole*," said Soufan. "Brother John is missing." He started to say something else, but he choked up. General Qamish's eyes also filled with tears. There was a long silence filled with the immense vacancy of O'Neill's passing.

General Qamish said that the prisoner was in Aden and there was only one last flight that evening into the capital. He picked up the phone to his subordinates and began shouting into it, "I want Quso flown in here tonight!" The Americans could almost hear the heels clicking on the other end. Then the general called the airport and demanded to be patched through to the pilot. "You will not take off until my prisoner is aboard," he ordered.

At midnight, Quso sat in the PSO office. He was in a petulant frame of mind. "Just because something happens in New York or Washington, you don't need to talk to me," he said. Soufan showed him three surveillance photos, which included the hijackers Mihdhar and Hazmi, but Quso denied that he was in any of the pictures.

The next day the CIA finally gave Soufan the fourth photo of the Malaysia meeting, which it had buried until now. Quso grudgingly identified the figure in the picture as Khallad, although Soufan already knew who he was. He was the mastermind of the *Cole*. The photo was the first link between al-Qaeda and 9/11.

Soufan interrogated Quso for three nights, then wrote reports and did research all day. On the fourth night, Soufan collapsed from exhaustion and was taken to the hospital. The next morning, however, he was back in the PSO office. Quso identified Marwan al-Shehhi, the pilot of United Airlines Flight

175, which crashed into the second tower. He had met Shehhi in a Kandahar guesthouse. He remembered that Shehhi had been ill during Ramadan, and that the emir of the guesthouse had taken care of him. The emir's name was Abu Jandal. As it happened, Abu Jandal was also in Yemeni custody.

He was a large man for a Yemeni, powerful, with a dark full beard, although he had softened up after months in jail. Soufan immediately recognized him as bin Laden's bodyguard.

Abu Jandal scowled at the Americans. "What are these infidels doing here?" he demanded. He took one of the plastic chairs and turned it around, sitting with his arms crossed and his back to the interrogators.

After some coaxing, Soufan got Abu Jandal to face him, but he still refused to look him in the eye. Abu Jandal did want to talk, however; he delivered a lengthy rant against America in rapid-fire Hijazi dialect. He also complained about the fact that he had never been charged. "Why am I in jail?" he kept demanding.

"Why is he in jail?" the Americans asked their Yemeni counterparts during a break.

"Suspicion."

"Suspicion of what?"

"You know, *suspicion*," the Yemeni officer responded.

Soufan realized that the prisoner was well trained in counter-interrogation techniques, since he easily agreed to things that Soufan already knew—that he had fought in Bosnia, Somalia, and Afghanistan, for instance—and denied everything else. The responses were designed to make the interrogators question their assumptions. Abu Jandal portrayed himself as a good Muslim who had flirted with jihad but had become disillusioned. He didn't think of himself as a killer but as a revolutionary who was trying to rid the world of evil, which he believed mainly came from the United States of America, a country he knew practically nothing about.

As the nights passed, Abu Jandal warmed to the sport of the interrogation. He was in his early thirties, older than most jihadis. He had grown up in Jeddah, bin Laden's hometown, and he was well read in religion. He enjoyed drinking tea and lecturing the Americans on the radical Islamist view of history; his sociability was his weak spot. Soufan flattered him and engaged him in theological debate. Within Abu Jandal's diatribes, Soufan picked up several useful details—that he had grown tired of fighting, that he was troubled by the fact that bin Laden had sworn *bayat* to Mullah Omar, that he worried about his two children, one of whom had a bone disease. Soufan also noted that Abu Jandal declined the pastries that came with the coffee, admitting he was a diabetic. These were small revelations that Soufan could use in getting him to identify the hijackers.

The next night, the Americans brought some sugarless wafers, a courtesy that Abu Jandal acknowledged. Soufan also brought him a history of America in Arabic.

Abu Jandal was confounded by Soufan and what he represented: a Muslim who could argue religion with him, who was in the FBI, who loved America. He quickly consumed the history that Soufan gave him and was shocked to learn of the American Revolution and the passionate struggle against tyranny that was woven into the American heritage. His worldview depended on the assumption that the United States was the wellspring of evil in the world.

Soufan, meanwhile, was trying to determine the boundaries of Abu Jandal's moral landscape. He asked about the proper way to wage jihad. Abu Jandal eagerly talked about how a warrior should treat his adversary in battle. The Quran and hadith are full of instructions concerning the honorable conduct of warfare.

Where does it sanction suicide bombing? Soufan wanted to know.

Abu Jandal said the enemy had an advantage in weapons, but the suicide bombers evened the score. "These are our missiles," he said.

What about women and children? Soufan asked. Aren't they supposed to be protected? He pointed to the bombings of the American embassies in East Africa. He recalled a woman on a bus in front of the Nairobi embassy, who was found clutching her baby, trying to protect him from the flames. Both had been incinerated. What sin had the mother committed? What about the soul of her child?

"God will give them their rewards in the Hereafter," said Abu Jandal. Besides, he added, "can you imagine how many joined bin Laden after the embassy bombings? Hundreds came and asked to be martyrs."

But many of the East African victims, perhaps most of them, were Muslims, said Soufan. The discussion was growing heated. Several times Abu Jandal resorted to quoting certain clerical authorities or suras from the Quran, but he found that Soufan was more than a match for him on theological matters. Now Abu Jandal asserted that, because the embassy bombings were on a Friday, when the victims should have been in the mosque, they were not real Muslims. It was the usual *takfir* view, but at least Soufan knew where the moral lines were drawn.

On the fifth night, Soufan slammed a news magazine on the table between them. There were photographs of the airplanes crashing into the towers and the Pentagon, graphic shots of people trapped in the towers and jumpers falling a hundred stories. "Bin Laden did this," Soufan told him.

Abu Jandal had heard about the attacks, but he didn't know many details. He studied the pictures in amazement. He said it looked like a "Hollywood production," but the scale of the atrocity visibly shook him. At that time the casualties were thought to be in the tens of thousands.

Besides Soufan and Abu Jandal, the small interrogation room held McFadden and two Yemeni investigators. Everyone sensed that Soufan was closing in. American and allied troops were preparing to go to war in Afghanistan, but they were waiting for information about the structure of al-Qaeda, the locations of hideouts, and the plans for escape, all of which American intelligence officials hoped Soufan and the other investigators could supply.

Coincidentally, there was a local Yemeni paper sitting on a shelf under the coffee table. Soufan showed it to Abu Jandal. The headline read, "Two Hundred Yemeni Souls Perish in New York Attack."

Abu Jandal read the headline and drew a breath. "God help us," he muttered.

Soufan asked what kind of Muslim would do such a thing. Abu Jandal insisted that the Israelis must have committed the attacks on New York and Washington, not bin Laden. "The Sheikh is not that crazy," he said.

Soufan took out a book of mug shots containing photos of known al-Qaeda members and various pictures of the hijackers. He asked Abu Jandal to identify them. The Yemeni flipped through them quickly and closed the book.

Soufan opened the book again and told him to take his time. "Some of them I have in custody," he said, hoping that Abu Jandal wouldn't realize that the hijackers were all dead.

Abu Jandal paused a fraction of a second on the picture of Marwan al-Shehhi before he started to turn the page. "You're not done with this one," Soufan observed. "Ramadan, 1999. He's sick. You're his emir and you take care of him."

Abu Jandal looked at Soufan in surprise.

"When I ask you a question, I already know the answer," said Soufan. "If you're smart, you'll tell me the truth."

Abu Jandal conceded that he knew Shehhi and gave his Qaeda name, Abdullah al-Sharqi. He did the same with Mohammed Atta, Khaled al-Mihdhar, and four others. But he still insisted that bin Laden would never commit such an action. It was the Israelis, he maintained.

"I know for sure that the people who did this were Qaeda guys," said Soufan. He took seven photos out of the book and laid them on the table.

"How do you know?" asked Abu Jandal. "Who told you?"

"You did," said Soufan. "These are the hijackers. You just identified them."

Abu Jandal blanched. He covered his face with his hands. "Give me a moment," he pleaded.

Soufan walked out of the room. When he came back he asked Abu Jandal what he thought now.

"I think the Sheikh went crazy," he said. And then he told Soufan everything he knew.

.   .   .

MARK ROSSINI had been told that John O'Neill was safe, and so he had spent much of that day and the next calling O'Neill's friends around the world, reassuring them that O'Neill was fine. Now he had to call them again, one by one. He was so angry with O'Neill. "Fucking bastard. Why didn't he run away?" For weeks, when he went home, Rossini would sit in his car and weep before he went into his house. Some of the agents had breakdowns. Some, like Dan Coleman, suffered permanent damage to their lungs because of the dust they inhaled that day.

The Trade Center burned for a hundred days. All during that time, the acrid stench penetrated the office of the FBI, a sickening reminder of their failure to stop the attack and their own narrow escape from death. One active agent, Leonard Hatton, a bomb technician, did not survive. He had worked the embassy bombings and the *Cole* with O'Neill, and he died trying to rescue victims in the towers. In the hectic, endless months following 9/11, the members of the I-49 squad were sorting through their shock, their grief, and their shame. Better than anyone in the country, they had known the danger America faced. And yet the I-49 squad had been largely alone in its efforts. Since the embassy bombings they had labored tirelessly, spending months and even years out of the country, many of them losing marriages or significant relationships because of the toll the investigations had taken. They were exhausted even before 9/11. Now their trauma was compounded by the stigma that was assigned to them because they had not prevented the tragedy they had known was coming.

O'Neill's face was one of thousands on the handmade posters plastering the walls of the Port Authority and Grand Central Terminal and telephone poles all over Manhattan. Against all odds, Valerie's brother, John McKillop, a paramedic in Chicago, vowed to find O'Neill. He and twenty-five of his colleagues drove to New York, with a police escort all the way. They were one of many spontaneous caravans of emergency services that poured into the city from all over the country. It was strange to see military forces on the streets of an American city, with gun emplacements protecting the bridges and significant buildings. Airports were shut down everywhere in America, but military jets scurried about like angry hornets.

When McKillop got to Ground Zero, he was staggered by the immense burning mountain of debris. Rescue workers were digging night and day hoping to find survivors, but the sight sucked the hope out of McKillop. "All I could think of was, What am I going to tell my sister?"

Many of the bodies of the people who died in the Trade Center were never found, but on September 21 rescuers digging in the rubble near the corner of Liberty and Greenwich streets found the corpse of a man in a blue suit. His wallet was in his breast pocket. It was John.

In so many respects, the Trade Center dead formed a kind of universal parliament, representing sixty-two countries and nearly every ethnic group and religion in the world. There was an ex-hippie stockbroker, the gay Catholic chaplain of the New York City Fire Department, a Japanese hockey player, an Ecuadoran sous chef, a Barbie Doll collector, a vegetarian calligrapher, a Palestinian accountant. . . . The manifold ways in which they attached to life testified to the Quranic injunction that the taking of a single life destroys a universe. Al-Qaeda had aimed its attacks at America, but it struck all of humanity.

As bits and pieces of the dead were extracted from the site, they were cataloged and identified, often using DNA that emergency workers had secured from family members who supplied strands of hair from a victim's brush, for instance. Each part of each body was given the same treatment, with one exception: When anyone of the more than four hundred deceased members of the uniformed services was discovered, there was a special protocol, which was accorded O'Neill. An American flag was draped over his body, and the New York City policemen and firemen who were digging through the rubble stood at attention as his body was carried to the ambulance.

When he was growing up in Atlantic City, John O'Neill had been an altar boy at St. Nicholas of Tolentine Church. On

September 28, a thousand mourners gathered at St. Nicholas to say farewell. Many of them were agents and policemen and members of foreign intelligence services who had followed O'Neill into the war against terrorism long before it had become a rallying cry. In the nervous days after the attacks, the streets around the church were barricaded and an army helicopter prowled overhead.

Dick Clarke had not shed a tear since 9/11, but when the bagpipes played and the casket passed by, he suddenly broke down. He remembered the last conversation he had with O'Neill, when he had turned down the job. "Look on the bright side," O'Neill had told him. "Whenever you come to New York, you can come up to Windows on the World." Then he had said, "Wherever we wind up, we'll always be brothers."

O'Neill's funeral was the catastrophe of coincidence that he had always been dreading. His wife and two children, and Valerie James and her two children, and Anna DiBattista encountered each other for the first time. All his secrets were revealed at once. But redemption was also present. O'Neill's greatest regrets had to do with his failings as a father. In May he had been given another chance: He was presented with his first grandchild. Ironically, O'Neill, who had been so nurturing to Valerie's grandchild, had trouble accepting his own status as grandfather, which always rings a mortal bell. It took him two months to get around to going to see the child. But afterward, the man who never kept family pictures in his office placed a photo of his grandson on his trophy wall. "You have been born in the greatest country in the world," O'Neill wrote to his grandson, in a letter that his brokenhearted son read at the funeral service. "It is well to learn the ethnic backgrounds of your parents, to love and cherish the ancient folklore. But never, never forget, you are an American first. And millions of Americans before you have fought for your freedom. The Nation holds all the terms of our endearment. Support, defend and honor those whose duty it is to keep it safe."

WHILE THEY WAITED for the mujahideen to rise up across Muslim lands and rush to Afghanistan, bin Laden and Zawahiri gloated over the success of the operation. "There is America, hit by God in one of its softest spots," bin Laden boasted in a pre-recorded videotape on al-Jazeera on October 7, the day after American and British bombers launched their first attacks on Taliban positions. "Its greatest buildings were destroyed, thank God for that. There is America, full of fear from its north to its south, from its west to its east. Thank God for that." Then he issued his call. "These events have divided the whole world into two sides—the side of believers and the side of infidels. May God keep you away from them. Every Muslim has to rush to make his religion victorious. The winds of faith have come."

One evening bin Laden and Zawahiri sat in a guesthouse in Kandahar. They were hosted by a paralyzed Saudi cleric named Khaled bin Ouda bin Mohammed al-Harby. "We planned and made calculations," bin Laden recounted. "We sat and estimated the casualties of the enemy. We figured the passengers in the planes, those will die. As regards the towers, we assumed they would include the people in the three or four floors the planes would crash into. That was all we estimated. I was the most optimistic. Due to the nature of my profession and work [i.e., construction], I figured that the fuel in the plane would raise the temperature in the steel to the point that it becomes red and almost loses its properties. So if the plane hits the building here"—he gestured with his hands—"the portion of the building above will collapse. That was the most we could hope for."

Many of the families of al-Qaeda had evacuated right after the attacks. Maha Elsamneh, the wife of Zawahiri's friend Ahmed Khadr, packed some clothes and food and took her children to an orphanage in Lowgar, fifty kilometers south of Kabul. They hid there for a couple of months. There was a well and indoor bathrooms. In mid-November, two nights after the fall of Kabul, Zawahiri's family appeared at the door. They looked awful. The children were barefoot and one of the daughters was not properly covered. Zawahiri's wife, Azza, was seriously ill. She explained that they had fled first to Khost, but then had returned to Kabul to pick up some supplies. That's when the American bombardment began.

In her feverish condition, Azza said that she had never realized who her husband actually was. "I never knew he was an emir," she said. "I can't believe it." It seemed strange to Maha, because everyone else knew.

Azza was carrying her youngest, Aisha, the Down syndrome child, who was still in diapers although she was four years old. Azza worried that if she died no one else could take care of Aisha. The girl was wide-eyed and so small and needful.

By now it had gotten bitterly cold. Although the war was still in the cities, the men of al-Qaeda were making their stand in Tora Bora, and their families decided to head to Pakistan. A large convoy formed and they made a slow drive through the mountains. Azza and her children stopped in Gardez at the guesthouse of Jalaladin Haqqanni, a Taliban government official, but Maha's family went on to Khost. That night there were two thundering explosions, so great that some of the children vomited and others had diarrhea. In the morning, one of Maha's sons went to check on the Zawahiris. He found that the house they were in had been struck. The cement roof had collapsed, pinning Azza underneath. The rescuers had found little Aisha injured but still alive, and they set her outside on a bed while they tried to save Azza. She was still alive, but she refused to be excavated because of her fear that men would see her face. Eventually, her cries stopped. When the rescuers finally returned to take care of the child, they discovered that she had frozen to death.

IN THE CAVES OF TORA BORA, bin Laden and Zawahiri visited the remaining al-Qaeda fighters and urged them to hold their positions and wait for the Americans. Instead, the al-Qaeda warriors found themselves fighting Afghans in the first two weeks of December, while the Americans flew overhead in B-52s, so far out of reach, dropping Daisy Cutter bombs on their caverns. "We were about three hundred mujahideen," bin Laden recounted. "We dug one hundred trenches that were spread in an area that does not exceed one square mile, one trench for every three brothers, so as to avoid the huge human losses resulting from the bombardment." Despite his preparations, on December 3, after American bombers struck a cave complex, Afghan ground troops uncovered more than a hundred bodies; they were able to identify eighteen of them as top al-Qaeda lieutenants.

Bin Laden felt betrayed by the Muslims who had failed to join him. Even the Taliban slipped away. "Only a few remained steadfast," he complained. "The rest surrendered or fled before they encountered the enemy." He wrote this on December 17. The brief battle of Tora Bora was over—a crushing loss for al-Qaeda, but also for the United States and its allies, who failed to nab their quarry. Bin Laden and the remaining al-Qaeda fighters had escaped into Pakistan, getting away with their lives but losing Afghanistan. Bin Laden chose this time to write what he described as his final bequest.

In his will, bin Laden tried to salvage his legacy. "I consider all Muslims in this immensely miserable time as my relatives," he wrote. He pointed to the bombings of the embassies in East Africa, the destruction of the World Trade Center, and the attack on the Pentagon: They were great victories. "Despite the setbacks that God has inflicted upon us, these painful blows will mark the beginning of the wiping out of America and the infidel West after the passing of tens of years, God willing."

Then he addressed his own family. "My wives, may God bestow His blessings on you," he wrote. "You knew from the very first day that the road is surrounded with thorns and mines. You have given up the pleasures of life, your families, and chosen the hardship of living by my side." He adjured them not to think of marrying again. "My sons, forgive me because I have given you very little of my time ever since I have chosen the path of jihad. . . . I have chosen a perilous course, filled with all sorts of tribulations that ruffle one's life. . . . If it were not for treason I would have triumphed." He then advised them not to join al-Qaeda. "In that I follow the example of Omar bin al-Khatab, the commandant of the faithful, who directed his son Abdullah not to proceed to the caliphate after his death. He said, 'If it is good we have had enough of it; if not, then Omar's suffering was enough.' "

. . .

IN MARCH 2002 AL-QAEDA REGROUPED in the mountains
near Khost, close to the Lion's Den. Predator drones were circling
the skies and American and Afghan troops, along with soldiers
from Canada, Australia, Denmark, France, Germany, and Nor-
way, were sweeping through the mountains in an operation called
Anaconda. The fighting had narrowed down to the Shah-e-Kot
valley on the ragged eastern edge of Afghanistan. Regional warlords had been bought off, the borders supposedly sealed, and the
al-Qaeda fighters were under constant bombardment. And yet a
band of horsemen rode unhindered to Pakistan.

They came to the village of a local militia leader named Gula
Jan, whose long beard and black turban might have signaled that
he was a Taliban sympathizer. "I saw a heavy, older man, an Arab,
who wore dark glasses and had a white turban," Jan said four
days later. "He was dressed like an Afghan, but he had a beautiful
coat, and he was with two other Arabs who had masks on." The
man in the beautiful coat dismounted and began talking in a
polite and humorous manner. He asked Jan and an Afghan companion about the location of American and Northern Alliance
troops. "We are afraid we will encounter them," he said. "Show us
the right way."

While the men were talking, Jan slipped off to examine a flyer
that had been dropped into the area by American airplanes. It
showed a photograph of a man in a white turban and glasses. His
face was broad and meaty, with a strong, prominent nose and full
lips. His untrimmed beard was gray at the temples and ran in
milky streaks below his chin. On his high forehead, framed by the
swaths of his turban, was a darkened callus formed by many
hours of prayerful prostration. His eyes reflected the sort of decisiveness one might expect in a medical man, but they also showed
a measure of serenity that seemed oddly out of place in a Wanted
poster. The flyer noted that Zawahiri had a price of $25 million on
his head.

Jan returned to the conversation. The man he now believed to be Zawahiri said to him, "May God bless you and keep you from the enemies of Islam. Try not to tell them where we came from and where we are going."

There was a telephone number on the Wanted poster, but Gula Jan did not have a phone. Zawahiri and the masked Arabs disappeared into the mountains.

AFTERWORD TO THE
VINTAGE BOOKS EDITION
(2011)

ON MAY 2, 2011, Osama bin Laden, a prisoner of his own renown (and perhaps of Pakistani intelligence as well), was slain by members of the United States Navy Seal Team Six at a three-story villa near an elite military academy in northern Pakistan. The most exhaustive manhunt in history concluded with a shot to the head and one to the chest. His body was flown to the *U.S.S. Carl Vinson*, where it was washed and swathed in burial clothes then dumped into the trackless North Arabian Sea. It was the end of a man, if not yet of his movement.

Fifteen years had passed since FBI Special Agent Daniel Coleman walked into the CIA's Alec Station in Tysons Corner, Virginia, to open a case on a man few people in the West, and even in American intelligence, had ever heard of. In the span of time between that moment and the actions that brought the case to a close, Osama bin Laden defined an era. The nearly three thousand Americans who died on 9/11 were only a fraction of the toll al-Qaeda inflicted in its global rampage.

This story might have ended in November 2001, when some four hundred American soldiers and intelligence officers on the ground, coupled with massive American airpower and the indigenous forces of the Northern Alliance, swept aside the Taliban and pummeled al-Qaeda in Tora Bora. A crucial miscalculation on the part of the American commanders not to reinforce combat units on the ground allowed bin Laden and most of his inner circle to slip into the Tribal Areas of Pakistan. Even so, al-Qaeda was essentially finished. According to accounts of its own insiders, eighty percent of bin Laden's followers were captured or killed. The movement was shattered. The leaders were alive, but they were dispersed, impoverished, humiliated, and discredited all over the world—including the Muslim world. From their hiding places in Yemen, Iran, Iraq, and Pakistan, al-Qaeda survivors lamented their failed strategy. Abu al-Walid al-Masri, a senior leader of al-Qaeda's inner council, later wrote that the experience in Afghanistan was "a tragic example of an Islamic movement managed in an alarmingly meaningless way." He added, "Everyone knew that their leader was leading them to the abyss and even the entire country to utter destruction, but they continued to carry out his orders faithfully and with bitterness."

The fateful decision of the Bush administration to invade and occupy Iraq in 2003 revivified the radical Islamist agenda. Simultaneous wars in two Muslim countries lent substance to bin Laden's narrative that the West was at war with Islam. New terrorist leaders came to prominence in Iraq—most notably Abu Musab al-Zarqawi, who slaughtered many more Muslims in Iraq alone during his three-year killing spree than the sum of all other al-Qaeda attacks around the world. By pledging allegiance to bin Laden in October 2004, Zarqawi established a pattern for other insurgent groups, previously nationalistic in their designs, to enlist in the universal jihad that al-Qaeda sought to wage. Although bin Laden and his cohort were essentially reduced to virtual presences on the Internet and smuggled tape recordings, the apocalyptic al-Qaeda idea took root, not only in Muslim countries but also among Muslim communities in the cities of Europe and eventually even in the United States.

As early as 1998, following the bombing of the American embassies in East Africa, al-Qaeda strategists began envisioning a less hierarchical organization than the one that bin Laden, the businessman, had designed. His al-Qaeda was a top-down terrorist bureaucracy, but it offered its members health care and paid vacations—it was a good job for a lot of rootless young men. The new al-Qaeda was entrepreneurial, spontaneous, and opportunistic, with the flattened structure of street gangs—what one al-Qaeda strategist, Abu Musab al-Suri, termed "leaderless resistance." Such were the men who killed 191 commuters in Madrid, on March 11, 2004, and the bombers in London on July 7, 2005, who killed fifty-two people, not counting the four bombers, and injured about seven hundred. The relationship of these emulators to the core group of al-Qaeda was tangential at best, but they had been inspired by its example and acted in its name. They were tied together by the Internet, which offered them a safe place to conspire. Al-Qaeda's leaders began supplying this new, online generation with a legacy of plans, targets, ideology, and methods.

Meantime, the War on Terror was transforming Western societies into security states with massive intelligence budgets and intrusive new laws. The American intelligence community became even more deeply entrenched with the worst despots of the Arab world and grimly mirrored some of their most appalling practices—indiscriminate and often illegal arrests, indefinite detentions, and ruthless interrogation techniques. That reinforced al-Qaeda's allegations that such tyrants only existed at the whim of the West and that Muslims were under siege everywhere because of their religion. The audacity of al-Qaeda's attacks had given radical Islamists credibility among people who were desperate for change. And yet the worldwide effort to contain al-Qaeda prevented the organization from repeating the spectacle of 9/11 and thwarted its aim of taking over a Muslim country.

The years immediately after 9/11 had offered an opportunity for the Islamists to offer their vision of a redeemed political system that would bring about real improvements in people's lives. Instead, they continued to propagate fantasies of theocracy and a caliphate, which had little chance of happening and did nothing to address the actual problems of Muslim youth—illiteracy, poverty, joblessness, and the desperation that comes from watching the rest of the world pass them by.

Al-Qaeda's tactical and political failures gave rise to a devastating philosophical challenge from the heart of political Islam.

This became evident in 2007, when Noman Benotman, the former head of the Libyan Fighting Group, an al-Qaeda ally, published an open letter to Ayman al-Zawahiri, bin Laden's chief lieutenant, demanding that the organization suspend its operations, saying that such actions had accomplished nothing and were now being used mainly as a subterfuge by Western interests to extend their influence in Muslim countries. That same year, Saudi cleric Salman al-Awdah, previously one of bin Laden's heroes, publicly denounced him on the sixth anniversary of 9/11, accusing him of "making terror a synonym for Islam," and asking, "Brother Osama, how much blood has been spilt? How many innocents among children, elderly, the weak and women have been killed and made homeless in the name of al-Qaeda?"

The most notable defection from al-Qaeda's philosophy was on the part of a man who wrote much of it: Sayyid Imam al-Sharif, also known as Dr. Fadl. He had been Zawahiri's classmate at Cairo University's medical school in the late 1960s; he then became the emir of Zawahiri's terror organization, al-Jihad, in Peshawar, Pakistan, in the mid-eighties, when the two men worked together at the Red Crescent hospital. There, they sought to enlist young Egyptians who were coming to fight in the jihad against the Soviets in Afghanistan into al-Jihad. Upon the founding of al-Qaeda in 1988, Dr. Fadl became the organization's principle ideologue. That year he wrote the first of two books that would lay the foundation of the organization's philosophy, *Essential Guide for Preparation*. The book asserted that jihad is the natural state of Islam, and that Muslims must always be in conflict with nonbelievers. His second book, *Compendium of the Pursuit of Divine Knowledge*, written in Khartoum in 1994, began with the proposition that salvation is only possible to a perfect Muslim. "A man may enter the faith in many ways, yet be expelled from it by just one deed," Fadl cautioned. He wrote that the rulers of Egypt and other Arab countries are apostates of Islam and that Muslims have a duty to wage jihad against such leaders; moreover, Muslims who submit to an infidel ruler are infidels themselves and doomed to damnation. The same punishment awaits those who serve in the government, the police, and the courts, and those who participate in democratic elections. "I say to Muslims in all candor that secular, nationalist democracy opposes your religion and your doctrine, and in submitting to it you leave God's book behind," he wrote. Anyone who believes otherwise is a heretic and should be slaughtered. Fadl was articulating a central doctrine of al-Qaeda philosophy, that of *takfir*—the excommunication of one Muslim by another. His books gave al-Qaeda and its allies a warrant to murder anyone who stood in their way.

Following 9/11, Fadl was arrested in Yemen and sent to Egypt, where he remains in prison. In November 2007, he published a manifesto that ran in newspapers in Egypt and Kuwait, titled "Rationalizing Jihad in Egypt and the World." It is a sweeping renunciation of his previous views. The opening proposition is that "There is nothing that provokes the anger of God and His wrath like the unwarranted spilling of blood and wrecking of property." Fadl then establishes a new set of highly restrictive rules for jihad. He castigates Muslims who resort to theft or kidnapping to finance jihad: "There is no such thing in Islam as ends justifying the means." One must gain permission from one's parents and creditors before waging jihad. Nor is jihad required if the enemy is twice as powerful as the Muslims; in an unequal contest, God permits peace treaties and cease-fires. Fadl repeatedly emphasizes that it is forbidden to kill civilians. Indiscriminate bombing—"such as blowing up of hotels, buildings, and public transportation"—is not permitted, because innocents will surely die. The most unexpected argument in this document is Fadl's assertion that the hijackers of 9/11 "betrayed the enemy," because they had been given U.S. visas, which are a contract of protection. "The followers of bin Laden entered the United States with his knowledge, and on his orders double-crossed its population, killing and destroying," Fadl writes. "The Prophet—God's prayer and peace be upon him—said, 'On the Day of Judgment, every double-crosser will have a banner up his anus proportionate to his treachery.'"

At one point, Fadl observes, "People hate America, and the Islamist movements feel their hatred and their impotence. Ramming America has become the shortest road to fame and leadership among the Arabs and Muslims. But what good is it if you destroy one of your enemy's buildings, and he destroys one of your countries? What good is it if you kill one of his people, and he kills a thousand of yours? . . . That, in short, is my evaluation of 9/11."

Fadl's manifesto was initially faxed from Tora prison, where he is being held, to the London office of the Arabic newspaper *Asharq al-Awsat*. "Do they now have fax machines in Egyptian jail cells?" Zawahiri joked. "I wonder if they're connected to the same line as the electric-shock machines." But Fadl's reasoning was devastating and the attack was far-reaching; moreover, many of Zawahiri's former colleagues signed the document. Worried that Fadl's statement signaled the death of the terrorist movement in Egypt, Zawahiri published a lengthy rejoinder on the Internet entitled "The Exoneration." "I'm warning those Islamist groups who welcome the document that they are giving the government the knife with which it can slaughter them," he wrote in 2008. America is torturing people in its military prisons and in Guantánamo Bay, Cuba, Zawahiri observes. "The U.S. gives itself the right to take any Muslim without respect to his visa," he argues. "If the U.S. and Westerners don't respect visas, why should we?" He reminded his readers of a well-known verse in the Quran supporting the divine mandate for jihad: "When the sacred months are drawn away, slay the idolaters wherever you find them, and take them, and confine them, and lie in wait for them at every place of ambush." This note, sounded so successfully in the past, failed to enlist much resonance.

Although al-Qaeda was unvanquished it was also unable to repeat its startling triumph. America was sinking ever more deeply into unpromising, fantastically expensive wars in the Muslim world—following the script that had been written by bin Laden. Repeatedly, he had outlined his goal of drawing America into such conflicts with the goal of bleeding the U.S. economically and turning the War on Terror into a genuine clash of civilizations. His attacks, from the twin U.S. Embassy bombings in East Africa in 1998, to the bombing of the USS Cole in 2000, and ultimately to 9/11, were designed to goad the United States into Afghanistan, where he expected that America would experience the same catastrophe that befell the Soviet Union in 1989, when it withdrew in defeat and then simply fell apart. Bin Laden's plan was that the sole remaining superpower would dissolve, the United States would become disunited states, and the way would be open for Islam to regain its natural place as the dominant force in the world.

Ten years after 9/11, al-Qaeda is not defeated. It has shown itself to be an adaptable, flexible, evolutionary organization, one that has outlasted most terrorist enterprises in history. One day, al-Qaeda will disappear, as all terrorist movements eventually do. But the template of asymmetrical warfare and mass murder that bin Laden and his confederates have created will inspire future terrorists flying other banners. The legacy of bin Laden is a future of suspicion, grief, and the loss of certain liberties that are already disappearing from memory.

Bin Laden failed in his central goal, however: to take over a Muslim country and establish a caliphate. Most of his plots were thwarted. More important, his pronouncements seemed increasingly irrelevant to the longings that were being awakened in the Muslim world. For a decade, bin Laden's main victory was to remain alive. And yet the War on Terror could not really end as long as he remained on the board.

WHEN I WAS a young man, I taught English at the American University in Cairo, and since then I've watched the vast, moody city go through wrenching changes. I was living there when Gamal Abdul Nasser died, in 1970. At the time, there were no diplomatic relations between the U.S. and Egypt, and only a few hundred Americans lived in the country, but the Egyptian people loved America and what it stood for. When I visited the country a few months after 9/11, to research this book, and many times since, I found the situation utterly reversed. The U.S. and Egyptian governments were close, but the Egyptian people were alienated and angry.

When I lived in Cairo, the population was about six million. Now it is three times that. The unbearable congestion of the city reflects the ungoverned quality of life that is the legacy of Hosni Mubarak's Egypt; pedestrians plunge into the anarchic traffic, their faces masked by fright or resignation. The absence of any attempt to impose order—in the form of streetlights or cross-walks—was characteristic of a government that had no sense of obligation to its people and sought only to protect itself.

During a visit in 2008, I went to Cairo University. The campus was intensely congested—over two hundred thousand students—and the buildings were crumbling from neglect. Although the campus was quiet, the mood of the students was troubled. Their professors had been on strike because of low pay; in Cairo's poorer neighborhoods, riots had broken out over the cost of bread, and, in a middle-class area, residents had marched against pollution. The government's response to the desperation had been to round up eight hundred members of the Muslim Brothers and throw them in jail.

Several faculty members I spoke with repeated the exhausted and confused formulations that were then so common among Egyptian intellectuals—that terrorism was the consequence of American meddling in the Middle East, but at the same time, the attacks of 9/11 were an inside job. The defeatism that has always hung over this city continued to undermine the voices for reform, and the cynicism that reflected the broken Egyptian spirit was still the prevailing mood.

The students were more cordial and less doctrinaire. They were impatient with Islamist dogma, which had done nothing to help ordinary Egyptians, and they expressed interest in the U.S. Presidential campaign, which provided such a contrast to their own smothered lives. The fact that a black man and a woman were contending for the Democratic nomination unsettled prejudices about America and the capacity of democracy to bring about profound social change. The students seemed eager for fresh thinking—a way to escape the dead end of radical Islam. One sensed a moment was coming when an overwhelming demand for reform might finally surge through the clotted arteries of the Arab political system. That moment, so long delayed, was finally approaching.

During the same visit, I had the opportunity to speak at the American University in Cairo, at its historic campus on Tahrir Square. Physically, the place was little changed from my days there; what struck me most strongly was the preponderance of young women who had covered themselves with hijabs. Egypt had always been a conservative society, but the striking increase in the outward display of piety, even in the more tolerant confines of the American University, marked a social shift that seemed to be at odds with the retreat of religious radicalism.

One of those young, covered women asked, in a tone that seemed close to despair, what was wrong with Egypt. Why hadn't it progressed? When I lived there, Egypt was an "underdeveloped country" on a par with South Korea and India and well ahead of China. In the nearly four decades that had passed since then, those countries had galloped ahead. Turkey, with a similar population, now has an economy four times the size of Egypt's. I reflected that, when dynamic, positive change happens, it is usually because of a generational commitment to social transformation. I mentioned my father, an impoverished farm boy from Kansas during the Dust Bowl, who became part of the generation that won World War II and created the most powerful economy in history. I had begun my own reporting career by covering the Civil Rights Movement, which came out of the black colleges of the American South. Similar generations are at work now, transforming the societies of Southeast Asia, Brazil, and the liberated satellites of the former Soviet Union. I didn't realize, as I spoke to those young Egyptians, that they would be the generation that would finally take on the task for their country.

On December 17, 2010, a twenty-six-year-old fruit vendor named Mohammed Bouazizi, a university graduate supporting eight family members, poured two liters of gasoline over himself and lit a match that set the entire Arab world afire. Within weeks, the Tunisian dictator had taken flight, and millions of young Egyptians filled Tahrir Square, seeking to spread the contagion of freedom.

I was deeply stirred as I watched that drama play out. Freedom has been postponed for so many decades. So many lives have been stunted. And yet rapid change brings chaos as well as progress. Certainly al-Qaeda and its kin will seek to exploit the turbulence that is bound to ensue. Perhaps the generation that will genuinely transform the Arab world has not yet arrived. The daunting problems within those societies will certainly frustrate the reformers, if not defeat them. But radical Islam has encountered a force far larger than itself and much more deeply rooted in the longings of Arabs to be a part of the future, rather than the past.

Lawrence Wright
Austin, Texas

PRINCIPAL CHARACTERS

Abu Hafs al-Masri: Former Egyptian policeman and member of al-Jihad who was al-Qaeda's military commander after the death of Abu Ubaydah. His real name is Mohammed Atef. One of bin Laden's closest advisors, he was killed by an American air strike in November 2001.

Abu Hajer al-Iraqi: Former Iraqi military officer and electrical engineer who joined the jihad in Afghanistan and became a close advisor of bin Laden's in Sudan. Although not theologically trained, he was head of the al-Qaeda fatwa committee and rendered two opinions that justified violence against American forces and the killing of innocents. Currently in an American prison after stabbing a prison guard with a sharpened comb. His real name is Mamdouh Mahmoud Salem.

Abu Jandal: Like bin Laden, Abu Jandal is a Saudi citizen of Yemeni extraction. In 2000, he became bin Laden's chief bodyguard in Afghanistan. Delivered the bride price to Yemen to secure bin Laden's fifth wife. Captured by Yemeni authorities after the USS *Cole* bombing, he became a significant source for the FBI. He released a memoir, *In the Shadow of Bin Laden*, (with French journalist Georges Mabrunot), in 2010. That same year, he was the subject of a documentary film, *The Oath*. Currently free from custody, he lives in Yemen. His real name is Nasser al-Bahri.

Abu Rida al-Suri: Businessman from Damascus who immigrated to Kansas City, then joined the jihad in Afghanistan in 1985. He is allegedly the author of the handwritten notes of the August 11, 1988, meeting in which the organization of al-Qaeda is first openly discussed. Later, he became bin Laden's friend and business advisor in Khartoum, where he still lives and operates a candy factory. His real name is Mohammed Loay Baizid.

Abu Ubaydah al-Banshiri: Former Egyptian policeman who gained a reputation on the battlefield in Afghanistan before Zawahiri introduced him to bin Laden. He became al-Qaeda's first military commander. Died in a ferry accident in Lake Victoria in May 1996. His real name is Amin Ali al-Rashidi.

Saif al-Adl: Al-Qaeda's military commander since 2002. It is unclear what his real name is. He may be Mohammed Ibrahim Makkawi, a former Egyptian military officer. He was a source for *Al-Zarqawi: The Second Generation of Al-Qaeda*, by Jordanian journalist Fouad Hussein. After the American-led invasion of Afghanistan in 2001, Adl took refuge in Iran. He was named as a placeholder leader of al-Qaeda following the death of bin Laden, until Ayman al-Zawahiri was formally chosen as the organization's leader.

Abdullah Anas: Algerian mujahid who fought with Ahmed Shah Massoud and married Abdullah Azzam's daughter. Worked in the Services Bureau with Osama bin Laden and Jamal Khalifa. Perhaps the greatest warrior of the Arab Afghans. His real name is Boudejema Bounoua. Currently lives in London, where he serves as an imam at the Finsbury Park mosque. He runs the Truf conflict-resolution consultancy, where he works toward ending the Afghan conflict with the Taliban.

John Anticev: FBI agent on the I-49 squad who obtained the crucial telephone number in Yemen belonging to Ahmed al-Hada, which served as an al-Qaeda switchboard. He is still with the FBI. He is now involved in outreach programs aimed at Muslim and Jewish communities.

Mohammed Atta: The Egyptian leader of the 9/11 hijacking team; pilot of American Airlines Flight #11 that struck the World Trade Center.

Abdullah Azzam: Charismatic Palestinian cleric who founded the Services Bureau in Peshawar in 1984. His fatwa summoning Muslims to repel the Soviet invasion of Afghanistan began the Arab involvement in that war. He was assassinated on November 24, 1989, a crime that has never been solved.

Mahfouz Azzam: Ayman al-Zawahiri's mother's uncle; the family patriarch and longtime lawyer and political figure in Cairo. He was Sayyid Qutb's protégé and later his attorney. He still lives in Helwan, Egypt.

Umayma Azzam: Ayman al-Zawahiri's mother. She died in Cairo in 2009.

Ahmed Badeeb: Osama bin Laden's former teacher at the Thagr School, Badeeb became Prince Turki's chief of staff. After the Afghan jihad, Badeeb became chairman of the board of United Press International. He is now a businessman in Jeddah and ran a losing campaign in the first municipal elections in that country in 2005.

Saeed Badeeb: Prince Turki's director of analysis and Ahmed Badeeb's brother; now retired and living in Jeddah and Washington, D.C.

Hasan al-Banna: Founder and Supreme Guide of the Muslim Brotherhood; murdered by Egyptian authorities in 1949.

Khaled Batarfi: Neighbor and boyhood friend of Osama bin Laden in Jeddah; now retired as an editor at *Al-Medina* newspaper, he teaches communication at Prince Sultan College in Jeddah.

Ramzi bin al-Shibh: Member of the Hamburg cell who oversaw the 9/11 plot. Captured in Karachi, Pakistan, on September 11, 2002, and is now in American custody in Guantánamo Bay, Cuba.

Abdullah bin Laden: Osama's oldest child, now living in Jeddah, with his wife Tiayba Mohammed bin Laden, a cousin, and their children. He runs an advertising business called Fame.

Abdul Rahman bin Laden: Son of bin Laden and Umm Abdullah and born with a birth defect called hydrocephalus, which has caused him permanent mental damage. He now lives with his mother in Syria.

Mohammed bin Laden: Creator of the Saudi Binladin Group and father of the bin Laden dynasty. Born in Rubat, in the Hadramout section of Yemen; as a young man left Yemen for Ethiopia and made his way to Arabia in 1931. Died in 1967 at the age of fifty-nine in an air crash in southern Saudi Arabia.

Osama bin Laden: Born in Riyadh in January 1958; became a fund-raiser for the Afghan jihad after the Soviet invasion in 1979; founded al-Qaeda in 1988. Killed by American special forces in Abbottabad, Pakistan, on May 2, 2011.

Steven Bongardt: FBI agent and member of the I-49 squad, now teaching at the FBI Academy in Quantico, Virginia.

Richard A. Clarke: Former counterterrorism coordinator in the National Security Council. Clarke retired from government in 2003 and became the best-selling author of *Against All Enemies*. He is also the founder of Good Harbor Consulting.

Jack Cloonan: Former member of the I-49 squad who handled Jamal al-Fadl and Ali Mohammed. Now head of Specialty Risks for red24, a firm based in London. He manages the Kidnap for Ransom response team.

Daniel Coleman: FBI agent and member of the I-49 squad who became the representative of the New York office of the FBI at the CIA's Alec Station in 1996. There he opened the first case on bin Laden in 1996, and his interrogation of Jamal al-Fadl exposed the al-Qaeda network. Now an FBI Fellow at the United States Military Academy Combating Terrorism Center.

Essam Deraz: Egyptian filmmaker and bin Laden biographer who chronicled the Arab Afghans in 1988. Currently lives in Cairo.

Anna DiBattista: Former girlfriend of John O'Neill; now director of Worldwide Accounts for the Hyatt Corporation.

Dr. Fadl: Titular leader of al-Jihad during Zawahiri's imprisonment and later in Afghanistan, until he resigned in 1993—reputedly to become a shepherd in Yemen. His real name is Sayyid Imam al-Sharif, although he writes under the name Dr. Abdul Aziz bin Abdul Salam. He is now in prison in Egypt.

Jamal al-Fadl: Sudanese secretary for bin Laden in Khartoum who became al-Qaeda's first defector when he stole $110,000 and fled into the embrace of American authorities. Testified in the New York trial of four al-Qaeda members in the embassy bombings case, *United States v. Usama bin Laden, et al.* Currently in the witness protection program somewhere in the United States.

Turki al-Faisal: Born February 15, 1945, youngest son of King Faisal bin Abdul Aziz. Educated primarily at the Lawrenceville School and Georgetown University, although he dropped out after the 1967 Six Day War. Became head of Saudi intelligence, where he held the Afghan file during the jihad against the Soviets. Served as the Saudi ambassador to the United Kingdom before assuming the same role in Washington. He retired in 2007. He is a trustee of the Oxford Islamic Center as well as the Center for Contemporary Arab Studies at Georgetown University, where he serves as a visiting distinguished professor.

Patrick Fitzgerald: Former assistant U.S. attorney for the Southern District of New York, involved in the prosecution of Sheikh Omar Abdul Rahman and the 1993 bombers of the World Trade Center, and was chief counsel in the successful prosecution of al-Qaeda members involved in the 1998 bombings of U.S. embassies in East Africa. Currently the U.S. attorney for the Northern District of Illinois, he is best known for his investigation of the Valerie Plame affair.

Louis Freeh: Director of the FBI from 1993 to 2001; now runs Freeh Group International, an independent global risk management firm.

Stephen Gaudin: FBI agent and member of the I-49 squad who interrogated Mohammed al-'Owhali. He is now a legal attaché for the FBI in Vienna.

Ahmed al-Hada: Yemeni mujahid who fought in Afghanistan and later provided the telephone in Sanaa that became the al-Qaeda switchboard. His daughter Hoda married Khaled al-Mihdhar. Currently in Yemeni custody.

Nawaf al-Hazmi: 9/11 hijacker who died at the age of twenty-five on American Airlines Flight 77, which crashed into the Pentagon. A wealthy Saudi who grew up in Mecca, Hazmi trained in al-Qaeda camps in Afghanistan and fought in Bosnia and Chechnya before becoming a part of the 9/11 plot. He attended the January 2000 meeting in Malaysia and entered the United States on January 15, 2001.

Gulbuddin Hekmatyar: Afghan Pashtun commander during the anti-Soviet jihad who initiated the Afghan civil war in 1992. Took refuge in Iran after the Taliban took power in 1996. Currently leading an insurgency against the Afghan government, which has charged him with war crimes.

Valerie James: Former girlfriend of John O'Neill; lives in New York City, where she is president of Valerie James Showroom, Inc., representing fashion designers.

Wa'el Julaidan: Close ally of Abdullah Azzam in the Services Bureau in Peshawar. Born in Medina in 1958, he studied at the University of Arizona. Became very close to bin Laden. Later worked for a Saudi charity, the Muslim World League, that was established to help Afghan refugees. Now lives in Jeddah.

Zaynab Ahmed Khadr: Daughter of Zawahiri's friend Ahmed Saeed Khadr and Maha Elsamneh, Zaynab grew up in Peshawar and Afghanistan with the bin Laden and Zawahiri children. In 2009 she married for the third time, to Joshua Boyle, son of a Canadian judge. They live in Toronto with Khadr's daughter from a previous marriage.

Jamal Khalifa: Born September 1, 1956, in Medina, Khalifa became friends with bin Laden while they were both students at King Abdul Aziz University in Jeddah. After graduation, Khalifa became a biology teacher in Medina, until he decided to join the jihad in Afghanistan in 1985. The following year he married bin Laden's older half-sister Sheikha. In 1988, he moved to Manila to establish a branch of the International Islamic Relief Organization. The FBI alleges that he raised money for the Abu Sayyaf terrorist group in the Philippines, but he was never charged. He was acquitted in Jordan of involvement in various terrorist plots. He was murdered in Madagascar in January 2007–apparently by bandits, although his family suspects that he was killed by American special forces. No one has been charged in the crime.

Khallad: Mastermind of the USS *Cole* bombing. His family is from Yemen, but he grew up in Saudi Arabia, where he knew bin Laden. He joined the jihad in Afghanistan at the age of fifteen, eventually losing a foot in a battle against the Northern Alliance. He became a part of the al-Qaeda security team. His real name is Tewfiq bin Attash. Now in U.S. custody in Guantánamo Bay, Cuba.

Jamal Khashoggi: Longtime Saudi journalist and former member of the Muslim Brotherhood who covered the Arab Afghans in the jihad against the Soviet occupation. Khashoggi served as an emissary from bin Laden's extended family, who were seeking to have him renounce violence and return to the Kingdom during his Sudanese exile. After 9/11, Khashoggi distinguished himself by being one of the few Saudis to acknowledge the cultural responsibility that led to the tragedy; later, he was appointed editor of *Al-Watan*, the Kingdom's largest daily, but was fired after publishing articles and cartoons that criticized the religious establishment for supporting violence. After serving as Prince Turki's media advisor in Washington, he returned to Saudi Arabia. He is currently building a television network for Prince Waleed bin Talal in Riyadh.

Ahmed Shah Massoud: Tajik warlord who was the finest strategist of the Afghan cause. After helping to drive the Soviets out of Afghanistan, he joined the government of President Burhanuddin Rabbani as defense minister in 1992. When Rabbani's government collapsed and the Afghan civil war began, Massoud became head of the Northern Alliance, a group of mujahideen leaders who opposed the Taliban. Bin Laden arranged to have him assassinated on September 9, 2001.

Khaled al-Mihdhar: A member of a distinguished family from the Hadramout that traces its lineage back to the Prophet Mohammed, Mihdhar grew up in Mecca. He married Hoda al-Hada, the daughter of the mujahid whose phone in Sanaa would prove to be so critical in understanding the scope of al-Qaeda. Mihdhar came to the United States in January 2000; he left for a period of time, presumably to shepherd the remaining 9/11 hijackers coming from Saudi Arabia; then he returned to the United States on July 4, 2001. He died in the crash of American Airlines Flight 77 when it struck the Pentagon on September 11, 2001. He was twenty-six years old.

Ali Mohammed: Egyptian double agent who joined al-Jihad while he was in the Egyptian army. Ordered by Zawahiri to penetrate American intelligence, he worked briefly for the CIA in Hamburg, Germany, before joining the U.S. Army, where he was stationed at the John F. Kennedy Special Warfare Center and School. The manuals he smuggled out of there became the foundation of al-Qaeda's training and tactics. Mohammed cased the U.S. embassies in East Africa and trained bin Laden's bodyguards. He is now a cooperative witness in U.S. custody, awaiting sentencing in his guilty plea in the embassy bombings case.

Khaled Sheikh Mohammed: The architect of the 9/11 attacks, Mohammed is uncle of Ramzi Yousef, the mastermind of the 1993 World Trade Center bombing. After growing up in Kuwait, Mohammed earned a bachelor's degree in mechanical engineering at North Carolina A&T in 1986. He then went to Peshawar, where he became a secretary of Abdul Rasul Sayyaf, the Afghan warlord favored by the Saudis. Met bin Laden in 1996, where he presented a portfolio of plans for attacking the United States. Captured in Pakistan in 2003, he is now being held by American authorities in an undisclosed location.

Zacarias Moussaoui: French Moroccan al-Qaeda operative sent to the United States to participate in an unspecified operation. Pleaded guilty to six counts of conspiracy and was sentenced to a lifetime of solitary confinement in a maximum-security prison.

Imad Mugniyah: Head of Hezbollah's security service who designed the 1983 suicide car bombings of the U.S. Embassy and the U.S. Marine Corps and French paratrooper barracks in Beirut in 1983; met with Zawahiri and bin Laden in Sudan and provided training for al-Qaeda. He died in a car bombing on Febrary 12, 2008, in Damascus, Syria, a killing thought to have been orchestrated by Mossad, but Israel denies involvement.

Hosni Mubarak: Was president of Egypt from 1981, until he was forced out of office during the 2011 Egyptian revolution. He is in ill health and under indictment for the premeditated murder of protesters.

Shukri Mustafa: Leader of the Takfir wa Hejira movement in Egypt. Executed in 1978.

Wakil Ahmed Muttawakil: Taliban foreign minister who later surrendered to American forces and then joined the government of Hamid Karzai.

Gamal Abdul Nasser: Leader of the 1952 Egyptian revolution; fiery nationalist who transformed politics in the Arab world. He and Sayyid Qutb had radically differing views on the future of Egypt—a difference that eventually led Nasser to have Qutb executed in 1966. Nasser died of a heart attack four years later.

Azza Nowair: Ayman al-Zawahiri's wife. She died in an American air strike in November 2001.

Mullah Mohammed Omar: One-eyed mystic who founded the Taliban in 1992 and essentially ruled Afghanistan from 1996 until the invasion by allied forces in 2001. His whereabouts are unknown, but he is thought to be living under the protection of Pakistani intelligence in the town of Quetta.

John O'Neill: A native of Atlantic City, New Jersey, O'Neill became a special agent of the FBI in July 1976, assigned to the Baltimore office. He went to FBI headquarters in April 1987, where he supervised investigations of white-collar crime. In 1991, he was appointed assistant special agent in charge of the Chicago office of the bureau; then in 1995 he returned to headquarters to be the chief of the counterterrorism section. He was appointed special agent in charge of the National Security Division in the FBI's New York office on January 1, 1997. He resigned from the FBI on August 22, 2001; the next day he started work as the World Trade Center's chief of security. He was forty-nine years old when he died on 9/11.

Mohammed al-'Owhali: Convicted bomber of the U.S. Embassy in Nairobi; now in an American prison serving a life sentence.

Thomas Pickard: Acting director of the FBI from June 25, 2001, until September 4, 2001. He retired two months later.

Mohammed Qutb: Sayyid Qutb's brother, also a widely read author and thinker; took refuge with other members of the Muslim Brotherhood in Saudi Arabia after spending time in Egyptian prisons. Became a popular speaker at forums where bin Laden was exposed to his teachings. Still lives in Mecca.

Sayyid Qutb: Islamist writer and educator who wrote *Milestones,* among many other important works. Nasser hanged him in 1966.

Burhanuddin Rabbani: Islamic scholar who served as president of Afghanistan from 1992 until 1996, when the Taliban took over. He briefly seized office again after the Taliban were deposed, but handed over power to Hamid Karzai's interim government in December 2001. He is the leader of the Afghanistan National Front, the country's largest opposition party.

Sheikh Omar Abdul Rahman: The "blind sheikh" who led the Islamic Group in Egypt and was the spiritual leader of al-Jihad. Imprisoned with Zawahiri and other Egyptian militants following the assassination of Anwar Sadat in 1981. Eventually convicted of plotting to destroy New York City landmarks, he is now serving a life sentence in a U.S. prison.

Ahmed Ressam: Algerian who trained in al-Qaeda camps in Afghanistan; captured in December 1999 as he tried to enter the United States from Canada carrying a load of explosives in his trunk. His evident goal was to blow up the Los Angeles airport. After his conviction in 2001, he began cooperating with U.S. authorities; but two years later, he stopped cooperating and recanted previous statements. He was sentenced to twenty-two years in prison. A federal appeals court found that sentence too lenient; it is now under review.

Mark T. Rossini: Former actor from the Bronx who became a private detective before joining the FBI. Assigned to the I-49 squad, he replaced Dan Coleman at Alec Station. He pleaded guilty in December 2008 for accessing FBI computers for personal purposes. He received a suspended sentence and agreed to resign from the FBI. He now is the president of MTR Associates LLC, a corporate security and consulting agency in New York City.

Amal al-Sada: Osama bin Laden's fifth wife. They married in 2001 when she was fifteen. She was shot in the leg as she rushed U.S. Navy Seals during the raid in Abbottabad on May 2, 2011, in an apparent attempt to protect bin Laden. She and her daughter are in Pakistani custody, along with two other bin Laden wives.

Anwar al-Sadat: Former president of Egypt, assassinated by al-Jihad in 1981.

Abdul Rasul Sayyaf: Afghan warlord who trained as a cleric at Cairo's al-Azhar university. Was bin Laden's Afghan sponsor and the Saudis' favored commander. He narrowly escaped an assassination attempt in a bombing that killed five of his bodyguards in 2009. He is currently a member of the Afghan parliament and is working to create amnesty for former mujahideen.

Michael Scheuer: CIA veteran who opened Alec Station in 1996 and ran it until he was relieved of duty in 1999. Writing anonymously after his retirement, he penned the exposés *Through Our Enemies' Eyes* and *Imperial Hubris*. He says he was fired from his position as a Senior Fellow with the Jamestown Foundation after asserting that the U.S. relationship with Israel undermined American security interests.

Shafiq: Teenage mujahid who saved bin Laden's life in the battle of Jalalabad.

Ali Soufan: Lebanese American FBI agent who was the case agent on the USS *Cole* bombing. His interrogation of Abu Jandal in Yemen after 9/11 led to the identification of the hijackers. He is now the CEO of the Soufan Group, an international security consulting firm, and the author of *Black Banners: The Inside Story of 9/11 and the War against Al Qaeda*.

Mary Lynn Stevens: Former girlfriend of John O'Neill, she is now the vice president of the Pentagon Federal Credit Union Foundation, an organization that assists soldiers and marines who have been wounded in Iraq and Afghanistan.

Yazid Sufaat: Malaysian businessman who worked with Zawahiri in Afghanistan to propagate anthrax spores. The January 2000 meeting between the USS *Cole* bombers and the 9/11 hijackers took place in his condominium in Kuala Lumpur. He also wrote a letter of recommendation for Zacarias Moussaoui. He was detained by Malaysian authorities after 9/11, but was released in 2008, with assurances that he will be "watched closely."

Medani al-Tayeb: Former treasurer of al-Qaeda. He married bin Laden's niece; lost a leg in Afghanistan; quit al-Qaeda in the early nineties and returned to live in Jeddah.

Hassan al-Turabi: Ideological leader of the 1989 Islamic revolution in Sudan. In and out of confinement since then, he now lives at home in Khartoum.

Issam Eldin al-Turabi: Son of Hassan al-Turabi, and bin Laden's friend during his stay in Sudan, Issam is a businessman and well-known horse breeder in Khartoum.

Umm Abdullah: Osama bin Laden's first wife, whom he married in 1974 when she was fourteen. She is from Syria, the daughter of bin Laden's mother's first cousin. She is the mother of eleven of his children. Her given name is Najwa Ghanem. She and her son Omar bin Laden published a memoir in 2009 with (with Jean Sasson), *Growing Up Bin Laden*.

She lives in Syria with her son Abdul Rahman and her two youngest daughters.

Umm Ali: Osama's wife from the Gilaini family in Mecca. She bore him three children. She asked for a divorce in 1996 and now lives in Saudi Arabia. Her given name is Khadijah Sharif. Her eldest son, Ali, is serving fifteen years in prison in Saudi Arabia for the illegal possession of a weapon.

Umm Hamza: Married Osama in 1982 and bore him one child. She is from a distinguished family in Jeddah and has a Ph.D. in child psychology. Her given name is Khairiah Sabar. After reportedly fleeing to Iran following 9/11, she returned to Saudi Arabia, and eventually slipped back into Pakistan to rejoin her husband and son. She was arrested following the raid in Abbottabad. Hamza, her only child (and thought by some to have been groomed by bin Laden to succeed him), escaped the raid.

Umm Khaled: From the Sharif family in Medina, she holds a Ph.D. in Arabic grammar and taught at the city's Education College. She and Osama have three daughters and a son. Her given name is Siham Sabar. She was captured in the Abbottabad raid.

Dr. Ahmed el-Wed: Takfiri Algerian doctor who worked in the Kuwaiti Red Crescent hospital in Peshawar with Zawahiri and Dr. Fadl; went back to Algeria and was killed during the civil war there.

Mary Jo White: Former U.S. attorney for the Southern District of New York. She is head of litigation for Debevoise & Plimpton, a New York law firm.

Ramzi Yousef: Mastermind of the 1993 World Trade Center bombing. The nephew of Khaled Sheikh Mohammed, Yousef was born in Kuwait in 1968; studied electrical engineering in Wales. Created elaborate plots to assassinate Pope John Paul II and President Bill Clinton and to blow up eleven American airliners simultaneously. Finally captured in Pakistan in 1995, he is in an American prison serving a life sentence plus 240 years.

Dr. Ayman al-Zawahiri: Leader of al-Jihad and the ideological leader of al-Qaeda. Born in Cairo on June 19, 1951, Zawahiri started a cell to overthrow the Egyptian government when he was fifteen years old. Imprisoned after Sadat's assassination in 1981 and convicted of dealing in weapons, he was released three years later. He fled to Saudi Arabia in 1985, and the following year moved to Peshawar, where he and Dr. Fadl rebuilt al-Jihad. After the end of the war against the Soviet occupation,

Zawahiri relocated his movement to Sudan, where he waged a campaign against the Egyptian government, resulting in the near total destruction of his organization. In 1996 he moved to Afghanistan and engineered a merger of al-Jihad with al-Qaeda. He is the author of several books, notably *Bitter Harvest* and *Knights Under the Prophet's Banner*. He was chosen as the leader of al-Qaeda on June 16, 2011.

Hussein al-Zawahiri: Ayman's youngest brother, an architect, was rendered by the CIA and the FBI to Egypt, where he was questioned and eventually released in August 2000. He now lives in Cairo.

Mohammed al-Zawahiri: Ayman's younger brother, who became deputy emir of al-Jihad. An architect by training, he set up the al-Jihad cell in Albania. He resigned from the organization in 1998. He was reputedly captured by Egyptian authorities in Dubai in 2000 and thought to have been executed in prison; however, the pan-Arab newspaper *Al-Sharq Al-Awsat* discovered that he was alive and being held in Tora Prison in Egypt in 2004. He was released from prison in March 2011, but rearrested shortly thereafter.

Dr. Mohammed Rabie al-Zawahiri: Ayman al-Zawahiri's father, a professor of pharmacology at Ain Shams University, who died in 1995.

Montassir al-Zayyat: Islamist lawyer in Cairo who was imprisoned with Zawahiri. He eventually wrote a biography of Zawahiri, *The Road to al-Qaeda*.

NOTES

Where there are attributed quotes in the text that are not cited in the notes, they derive from personal interviews.

1. The Martyr

9 **Sayyid Qutb:** I am especially indebted to Mohammed Qutb for his generous recollections of his brother. My views of Qutb's life have also been shaped by communications with John Calvert and Gilles Kepel.

   "Should I go": al-Khaledi, *Sayyid Qutb: min al-milad*, 194.

   Powerful and sympathetic friends: interview with Mohammed Qutb. Qutb names in particular Mahmud Fahmi Nugrashi Pasha, the Egyptian prime minister.

10 **not even a very religious man:** Shepard, *Sayyid Qutb*, xv. Mohammed Qutb told me, "For a while, he became more secular."

   he had memorized the Quran: Mohammed Qutb, personal communication.

   He had read: al-Khaledi, *Sayyid Qutb: min al-milad*, 139.

11 **"I hate those Westerners":** Qutb, "Al-dhamir al-amrikani."

   "dishonorable" women: John Calvert, " 'Undutiful Boy,' " 98.

   The dearest relationship: Mohammed Qutb, personal communication.

   "I have decided": al-Khaledi, *Amrika min al-dakhil*, 27.

12 **"half-naked":** al-Khaledi, *Sayyid Qutb: min al-milad*, 195. Later Qutb would claim that the woman was an agent of the American Central Intelligence Agency, sent to seduce him.

   the most prosperous holiday: McCullough, *Truman*, 621.

13 **Half of the world's:** Johnson, *Modern Times*, 441.

13 **Fully a fourth:** White, *Here Is New York,* 46.

14 **never met one:** Mohammed Qutb, personal communication.
   English was rudimentary: interview with Mohammed Qutb.
   "Here in this strange place": Sayyid Qutb, letter to Anwar el-Maadawi, in al-Khaledi, *Sayyid Qutb: al-adib,* 157–58.
   "black elevator operator": Ibid., 195–96.

15 **Kinsey researcher:** Manchester, *The Glory and the Dream,* 479.
   Qutb was familiar: Qutb, *Shade of the Qur'an,* 6:143. The Kinsey Report is rendered "McKenzie" in this translation.
   "a reckless": Qutb, *Majallat al-kitab,* 666–69.
   "Every time a husband": al-Khaledi, *Amrika min al-dakhil,* 185–86.
   "Communism is creeping": Frady, *Billy Graham,* 236.

16 **one of every 1,814 people:** Oshinsky, *A Conspiracy So Immense,* 96.
   "They are everywhere": ibid., 97.
   "Either Communism must die": Frady, *Billy Graham,* 237.
   "Either we shall walk": Shepard, *Sayyid Qutb,* 354.

17 **he saw in the party of Lenin:** interview with Gamal al-Banna.
   "like a vision": ibid., 34.
   "a complete system": ibid., 51.
   "The city": White, *Here Is New York,* 54.
   Qutb moved to Washington: Calvert, " 'Undutiful Boy,' " 93.

18 **"Life in Washington":** ibid., 94.
   "a primitiveness": Qutb, "Amrika allati ra'ayt" (b).
   "I'm here at a restaurant": Sayyid Qutb, letter to Tewfiq al-Hakeem, in al-Khaledi, *Amrika min al-dakhil,* 154.
   "Whenever I go": Qutb, "Amrika allati ra'ayt" (c).
   "who knows full well": Qutb, "Amrika allati ra'ayt" (b).

19 **"Today the enemy":** Mohammed Qutb, personal communication. Qutb attributes the quote to "the doctors themselves" and says, "We, the members of the family, heard it from my brother personally."
   "Sheikh Hasan's followers": Albion Ross, "Moslem Brotherhood Leader Slain as He Enters Taxi in Cairo Street," *New York Times,* February 13, 1949.
   a profound shock: interview with Mohammed Qutb.
   they had never met: Mohammed Qutb, personal communication.
   "If the Brothers succeed": Azzam, "Martyr Sayyid Qutb."

20 **pay him a fee:** al-Khaledi, *Sayyid Qutb: al-adib,* 149.
   "I decided to enter": Azzam, "Martyr Sayyid Qutb." Qutb himself writes, however, that he didn't formally join the Brotherhood until 1953. Qutb, *Limadah 'azdamunee.*
   Summer courses: interview with Michael Welsh, who is the source of much of the information on the history of Greeley; interviews

with Peggy A. Ford, Janet Waters, Ken McConnellogue, Jaime McClendon, Ibrahim Insari, and Frank and Donna Lee Lakin.

20 **greatest civilizations:** Peggy A. Ford, personal communication.

21 **highly publicized:** Larson, *Shaping Educational Change*, 5.
mandatory virtues: ibid.
James Michener: Peggy A. Ford, personal communication.

22 **"small city":** Qutb, "Hamaim fi New York," 666.
Garden City: interview with Michael Welsh.
"They were kicking": al-Khaledi, *Amrika min al-dakhil*, 181.
Meeker: Geffs, *Under Ten Flags*, 156–57; interview with Michael Welsh.
Middle Eastern community: interview with Sa'eb Dajani.

23 **"But we're Egyptians":** interview with Sa'eb Dajani.
several of the Arab students: interview with Ibrahim Insari.
"racism had brought": al-Khaledi, *Amrika min al-dakhil*, 169.
"The foot does not": Qutb, "Amrika allati ra'ayt" (b), 1301–2.

24 **"simply biological":** al-Khaledi, *Amrika min al-dakhil*, 194.

26 **Qutb acted as host:** interview with Ibrahim Insari.
classical records: interview with Sa'eb Dajani.
"Jazz is": Qutb, "Amrika allati ra'ayt" (b), 1301.
"dancing hall": ibid., 1301–6.

27 **"estrangement":** al-Khaledi, *Amrika min al-dakhil*, 157.
"The soul has": Sayyid Qutb, letter to Tewfig al-Hakeem, in al-Khaledi, *Amrika min al-dakhil*, 196–97.
"white man": ibid., 39.

28 **Islam and modernity:** Abu-Rabi, *Intellectual Origins*, 156; Berman, *Terror and Liberalism*, 87ff.
Qutb returned: interview with Mohammed Qutb; al-Khaledi, *Sayyid Qutb: al-adib*, 152.

29 **two hundred red automobiles:** Rodenbeck, *Cairo*, 152.
"It is the nature": Neil MacFarquhar, "Egyptian Group Patiently Pursues Dream of Islamic State," *New York Times*, January 20, 2002.
lower-middle class: Ibrahim, *Egypt Islam and Democracy*, 36.

30 **more than a million:** interview with Saad Eddin Ibrahim.
intimately organized: Mitchell, *Society of the Muslim Brothers*, 32.
In retaliation: Abdel-Malek, *Egypt*, 34; Rodenbeck, *Cairo*, 155. Nutting, *Nasser*, 31, gives the alternative figure of forty-three policemen dead and seventy-two wounded.
led by members: Abdel-Malek, *Egypt*, 35.

31 **classical music albums:** interview with Fahmi Howeidi. Other observations of Qutb's villa were made during a tour of Helwan with Mahfouz Azzam.

31 **Some of the planning:** interview with Gamal al-Banna; al-Khaledi, *Sayyid Qutb: al-shaheed,* 140–41; al-Khaledi, *Sayyid Qutb: al-adib,* 159. Members of the Free Officers who were in the society are listed in Abdel-Malek, *Egypt,* 94, 210–11.
"just dictatorship": Sivan, *Radical Islam,* 73.
Nasser then invited: Mohammed Qutb, personal communication.
he was offered: al-Khaledi, *Sayyid Qutb: al-shaheed,* 142.

32 **The Islamists wanted:** interview with Olivier Roy; Roy, *Afghanistan,* 37–39.
opposed egalitarianism: Heikal, *Autumn of Fury,* 127.

33 **secret alliance:** Ibid., 141.
"Let them kill": nasser.bibalex.org
placing thousands: ibid.; figures range from "dozens" (Calvert, " 'Undutiful Boy,' " 101) to "seven thousand" (Abdel-Malek, *Egypt,* 96).
Qutb was charged: Hannonen, "Egyptian Islamic Discourse," 43.
high fever: Moussalli, *Radical Islamic Fundamentalism,* 34. Al-Khaledi, *Sayyid Qutb: al-shaheed,* 145, also mentions the use of dogs during the torture of Sayyid Qutb.
"principles of the revolution": al-Khaledi, *Sayyid Qutb: al-shaheed,* 154.
planned takeover: Mitchell, *Society of the Muslim Brothers,* 152.

34 **always frail:** Mohammed Qutb, personal communication; Moussalli, *Radical Islamic Fundamentalism,* 34, 62 n.
tuberculosis: Fouad Allam, personal interview.
in the prison hospital: Moussalli, *Radical Islamic Fundamentalism,* 36.

35 **"Mankind today":** Qutb, *Milestones,* 5ff.

36 **government of Saudi Arabia:** al-Aroosi, *Muhakamat Sayyid Qutb,* 80–82.
plot to overthrow: interview with Fouad Allam; al-Aroosi, *Muhakamat Sayyid Qutb,* 43.
security police: interview with Fouad Allam.
"time has come": al-Khaledi, *Sayyid Qutb: al-shaheed,* 154.
"Thank God": ibid., 156.
He dispatched Sadat: interview with Mahfouz Azzam.
minister of education: al-Khaledi, *Sayyid Qutb: al-shaheed,* 154.

37 **"Write the words":** interview with Mahfouz Azzam.
government refused: interview with Mohammed Qutb.

2. The Sporting Club

38 **Maadi:** Much of the history and sociology of Maadi comes from interviews with Samir W. Raafat and from his book, *Maadi.*

39 **Dr. Mohammed Rabie al-Zawahiri:** Information about the Zawahiri family is largely drawn from interviews and personal communications with Mahfouz Azzam and Omar Azzam.

40 **highly unpopular:** Yunan Rizk, "Al-Azhar's 1934," *Al-Ahram Weekly,* May 13–19, 2004.
private medical clinic: interview with Khaled Abou el-Fadl.

41 **Michel Chalhub:** Raafat, *Maadi,* 185.

42 **"inhumane":** interview with Mahfouz Azzam.
"genius": interview with Zaki Mohamed Zaki.
"From tomorrow": interview with Mahfouz Azzam.

43 **"We don't want":** interview with Omar Azzam.

44 **"Nasserite regime":** al-Zawahiri, "Knights Under the Prophet's Banner," part 3.
Parents were fearful: interview with Zaki Mohamed Zaki.

46 **"Then history":** al-Zawahiri, "Knights Under the Prophet's Banner," part 6.
In return for their support: interview with Saad Eddin Ibrahim.

47 **even to his family:** Chanaa Rostom, "li awil mara shaqiqat al-Zawahiri tatahadith" [For the First Time Zawahiri's Sister Speaks], *Akher Sa'a,* October 24, 2001.
A joke: interview with Mahfouz Azzam and Omar Azzam.

48 **provided them with arms:** interview with Hisham Kassem.
in small cells: Cooley, *Unholy Wars,* 40.

50 **fewer than ten members:** interview with Abdul Haleem Mandour.
Four of these cells: interview with Kamal Habib.
"Before that": interview with Essam Nowair.

51 **become a martyr:** interview with Omar Azzam.

52 **"My connection":** al-Zawahiri, "Knights Under the Prophet's Banner," part 2.

53 **had to use honey:** interview with Mahfouz Azzam.
Writing to his mother: interview with Omar Azzam; Robert Marquand, "The Tenets of Terror," *Christian Science Monitor,* October 18, 2001.
Through his connection: interview with Omar Azzam.
recruiting for jihad: interview with Mahmoun Fandy.

54 **"a training course":** al-Zawahiri, "Knights Under the Prophet's Banner," part 2.

55 **"lunatic madman":** Ibrahim, *Egypt Islam and Democracy,* 30 n.
"Yes, we are reactionaries": Ayatollah Ruhollah Khomeini, "Speech at Feyziyeh Theological School," August 24, 1979; reproduced in Rubin and Rubin, *Anti-American Terrorism,* 34.
"Islam says": Taheri, *Holy Terror,* 226–27.

56 **Iranian revolution:** Abdelnasser, *Islamic Movement,* 73.

  five hundred Quranic verses: Roy Mottahedeh, personal communication.

57 **final speech:** Guenena, " 'Jihad' an 'Islamic Alternative,' " 80–81.

  Sadat dissolved: Kepel, *Jihad,* 85.

  "No politics in religion": Abdo, *No God but God,* 54.

  Zumar's plan: 1981 interrogation of Ayman al-Zawahiri.

58 **"a noble person":** al-Zawahiri, "Knights Under the Prophet's Banner," part 5.

  "something missing": interview with Yassir al-Sirri.

59 **Essam al-Qamari came out:** 1981 interrogation of Ayman al-Zawahiri.

60 **Citadel:** interview with Montassir al-Zayyat.

61 **Two weeks later:** interview with Fouad Allam.

62 **"Let him pray":** interview with Omar Azzam.

  Zawahiri went to the mosque: interview with Mahfouz Azzam.

  "The toughest thing": al-Zawahiri, "Knights Under the Prophet's Banner," part 11.

  Qamari was shot: interview with Kamal Habib.

64 **marks of torture:** Fouad Allam, who allegedly oversaw the torture personally, claims that no torture took place; it's all a legend, he says. There may be some truth in that; many of the stories that prisoners tell are so gothic that they have the ring of fantasy, and certainly they have been hawked to reporters in order to discredit the regime and enhance the standing of the Islamists. Allam gave me a 1982 video of a young Montassir al-Zayyat (who had told me of being repeatedly beaten and given electroshock) buoyantly greeting incoming prisoners at Torah Prison and telling them how well he had been treated. "They even gave me this Quran," he says, holding up a pocket-size book. Zayyat now maintains that he was tortured into making the statement, although Kamal Habib, whose hands are spotted with scars from cigarette burns, says that Zayyat was never tortured. "It's just something he says to the media," he told me.

  The question is what happened to Zawahiri. "The higher you were in the organization, the more you were tortured," Habib says. "Ayman knew a number of officers and had some weapons. He was subjected to severe torture." Several former prisoners told me that the most common form of torture was to have one's hands tied behind him and then to be hoisted onto a doorjamb—hanging, sometimes for hours, by one's hands behind one's back. For Habib, it took years to lose the numbness in his arms. Zawahiri himself never talks about his own experience, but he writes, "The brutal treadmill of torture broke bones, flayed skins, shocked nerves, and killed souls. Its methods were lowly. It detained women, committed sexual assaults, called men feminine names, starved prisoners, gave them bad food, cut off water, and prevented visits to humiliate the detainees" (al-Zawahiri, "Knights Under the Prophet's Banner," part 4). One can imagine that the humiliation was all the greater for a man as prideful as Dr. Zawahiri.

Zawahiri's reference to the use of "wild dogs" as a form of torture is a frequent allegation by ex-prisoners. Sayyid Qutb was allegedly mauled by dogs during his second arrest. Dogs are lowly outcasts in Islamic culture, so such a punishment is particularly degrading.

65 **"We were defeated":** interview with Usama Rushdi.
driver arrived: ibid.
67 **Zawahiri pointed out:** interview with Montassir al-Zayyat.
they had had visions: Ibrahim, *Egypt Islam and Democracy,* 20.
68 **"model young Egyptians":** ibid., 19.
"You have trivialized": interview with Saad Eddin Ibrahim.
worried about the political consequences: interview with Mahfouz Azzam.
a surgery fellowship: Heba al-Zawahiri, personal communication.
a tourist visa to Tunisia: interview with Usama Rushdi.

3. The Founder

69 **arrived in the Kingdom in 1985:** interview with Ahmed Badeeb.
"scars left on his body": al-Zayyat, *The Road to al-Qaeda,* 31.
testifying against his comrades: ibid., 49.
70 **"situation in Egypt":** *Tahta al-Mijhar* [Under the Microscope], al-Jazeera, February 20, 2003.
Zawahiri and bin Laden met: al-Zayyat, "Islamic Groups," part 4, *Al-Hayat,* January 12, 2005. Zayyat claims that Zawahiri gave him this information, although Zayyat did not tell me this when we spoke in 2002. At that time, he said that Zawahiri and bin Laden probably met in 1986 in Peshawar. This new information, he contends, is based on subsequent conversations with Zawahiri. Mohammed Salaah, the *Al-Hayat* correspondent in Cairo, told me that, according to his sources, the two men met in 1985, which would have been in Jeddah. Others speculate that the first meeting of Zawahiri and bin Laden took place in Pakistan; for instance, Jamal Ismail told Peter Bergen that the first meeting of the two men was in Peshawar in 1986. Bergen, *The Osama bin Laden I Know,* 63.

70 **"If our first parent":** Burton, *Personal Narrative*, 2:274.

71 **bin Laden's father was buried here:** interview with anonymous bin Laden family spokesperson.
death in an air crash in 1967: Othman Milyabaree and Abdullah Hassanein, "Al-Isamee al-Kabeer Alathee Faqadathoo al-Bilad" [The Big Self-Made Man the Country Has Lost], *Okaz*, September 7, 1967.
builders and architects: Eric Watkins, personal communication.
Ethiopia: interview with bin Laden family spokesperson.
boat to Jizan: interview with Saleh M. Binladin.

72 **massacring thousands:** Aburish, *The Rise, Corruption, and Coming Fall*, 24. According to Aburish, "No fewer than 400,000 people were killed and wounded, for the Ikhwan did not take prisoners, but mostly killed the vanquished. Well over a million inhabitants of the territories conquered by Ibn Saud fled to other countries." The Saudi historian Madawi al-Rasheed notes that such figures are hard to credit, since there was no one doing the counting, but she writes, in personal communication, "The scale of Saudi atrocities in the name of unifying the country is massive." She adds, "The Ikhwan were nothing but a mercenary force mobilised by Ibn Saud to fight his own wars and to serve his own purposes. Once they did the job for him he massacred them using other mercenaries, this time the sedentary population of southern Najd, other tribes, and the British Royal Air force stationed in Kuwait and Iraq at the time."
theological innovations: Schwartz, *Two Faces of Islam*, 69ff.

73 **they could kill:** Khaled Abou el Fadl, "The Ugly Modern and the Modern Ugly," 33–77.
Karl Twitchell: Lacey, *The Kingdom*, 231ff; Lippman, *Inside the Mirage*, 15ff.

74 **had begun as a dockworker:** interview with Nawaf Obaid.
one glass eye: interview with anonymous bin Laden family spokesperson.
the result of a blow: interview with Jamal Khalifa. A bin Laden family spokesperson disputes the story about the teacher hitting Mohammed bin Laden; he says the eye was lost in an accident in Ethiopia. Before protective goggles were commonly used, bricklayers and stonecutters often were blinded by chips of rock or mortar. I rely on the school-teacher story because Khalifa heard it from his wife, who was close to her father. Other bin Laden brothers I've spoken to admit they have no special knowledge about the loss of their father's vision.
"his signature": interview with Saleh M. Binladin.
"dark, friendly, and energetic": interview with Michael M. Ameen, Jr.

74 **Aramco began a program:** Thomas C. Barger, "Birth of a Dream,"
   Saudi Aramco World 35, no. 3 (May/June 1984).
   Aramco sponsorship: interview with Prince Turki al-Faisal.
   "Aramco was really the only institution that built things," Prince
   Turki told me. "When King Abdul Aziz wanted something done he
   would ask Aramco to do it, or get their advice. That was how bin
   Laden came into the picture. He was recommended."
75 **"raised as a laborer":** Othman Milyabaree and Abdullah Hassanein,
   "Al-Isamee al-Kabeer Alathee Faqadathoo al-Bilad" [The Big Self-
   Made Man the Country Has Lost], *Okaz*, September 7, 1967.
   unprofitable projects: interview with anonymous Saudi source.
   They called him *mu'alim*: interview with Jamal Khalifa.
   renovating houses: interview with anonymous bin Laden family
   spokesperson.
   minister of finance: Mohammed Besalama, "Al-Sheikh Mohammed
   Awad bin Laden al-Mu'alem" [Sheikh Mohammed Awad bin Laden,
   the Teacher], *Okaz*, June 2, 1984.
   Osama bin Laden would recall: interview with Ali Soufan.
   drove the king's car: interview with anonymous bin Laden family
   spokesman.
   first concrete building: anonymous Saudi source.
   minister of public works: Mohammed Besalama, "Al-Sheikh
   Mohammed Awad bin Laden al-Mu'alem" [Sheikh Mohammed
   Awad bin Laden, the Teacher], *Okaz*, June 2, 1984; interview with
   anonymous bin Laden family spokesman.
   pay the same fee: Mohammed Besalama, "Al-Sheikh Mohammed
   Awad bin Laden al-Mu'alem" [Sheikh Mohammed Awad bin Laden,
   the Teacher], *Okaz*, June 2, 1984.
   one well-paved road: Mayer, "The House of bin Laden."
   largest customer: anonymous Saudi source. A spokesperson for the
   Caterpillar Corporation refused comment.
76 **donated the asphalt:** Lippman, *Inside the Mirage*, 49.
   Umm Kalthoum: interview with Khaled Batarfi.
   "We have to organize": interview with Prince Talal bin Abdul Aziz.
   throwing money: Lacey, *The Kingdom*, 302.
77 **Hotel al-Yamama:** interview with Michael M. Ameen, Jr.
   bin Laden began diversifying: Aramco, *Binladen Brothers for Contracting and Industry* (N.p., n.d.)
   Grand Mosque: figures from Abbas, *Story of the Great Expansion*,
   364ff., and a Saudi Binladin Group promotional film.
78 **less than a hundred dollars:** Lacey, *The Kingdom*, 323.
   fronted the money: interview with anonymous Saudi source.

79 **special permission:** Lippman, *Inside the Mirage,* 127. At the time, the
king also had to personally approve every takeoff and landing of
flights in the Kingdom.

training Saudi forces in 1953: Rachel Bronson, personal communication. According to Bronson, the Saudis permitted the Americans to
build an air base in 1945, which was designed to facilitate troop
movement to the Pacific theater during World War II. The American
presence was renegotiated after the war, and the Americans conducted a survey to determine Saudi military needs. In 1953 the
United States and the Saudis signed the agreement that allowed
American forces to train Saudi units. It has served as the basis for all
subsequent military cooperation.

view the ruins: interview with Stanley Guess.

80 **al-Qaeda would use this:** Wiktorowicz and Kaltner, "Killing in the
Name of Islam."

surrendered to the Ikhwan: Champion, *The Paradoxical Kingdom,* 49ff.;
al-Rasheed, *A History of Saudi Arabia,* 66; Lacey, *The Kingdom,* 188.

He had a vision: interview with Prince Turki al-Faisal.

81 **Bin Laden's brilliant solution:** anonymous bin Laden family
spokesman, personal communication.

bin Laden pushed a donkey: interview with Mahmoud Alim.
According to Ali Soufan, Osama bin Laden often recounted the same
story.

For twenty months: anonymous bin Laden family spokesman, personal communication.

beginning in 1961: Saudi Binladin Group brochure.

dynamite charges: interview with Khaled Batarfi.

marking the path: interview with Jamal Khalifa.

unbudgeted expenses: interview with Prince Turki al-Faisal.

82 **He paid for the operation:** Othman Milyabaree and Abdullah Hassanein, "Al-Isamee al-Kabeer Alathee Faqadathoo al-Bilad" [The Big
Self-Made Man the Country Has Lost], *Okaz,* September 7, 1967.

"What I remember": "Walidee Ramama al-Aqsa Bilkhasara" [My
Father Renovated Al Aqsa Mosque, with a Loss], *Al-Umma al-
Islamiyya,* October 18, 1991.

fathered fifty-four children: interview with anonymous bin Laden
family spokesman, who told me there were twenty-nine daughters
and twenty-five sons. National Commission on Terrorist Attacks
Upon the United States, *The 9/11 Commission Report* (55), puts the
total number of children at fifty-seven.

The total number of wives: interview with anonymous bin Laden
family spokesman.

82 **An assistant followed:** interview with anonymous bin Laden family spokesman.

concubines: bin Ladin, *Inside the Kingdom*, 69.

"My father used to say": Anonymous, *Through Our Enemies' Eyes*, 82.

his seventeenth son, Osama: *The 9/11 Commission Report*, 55.

Syrian wife: "Ashiqaa' Wa Shaqiqat Oola Zawjat Bin Laden Bilathiqiya Khaifoon 'Alayha wa 'ala Atfaliha al 11 Fee Afghanistan" [The Brothers and Sisters of the First Wife of bin Laden in Latakya Are Afraid for Her and Her 11 Children in Afghanistan], *Al-Sharq al-Awsat*, November 14, 2001.

fourteen-year-old girl: interview with Khaled Batarfi.

Alia Ghanem: Ali Taha and Emad Sara, "Al-Majellah Fee Qaryat Akhwal Osama bin Laden Fee Suria" [Al-Majellah in the Village of the Uncles, of Osama bin Laden's in Syria], *Al-Majellah*, December 8, 2001.

the Alawite sect: Joseph Bahout, personal communication. Whether Alia Ghanem herself was an Alawi is a subject of dispute. Ahmed Badeeb, an assistant to Prince Turki when he was head of Saudi intelligence, told me that she was an Alawite, as did Osama bin Laden's brother-in-law, Jamal Khalifa, and his friend Jamal Khashoggi. The family has denied it—which, of course, could be religious dissimulation. Ahmed Zaidan told me that he had asked the guests at the wedding of Osama's son in Jalalabad in 2001 if Alia was an Alawite and was told that she was not. Wahib Ghanem, an Alawite from Lattakia in the 1940s, was a founder of the Baath Party. There are, however, Ghanems who are Christian or Sunni Islam, especially in Lebanon.

83 **Alia joined bin Laden's household:** Nawaf Obaid says that Alia was actually a concubine, a point that is reinforced by Carmen bin Ladin. Jamal Khashoggi says, "The fact that she gave birth to Osama meant that they were married, but there was the business of buying concubines—it was a thing of that time, the 1950s, particularly from the Alawi sect."

Alia was modern and secular: interview with Jamal Khalifa.

January 1958: Bin Laden says, "I was born in the month of Ragab in Hejira 1377." "Walidee Ramama al-Aqsa Bilkhasara" [My Father Renovated al-Aqsa Mosque, with a Loss], *Al-Umma al-Islamiyya*, October 18, 1991. He told Jamal Ismail, "God Almighty was gracious enough for me to be born to Muslim parents in the Arabian Peninsula, in al-Malazz neighborhood in al-Riyadh, in 1377 Hejira"—which could be 1957 or 1958, depending on the month. Jamal Ismail, "Osama bin Laden: The Destruction of the Base," presented by Salah

Najm, al-Jazeera, June 10, 1999. Bin Laden allegedly gave his birth date as March 10, 1957, during that interview, but it was not a part of the transcript. Moreover, Saudi men of his age typically do not know their actual date of birth, since birthdays are not celebrated. Saudi authorities arbitrarily assigned many men the same birth date for passports and other official documents. For instance, bin Laden's friend Jamal Khalifa was "officially" born on February 1, 1957; by chance, he found a notation in a family diary that he was actually born on September 1, 1956. The bin Laden family records, such as they are, do not give a particular date of his birth.

83 **"Rest his soul":** "Walidee Ramama al-Aqsa Bilkhasara" [My Father Renovated al-Aqsa Mosque, with a Loss], *Al-Umma al-Islamiyya*, October 18, 1991.

84 **The children rarely saw:** interview with Ali Soufan, who says, "His brothers told me he never saw his father more than three or four times."

he would call them: interview with Jamal Khalifa.

gold coin: interview with anonymous Saudi source.

he rarely spoke: "Half-brother Will Pay to Defend bin Laden," AP, July 5, 2005. Yeslam bin Laden spoke of being afraid of his father on the al-Arabiya satellite channel, but his comments were misinterpreted in an English-language AP story to say that he had been beaten.

"I remember reciting": "Walidee Ramama al-Aqsa Bilkhasara" [My Father Renovated al-Aqsa Mosque, with a Loss], *Al-Umma al-Islamiyya*, October 18, 1991.

religious debates: Reeve, *The New Jackals*, 159.

"He gathered his engineers": Salah Najm and Jamal Ismail, "Osama bin Laden: The Destruction of the Base," al-Jazeera, June 10, 1999.

marrying off ex-wives: interview with anonymous bin Laden family spokesperson.

Mohammed al-Attas: interview with Khaled Batarfi.

85 **Osama was four or five:** interview with Jamal Khalifa.

another teenage bride: interview with Michael M. Ameen, Jr.

so charred: interview with bin Laden family spokesperson. Bin Ladin, *Inside the Kingdom*, 65.

"King Faisal said": Reeve, *The New Jackals*, 159.

for the next ten years: Mohammed Besalama, "Al-Sheikh Mohammed Awad bin Laden al-Mu'alem" [Sheikh Mohammed Awad bin Laden, the Teacher], *Okaz*, June 2, 1984.

86 **Only Osama remained behind:** interview with anonymous Saudi source.

86 **al-Thagr:** interview with Prince Amr Mohammed al-Faisal.

class of sixty-eight students: interview with Ahmed Badeeb. The two princes were Abdul Aziz bin Mishal bin Abdul Aziz and Abdul Aziz bin Ahmed bin Abdul Rahman.

87 **found him shy:** Brian Fyfield-Shayler, quoted in "Meeting Osama bin Laden," PBS, January 12, 2005.

Some ascribe the change: interviews with Tarik Ali Alireza and Ahmed Badeeb.

Osama stopped watching: "Half Brother Says bin Laden Is Alive and Well," www.cnn.com/2000/WORLD/meast/03/18/osama.brother, March 19, 2002.

"In his teenage years": Khaled Batarfi, "An Interview With Osama bin Laden's Mother," *The Mail on Sunday,* December 23, 2001.

right after *isha*: interview with Khaled Batarfi.

88 **"beginning of his path":** Michael Slackman, "Bin Laden's Mother Tried to Stop Him, Syrian Kin Say," *Chicago Tribune,* November 13, 2001.

89 **companions of the Prophet:** Rahimullah Yusufzai, "Terror Suspect: An Interview with Osama bin Laden," ABCNews.com, December 1988.

"The Abu Bakr group": interview with Khaled Batarfi.

"I decided to drop out": "Walidee Ramama al-Aqsa Bilkhasara" [My Father Renovated al-Aqsa Mosque, with a Loss], *Al-Umma al-Islamiyya,* October 18, 1991.

90 **wedding party:** interview with Khaled Batarfi.

"constantly pregnant": bin Ladin, *Inside the Kingdom,* 160.

"Only nerds": interview with Jamal Khashoggi.

He studied economics: interview with Jamal Khalifa, who is the source of much of the information about bin Laden's university experience.

"I formed a religious charity": "Walidee Ramama al-Aqsa Bilkhasara" [My Father Renovated al-Aqsa Mosque, with a Loss], *Al-Umma al-Islamiyya,* October 18, 1991.

91 **walk barefoot:** interview with Jamal Khalifa.

Mohammad Qutb . . . would lecture: interviews with Khaled Batarfi, Jamal Khalifa, and Mohammed Qutb.

92 **eleven children:** interview with Khaled Batarfi; Douglas Farah and Dana Priest, "Bin Laden Son Plays Key Role in al-Qaeda," *Washington Post,* October 14, 2003.

sleep under the stars: interview with Khaled Batarfi.

refused to let them attend school: interview with Jamal Khalifa.

Abdul Rahman: ibid.

93 **using honey:** interview with Zaynab Ahmed Khadr, who has a child with a similar disability. She discussed the problem with Abdul Rahman's mother.

94 **Umm Hamza:** interviews with Zaynab Ahmed Khadr (who also supplied the tallies of bin Laden's children) and with Maha Elsamneh.

house on Macaroni Street: tour and interview with Jamal Khalifa.

95 **"I want to be":** interview with Jamal Khalifa.

"I recall, with pride": "Walidee Ramama al-Aqsa Bilkhasara" [My Father Renovated al-Aqsa Mosque, with a Loss], *Al-Umma al-Islamiyya,* October 18, 1991.

just over six feet tall: *The 9/11 Commission Report,* 55, drawing from American intelligence, places bin Laden's height at 6'5". According to Michael Scheuer, that estimate derived from Essam Deraz, bin Laden's first biographer, who told me bin Laden was "more than two meters tall, maybe two-five or two-four"—over 6'8" tall. John Miller, who interviewed bin Laden for ABC television, described him as 6'5", but he saw him on only one occasion. Ahmad Zaidan, the al-Jazeera bureau chief in Islamabad who met bin Laden several times, estimates his height at 180 cm., about 5'11". Bin Laden's friends, however, closely agree on his height. Jamal Khashoggi told me that bin Laden was "exactly my height"—182 cm., nearly 6'. Bin Laden's friend in Sudan, Issam Turabi, told me that bin Laden was 183 or 184 cm., about 6'. His college friend and housemate, Jamal Khalifa, places his height at 185 cm., just over 6'1". That is the actual height of bin Laden's son Abdullah, who says his father is about two inches taller than he. Bin Laden's friend Mohammed Loay Baizid also says that bin Laden is two inches taller than he is, but Baizid stands only 5'7". One could theorize about the wide disparity in perceptions; I only include this survey as an example of one reporter's frustration in trying to get an answer to a single simple question—among many that had conflicting responses.

4. Change

97 **"Thanksgiving turkey?"** Prince Turki al-Faisal speech to Contemporary Arab Studies Department, Georgetown University, February 3, 2002.

Turk or Feaslesticks: "The Lawrence," yearbook for the Lawrenceville School, Lawrenceville, New Jersey, May 4, 1962, 5.

97 **"Did you hear"**: Prince Turki al-Faisal speech to Contemporary Arab Studies Department, Georgetown University, February 3, 2002.

98 **Bill Clinton:** Clinton, *My Life*, 110.
"Look, I didn't give": interview with Prince Turki al-Faisal.

99 **average Saudi income:** Wright, "Kingdom of Silence." It became equal to the United States in 1981.

100 **30 or 40 percent:** Wright, "Kingdom of Silence"; interview with Berhan Hailu.

101 **co-opt the ulema:** al-Rasheed, *A History of Saudi Arabia*, 124; also, Teitelbaum, *Holier Than Thou*, 17ff.
fifty thousand Muslims: Lacey, *The Kingdom*, 478. Much of this account comes from Lacey and from James Buchan, "The Return of the Ikhwan," in Holden and Johns, *The House of Saud*, 511–26.

102 **"Your attention, O Muslims!":** Heikal, *Iran*, 197. Kechichian claims that none of the thousands of pilgrims in the mosque that day heard Qahtani, "or anyone else for that matter," invoke the Mahdi. Kechichian, "Islamic Revivalism," 15. I could find no other sources to support this assertion.

103 **an employee of the bin Laden organization:** bin Ladin, *Inside the Kingdom*, 123–24.

104 **sun rotated:** AbuKhalil, *Bin Laden, Islam, and America's New "War on Terrorism,"* 64.
Oteibi had been his student: Holden and Johns, *The House of Saud*, 517.
four or five hundred insurgents: al-Rasheed, *A History of Saudi Arabia*, 144; Lacey suggests 200, in *The Kingdom*, 484; Aburish estimates 300, in *The Rise, Corruption, and Coming Fall*, 108. Arab sources place the figure in the thousands. Captain Paul Barril says there were 1,500 insurgents, in *Commando*, October/November 2002.
some American Black Muslims: Holden and Johns, *The House of Saud*, 520.
armory of the National Guard: Mackey, *The Saudis*, 231.
on biers: Lacey, *The Kingdom*, 484.

105 **Salem . . . arrived:** interview with Jamal Khalifa.

106 **jaw was blown away:** Holden and Johns, *The House of Saud*, 525.

107 **recommended gas:** interview with Prince Turki al-Faisal.
they converted to Islam: The history of this event is full of contradictory claims. Da Lage cites Captain Paul Barril, who led three French policemen to Mecca, where they "converted" on the spot to Islam, so that they could direct the assault on the Grand Mosque. Olivier Da Lage, "Il y a quinze ans: La prise de la Grande Mosquée

de La Mecque," *Le Monde*, November 20–21, 1994. Aburish claims that the rebels were put down by French paratroopers, who actually did flood and electrify the chambers. Aburish, *The Rise, Corruption, and Coming Fall*, 108.

Turki denies that the French converted or entered Mecca. De Marenches also denies that the French entered Mecca. De Marenches and Ockrent, *The Evil Empire*, 112. I have chosen to credit the account of Captain Barril on the authority of an anonymous Saudi intelligence source.

108 **more than 4,000:** Theroux, *Sandstorms*, 90.

Osama bin Laden and his brother Mahrous: interview with Jamal Khalifa.

109 **Oteibi and his followers were true Muslims:** Burke, *Al-Qaeda*, 55.

"I was enraged": Robert Fisk, "Anti-Soviet Warrior Puts His Army on the Road to Peace," *Independent*, December 6, 1993.

"a big secret": "Walidee Ramama al-Aqsa Bilkhasara" [My Father Renovated al-Aqsa Mosque, with a Loss], *Al-Umma al-Islamiyya*, October 18, 1991.

"hand over the money": ibid.

his friend Omar Abdul Rahman: Weaver, *A Portrait of Egypt*, 180.

got him dismissed in 1980: *Tahta al-Mijhar* [Under the Microscope], al-Jazeera, February 20, 2003.

110 **"Jihad and the rifle alone":** Abdullah bin Omar, "The Striving Sheik: Abdullah Azzam," *Nida'ul Islam*, trans. Mohammed Saeed, July–September 1996, www.islam.org.au/articles/14/AZZAM.HTM.

"Jihad for him": Mohammed al-Shafey, "Al-Sharq al-Awsat Interviews Umm Mohammed," *Al-Sharq al-Aswat*, April 30, 2006.

spotted an announcement: *Tahta al-Mijhar* [Under the Microscope], al-Jazeera, February 20, 2003.

in November 1981: Mohammed, *Al-Ansar al-Arab fi Afghanistan*, 37.

"I reached Afghanistan": untitled Abdullah Azzam recruitment video, 1988.

birds functioned as an early-warning radar system: interview with Jamal Khalifa.

111 **"He lives in his house":** Azzam, *The Lofty Mountain*, 150.

"If you have it": interview with Jamal Khalifa.

Paid agents rounded up: Salah, *Waqai' Sanawat al-Jihad*.

112 **office in Cairo:** Dr. Gehad Auda and Dr. Ammar Ali Hasan, "Strategic Papers: The Globalization of the Radical Islamic Movement: The Case of Egypt," www.ahram.org.eg/acpss/eng/ahram/2004/7/5/SPAP5.htm.

Bin Laden opened a halfway house: interview with Essam Deraz.

112 **he ran special military camps:** Mohammed Sadeeq, "The Story of Saudi Afghans: They Participated in Jihad and Violent Fighting," *Al-Majellah,* May 11, 1996.

dozens of trucks: Shadid, *Legacy of the Prophet,* 83.

113 **"The Saudi government asked me":** Osama bin Laden, interviewed by al-Jazeera, October 7, 2001. Bin Laden dates this conversation to 1979, which is when he says he first went to Afghanistan.

"won't even get near": interview with Khaled Batarfi.

5. The Miracles

114 **"Now we can give the USSR":** Cooley, *Unholy Wars,* 19.

115 **170 armed Afghan militias in the mid-**1980s: ibid., 232.

800,000 people . . . under their authority: interview with Abdullah Anas.

Abdul Rasul Sayyaf: Jon Lee Anderson, "Letter from Kabul: The Assassins," *New Yorker,* June 10, 2002.

lock them up in a jail: Coll, *Ghost Wars,* 83.

116 **"Fear of bodily participation":** Mohammed, *Al-Ansar al-Arab fi Afghanistan,* 85.

he forfeited his share of the profit: Azzam, *The Lofty Mountain,* 150.

"surprised by the sad state": ibid.

"mountains were shaking": ibid.

117 **"between five and ten million dollars":** ibid., 88.

three hundred dollars per month: Bergen, *Holy War,* 56.

119 **house bin Laden was renting:** Mohammed, *Al-Ansar al-Arab fi Afghanistan,* 119.

twenty-five thousand dollars a month: Anonymous, *Through Our Enemies' Eyes,* 99; Mohammed, *Al-Ansar al-Arab fi Afghanistan,* 198.

"this heaven-sent man": Bernstein, *Out of the Blue,* 45.

to deliver cash: interview with Ahmed Badeeb and Sayeed Badeeb. According to Sayeed Badeeb, the Saudi government continued its support until bin Laden left Afghanistan in 1989.

$350 to $500 million per year: private communication with Marc Sageman, who was a CIA case officer in Afghanistan at the time.

120 **he first met bin Laden in** 1985: Elsewhere, he says, "Our first meeting must have taken place around 1984." "And then Mullah Omar Screamed at Me," *Der Spiegel,* November 2004.

Turki could recruit: Clarke, *Against All Enemies,* 52.

cashews and chocolate: Jason Burke, "The Making of bin Laden: Part 2," *Observer,* October 28, 2001.

120 **He built a theological library:** Anonymous, *Through Our Enemies' Eyes*, 98.

tutored at least one young Afghan warrior: Jason Burke, "The Making of bin Laden: Part 2," *Observer*, October 28, 2001.

University of Dawa al-Jihad: Fouda and Fielding, *Masterminds of Terror*, 91; Cooley, *Unholy Wars*, 238.

pitched in at *Jihad*, the Arabic-language magazine: Burke, *Al-Qaeda*, 56.

"small smile": interview with Khaled Khawaja.

121 **"November 1985":** interview with anonymous al-Qaeda source.

"Brigade of the Strangers": Mohammed, *Al-Ansar al-Arab fi Afghanistan*, 177.

modern conveniences: interview with Zaynab Abdul Khadr.

never more than three thousand: interview with Abdullah Anas. Milt Bearden, who was the CIA chief of station in Afghanistan at the time, says, "We figured there were about two thousand Arab Afghans at any one time, plus a couple thousand Arab Afghans who treated it as a Club Med"—i.e., they came for brief holidays. "This compares with about a quarter million full- or part-time Afghans, and 125,000 Soviets," Bearden says.

122 **father's real identity:** interview with Zayneb Ahmed Khadr.

"I traveled to acquaint people": untitled Abdullah Azzam recruitment video, 1988.

stories of the mujahideen: For instance, see Abdullah Yusuf Azzam, "The Signs of ar-Rahmaan in the Jihad of the Afghan," www.islamic awakening.com/viewarticle.php?articleID=877&.

When one beloved mujahid expired: Abdullah Yusuf Azzam, "Abul-Mundhir ash-Shareef," www.islamicawakening.com/viewarticle.php ?articleID=30&.

123 **was paying for mujahids:** interview with Mohammed Loay Baizid.

if one subtracted the oil revenue: James R. Woolsey, "Defeating the Oil Weapon," *Commentary*, Sept. 2002. The figure is for the mid-1990s. Other statistics have been extrapolated from the authoritative Arab Human Development Report 2002.

124 **"raid and be slain":** Osama bin Laden, "Message to the Iraqi People," al-Jazeera, October 18, 2003.

125 **"He who dies,"** Mitchell, *Society of the Muslim Brothers*, 207.

"Islam is not merely 'belief' ": Qutb, *Milestones*, 58ff.; includes other Qutb quotes that follow.

life without Islam is slavery: This argument is more fully developed in Roxanne L. Euben, "Comparative Political Theory: An Islamic

Fundamentalist Critique of Rationalism," *Journal of Politics* 59, no. 1 (February 1997): 28–55.

125 **Muslim Brotherhood refuted:** interview with Jamal Khashoggi.
    concerned Saudi fathers: interview with Mohammed al-Hulwah.

127 **"Your presence is no longer needed":** Mohammed, *Al-Ansar al-Arab fi Afghanistan,* 178.
    In 1986 bin Laden brought his wives and children: This is according to Essam Deraz, although Mohammed Loay Baizid places the date of the move in 1988.

128 **Bin Laden expanded the caverns:** interview with Marc Sageman.
    "God is great! God is great!": Mohammed, *Al-Ansar al-Arab fi Afghanistan,* 185.
    bin Laden financed: Jamal Ismail, "Usama bin Laden, the Destruction of the Base," al-Jazeera, June 10, 1999.

129 **inspired by the lines:** Mohammed, *Al-Ansar al-Arab fi Afghanistan,* 241.
    Soviet base: ibid., 233.
    single car: ibid., 216.

131 **"I began thinking":** "Walidee Ramama al-Aqsa Bilkhasara" [My Father Renovated al-Aqsa Mosque, with a Loss], *Al-Umma al-Islamiyya,* October 18, 1991.
    skilled engineers: interview with anonymous bin Laden family spokesman.
    seven man-made caverns: interview with Essam Deraz.
    Sheikh Tameem: interviews with Bassim A. Alim and Mohammed Loay Baizid.
    not over eighteen years old: Mohammed, *Al-Ansar al-Arab fi Afghanistan,* 211.

132 **"Tell him that I will not return":** Azzam, *The Lofty Mountain,* 23. Sheikh Tameem never did find his martyrdom. He died the following year of a heart attack while on a speaking tour in Orlando, Florida.

133 **"afraid that some of the brothers":** Mohammed, *Al-Ansar al-Arab fi Afghanistan,* 261.
    force of 120: Abu Muhammed in Azzam, *The Lofty Mountain,* 97.
    He chose to attack on a Friday: Mohammed, *Al-Ansar al-Arab fi Afghanistan,*265.

134 **closing down the Arab guesthouses:** interview with Mohammed Loay Baizid.
    "There were nine": Azzam, *The Lofty Mountain,* 109.
    nine or ten thousand troops: ibid., 100ff., which is the source for

464   *Notes*

much of this account, along with Mohammed, *Al-Ansar al-Arab fi Afghanistan*, 310ff., and "Walidee Ramama al-Aqsa Bilkhasara" [My Father Renovated al-Aqsa Mosque, with a Loss], *Al-Umma al-Islamiyya*, October 18, 1991.

135 **"shouted at me":** Mohammed, *Al-Ansar al-Arab fi Afghanistan*, 316.
 "thought he was possessed": Azzam, *The Lofty Mountain*, 30.

136 **"very tired":** "Walidee Ramama al-Aqsa Bilkhasara" [My Father Renovated al-Aqsa Mosque, with a Loss], *Al-Umma al-Islamiyya*, October 18, 1991.
 "guard the left side:" Mohammed, *Al-Ansar al-Arab fi Afghanistan*, 326.

137 **"It passed by me":** Osama bin Laden in Azzam, *The Lofty Mountain*, 112, 113.
 "There was a terrible battle": "Walidee Ramama al-Aqsa Bilkhasara" [My Father Renovated al-Aqsa Mosque, with a Loss], *Al-Umma al-Islamiyya*, October 18, 1991.
 "I was only thirty meters from the Russians": Robert Fisk, "The Saudi Businessman Who Recruited Mujahideen Now Uses Them for Large-Scale Building Projects in Sudan," *Independent*, December 6, 1993.
 bag of salt: interview with Jamal Khashoggi, who also spoke about bin Laden's episodes of malaria and pneumonia. There is a link between low blood pressure and diabetes, for which some have said bin Laden received insulin shots. Bergen, *Holy War*, 57; also, Hasin al-Binayyan, "Al-Qaeda Man Freed from Riyadh Jail Reveals It All," *Arab News*, November 26, 2001. However, Jamal Khalifa says that bin Laden was not diabetic.
 "only nine brothers": Osama bin Laden in Azzam, *The Lofty Mountain*, 114. (The quote has been slightly corrected for grammatical reasons that may have been caused by the translation.)
 gave bin Laden a trophy: interview with Mohammed Loay Baizid.

6. The Base

139 **treasures of the Afghan national museum:** interviews with Mohammed Sarwar and Rahimullah Yusufzai.
 skimming off the subsidies: interview with Marc Sageman. Sageman disputes the common assertion that the commanders were enriching themselves from the heroin trade.
 Their murderous rivalries: interview with Rahimullah Yusufzai.

140 **"second home":** interview with Jamal Ismail.

140 **Mohammed set up al-Jihad's financial pipeline:** unpublished CIA document, "Report on Mohammed al-Zawahiri" (no date, no author).

Bitter Harvest: Some members of al-Jihad believed that Zawahiri had plagiarized this book, which they say was actually written by Sayyid Imam al-Sharif (also known as Dr. Fadl).

"available free": interview with Kemal Helbawi.

141 **Dr. Fadl:** interview with Yasser al-Sirri, also Hamdi Rizq, "Confessions of Those 'Returning from Albania' Mark the End of the Egyptian 'Jihad Organization,' " *Al-Wasat,* April 19, 1999. Translated by FBIS.

Kuwaiti-backed Red Crescent hospital: interviews with Jamal Khashoggi and Osama Rushdi.

Dr. Ahmed el-Wed: interviews with Kamal Helbawy and Abdullah Anas.

Takfir wa Hijira: Kepel, *Muslim Extremism in Egypt,* 73–78.

142 **mosque Zawahiri had frequented:** interview with Khaled Abou El-Fadl.

Remnants of the group: Heikal, *Autumn of Fury,* 251.

143 **blood of Muslims cannot be shed:** *Sahih Bukhari,* vol. 9, bk. 83, no. 17.

entitled to kill practically anyone: interview with Usama Rushdi.

144 **Fisher-Price:** interview with Maha Elsamneh.

145 **"unusually close family":** Chanaa Rostom, "Al-Zawahiri's Latest Victims," *Akher Sa'a,* December 12, 2001.

146 **"As of now":** al-Zawahiri, "Knights Under the Prophet's Banner," part 2.

147 **on his payroll:** exhibit from "Tareek Osama" document presented in *United States v. Enaam M. Arnaout.*

Abu Ubaydah: interviews with Jamal Khashoggi and Essam Deraz.

Zawahiri had introduced: "Bin-Ladin Associate Interrogated," *Al-Sharq al-Awsat,* June 24, 1999.

148 **Abu Hafs:** interview with Essam Deraz.

Mohammed Ibrahim Makkawi: Nabil Sharaf El Din, "Details on the Man Who Carved the Story of bin Laden (Part III)," *Al-Watan,* September 29, 2001. Translated by FBIS. According to Abduh Zinah, "Report Profiling Five Egyptian Terrorists on US Most Wanted List," *Al-Sharq al-Awsat,* December 20, 2001, Makkawi went to Saudi Arabia in 1998, then to Afghanistan.

clean-shaven: interview with Montassir al-Zayyat, who was Makkawi's lawyer.

dangerously unbalanced: interviews with Kamal Habib and Mohammed Salah.

148 **crash an airliner:** interview with anonymous Cairo political figure. "I believe he is the true father of September 11," the source told me. He also described Makkawi as a "psychopath."

Saif al-Adl: There is a controversy over whether the al-Qaeda figure who goes by this name is the same man as Mohammed Makkawi. He is identified this way on the U.S. indictment, but according to Ali Soufan, "We don't really know Saif al-Adl's real name, not even the Egyptian service knows who he is. But he fought against the Russians in Afghanistan." Nu'man bin Uthman, a Libyan Islamist who fought in Afghanistan and claims to know both Makkawi and Saif al-Adl, contends that they are different men. Mohammed el-Shafey, "Libyan Islamist bin-Uthman Discusses Identity of al-Qa'ida Operative Sayf-al-Adl," *Al-Sharq al-Awsat,* May 30, 2005. On the other hand, Jordanian author Fu'ad Husayn recently interviewed Saif al-Adl and says that he is Makkawi. Fu'ad Husayn, "Al-Zarqawi . . . The Second Generation of al-Qaida, Part 2," *Al-Quds al-Arabi,* June 16, 2005. Translated by FBIS. Jamal Ismail, who was a reporter for an Islamist paper in Peshawar during the 1980s, says that Saif al-Adl is not Makkawi but another Egyptian currently living in Iran; Makkawi, says Ismail, is a refugee in Europe.

149 **position papers:** interview with Jamal Khalifa.

"Dr. Ayman was giving him a class": interview with Mohammed Loay Baizid.

"I don't know what some people": interview with Abdullah Anas.

issued a fatwa: Gunaratna, *Inside al-Qaeda,* 22.

"pioneering vanguard": Azzam, "The Solid Base."

150 **train brigades of Hamas fighters:** Jamal Ismail, personal communication.

hated Yasser Arafat: Abdel Bari Atwan in Bergen, *The Osama bin Laden I Know,* 170.

moving the struggle to Kashmir: interview with Jamal Khashoggi. Notably, Bosnia was also not on bin Laden's list of prospective targets for jihad.

One fateful day: interviews with Mohammed Loay Baizid (Abu Rida al-Suri) and Wa'el Julaidan through an intermediary. Baizid claims he was out of the country at the time of the meeting, and that Abu Hajer later told him about it. The court in Chicago contends that the handwritten notes of the meeting are actually Baizid's. Wa'el Julaidan, who was present, told me through an intermediary that Abdullah Azzam was there as well.

151 **sketchy handwritten notes:** exhibit from "Tareek Osama" document presented in *United States v. Enaam M. Arnaout.* The translation I

have provided differs in several respects from what was provided to the court.

152 **Medani al-Tayeb:** interview with Jamal Khalifa.

al-Qaeda al-Askariya: exhibit from "Tareek Osama" document presented in *United States v. Enaam M. Arnaout.*

153 **"Brother Abu Ubaydah":** Ahmad Zaydan, "The Search for al-Qa'ida," *Tahta al-Mijhar* [Under the Microscope], al-Jazeera, trans. FBIS, September 10, 2004.

"Sixty": interview with Mohammed Loay Baizid.

154 **"independent body":** interview with Abdullah Anas.

155 **"The Saudi authorities":** ibid.

"Say something": ibid.

"Osama is limited": ibid.

156 **Abu Abdul Rahman:** His real name is Ahmed Sayed Khadr. Interviews with Zaynab Ahmed Khadr, Maha Elsamneh, and Mohammed Loay Baizid. Details of the trial come from Wa'el Julaidan, who responded to questions through an intermediary, and "Tareek Osama" document presented in *United States v. Enaam M. Arnaout.*

expel him from the leadership: "The Story of the Arab Afghans from the Time of Their Arrival in Afghanistan Until Their Departure with the Taliban," Part 5, *Al-Sharq al-Awsat,* December 12, 2004.

"Soon we will see the hand": interview with Abdullah Anas.

"cannot trust the Egyptians": interview with Jamal Khalifa.

157 **"not a single Soviet soldier":** Cordovez and Harrison, *Out of Afghanistan,* 384.

fifteen thousand lives: Borovik, *The Hidden War,* 12–13.

Between a million: William T. Vollmann, "Letter from Afghanistan: Across the Divide," *New Yorker,* May 15, 2000.

third of the population: interview with Prince Turki al-Faisal.

six thousand Arabs: Ismail Khan, "Crackdown Against Arabs in Peshawar," *Islamabad the News,* April 7, 1993.

"men with large amounts of money": from "Chats from the Top of the World," no. 6, from the Harmony Documents.

air-conditioned cargo containers: Benjamin and Simon, *The Age of Sacred Terror,* 101.

takfiris even held up a truck: interview with Jamal Khashoggi.

158 **sold arms for gold:** Raphaeli, "Ayman Muhammed Rab'i al-Zawahiri."

"The Blind Leader": interview with Usama Rushdi.

awarding $100,000: Bergen, *The Osama bin Laden I Knew,* 70.

Jalalabad: The account that follows is based on a number of interviews, but they include some contradictory stories that are worth noting. Marc Sageman, who was a CIA case officer in Pakistan at the time, told me that the garrison of Afghan soldiers—450 men—who were guarding the airport quickly surrendered. Given the jealousy and divisiveness of the mujahideen factions, it was decided that the prisoners would be parceled out among them. The Arabs got a one-ninth share—49 men. The Arabs murdered them, cut their bodies to pieces, and packed them into crates. Then they loaded the boxes onto a supply truck, which they sent into the beleaguered city, with a sign that said, "This is what happens to apostates." At that point the war abruptly changed. The Afghan troops inside Jalalabad stopped negotiating their surrender and began fighting back. Within days, the Afghan air force drove the mujahideen away from the airport and back into the mountains. If this account is true, this was the first evidence of bin Laden's appetite for slaughter. Olivier Roy, the great French scholar and student of Afghanistan, said that he had heard essentially the same account from Afghans who were inside the garrisoned city. Neither Sageman nor Roy was present at the battle, however. Essam Deraz, who was there, denies that such an event ever occurred, as does Ahmed Zaidan, who covered the battle as a reporter. Indiscriminate slaughter of prisoners was common on both sides in that war.

Another issue about the battle of Jalalabad is whether bin Laden was injured. Michael Scheuer, who was head of the CIA's Alec Station, says that bin Laden was injured twice in the jihad against the Soviet Union: once in Jaji, a foot wound, and once in the shoulder from a piece of shrapnel. Essam Deraz, again, says that bin Laden was never injured during that war, as does Jamal Khalifa.

158 **five to seven thousand Afghan mujahideen:** Yousaf and Adkin, *The Bear Trap*, 227–28.

159 **four kilometers above the city:** interview with Essam Deraz.
fewer than two hundred men: interview with Abdullah Anas.
malaria . . . pneumonia: interview with Jamal Khashoggi.
medical genius: interview with Essam Deraz.
Addison's disease: I'm grateful to Dr. Jeanne Ryan, who consulted with me on these matters and provided the diagnosis. Although the CIA, among others, has speculated that bin Laden suffers from kidney disease, he would probably have died by now without frequent dialysis, and the symptoms are not the same as the ones described here. Dr. Ryan points out that patients with kidney disease cannot tolerate extra salt. Everyone who knew bin Laden well was acquainted with his constant dipping into his salt supply. One of the

key indicators of Addison's is the eventual darkening of the skin, which has become apparent in bin Laden's later video appearances.

160 **twenty sorties a day:** Yousaf and Adkin, *The Bear Trap*, 230.

glucose transfusion: Details of this episode come from an interview with Essam Deraz and from his account that is rendered in Azzam, *The Lofty Mountain*, 80ff.

161 **Shafiq:** interviews with Abdullah Anas and Jamal Khalifa.

162 **Eighty other Arabs:** interview with Abdullah Anas. Other accounts place the figure as high as five hundred. "The Story of the Arab Afghans from the Time of Arrival in Afghanistan Until Their Departure with the Taliban," part 6, *Al-Sharq al-Awsat*, December 13, 2004.

Farouk was a *takfir* camp: interview with Abdullah Anas.

Those chosen: Hasan al-Banyan, "The Oldest Arab Afghan Talks to 'Al-Sharq al-Awsat' About His Career That Finally Landed Him in Prison in Saudi Arabia," *Al-Sharq al-Awsat*, November 25, 2001.

in triplicate: Gunaratna, *Inside al-Qaeda*, 56.

$1,000 a month: interview with Jack Cloonan.

round-trip ticket home: Details of the al-Qaeda employment contract can be found in the Harmony Documents, drawn from a United States Department of Defense database. www.ctc.usma.edu/aq_harmonylist.asp.

constitution and by-laws: ibid.

163 **"We are your soldiers":** interview with Abdullah Anas.

164 **discovered and disarmed a powerful bomb:** "Saudi 'Afghan' Talks About Involvement with al-Qa'ida, bin Ladin," *Al-Sharq al-Awsat*, November 25, 2001.

"It's better to leave": interview with Ahmed Badeeb.

They embraced for a long time: *Tahta al-Mijhar* [Under the Microscope], al-Jazeera, Feb. 20, 2003.

twenty kilograms of TNT: Gunaratna, *Inside al-Qaeda*, 23.

spreading rumors: interview with Usama Rushdi.

7. *Return of the Hero*

165 **27 million Saudi riyals:** interview with bin Laden family spokesperson. Jamal Khalifa, who is married to one of bin Laden's half sisters, told me the annual share is "not even a million riyals"—$266,000, a figure that was confirmed by the bin Laden family spokesperson. That amount is considerably less than even the downsized figure given by the 9/11 Commission, which states: "from 1970 through 1994, bin Ladin received about $1 million per year—a significant sum, to be sure, but not a $300 million fortune that could be used to

fund jihad." National Commission on Terrorist Attacks Upon the United States, *The 9/11 Commission Report*, 170. Jamal Khashoggi told me that when bin Laden returned from Afghanistan, he informed his brothers that he had spent his share of his inheritance on the jihad, and that they made it up to him out of their own pockets; a bin Laden family spokesperson disputes this, however.

165 **build roads in Taif and Abha:** Robert Fisk, "The Saudi Businessman Who Recruited Mujahedin Now Uses Them for Large-Scale Building Projects in Sudan," *Independent*, December 6, 1993.

166 **"Othman of his age":** interview with Monsour al-Njadan.
482-foot yacht: Simons, *Saudi Arabia*, 28.
blackjack and roulette dealers: Marie Colvin, "The Squandering Sheikhs," *Sunday Times*, August 29, 1993.
"whores, pornography": David Leigh and David Pallister, "Murky Shadows Amid the Riviera Sunshine," *Guardian*, March 5, 1999.

167 **shooting at them:** interview with Mohammed al-Rasheed.
modest, one-story house: interview with Frank Anderson.
raised ostriches: Jamal Khashoggi, personal communication.

168 *White Knight*: *Petition by Despina Sahini v. Turki Saeed or Turki al-Faisal bin Abdulaziz al-Saud*, Court of First Instance, Athens, Greece, February 2, 2003.
banana daiquiri: Coll, *Ghost Wars*, 73.
"This man has defamed": interview with Ahmed Badeeb.

169 **ex-convicts:** ibid.
taught and studied in Mecca: interview with Sami Angawi.
forbade the Shia: Simons, *Saudi Arabia*, 34.

170 1 **percent of the world Muslim population:** Yamani, *To Be a Saudi*, 63.
90 **percent of the expenses:** Dawood al-Shirian, "What Is Saudi Arabia Going to Do?" *Al-Hayat*, May 19, 2003.

171 **"They have attacked our brothers":** Osama bin Laden speech in the bin Laden family mosque in Jeddah, April 1990, filmed by Essam Deraz.

172 **"when America permitted":** bin Laden videotape, al-Jazeera, October 29, 2004.
"Thank you": www.pbs.org/wgbh/pages/frontline/.

173 **America and Saudi Arabia:** cf. Lippman, *Inside the Mirage*.
more than thirty thousand: Peterson, *Saudi Arabia and the Illusion of Security*, 46.
more than 200,000 Americans: Prince Turki al-Faisal, address to Seton Hall University, October 14, 2003.
United States was the tenth: Aburish, *The Rise, Corruption, and Coming Fall*, 169.

173 **In 1989 bin Laden approached:** interviews with Saeed Badeeb and Ahmed Badeeb.

174 **Americans had a secret agreement:** interview with Jamal Khashoggi.

suitcases full of cash: Randal, *Osama*, 100.

175 **a number of trips to the new republic:** interviews with Ahmed Badeeb and Saeed Badeeb.

assassinate socialist leaders: The Yemeni government maintained that "Yemeni Afghan groups executed several socialist figures and mounted 158 operations . . . between 1990 and 2004 on the strength of fatwas issued by Osama bin Laden." Quoted in Anonymous, *Through Our Enemies' Eyes*, 112. The Yemenis apparently did not realize that a new organization, al-Qaeda, was responsible for these operations.

176 **"I was working":** interview with Ahmed Badeeb.

he immediately doubled the figure: interview with Nawaf E. Obaid.

a little over 5 million: Professor William B. Quandt, personal communication.

moved its foreign headquarters: Simons, *Saudi Arabia*, 214.

"I said many times": Osama bin Laden, interviewed by Peter L. Bergen and Peter Arnett, CNN, May 10, 1997.

177 **"burn half of Israel":** Amatzia Baram, "The Iraqi Invasion of Kuwait," in *The Saddam Hussein Reader*, edited by Turi Munthe, 259.

non-aggression pact: According to Leslie and Alexander Cockburn, "Royal Mess," *New Yorker*, November 28, 1994, the Saudis had also been funding Iraqi research into nuclear weapons. On the other hand, Richard A. Clarke contends, in an interview, that scenario is "quite unbelievable," since a nuclear-armed Saddam was Saudi Arabia's greatest fear.

no intention of invading Kuwait: www.kingfahdbinabdulaziz .com/main/1300.htm.

raid bin Laden's farm: "Biography of Usamah bin-Ladin, written by brother Mujahid with minor modifications," Islamic Observation Center, trans. FBIS, April 22, 2000.

One battalion: Woodward, *The Commanders*, 248.

178 **bin Laden wrote a letter:** Esposito, *Unholy War*, 12.

royal family itself was divided: Abir, *Saudi Arabia*, 174.

satellite images: Later press reports questioned the accuracy of these images, pointing out that commercial Russian satellite photos showed empty stretches of sand along the Saudi border. Scott Peterson, "In War, Some Facts Less Factual," *Christian Science Monitor*,

September 6, 2002. Richard A. Clarke, in an interview, says that the images General Schwarzkopf presented were not of the border area but of the Iraqi occupation of Kuwait.

178 **Cheney pledged:** Clarke, *Against All Enemies*, 58.
"Come with all": interview with Richard A. Clarke.
bin Laden spoke to Prince Sultan: Burke, *Al-Qaeda*, 124; also, Anonymous, *Through Our Enemies' Eyes*, 114; *Thomas E. Burnett, Sr., v. Al Baraka Investment and Development Corporation, et al., Final Third Amended Complaint.*

179 **"I am ready":** al-Hammadi, "The Inside Story of al-Qaʻida," part 8, March 26, 2005.
"no caves": Douglas Jehl, "Holy War Lured Saudis as Rulers Looked Away," *New York Times*, December 27, 2001.
proposals to the CIA: Prince Turki al-Faisal speech to Contemporary Arab Studies Department, Georgetown University, February 3, 2002.
in a theater: interviews with Ahmed Badeeb and Hassan Yassin.
fifty-eight thousand men: Abir, *Saudi Arabia*, 176.
"We pushed the Soviets": interview with Ahmed Badeeb.
The prince laughed: Arnaud de Borchgrave, "Osama's Saudi moles," *Washington Times*, August 1, 2003.
"radical changes": Jamal Khashoggi, "Osama Offered to Form Army to Challenge Saddam's Forces: Turki," *Arab News*, November 7, 2001.

180 **Prince Turki argued:** Jamal Khashoggi, "Kingdom Has a Big Role to Play in Afghanistan," *Arab News*, November 6, 2001.
that Caliph Omar: Lewis, *The Crisis of Islam*, xxix–xxx.
"inadmissible": al-Hammadi, "The Inside Story of al-Qaʻida," part 8, March 26, 2005.

181 **1,500 foreign journalists:** al-Rasheed, *A History of Saudi Arabia*, 166.
"infidels": Wright, "Kingdom of Silence."
"Letter of Demands": al-Rasheed, *A History of Saudi Arabia*, 170; also, Champion, *The Paradoxical Kingdom*, 218ff.; Abir, *Saudi Arabia*, 186ff.

182 **more shocked:** Champion, *The Paradoxical Kingdom*, 221.

183 **"There's a role":** interview with Jamal Khashoggi.
Worried about the influence: interview with Michael Scheuer, who talked to Turki during this period.

184 **Saudi Arabia had recruited:** Stephen Engelberg, "One Man and a Global Web of Violence," *New York Times*, January 14, 2001.

8. Paradise

185 **fifteen and twenty-five thousand:** interview with Steven Simon. Other estimates range from five to fifteen thousand. Reeve, *The New*

Jackals, 3; also, Halliday, *Two Hours That Shook the World,* 166. Marc Sageman cautions in a personal communication: "I wanted to zero in on the numbers myself. What I found out is that no one knew, and did not even know how to go about even estimating this number. So far, all the numbers are arbitrary, based on a very wild guess."

185 **directly to jail:** interview with Saeed Badeeb.

186 **"even with Red Indians":** interview with Hasan al-Turabi.
four trusted associates: testimony of Jamal al-Fadl, *U.S. v. Usama bin Laden, et al.*

187 **"it is Sudan!":** interview with Mohammed Loay Baizid.
gave Fadl $250,000: testimony of Jamal al-Fadl, *United States v. Usama bin Laden et al.*
which brought Osama: interview with Dr. Ghazi Salaheddin.
seventeen children: interview with Zaynab Abdul Khadr.
leader of Sudan greeted: Ahmad Zaydan, "The Search for al-Qaeda," al-Jazeera, September 10, 2004.
Nearly every month: interview with Ibrahim al-Sanoussi.

188 **heresy in bin Laden's eyes:** interview with Jamal Khalifa.
"art, music, singing": interview with Hasan al-Turabi.
"The Prophet himself": interview with Hasan al-Turabi.

190 **The neighbors claimed:** al-Nour Ahmed al-Nour, "His Neighbor Claims He Does Not Speak Much," *Al-Hayat,* November 19, 2001.
what his guests left: interview with Issam Eldin Turabi.
al-Qaeda soccer teams: interview with Jack Cloonan.
"great Islamic investor": "Part One of a Series of Reports on bin Ladin's Life in Sudan: Islamists Celebrated Arrival of 'Great Islamic Investor,' " *Al-Quds al-Arabi,* November 24, 2001. Translated by FBIS.

191 **$350 million:** Ibid.
$50 million: *Thomas E. Burnett, Sr. v. Al Baraka Investment and Development Corporation, et al.* Final Third Amended complaint.
"larger than Bahrain": interview with Dr. Khaled Batarfi.
leather for the Italian market: Bergen, *Holy War,* 81.
a million acres: Burr, *Revolutionary Sudan,* 71.
near monopoly: U.S. State Department fact sheet on Usama bin Laden, August 14, 1996.
filled out in triplicate: interview with Bruce Hoffman.
between $50 and $120: al-Hammadi, "The Inside Story of al-Qa'ida," part 9, March 28, 2005.
Saudis got more: interview with Dan Coleman.
five hundred people working: interview with Hassabulla Omer.

192 **a hundred of them who were active members:** ibid. The testimony of Jamal al-Fadl *(U.S. v. Usama bin Laden, et al.)* is confusing because

he apparently conflates the number of employees of bin Laden's companies with the actual number of people who had formally pledged *bayat* to bin Laden.

192 **$1 million a day:** Burr, *Revolutionary Sudan,* 36.

holy men . . . fasting: al-Nour Ahmed al-Nour, "His Neighbor Claims He Does Not Speak Much," *Al-Hayat,* November 19, 2001.

blessings of peace: interview with Ghazi Salah Eddin Atabani.

193 **Abu Hajer:** interviews with Tom Corrigan, Daniel Coleman, Allan P. Haber, Jamal Khalifa, and Mohammed Loay Baizid.

he deserted: interrogation of Mamdouh Mahmoud Salim Ahmed, Munich, September 17, 1998.

194 **made bin Laden weep:** interview with Daniel Coleman.

September 11: Belloc, *The Great Heresies,* 85.

195 **"Jihad against America?":** al-Hammadi, "The Inside Story of al-Qa'ida," part 8, March 26, 2005.

196 **"a large-scale front":** ibid., part 5, March 23, 2005.

nine hundred people: United States Department of State, *Country Reports on Terrorism, 2004,* April 2005.

Carlos the Jackal: interviews with Tim Niblock and Hassabullah Omer. Ken Silverstein, "Official Pariah Sudan Valuable to America's War on Terrorism," *Los Angeles Times,* April 29, 2005.

197 **in exchange for weapons:** Douglas Farah and Dana Priest, "Bin Laden Son Plays Key Role in al-Qaeda," *Washington Post,* October 14, 2003.

198 **Ibn Tamiyyah had issued a historic fatwa:** testimony of Jamal al-Fadl, *U.S. v. Usama bin Laden, et al.*

9. *The Silicon Valley*

200 **"awesome symbolic towers":** Osama bin Laden interview with Tayser Alouni, al-Jazeera, October 2001, translated by CNN.

201 **Little Egypt:** Kepel, *Jihad,* 301.

issued a fatwa: interview with Tom Corrigan.

"descendants of apes": Kohlmann, *Al-Qaida's Jihad in Europe,* 26.

"cut the transportation": ibid, 185.

hoped to paralyze New York: interviews with Frank Pellegrino, David Kelley, Lewis Schiliro, James Kallstrom, Joe Cantemessa, Richard A. Clarke, Thomas Pickard, Pascual "Pat" D'Amuro, Mark Rossini, Mary Galligan, and Tom Corrigan.

bin Laden was financially backing: interview with Tom Corrigan.

202 **sodium cyanide:** Reeve, *The New Jackals,* 43.

dirty bomb: ibid., 147.

202 **tourists felt:** ibid., 12.

hospital casualties: ibid., 15.

203 **Zawahiri appeared on the speaker circuit:** There is considerable dispute about the exact date of Zawahiri's trip to the United States, or whether there was more than one. Ali Mohammed, the FBI's main source on this matter, told investigators that Zawahiri traveled to Brooklyn in 1988 in the company of Abu Khaled al-Masri, which is an alias for Mohammed Shawki Islambouli, the brother of the assassin of Anwar al-Sadat, and who was on the *shura* council of al-Jihad. As for the California trip, Mohammed says it took place in 1993 before the World Trade Center bombing, which occurred on February 26. Zawahiri's host in California, Dr. Ali Zaki, however, says he met Zawahiri once, in 1989 or 1990. There is also court testimony in Egypt by Khaled Abu al-Dahab, another member of al-Jihad who lived in California. "Ayman al-Zawahiri came to America to collect donations," Abu al-Dahab told a court in Cairo in 1999. Abu al-Dahab gave the date of Zawahiri's trip as late 1994 or 1995. For this narrative, I have chosen to accept the FBI version of the travel dates.

According to Dan Coleman, Zawahiri paid a visit to the mujahideen's Services Bureau branch office in Brooklyn in 1988. The office on Atlantic Avenue was run by one of Zawahiri's men in al-Jihad, Mustafa Shalabi. Two years later, Shalabi got into a dispute with Zawahiri's old rival, Sheikh Omar Abdul Rahman, over money. The blind sheikh wanted to use the funds the center raised to support the international jihad. Shalabi wanted the money to go into the Islamist rebellion against Egypt. He refused to relinquish control of the account. In March 1991 someone entered Shalabi's apartment in Brooklyn, beat him, strangled him, and stabbed him more than thirty times—a murder that has never been solved.

Bern, Switzerland . . . real name: interview with Jack Cloonan.

204 **martial artist:** interview with Mark Rossini.

the government rightly suspected: Benjamin and Simon, *The Age of Sacred Terror,* 123.

already a member: plea, *U.S. v. Ali Mohamed.*

the Cairo station: interview with Jack Cloonan.

probably a plant: interview with Michael Scheuer.

205 **sponsored by the agency:** Paul Quinn-Judge and Charles M. Sennott, "Figure Cited in Terrorism Case Said to Enter US with CIA Help," *Boston Globe,* February 3, 1995.

the transatlantic flight: Peter Waldman, Gerald F. Seib, Jerry Markon, and Christopher Cooper, "The Infiltrator: Ali Mohamed

Served in the U.S. Army—and bin Laden's Circle," *Wall Street Journal*, November 26, 2001; Miller, Stone, and Mitchell, *The Cell*, 141.

205 **pursuing a doctorate:** Bergen, *Holy War*, 129.

Kinko's: interview with Jack Cloonan.

206 **members of al-Jihad:** interview with Tom Corrigan.

"kill Russians": Benjamin Weiser and James Risen, "The Masking of a Militant: A Special Report; a Soldier's Shadowy Trail in U.S. and in the Mideast," *New York Times*, December 1, 1998.

kidnappings, assassinations, and hijacking: "The Story of the Arab Afghans from the Time of Their Arrival in Afghanistan Until Their Departure with the Taliban," part 5, *Al-Sharq al-Awsat*, December 12, 2004.

triggering device: interview with Jack Cloonan.

"buy rugs": interview with Jack Cloonan.

name of Osama bin Laden: interview with Jack Cloonan. Bin Laden's name and his organization were already beginning to be known even in the media. There is an Agence France Presse article, "Jordanian Militants Train in Afghanistan to Confront Regime," dated May 30, 1993, in which a "27-year-old militant" admits that he has been "trained by Al-Ka'ida, a secret organization in Afghanistan that is financed by a wealthy Saudi businessman who owns a construction firm in Jeddah, Ossama bin Laden."

207 **"James Bond":** interview with Harlen L. Bell.

they had been lost: interview with Daniel Coleman.

German military attaché: confessions of Ahmed Ibrahim al-Sayed al-Najjar, "Returnees from Albania" case, September 1998.

208 **two thousand dollars:** interview with Jack Cloonan.

209 **Naguib Mahfouz:** interview with Naguib Mahfouz.

210 **"Vanguards of Conquest":** al-Zawahiri, "Knights Under the Prophet's Banner," part 6. There is an ongoing dispute about whether Zawahiri was in charge of the Vanguards. There were several articles in the press that described the Vanguards as a dissident, break-away group from al-Jihad, which was led by Ahmed Agazzi and Yasser el-Sirri. However, el-Sirri was evasive when I queried him on this. "In 1993 and 1994, many did not agree with what happened in Egypt," he said. "But Zawahiri had the money. This group did not." Mamdouh Ismail, an Islamist lawyer in Cairo, told me that "Vanguards" was a media name; in fact, the arrested persons were largely members of al-Jihad—a view echoed by Hisham Kassem, a human rights advocate and publisher in Cairo, and Montassir al-Zayyat. "There is nothing called 'Vanguards of Conquest,' " Zayyat asserts.

210 **judicial standards:** According to Hisham Kassem, a Cairo publisher and human rights worker, "Vanguards was accused of trying to overthrow the government. Part of the evidence was a baseball bat and an air rifle. The ones you think are dangerous, you hang; the rest you give life sentences. It was all staged."

"only solution": Andrew Higgins and Christopher Cooper, "Cloak and Dagger: A CIA-Backed Team Used Brutal Means to Crack Terror Cell," *Wall Street Journal,* November 20, 2001.

backs of camels: testimony of Jamal al-Fadl, *U.S. v. Usama bin Laden, et al.*

211 **"The Minister escaped":** "Al-Sharq al-Awsat Publishes Extracts from al-Jihad Leader al-Zawahiri's New Book," by FBIS, *Al-Sharq al-Awsat,* December 2, 2001.

been to Iran: "Confessions from Last Leader of al-Jihad Organization," *Rose el-Youssef,* February 2, 1997. Translated by FBIS.

Zawahiri distributed cassettes: Salah, *Waqai' Sanawat al-Jihad.*

"Terrorism is the enemy": "Egyptian Mourners Condemn Terrorists," *AP,* November 27, 1993.

212 **"The unintended death":** Ayman al-Zawahiri, "Al-Sharq al-Awsat Publishes Extracts from al-Jihad Leader al-Zawahiri's New Book," *Al-Sharq al-Awsat,* December 2, 2001. Translated by FBIS.

"This meant": ibid.

10. Paradise Lost

214 **350,000 lives:** Huband, *Warriors of the Prophet,* 36.

250 men: Anonymous, *Through Our Enemies' Eyes,* 136.

a handful: interview with Hassabulla Omer. The testimony of L'Houssaine Kherchtou mentions only a couple of al-Qaeda fighters, who were sent to Somalia because they were dark-skinned and could pass as natives. *U.S. v. Usama bin Laden et al.* The extent of al-Qaeda's involvement in Somalia remains unresolved. Mary Deborah Doran, who concentrated on the Somali question for the FBI, wrote me: "I think there's no doubt AQ played a role in Somalia, and I believe that AQ had a role in the killing of our Rangers in October 1993—that even if they weren't the ones to pull the trigger (something we won't know until we find the people who did pull the triggers or were there when they were pulled), I believe it wouldn't have happened without them."

"Somalis treated us": al-Hammadi, "The Inside Story of al-Qa'ida," part 2, March 24, 2005.

215 **"Based on the reports":** Taysir Aluni interview with Osama bin Laden, al-Jazeera, October 2001.

215 **Ali Mohammed, taught:** interview with Jack Cloonan.

216 **Qari el-Said:** interview with Abdullah Anas.

two months of 1994: Wiktorowicz, "The New Global Threat."

"Thank God": interview with Abdullah Anas.

217 **"better image":** Evan Kohlmann, "The Legacy of the Arab-Afghans: A Case Study" (international politics honors thesis, Georgetown University, 2001).

"too flexible": interview with Abdullah Anas.

More than a hundred thousand: Kepel, *Jihad*, 254.

chemical agents . . . smuggling: testimony of Jamal al-Fadl, *U.S. v. Usama bin Laden, et al.*

Jamal al-Fadl: interviews with Jack Cloonan and Mark Rossini.

The general wanted $1.5 million: testimony of Jamal al-Fadl, *U.S. v. Usama bin Laden, et al.* Mohammed Loay Baizid (Abu Rida al-Suri), who allegedly purchased the "uranium" for bin Laden, claims that this entire episode never happened. His statement is supported by Hassabulla Omer, who was working in Sudanese intelligence at the time. Both men say there were similar rumors and scams operating in Khartoum that might have been the basis for Fadl's testimony.

218 **red mercury:** personal correspondence with Roy Schwitters.

nuclear warheads: Anonymous, *Through Our Enemies' Eyes*, 125.

Ansar al-Sunnah Mosque: Details about the assassination attempt come from Mohammed Ibrahim Naqd, "The First Attempt to Assassinate bin Laden Was Attempted by a Libyan Who Was Trained in Lebanon," *Al-Hayat*, November 18, 2001; and Ibrahim Hassan Ardi, "Al-Watan Places the Period the Head of al-Qaeda Spent in Sudan," *Al-Watan*, October 25, 2001; "Ossama bin-Ladin: Muslims Who Live in Europe Are Kafirs," *Rose al-Yousef*, December 9, 1996; al-Hammadi, "The Inside Story of al-Qa'ida," part 3, March 21, 2005; and from interviews with Issam al-Turabi, Sadiq el-Mahdi, Hassabulla Omer, and Khaled Yusuf. A number of sources state that there were actually two assassination attempts on bin Laden, sometimes given as being several weeks apart, but those reports stem from bin Laden himself, who counts the shooting at the mosque the night before as an attempt on his life.

219 **suffered from asthma:** interview with Jamal Khalifa. Some of the details about bin Laden's son Abdullah come from al-Hammadi, "The Inside Story of al-Qa'ida," part 3, March 21, 2005.

"At that moment": "Ossama bin-Ladin: Muslims Who Live in Europe Are Kafirs," *Rose al-Yousef*, December 9, 1996.

219 **"They had targeted":** ibid.

"regimes in our Arabic region": Wright, "The Man Behind bin Laden."

220 **Egyptian intelligence:** interview with Jamal Khashoggi.

CIA believed: interview with Michael Scheuer.

kept their university jobs: interview with anonymous Sudanese source.

221 **"We have not been":** interview with Jamal Khalifa.

222 **It was Egypt:** ibid.

Fahd personally decided: interview with Saeed Badeeb.

"Take it,": "Walidee Ramama al-Aqsa Bilkhasara" [My Father Renovated al-Aqsa Mosque, with a Loss], *Al-Umma al-Islamiyya,* October 18, 1991.

seeking asylum: Daniel McGrory, "The Day When Osama bin Laden Applied for Asylum—in Britain," *Times,* September 29, 2005.

223 **about $7 million:** interview with bin Laden family spokesperson.

depended on the monthly stipend: interview with Jamal Khalifa.

spreading money around: interview with Hassabulla Omer.

rock-crushing machines: Benjamin Weiser, "Ex-Aide Tells of Plot to Kill bin Laden," *New York Times,* February 21, 2001.

"Business is very bad": testimony of Jamal al-Fadl, *U.S. v. Usama bin Laden, et al.* Interview with Mohammed Loay Baizid.

224 **"lost all my money":** testimony of L'Houssaine Kherchtou, *U.S. v. Usama bin Laden, et al.*

a billionaire: testimony of Jamal al-Fadl, *U.S. v. Usama bin Laden, et al.*

225 **nearly $1 million:** ibid. The actual amounts were $795,200.49 from the Witness Protection Program and $151,047.02 from the FBI. That does not include money that may have been given to Fadl by the CIA, who were the first to interview him.

New Jersey Lottery: interview with Jack Cloonan.

two cameras: ibid.

226 **"Bin Laden looked":** plea, *U.S. v. Ali Mohamed.*

"I am tired": Hasin al-Banyan, "The Oldest Arab Afghan Talks to 'Al-Sharq al-Awsat' About His Career That Finally Landed Him in Prison in Saudi Arabia," trans. FBIS, *Al-Sharq al-Awsat,* November 25, 2001.

Medani al-Tayeb: interview with Jamal Khalifa.

several delegations: Anonymous, *Through Our Enemies' Eyes,* 146.

227 **"It means that Abdullah":** interview with Mohammed Loay Baizid.

conciliatory note: interview with Jamal Khashoggi.

if he pledged to give up jihad: interview with Ahmed Badeeb.

11. The Prince of Darkness

230 **"O'Neill":** interview with Richard A. Clarke.
232 **"nightclub wardrobe":** interview with Steven Simon.
paint its jet: interview with Admiral Paul E. Busick.
$12 million: Naftali, *Blind Spot*, 242.
233 **Su-Casa:** Reeve, *New Jackals*, 104.
235 **"Sons of John":** interview with Mark Rossini.
237 **"This battle is not between al-Qaeda and the U.S.":** Taysir Aluni interview with Osama bin Laden, al-Jazeera, October 2001.
239 **new basing agreements:** interview with Richard A. Clarke.
240 **former Egyptian minister:** Alain Geresh, *From Index on Censorship*, www.geocities.com/saudhouse_p/endofan.htm, April 1996.
"Why would my car": Kevin Dennehy, "Cape Man Relives Close Call with Terrorist Bombing While in Saudi Arabia," *Cape Cod Times*, October 25, 2001.
torturing confessions: A vivid account of the roundup and torture of Arab Afghans following the 1995 bombing can be found in Jerichow, *The Saudi File*, 136–40.
241 **Farouk camp:** Kohlmann, *Al-Qaida's Jihad in Europe*, 158.
nearly identical confessions: Teitelbaum, *Holier Than Thou*, 76.
"heroes": Anonymous, *Through Our Enemies' Eyes*, 141.
fatwa urging jihad: Salah Najm and Jamal Ismail, "Osama bin Laden: The Destruction of the Base," al-Jazeera, June 10, 1999.
"first terrorist blow": Prince Turki al-Faisal speech to Seton Hall University, October 14, 2003.

12. The Boy Spies

242 **Egyptian intelligence learned:** *Al-Ahram*, July 5, 1995.
243 **married local women:** interview with David Shinn.
smuggled weapons: interview with Sadiq al-Mahdi.
motivational talk: *Al-Ahram*, July 5, 1995.
The plan: interview with Saeed Badeeb.
Mubarak's plane: interview with Hisham Kassem.
grenade launcher malfunctioned: interview with Mohammed el-Shafey.
return to the airport: interview with Saeed Badeeb.
244 **"The sons":** Petterson, *Inside Sudan*, 179.
Houses were burned: interview with Hisham Kassem.
thousands of suspects: Human-rights organizations estimate the

number of Islamists still incarcerated in Egypt at 15,000; Islamists put the figure at 60,000.

244 **fiendish plan:** interviews with Yassir el-Sirri, Montassir el-Zayyat, and Hani el-Sibai.

a senior member: Mohammed el-Shafey, "Al-Zawahiri's Secret Papers," part 6, *Al-Sharq al-Awsat,* December 18, 2002.

"It could even": interview with Yassir el-Sirri.

246 **"state within a state":** Mohammed el-Shafey, "Al-Zawahiri's Secret Papers," part 6, *Al-Sharq al-Awsat,* December 18, 2002.

fewer than a hundred: confessions of Ahmed Ibrahim al-Sayed al-Najjar, "Returnees from Albania" case, September 1998.

"These are bad times": ibid.

247 **November 19, 1995:** The account of the Egyptian Embassy bombing comes from al-Hammadi, "The Inside Story of al-Qa'ida," part 9, March 28, 2005.

cab driver: "Al-Qaida, Usama bin Laden's Vehicle for Action," unsigned CIA document, July 12, 2001. The document describes Abu Khabab as a "limousine driver," which in the Middle East is usually a euphemism for cab driver.

government rounded up: interview with Ismail Khan.

248 **there were no innocents:** Maha Azzam, "Al-Qaeda: The Misunderstood Wahhabi Connection and the Ideology of Violence," *Royal Institute of International Affairs Briefing Paper No. 1,* February 2003.

"A man may": *Sahih Bukhari,* vol. 8, bk. 77, no. 60.

"a generation of mujahideen": Mohammed el-Shafey, "Al-Zawahiri's Secret Papers," part 6, *Al-Sharq al-Awsat,* December 18, 2002.

249 **"Do you remember":** interview with Issam al-Turabi.

his right testicle: Randal, *Osama,* 147.

French had issued a similar indictment: interview with Ghazi Salah Eddin Atabani.

250 **"if he apologizes":** interview with Timothy Carney.

251 **"We are ready":** interview with Elfatih Erwa. Both Richard A. Clarke, who was the national coordinator for security, infrastructure protection, and counterterrorism at the time, and his deputy Steven Simon dispute the point that the Sudanese ever formally offered bin Laden to the United States, but neither man was in the meeting, and it seems clear that the director of national security at the time, Sandy Berger, did explore the possibility of accepting bin Laden. The 9/11 Commission, however, stated that it found "no credible evidence" that Erwa had made the offer. *9/11 Commission Report,* 110.

nurtured the fantasy: Barton Gellman, "U.S. Was Foiled Multiple

Times in Efforts to Capture bin Laden or Have Him Killed," *Washington Post*, October 3, 2001.

251 **Bashir offered:** "Arabs and Muslims Must Break Barriers, Contact Others: Turki," *Saudi Gazette*, November 11, 2002.

"Give us proof": interview with Ahmed Badeeb.

"Ask him to leave": interview with Ahmed Badeeb.

252 **Turabi and bin Laden argued:** al-Hammadi, "The Inside Story of al-Qa'ida," part 3, March 21, 2005.

Turabi did bin Laden the favor: Jason Burke, "The Making of bin Laden: Part 1," *Observer*, October 28, 2001.

253 **$12 million:** Robert Block, "In the War Against Terrorism, Sudan Struck a Blow by Fleecing bin Laden," *Wall Street Journal*, December 3, 2001.

"a mixture": ibid.

check for $2,400: testimony of L'Houssaine Kherchtou, *U.S. v. Usama bin Laden, et al.*

Tupolev jet: interview with Jack Cloonan.

Two of bin Laden's young sons: al-Hammadi, "The Inside Story of al-Qa'ida," part 3, March 21, 2005.

He held America responsible: interview with Jamal Khashoggi.

13. Hijira

254 **given him money:** interview with Ahmed Badeeb.

abducted children: interview with Rahimullah Yusufzai.

255 **disabled 4 percent:** Tim Friend, "Millions of Land Mines Hinder Afghan Recovery," *USA Today*, November 27, 2001.

most of them orphans: According to Thomas Gouttierre, director of the Center for Afghanistan Studies at the University of Nebraska-Omaha, 80 percent of the Taliban forces were orphans from the Soviet war. Anna Mulrine, "Unveiled Threat," *U.S. News and World Report*, October 15, 2001.

three former mujahideen: Burke, *Al-Qaeda*, 145.

Younis Khalis: interview with Rahimullah Yusufzai.

teenage brides: Coll, *Ghost Wars*, 327.

256 **hired pilots:** U.S. Embassy (Islamabad) confidential cable, "Finally, a Talkative Talib: Origins and Membership of the Religious Students' Movement," February 20, 1995.

four Talibs in a jeep: interview with anonymous Pakistani diplomat.

lost his right eye: Arnaud de Borchgrave, "Osama bin Laden—'Null and Void,' " *UPI*, June 14, 2001.

256 **crack marksman:** Ismail Khan, "Mojaddedi Opposes Elevation of Taliban's Omar," *Islamabad the News*, April 6, 1996.

passable Arabic: interview with Farraj Ismail.

257 **"Corruption and moral disintegration":** Zaidan, *Bin Laden Bila Qina'*.

vision of the Prophet: U.S. Embassy (Islamabad) confidential cable, "Finally, a Talkative Talib: Origins and Membership of the Religious Students' Movement," February 20, 1995.

2,500 men: Nojumi, *The Rise of the Taliban*, 118.

students in a vocational school: Coll, *Ghost Wars*, 294–95.

258 **three million Afghan refugees:** interview with Prince Turki al-Faisal.

Sufi shrines: Juan Cole, personal communication.

monthly stipend: Nojumi, *The Rise of the Taliban*, 119.

beggars and sissies: Lamb, *The Sewing Circles of Heart*, 105.

twelve thousand fighters: Burke, *Al-Qaeda*, 113.

259 **10 percent tax:** Nojumi, *The Rise of the Taliban*, 136.

tents for the wives: Robert Fisk, "Small Comfort in bin-Ladin's Dangerous Exile," *Independent*, July 11, 1996.

260 **former Soviet collective:** Jason Burke, "The Making of bin Laden: Part 1," *Observer*, October 28, 2001.

Najm al-Jihad: "The Story of the Arab Afghans from the Time of Arrival in Afghanistan Until Their Departure with the Taliban, part 3," *Al-Sharq al-Awsat*, December 10, 2004.

men bunked nearby: interview with Rahimullah Yusufzai.

trade in honey: interview with Peter L. Bergen.

Electricity: Mohammed el-Shafey, "Son of al-Qai'da Financier: 'Lived Next to bin Ladin's Family, Who Disliked Electricity and Called for Austerity,' " *Al-Sharq al-Awsat*, April 16, 2004.

no international telephone: Robert Fisk, "Small Comfort in bin-Ladin's Dangerous Exile," *Independent*, July 11, 1996.

Americans were monitoring: Actually, according to Jack Cloonan, U.S. intelligence did not learn about the phone until 1997.

He was suspicious: "Biography of Usamah bin-Ladin, Written by Brother Mujahid with Minor Modifications," Islamic Observation Center, April 22, 2000. Translated by FBIS.

killed in an ambush: Burke, *Al-Qaeda*, 156.

taught his wives: "The Story of the Arab Afghans from the Time of Arrival in Afghanistan Until Their Departure with the Taliban, Part 3," *Al-Sharq al-Awsat*, December 10, 2004. Translated by FBIS.

"We don't want subversive": Tim McGirk, "Home Away from Home," *Time*, December 16, 1996.

261 **beaten and tortured:** Rashid, *Taliban*, 49.

"Women you should": from appendix 1 of ibid., 217ff. Rashid reproduced the Taliban decrees that had been translated from Dari and passed to reporters. He left the grammar and spelling as in the original. Statistics of female employment come from Anna Mulrine, "Unveiled Threat," *U.S. News and World Report*, October 15, 2001.

"unclean things": Amy Waldman, "No TV, No Chess, No Kites: Taliban's Code, from A to Z," *New York Times*, November 22, 2001.

262 **"Beatle-ly" . . . "her home will be marked":** ibid.

only animals that survived: interview with Bahram Rahman.

"Throw reason": Burke, *Al-Qaeda*, 111.

263 **overloaded ferry:** testimony of Ashif Mohamed Juma, *U.S. v. Usama bin Laden, et al.*

265 **"You are not unaware":** Osama bin Laden, "Declaration of War Against the Americans Occupying the Land of the Two Holy Places," *Al-Quds al-Arabi*, August 23, 1996.

266 **secretary for . . . Sayyaf:** interview with Yosri Fouda.

267 **poorly trained:** Fouda and Fielding, *Masterminds of Terror*, 116.

month in the Philippines: interview with Frank Pellegrino.

"Bojinka": *9/11 Commission Report*, 488 n. Previous reports have erroneously stated that the term was a Serbo-Croatian word for "big bang."

Haruki Ikegami: Reeve, *The New Jackals*, 79.

did not know Yousef: interview with Jamal Khashoggi, who says bin Laden "swore" to him that he did not know Yousef. Yousef did spend time in al-Qaeda camps and safe houses in 1989, however, and may have been in Peshawar at the same time that bin Laden was mediating the civil war in Afghanistan. Coll, *Ghost Wars*, 249. Mohammed Saleh, the *Al-Hayat* correspondent in Cairo, told me that Ramzi Yousef and bin Laden met in Pakistan, but he would not reveal the source of this information.

sent a messenger: Reeve, *The New Jackals*, 76.

sent to bin Laden diagrams: interview with Michael Scheuer.

kill Pope John Paul II: Reeve, *The New Jackals*, 86.

268 **training pilots:** *9/11 Commission Report*, 149.

14. Going Operational

269 **Khobar Towers:** interviews with John Lipka, Dale Watson, Jack Cloonan, and anonymous political officer in Riyadh; Freeh, *My FBI*, 11ff. Kenneth M. Pollack, in personal communication, writes, "The Saudis fully concurred with our conclusion that Iran was behind

Khobar Towers. I never heard the slightest hint that they believed al-Qaʻeda was responsible. However, because they had begun their rapprochement with Tehran—and especially after Muhammad Khatemi's election in Iran—it was our strong sense that they did not want us to be able to reach that definitive conclusion for fear that we would either want to mount a retaliatory strike against the Iranians or feel compelled to do so." Richard A. Clarke and Steven Simon have expressed similar sentiments in interviews. The 9/11 Commission, however, leaves open the possibility of a connection between the Khobar Towers bombing and al-Qaeda, saying that there was "strong but indirect evidence" that the organization "did in fact play some as yet unknown role." Douglas Jehl, "No Saudi Payment to Qaeda Is Found," *New York Times,* June 19, 2004. That evidence has not been made public, however. According to Michael Scheuer, the link was made in a memorandum prepared by the CIA and turned over to the commission.

270 **"Wasn't that a great trip?":** interview with Richard A. Clarke. Freeh, in personal communication, denies this exchange took place. O'Neill told many others the same story, however.

271 **It was Naif who decided:** interview with anonymous former U.S. State Department official.
"Maybe you have": interview with Rihab Massoud.

272 **"go operational":** interview with John Lipka.
"got this town wired": interview with R. P. Eddy.

273 **TWA Flight 800**: interviews with Richard A. Clarke, Tom Corrigan, and Tom Lang.

274 **Alec Station:** interviews with Daniel Coleman and Michael Scheuer.

276 **"Send ten green papers":** exhibit from *U.S. v. Usama bin Laden, et al.*
six children: bail hearing, *U.S. v. Usama bin Laden, et al.*
Coleman put the women: interview with Daniel Coleman.

277 **"Would you like":** interview with Daniel Coleman.

15. Bread and Water

278 **They flattered him:** Abdel Bari Atwan, "Interview with Saudi oppositionist Usmah bin-Ladin," *Al-Quds al-Arabi,* November 27, 1996.
endorsed their rule: Burke, "The Making of bin Laden: Part 1," *Observer,* October 28, 2001.
television crew: Bergen, *Holy War,* 17ff.

280 **sent a helicopter:** al-Hammadi, "The Inside Story of al-Qaʻida," part 5, March 23, 2005.

281 **plot . . . to kidnap:** "Walidee Ramama al-Aqsa Bilkhasara" [My

Father Renovated al-Aqsa Mosque, with a Loss], *Al-Umma al-Islamiyya*, October 18, 1991.

281 **"We want a simple life":** al-Hammadi, "The Inside Story of al-Qa'ida," part 5, March 23, 2005.

about eighty mud-brick: Coll, *Ghost Wars*, 391.

"in perfect harmony": al-Hammadi, "The Inside Story of al-Qa'ida," part 6, March 24, 2005.

two T-55 Soviet tanks: Clarke, *Against All Enemies*, 149.

282 **"May God be praised":** al-Hammadi, "The Inside Story of al-Qa'ida," part 6, March 24, 2005.

Switzerland: "Secrets of Relations Among al-Zawaheri, ben Ladan, and Hezb ul-Tahrir in Terrorist Operations in Europe" [*sic*], *Al-Watan al-Arabi*, October 13, 1995. Translated by FBIS. One of Zawahiri's associates testified in Egypt that he had had telephone contacts with Zawahiri in Geneva. Khalid Sharaf-al-Din, "Surprises in the Trial of the Largest International Fundamentalist Organization in Egypt," *Al-Sharq al-Awsat*, March 6, 1999. Translated by FBIS. The **Swiss villa** is from "Al-Jihad Terrorist Claims Strong CIA-Terrorist Ties," *MENA*, September 8, 1996. Yassir al-Sirri, who was close to al-Jihad, maintained in an interview that Zawahiri never lived in Switzerland, but Zawahiri's cousin Maha Azzam says he did.

Bulgaria: interview with Saeed Badeeb.

Copenhagen: interview with Jesper Stein; Michael Taarnby Jensen, personal correspondence.

fake passport: Andrew Higgins and Alan Cullison, "Terrorist's Odyssey: Saga of Dr. Zawahri [*sic*] Illuminates Roots of al-Qaeda Terror," *Wall Street Journal*, July 2, 2002.

satellite television channel: Wright, "The Man Behind bin Laden," *New Yorker*, September 16, 2002.

283 **"Conditions there":** Andrew Higgins and Alan Cullison, "Terrorist's Odyssey: Saga of Dr. Zawahri [*sic*] Illuminates Roots of al-Qaeda Terror," *Wall Street Journal*, July 2, 2002.

"If the Chechens": al-Zawahiri, "Knights Under the Prophet's Banner," part 7.

four passports: C. J. Chivers and Steven Lee Myers, "Chechen Rebels Mainly Driven by Nationalism," *New York Times*, September 12, 2004.

284 **"God blinded them":** Andrew Higgins and Alan Cullison, "Terrorist's Odyssey: Saga of Dr. Zawahri [*sic*] Illuminates Roots of al-Qaeda Terror," *Wall Street Journal*, July 2, 2002.

ISI subsidizing: Benjamin and Simon, *The Age of Sacred Terror*, 146.

Notes

487

284 **purchase some expensive vehicles:** Vahid Mojdeh, in Bergen, *The Osama bin Laden I Know,* 164.

a hundred-dollar-per-month: confessions of Ahmed Ibrahim al-Sayed al-Najjar, "Returnees from Albania" case, September 1998.

250 people: Abdurrahman Khadr, in Bergen, *The Osama bin Laden I Know,* 173.

"This place is worse": Alan Cullison and Andrew Higgins, "Strained Alliance: Inside al-Qaeda's Afghan Turmoil," *Wall Street Journal,* August 2, 2002.

288 **play Nintendo:** Abdel Bari Atwan, in Bergen, *The Osama bin Laden I Know,* 170.

289 **Azza:** interview with Maha Elsamneh.

290 **nonviolence initiative:** interview with Montassir al-Zayyat.

twenty thousand Islamists: Weaver, *A Portrait of Egypt,* 264. Weaver estimates the number of Islamists slain to be between seven and eight thousand, 267.

released two thousand: Rubin, *Islamic Fundamentalism,* 161.

"The political translation": Mohammed el-Shafey, "Al-Zawahiri's Secret Papers," part 5, *Al-Sharq al-Awsat,* December 17, 2002. Translated by FBIS.

291 **bargaining chip:** interview with Hisham Kassem.

three thousand security: Weaver, *A Portrait of Egypt,* 272.

292 **red headbands:** Douglas Jehl, "70 Die in Attack at Egypt Temple," *New York Times,* November 18, 1997.

"No to tourists": Weaver, *A Portrait of Egypt,* 259.

dead included: Alan Cowell, "At a Swiss Airport, 36 Dead, Home from Luxor," *New York Times,* November 20, 1997; also, Douglas Jehl, "At Ancient Site Along the Nile, Modern Horror," *New York Times,* November 19, 1997.

293 **Rifai Taha said:** Anonymous, *Through Our Enemies' Eyes,* 199.

bin Laden had financed: Jailan Halawi, "Bin Laden Behind Luxor Massacre?" *Al-Ahram Weekly,* May 20–26, 1999.

"The young men": Lawrence Wright, "The Man Behind bin Laden," *New Yorker,* September 16, 2002.

"We thought we'd never": interview with Hisham Kassem.

294 **The main point:** Fu'ad Husayn, "Al-Zarqawi . . . The Second Generation of al-Qa'ida, Part Fourteen," *Al-Quds al-Arabi,* July 13, 2005.

who was responsible: al-Zawahiri, "Knights Under the Prophet's Banner," part 11.

Zawahiri began writing: Kenneth M. Karas summation, *U.S. v. Usama bin Laden, et al.*

295 **lamely explaining:** Zayyat, *The Road to al-Qaeda,* 89.

295 **"dark past":** Mohammed el-Shafey, "Al-Zawahiri's Secret Papers," part 2, trans. FBIS, *Al-Sharq al-Awsat,* December 14, 2002.
"If the Contractor": Mohammed el-Shafey, "Al-Qaeda's Secret Emails," part 2, trans. FBIS, June 13, 2005.

296 **pledged to resign:** al-Zayyat, *The Road to al-Qaeda,* 109.
Zawahiri's own brother: interview with Hani al-Sibai.
"I myself heard": confessions of Ahmed Ibrahim al-Sayed al-Najjar, "Returnees from Albania" case, September 1998.

16. *"Now It Begins"*

297 **thirty Algerians . . . Young men from Yemen:** Burke, *Al-Qaeda,* 186.
298 **staged and cartoonish:** interview with Ismail Khan.
"Let's talk": interview with Rahimullah Yusufzai.
"Terrorism can be commendable": www.pbs.org/frontline.

299 **he wouldn't speak:** al-Hammadi, "The Inside Story of al-Qa'ida," part 6, March 24, 2005.
kidney disease: interview with Rahimullah Yusufzai.

300 **'Owhali . . . Azzam:** testimony of Stephen Gaudin, *U.S. v. Usama bin Laden, et al.*
erased the Saudis' faces: Miller, Stone, and Mitchell, *The Cell,* 192.

301 **kidnap bin Laden:** interviews with Michael Scheuer, Dale Watson, Mark Rossini, Daniel Coleman, and Richard A. Clarke.
302 **"Finish this":** interview with Prince Turki al-Faisal.
303 **left town:** interview with Michael Scheuer.
"Are you agreed": The meeting with Mullah Omar is largely Turki's firsthand account. Michael Scheuer says, based on CIA coverage of the meeting, that Omar and Turki quarreled, with Omar reportedly saying, "Your highness, I have just one question: When did the royal family become lackeys of the Americans?"

304 **four hundred four-wheel-drive . . . Mazar-e-Sharif:** Rashid, *Taliban,* 72–73.
several hundred Arabs: ibid., 139.
Ahmed Salama Mabruk: interviews with Daniel Coleman, Mark Rossini, and Montassir al-Zayyat.

305 **tortured:** interview with Hafez Abu-Saada.
306 **Saleh:** His real name is Abdullah Ahmed Abdullah, also known as Abu Mohammed el-Masri. He has never been captured. Interview with Ali Soufan; also, testimony of Stephen Gaudin, *U.S. v. Usama bin Laden, et al.*
309 **"Now it begins":** interview with Daniel Coleman.

310 **Nairobi:** interviews with Pascuale "Pat" D'Amuro, Stephen Gaudin, Mark Rossini, and Kenneth Maxwell.
passports: interview with Ali Soufan.
Stephen Gaudin: interview with Stephen Gaudin.
311 **five American embassies:** interview with Mark Rossini.
315 **Ahmed al-Hada:** interviews with Pascuale "Pat" D'Amuro, Daniel Coleman, and Ali Soufan.
called the number: FBI document, "PENTBOM Major Case 182 AOT-IT," November 5, 2001.
316 **"Kissinger's Promise":** testimony of Stephen Gaudin, *U.S. v. Usama bin Laden, et al.*
317 **"connections":** interview with Mary Lynn Stevens.
issuing threats: interview with Grant Ashley.
318 **raising money:** interview with Michael Rolince.
bypass surgery: interview with Paul Garmirian.
320 **Jamal al-Fadl:** interview with Mark Rossini.
hired a spy: interview with Milt Bearden. Bearden thinks the foreign asset was either Egyptian or Tunisian.
321 **If surveillance aircraft:** interview with Admiral Bob Inman.
refused to share the raw data: interview with Michael Scheuer.
322 **"Where do you think":** al-Hammadi, "The Inside Story of al-Qa'ida," part 9, March 28, 2005.
"Can you at least": interview with Abdul Rahman Khadr.
323 **twenty-two Afghans:** U.S. Department of State confidential cable, "Osama bin Laden: Taliban Spokesman Seeks New Proposal for Resolving bin Laden Problem," November 28, 1998. Hospital sources and Pakistani officials counted eleven dead, and fifty-three wounded. Ismail Khan, "Varying versions," *Islamabad the News,* August 30, 1998.
"Each house": al-Hammadi, "The Inside Story of al-Qa'ida," part 9, March 28, 2005.
bin Laden sold the unexploded missiles: Murad Ahmad, "Report Cites Russian 'Documents' on bin Ladin's Past," *Al-Majellah,* December 23, 2001.
324 **"survived the attack":** interview with Rahimullah Yusufzai.

17. The New Millennium

325 **Mullah Omar placed a secret call:** U.S. Department of State confidential cable, "Afghanistan: Taliban's Mullah Omar's 8/22 Contact with State Department," August 22, 1998.
326 **furious:** interview with Rahimullah Yusufzai.

326 **He judged:** U.S. Embassy (Islamabad) cable, "SITREP 6: Pakistan/ Afghanistan Reaction to U.S. Strikes," August 25, 1998.
"I shed tears": Robert Fisk, "Bin Laden's Secrets Are Revealed by al-Jazeera Journalist," *Independent*, October 23, 2002.
"We consider you": Burke, *Al-Qaeda*, 168.
fishing: Stephen Braun and Judy Pasternak, "Long Before Sept. 11, bin Laden Aircraft Flew Under the Radar," *Los Angeles Times*, November 18, 2001.
"This time": interview with Prince Turki al-Faisal.

327 **on drugs:** "Spiegel Interview: 'And Then Mullah Omar Screamed at Me,' " *Der Spiegel*, March 8, 2004. Translated by Christopher Sultan.
they were easily relocated: interview with Abdul Rahman Khadr.

328 **"There is no need":** al-Hammadi, "The Inside Story of al-Qa'ida," part 6, March 24, 2005.
"Did you expect": ibid.

330 **military objected:** *9/11 Commission Report*, 131.
"burned out": interview with Michael Scheuer.

333 **"Catholic thing":** interview with Grant Ashley.

334 **"Gee, John":** interview with anonymous FBI agent.
paying the mortgage: Weiss, *The Man Who Warned America*, 279.
borrowing money: interview with Joe Cantemessa.
"common strategy": Anonymous, *Through Our Enemies' Eyes*, 124.

335 **the prophesied Mahdi:** interview with Ahmed Badeeb.
stop backing anti-Saddam insurgents: *9/11 Commission Report*, 61.
met the Iraqi dictator: Jeffrey Goldberg, "The Great Terror," *New Yorker*, March 25, 2002.
Iraqi intelligence officials flew: *9/11 Commission Report*, 66.
Zawahiri went to Baghdad: "Iraq: Former PM Reveals Secret Service Data on Birth of al-Qaeda in Iraq," *Aki*, May 23, 2005.

336 **piece of the infrastructure:** interview with Lewis Schiliro.
The CIA warned: statement of Samuel R. Berger, *Joint Congressional Inquiry*, September 19, 2002.
"Hey, we've got something": Robert Draper, "The Plot to Blow Up LAX," *GQ*, December 2001.

338 **Times Square:** interviews with Joseph Dunne and Mark Rossini.
"If they're gonna": Clarke, *Against All Enemies*, 214.
Night of Power: interview with Robert McFadden.

18. Boom

340 **middle or upper:** interview with Marc Sageman. Many of the statistics derive from his important study, *Understanding Terror Networks*.

340 **mental disorders:** Sageman remarks that "only four of the 400 men [in his sample] had any hint of a disorder. This is below the world-wide base rate for thought disorders." Marc Sageman, "Understanding Terror Networks," *E-Notes,* Foreign Policy Research Institute, November 1, 2004.

middle-class professionals: Nick Fielding, "Osama's Recruits Well-Schooled," *Sunday Times,* April 3, 2005.

young, single men: interview with Abdullah Anas.

Shia Muslims had participated: interview with Abdullah Anas.

341 **ten and twenty thousand trainees:** *9/11 Commission Report,* 66. Sageman privately estimates the number of recruits during this period was no more than five thousand.

utopian goals: Bernstein, *Out of the Blue,* 86.

three main stages: al-Hammadi, "The Inside Story of al-Qaʻida," part 5, March 23, 2005.

342 **"enemies of Islam":** interview with Ali Soufan.

"shooting the personality": David Rohde and C. J. Chivers, "Al-Qaeda's Grocery Lists and Manuals of Killing," *New York Times,* March 17, 2002.

Kamikaze Camp: Abu Zayd, "After Ben Ladan's Return to Afghanistan and Revival of Fundamentalist Alliance," *Al-Watan al-Arabi,* June 7, 1996.

343 **Arnold Schwarzenegger:** interview with Jack Cloonan. The author's own movie, *The Siege,* was also viewed by al-Qaeda members.

"the destructive power": Alan Cullison and Andrew Higgins, "Computer in Kabul Holds Chilling Memos," *Wall Street Journal,* December 31, 2001.

five hours to die: undated, unsigned document, "CIA Report on the Zawahiri Brothers."

Yazid Sufaat: "Is al-Qaeda Making Anthrax?" *CBS News,* October 9, 2003; Eric Lipton, "Qaeda Letters Are Said to Show Pre-9/11 Anthrax Plans," *New York Times,* May 21, 2005.

preferred nuclear bombs: "The Story of the Afghan Arabs," *Al-Sharq al-Awsat,* part 1, December 8, 2004.

344 **Hamburg:** interviews with Georg Mascolo, Josef Joffe, Jochen Bittner, Manfred Murck, and Cordula Meyer.

about 200,000: "The Hamburg Connection," *BBC News,* August 19, 2005.

346 **"a good man":** *9/11 Commission Report,* 165.

"elegant": John Crewdson, "From Kind Teacher to Murderous Zealot," *Chicago Tribune,* September 11, 2004.

"I had a difficult": Brian Ross, "Face to Face with a Terrorist," ABC News, June 6, 2002.

347 **signed a standardized will:** Fouda and Fielding, *Masterminds of Terror*, 82.

Atta was enraged: Nicholas Hellen, John Goetz, Ben Smalley, and Jonathan Ungoed-Thomas, "God's Warrior," *Sunday Times*, January 13, 2002.

"planes operation": 9/11 Commission Report, 154.

348 **spring of 1999:** "Substitution for the Testimony of Khalid Sheikh Mohammed," *U.S. v. Moussaoui*.

only ones involved: *9/11 Commission Report*, 155.

"America is": "Bin Laden's Sermon for the Feast of the Sacrifice," MEMRI Special Dispatch Series—No. 476, www.memri.org, March 5, 2003.

Sears Tower: Paul Martin, "Chicago, L.A. Towers Were Next Targets," *Washington Times*, March 30, 2004.

349 **Nawaf al-Hazmi:** *Joint Inquiry into Intelligence Community Activities Before and After the Terrorist Attacks of September 11, 2001*, 131; and *Der Spiegel, Inside 9-11*, 16.

Khaled al-Mihdhar: *Joint Inquiry into Intelligence Community Activities Before and After the Terrorist Attacks of September 11, 2001*, 131; interview with Ali Soufan; and Eric Watkins, personal communication.

Ramadan: Georg Mascolo, "Operation Holy Tuesday," *Der Spiegel*, October 27, 2003.

350 **bin al-Shibh:** interview with Ali Soufan.

351 **"Something nefarious":** *9/11 Commission Report*, 353.

CIA already had the names: interview with Saeed Badeeb.

"We need to continue the effort": "Three 9/11 Hijackers: Identification, Watchlisting, and Tracking," *Staff Statement No. 2*, 4, National Commission on Terrorist Attacks upon the United States.

352 **"This is not a matter":** interview with Mark Rossini.

"Is this a no go": Miller is identified as "Dwight" in "A Review of the FBI's Handling of Intelligence Information Related to the September 11 Attacks," Department of Justice, Office of the Inspector General, November 2004, 233.

353 **drowning in a flood of threats:** interview with an anonymous CIA employee of Alec Station, who told me, "The real miracle is that there was only one major failure."

twelve employees: *The 9/11 Commission Report*, 479.

354 **"Manson Family":** Steve Coll, "A Secret Hunt Unravels in Afghanistan," *Washington Post*, February 22, 2004.

Bayoumi: Michael Isikoff and Evan Thomas, "The Saudi Money Trail," *Newsweek*, December 2, 2002; *9/11 Commission Report*, 215–18; *Joint Inquiry into Intelligence Community Activities Before and After the*

Terrorist Attacks of September 11, 2001, 172–74; "A Review of the FBI's Handling of Intelligence Information Related to the September 11 Attacks," Department of Justice, Office of the Inspector General, November 2004, 325.

356 **going nowhere:** interview with Jack Cloonan.

359 **"centralization":** al-Hammadi, "The Inside Story of al-Qaʻida," part 4, March 22, 2005.

USS *The Sullivans:* *9/11 Commission Report,* 190–91.

360 **shaped charges:** Benjamin and Simon, *The Age of Sacred Terror,* 323.

"Enough of words": Bergen, *Holy War,* 186.

Aden: interview with anonymous former CIA officer.

USS *Cole:* interviews with Barbara Bodine, Kenneth Maxwell, Thomas Pickard, Pascuale "Pat" D'Amuro, Jim Rhody, Tom Donlon, Ali Soufan, Kevin Giblin, Barry Mawn, David Kelley, Mark Rossini, and Kevin Donovan; also, John O'Neill, "The Bombing of the U.S.S. Cole," speech given at 19th Annual Government/Industry Conference on Global Terrorism, Political Instability, and International Crime, March 2001; Graham, *Intelligence Matters,* 60–61; Bergen, *Holy War,* 184–92; Weiss, *The Man Who Warned America,* 287–312; "The Man Who Knew," www.pbs.org.¨

366 **clear directives:** interview with Michael Sheehan.

372 **"errand boy":** interview with Ali Soufan.

Soufan sent Khallad's photo: According to Soufan, "the agency went behind my back" to interview his source in Afghanistan in December 2000. The agency was sharing his source at this time, but in accordance with protocol, brought along the FBI legal attaché from Islamabad. At this time, the CIA officer had the source identify a surveillance photo of Khallad from the Malaysia meeting. This allowed the agency to correctly say that the FBI was present when the picture was shown; however, the interview was conducted in Arabic, a language that the FBI attaché didn't speak, so he was unaware of what was actually transpiring.

374 **Samsonite suitcases:** "The Story of the Afghan Arabs," *Al-Sharq al-Awsat,* part 4, December 12, 2004.

Bin Laden separated: *9/11 Commission Report,* 191.

launching another missile: Clinton, *My Life,* 925.

hoped to lure: interview with Ali Soufan.

19. The Big Wedding

376 **marriage:** interviews with Ahmed Zaidan, Jamal Khalifa, and Maha Elsamneh; Zeidan, *Bin Laden Bila Qinaʻ,* 109–58.

376 *A destroyer:* "Bin Laden Verses Honor *Cole* Attack," *Reuters,* March 2, 2001.

377 **sleeplessness:** Abdullah bin Osama bin Laden says that his father was only sleeping two or three hours a night. "Bin Laden's Son Defiant," BBC, October 14, 2001.
Our men are in revolt: government exhibit, *U.S. v. Moussaoui.*

378 **Dick Clarke:** interview with Richard A. Clarke; also, Clarke, *Against All Enemies,* 225–34. *The 9/11 Commission Report* says that Clarke told Rice he wanted to be reassigned in May or June; he told me March.
Rice demurred: Philip Shenon and Eric Schmitt, "Bush and Clinton Aides Grilled by Panel," *New York Times,* March 24, 2004.

379 **eighty thousand dollars:** interview with Valerie James. O'Neill's base salary was $120,336.
"hot-blooded revolutionary": Mohammed el-Shafey, "UBL's Aide al-Zawahiri Attacks Jihad Members 'Taking Refuge in Europe,' " *Al-Sharq al-Awsat,* April 23, 2001. Translated by FBIS.

380 **Ahmed Shah Massoud:** interview with Abdullah Anas; Kathy Gannon, "Osama Ordered Assassination," *Advertiser,* August 16, 2002; Jon Lee Anderson, "Letter from Kabul: The Assassins," *New Yorker,* June 10, 2002; Burke, *Al-Qaeda,* 177; Mike Boettcher and Henry Schuster, "How Much Did Afghan Leader Know?" CNN, November 6, 2003; *9/11 Commission Report,* 139; Defense Intelligence Agency confidential cable, "IIR [Excised]/The Assassination of Massoud Related to 11 September 2001 Attack," November 21, 2001; Benjamin and Simon, *The Age of Sacred Terror,* 338; Coll, *Ghost Wars,* 568.

381 **"using an airplane":** Sam Tannehaus, "The C.I.A.'s Blind Ambition," *Vanity Fair,* January 2002. Tannehaus reports the attack was going to be on the G-8 in Genoa, but Clarke told me that the tip involved a presidential assassination in Rome.
Wakil Ahmed Muttawakil: "Newspaper Says U.S. Ignored Terror Warning," *Reuters,* September 7, 2002.
Jordanian intelligence: John K. Cooley, "Other Unheeded Warnings Before 9/11?" *Christian Science Monitor,* May 23, 2002.

382 **Amal al-Sada:** interview with Ali Soufan.
"Songs and merriment": al-Hammadi, "The Inside Story of al-Qa'ida," part 6, March 24, 2005.
mother chastised: interview with Ali Soufan.

383 **"We're going to kill":** interview with Richard A. Clarke.

384 **"Something bad":** Dana Priest, "Panel Says Bush Saw Repeated Warnings," *Washington Post,* April 13, 2004.
Intelink: Intelink is a handicapped system available to other intelligence agencies. It would have shown Gillespie only what was avail-

able to FBI intelligence. Had she looked on the Hercules system, the powerful CIA database that contained all the cables and NSA traffic and which was available to her, she would have gotten a complete picture of the agency's knowledge of Mihdhar and Hazmi.

384 **June 11**: interviews with Dina Corsi, Steven Bongardt, Ali Soufan, and Mark Rossini. Miller, Stone, and Mitchell, *The Cell*, 305; Cofer Black statement, September 20, 2002, *Joint Inquiry into Intelligence Community Activities Before and After the Terrorist Attacks of September 11, 2001*. Dina Corsi told me that she had written the names of Mihdhar and Hazmi on the backs of the photographs, so that the names were made available to the criminal agents on the I-49 squad, but Bongardt says he never saw them.

387 **"the Wall"**: interviews with Jack Cloonan, Ali Soufan, Pascuale "Pat" D'Amuro, Daniel Coleman, Admiral Bob Inman; *9/11 Commission Report*, 78–80.

388 **given birth:** *9/11 Commission Report*, 222.
Pink Floyd: interview with Ali Soufan.

389 **O'Neill . . . in Spain:** interviews with Mark Rossini, Valerie James, Enrique García, Emiliano Burdiel Pascual, and Teodoro Gómez Domínguez.

390 **Atta . . . also in the country:** interviews with José Maria Irujo, Keith Johnson, and Ramón Pérez Maura; *Joint Congressional Inquiry*, 139; Fouda and Fielding, *Masterminds of Terror*, 137.
Irish Republican Army: interview with Dan Coleman.

394 **"The duties of this religion":** "Rede des Scheich usamma Bin LADEN anläßlich des Fitr-Festes erster schawal 1420." [Speech of Sheikh Osama Bin Laden on the occasion of the Fitr celebration of the first schawal 1420], Motassadeq Document, Trans. Chester Rosson. I have modified some of the grammar and the stilted language, which was translated from Arabic to German to English.

395 **alarming electronic communication:** interviews with Jack Cloonan, Mark Rossini, and Daniel Coleman; Miller, Mitchell, and Stone, *The Cell*, 289; *Joint Congressional Inquiry*, 20. In FBI vernacular, an "electronic communication" is an e-mail that requires a response; it is not an informal document. It has superseded teletypes as a formal communication.

396 **Zacarias Moussaoui:** interviews with Richard A. Clarke and Michael Rolince; *9/11 Commission Report*, 273–76.

397 **Yazid Sufaat:** *9/11 Commission Report*, 151; "Entrepreneurs of Terrorism," *Weekend Australian*, July 24, 2004.
"Today is": Weiss, *The Man Who Warned America*, 350.

398 **INS:** interviews with Ali Soufan, Jack Cloonan, Mark Rossini, and

Daniel Coleman; Eleanor Hill, "The Intelligence Community's Knowledge of the September 11 Hijackers Prior to September 11, 2001," Joint Inquiry Staff Statement, *Joint Congressional Inquiry*, September 20, 2002.

400 **"I left because":** Roula Khalaf, "Dinner with the FT: Turki al-Faisal," *Financial Times*, November 1, 2003.

"over-ripened fruit": Paul Mcgeough, "The Puppeteer," *Sydney Morning Herald*, October 8, 2002.

"huge burden": Weiss, *The Man Who Warned America*, 359.

Massoud: Jon Lee Anderson, "Letter from Kabul: The Assassins," *New Yorker*, June 10, 2002.

401 **Mullah Mohammed Khaksar:** Kathy Gannon, "Osama 'Ordered Assassination,' " *Advertiser*, August 17, 2002.

"We're overdue": interviews with Jerome Hauer and Robert Tucker.

402 **mountains above Khost:** interview with Ali Soufan.

"We were playing": videotape of bin Laden's dinner with Sheikh Ali Saeed al-Ghamdi.

banned all talk of dreams: Sageman, *Understanding Terror Networks*, 117.

403 **America in ashes:** Peter Finn, "Hamburg's Cauldron of Terror," *Washington Post*, September 11, 2002.

nine thousand gallons: Der Spiegel, *Inside 9-11*, 50.

O'Neill helped usher: Weiss, *The Man Who Warned America*, 366.

404 **"Wait, wait":** interview with Ali Soufan.

held up three fingers: Mike Boettcher, "Detainees Reveal bin Laden's Reaction to Attacks," CNN.com, September 10, 2002.

405 **north tower:** Details of the scene inside come from interviews with Kurt Kjeldsen and Michael Hingson; the video footage shot by Jules and Gedeon Naudet; Murphy, *September 11*; Fink and Mathias, *Never Forget*; and Smith, *Report from Ground Zero*.

406 **"Is it true":** interview with Wesley Wong.

407 **dust was a compound:** Anthony DePalma, "What Happened to That Cloud of Dust?" *New York Times*, November 2, 2005.

20. Revelations

409 **Quso and Abu Jandal interrogations:** interviews with Ali Soufan and Robert McFadden.

417 **special protocol:** Weiss, *The Man Who Warned America*, 383.

"We planned": John R. Bradley, "Definitive Translation of 'Smoking Gun' Tape." www.johnrbradley.com/art_27.html, July 15, 2004. translated by Ali al-Ahmed.

418 **"I never knew":** interview with Maha Elsamneh.

Tora Bora: Smucker, *Al-Qaeda's Great Escape*, 119–20.

"We were about": bin Laden audiotape: "Message to Our Muslim Brothers in Iraq," BBCNews.com, February 12, 2003.

419 **"Only a few":** "Al-Majellah Obtains bin Ladin's Will," *Al-Majellah*, October 27, 2002. Translated by FBIS.

420 **"I saw a heavy":** Ilene R. Prusher, "Two Top al-Qaeda Leaders Spotted," *Christian Science Monitor*, March 26, 2002.

BIBLIOGRAPHY

Abbas, Hamid. *Story of the Great Expansion.* Jeddah: Saudi Bin Ladin Group [*sic*], 1996.

Abdel-Malek, Anouar. *Egypt: Military Society.* Translated by Charles Lam Markmann. New York: Random House, 1968.

Abdelnasser, Walid Mahmoud. *The Islamic Movement in Egypt: Perceptions of International Relations, 1967–81.* London: Kegan Paul International, 1994.

Abdo, Geneive. *No God but God: Egypt and the Triumph of Islam.* Oxford: Oxford University Press, 2000.

Abdullah, Isam. "Al-Majellah Tuhawir Shahid Ayan Arabi ala Hisar Kandahar" [*Al-Majellah* Interviews an Arab Witness to the Siege of Kandahar]. Translated by May Ibrahim. *Al-Majellah,* December 3, 2001.

Abir, Mordechai. *Saudi Arabia: Government, Society, and the Gulf Crisis.* New York: Routledge, 1993.

Abou El Fadl, Khaled. "The Ugly Modern and the Modern Ugly: Reclaiming the Beautiful in Islam." In *Progressive Muslims: On Justice, Gender, and Pluralism,* edited by Omid Safi. Oxford: Oneworld Publications, 2003.

——— et al. *The Place of Tolerance in Islam.* Boston: Beacon Press, 2002.

AbuKhalil, As'ad. *Bin Laden, Islam, and America's New "War on Terrorism."* New York: Seven Stories, 2002.

Abu-Rabi, Ibrahim M. *Intellectual Origins of Islamic Resurgence in the Modern Arab World.* Albany: State University of New York Press, 1996.

Aburish, Saïd K. *The Rise, Corruption, and Coming Fall of the House of Saud.* New York: St. Martin's, 1996.

Ajami, Fouad. *The Arab Predicament: Arab Political Thought and Practice Since 1967.* Cambridge: Cambridge University Press, 1981.

———. *The Dream Palace of the Arabs: A Generation's Odyssey.* New York: Pantheon Books, 1998.

Algar, Hamid. *Wahhabism: A Critical Essay.* New York: Islamic Publications International, 2002.

Amin, Mohamed. *The Beauty of Makkah and Madinah.* Nairobi: Camerapix Publishers International, 1999.

"Amreeka Tantaqim wa bin Laden Yuhadid" [America Avenges and bin Laden Threatens]. Translated by Dina Ibrahim. *Akhbar al-Hawadith,* October 11, 2001, no. 497.

Anas, Abdullah. *Wiladat al-Afghan al-Arab: Seerat Abdulla Anas bayna masood wa Abdulla Azzam* [The Birth of the Arab Afghans: The Memoirs of Abdullah Anas: Between Masood and Abdullah Azzam]. Beirut: Dar al-Saqee, 2002.

Anonymous. *Through Our Enemies' Eyes: Osama bin Laden, Radical Islam, and the Future of America.* Washington, D.C.: Brassey's, 2002.

"Aqdam al-Afghan al-Arab Yatahadath lilSharq al-Awsat 'an Maseeratihi alatee Awsalat'hoo fee al-Nihayya ila al-Sijn fee al-Saudia" [The Oldest of Arab Afghans Speaks to al-Sharq al-Awsat About His Journey That Led Him in the End to a Saudi Arabian Prison]. Translated by Amjad M. Abu Nseir. *Al-Sharq al-Awsat,* November 25, 2001.

Armstrong, Karen. *Muhammad: A Biography of the Prophet.* New York: HarperCollins, 1992.

al-Aroosi, Mahmoud Kamel. *Muhakamat Sayyid Qutb.* Translated by Nidal Daraiseh. Cairo: Matba'at al-Jamhooriya al-Hadeetha, 1995.

Asaad, Khalid Khalil. *Mukatil Min Mecca* [A Warrior from Mecca]. Translated by Nidal Daraiseh. London: al-I'lam, 2001.

Atwan, Abdel Bari. *The Secret History of al-Qa'ida.* London; Saqi, 2006.

"Ayna Thahaba Qatalat al-Sadat?" [Where Have the Killers of Sadat Gone?]. Translated by Mandi Fahmy. *Akhir Sa'ah* [The Last Hour], October 24, 2001, pp. 36–39.

Azzam, Abdullah. *The Lofty Mountain.* London: Azzam Publications, 2003.

———. "Martyr Sayyid Qutb: A Giant of Islamic Thought." www.azzam .com (now defunct).

———. "The Solid Base" [Al-Qaeda]. *Al-Jihad,* April 1988, no. 41.

Badeeb, Saeed M. *The Saudi-Egyptian Conflict Over North Yemen, 1962–1970.* Boulder, Col.: Westview, 1986.

Baer, Robert. *Sleeping with the Devil.* New York: Crown Publishers, 2003.

Bahmanyar, Mir. *Afghanistan Cave Complexes, 1979–2004.* Oxford: Osprey Publishing Group, 2004.

Baker, Raymond William. *Islam Without Fear: Egypt and the New Islamists.* Cambridge: Harvard University Press, 2003.

Bamford, James. *A Pretext for War: 9/11, Iraq, and the Abuse of America's Intelligence Agencies.* New York: Doubleday, 2004.

Bearden, Milt, and James Risen. *The Main Enemy: The Inside Story of the CIA's Final Showdown with the KGB.* New York: Random House, 2003.

Bell, J. Bower. *Murders on the Nile.* San Francisco: Encounter Books, 2003.

Belloc, Hilaire. *The Great Heresies.* Manassas, Va.: Trinity Communications, 1987.

Benjamin, Daniel, and Steven Simon. *The Age of Sacred Terror.* New York: Random House, 2003.

Bergen, Peter L. *Holy War: Inside the Secret World of Osama bin Laden.* New York: Free Press, 2001.

———. *The Osama bin Laden I Know: An Oral History of al-Qaeda's Leader.* New York: Free Press, 2006.

Berman, Paul. *Terror and Liberalism.* New York: Norton, 2003.

Bernstein, Richard. *Out of the Blue: The Story of September 11, 2001, from Jihad to Ground Zero.* New York: Times Books, 2002.

Bin Ladin, Carmen. *Inside the Kingdom: My Life in Saudi Arabia.* New York: Warner Books, 2004.

Blum, Howard. *The Eve of Destruction: The Untold Story of the Yom Kippur War.* New York: HarperCollins, 2003.

Borovik, Artyom. *The Hidden War: A Russian Journalist's Account of the Soviet War in Afghanistan.* New York: Grove Press, 1990.

Brogan, Daniel. "Al-Qaeda's Greeley Roots." *5280* (June/July 2003): 158–65.

Burke, Jason. *Al-Qaeda: Casting a Shadow of Terror.* London: I. B. Taurus, 2003.

Burr, J. Millard, and Robert O. Collins. *Revolutionary Sudan: Hasan al-Turabi and the Islamist State, 1989–2000.* Leiden: Brill, 2003.

Burton, Richard F. *Personal Narrative of a Pilgrimage to al-Madina and Meccah.* Vols. 1 and 2. Edited by Isabel Burton. New York: Dover, 1964.

Calvert, John. " 'The World Is an Undutiful Boy!': Sayyid Qutb's American Experience." *Islam and Christian-Muslim Relations* 11, no. 1 (2000).

Campbell, Kurt M., and Michèle A. Flournoy. *To Prevail: An American Strategy for the Campaign Against Terrorism.* Washington, D.C.: Center for Strategic and International Studies, 2001.

Carré, Oliver. *Mysticism and Politics: A Critical Reading of Fi Zilal al-Qur'an by Sayyid Qutb (1906–1966).* Translated from the French by Carol Artigues and revised by W. Shepard. Leiden: Brill, 2003.

Champion, Daryl. *The Paradoxical Kingdom: Saudi Arabia and the Momentum of Reform.* New York: Columbia University Press, 2002.

Clarke, Richard A. *Against All Enemies: Inside America's War on Terror.* New York: Free Press, 2004.

Clinton, Bill. *My Life*. New York: Knopf, 2004.

Coll, Steve. *Ghost Wars: The Secret History of the CIA, Afghanistan, and bin Laden, from the Soviet Invasion to September 10, 2001*. New York: Penguin, 2004.

Cooley, John K. *Unholy Wars*. London: Pluto Press, 2000.

Corbin, Jane. *Al-Qaeda: In Search of the Terror Network That Threatens the World*. New York: Thunder's Mouth Press / Nation Books, 2002.

Cordovez, Diego, and Selig S. Harrison. *Out of Afghanistan: The Inside Story of the Soviet Withdrawal*. New York: Oxford University Press, 1995.

Country Reports on Terrorism 2004. [no city]: U.S. Department of State, 2005.

Crile, George. *Charlie Wilson's War: The Extraordinary Story of the Largest Covert Operation in History*. New York: Atlantic Monthly Press, 2003.

Der Spiegel Reporters, Writers, and Editors. *Inside 9-11: What Really Happened*. Translated by Paul De Angelis and Elisabeth Koestner. New York: St. Martin's, 2001.

Esposito, John. *Unholy War: Terror in the Name of Islam*. Oxford: Oxford University Press, 2002.

Euben, Roxanne L. *Enemy in the Mirror: Islamic Fundamentalism and the Limits of Modern Rationalism*. Princeton, N.J.: Princeton University Press, 1999.

Fandy, Mamoun. *Saudi Arabia and the Politics of Dissent*. London: Palgrave, 2001.

Feininger, Andreas. *New York in the Forties*. New York: Dover, 1978.

Fernea, Elizabeth Warnock, and Robert A. Fernea. *The Arab World: Forty Years of Change*. New York: Doubleday, 1997.

Fink, Mitchell, and Lois Mathias. *Never Forget: An Oral History of September 11, 2001*. New York: HarperCollins, 2002.

Fouda, Yosri, and Nick Fielding. *Masterminds of Terror: The Truth Behind the Most Devastating Terrorist Attack the World Has Ever Seen*. New York: Arcade, 2003.

Frady, Marshall. *Billy Graham: A Parable of American Righteousness*. Boston: Little, Brown, 1979.

Freeh, Louis J., with Howard Means. *My FBI: Bringing Down the Mafia, Investigating Bill Clinton, and Fighting the War on Terror*. New York: St. Martin's, 2005.

Friedman, Thomas L. *From Beirut to Jerusalem*. New York: Doubleday, 1989.

Geffs, Mary L. *Under Ten Flags: A History of Weld County, Colorado*. Greeley: McVey Printery, 1938.

Gold, Dore. *Hatred's Kingdom.* Washington, D.C.: Regnery Publishing, 2003.

Goldschmidt, Arthur Jr. *Biographical Dictionary of Modern Egypt.* Cairo: American University in Cairo Press, 2000.

Graham, Bob, with Jeff Nussbaum. *Intelligence Matters: The CIA, the FBI, Saudi Arabia, and the Failure of America's War on Terror.* New York: Random House, 2004.

Griffin, Michael. *Reaping the Whirlwind: The Taliban Movement in Afghanistan.* London: Pluto Press, 2001.

Guenena, Nemat. "The 'Jihad': An 'Islamic Alternative' in Egypt." Master's thesis, American University in Cairo Press, 1985.

Gunaratna, Rohan. *Inside al-Qaeda: Global Network of Terror.* London: Hurst, 2002.

Habeeb, Kamal Saeed. *Al-Haraka al-Islamiyya min al-Muqwajaha ila al-Muraja'a* [The Islamic Movement from Confrontation to Revision]. Translated by Mandi Fahmy. Cairo: Maktabat Madbooly, 2002.

Halliday, Fred. *Two Hours That Shook the World.* London: Saqi, 2002.

al-Hammadi, Khalid. "The Inside Story of al-Qa'ida, as Told by Abu-Jandal (Nasir al-Bahri), bin Ladin's Personal Guard." Translated by FBIS. *Al-Quds al-Arabi.*

Hamza, Khaled. "Al-Doctor—al-Khaleefa al-Muntathar: Qisat Ayman al-Zawahiri min al-Tafawuq fee al-Tib li-Qiadat Tantheemat Irhabiyya" [The Doctor—the Awaited Khalif: Ayman al-Zawahiri's Story from Excelling in Medicine to Leading Terrorist Groups]. Translated by Mandi Fahmy. *Akhir Sa'ah* [The Last Hour], October 2001, no. 3495, pp. 8–9.

Hannonen, Sanna. "Egyptian Islamist Discourse: On Political and Social Thought of Hasan al-Banna (1906–1949) and Sayyid Qutb (1906–1966)." Master's thesis, University of Helsinki, 1999.

Harmony Documents. United States Department of Defense database. www.ctc .usma.edu/aq_harmonylist.asp

Heikal, Mohammed. *Autumn of Fury: The Assassination of Sadat.* New York: Random House, 1983.

———. *Iran: The Untold Story.* New York: Pantheon, 1982.

Holden, David, and Richard Johns. *The House of Saud: The Rise and Rule of the Most Powerful Dynasty in the Arab World.* New York: Holt, Rinehart, and Winston, 1981.

Hourani, Albert. *A History of the Arab Peoples.* Cambridge: Belknap Press of Harvard University Press, 2002.

Huband, Mark. *Warriors of the Prophet: The Struggle for Islam.* Boulder: Westview, 1998.

Ibrahim, Saad Eddin. *Egypt Islam and Democracy: Critical Essays.* Cairo: American University in Cairo Press, 1996.

Ismail, Faraj. "Fee Awal Hadeeth Lahoo Baʻd al-Harb: Ayman Zawahiri Yatahadath LilMajalla ʻan Ikhtifa bin Laden wa Qisat al-Khiana wa al-Huroob min Afghanistan!" [In His First Interview After the War: Ayman Zawahiri Speaks to al-Majalla on the Disappearance of bin Laden, the Story of Betrayal, and Fleeing from Afghanistan]. Translated by Mandi Fahmy. *Al-Majalla,* December 2001, no. 1140, pp. 12–13.

Ismail, Jamal Abdul Latif. "Bin Laden wa al-Jazeera wa . . . Anaa" [Bin Laden, al-Jazeera and . . . Me]. Translated by Amjad M. Abu Nseir. London: Islamic Observation Centre, 2001.

Jacquard, Roland. *In the Name of Osama bin Laden: Global Terrorism and the bin Laden Brotherhood.* Translated by George Holoch. Durham: Duke University Press, 2002.

Jerichow, Anders. *The Saudi File: People, Power, Politics.* New York: St. Martin's, 1998.

Johnson, Paul. *Modern Times.* New York: Harper and Row, 1983.

Joint Inquiry Into Intelligence Community Activities Before and After the Terrorist Attacks of September 11, 2001: Report of the U.S. Senate Select Committee on Intelligence and U.S. House Permanent Select Committee on Intelligence. Washington, D.C., December 2002.

Jordán, Javier. *Profetas del miedo: Aproximación al terrorismo islamista.* Pamplona: EUNSA, 2004.

Kechichian, Joseph A. "Islamic Revivalism and Change in Saudi Arabia." *The Muslim World* 80, no. 1 (January 1990): 1–16.

Kepel, Gilles. *Jihad: The Trail of Political Islam.* Translated by Anthony F. Roberts. Cambridge: Belknap Press of Harvard University Press, 2002.

———. *Muslim Extremism in Egypt: The Prophet and Pharaoh.* Berkeley: University of California Press, 1993.

al-Khaledi, Salah Abdel Fatah. *Amrika min al-dakhil bi minzar Sayyid Qutb* [America from the Inside from the Viewpoint of Sayyid Qutb]. 2d ed. Translated by Nidal Daraiseh. Jiddah: Dar al-Minara, 1986.

———. *Sayyid Qutb: al-adib, al-naqid, wa-al-daʻiyah al-mujahid, wa-al-mufakkir al-mufassir al-raiʼid* [Sayyid Qutb: The Scholar, the Critic, the Preacher, the Warrior, the Explainer, the Pioneer]. Translated by Nidal Daraiseh. Damascus: Dar al-Qalam, 2000.

———. *Sayyid Qutb: al-shaheed al-hay* [Sayyid Qutb: The Living Martyr]. Translated by Nidal Daraiseh. Amman: Maktabat al-Aqsa, 1981.

———. *Sayyid Qutb: min al-milad ila al-istishihad* [Sayyid Qutb: From Birth to Martyrdom]. Translated by Nidal Daraiseh. Damascus: Dar al-Qalam, 1991.

Kinsey, Alfred C., et al. *Sexual Behavior in the Human Male*. Philadelphia: W. B. Saunders, 1948.

Kohlmann, Evan F. *Al-Qaida's Jihad in Europe: The Afghan-Bosnian Network*. Oxford: Berg, 2004.

Lacey, Robert. *The Kingdom: Saudi Arabia and the House of Sa'ud*. New York: Harcourt Brace Jovanovich, 1981.

Lamb, Christina. *The Sewing Circles of Heart: My Afghan Years*. London: Flamingo, 2003.

Larson, Robert W. *Shaping Educational Change: The First Century of the University of Northern Colorado at Greeley*. Boulder: Colorado Associated University Press, 1989.

Lawrence, T. E. *Seven Pillars of Wisdom*. New York: Doubleday, 1926.

Lewis, Bernard. *The Crisis of Islam: Holy War and Unholy Terror*. New York: Modern Library, 2003.

Lippman, Thomas W. *Inside the Mirage: America's Fragile Partnership with Saudi Arabia*. Boulder, Col.: Westview, 2004.

Long, David E. *The Kingdom of Saudi Arabia*. Gainesville: University Press of Florida, 1997.

"Looking for Answers." *Frontline*. www.pbs.org/frontline.

Mackey, Sandra. *The Saudis: Inside the Desert Kingdom*. New York: Norton, 2002.

Mackintosh-Smith, Tim. *Yemen: The Unknown Arabia*. Woodstock: Overlook Press, 2000.

Manchester, William. *The Glory and the Dream*. Boston: Little, Brown, 1974.

Mansfield, Peter. *The Arabs*. London: Penguin Books, 1992.

de Marenches, [Alexandre], interviewed by Christine Ockrent. *The Evil Empire: The Third World War Now*. Translated by Simon Lee and Jonathan Marks. London: Sidgwick and Jackson, 1988.

Matar, 'Ala. "Matha Ba'd al-Mawaqif al-Jadeeda Liqada al-Gama'a al-Islamiyya?" [What After the New Positions of the Leadership of the Islamic Group?]. Translated by Mandi Fahmy. *Akhir Sa'ah*, February 2002, no. 3512, pp. 30–31.

McCullough, David. *Truman*. New York: Simon and Schuster, 1992.

Mayer, Jane. "The House of bin Laden." *New Yorker*, November 12, 2001.

Miller, John, and Michael Stone, with Chris Mitchell. *The Cell: Inside the 9/11 Plot, and Why the FBI and CIA Failed to Stop It*. New York: Hyperion, 2002.

"Min Ayman ila Walidataho" [From Ayman to His Mother]. Translated by Mandi Fahmy. *Al-Wasat*, February 21, 1994.

Mitchell, Richard P. *The Society of the Muslim Brothers.* New York: Oxford University Press, 1993.

Mohammed, Basil. *Al-Ansar al-Arab fi Afganistan.* [Pages from the Registry of Arab Cohorts in Afghanistan]. No translator given. Jeddah: House of Learning, 1991.

Moore, Robin. *The Hunt for bin Laden: Task Force Dagger.* New York: Random House, 2003.

Morris, Benny. *The Road to Jerusalem: Glubb Pasha, Palestine, and the Jews.* London: I.B. Taurus, 2002.

Moussalli, Ahmad S. *Radical Islamic Fundamentalism: The Ideological and Political Discourse of Sayyid Qutb.* Beirut: American University of Beirut, 1992.

Mubarak, Hisham. *Al-Irhabiyoon Qadimoon! Dirasa Muqarana Bayna Mawqif al-khwan al-Muslimoon wa Gama'at al-Gihad min Qadiat al-Unf 1938–1994* [The Terrorists Are Coming: A Comparative Study Between the Positions of the Muslim Brothers and the Jihad Groups on Violence 1938–1994]. Translated by Mandi Fahmy. Cairo, 1995.

Munthe, Turi. *The Saddam Hussein Reader.* New York: Thunder's Mouth Press, 2002.

Murphy, Dean E. *September 11: An Oral History.* New York: Doubleday, 2002.

Naftali, Timothy. *Blind Spot: The Secret History of American Counterterrorism.* New York: Basic Books, 2005.

Naguib, Sameh Khairy. "The Political Ideology of the Jihad Movement." Master's thesis, American University in Cairo, 1994.

Najm, Salah, and Jamal Ismail. "Osama bin Laden: Tadmeer al-Qaeda" [Osama bin Laden: The Destruction of the Base]. Translated by Dina Ibrahim. Al-Jazeera, June 10, 1999.

Nasr, Seyyed Hossein. *Islam: Religion, History, and Civilization.* San Francisco: HarperSanFrancisco, 2003.

Nasser, Khaled. "Zawjat bin Laden Tatahadath LilMajalla: Qisataho ma' Taliban wa Marath al-Kila wa Um Awad" [Bin Laden's Wife Speaks to Al-Majalla: Bin Laden's Story With the Taliban, Kidney Disease, and Um Awad]. Translated by Dina Ibrahim. *Al-Majalla,* March 2002, no. 1152, pp. 16–19.

National Commission on Terrorist Attacks Upon the United States. *The 9/11 Commission Report.* New York: Norton, 2004.

Nielsen, Jorgen. *Muslims in Western Europe.* Edinburgh: Edinburgh University Press, 1992.

Nojumi, Neamatollah. *The Rise of the Taliban in Afghanistan: Mass Mobilization, Civil War, and the Future of the Region.* New York: Palgrave, 2002.

Nutting, Antony. *Nasser.* New York: Dutton, 1972.

Obaid, Nawaf E. *The Oil Kingdom at 100: Petroleum Policymaking in Saudi Arabia.* Washington, D.C.: Washington Institute for Near East Policy, 2000.

Oshinsky, David M. *A Conspiracy So Immense: The World of Joe McCarthy.* New York: Macmillan, 1983.

Pesce, Angelo. *Jiddah: Portrait of an Arabian City.* Napoli: Falcon Press, 1977.

———. *Taif: The Summer Capital of Saudi Arabia.* Jeddah: Immel Publishing, 1984.

Peterson, J. E. *Saudi Arabia and the Illusion of Security.* New York: International Institute for Strategic Studies / Oxford University Press, 2002.

Petterson, Donald. *Inside Sudan: Political Islam, Conflict, and Catastrophe.* Boulder, Col.: Westview, 1999.

Posner, Gerald. *Why America Slept: The Failure to Prevent 9/11.* New York: Random House, 2003.

Qutb, Sayyid. *A Child from the Village.* Translated, edited, and introduced by John Calvert and William E. Shephard. Syracuse, N.Y.: Syracuse University Press, 2004.

———. "Al-dhamir al-amrikani wa qadiat filistin." Translated by Reham al-Sherif. *Al-Resala* 2 (October 21, 1946): 16–19.

———. "Amrika allati ra'ayt: fi mizan al-insaniyya." Translated by Reham al-Sherif. *Al-Resala* 957 (November 1951 [a]): 1245–46.

———. "Amrika allati ra'ayt: fi mizan al-insaniyya." Translated by Reham al-Sherif. *Al-Resala* 959 (November 1951 [b]): 1301–6.

———. "Amrika allati ra'ayt: fi mizan al-insaniyya." Translated by Reham al-Sherif. *Al-Resala* 961 (November 1951 [c]): 1357–60.

———. "Hamaim fi New York." Translated by Dina Ibrahim. *Majallat al-kitab* 8 (December 1949): 666–69.

———. *In the Shade of the Qur'an.* Translated by Adil Salahi. Vol. 6. Leicester: Islamic Foundation, 2002.

———. *Limadah 'azdamunee* [Why Do They Execute Me?]. Translated by Amjad M. Abu Nseir. www.hanein.net/modules.php?name=News&file=article&sid=162.

———. *Milestones.* Indianapolis, Ind.: American Trust Publications, 1990.

Raafat, Samir W. *Maadi 1904–1962: Society and History in a Cairo Suburb.* Cairo: Palm Press, 1994.

Raphaeli, Nimrod. "Ayman Muhammed Rab'i al-Zawahiri: Inquiry and Analysis." Middle East Media Research Institute. MEMRI.org, November 26, 2001.

Randal, Jonathan. *Osama: The Making of a Terrorist.* New York: Knopf, 2004.

al-Rasheed, Madawi. *A History of Saudi Arabia.* Cambridge: Cambridge University Press, 2002.

Rashid, Ahmed. *Taliban: The Story of the Afghan Warlords.* London: Pan Books, 2000.

———. *Jihad: The Rise of Militant Islam in Central Asia.* New Haven: Yale University Press, 2002.

Raymond, André. *Cairo.* Cambridge: Harvard University Press, 2000.

Reed, Betsy, ed. *Nothing Sacred: Women Respond to Religious Fundamentalism and Terror.* New York: Thunder's Mouth Press / Nation Books, 2002.

Reeve, Simon. *The New Jackals: Ramzi Yousef, Osama bin Laden, and the Future of Terrorism.* Boston: Northeastern University Press, 1999.

Rodenbeck, Max. *Cairo: The City Victorious.* New York: Knopf, 1999.

Roy, Olivier. *Afghanistan: From Holy War to Civil War.* Princeton, N.J.: Darwin Press, 1995.

Rubin, Barry. *Islamic Fundamentalism in Egyptian Politics.* London: Palgrave Macmillan, 2002.

———, ed. *Revolutionaries and Reformers: Contemporary Islamist Movements in the Middle East.* Albany: State University of New York Press, 2003.

Rubin, Barry, and Judith Colp Rubin. *Anti-American Terrorism and the Middle East: A Documentary Reader.* Oxford: Oxford University Press, 2002.

Sachar, Howard M. *A History of Israel: From the Rise of Zionism to Our Time.* New York: Knopf, 1996.

Sageman, Marc. *Understanding Terror Networks.* Philadelphia: University of Pennsylvania Press, 2004.

Salaah, Muhammad. "Al-Ahkam Fee Qadiat Sidqee Tasdur Ghadan al-Khamees" [The Verdict in Salah's Case Will Be Announced Tomorrow, Thursday]. Translated by May Ibrahim. *Al-Hayat,* March 15, 1994.

———. *Waqai' Sanawat al-Jihad: Rihlat al-Afghan al-Arab* [Years of Jihad: The Journey of the Arab-Afghans]. Translated by Mandi Fahmy. Cairo: Khuloud Publishing, 2001.

Schwartz, Stephen. *The Two Faces of Islam: The House of Sa'ud from Tradition to Terror.* New York: Doubleday, 2002.

Shadid, Anthony. *Legacy of the Prophet: Despots, Democrats, and the New Politics of Islam.* Boulder, Col.: Westview, 2002.

al-Shathilee, Farouk. "Juthoor al-Irhab" [The Roots of Terrorism]. Translated by May Ibrahim. *Akhbar al-Hawadath,* October 22, 1998, no. 342, pp. 34–35.

Shepard, William E. *Sayyid Qutb and Islamic Activism: A Translation and Critical Analysis of Social Justice in Islam.* Leiden: Brill, 1996.

Simons, Geoff. *Saudi Arabia: The Shape of a Client Feudalism.* New York: St. Martin's, 1998.

Sivan, Emmanuel. *Radical Islam: Medieval Technology and Modern Politics.* New Haven, Conn.: Yale University Press, 1985.

Smith, Dennis. *Report from Ground Zero.* New York: Viking, 2002.

Smucker, Philip. *Al-Qaeda's Great Escape: The Military and the Media on Terror's Trail.* Washington, D.C.: Brassey's, 2004.

Taheri, Amir. *Holy Terror.* London: Adler and Adler, 1987.

Tanner, Stephen. *Afghanistan: A Military History from Alexander the Great to the Fall of the Taliban.* New York: Da Capo Press, 2002.

Al-Tareeq ila 11 september [The Road to September 11]. A two-series documentary from the program *Siree Lilghaya* [*Top* Secret]. Translated by Dina Ibrahim. Al- Jazeera Satellite Channel, September 11, 2002.

Teitelbaum, Joshua. *Holier Than Thou: Saudi Arabia's Islamic Opposition.* Washington, D.C.: Washington Institute for Near East Policy, 2000.

Theroux, Paul. *The Pillars of Hercules: A Grand Tour of the Mediterranean.* New York: Putnam, 1995.

Theroux, Peter. *Sandstorms: Days and Nights in Arabia.* New York: Norton, 1990.

Thomas E. Burnett, Sr. v. al-Baraka Investment and Development Corporation, et al., Final Third Amended Complaint. Case Number 1:02CV01616 (JR) U.S. District Court for the District of Columbia, November 22, 2002.

The Two Holy Mosques. Riyadh: National Offset Printing Press, 1994.

Unger, Craig. *House of Bush, House of Saud.* New York: Scribner, 2004.

United Nations Development Programme. Regional Bureau for Arab States. *Arab Human Development Report 2002: Creating Opportunities for Future Generations.* 2002.

Wathaaiq Hizb al-Sharee'a [Al-Sharee'a Party's Documents]. Translated by Dina Ibrahim. Cairo: Markaz Yafa Lildirasat wa al-Abhath, 2000.

Weaver, Mary Anne. *A Portrait of Egypt: A Journey Through the World of Militant Islam.* New York: Farrar, Straus, and Giroux, 1999.

Weiss, Murray. *The Man Who Warned America: The Life and Death of John O'Neill, the FBI's Embattled Counterterror Warrior.* New York: Regan Books, 2003.

White, E. B. *Here Is New York.* New York: Little Bookroom, 1999.

Wiktorowicz, Quintan. "The New Global Threat: Transnational Salafis and Jihad." *Middle East Policy* 8, no. 4 (December 2001).

———, and John Kaltner. "Killing in the Name of Islam: Al-Qaeda's Justification for September 11." *Middle East Policy Council Journal* 10, no. 2 (Summer 2003).

Woodward, Bob. *The Commanders.* New York: Touchstone, 1991.

Wright, Lawrence. "The Counterterrorist." *New Yorker,* January 14, 2002.

———. "Kingdom of Silence." *New Yorker,* January 5, 2004.

———. "The Man Behind bin Laden." *New Yorker,* September 16, 2002.

Yamani, Hani A. Z. *To Be a Saudi.* London: Janus, 1997.

Yousaf, Mohammad, and Mark Adkin, *The Bear Trap: Afghanistan's Untold Story.* London: Leo Cooper, 1992.

Zaidan, Muwafak Ahmad. *Bin Laden Bila Qina'* [Bin Laden Unmasked]. Translated by Nidal Daraiseh. Beirut: Al-Sharika al-Alamiyya Lilkitab, 2003.

———. "Al-Natiq Alrasmee bi Ism Tala'I al-fath Ya'tarif BiMuhawalat Ightiyyal Ghali [The Official Spokesman for Fath Admits the Group Attempted to Assassinate Ghali]. Translated by Dina Ibrahim. *Al-Hayat,* May 15, 1994, no. 1135, p. 6.

Zaki, Mohamed Zaki. "Al-Zawahiri Kana Zameelee Fee al-Madrasa" [Al-Zawahiri Was My Classmate in School]. Translated by Mandi Fahmy. *Akhir Sa'ah,* October 2001, no. 3495, pp. 10–12.

Zarie, Mohammed. *In Defense of Prisoners' Rights: HRCAP Reports from 1997 to 2000.* Cairo: Human Rights Center for the Assistance of Prisoners, 1997.

al-Zawahiri, Ayman. *Fursan Taht Rayah al-Nabi* [Knights Under the Prophet's Banner]. Translated by Amjad M. Abu Nseir. Casablanca: Dar-al-Najaah al-Jadeedah, 2001.

———. *Al-Hasad al-Murr: al-Ikhwan al-Muslimonn Fee Sitoon* [Bitter Harvest: The Muslim Brothers in Sixty Years]. Translated by Mandi Fahmy. Dar al-Bayariq. No city, no date.

———. "Knights Under the Prophet's Banner." Translated by FBIS. *Al-Sharq al-Awsat,* December 2–12, 2001.

"Al-Zawahiri Yarud 'Ala Bush Bibayan Khasa bihee Filisteen" [Al-Zawahiri Responds to Bush in a Statement Specific on Palestine]. Translated by Amjad M. Abu Nseir. Al-Jazeera Satellite Channel. www.aljazeera.net/news/asia/2001/11/11-10-3.htm.

al-Zayyat, Montassir. *Al-Jamaat al-Islamiyya: Nathra Dakhiliyah* [Islamic Groups: An Internal View]. Translated by Amjad M. Abu Nseir. *Al-Hayat,* January 10–14, 2005.

———. *Ayman al-Zawahiri Kama 'Araftahoo* [Ayman al-Zawahiri as I Knew Him]. Translated by Amjad M. Abu Nseir. Cairo: Dar Misr al-Mahroosa, 2002.

———. *The Road to al-Qaeda: The Story of bin Laden's Right-Hand Man.* London: Pluto Press, 2004.

AUTHOR INTERVIEWS

Nicholas Abbott
Abdelaziz Osman Abdelaziz
Tourabi Abdellah
Genieve Abdo
Khaled S. Abu Rashid
Hafez Abu Saada
Victor Abu Said
Asma Afsaruddin
Iftikhar Ahmad
Ali al-Ahmed
Reem Akkad
Abu Ala-Mady
Alaweed bin Talal
Mohammed Alawwan
Hamid Algar
Mirza Ali
Mohammed Jasim el-Ali
Bassim A. Alim
Mohammed Alim
Tariq Ali Alireza
Fouad Allam
Jeff Allen
Graham Allison
Rogelio Alonzo
Abdel Monem Said Aly
Faiza Salah Ambah
Michael Ameen Jr.
Abdullah Anas
Frank Anderson

Lars Erslev Anderson
Sami Angawi
John M. Anticev
Michael Anticev
R. Scott Appleby
Gustavo de Aristegui
Grant Ashley
Saad Asswailim
Ghazi Salah Eddin Atabani
Abdel Bari Atwan
Gerald L. Auerbach
Juan Avilés
Mohammed Saleem al-Awa
Mohsin al-Awaji
Mohammed al-Awwam
Hussein al-Aydi
Javed Aziz
Sahar Aziz
Talal bin Abdul Aziz
Mahfouz Azzam
Maha Azzam
Omar Mahfouz Azzam
Nadia ba-Ashen
Yahia Hussein Babiker
Ahmed M. Badeeb
Saeed Badeeb
Robert Baer
Omar Bagour
Faisel Bajaber

Ramesh Balon
Gamal al-Banna
Shmuel Bar
Tom Barfield
Michael Barrett
Hasan Basweid
Khaled Batarfi
Faisal Batewil
Mohammed Loay Baizid
Milt Bearden
Waquih Bector
Mohammed bin Nasser Belfas
Harlen L. Bell
Daniel Benjamin
Robert Bentley
Peter L. Bergen
Sandy Berger
James Bernazzani, Jr.
Khaled al-Berri
Abdullah M. Binladen
Saleh M. Binladen
Mohammed A. bin Mahfooz
Sultan bin Salman
Alaweed bin Talal
Ghazi Faisal Binzagr
Jochen Bittner
Robert Blitzer
Philip Bobbitt
Waguih Boctor
Barbara Bodine
Steven A. Bongardt
Arnaud de Borchgrave
Theron Bouman
H. Braxton
Jean-Charles Brisard
Peter T. R. Brooks
Rachel Bronson
Jean-Louis Bruguiere
Ihsan Ali bu-Hulaiga
Paul Busick
Malik A. Ruiz Callejas
Robert Callus

John Calvert
Greg Campbell
Antonio Cañizares
Vincent Cannistraro
Joseph Cantemessa
Yigal Carmon
Timothy Carney
Jacobo Teijelo Casanova
Sharon Chadha
David Chambers
Robert Chambers
Gary Chapman
Françoise Chipaux
Frank Cilluffo
Richard A. Clarke
Jack Cloonan
Ray Close
Charles Cogan
Daniel J. Coleman
Denis Collins
Elizabeth O. Colton
John Cooley
Thomas F. Corrigan
Dina Corsi
Juan Cotino
Roger Cressey
Dominik Cziesche
Pasquale D'Amuro
Saeb Dajani
Thomas G. Donlon
Essam Deraz
Aida Self el-Dawla
Sarah al-Deeb
Agustín Diaz
Anna DiBattista
Tom Dillon
Teodoro Gómez Domínguez
Kevin Donovan
Joseph Doorley
Mary Deborah Doran
Eleanor Doumato
Joshua L. Dratel

Abdel Aziz al-Dukheil
Carson Dunbar
Charles Dunbar
Joseph Dunne
Elizabeth Durkee
Jack Eckenroad
Mohamed Salah Eddin
R. P. Eddy
Mohamed al-Edrisi
Paul Eedle
Abdel Wahab el-Effendi
Michael E. Elsner
Steven Emerson
Javier Jordán Enamorado
Elfatih Erwa
Emilio Lamo de Espinosa
Essam el-Eryan
John Esposito
Khaled Abou el-Fadl
Abdulaziz H. Fahad
Mandi Fahmy
Amr Mohamed al-Faisal
Reem al-Faisal
Saud al-Faisal
Turki al-Faisal
Mahmoun Fandy
Saad al-Faqih
Juan Avilés Farré
Jamil Farsi
Najla Fathi
Haizam Amirah Fernández
Elizabeth Fernea
Robert Fernea
Al Finch
Walid A. Fitaihi
Patrick Fitzgerald
Peggy A. Ford
Yosri Fouda
Wyche Fowler
Charles E. Frahm
Stephen Franklin
Louis J. Freeh

Alan Fry
Graham Fuller
Abdel Moneim Abdel Futuh
Neal Gallagher
Mary E. Galligan
Kathy Gannon
Antonio Maldonado García
Benigno Pendás García
Enrique García
Mike Garcia
Paul Garmirian
Diego López Garrido
Baltazar Garzón
Stephen J. Gaudin
F. Gregory Gause III
Fawaz Gerges
Hussein Abdel Ghani
Kevin P. Giblin
Hao Gilbertson
Heather Gregg
Klaus Grünewald
Stanley Guess
Hosnya Guindy
Hamid Gul
Rohan Gunaratna
Lou Gunn
Allan P. Haber
Kamal al-Sayyid Habib
Herb Haddad
Deborah Hadwell
Sayeed Abdul Hafez
Mohammed M. Hafez
Ali el-Haj
Lisa Gordon Haggerty
Abdul Rahman Haggog
Berhan Hailu
Yousef A. al-Hamdan
Khaled al-Hammadi
Andrew Hammond
Hussein Haqqani
Hasan al-Harithi
Mamdouh al-Harithi

Mohamed Haroun
Elias Harfouche
Peter Harrigan
Tom Hartwell
Saad Hasaballah
Khalid Hasan
Janullah Hashimzada
Badreldin Hassan
Hamza al-Hassan
Sulaiman al-Hatlan
Suliman Hathout
Hasan Hatrash
Jerome Hauer
Thomas Hegghammer
Kamal Helbawy
Clement Henry
Neil Herman
Ibrahim Hilal
Michael Hingson
Frank Hodgkins
Bruce Hoffman
Tariq al-Homayed
Ibrahim Hooper
Fahmi Howeidi
Steven Hughes
Mohammed I. al-Hulwah
Malik Hussein
Len Hutton
Hussein Ibish
Abdel Wahab Ibrahim
Dina Ibrahim
Saad Eddin Ibrahim
Bob Inman
Ibrahim Insari
José María Irujo
Christopher Isham
Farraj Ismail
Jamal Ismail
Mamdouh Ismail
Mahnaz Ispahani
Edward Jajko
Ali A. Jalali

Kevin James
Valerie James
Edward Jeep
Josef Joffe
Chris Johnson
Keith Johnson
Rocio Millán Johnson
Robert Jordan
Adl al-Jubair
Nail al-Jubair
James K. Kallstrom
Salah Abd al-Kareem
Hisham Kassem
Mahmoud Kassem
Theodore Kattouf
Rita Katz
Elaine Kaufman
Joseph Kechichian
David Kelley
Gilles Kepel
Abdul Rahman Khadr
Zaynab Ahmed Khadr
Jamal Khalifa
Ashraf Khalil
Imran Khan
Ismail Khan
Javed Aziz Khan
Jamal Ahmad Khashoggi
Khalid Khawaja
Mohammed al-Khereiji
Ramzi Khouri
Kathryn Kilgore
Daniel Kimmage
Judith Kipper
Kirk Kjeldsen
Bernard Kleinman
Bassma Kodmani
Evan Kohlmann
Michael Kortan
May Kutbi
Ben Kuth
Robert Lacey

Stéphane Lacroix
Donna Lee Lakin
Frank Lakin
Salah Lamei
Ted Landreth
Thomas F. Lang
Mohamed abd al-Latif
Fernando Lázaro
Rodney Leibowitz
Eric Lewis
Richard Lind
James Lindley
John Lipka
John J. Liguori
David Long
Bernabe López García
Douglas MacEachin
Petros Machas
Dittmar Machele
Khaled al-Maeena
Naguib Mahfouz
Wissal al-Mahdi
Saddiq al-Mahdi
Abdulaziz I. al-Mana
Abd al-Haleem Mandour
Jay C. Manning
Manuela Marín
Saad M. Mariq
Jonathan Marshall
Bobby Martin
Georg Mascolo
Rihab M. Massoud
Barry Mawn
Kenneth J. Maxwell
Ernest May
Andrew McCarthy
Pete McCloskey Jr.
Ken McConnellogue
Janet McElligot
Robert McFadden
John McKillop
Jaime McLendon

Frances Meade
Richard A. Meade
Dominic Medley
Amin el-Mehdi
Roel Meijer
Moneir Mahmoud Aly el-Messery
Cordula Meyer
John J. Miller
Marty Miller
John Mintz
Hamid Mir
Mustafa al-Mirabet
Hafez al-Mirazi
Assaf Moghadem
Mohammed el-Affi Mohammed
Rustam Shah Mohmand
Abdul Mohsin Mosallam
Rashid al-Mubarek
Ursulla Mueller
Manfred Murck
Kim Murphy
Richard Murphy
Virginia Murr
Ali al-Musa
Izzud-din Omar Musa
Khaled Musa
Mustapha el-M'Rabet
Ibrahim Nafie
Timothy Naftali
Hani Nagshabandi
Adil Najam
Louis A. Napoli
Octavia E. Nasr
Dona Abdel Nasser
Sami Saleh Nawar
Hisham Nazer
Sanna Negus
Soraya Sarhaddi Nelson
Salameh Nematt
Petter Nesser
Tim Niblock
Monsour al-Njadan

Yusuf Mohammed Noorwali
M. Arif Noorzai
Essam Noweira
Ayman Nur
Christine O'Neill
J. P. O'Neill
Hugh O'Rourke
Nawaf Obaid
Mohammed S. al-Odadi
Hassabulla Omer
Fathi Osman
George Pagoulatis
Emiliano Burdiel Pascual
Reuven Paz
Ami Pedahzur
Gareth Peirce
Francis J. Pellegrino
Benigno Pendás
Ramón Pérez-Maura
Thomas J. Pickard
William Ryan Plunkett
Javier Pogalan
Josh Pollack
Florentino Portero
Joachim Preuss
Jim Quilty
Mohammed Qutb
Khaled Rabah
Samir Rafaat
Nimrod Rafaeli
Abdullah Omar Abdul Rahman
Ahmed Abdul Rahman
Bahran Rahman
Osama Rajkhan
David C. Rapoport
Madawi al-Rasheed
Abdel Rahman al-Rashid
Mohamed Rashid
Diaa Rashwan
Ross Reiss
Jim Rhody
Hamid bin Ahmed al-Rifai

Lawrence K. Robinson
Jorge Rodríguez
Michael A. Rolince
Ken Rosenthal
James J. Rossini
Mark T. Rossini
Jim Roth
Olivier Roy
Michael Rubin
William Rugh
Usama Rushdi
Jeanne Ryan
Hafez Abu Saada
Mahmoud Sabit
Abdul Rahman al-Saeed
Marc Sageman
Muhammed Salaah
Salama Ahmed Salama
Ali Salem
Ysura Salim
Mohammed Salmawy
Maha Elsamneh
Bob Sama
Mujahid M. al-Sawwaf
Mohammed Sayed Tayib
Michael Scheuer
Lewis Schiliro
Abdallah Schleifer
Yoram Schweitzer
Deborah Scroggins
Abdul Aziz al-Sebail
Mohammed el-Shafey
Restum Shah
Rafiq Shaheed
Emad Eldeen Shahin
Mohammed Ali Al al-Shaikh
Said al-Shaikh
Ron Shapiro
Mohammed A. al-Sharif
Michael Sheehan
Abdullah al-Shehri
Virginia Sherry

Aziz Shihab
Myrna Shinbaum
David Shinn
Ekram Shinwari
Allen Shivers
Hussein Shobokshi
Mohammed Shoukany
Mahmoud Shukri
Asma Siddiki
Mazhar Siddiqi
Sabahat Siddiqi
Hani al-Siba'iy
Steven Simon
Yassir el-Sirri
Marvin Smilon
Philip Smucker
Ibrahim al-Sonousi
Ali H. Soufan
Jesper Stein
Guido Steinberg
Jessica Stern
Mary Lynn Stevens
Raymond Stock
Dominic Streatfeild
Abdullah Subhi
Ghassan al-Sulaiman
Gamal Sultan
Joseph Szlavik Jr.
Michael Taarnby
Nahed M. Taher
Azzam Tamimi
Lorraine di Taranto
Mohamed Saeed Tayeb
Jacobo Teijello
Joshua Teitelbaum
Peter Theroux
Omar Toor
Aldo J. Tos
Owais Towhid
Greg Treverton
Robert Tucker

Matthew Tueller
Hassan al-Turabi
Issam Eldin al-Turabi
Thomas Twetten
Abu Ubeida
Joe Valiquette
Reuben Vélez
Lorenzo Vidino
Bob Walsh
Janet Waters
Eric Watkins
Dale Watson
William F. Wechsler
Gabriel Weimann
Benjamin Weiser
Michael Welsh
Jeff Wharton
John V. Whitbeck
Mary Jo White
Wayne White
Robert Whithead
Larry Whittington
Quintan Wiktorowicz
Gina Abercrombie-Winstanley
Kelly Wojda
Wesley Wong
Hani Yamani
Mai Yamani
Hassan Yassin
Yehia J. Yehia
Khaled Yusuf
Rahimullah Yusufzai
Mark Zaid
Ali Zaki
Ezzat Zaki
Zaki Mohammed Zaki
Heba al-Zawahiri
Montasser al-Zayat
Ahmad Muaffaq Zaidan
Mohammed Zohair
Abdou Zuma

ACKNOWLEDGMENTS AND
NOTES ON SOURCES

LIES AND DECEPTION always pose a problem to a journalist who is trying to construct a truthful narrative, and in a project that largely relies on interviews with jihadis and intelligence operatives, the reader can suppose that there is a danger in placing too much trust in such sources. To complicate matters further, the early scholarship on the subject of al-Qaeda and the personalities that populate it was often shoddy and misleading. The Arabic press, which is essential to a chronicler of the lives of Zawahiri and bin Laden, is bridled by the autocratic governments in the region. Nor can one put too much faith in sworn testimony by witnesses who have already proved themselves to be crooks, liars, and double agents. How, then, does the writer choose which story to tell among so many conflicting and untrustworthy accounts?

Fortunately, some useful documents have surfaced in the five years since 9/11 that provide a reference for journalists who are looking for solid footing. Particularly helpful are "Tareek Osama" (the history of Osama), a collection of memos, letters, and notes that were taken from an al-Qaeda computer captured in Bosnia and entered into evidence in *United States v. Enaam Arnout;* a trove of e-mails and other correspondence that *Wall Street Journal* reporter Alan Cullison fortuitously acquired when he purchased what turned out to be a looted al-Qaeda computer in Kabul; and the important official papers of al-Qaeda, including its constitution and bylaws, many of which were gathered by the United States Department of Defense after the war in Afghanistan and form what is called the Harmony Documents. These items provide a bedrock of reliable information that can be useful in testing the trustworthiness of other sources.

Even these valuable materials can be misleading, however. For instance, the handwritten notes in "Tareek Osama" that record the critical meeting on August 11, 1988, when the term al-Qaeda first surfaces, give us a peek at what appears to be the moment of creation. As such, it is an essential scene in my narrative. However, the English translation that was provided to the court is often confounding. "I see that we should think in the origin of the idea we came for from the beginning," it says early on. "All this to start a new fruit from below zero." A better translation of this passage would be: "We should focus on the idea that brought us here in the first place. All this to start a new project from scratch." According to the document, the secretary who recorded these notes was bin Laden's friend Abu Rida al-Suri (Mohammed Loay Baizid), but when I interviewed him in Khartoum, he denied that he was even in Afghanistan or Pakistan in 1988. I don't know the truth of his assertion, but his name is on the document. Wa'el Julaidan, who refused to talk to me face-to-face, was in this meeting, and he agreed to answer my questions through an intermediary. He provided the surprising information that it was Abdullah Azzam who called it in the first place; he also gave me the names of the participants and described a vote that was taken at the end of the meeting on the formation of al-Qaeda. None of that is in the court documents. Medani al-Tayeb, who was al-Qaeda's treasurer, told me through an intermediary that the organization had already been formed before the August 11 meeting—he had joined the previous May—so the vote appears to have formalized the creation of an organization that already existed underground. I believe that the reader can begin to appreciate the murky nature of the world in which al-Qaeda operates and the imperfect means I have sometimes employed in order to gain information.

Similarly, I have had to compromise on reporting things I believe to be true but cannot prove. One tantalizing example is the fact that Prince Turki disclosed to the Associated Press on October 17, 2003, that as head of Saudi intelligence he had personally provided the names of two of the eventual September 11 hijackers, Nawaf al-Hazmi and Khaled al-Mihdhar, to the CIA in late 1999 or early 2000. "What we told them was these people were on our watch list from previous activities of al-Qaeda, in both the embassy bombings and attempts to smuggle arms into the kingdom in 1997," Turki said at the time. This would explain the CIA's sudden interest in those men around the date of the meeting in Malaysia of the hijackers and the USS *Cole* bombers. The CIA furiously rejected Turki's comments, and the Saudi ambassador to the United States, Prince Bandar bin Sultan, clarified his cousin's statement by saying that there were "no documents" sent by Saudi Arabia regarding the hijackers to American intelligence. At the time, Turki stood by his statement, maintaining that he had passed the information, at least orally. I had confirmation of his claim from Nawaf Obaid, a security consultant for the Saudi government, who told me that the names of the future hijackers were given to the CIA's chief of station in Riyadh. Now, however, Turki, who has replaced Bandar at the Saudi embassy in Washington, says that, after reviewing his notes, he was wrong; he himself never gave information about any hijackers to the Americans. Because of his outright denial, I removed this version of the story from the text. I cite it here to address the questions that might pose themselves to readers who know about this episode, and also to acknowledge the crosscurrents of politics and diplomacy that sometimes pull the real story, whatever it may be, frustratingly out of reach.

The reporting of this book has required constant checking of hundreds of sources against each other, and it is in this back-and-forth inquiry that the approximate truth—the most reliable facts—can be found. One might call this horizontal reporting, since it takes into account the views of as many participants as are willing to talk. Although the list is long, it is certainly not complete. There are key people in the American intelligence community, particularly in the CIA, who declined to meet with me; moreover, many of the best sources in al-Qaeda are being held by American authorities, not only secretly but also in U.S. prisons, where they are kept apart from any contact with the press, despite my pleas to their wardens and the judges in their cases. A full history of al-Qaeda cannot be told until they are allowed to talk.

There is another axis of reporting, a vertical one, that has more to do with understanding than with simple facts. Some of the people in this book I have interviewed in depth dozens of times. Invariably, the most profitable conversations are ones that come after a degree of trust has developed between the journalist and his source. This relationship is fraught with problems, since trust and friendship go hand in hand. Knowledge is seductive; the reporter wants to know, and the more he knows, the more interesting he becomes to the source. There are few forces in human nature more powerful than the desire to be understood; journalism couldn't exist without it. But the intimacy that comes with sharing secrets and unburdening profound feelings invites a reciprocal degree of friendly protection that a reporter cannot always offer. By the conspicuous use of a tape recorder and extensive note-taking, I try to remind both of us that there is a third party in the room, the eventual reader.

I have strained to keep the use of anonymous sources to a minimum. As a reader, I often question the reliability of unsourced information, and so I've dragged as many of my informants into the light as possible. Some sources habitually start an interview by saying it is off the record, but they may later approve specific quotes or intelligence when asked. Where there remain items that are not tied to specific individuals or documents, they represent vital information that I have good reason to accept as true.

THIS BOOK comes heavily mortgaged to the generosity of hundreds of people. Although I can never repay their kindness, I hope they will feel that I have honored their trust.

Sayyid Qutb may have been miserable in Greeley, Colorado, but he did not have the advantage of meeting Peggy A. Ford, the archives and research coordinator at the City of Greeley Museum, or Janet Waters, the head of archival services at the James A. Michener Library of the University of Northern Colorado, who made themselves and their useful files available. Ken McConnellogue, the vice president for university advancement at the same institution, graciously provided vital background information; and Michael Welsh, a professor of history, took me around the campus and the town and gave me such an insightful and delightful tour that I came away envying his students.

Foreign correspondents rely on "fixers" to guide them through cultures they barely understand. Fixers make appointments, translate, and often provide context that a stranger could never grasp on his own. In Cairo, I was especially blessed by the delightful company of Mandi Fahmy, as well as Rola Mahmoud and Jailan Zayan. Samir Rafaat was an invaluable escort into the Maadi childhood of Dr. Ayman al-Zawahiri. I am deeply indebted to Mahfouz Azzam and Omar Azzam for their patient and gracious responses to my endless queries. Gamal al-Banna and Essam el-Eryan provided invaluable insights on the Muslim Brotherhood, and Kamal Habib was highly informative about the origins of al-Jihad. Mamdouh Ismail, Gamal Sultan, and Montassir al-Zayyat were indispensable informants on Islamic movements, and Fouad Allam helped me understand the government's response to the challenges such organizations posed. Abdallah Schleifer was a source of great insight and amusement, and a surprisingly fine cook to boot. Saad Eddin Ibrahim, fresh from prison and still suffering the effects of that ordeal, was kind enough to give me the benefit of his invaluable research. For their friendship and hospitality, I particularly thank Jan and Safwat Montassir, Sanna Hannonen Negus, Dr. Abdul Wahab Ibrahim and Aida el-Bermawy, Raymond Stock, Jim Pringle and Samia el-Bermawy, Essam Deraz, Ali Salem, and my old professor Dr. Yehia el-Ezabi.

I spent more than a year after 9/11 seeking a visa from the Kingdom of Saudi Arabia. Finally, realizing that I wasn't going to get in as a reporter, I took a job "mentoring" young reporters at the *Saudi Gazette* in Jeddah, bin Laden's hometown. This serendipitous ploy permitted me an understanding of Saudi society that I could never have gained from the journalist's lofty vantage. For that, I have to thank Dr. Ahmed al-Yousef, the editor in chief; Dr. Mohammed Shoukany, the editor who invited me into his newsroom in the first place; and my colleagues Iftikar Ahmed, Ramesh Balon, Ramzi Khouri, and Mazhar Siddiqi. My greatest teachers, however, were my reporters: Faisal Bajaber, Hasan Basweid, Najla Fathi, Mamdouh al-Harithi, Hasan Hatrash, Mohammed Zoheb Patel, Mahmoud Shukri, and Sabahat Siddiqi. I owe a great debt to the generous spirits of Faiza Ambah, Elizabeth O. Colton, Dr. Khaled Batarfi, Berhan Hailu, Peter Harrigan, Jamal Khalifa, Jamal Khashoggi, Khaled al-Maeena, Dr. Abdullah al-Shehri, Hussein Shobokshi, and Gina Abercrombie-Winstanley, who made my journeys to the Kingdom both productive and enjoyable.

In Pakistan, I shamelessly milked my colleagues for their experiences in covering the jihad. I thank Kathy Gannon of Associated Press, Françoise Chipaux at *Le Monde,* Jamal Ismail at Abu Dhabi television, Ismail Khan at *Dawn,* Rahimullah Yusufzai at the *News of Islamabad,* and Ahmed Muaffaq Zaidan at al-Jazeera. Mahnaz Ispahani provided a very useful overview of the country and some invaluable sources as well. Despite the vast difference that separated our views of the world, Khaled Khawaja went to great lengths to help me understand his perspective. I am particularly indebted to Zaynab Ahmed Khadr for sharing her intimate memories of life in the al-Qaeda community during our many conversations in Pakistan and Canada. Bahram Rahman guided me through Afghanistan, and his company was always a pleasure. I think I still owe Dominic Medley a drink at the Hotel Mustafa.

Issam Eldin al-Turabi was a very entertaining and enlightening host during my several trips to Sudan. I'm also grateful to Mohammed Loay Baizid for entrusting me with his recollections, and to Hassabulla Omer for candidly discussing the dilemma bin Laden posed to Sudanese intelligence.

Georg Mascolo and his investigative team at *Der Spiegel* did first-rate work uncovering the secret life of the Hamburg cell. Georg lent me one of his finest reporters, Cordula Meyer, to be my guide during my time in Hamburg, and I depended on her insights for my portrait of the hijackers in Germany. I am also grateful to Dr. Guido Steinberg in Berlin, the former head of counterterrorism for the chancellor's office, whose expertise on terrorism helped shape my understanding. In Spain, I was assisted by Rocio Millán Johnson, an enterprising reporter and a wonderful spirit. I am also grateful to Emilio Lamo de Espinosa and Haizam Amirah Fernández of the Real Instituto Elcano. Gustavo de Aristegui was a challenging intellectual companion during my time in Madrid. Juan Cotino, Enrique García, Emiliano Burdiel Pascual, and Teodoro Gómez Domínguez of the national police were extremely accommodating. I also want to acknowledge my colleagues: Fernando Lázaro at *El Mundo,* José María Irujo at *El País,* Ramón Pérez Maura at *ABC,* and especially Keith Johnson at the *Wall Street Journal,* each of whom generously helped me with sources and information.

The first time I went to interview Gilles Kepel, professor of Middle East Studies at the Institute for Political Studies in Paris, he asked me to teach his class instead. It turned out to be the best introduction to a man whose groundbreaking work on Islamism in Egypt has shaped the scholarship of this movement. His students are a powerful and enduring reflection of his influence. I am also very much indebted to the hospitality of my former editor at *The New Yorker,* Lee Aitken, and to my friends Christopher and Carol Dickey, who made my trips to Paris so much more enjoyable than they would have been without their delightful company. Olivier Roy, a profound scholar, was kind enough to share his thoughts with me on several occasions; and the courageous counterterrorism judge Jean-Louis Bruguière gave me the benefit of his unique understanding of al-Qaeda.

London is a special stop for any reporter interested in Islamism and jihad. Some of my best sources have been granted political asylum, and they willingly talked to me despite the threat that their status might be changed at any time. I'm particularly thankful to Yassir el-Sirri, Usama Rushdi, and Hani el-Siba'iy. Abdullah Anas and Kemal Helbawi were great friends to me during my visits and made important contributions to my understanding of the Arab Afghan experience. Alan Fry of Scotland Yard shared the British counterterrorist perspective with me. Yosri Fouda, the star reporter for al-Jazeera, was a welcome companion on several very memorable evenings. Abdul Rahman al-Rashid, the former editor of *Al-Sharq al-Awsat,* was a generous informant, and his successor in that chair, Tariq al-Homayed, has been a kindred spirit since we first met in Jeddah. I want to pay especial tribute to Mohammed el-Shafey, a great reporter who has covered terrorism and radical Islam for years at *Al-Sharq al-Awsat.* Many thanks to him for his kindness.

I owe a particular debt to Richard A. Clarke, who was a very patient tutor in the ways of Washington. At the FBI, I will always appreciate the candor of the members of the I-49 squad, especially Jack Cloonan, Daniel Coleman, Mark Rossini, and Ali Soufan, each of whom I interviewed countless times. Without them, there would be no book, it's that simple. Pasquale D'Amuro made sure that the New York office was open to me, and for his trust, I am deeply grateful. Joe Valiquette and Jim Margolin assisted me by arranging interviews that often went on long after the offices closed. At headquarters, I would like to thank John Miller, Michael Kortan, and Angela Bell, who were very helpful in setting up interviews and providing information. Michael Scheuer was a candid guide to the culture of Alec Station and the CIA. His scholarship on bin Laden and al-Qaeda are unsurpassed. There are other people in the American intelligence community I cannot name who have been extremely helpful.

Three women—Anna DiBattista, Valerie James, and Mary Lynn Stevens—shared their often painful memories of John O'Neill, and I was privileged to be entrusted with their stories.

Languages naturally posed a barrier, so I would like to thank the translators that I have hired all over the world. In Arabic: my former assistant Dina Ibrahim was absolutely invaluable, not just because of her skillful translation; also Dina's sister May, and on occasion their mother Aida; my Arabic instructor, Amjad M. Abu Nseir; Jilan Kamel; Nidal Daraiseh, another valued assistant; and Reham al-Sharif in Cairo. In German: Ralf Jaeger and Chester Rosson. In French and Italian: Caroline Wright. In Spanish: Rocio Millán Johnson, Frank Hodgkins, and Major Edward Jeep.

Portions of this book appeared in *The New Yorker;* indeed, this project began on September 11, 2001, when I asked the editor, David Remnick, to put me to work. Since then I have had the benefit of that magazine's exacting editorial assistance. Jeffrey Frank, Charles Michener, and Daniel Zalewski have each handled articles that contribute to the final product. I am always indebted to *The New Yorker*'s fact-checkers, my favorite department of the magazine, which is overseen by Peter Canby. Checkers who have assisted me on this project include Gita Daneshjoo, Boris Fishman, Jacob Goldstein, Marina Harss, Austin Kelley, Nandi Rodrigo, Andy Young, and particularly Nana Asfour, who also served as the Arabic translator for several important interviews. I owe a huge debt to Natasha Lunn, the magazine's photo editor, who drew together many of the images that have been included in this book.

Many people assisted in getting me visas or access to people that I could never have approached on my own. Janet McElligot and Milt Bearden were extremely kind in this regard. In addition to helping to shape the ideas for this book, Elizabeth Fernea actually found me the job in Saudi Arabia. Her contribution is apparent all through this work.

There is a small group of private scholars whose work on terrorism has been of great assistance to journalists, and I want to thank Rita Katz and the SITE Institute, Steven Emerson and Lorenzo Vidino of the Investigative Project, and Evan F. Kohlmann for making materials available from their collections. I'm also indebted to Michael Elsner at the Motley Rice law firm, who generously let me prowl through their impressive archive. Karen Greenburg and the staff of the Center on Law and Security at the New York University School of Law have provided an intellectual testing ground for many of the ideas explored in this book.

I am fortunate to be a part of a virtual community, Gulf 2000, created by Gary Sick, adjunct professor of international affairs and the former director of the Middle East Institute at Columbia University. G2K, as its members call it, has proved to be an absolutely invaluable resource of scholarship and shared ideas.

Journalists count on each other even when they are competing. In addition to the colleagues I've already mentioned, I would particularly like to acknowledge the assistance of CNN's terrorism analyst, Peter L. Bergen, John Burnett with National Public Radio, Chris Isham of ABC News, Stephen Franklin at the *Chicago Tribune,* Jonathan Ledgard at *The Economist,* and Philip Smucker at *Time,* each of whom gave me the benefit of their greater experience and many valuable contacts. They are courageous souls and valued friends.

Kirk Kjeldsen, who on 9/11 was a reporter for *Waters* magazine, happened to be late for a meeting in the World Trade Center that morning, and because he fell asleep on the subway he survived to tell me his story, which became a part of *The New Yorker*'s now-famous black issue of September 24, 2001. Kirk also did me the favor, as a colleague, of attending John O'Neill's memorial service and interviewing some of O'Neill's friends and coworkers on that occasion.

Will Haber gave me valued assistance, as did Mona Abdel-Halim, who has become a trusted sounding board. Jan McInroy has been my preferred copy editor for many years, and I always count on her judgment. I am especially reliant on Nora Ankrum, who helped me organize the mass of information into fourteen boxes of note cards. Her cheerful presence lightened this sometimes daunting task.

I owe a special debt to Stephen Harrigan and Gregory Curtis, dear friends, who read the book in its rawest form and made extremely helpful suggestions. It was Steve who suggested writing this book in the first place. Peter Bergen, Rachel Bronson, John Calvert, Steve Coll, Mary Deborah Doran, Thomas Hegghammer, Michael Rolince, Marc Sageman, and Michael Welsh read all or portions of the book and gave me the benefit of their expertise. The errors that remain in the book are my responsibility, but there are fewer of them thanks to the generosity of these patient readers.

My friend and agent, Wendy Weil, campaigned for this project; fortunately, Ann Close, who edited three of my previous books, reunited with me on this one. I am grateful to have my team back together! My wife, Roberta, supported my decision to do this book, although it meant that we were apart for much of the nearly five years that it has taken to accomplish. I'm so happy to be home.

INDEX

ABC news, 299, 300, 306
Abdel-Halim, Shayma, 211
Abdu, Mohammed, 208
Abdul Aziz, King of Saudi
    Arabia, 72–3, 75, 76, 80, 103,
    167, 453n
Abdullah, Ahmed (Ahmed the
    German), 306–7, 308
Abdullah, King of Saudi Arabia,
    112, 177–8, 227, 239, 251, 302,
    400
Abdul Rahman, Sheikh Omar,
    (the "blind sheikh"), 65, 109,
    196, 203, 209, 244, 251, 273, 314,
    357, 387, 475n; fatwas issued
    by, 66, 201, 209; as leader of
    Islamic Group, 66; recruitment
    by, 200–201; rivalry with
    Zawahiri, 158; sponsors of, 66;
    tactical disagreements with
    Zawahiri, 67; and Sadat
    assassination, 65; U.S. asylum
    sought by, 201; in U.S. prison,
    291, 293, 296
Abu Abdul Rahman, 156
Abu Hafs al-Masri (Mohammed
    Atef), 130, 148, 150, 162, 284,
    343, 348–9, 374, 375
Abu Hajer al-Iraqi (Mamdouh
    Mahmoud Salem), 132, 150–1,

152, 193–4, 195, 197, 198–9,
    227, 263, 466n
Abu Jandal, 281–2, 328, 382,
    410–13
Abu Khabab, 343
Abu Nidal Organization, 196
Abu Rida al-Suri (Mohammed
    Loay Baizid), 126, 133, 151–2,
    153, 214, 224, 227, 253n, 433n,
    466n, 478n
Abu Ubaydah al-Banshiri (Amin
    Ali al-Rashidi), 130, 134,
    136–7, 147–8, 150, 153, 162,
    262–3, 284, 375
Adham, Sheikh Kamal, 98
al-Adl, Saif, 253, 328, 375, 466n
al-Adnani, Sheikh Tameem,
    131–3, 134, 135–6, 155
Afghanistan, 163, 171, 183, 193,
    206, 208, 227, 231, 240, 246,
    252, 255–62, 266, 276, 278, 316,
    320, 340, 365, 372, 374, 410,
    461n–2n; al-Qaeda base and
    operations in, 284–90, 349–50,
    418–21; anti-Soviet jihad in, 4,
    53–4, 70, 109–13, 117–38, 194,
    325; bin Laden's retreat to,
    252–3; civil war in, 254–5,
    255–6, 400; opium trade in, 53,
    259; refugees from, 52, 53;

530   *Index*

Afghanistan *(continued)*
Soviet occupation of, 4, 55, 109–13, 114–15, 148, 157, 179, 256–7; U.S. attacks on al-Qaeda in, 309, 416, 418–19, 420
Ahmed the German, *see* Abdullah, Ahmed
Ahmed, Siddiq, 328
Alec Station, 3–6, 273, 274–5, 301, 351, 353–4, 358, 395, 435n
al-Alfi, Hasan, 211
Algeria, 41, 142, 162, 215–17, 221
Ali, Fourth Caliph, 56n, 141
Allam, Fouad, 62, 450n–1n
Anas, Abdullah, 120, 149, 154–5, 163, 216
Al-Ansar (GIA newspaper), 216
Ansar al-Islam, 335
Anticev, John, 272–3, 314
Anticev, Mike, 272–3
al-Aqsa Mosque, 84
Arab Afghans, 121–4, 126, 141, 147, 149, 153–4, 239, 240, 462n
Arab world; dismay at embassy bombings of, 308–9, 323; Israeli military dominance as humiliation for, 11, 28, 45, 46; view of anti-Soviet jihad within, 53–4; views of U.S. in, 10–11, 27
Arafat, Yasser, 150
Aramco, 74, 75, 453n
Aref, Abdul Salam, 35–6
Army, U.S., al-Qaeda members in, 204–6
Army Corps of Engineers, U.S., 173, 176
Arnett, Peter, 279–80
Atef, Khadija, 376–8
Atef, Mohammed, *see* Abu Hafs al-Masri
Atta, Mohammed, 345–7, 349–50, 390, 413
al-Attas, Mohammed, 84–5

Attash, Tewfiq bin, *see* Khallad
Attorney's Office, U.S., 5–6, 300, 383, 389
Atwan, Abdel Bari, 279
al-Awdah, Salman, 426
Azerbaijan, 283–4, 304
al-Azhar University, 40, 109, 115, 208
Azzam, Abdullah, 109–12, 116–19, 120, 125, 126–7, 128, 131, 134–5, 149, 163–4, 256–7, 266, 314, 375, 466n; assassination of, 164; future of jihad and, 150–1; jihad recruitment by, 121–4; as obstacle to Egyptian inner circle, 154–7; rivalry with Zawahiri of, 149–50; U.S. fundraising by, 204
Azzam, Abdul Wahhab, 40
Azzam, Ibrahim, 164
Azzam, "Jihad Ali," 300, 306, 307
Azzam, Mahfouz, 42–3, 48, 53–4, 62
Azzam, Mohammed, 164
Azzam, Omar, 60
Azzam, Umayma (Ayman al-Zawahiri's mother), 39, 40, 42, 69

Badeeb, Ahmed, 86, 89, 115, 164, 174–5, 251, 258, 455n
Badeeb, Saeed, 220, 351
Bahareth, Sheikh Mohammed Salah, 85, 86
Baizid, Mohammed Loay, *see* Abu Rida al-Suri
Bandar bin Sultan, Prince of Saudi Arabia, 172
Bangladesh, 284, 295, 340
al-Banna, Hasan, 18–19, 125
Bashar, Haji, 257
al-Bashir, Omar Hasan, 186, 251
Batarfi, Khaled, 85–6

Bayoumi, Omar, 354–5
Bechtel, 74, 75, 173
Benotman, Noman, 426
Beirut, 197, 211
Bergen, Peter, 279, 451*n*
Berger, Sandy, 323
bin Baz, Abdul Aziz, 104, 118,
181, 222
bin al-Khatab, Omar, 419
bin Laden, Abdullah, 92, 219,
220–1, 458*n*
bin Laden, Abdul Rahman, 92–3,
220–1, 288, 382
bin Laden, Ali, 94, 221
bin Laden, Bakr, 222
bin Laden, Carmen, 90, 455*n*
bin Laden, Fatima, 285–6, 287
bin Laden, Hamza, 94, 377
bin Laden, Iman, 287
bin Laden, Khadija, 285, 286
bin Laden, Khaled, 94
bin Laden, Mahrous, 108–9
bin Laden, Mohammed (son),
376–7, 382
bin Laden, Mohammed bin
Awahd, 175–6, 452*n*;
background of, 71, 73;
business success of, 73–6,
77–82; children of, 82, 84, 85,
86, 94; death of, 85, 86;
divorces of, 82, 84; as idolized
by Osama, 71; illiteracy of,
74, 94–5; personality and
appearance of, 74, 82, 83–4;
ties to Saudi royal family of,
75, 77, 78–9, 97–8; wives of,
82–4; work habits and
reputation of, 71, 74–5, 76, 81
bin Laden, Omar, 220, 253
bin Laden, Osama, 88–9, 106,
108–9, 115, 126–7, 186, 189–90,
198, 293, 295, 296, 314–15, 451*n*,
468*n*, 484*n*; and Afghan civil
war, 183–4; Algerian support

withdrawn from, 217; analysis
of U.S. by, 213–15, 391; as anti-
Communist, 173–5; and anti-
Soviet jihad, 4, 70, 108–13,
115–21; Arab Afghans'
dependence on, 247; Azzam's
influence on, 109–10, 111–12;
assassination attempts on, 184,
218–20, 321–2, 327–9, 478*n*;
athletic interests of, 86, 89,
90–1, 288; attacks led by, 126–7,
128, 133–4; attempt to
assassinate Clinton of, 267;
bodyguards of, 220, 253, 298,
328, 410; and break with
Khalifa, 129–31; business
failures of, 223–4, 226; cave
imagery and tactics of, 131,
142, 264–5, 266; childhood and
adolescence of, 70–1, 83–90;
children of, 92–3, 94, 190,
219–21, 286, 287–8, 298; CIA
plans to neutralize, 274–5,
301–2, 330; on coalition troops,
182; concerns about Azzam of,
164; consultation with Saudi
intelligence of, 164; courted by
Sudan, 186–7; criminal case
against, 5, 277, 301–2, 309,
372–4; Crusades invoked by, 4,
237–8; daily life in Sudan of,
187–92, 218–21; death of, 423;
deprivation sought by, 87, 281;
desire to return home of, 226–7,
228–9; dream interpretation
by, 402–3; dream of Islamic
peninsula, 180; early
conservatism on sex of, 87;
early relations with family of,
85–6, 87; education of, 86–7,
89–90, 94–5; Egyptians in inner
circle of, 130, 148–9, 154–7, 161,
162, 220, 228–9, 328; as emir,
158; Fahd loathed by, 227; fame

bin Laden, Osama *(continued)*
and position in Saudi Arabia
of, 165, 170–1, 172–3, 175–6;
family condemnation of, 222;
and family firm, 88–9, 95;
family reconciliation attempts
of, 227–9; farming interests of,
91, 92, 108, 191–2, 228; fatwas
issued by, 4, 265–6, 279, 307;
final will and bequests of, 419;
finances and wealth of, 254,
282, 284, 298, 306, 469n–70n;
"frank manifesto" of, 238–9; on
future of jihad after
Afghanistan, 152; future of
jihad envisioned by, 128;
generosity to friends of, 93;
global pressure on Saudis to
stop, 221–2; goals of, 150;
health of, 136, 137, 159–61, 184,
288, 299, 301, 464n, 468n–9n;
horses as interest of, 189, 288;
identification with Prophet of,
263–5; image management by,
217, 377; increased al-Qaeda
status of, 218, 375; interviews
of, 278–80, 297–300, 303, 306;
and Iraqi invasion of Kuwait,
178–80; jihadist leadership
taken by, 155; as key to al-
Qaeda formation, 375; in
leadership of anti-Soviet jihad,
117–21, 126–38; links to A. Q.
Khan of, 300; Lion's Den
defended by, 134–8; loss of
followers of, 263; loyalty
pledge to Mullah Omar by,
326, 411; loyalty valued by, 221;
management style of, 190–2,
424–5; and martyrdom, 124; M.
bin Laden recalled by, 71, 75,
82–4, 85, 94–5; meeting with
Khaled Sheikh Mohammed,
266–7; merging of Islamist

groups under, 208–9, 215;
mother of, *see* Ghanem, Alia;
Muslim Brotherhood joined by,
90; at Najm al-Jihad, 259–60;
9/11 assignments made by,
348, 350; 9/11 monitored by,
403–4, 416–17; offered to U.S.
by Sudan, 251, 481n; oil wealth
seen as westernizing by, 195–6;
O'Neill's focus on, 237, 274,
275, 390; 'Owhali meeting
with, 316; in Pakistan, 183–4,
419–20; parents' divorce and,
84–5; passport returned to, 183;
passport revoked of, 222;
personality and appearance of,
87, 91, 95–6, 120–1, 171, 179–80,
189, 190, 249, 250, 458n;
philosophy of terrorism of,
298; polygamy practiced by,
93–4; popular support of,
323–4; press conferences given
by, 297–300; primitive persona
adopted by, 266; private army
of, 161–2, 165, 179; publicity as
currency for, 297–8; Qutb's
influence on, 91–2; raised
international profile of, 297–8;
recruitment for jihad by, 120,
375, 382; reframing of hijira by,
263–5; relations with Iraq of,
176–7, 178, 335; religious and
political awakening of, 87–90;
on religious duties, 394–5;
risk-taking of, 89, 91; rivalries
of, 131–3, 187–8, 197; satellite
phones of, 321, 388; Saudi
and Taliban cooperation on,
302–4; Saudi attempt to
reconcile with, 227; Saudi
citizenship revoked, 222; Saudi
complicity with, 172–3; Saudi
reforms demanded by, 238–9;
Saudi refusal to deal with, 251;

Saudi royal family anger with, 175–6, 177; Saudi royal family denounced by, 222, 229, 238–9, 278, 279; seizure of assets of, 223; self-created mythos of, 183, 265–6, 280; Sheik Omar Abdul Rahman financed by, 201; standing in social circle of, 88; Sudanese investments of, 188, 190–1, 253*n*, 260, 275; Sudan expulsion of, 249, 250–3; support of clergy against royal family sought by, 180; suspicions of Islamists about, 295; as symbolic figure of resistance, 323–4; Taliban relations with, 260, 280–1, 325–6, 336, 374, 401; on technology, 228; and terrorist attacks in Pakistan, 247; Tomahawk missiles acquired by, 323; UAE princes visits with, 329–30; in United Kingdom, 93; uranium sought by, 217–18; U.S. intelligence on, 3–7, 207, 273, 309–10, 311–12, 329–30; U.S. seen as enemy by, 146, 170–3, 213–14, 237–8, 298, 299; and U.S. support in Afghanistan, 172; on violence within Saudi Arabia, 227–8, 228, 241; war on U.S. declared by, 4, 279, 307; wives of, 90, 93–4, 220–1, 260, 281, 285, 286–7, 298, 332, 377, 382; *see also specific wives* (Umm Abdullah, Umm Ali, Umm Hamza, Umm Khaled, and Amal al-Sada); Yemeni guerrilla war financed by, 173–5; Zawahiri's alliance and relationship with, 70, 146–50, 159–61, 220, 284, 296, 380; *see also* Afghanistan; al-Qaeda

bin Laden, Othman, 382
bin Laden, Saad, 253
bin Laden, Salem, 105, 106
bin Laden, Sheikha, 112
bin Rasheed, Khaled Saleem, *see* al-'Owhali, Mohammed
bin Suleiman, Sheikh Abdullah, 75
Bleakley, Albert M., 240
Bodine, Barbara, 364–7, 369–71, 372, 404
Bongardt, Steven, 385, 399, 403, 405
Bosnia, 149, 185, 240, 262, 341, 346, 349, 410
Bouazizi, Mohammed, 431
"Brigade of the Strangers," 121, 126
Britain, 222, 294, 344, 375; Egyptian occupation by, 10, 29–31, 38; Nasser's negotiation with, 32; weapon sales in Saudi Arabia of, 176
Brown, Marion, 276–7
Bulgaria, 252, 282
Bush, George H. W., 182
Bush, George W., 378, 381
Bushnell, Prudence, 307

Cairo, Egypt, 11–12, 13, 14, 45, 53–4
Cairo University, 29–30, 40, 47, 69
Canada, 338, 420
Carney, Timothy, 250
cells, terrorist, 6, 30, 44–5, 47, 48, 58, 69, 241, 297, 336, 337; *see also specific organizations*
Central Intelligence Agency (CIA), 3, 20, 107, 115, 154, 203, 206, 220, 235, 250, 269, 274, 304, 352, 353, 357, 383–4; dismissal of warnings on embassy bombings by, 311–12; information withheld by, 386,

Central Intelligence Agency (CIA) *(continued)* 395, 408–9; Islamists cells penetrated by, 204–5; lack of information on al-Qaeda of, 301, 353; plans to neutralize bin Laden of, 274–5, 301–2, 330; Saudi cooperation with, 351, 353; terror warnings given by, 336; Turki's work with, 168–9, 179; *see also* Alec Station; intelligence, U.S.

Chalhub, Michel, *see* Sharif, Omar, 41

Chechnya, 185, 262, 283, 297, 341, 346

chemical weapons, 217–18, 319–20, 343–4

Cheney, Dick, 178, 239

China, 16, 176

Christianity, 16, 17, 45, 66, 78, 83, 180, 194

Clark, Tom, 16

Clarke, Richard A., 230, 233–5, 275, 310, 319, 321, 330, 338, 378–79, 380, 383, 386, 389–90, 416, 471*n*, 481*n*, 484*n*

Clinton, Bill, 98, 203, 215, 251, 267, 300, 305, 319–20, 325, 346, 367, 374, 387, 391

Cloonan, Jack, 273, 317, 319, 337, 395

CNN, bin Laden interview with, 278–80

Cole, USS, 350, 351, 352, 384–5, 397, 398, 408, 414, 428; attack on, 360–1; bin Laden's poem about, 376; investigation of attack on, 361–74, 390; repairs made to, 369; U.S. retaliation for, 374

Coleman, Daniel, 3–6, 273, 274–7, 301–2, 304, 309, 317–18, 329, 407, 414, 423, 475*n*

Collins, Michael, 390, 392

Colorado State College of Education, 20, 23, 24–6

communism, communists, 15–17, 112, 146, 174, 197, 199, 260

Compendium of the Pursuit of Divine Knowledge (Dr. Fadl), 426

Coptic Christians, 58, 66

Corsi, Dina, 384–5, 398–9, 408, 485*n*

Cruise, Kevin, 273

Crusades, 4, 194, 237–8

D'Amuro, Pascuale, "Pat," 312

Dar al-Ulum school, 19

Dar es Salaam, Tanzania, 306, 308

Dawa al-Jihad, University of, 120

Defense Department, U.S., 207, 232, 234; *see also* Pentagon

Denmark, 210, 420

Deraz, Essam, 147–8, 159, 160, 458*n*, 468*n*

al-Dhahabi, Sheikh Mohammed, 142

Dhahran, 75, 131, 279

DiBattista, Anna, 332, 333, 400, 404, 416

di Taranto, Lorraine, 272

Doran, Mary Deborah, 273, 407, 477*n*

Egypt, 141–2, 144, 145, 197*n*, 201, 209, 244, 252, 279, 340, 379, 475*n*; al-Jihad arrests in, 210; anti-British resistance in, 29–31; background of political prisoners in, 67–8; British occupation of, 10, 29, 38; child spies used by, 244–5; communist influence in, 15–17; deal between government and Islamists in, 290–1; as focus of al-Jihad, 57, 209–11, 242–3, 295, 380;

ideological struggle of revolution in, 33; Islamic movement and political radicalization in, 19–20, 29–30, 34–7, 46–50, 242–3, 296; Islamist movement overlap with fascism in, 45; Israeli defeats of, 11, 29, 47, 57, 59; political humor in, 47; popular outrage against terrorism in, 211–12, 293–4; radicalization of universities in, 47, 48; revolution in, 30–37, 44, 431; Saudis pressured to stop bin Laden by, 222; secularization of, 19–20, 38–9, 46; Shah in residence in, 55; terrorist attacks in, 291–3; tourism in industry in, 291–3; women's rights in, 57; Zawahiri's desire for revenge on, 246–7
Elsamneh, Maha, 287, 417
Eritrea, 149, 225
Erwa, Elfatih, 250–1, 481n
Essential Guide for Preparation (Dr. Fadl), 426
Ethiopia, 71, 243, 452n

al-Fadl, Jamal, 5–6, 142, 143, 150, 156, 162, 187, 217, 223, 224–5, 275, 277, 320, 426–8
Fahd, King of Saudi Arabia, 101, 166, 175, 177, 192, 221–2, 238–9, 302
Faisal, King of Saudi Arabia, 78–9, 80–1, 97, 98, 100–101, 167, 176
Farouk, King of Egypt, 9, 10, 29, 30
Farouk camp, 162, 322
Farouk Mosque, 49
fatwas, 4, 66, 194, 201, 209, 265–6, 279, 295–6, 307
al-Fawwaz, Khaled, 222

Federal Aviation Administration (FAA), 336, 389
Federal Bureau of Investigation (FBI), 3, 201, 206, 300, 307, 357–8; Annual Field Office Report of, 358; authority of, 353; *Cole* attack investigated by, 360–74; connection with foreign police of, 235–6; counterterrorism section of, 230–7; embassy bombing investigations by, 309–17, 349; evacuation from Yemen of, 408; I-49 division of, 272–3, 314, 317, 353, 358, 363, 383, 386, 387, 398, 407; initial disinterest in al-Qaeda by, 5–7; internal culture of, 236; Most Wanted list of, 336; narrow leadership of, 236; outdated technology at, 269; *see also* Alec Station; intelligence, U.S.
Fitzgerald, Patrick, 5, 300, 309, 316, 383
Foda, Farag, 209
Foreign Intelligence Surveillance Act (FISA), 388
Frahm, Charles E., 354
France, 176, 249, 294, 344, 420
Freeh, Louis, 232, 269–71, 330, 336, 354, 362, 374, 378
Friendship Bridge, 157
Front Islamique du Salut (FIS), 215–16
Fuller, Rob, 399

Galal, Nabila, 144–5
al-Gama'a al-Islamiyya, *see* Islamic Group
Gandhi, Mahatma, invoked by bin Laden, 172
Gaudin, Steven, 310–17, 383, 406
Germany, 176, 344–6, 350, 362, 420

Ghanem, Alia, 82–3, 84–5, 88, 90, 113, 455*n*
Ghanem, Leila, 88
Ghanem, Najwa, *see* Umm Abdullah
Gillespie, Margarette, 384–6, 398, 494*n*–5*n*
Giuliani, Rudy, 357
Golan Heights, 45, 47
Graham, Mary Margaret, 386
Grand Mosque, Mecca, 77–8, 101–8, 167, 170, 459*n*–60*n*
Greeley, Colo., 20–7, 38
Gromov, Boris V., 157
Ground Zero, 415
Groupe Islamique Armé (GIA), 216
Gul, Hamid, 323
Gulf Cooperation Council, 238
Gulf War (1991), 4, 182, 214, 238, 294
Gunn, Lou, 397

al-Hada, Ahmal, 350
al-Hada, Ahmed, 315, 387
al-Hada, Hoda, 349
Hadley, Stephen, 378
Hadramout, 71, 86, 175, 364
el-Hage, Wadih, 275–7, 302
hajj, 73, 78, 84, 101–2, 104, 117, 251
Hamas, 149–50, 196, 306, 309
Hamburg cell, 344–7, 349–50, 394
Hamza, Mustafa, 243, 291
Hamzah, Sheikh Mir, 295
Hanjour, Hani, 341, 396
Haqqanni, Jalaladin, 418
al-Harby, Khaled bin Ouda bin Mohammed, 417
Hatton, Leonard, 414
Hauer, Jerome, "Jerry," 401
al-Hawali, Sheikh Safar, 316
Al-Hayat (newspaper), 305–6
Hayatabad, Pakistan, 121, 144

al-Hazmi, Nawaf, 349–51, 352–3, 354–5, 373–4, 384–6, 388, 398–9, 409, 494*n*–5*n*
Hekmatyar, Gulbuddin, 115, 126–7, 133, 163, 164, 183
Helwan, Egypt, 12, 31
al-Hennawi, Mahmoud Hisham, 283
Heyworth-Dunne, James, 20
Hezbollah, 196–7, 211, 271, 306, 309, 335
Hijaz, *see* Saudi Arabia
al-Hijira (construction co.), 191
Hoover, J. Edgar, 16, 175, 273, 317
Hudaybi, Hasan, 92
al-Hudhaif, Abdullah, 239–40
Hussein, King of Jordan, 41
Hussein, Saddam, 176, 177, 178, 193, 214, 334–5
Hussein Sidki Mosque, 42

ibn Abdul Wahhab, Mohammed, 72
Ibn al-Nafees clinic, 68, 69
Ibn Tamiyyah, 198, 208
Ibn Thabit, Hassan, 129
Ibrahim, Prophet, 78
Ibrahim, Saad Eddin, 67–8, 340
Ikegami, Haruki, 267
Ikhwan, 72, 80, 103, 452*n*
Al-Ikhwan al-Muslimin (magazine), 32, 43
Imam, Sayyid, 140–1
Immigration and Naturalization Service (INS), 349, 389, 396, 398
innocents, death of, 198–9, 248, 324
Intelink, 384, 494*n*–5*n*
intelligence, U.S.: Cold War era, 4; failures of, 201–2, 207, 275, 305, 320, 350–4, 371, 381, 382–9; interagency conflicts of, 301–2, 304–5, 321, 351–4, 355–6, 372, 373–4, 384–5, 387,

396–7, 398–400; investigation of 9/11 by, 408–13; Saudi cooperation with, 168–9, 179, 302; Sudanese cooperation with, 250–1, 319–20; *see also specific intelligence agencies*

Intelligence Unit 75, 60–2, 64, 68

Interior Ministry, Egyptian, 61–2

Interior Ministry, Saudi Arabia, 169, 175, 223

International Islamic Front for Jihad Against Jews and Crusaders, 295–6; formation of, 304

Inter-Services Intelligence (ISI), Pakistan, 114–15, 120, 127, 154, 163, 284, 323

International Islamic University, 110

In the Shade of the Quran (Qutb), 34, 91

Iran, 55–6, 114, 173, 177, 193, 196–7, 211, 254, 258, 271, 484n–5n

Iraq, 35–6, 114, 176–7, 179, 198, 239, 269, 452n; al-Qaeda communications with, 334–5; American embassy in, 365; insurgency in, 335; Kuwait invaded by, 177–82, 365; military capabilities of, 179; Shiites as dominant in, 56; in Six Day War, 45; U.S. operations in, 294–5

Isham, Christopher, 300

Islam, 48, 78, 91, 142; Arabian consolidation under, 80; call for revival of traditional, 35, 44, 45; Christianity as rival of, 194–5; as comfort to expat Muslims, 344; as "complete" system or way of life, 17, 22, 28, 91; divorce in, 57, 82, 221; evil omens as forbidden in,

161; ideological conflicts within, 34, 55, 56n, 92; jurisprudence in, 169; lack of U.S. understanding of, 236; materialism vs., 17; modernity vs., 28, 35, 195–6; political uses of, 19; prayer schedules in, 393; rise of anti-Semitism in, 45–6; Saudi intolerance for range of views on, 73, 88; seen by Banna as dominant, 29; Sharia seen as outdated by modernist, 57; spread of, 263; suicide as taboo in, 211, 248–9, 411; U.S. culture seen as threat to, 195–6; *see also* Islamism, Islamist movement; *specific branches and traditions*

Islamabad, Pakistan, 110, 116, 230, 307

al-Islambouli, Khaled, 58–9, 63, 204

Islamic Group (al-Gama'a al-Islamiyya), 63, 158, 196, 209, 211, 243, 284; formation and structure of, 48; operations undertaken by, 209, 290–3; opposition to global anti-U.S. fatwa of, 295–6; Sheikh Omar Abdul Rahman as leader of, 66; tactics of, 66–7

Islamic Jihad, *see* al-Jihad

Islamic People's Congress, 335

Islamism, Islamist movement: Coptic Christians targeted by, 66; in Egypt, 19–20, 28, 34–7, 45–50; in Egyptian custody, 290; FBI lack of understanding of, 236; fractured core of, 63; grievances against U.S. of, 294–6; ideological split among, 290–1; imposition of Sharia law as goal of, 56;

Islamism, Islamist movement
(*continued*):
  international revulsion at
    tactics of Algerian, 216–17;
    Israeli victory in Six Day War
    as call to, 45; jihad as
    neverending for, 124–5;
    Muslim Brotherhood and
    roots of, 30; origins of, 10;
    Qutb's ideas at core of, 12,
    16–17, 28, 35, 44; recruiting
    success of, 67–8; rise of, 45;
    Sadat's ties to, 46–7, 48;
    Saddam's attempts for alliance
    with, 334–5; secular
    government as target of, 30,
    43, 61; Sheikh Omar Abdul
    Rahman's influence on, 65–6;
    shift from regional to global
    goals of, 294; tactical split
    within, 50, 56, 66–7; united by
    bin Laden's vision, 375
Ismail, Jamal, 451n, 455n–6n,
    466n
Israel, 118n, 150, 196, 225, 293,
    296, 347, 374; establishment of,
    11, 46, 295; military
    dominance of, 11, 29, 45, 46;
    1973 attack on, 47, 57, 59;
    Sadat's peace treaty with, 57,
    59; U.S. support for, 11, 171,
    280, 315; victory in Six Day
    War of, 45, 98
Ittihad-e-Islami (Islamic Union),
    115

jahiliyya (period before
    Mohammed), 32, 35, 46, 111,
    125
Jaji, Afghanistan, 116, 128, 129
Jalalabad, Afghanistan, 158–62,
    163–4, 255, 262, 467n–8n
James, Jay, 390, 416
James, Valerie, 331–3, 356, 358,

372, 389–90, 391–3, 400, 401–2,
    404, 407, 414, 416
Jamiat-ul-Ulema of Pakistan, 295
Jammat al-Jihad, *see* al-Jihad
Jan, Gula, 420–1
Jarrah, Ziad, 347, 350
al-Jazeera, 215, 282, 417
Jeddah, Saudi Arabia, 68, 77,
    145, 219, 254; arrival of M. bin
    Laden in, 71, 74; bin Laden
    family move to, 76;
    Zawahiri/bin Laden meeting
    in, 69–71
Jews, 14, 38, 45, 46, 180, 196, 201,
    346
jihad, 124, 258; anti-Soviet, 4,
    53–5, 70, 108–13, 115–38, 195,
    325; conflicts on conduct and
    definition of, 150–2, 247–8;
    death of innocents in, 248;
    distant vs. near enemy in, 46;
    as duty to God, 72; fatwas
    required by, 66; as internal
    struggle v. holy war, 89;
    Qutb's call for anti-British, 32;
    see also fatwas
al-Jihad, 129, 141, 142–3, 144,
    158, 187, 196, 197n, 203–4, 222,
    242, 244, 252, 262, 282, 290,
    295, 335, 365, 375, 475n, 476n;
    Brotherhood's tactical split
    with, 50, 56; children tried and
    executed by, 245–6; CIA
    operations against, 304, 305;
    Egypt as focus of, 57, 209–11,
    242, 295, 379; finances of,
    207–8, 210, 295; formation and
    structure of, 50, 57, 69–70,
    207–9, 210, 380; operations
    and tactics of, 58–60, 62–3, 66,
    209, 210, 247; Sadat
    assassination and, 58–9, 62–3;
    Sadat's round up of, 58; *shura*
    council of, 245; splits within,

245–6, 284, 295–6, 379–80;
support for Iranian Revolution
in, 56; suspicions of bin Laden
in, 210, 379; U.S. intelligence
on, 304
Jihad Movement, Bangladesh,
295
Jihad Wal, 126, 322
Jizan, Saudi Arabia, 71
John Paul II, Pope, 203, 267
Joint Terrorism Task Force, 272,
338, 357
Jordan, 45, 79, 109, 246, 336, 338,
381
Julaidan, Wa'el, 150, 214, 466*n*
Juma, Ashif Mohammed, 263
Justice Department, U.S., 234,
358, 379, 387, 389

Kalthoum, Umm, 76, 88, 170
Kamikaze Camp, 342
Kandahar, Afghanistan, 258–9,
280–1, 284–9, 302, 417; *see also*
Afghanistan
Karas, Kenneth, 5, 383
Karim, Abdul Basit Mahmoud
Abdul, *see* Yousef, Ramzi
Karniewicz, Richard, 273
Kashmir, 149, 150, 185, 262, 297
Kenya, 224, 250, 262–3, 275–7;
FBI investigation in, 310–17,
312, 349, 414; U.S. embassy
bombing in, 225–6, 306–8, 312,
324, 338, 383, 407, 411–12,
419
Khadr, Abdul Kareem, 289
Khadr, Abdul Rahman, 288, 322
Khadr, Ahmed Sayed, 417, 467*n*
Khadr, Zaynab Ahmed, 284–90
Khaksar, Mullah Mohammed,
401
Khaldan camp, 297, 316
Khaled, King of Saudi Arabia,
101, 103, 104, 105

Khalifa, Jamal, 90–1, 92, 93–4,
102, 109, 112, 119, 129–31, 161,
221, 452*n*, 455*n*, 456*n*, 458*n*,
468*n*, 469*n*
Khalis, Younis, 255
Khallad, 350, 352, 371–2, 373,
384–6, 409
Khan, Wali, *see* Shah, Walikhan
Amin
Khashoggi, Jamal, 90, 220, 227,
455*n*, 457*n*, 464*n*, 470*n*
al-Khatab, Abdullah, 419
Kherchtou, L'Houssaine, 224
al-Khilaifi, Mohammed
Abdullah, 219–20
Khobar Towers, 269–71, 273, 279,
484*n*–5*n*
Khomeini, Ayatollah Ruhollah, 55
Khost, Afghanistan, 320–2
Khozam Palace, 75
King Abdul Aziz University, 90,
93–4, 109
King Saud University, 40, 181
*Knights Under the Prophet's
Banner* (Zawahiri), 52
Kosovo, 185, 346
Kuwait, 114, 164, 177–82, 344,
365, 452*n*, 471*n*

Lahore, Pakistan, 116
Lang, Tom, 273
law enforcement,
internationalization of, 235–6,
271–2, 383
Lebanon, 86, 196, 197, 211, 213,
220, 271, 277, 347, 455*n*
Lewinsky, Monica, 319, 346
Lion's Den, 129–30, 131–2, 133–8,
136, 147, 151, 162, 262, 340–1,
420
Lopez, Kathy, 362–3
Los Angeles International
Airport, 297, 337, 398
Luxor, Egypt, 291–3, 294, 295

540 *Index*

Maadi, Egypt, 38–41, 44, 49, 69
Maasada training camp, *see* Lion's Den
Mabruk, Ahmed Salama, 283, 304
McClendon, Jaime, 23
McFadden, Robert, 408
McKillop, John, 414–15
madrassas, 257, 258, 297
Mafia, 236, 317, 383
Mahdi ("one who guides"), 102
Mahfouz, Naguib, 209
Mahir, Ahmed, 43
Makkawi, Mohammed Ibrahim, 148, 455n–6n
Malaysia, 350, 351–2, 372–3, 384–8, 398, 408–9
Malinowski, Michael E., 325
Manila, Philippines, 203, 267, 300
Marenches, Count Claude Alexandre de, 107, 460n
martyrdom, 122, 123–4, 130–131, 211, 308, 316
Marxism, Marxists, 35, 48, 49, 58
Masjid al-Nur, 142
al-Masri, Abu al-Walid, 424
Massoud, Ahmed Shah, 155, 163–4, 183, 256, 288, 349, 378, 380–1, 400–1
Mawn, Barry, 356, 358–9, 361–2, 370–1, 372, 379, 389, 406
Mazar-e-Sharif, 304, 306
Mecca, 77–8, 80–1, 117, 180, 254, 263, 264; 1979 seizure of Grand Mosque in, 101–8
Medina, 46, 69, 76, 83, 116, 180, 263
Meeker, Nathan, 20–1, 22, 38
Meskini, Abdul Ghani, 337
al-Mihdhar, Khaled, 349, 350–3, 354–5, 373–4, 384–8, 398–9, 409, 413, 495n

Milestones (Ma'alim fi al-Tariq) (Qutb), 34–5, 36, 91, 92
Millennium After-Action Review, 338
Miller, Doug, 351–2
Miller, John, 299–300, 458n
modernity, 28, 35, 195–6, 266
Mohammed, Ali Abdelsoud, 197n, 204–7, 208, 209, 211, 214, 215, 220, 225, 475n
Mohammed, Khaled Sheikh, 266, 267–8, 347–8, 388, 417
Mohammed, Prince of Saudi Arabia, 166
Mohammed, Prophet, 35, 46, 56n, 56, 72–3, 80, 143, 188, 248, 259, 263–4, 338, 394
Mohammed bin Laden Company, 74, 77, 84, 89, 95
Mongols, 198
al-Motassadeq, Munir, 345–6
Moussaoui, Zacarias, 297, 396–7
Mövenpick Hotel, 198
Mubarak, Hosni, 201, 242–4, 381, 430; anti-Islamist operations of, 60, 242, 244; attempted assassination of, 243, 250, 251, 341
Mubarak, Suzanne, 291
Mugniyah, Imad, 197
al-Muhasibi, Harith, 208
Mu'iz, Abdul, *see* al-Zawahiri, Ayman
mujahideen, 53–5, 110–11, 115, 116–17, 127, 220, 256, 468n; internal conflicts within, 163, 183; romanticized by U.S., 194
Al-Mujahideen (newspaper), 282
music, 88, 170, 188
Muslim Brotherhood (al-Ikhwan al-Muslimin), 18–19, 102, 119, 125, 140, 149–50, 154–5, 170, 242; British occupation resisted

by, 29; core membership of, 29; Egyptian government actions against, 29–30; Egyptian prison strike by, 34; imprisonment of, 33–4; medical clinics run by, 52; Nasser assassination attempted by, 33; and overthrow of Farouk, 30–1; politicized Islam spread by, 91; radicalization of younger members in, 46–7; roots of Islamist movement and, 30; Sadat's ties to, 31; Saudi support for, 36; secret apparatus of, 30, 33, 36; social welfare structure created by, 29, 52; structure of, 30, 48; Supreme Guide of, 92; tactical split with al-Jihad of, 50, 56; as teachers in Saudi schools, 87, 91; as underground in Saudi Arabia, 90

muttawa, 167, 169

Muttawakil, Wakil Ahmed, 327, 381

Mwangi, Roselyn Wanjiku, 311, 407

Naif, Prince of Saudi Arabia, 169, 175, 178, 181, 183, 239, 271

Naji, Hamoud, 368

Najibullah, 261

al-Najjar, Ahmed, 296

Najm al-Jihad farm, 260

Napoli, Louis, 272

al-Nashiri, Abdul Rahim, 359–60

Nasser, Gamal Abdul, 30–36, 45; assassination attempt on, 33; death of, 46, 66, 429; as Islamist target, 32–3, 46, 65; Qutb and, 31, 32, 35–6; seen as threat by Saudi Arabia, 36; treaty negotiation with British of, 32

National Guard, Saudi Arabia, 176, 177, 270

National Security Agency (NSA), 4, 321, 350–1, 381, 384, 388

National Security Council (NSC), 233–4, 319, 389

News (Islamabad), 124, 298, 321

New York, N.Y., 12–14, 17, 21, 272–4, 353; *see also* September 11, 2001, terrorist attacks of; World Trade Center

New York Times, 19, 389, 394

9/11 Commission, 469*n*–70*n*, 481*n*, 485*n*

9/11 *Commission Report, The*, 458*n*, 470*n*

Northern Alliance, 349, 350, 378, 380, 401

Nowair, Essam, 50–1, 144

al-Nur Mosque, 207

Obaid, Nawaf, 455*n*, 511

oil, oil wealth, 73–4, 99, 170, 173, 176, 195, 238, 266

Oklahoma City bombing, 235, 270

Oman, 114, 162

Omar, Caliph, 180

Omar, Mullah Mohammed, 256–7, 278, 284, 297; bin Laden's relations with, 260, 280–1, 298–9, 325–7; political authority gained by, 259; Taliban created by, 257, 259; Turki's meeting with, 302–4, 326–7, 328

Omer, Hassabulla, 253*n*, 477*n*–8*n*

O'Neill, Carol, 331, 416

O'Neill, Christine, 331, 333, 392, 416

O'Neill, John, 230–7, 241, 275, 300, 305, 331, 378–9, 383, 386; al-Qaeda threat recognized by, 395; attack on U.S. homeland anticipated by, 335–8; background of, 318; bin Laden as focus of, 237, 274, 275, 301, 390; censure and reprimands of, 334, 358; changing nature of terrorism understood by, 236–7, 395; Clarke as ally of, 234–5; *Cole* investigation of, 362–74, 390, 397; death of, 407, 409, 414; embassy bombing investigation of, 309–18; financial strain on, 334; funeral of, 415–16; Justice Department inquiry on, 358, 389–90; and Khobar Towers bombing, 269–72; millennium concerns of, 335–8; during 9/11 attacks, 403, 404, 405–6, 407; in New York office, 272–4; personality and appearance of, 231–2, 318–19; religious and philosophical views of, 391–2; reputation and work habits of, 231–2, 235–6, 271, 317–19, 356, 357–8, 390–391; retirement from FBI of, 389–91, 397–8; romantic relationships of, 331–4, 356; Saudi non-cooperation with, 270–1; Scheuer and, 274, 275, 352–4; terrorist mind understood by, 390
O'Neill, John, Jr., 331, 403, 416
OPEC, 197
Operation al-Aqsa, 308
Operation Anaconda, 420
Operation "Bojinka," 267
Operation Gomorrah, 346
Operation Grapes of Wrath, 347
Operation Holy Kaaba, 308

Operation Infinite Reach, 320–4, 327–8, 330, 361
Operation Restore Hope, 198, 225
opium trade, 53, 259, 380
al-Oteibi, Juhayman, 102–3, 105–6, 108–9
Othman, Caliph, 166, 188
Ottoman Empire, 73, 294
al-'Owhali, Mohammed, 300, 306, 312–17, 383

Pakistan, 40, 52–4, 60, 105, 109, 114–15, 116, 119, 127, 185, 231, 261, 284, 297, 340, 357, 385; Afghan refugees in, 52, 53; bin Laden in, 183–4, 419–20; Egyptian embassy bombing in, 247–8; FBI in, 232–3; as Taliban ally, 255, 256, 257, 326–7; terrorist attacks in, 247–8; Zawahiri in, 140–1, 143–7, 420–1; *see also* Peshawar, Islamabad
Palestine, Palestinians, 22–3, 45, 87, 109, 118n, 149–50, 171, 180, 196, 211, 294, 346, 374
Pentagon, 348, 406, 419
Perkins, Abby, 407
Perry, William, 4, 266
Peshawar, Pakistan, 109, 115, 163, 231, 285, 381; as base of anti-Soviet jihad, 110–11, 119–20, 139–40; money funneled through, 154
Philippines, 149, 150, 267; *see also* Manila
Pickard, Thomas, 310, 356, 362
"planes operation," *see* September 11, 2001, terrorist attacks of
Political Security Organization (PSO), Yemen, 367–8, 371, 373, 409

polygamy, 82, 93–4
Port Sudan, 187, 191, 252
Preachers Not Judges (Hudaybi), 92
Prophet's Mosque, Medina, 76, 78, 83, 116, 165

al-Qadurat (import co.), 191
al-Qaeda, 141, 144, 146, 245, 262–4; 9/11 planning and monitored by, 266–8, 347–50, 403–4; al-Fadl's testimony about, 5; al-Jihad supported and absorbed by, 210, 380; bin Laden's resolve to quit, 192; chemical weapons pursued by, 217–18, 319–20, 343–4; *Cole* attack considered victory by, 374; daily life at Afghan base of, 284–90; death cult at core of, 124; diversity of enemies of, 342; Egyptian inner circle of, 147, 284, 293–4, 375, 380; embassy bombings links to, 247, 308, 321, 325, 326, 350, 359; employed at bin Laden businesses, 191–2; evolution of, 152–4, 190, 193–4, 198–9, 375; fanaticism of, 6–7; fatwa committee of, 194; finances of, 223, 224–5, 226, 253, 282, 284, 306; first documented strike of, 306–7; freelance terrorists and, 337; growth and public profile of, 6–7, 152, 218, 295, 297–8, 306; inexperience with operations of, 307; innocent deaths accepted by, 198–9, 324; international profile of, 306; introspection after Luxor within, 293–4; involvement in Somalia of, 477*n*; Iranian links of, 197*n*; Iraq communications with, 334–5; Khobar Towers and, 484*n*–5*n*; as law enforcement challenge, 383; links to *Cole* attack of, 372; loss of followers of, 282; loyalty oaths of, 326; membership benefits and requirement of, 153, 162; modern methods and tools used by, 7; Mubarak assassination attempts by, 243; mythologies created by, 138, 264–5; network map of, 6, 387–8; as one of many bin Laden enterprises, 218; operatives in U.S. of, 336, 337, 352, 373–4, 384, 388; playbook of, 205; preferred by Saudis to Brotherhood, 155; as private army, 199; Saudi surveillance in U.S. of, 355; seen as manageable threat by early U.S. intelligence, 6–7, 338; Shura council of, 216, 328; structure and management of, 6, 162–3, 214, 215–16, 241, 327–8, 359, 412; Sudanese links of, 187, 217; Sunni and Shiite reunification and, 197; tactical disagreements within, 343; Taif siege invoked by, 80; training and recruitment in, 6–7, 162, 194, 340–4, 374; training camps of, *see* training camps, *specific camps*; traitors to, 5–6, 225; U.S. attack in Afghanistan on, 309, 416, 418–19, 420; U.S. homeland strikes planned by, 347–8, 381; U.S. intelligence lacking on, 301, 311; U.S. intelligence on, 4–7, 207, 225, 275, 276, 304–5, 310, 315; U.S. seen as main threat by, 193, 194, 213–14; U.S. troops in Persian Gulf targeted by, 193, 197, 360; and Yemeni guerilla war, 175; Zabadi program of, 343–4

al-Qahtani, Mohammed Abdullah, 102, 106
al-Qamari, Essam, 58, 59–60, 61–2, 67, 246
Qamish, Ghalib, 371, 409
Al-Quds al-Arabi (newspaper), 241, 278, 295
al-Quds mosque, 345, 347
Queen Hatshepsut's temple, 291–3
Quran, 99, 102, 124–5, 142–3, 258
al-Quso, Fahd, 361, 371, 373, 384–5, 408–9
Qutb, Fatima, 11
Qutb, Hamida, 36
Qutb, Mohammed, 91–2
Qutb, Sayyid, 9–37, 43–4, 91–2, 111, 125, 141, 144, 149, 209, 314, 344, 375, 451n; anti-British jihad called for by, 32; anticommunism of, 16–17; appearance and personality of, 9, 28, 43; Banna as intellectual rival to, 19; darkening political views of, 34; early politics of, 9–10, 16–17; and Egyptian Islamic movement, 31–7; imprisonment and torture of, 32, 33–6, 61, 62; Islamic fundamentalism built on ideas of, 12, 16–17, 28, 35; Islamic government espoused by, 32–3, 35; martyrdom embraced by, 36, 43; Nasser and, 31, 32, 35–6; poor health of, 34; radicalized by trip to U.S., 27–8; religious background and deliberations of, 10, 12; revival of Islam sought by, 35; student life in Greeley, 23–4; trial and execution of, 36–7, 43, 44; in U.S., 9, 11–28; Western civilization seen as all-engulfing by, 10; women and, 11, 18, 23–4; writings from prison of, 34–5, 47

Rabbani, Burhanuddin, 115, 256
racism, 13, 23, 27–8
Rahman, Abu Abdul, 155–6
Rahman, Fazlul, 295
Rahman, Sheikh Omar Abdul, 65, 109, 196, 203, 209, 244, 251, 273, 314, 357, 387, 475n; fatwas issued by, 66, 201, 209; as leader of Islamic Group, 66; recruitment by, 200–201; rivalry with Zawahiri of, 158; tactical disagreements with Zawahiri of, 67; trial and imprisonment over Sadat assassination of, 65; U.S. asylum sought by, 201; in U.S. prison, 291, 293, 296; wealthy sponsors of, 66
Ramadan, 47, 82, 117, 135, 136, 152, 338, 359
al-Rashidi, Amin Ali, *see* Abu Ubaydah al-Banshiri
Red Crescent Society, 52–3, 54, 140, 141, 156, 204
red mercury, 218
renditions, 231, 232–3, 357, 362
Reno, Janet, 232, 301, 310, 319
Ressam, Ahmed, 297, 336–8, 398
Reza Pahlavi, Mohammed, Shah of Iran, 55, 197n
Rice, Condoleezza, 378
Riyadh, Saudi Arabia, 75, 77, 168, 182, 279
Ross, William, 25
Rossini, Mark, 358, 390, 391, 414
Rushdi, Osama, 140

al-Sada, Amal, wife of bin Laden, 382

al-Sadat, Anwar, 34, 36, 142, 247,
475*n;* anti-Islamist actions of,
57–8, 66; assassination of,
58–9, 242; Brotherhood ties of,
31, 46; dissident roundup
ordered by, 58; Israeli peace
treaty with, 57; lip service on
Sharia of, 57; peace made with
Islamists by, 46–7, 48; Shah
invited to Egypt by, 55
al-Sadat, Jihan, 57
Sageman, Marc, 468*n,* 473*n*
el-Said, Qari, 216
Salafist Islam, 49, 72, 73, 109,
143, 146, 155, 196, 208, 375
Saleh, Ali Abdullah, 175, 367
Salim, Mamdouh, *see* Abu Hajer
al-Iraqi
Salman, Prince of Saudi Arabia,
328
Sanchez, Linda, 205
al-Sarawat Range, 78, 79, 254
al-Saud family, bin Laden family
ties to, 75, 77, 78–9
Saud, King of Saudi Arabia,
76–7, 101, 106
Saudi Arabia, 40, 114, 163, 164,
261, 278, 297, 316, 340, 344; al-
Qaeda attacks within, 240–1;
bin Laden family success in,
73–6, 77–82; census figures on,
176; citizenship as valuable in,
222; cooperation with U.S.
intelligence of, 168–9, 179, 302;
creation of third state of, 73;
defense spending and military
of, 103, 107, 176; economy of,
73, 170, 238; entertainment in,
170; female driving ban in, 181;
financial support of Islamic
world by, 170, 344; first state of,
73; flight restrictions in, 79;
geography of, 79–80;
government control of media

in, 177; Hijaz, 71, 79, 80;
intelligence department in, 86,
164, 302; international standing
of, 177–8, 327; intolerance for
range of views on Islam in, 73,
88; Iraq as threat to, 176–7;
jihad financing from, 118;
Khobar Towers bombing in,
269–71; Kuwaiti refugees in,
182; military of, 79, 103, 107,
179, 240, 454*n;* Muslim
Brotherhood supported by, 36;
Najd, 73, 86; non-Muslims in
defense forces of, 180–1; oil and
oil wealth of, 74, 170, 173, 176,
238, 266; opposition to Fahd's
reforms in, 238; political
isolation in Arab world of,
177–8, 327; population claims
of, 176; power struggle and
reforms in, 181–2, 238, 270; as
pressured to deal with bin
Laden, 251; public image of
royal family in, 166–7; relations
with South Yemen of, 174;
religion in daily life of, 90,
169–70; request to Taliban for
bin Laden by, 326–7; return of
Afghan jihadists to, 185; rise of
radicalism in, 123; second state
of, 73; Sharia law in, 271,
279–80; Taliban links of, 302–3,
326–7; tension between royal
and religious power in, 72;
transformation of
infrastructure in, 73, 75–6,
79–82; uneven development
across, 79; U.S. military
presence in, 4, 79, 176, 178–82,
192–3, 238–9, 240, 241, 294, 306,
327; U.S. relations with, 173,
178, 302, 355; U.S. training of
military for, 79, 240, 454*n;*
Wahhabism as dominant in, 71;

Saudi Arabia *(continued)*
worldwide Islam supported
by, 170
Saudi Binladin Group, 77, 78–9,
112, 116, 131, 178–9, 187
Sayyaf, Abdul Rasul, 115–16,
116, 120, 128, 129, 133, 136,
138, 147, 266, 381
Saznoor, Maulvi, 260
Scheuer, Michael, 274–5, 301,
305, 317, 329–30, 351, 352, 354,
458*n*, 468*n*, 485*n*
Schiliro, Lewis, 203, 356, 400
Schleifer, Abdallah, 48–50, 51–2,
54, 68
Schwarzkopf, H. Norman, 178,
462*n*
September 11, 2001, terrorist
attacks of, 61, 80, 374–5, 386,
403–7; al-Qaeda planning of,
266–8, 347–50, 351–2, 390,
402–3; financing of, 373;
intended targets of, 347–8;
search and rescue after,
414–15; U.S. intelligence
investigation into, 408–13
Services Bureau (Makhtab al-
Khadamat), 119, 120, 154, 155,
193; U.S. branches of, 204, 217,
475*n*
sex, 14–15, 27, 87
al-Shaffei, Hussein, 43
Shafiq, 161–2
Shah, Wali Khan Amin, 130, 300
al-Shamrani, Muslih, 240–1
Sharia, 56, 143, 182, 188, 195, 258,
271, 279
Sharif, Nawaz, 183
Sharif, Omar (Michel Chalhub),
41
al-Sharqi, Abdullah, *see* al-
Shehhi, Marwan
Sharraf, Ahmed, 244–5

Sharraf, Mohammed, 244
al-Sha'tha, Abu, 328
al-Shehhi, Marwan, 347, 350,
409–10, 413
Shepheard's Hotel, 30, 54
al-Shibh, Ramzi bin, 347, 350,
390, 413
al-Shifa pharmaceutical plant,
320
Shiites, 56, 82, 169, 197, 211, 304,
342
Sidqi, Atef, 211
Simon, Steven, 481*n*, 485*n*
Six Day War, 45, 98
Social Justice in Islam (Qutb), 19
Somalia, 149, 198, 218, 226, 228,
308, 410, 477*n*; al-Qaeda
connection in, 302; famine in,
192–3, 214; U.S. helicopters
shot down in, 6, 214–15, 279
Soufan, Ali, 309–10, 363, 384–5,
397, 401, 404, 406, 466*n*, 493*n*;
in 9/11 investigation, 408–13;
in Cole investigation, 363–4,
367, 368–9, 370, 372, 373, 374
Soviet Union, 150, 171, 182, 199,
204, 299, 340, 375; Afghanistan
occupied by, 4, 55, 109–15, 148,
157, 179, 256–7; Afghan jihad
against, 4, 53–4, 70, 109–13,
116–38, 194, 325; withdrawal
from Afghanistan of, 127, 153,
157, 179, 257
Spain, 149, 389, 395
State Department, U.S., 205, 231,
233, 234, 250, 325, 366; terror
watch lists of, 319, 320, 352,
385, 386, 398
Stevens, Mary Lynn, 331–2,
333
Strategic Information and
Operations Center (SIOC),
230–1, 232–3, 309

al-Subayil, Sheikh Mohammed, 101

Sudan, 193, 206, 210, 215, 222, 242, 245, 284, 297, 308, 340, 481*n;* al-Jihad expelled from, 246, 249; bin Laden courted by, 186–7; bin Laden offered to U.S. by, 251, 481*n;* bin Laden's investments in, 188, 190–1, 253*n,* 260, 275; bin Laden's life in, 187–92, 218–21; chemical weapons rumors in, 319–20; Christian population in, 188, 190; civil war in, 186, 190, 192; complicity in attack on Mubarak of, 243–4; economy of, 190–1, 223–4, 320; expulsion of bin Laden from, 249, 250–3; horse racing in, 189; and independence of al-Jihad, 208; intelligence cooperation with U.S. by, 250–1, 319–20; Salafist movements in, 196–7; on state sponsored terror list, 250; terrorists in, 196–7; UN sanctions on, 243; U.S. Embassy removed from, 250; Zawahiri expelled from, 282

Sufaat, Yazid, 343, 351, 397

Sufi Islam, 48, 49, 115, 125, 208, 258

suicide, suicide bombers, 197, 248–9, 293, 307–8, 359, 382; as taboo in Islam, 211, 248–9, 411

Sultan, Prince of Saudi Arabia, 103, 104, 105

Summerlin, Carl, 273

Sunnis, 56, 211, 342

al-Suri, Abu Musab, 425

Syria, 45, 47, 82, 180, 382

Taha, Ali Othman, 250

Taha, Rifai Ahmed, 291, 293, 295

Taif, Saudi Arabia, 80–2, 107, 116, 165

takfir, 34, 141–4, 149, 150–1, 156, 162, 216, 218, 220, 238, 412, 427

Takfir wa Hijira (Excommunication and Withdrawal), 141–2

Talal, Prince of Saudi Arabia, 76

Taliban, 167, 278, 280, 284, 294, 297, 302, 316, 323, 349, 350, 376, 378, 380, 400; Afghan acceptance of, 255–6, 257, 264; bin Laden's relations with, 260, 336, 419; code of behavior dictated by, 261–2; formation of, 257; Pakistani support for, 255, 256, 257, 326–7; recognition as legitimate government of, 261; Saudi links to, 302–3; Saudi support for, 256, 257; split over bin Laden within, 325–6, 374; and U.S. attack on Afghanistan, 417; withdrawn support for bin Laden of, 419

Tanzania, 263, 277; U.S. embassy bombing in, 306, 308, 311, 321, 324, 338, 382, 411–12, 419

Tarnak Farms, *see* Kandahar

al-Tayeb, Medani, 152, 226

Tenet, George, 302, 330, 354

al-Thimar al-Mubaraka (bin Laden agricultural co.), 191

al-Thagr school, 86

The Sullivans, USS, 339, 350, 359

Tora Bora, Afghanistan, 127–8, 215, 260, 265, 347, 418

torture: of Qutb, 33, 34, 61, 62; religious intensity in response to, 67; used by Intelligence Unit 75, 61, 62, 64–5, 67–8, 69

tourism, as terrorist target, 291–3

training camps, 6, 112, 125, 128, 129–30, 162, 206, 213, 240–1, 279, 284, 297, 300, 306, 316, 322–3, 327, 337, 340–1, 342, 360, 403
Tucker, Robert, 401
al-Turabi, Hasan, 186, 187, 190, 242, 244, 246, 249, 252, 334; form of Islam espoused by, 187–8; rivalry with bin Laden of, 187–8, 197
al-Turabi, Issam, 188, 192, 249–50, 458*n*
Turkey, 142, 297, 340
Turki, Prince of Saudi Arabia, 101, 114–16, 164, 167–9, 176, 220, 222, 241, 251, 258, 278, 302–3, 351, 453*n*, 455*n*, 460*n*; and Afghan civil war, 183–4; bin Laden's meetings with, 173–4, 179–80; and bin Laden's money for jihad, 119–20; conflict with clergy of, 168–9; education of, 97–8; lifestyle of, 167–8; meetings with Taliban, 302–3, 326–7, 328; personality and appearance of, 97; Saddam seen as threat by, 179; in Saudi Foreign Liaison Bureau, 98; and seizure of Grand Mosque, 101–9; work with CIA of, 168–9, 179
Turki, Sheikh Abdullah, 303
TWA Flight 800, crash of, 273
Twitchell, Karl, 73

Umm Abdullah (Najwa Ghanem), wife of bin Laden, 90, 92, 220–1, 285, 286, 287, 382
Umm Ali, wife of bin Laden, 94, 221
Umm Hamza, wife of bin Laden, 94, 220, 286–7, 377

Umm Khaled, wife of bin Laden, 94, 220, 285, 286, 288
United Airlines Flight 175, 409–10
United Arab Emirates, 197*n*, 254, 261, 329–30
United Nations, 3, 13, 16, 47, 59, 182, 193, 201, 214, 243, 294, 381
United States, 12–13, 14, 16–17, 18, 22–3, 27, 105, 150, 163, 170, 176, 210, 296; al-Qaeda attacked in Afghanistan by, 309, 416, 418–19, 420; anticommunism of, 15–16; anti-Soviet jihad supported by, 194, 325; bin Laden's declaration of war on, 4, 265–6, 279, 307; capitalism of, 17; domestic terrorism in, 235, 237, 270, 335–8; first Islamist attack on, 202–3; flight schools in, 341, 348–9, 350, 354, 395; as immigrant nation, 11; impact of Kinsey Report on, 14–15; influence in Persian Gulf of, 192–3; intelligence in, *see* intelligence, U.S.; Islamist scope of activity in, 237; Israel supported by, 11, 171, 280, 315; materialism of, 17, 27; military presence in Saudi Arabia of, 4, 79, 176, 178–82, 192–3, 238–9, 240, 241, 294, 306, 327; Saudi surveillance of al-Qaeda in, 355; Saudis as ally of, 173, 355; Saudi troops trained by, 79, 240, 444*n*; seen as threat by Islamists, 146, 170–3, 198–9, 213–14, 237–8, 298, 299; Sudan's offer of bin Laden to, 251, 471*n*; terror cells and fundraising within, 122, 201–2, 203–4, 465*n*; warnings of attacks within, 335–8, 381–2; Yemeni relations of, 366
uranium, 217–18, 478*n*

"Vanguards of Conquest," 210, 466*n; see also* al-Jihad
Vinnell Corporation, 240

Wadi El Aqiq, 188, 219
Wahhabism, 99, 100, 102, 115, 198, 258; core beliefs of, 71, 72–3; as dominant power in Saudi Arabia, 71, 72; intolerance for other forms of Islam in, 73, 88; in Saudi Arabia, 168, 169–70; as Saudi state religion, 73; as term rejected by Saudis, 72
Washington D.C., 17–18, 348, 406, 419
Watson, Dale, 338, 372
el-Wed, Ahmed, 141, 142, 143, 156
White, Mary Jo, 357–8, 382–3
White House, 230, 234, 348
Williams, Kenneth, 395
Wilshire, Tom, 383–4
women, 11, 18, 23–4, 347; equality under Islam of, 188; rights granted in Egypt to, 57; in Saudi Arabia, 168–9, 180–1; under Taliban rule, 261; traditional Islamic dress of, 49, 51, 57
Wong, Wesley, 405–6
"World Is an Undutiful Boy, The" (Qutb), 25
World Trade Center, 200–201, 357, 386; chosen as target for 9/11, 348, 419; FBI offices in, 414; 1993 bombing of, 201–3, 230, 236, 266–7, 279, 383, 387; O'Neill as security chief at, 389–90, 391, 398, 401; *see also* September 11, 2001, terrorist attacks of
World War II, 12–13, 17, 27, 38, 45, 346

Yemen, 40, 79, 86, 100, 184, 192, 193, 198, 207, 210, 221, 228, 246, 297, 312, 315, 338–9, 349, 359, 401; attack on *Cole* in, 360–75; cells in, 365, 387–8; 1992 bombing in, 6; Saudi relations with, 174–5; U.S. relations with, 365–6
Yousef, Ramzi, 201–2, 203, 230, 266–7, 279, 348, 484*n*; rendition of, 231, 232–3, 357, 362
Yusufzai, Rahimullah, 124, 298, 320, 324

Zabadi program, 343–4
Zaidan, Ahmed, 455*n*, 458*n*, 468*n*
Zaki, Ali, 207–8, 475*n*
Zaki, Salim, 29–30
al-Zarqawi, Abu Musab, 335, 336, 424
al-Zawahiri, Aisha, 290, 418
al-Zawahiri, Ayman, 38–68, 109*n*, 112, 129, 140, 142–4, 147–8, 155–6, 162, 164, 184, 186, 195, 196, 197*n*, 242, 244, 252, 262, 279, 293, 299, 305, 307, 320–1, 324, 351, 374, 375, 400, 426, 428, 450*n*–1*n*, 475*n*, 476*n*; during anti-Soviet jihad, 52–3, 54–5, 70; arrest in Russia of, 283–4; assassination attempts on, 245–6; Mahfouz Azzam's influence on, 42–3; background and childhood of, 40, 41–4, 65; bin Laden's alliance and meetings with, 70, 146–50, 159–61, 220, 284, 296, 380; children of, 289–90; concerns about attack on U.S. of, 146; and conflicts within al-Jihad, 50, 66–7, 245–6; conservative views on women of, 51;

al-Zawahiri, Ayman *(continued)* courtship and marriage of, 50–2; declaration of unity drafted by, 294–6; devout reputation of, 42; and Egyptian nonviolence initiative, 290–1; escape from Egypt of, 68, 69–70; evolution of activism of, 47, 60, 66–7; expelled from Sudan, 282; followers alienated by, 246–8; interrogation and torture by Intelligence Unit 75 of, 60, 64, 68, 69; Islamist cells developed by, 44–5, 47, 57, 69, 209–10; medical practice and reputation of, 52, 53, 54, 55, 58, 59, 68, 69, 159; nom de guerres of, 203–4, 207; as overshadowed by bin Laden, 207–9; in Pakistan, 140–1, 144–7, 420–1; personality and appearance of, 42–4, 69, 420; Qamari entrapped by, 61–2; raised visibility of, 304; as real power of al-Qaeda, 299; recruitment by, 53, 57, 68, 147; resignation from al-Jihad of, 379; revenge on Egypt sought by, 246; rivalries of, 149–50, 158; and Sadat assassination, 59–68; suicide operations rationalized by, 248–9; travels to Iraq of, 334–5; trips to U.S. of, 203–4, 207–8, 475n; *see also* al-Jihad

al-Zawahiri, Azza, 50–1, 144–5, 289–90, 417

al-Zawahiri, Fatima, 145

al-Zawahiri, Heba, 40, 69

al-Zawahiri, Hussein, 40, 60, 63n

al-Zawahiri, Kashif, 39

al-Zawahiri, Khadija, 145

al-Zawahiri, Mohammed (Ayman's brother), 40, 43, 63n, 69, 140, 296, 305

al-Zawahiri, Mohammed (Ayman's son), 145, 289

al-Zawahiri, Mohammed al-Ahmadi, 40

al-Zawahiri, Mohammed Rabie (Ayman's father), 39–41, 42

al-Zawahiri, Nabila, 289

al-Zawahiri, Umayma (Ayman's daughter), 145, 289

al-Zawahiri, Umnya, 40

Zawya Mosque, 62

al-Zayyat, Montassir, 61, 65, 67, 69, 70, 290, 450n, 476n

Zent, John, 206–7

al-Zumar, Aboud, 57, 59–60

Organized by page for clarity; actual section does not include page numbers.

Grateful acknowledgement is made to the following for permission to reprint photographs:

page 1: Sayyid Qutb with Colorado State College president: Michener Library, University of Northern Colorado. Aerial view of Greeley, Colorado: Greeley Museum. Qutb on trial: al-Ahram

page 2: Zawahiri as a child: the Azzam family, AFP/HO/*Al-Hayat.* Zawahiri in medical school: the Azzam family, AFP/Getty

page 3: Prisoners on trial: AP. Sheikh Omar Abdul Rahman: Aladin Abdel/ Reuters/Corbis. Zawahiri on trial: Getty

page 4: Mohammed bin Laden with Prince Talal in the Grand Mosque: courtesy of Prince Talal. Mohammed bin Laden and King Faisal: courtesy Saudi Binladin Group. Grand Mosque: Abbas/Magnum. Juhayman al-Oteibi: courtesy of Saudi Embassy

page 5: Jamal Khalifa: author's collection. Osama bin Laden's first house in Jeddah: author's collection. Osama bin Laden's second house in Jeddah: author's collection;

page 6: Abdullah Azzam: courtesy of Abdullah Anas. Young Osama bin Laden: EPA/Corbis. Azzam and Massoud: courtesy of Abdullah Anas

page 7: General Hamid Gul: author's collection. Prince Turki: Corbis. Prince Turki negotiating among warring mujahideen: courtesy of Jamal Khashoggi

page 8: World Trade Center: Getty. Ramzi Yousef: courtesy of the FBI

page 9: Hasan al-Turabi: author's collection. Osama bin Laden: courtesy of Scott MacLeod. Osama bin Laden's mosque: author's collection

page 10: Osama bin Laden with gun: AFP/Getty. Taliban fighters on tank: Sayed Salahuddin/Reuters/Corbis

page 11: Bin Laden and Zawahiri at a press conference: CNN via Getty. Dar-ul-Aman Palace ruins: author's collection

page 12: Ruins of the American Embassy in Nairobi, Kenya: Reuters. Ruins of the American Embassy in Tanzania: courtesy of the FBI. Pharmaceutical plant ruins: author's collection

page 13: USS *Cole:* Getty. Michael Scheuer: AP. Richard Clarke: AP

page 14: Valerie James and John O'Neill: courtesy of Valerie James. Mary Lynn Stevens and John O'Neill: courtesy of Mary Lynn Stevens. Anna DiBattista and John O'Neill: courtesy of Anna DiBattista

page 15: John O'Neill and Daniel Coleman: courtesy of Daniel Coleman. Ruins of bin Laden's hideout in Afghanistan: courtesy of the FBI. John O'Neill's mother and wife at his funeral: AP

page 16: World Trade Center ruins: Hale Gurland/Contact Press Images